AF225977

An Exposition Of John Seventeen

An
Exposition
Of
John
Seventeen

Thomas Manton

Sovereign Grace Publishers, Inc.
P.O. Box 4998
Lafayette, IN 47903

Printed In the United States of America
By Lightning Source, Inc.

FOREWORD

The stores of Puritan exposition have recently been thrown open widely to the Church of Christ by the publication of religious classics by the Sovereign Grace Book Club. Volumes, once scarce, are now available to the diligent preacher of the Word. The minister who would prevent his sermons from being vapid and superficial would do well to become acquainted with the Puritans who have enriched the Church with their writings. Charles Spurgeon acknowledged his debt to the works of the divines and learned men who labored before him and his sermons reflect his study of them. The Puritans have left behind them a vast treasure of expository works and wise is the minister who makes use of this treasury.

One cannot begin better in acquiring a taste for Puritan writings than with those of Thomas Manton (1620-1677). His writing is natural, clear and eloquent. His expressions possess a warmth of genuine piety and reveal a close walk with his Lord and Soviour. Like many of his generation he entered deeply into the question of Christian experience as well as theology.

One of his contemporaries, William Bates, writes of Manton, "God had furnished him with a rare union of those parts that are requisite to form an excellent minister of his Word. A clear judgment, rich fancy, strong memory, and happy elocution, met in him, and were excellently improved by his diligent study . . . one that always had before his eyes the great end of the ministry, the glory of God and the salvation of men."

A common fault with Puritan writers is that they reflected the influence of the Scholastics. Their sermons contained a multitude of divisions and subdivisions. Each word of the text was carefully expounded and its theological and practical implications related with great detail. This sometimes makes for tedious and laborious reading. But golden nuggets are to be found in their works and worth all the effort and labor that goes into extracting them.

The works of Thomas Manton, however, are not dull nor are they difficult to read. F. R. Webber reveals the reason for this in his recent book, "A History of Preaching." He relates how on one occasion Manton was asked to preach before the Lord Mayor and aldermen. He delivered a sermon that was notable for its display of learning, but lacking in the doctrines of grace. As he left the building, a shabby man seized him by the sleeve of his preaching robe and said, "Sir, I came hoping to get some good for my soul, but I could understand very little of what you said." Manton looked at the ragged man for a moment and then said, "My friend, it was not I who gave you a sermon. You have given me one; and with the help of the Living God I shall never be so great a fool again." Undoubtedly, this explains the simplicity and clarity of Manton's style in comparison with others of his generation.

Manton's commentary on the epistle of James still continues to be popular and is his best known work. He also wrote commentaries on Isaiah 53, Matthew 25, and Jude. Actually they consist of sermons delivered to his congregation and later published. He preached 190 sermons on Psalm 119. Each sermon seeks to exhaust the text and reveals both the learning of the preacher and depth of piety of the congregation that loved such exposition.

The present volume consists of a series of sermons on the high priestly prayer of our Lord revealed in John 17. How important this prayer is for the Church! Christ supplicates for himself, his disciples and all who believe on his name. He has left a pattern of his perpetual intercession for the ministry and the Church. He who would know the mind and heart of the Lord must study this chapter. With love and deep reverence Manton opens up for us the glorious and blessed truths of this intercessory passage.

J. Marcellus Kik

CONTENTS

SERMONS UPON JOHN XVII.

SERMON I.

These words spake Jesus, and lift up his eyes to heaven, and said, Father, the hour is come; glorify thy Son, that thy Son also may glorify thee.—JOHN XVII. 1.

I SHALL, in the following exercises, open to you Christ's solemn prayer recorded in this chapter—a subject worthy of our reverence and serious meditations. The Holy Ghost seemeth to put a mark of respect upon this prayer above other prayers which Christ conceived in the days of his flesh. Elsewhere the scripture telleth us that Christ prayed; but the form is not expressed, or else only brief hints are delivered, but this is expressed at large. This was, as it were, his dying blaze. Natural motion is swifter and stronger in the end; so was Christ's love hottest and strongest in the close of his life; and here you have the eruption and flame of it. He would now open to us the bottom of his heart, and give us a copy of his continual intercession. This prayer is a standing monument of Christ's affection to the church; it did not pass away with the external sound, or as soon as Christ ascended into heaven, and sat at the right hand of the Father; it retaineth a perpetual efficacy; the virtue remaineth, though the words be over. As the word of creation hath retained its vigour these five or six thousand years: 'Increase and multiply, and let the earth bring forth after its kind;' so the voice of this turtle is ever heard, and Christ's prayers retain their vigour and force, as if but newly spoken.

In this prayer he mentions all blessings and privileges necessary for the church. He prayeth for himself, for the apostles, for all believers. He beginneth with his own glorification, as the foundation; and goeth on to seek the welfare of the apostles, as the means; and then the comfort of believers, as the fruit of his administrations in the world. Christ's merit, the apostles' word, the believers' comfort, are three things of the highest consideration in religion. I shall open these in the order and method in which they are laid down.

In the first verse we have :—

1. The preface to the whole prayer, *these things said Jesus,* &c.

2. Christ's free request, *glorify thy Son;* which is backed with reasons taken from—

[1.] His special relation, *Father,* and *thy Son.*

[2.] His present necessity, *the hour is come.*

[3.] The aim of his request, *that thy Son also may glorify thee.*

I shall go over the phrases as they are offered in the order of the words.

'These things spake Jesus;' that is, when he had spoken these things. This clause serveth—

1. To show the order of the history; his prayer followed his farewell sermon.

2. The suitableness of his prayers to the sermon. The points there enforced are here commended to God in prayer. It were easy to suit the requests to the consolations and instructions of that sermon. From hence—

[1.] Observe how fitly Christ dischargeth the office of a mediator. The office of a mediator, or day's-man, is 'to lay his hand upon both,' Job ix. 33; to treat and deal with both parties. Hitherto Christ hath dealt with men in the name of God, opening his counsel to us; now he dealeth with God in the name of men, opening our case to him. As Moses, the typical mediator, was to speak to God, Exod. xix. 19, and from God, Exod. xx. 19, so did our Lord speak from God and to God. He still performeth the same work and office. He speaketh to us in the word, and for us in prayer. The word never works till we hear Christ speaking in it: 2 Cor. xiii. 3, 'Since ye seek a proof of Christ speaking in me;' and our prayers are not accepted, but by virtue of Christ's intercession. Those that made their addresses to King Admetus, brought the prince with them in their arms; or as Joseph charged his brethren that they should not see his face unless they brought Benjamin with them, their brother; we cannot see God's face unless we bring our elder brother with us. Acts xii. 20, when Herod was displeased with the men of Tyre, they made Blastus, the king's chamberlain, their friend. It is good to have a favourite in heaven. Among all the favourites, none so acceptable as Christ; get him to make intercession for you. Out of the whole, learn to see Christ in the word, to use Christ in prayer; he is the golden pipe by which our prayers ascend, and the influences of heaven are conveyed to us: 1 Cor. viii. 6, 'One Lord, Jesus Christ, by whom are all things, and we by him.' All things come from God to us through Christ.

[2.] Observe Christ's order and method. From preaching he descendeth to prayer; the word worketh not without the divine grace. We may open the word, but God must open the understanding, Luke xxiv. 28, with 45. Christ himself, you see, sealeth his doctrine with the seal of prayer. Moral suasion worketh not without a divine and real efficacy. The apostles said, Acts vi. 4, 'We will give ourselves continually to prayer, and the ministry of the word.' When God hath spoken to us, we must speak to God again. Prayer is the best key to open the heart, because it first openeth heaven. Those that hear a sermon, and do not pray for a blessing, see nothing of God in his ordinances, nothing but what is of man's oratory and argument. Efficacy is quite another thing, and when God speaketh in his word with

Samuel, they think it is Eli. It reproveth them that, when the sermon is ended, go out, and turn their backs upon prayer ; this is to neglect Christ's method. And it presseth you still to help on the word by your prayers: Rom. xv. 30, 'I beseech you, brethren, for the Lord Jesus Christ's sake, and for the love of the Spirit, that ye strive together with me in your prayers.' If you would have Christ's glory and the Spirit's efficacy promoted, you must take this course.

[3.] Observe the industry and diligence of the Lord Jesus in holy things. He letteth no time pass without some saving work ; from doctrine he turneth himself to prayer. He began with the supper, and goeth on with discourse, and finisheth all with prayer. It upbraideth us that are soon weary of holy things. We are like foolish birds that leave the nest, and are often straggling, and let the eggs cool before they are hatched. Our religion cometh by flashes, which are never perfected and ripened. Now especially should we imitate Christ upon solemn days of worship ; as the Lord's-day, our whole time should be parted into meditation and prayer and conference. And yet more especially after the Lord's supper we should continue the devotion, and make the whole day a post-communion, as civet-boxes retain their scent when the civet is taken out ; and when the act is over, our thoughts and discourse and actions should still savour of the solemnity. Certainly it is an argument of much weakness to be all for flashes and sudden starts. If we would refresh ourselves with change, it should be with change of exercise, and not of affection. If it seem irksome, consider, it is more easy to persevere in a heavenly frame than to begin again ; and when the heart is warm, we should take heed we do not lose the present advantage. A bell is kept up with less difficulty than raised ; and when a horse is warm in his gears he continues his journey with more ease than if he should stand still a while and grow stiff. If we yield to weariness, how shall we hope to raise the heart again, and to get it to this advantage ? Corruption doth but cheat thee if thou thinkest to get a fresh start by intermission. As I said before, there is refreshment in change of exercise ; and when one teat is drawn dry, we may, as the lamb, suck another that will yield new supply and sweetness.

'And lift up his eyes to heaven.'—The scripture taketh notice of the gesture. Christ's gestures are notable, because real significations of the motions of his heart. In the garden, when he began his passion, he fell on his face and prayed, Mat. xxvi. 39 ; but here he lifted up his eyes. When he travailed under the greatness of our sins, his posture is humble ; but now, when he is treating with God for our mercies, he useth a gesture that implieth a more elevated and generous confidence. Gestures, being actions suited to the affections, are significant, and imply the dispositions of the heart. Let us see what may be collected out of this gesture, lifting the eyes to heaven.

1. The raising of the heart to God in prayer. Prayer is ἀνάβασις τοῦ νοῦ πρὸς τόν Θεόν, the ascension or elevation of the heart to God, the motion of the body suiting with that of the soul ; so David expresseth it, Ps. xxv. 1, 'I lift my heart to thee.' When you pray, know what is your work. If you would converse with God, you need not change place, but raise the affection. God boweth the heavens, and you lift up the heart ; it is not the lifting up the voice, but of the

spirit. The lifting up of the voice, or of the eye are good, as outward significations, but the chief work is to lift up the heart; the understanding in raised thoughts of God, the affections by strong operations of desire and love. Usually our hearts are heavy, and sink as lead within us; it is a work of difficulty to raise them. We must pull up the weights, προσκαρτεροῦντες τῇ προσευχῇ, 'continuing in prayer,' Acts i. 14. As Moses his hands easily fell and sunk, so do our hearts, Exod. xvii. There are plummets and weights of sin hang upon us, which must be cut off if we intend to get up the heart in prayer.

2. Spiritual reverence of God: 'The heavens are his throne and dwelling-place,' Ps. ciii. 19. There his majesty and power shineth forth, there we behold his majesty, in that sublime and stately fabric. Earthly kings, that their majesty may appear the greater to their subjects, have their thrones exalted, and made of precious matter, with cunning and curious artifice. But what are these to that sublime and admirable fabric of the heavens? The very sight of the heavens show how excellent God is. So that looking up to heaven noteth the raising the heart in the reverent consideration of God's majesty and excellency. We may come with hope; we speak to our Father: but we must speak with reverence; we speak to our Father in heaven. When we lift up our eyes, and look upon that stately fabric, the awe of God should fall upon us. We are poor worms crawling at God's footstool. By looking up to heaven we do most seriously set God before us. So when Solomon speaketh against the slightness of our addresses to God, he propoundeth this remedy, Eccles. v. 2, 'Be not rash with thy mouth, and let not thine heart be hasty to utter anything before God; for God is in heaven, and thou upon earth.' There is a distance; there God appeareth in his royalty. We tremble to come before the thrones of earthly princes; they are but thy fellow clay: how far do the stars of heaven excel their richest jewels! What is all their state to the pure matter of the heavens, to that blaze of light wherewith he is clothed? Ps. civ. 2, 'Who coverest thyself with light as with a garment, who stretchest out the heavens like a curtain.' What are the coaches of princes to the chariots of the clouds, and wings of the wind, and that majesty and state that God keepeth in the heavens?

3. It noteth confidence in God, or a disclaiming of all sublunary confidence. The godly, in all their prayers and cries, look up unto the heavens, to note their confidence in God, and not in fleshly aids; as Ps. cxxi. 1, 'I will lift up mine eyes unto the hills, from whence cometh my help;' meaning, his relief and deliverance should come from God alone. A christian looketh round about him, and seeth no ground of help but in the tops of the hills. So Ps. cxxiii. 1, 'Unto thee I lift up mine eyes, O thou that dwellest in the heavens.' The thrones of princes are places slippery and unsafe; but our supports are out of gunshot: Lam. iii. 41, 'Let us lift up our heart with our hands unto God in the heavens.' We must not rest upon anything in the world. He that made the heavens can accomplish our desires. The constant course of the heavens noteth God's faithfulness. A man may foresee some natural events some hundred years before. The glorious fabric of the heavens is a monument of his power.

4. To show that their hearts are taken off from the world, and from

carnal desires. Christ's eyes were to heaven; there his Father was : and christians lift up their eyes to heaven, because they mainly 'seek those things that are above,' where God's throne is, and 'where Christ is now sitting at his right hand,' Col. iii. 1. It is for beasts to grovel and look downward. Our home is above, in those upper regions; there is our Christ, our pure and sweet companions. Their heart cannot be severed from their head. When we expect one, we turn our eyes that way ; as the wife looks towards the seas when she expects her husband's return. It doth them good to look towards these visible heavens, remembering that one day they shall have a place of rest there. God hath fixed his throne, and Christ hath removed his body out of the world, that we may look upward. These things from the gesture.

'And said.'—The word noteth a vocal expression of the prayer. Moses cried, Exod. xiv. 15, which noteth an inward fervency. There are no words mentioned, but Christ ' said ; ' that is, with an audible voice.

I shall from this word inquire—(1.) Why he prayed; (2.) Why he pronounced his prayers in the hearing of the apostles.

First, Why he prayed ; for it seems strange that Christ should be brought upon his knees, and that he, who was the express image of his Father's glory, should need the comfort of prayer, and that the heir of heaven, who hath the key of David, and openeth and no man shutteth, should stand knocking at the Father's door. I answer—

1. This was the agreement between God and him, that he was first to establish a right, and then to sue it out in court: Ps. ii. 8, ' Ask of me, and I will give thee the heathen for thine inheritance, and the utmost parts of the earth for thy possession.' This prayer is nothing else but Christ presenting his merits before the tribunal of God. In the whole transaction of man's salvation, God the Father would sustain the person of the ruler and governor of the world ; and Christ was to come and make his plea before him, to give an account of his work, and to sue out his own right, and the right of his members. Oh ! wonder at the business of our salvation, the love of God, the condescension of Christ, when he took the quality of our surety upon him. He is to make a formal process, to plead his own merits and our interest ; for so he is less than the Father as mediator : ' My Father is greater than I.' Not only as man, but as mediator, Christ sustained a lesser place.

2. That we might have a copy of his intercession. Christ is good at interceding ; he gave the world a taste in his last prayer. It is a pledge of those continual groans which, as a mediator of the church, he putteth up for us in heaven. We have an excellent advocate : 1 John ii. 2, ' If any man sin, we have an advocate with the Father, Jesus Christ the righteous.' When thou art in danger of temptation, he saith, ' They are in the world; keep them from the evil of the world.' When thou art practising holinesss, Christ speaketh a good word of thee behind thy back: 'Father, they keep thy word.' He is a good shepherd, that knoweth the state of his flock, and readily giveth an account to the Father.

3. That these prayers might be a constant fountain and foundation of spiritual blessings. Christ's prayers are as good as so many pro-

mises; for he is always heard, John xi. 42. In this prayer, Christ speaketh as God-man. There is not any ἐρωτῶ, I ask, but θέλω, I will. Ver. 24, 'Father, I will that they also be with me where I am.' A word, not of request, but of authority. The divine nature giveth a force and efficacy to these prayers. When he prayeth, whole Christ prayeth, God-man; and as his passion received efficacy from his godhead, so did his prayers: Acts xx. 28, 'Feed the church of God, which he hath purchased with his own blood.' As it was the blood of God, so it is the prayer of God. The godhead is interested in all these actions; it is the prayer of the Son of God made flesh. The things which he asketh belong to the human nature, yet he prayeth as God. He that heareth with the Father, will be heard by the Father. Christ's prayer is not like the prayers of other holy men recorded in scripture for a form and pattern, but as a fountain of comfort and blessing. This should beget a confidence in the accomplishment of all these promises, the safety of the elect, the success of the word, the unity of the church, and the possession of glory.

4. To commend the duty of prayer. He commanded it before, and commended it by promise: John xiv. 13, 14, 'Whatsoever ye shall ask of the Father in my name, that will I do, that the Father may be glorified in the Son. If ye shall ask anything in my name, I will do it;' John xv. 16, 'That whatsoever ye shall ask of the Father in my name, he may give it you.' Now, to precept and promise he would add his own example. Certainly there are none above ordinances, if Christ the eternal Son of God was not. If Christ, who was of the same majesty and power with his Father, did pray so earnestly and seriously, when, in the light of omnisciency, he saw the fruit of his passion, how much more are prayers necessary for us, under such infirmity of flesh to which we are subject, and such rage of Satan and the world! In all cases we must use this remedy. They that are above prayer are beyond religion. In his greatest works Christ despised not this remedy. Christ knew his own deliverance, and was sure of it; yet he will not have it but by prayer. He had an eternal right to heaven and glory, and a new right by purchase, yet he would have his charter confirmed by prayer. And so, though we have assurance of mercy, we must take this course to get it accomplished; though we have large possessions and a liberal supply, when it is at the table we must receive it as a boon from grace: 'Give us this day our daily bread.' If for no other reason, prayer is necessary for submission to God, and that we may renew the sense of that tenure by which we hold a charter of grace, that by asking we may still take it out of free grace's hands. Christ had a right, yet, because of that mixture of grace with justice in all divine dispensations, he is to ask.

5. That our prayers might be effectual. Christ's prayer is large and comprehensive. We can mention nothing but he has begged it already *in terminis*, or by consequence. The prayers of the saints have their efficacy, but not from any virtue in them, but by Christ's merits, by virtue of his prayers. Now Christ hath consecrated the way, it is like to be successful; no prayer can miscarry. God may cast out the dross, but he will be sure to receive the prayer. Now he doth not refuse your money, but rubbeth off the filth of it. It is very

notable that Christ consecrated all ordinances, and made them successful by his own obedience.   Baptism; he made the waters of baptism salutary.   Hearing; Christ was one of John's auditors: 'Behold the Lamb of God,' John i. 29.   Singing, prayer, receiving the supper; he loveth the society, ever since he himself was a communicant: Mat. xxvi. 29, 'I will not drink henceforth of the fruit of this vine, until the day when I drink it new with you in my Father's kingdom.' Christ doth but act over that ordinance in heaven.   So for prayer.

Secondly, The next thing is why Christ spake aloud in prayer.

I answer—He might have prayed in silence, but he would be our advocate, but so that he might be our teacher.   When he prayed for us, he prayed publicly and with a loud voice, for our comfort and instruction, and to give vent to the strength of his affection by leaving this monument in the church: ver. 13, ' These things I speak in the world, that they may have my joy fulfilled in themselves;' that in all trials and afflictions we might draw consolation from the matter of this prayer.   You may observe hence, that it is of advantage to use vocal prayer, not only in public, when we may quicken others, as one bird setting all the rest a-chirping, and we profess we are not ashamed of God or his worship, but in private also.   God made body and soul, and will be served by both.   Words are as giving vent to, or as the broaching of, a full vessel.   Strong affections cannot be confined to thoughts: Ps. xxxix. 2, 3, ' My heart was hot within me; while I was musing, the fire burned; then spake I with my tongue.'   Musing makes the fire to burn.   There is a continual prayer by ejaculations' and thoughts; but words become solemn and stated times of duty.   Words are a boundary to the mind, and fix it more than thoughts, which are usually light and skipping.   The mind may wander, but words are as a trumpet to summon them again into the presence of God.   Our roving madness will be sooner discerned in words than in thoughts. When a word is lost or misplaced, we are more ashamed; and by words, a dull sluggish heart is sometimes quickened and awakened. It is good to use this help.

Now I come to the prayer itself.

' Father.'—It is a word of confidence and sweet relation, in which there is much of argument, in that Christ, as God's only Son, speaketh to his own Father: ' Father, glorify thy Son.'   A father is wont to be delighted with the glory and honour of a son, as the mother of Zebedee's children sought their preferment, Mat. xx. 20.   It is good to observe that Christ doth not say, ' Our Father,' as involving our interest with his, because it is of a distinct kind.   Christ would observe the distinction between us and himself: he is a Son that is equal with the Father, co-eternal with his Father; but we are adopted sons, made so.   When he speaketh to his disciples, he saith not, Our heavenly Father, but ' Your heavenly Father knoweth that ye have need of all these things,' Mat. vi. 32; and John xx. 17, ' I ascend unto my Father and your Father, and to my God and your God;' clearly distinguishing his own interest from ours.   And mark, Christ useth the argument of son and father to show that he was not therefore glorified because a son, but therefore a son because glorified. We may note hence—

1. That it is very sweet and comfortable in prayer when we can come and call God Father. It is a word of affection, reverence, and confidence; in all which the excellency of prayer consisteth. So Christ in all his addresses: 'Father, if it be possible, let this cup pass from me,' Mat. xxvi. 39. So also all his prayers are bottomed on this relation; ver. 5, 'And now, O Father, glorify thou me with thine own self;' Mat. xi. 25, 'I thank thee, O Father, Lord of heaven and earth,' &c. He hath taught us the same, to pray, 'Our Father which art in heaven,' Mat. vi. 9. The great work of the Spirit is to help us to speak thus to God; not with lips that feign, but from our hearts: Rom. viii. 15, 'Ye have received the spirit of adoption, whereby we cry, Abba, Father.' We confine the Spirit's assistance to earnest tendencies and vigorous motions; the main work is, to help us to cry, Father, with a proper and genuine confidence. Now all cannot do this: a wicked man cannot say safely to God, My Father. Whosoever claims kindred of God, while he is unjust and filthy, it is not a prayer, but a contumely and slander : 'He that sanctifieth, and those that are sanctified, are all of one; for which cause he is not ashamed to call them brethren,' Heb. ii. 11. Christ counteth none to be of his kindred but the regenerate. Pagans are strangers, and carnal men in the church are bastards; they had need study holiness that would claim kindred of Christ. Consider then what claim and interest have you in God ? It is sad if we can only come as creatures, cry as ravens for food, out of a general title to his providence, or to cry, Father, and lie; to take his name in vain. It is sweeter to speak to God as a son than as a creature ; 'Lord, Lord,' is not half so sweet as, 'Our Father.' This is a sweet invitation to prayer : Mat. vii. 9, 'What man of you, who if his son ask bread, will he give him a stone?' Ver. 11, 'If ye then, that are evil, know how to give good gifts to your children, how much more will your heavenly Father give good things to them that ask him ?' It is a consolation in prayer: Gal. iv. 6, 'Because ye are sons, he hath sent forth the Spirit of his Son into your hearts, crying, Abba, Father.' It is a ground of hope and expectation after prayer : 'Ye have received the spirit of adoption, to call God, Father.'

2. Christ was about to suffer bitter things from the hand of God, and yet he calleth him Father. In afflictions, we must still look upon God as a Father, and behave ourselves as children. Christ felt him a judge, yet counts him a father. God, as a judge, was now about to lay on him the sufferings of all the elect, yet Christ calls him Father, to declare his obedience and trust. The hour was come in which the whole weight of God's displeasure was to be laid upon him; yet, in this relative term, he acknowledgeth his Father's love, and manifesteth his own obedience. We should do so in all our afflictions :—(1.) Maintain the comfort of adoption; (2.) Behave ourselves as children.

1. Maintain the comfort of adoption. It is the folly of the children of God to question his love because of the greatness of their afflictions, as if their interest did change with their condition, and God were not the God of the valleys as well as the God of the hills. We have more cause to discern love than to question it. Bastards are left to a looser discipline : Heb. xii. 8, 'If ye are without chastisement, whereof all are partakers, then are ye bastards and not sons.' To be exempted

from the cross is to be put out of the roll of children. The bramble of the wilderness is suffered to grow wild, but the vine is pruned. The stones that are designed for a noble structure or building are hewed and squared when others lie by neglected.

2. Behave ourselves as children, with patience and hope.

[1.] With a submissive patience. 'Father' is a word that implieth authority and love and care, all which are arguments of patience. Fathers have a natural right to rule; we must take it quietly and patiently at their hands. Isaac yielded to his father when he went to be sacrificed. It is said, Gen. xxii. 8, 'They both went together;' which noteth his quiet submission. But fatherly acts are not only managed with authority, but with love and care. Slaves may be corrected out of cruelty and hatred by their masters, but fathers do not deal so with children: Heb. xii. 9, 10, 'Furthermore, we have had fathers of our flesh which corrected us, and we gave them reverence; shall we not much rather be in subjection to the Father of spirits, and live? For they verily for a few days chastened us after their own pleasure; but he for our profit, that we might be partakers of his holiness.' The apostle argueth *a minori ad majus*. None can be such a father as the Lord, so wise as he, so loving as he. God putteth on all relations: he hath the bowels of a mother, the wisdom of a father. He is a mother for tenderness of love: Isa. xlix. 15, 'Can a woman forget her sucking child, that she should not have compassion on the son of her womb? Yea, they may forget, yet will I not forget thee.' A father for wisdom and care: Mat. vi. 31, 32, 'Take no thought, saying, What shall we eat? &c., for your heavenly Father knoweth that you have need of all these things.' Earthly parents sometimes chastise their children out of mere passion, at least there is some mixture of corruption; but the Lord's dispensations are managed with much love and judgment. Therefore say, as Christ, John xviii. 11, 'The cup which my Father hath given me, shall I not drink of it?' It is a bitter cup, but it cometh from the hand of a father: our Father gave it us, and our elder brother began it to us. We should love the cup the better ever since Christ's lips touched it.

[2.] With hope. When we are perplexed, we should not be in despair, but sustain ourselves under our great hopes: 1 John iii. 2, 'Now we are the sons of God, but it doth not yet appear what we shall be.' We have the right of children, though afflicted; our estate and patrimony is in the heavens. An heir in his nonage is under tutors and governors; he is born to a great possession, but kept under a severe discipline.

The hour is come, $\dot{\eta}$ $\ddot{\omega}\rho\alpha$, that hour.

1. That hour which was defined in God's decree, set down and appointed by the council of the Trinity; not by fate, or any necessity of the stars, but by God's wise providence and ordination. No man could take Christ till his hour was come: John vii. 30, 'Then they sought to take him; but no man laid hands on him, because his hour was not yet come.' But when this hour was come, the Son of God was brought under the power of men, and liable to the assaults of devils. Therefore he saith, Luke xxii. 53, 'This is your hour, and the power of darkness. No calamity can touch us without God's will.

The hour, the measure, all the circumstances of sufferings, fall under the ordination of God. It is not only a general ordinance that we shall suffer affliction; the apostle mentioneth that, 1 Thes. iii. 3, 'Let no man be moved by this affliction; for yourselves know that you were thereunto appointed.' It is the ordinance of God that the way to heaven should lie through a howling wilderness. All the saints in heaven knew no other road; afflictions seem one of the waymarks. But we speak now of another appointment, of determining all the circumstances of the affliction, the time, the measure, the instruments. It is the comfort of a christian that nothing can befall him but what his Father wills: 'A sparrow cannot fall to the ground without our heavenly Father,' Mat. x. 29. The wise Lord hath brewed our cup, and moulded and shaped every cross. All the ounces of gall and wormwood are weighed out by a wise decree, and our cup is tempered by God's own hand. We storm many times because of such and such accidents, and circumstances of the cross, as if we would have God ask our vote and advice, and as if our opinion were a better balance wherein to weigh things than divine providence. Providence reacheth to every particular accident. Your doom was long since written: such a vessel of mercy shall be thus and thus broached and pierced; every wound and sorrow is numbered.

2. That hour which was determined and foretold in the prophecies. God doth all things in fit seasons; he hath his days and hours. Daniel 'understood by books the number of the years,' Dan. ix. 2; Hab. ii. 3, 'The vision is for an appointed time.' It easeth the heart of much distraction when we consider there is a period fixed. There is a clock with which providence keepeth time and pace, and God himself setteth it. ' It is good for us to wait the Lord's leisure: ' God himself waiteth as well as we: Isa. xxx. 18, ' He waiteth that he may be gracious.' He letteth the course of causes run on till the fit hour and moment of execution be come, when he may discover himself with most advantage to his glory and the comfort of his servants; and God waiteth with as much earnestness as you do (I speak after the manner of men): Isa. xvi. 14, ' But now hath the Lord spoken, saying, Within three years, as the years of a hireling, and the glory of Moab shall be contemned,' &c.; as the hireling waiteth for the time of his freedom, and when he is to receive his wages. Moab was a bitter enemy. Therefore let us wait: John viii. 7, ' Your times are always ready, but my time is not yet come.' We draw draughts of providence with the pencil of fancy, and then confine God to the circle of our own thoughts, as if he must be always ready at our hours.

3. The hour is come; the sufferings of God's people are very short. To our sense and feeling they seem long, because carnal affections are soon tired; but the word doth not reckon by centuries and years, but moments: Ps. xxx. 5, ' Weeping may endure for a night, but joy cometh in the morning.' All temporal accidents are nothing compared to eternity. The sorrows of our whole life are but one night's darkness: ' This light affliction, that is but for a moment,' saith the apostle, 2 Cor. iv. 17. Set time against eternity, and we shall want words to declare the shortness of it. Our hour will be soon ended. Wait a while and we shall be beyond fears. The martyrs in heaven

do not think of flames, and wounds and saws; these were the sufferings of a moment: John xvi. 21, 'A woman when she is in travail hath sorrow, because her hour is come: but as soon as she is delivered of the child, she remembereth no more the anguish, for joy that a man is born into the world;' John xvi. 16, 'A little while, and ye shall not see me; and again, a little while, and ye shall see me.' To faith, the time between Christ's departure and his second coming is but as the time between his death and resurrection; for of that Christ also speaketh, as is clear by the subsequent context. We measure all by sense, and therefore cry, How long, how long; as men in pain will count minutes; but look to the endless glory within the veil, and it is nothing. We should especially take this comfort to ourselves in sickness and death; it is but an hour. Wink and thou shalt be in heaven, said a martyr.

4. The hour is come, saith Christ, and therefore prayeth. When the sad hour is come, the only remedy is prayer. We should not despond, but meet sorrows with a generous confidence. Now the only way is to pray. If we cannot look for a deliverance, we may pray for a mitigation, for shortening affliction: Mat. xxiv. 20, 'Pray that your flight be not in the winter, nor on the Sabbath-day,' when it may be tedious to body or soul. Pray that you may glorify God in sufferings, as Christ sueth out support in this request. Usually when evils are unavoidable we give over all addresses; yet our condition is capable of mercy. If the hour be come, beg that a spirit of glory may rest upon you.

5. Christ knew his hour. There was no traitor by; Judas was not present; the soldiers were not come to apprehend him; all was yet in the dark, and kept secret in the bosom of the priests and elders. It confirmeth us in the belief of the omnisciency of Christ. He knew the moment of his suffering before there was any appearance of it: 'All things are open and naked before him with whom we have to do;' and he 'seeth our thoughts afar off.'

6. Christ knew the hour was come, yet he seeketh not a hiding-place, or to avoid the storm by flight. How many natural and supernatural ways had Christ to escape! He could have smitten them with a beam of majesty. It noteth the willingness of Christ to suffer all this trouble and danger for our sakes as our conqueror. When Christ was to grapple with our enemies, he did not decline the battle, but with courage and confidence entered into the lists with death and hell. As our sacrifice, he went willingly to the altar, not like a swine, but like a sheep; not with howling and reluctancy, but with a ready patience.

7. The act of Christ's death was quickly over; it was but a short space of time; he calleth it an hour: Ps. cx. 7, *de torrente bibet*, 'He shall drink of the brook in the way;' a draught of death: 'He tasted death for every one,' Heb. ii. 9. At one draught he drunk hell dry as to the elect.

Object. But we were to suffer eternally, and Christ was to bear our sorrows.

I answer—Though Christ paid the same debt, yet, through the excellency of his person, it was done in a shorter time. A payment in gold is the same sum with a payment in silver or brass; only, through the excellency of the metal, it taketh up less room.

8. *The hour is come.* By way of argument, he showeth the occasion of his prayer in this hour of sadness and ignominy. I am to be betrayed, condemned, buffeted, crucified; my majesty will be obscured, and my death, like a veil, drawn upon my glory: now, glorify me in this hour. Indeed, thus it was in all Christ's weakness and abasement, there was some adjunct of glory. In his incarnation, he is thrust out into a manger, a place for horses; but there he is worshipped. A star in heaven is hung up for a sign of that inn where Christ lay; a new bonfire to welcome that great, but poor prince, into the world. He is apprehended by the soldiers, but they are driven back, and twice checked in their rude attempt by the beams and emissions of his divine glory. He is tempted by the devil in the wilderness, but angels are sent to minister to him. He had not wherewith to pay tribute to Cæsar, but the sea payeth tribute to him, and a fish bringeth the money. When he was crucified and scoffed at, heaven itself becometh a mourner, and puts on a veil of darkness; the high priest did not rend his clothes, but the veil of the temple was rent in twain, from the top to the bottom. One thief scoffed him, but another proclaimed him king. When man denied him, the creatures preached up his glory. Thus Christ, in the saddest hour, is still glorified. And thus it is with the children of God. Afflictions on wicked men are evil, and all evil; but to the saints, a mixed dispensation: sweet experiences they have in the midst of sad calamities, and mercy in the midst of wrath.

'Glorify thy Son.'—This is the request itself: what is the meaning of it? Origen understandeth it of the very ignominy of the cross itself, which was to Christ a glory; *Gloria salvatoris, patibulum triumphantis.* The cross was not a gibbet, but a throne of honour; and Calvary to Christ was as glorious as Olivet. It is expressed by lifting up. But certainly this cannot be intended here, because it was the lowest act of his humiliation and abasement. This is made the motive and reason of his request: 'The hour is come,' by which, as we have seen, he intendeth that sad ignominious hour. In short, it is meant either of God's glorifying him *in* his sufferings, or God's glorifying him *after* his sufferings; as will appear by the sequel and two parallel places.

1. Glory in his sufferings. It is said, John xiii. 31, 32, 'Therefore when he was gone out, Jesus said, Now is the Son of man glorified, and God is glorified in him. If God be glorified in him, God shall also glorify him in himself, and shall straightway glorify him.' The meaning is, now he is to show himself a glorious Saviour, by which God shall also be glorified, for which he will uphold and reward him. So, 'Glorify thy Son;' he intendeth those passages by which his glory is manifested to the world. And so he intends—

[1.] Miracles; while Christ suffered, the frame of nature seemed to be out of course: Mat. xxvii. 51, 'The veil of the temple was rent in twain, from the top to the bottom; and the earth did quake, and the rocks rent;' and ver. 54, 'When the centurion, and they that were with him, saw these things, they feared greatly, saying, Truly this was the Son of God.'

[2.] Support and strength. This was Christ's last combat, and he was to discover the strength and the power of the Godhead. Now he prayeth for those tokens and significations of the divine power in his death, to undeceive the world, and that the disciples might receive no scandal by his cross.

2. Glory after death; so it is said, John vii. 39, 'That the Spirit was not yet given, because Christ was not yet glorified.' Till his resurrection and ascension into heaven, he was not inaugurated into the headship of the church, and gave not out those royal largesses and gifts of the Spirit. So that by this prayer Christ intendeth the resurrection and all the consequents of it. ⎰ His resurrection, by which his divinity was declared: Rom. i. 4, 'And declared to be the Son of God, with power, according to the spirit of holiness, by the resurrection from the dead.' His ascension and invisible triumph: Col. ii. 15, 'Having spoiled principalities and powers, he made a show of them openly, triumphing over them in it;' Eph. iv. 8, 'When he ascended on high, he led captivity captive, and gave gifts unto men.' The reception of his humanity to heaven, and his sitting down at the right hand of God: Phil. ii. 9–11, 'Wherefore God also hath highly exalted him, and given him a name above every name; that at the name of Jesus every knee should bow, of things in heaven, and things in earth, and things under the earth: and that every tongue should confess that Jesus Christ is Lord, to the glory of God the Father.' His inauguration into the throne, and authority over all things. The preaching of the gospel in his name, together with the success of it: Isa. lv. 4, 5, 'Behold, I have given him for a witness to the people, a leader and commander to the people. Behold, thou shalt call a nation that thou knewest not; and nations that know not thee, shall run unto thee; because of the Lord thy God, and for the Holy One of Israel; for he hath glorified thee.' His return at the day of judgment, with power and great glory. The petition must be explained according to the event of all the glory that God put upon Christ after his passion. The meaning of the whole is, Hitherto I have laid aside my glory, and now lay down my life; sustain me by thine arm, that I may overcome death; and raise me again with triumph and honour, that I may go into glory, leading captivity captive, and receive the principality; that by the resurrection, publication of the gospel, and last judgment, the glory of my divinity may be known and acknowledged.

But how doth Christ pray, 'Glorify me,' when he saith elsewhere, John viii. 5, 'I seek not my own glory'?

I answer—Christ speaketh there of himself in the judgment of his adversaries, who thought him a mere man, and showeth that he came not as an impostor, to seek himself. God would well enough provide for his glory and esteem. There he disclaimeth all particular private aims, affections, and attempts; here he sueth out his right according to his Father's promise.

Observe hence—

1. Christ saith, 'The hour is come;' and then, 'Father, glorify me.' The true remedy of tribulation is to look to the succeeding glory, and to counterbalance future dangers with present hopes. In this prayer Christ reviveth the grounds of confidence. One is, 'Father, glorify

me.' This was comfort against that sad hour; and so it must be our course 'not to look to things which are seen, but to things that are not seen,' 2 Cor. iv. 17, to defeat sense by faith. When the mind is in heaven, it is fortified against the pains which the body feeleth on earth. Strong affections give us a kind of dedolency; a man will venture a knock that is in reach of a crown, 1 Tim. iv. 8. It is the folly of christians to let fancy work altogether upon present discouragements. Faith should be fixed in the contemplation of future hopes. It is a sad hour, but there is glory in the issue and close.

2. Observe again, first, Christ had his hour; then he saith, 'Glorify me.' Luke xxiv. 26, 'Ought not Christ to suffer, and then to enter into his glory?' Shame, sorrow, and death is the roadway to glory, joy, and life; the captain of our salvation was thus made perfect, Heb. ii. 10; and all the followers of the Lamb are brought in by that method. It is the folly of some that think to be in heaven before they have done anything for God's glory upon .earth. You would invert the method and stated course of heaven. None is crowned except he strive lawfully, 2 Tim. ii. 5, 6: and ver. 11, 12, 'It is a faithful saying; for if we be dead with him, we shall also live with him; if we suffer, we shall also reign with him.' It hath the seal of a constant dispensation, it is a faithful saying. All the promises run, 'To him that overcometh.' We must have communion with Christ in all estates: Rom. viii. 17, 'If so be that ye suffer with him, that ye may be also glorified together.' It is a necessary condition: 'We are heirs, if so be that we suffer with him,' &c. We are too delicate; we would have our path strewed with roses, and do not like this discipline. Abel signifies mourning, and Stephen a crown, they were the first martyrs of either testament. If you want afflictions, you want one of the necessary waymarks to heaven.

3. 'Glorify me.' Christ seeketh not the empty things of this world, but to be glorified with the Father. We want some spiritual ambition, and are too low and grovelling in our desires and hopes: 'If you be risen with Christ, seek those things that are above, where Christ sitteth at the right hand of God,' Col. iii. 1. It is no treason to aspire to the heavenly kingdom: Mat. vi. 33, 'Seek first the kingdom of God, and the righteousness thereof;' and to seek a place on Christ's own throne. Neither is it any culpable self-seeking to seek self in God: John v. 44, 'How can ye believe, that receive honour one of another, and seek not the honour that cometh from God alone?' John xii. 43 · They 'loved the praise of men more than the praise of God.' Here we may seek our own honour and glory without a crime. Oh! behold the liberality and indulgence of grace! God hath set no stint to our spiritual desires; we may seek not only grace, but glory.

4. Christ himself prayeth to be glorified; it noteth the truth of his abasement. He is the Lord of glory, 1 Cor. ii. 8, and had a natural and eternal right: 'He thought it no robbery to be equal with God;' and yet Christ himself is now upon his knees. If he had said, Let them be glorified, that had been much, that he would open his mouth to plead for sinners; but he saith, 'Glorify me,' or 'Glorify thy Son;' which is a strange condescension, that he that had the key of David should now be knocking at the Father's gate, and receive his own

heaven by gift and entreaty.   He might take, without robbery, glory as his due; yet, as our mediator, he is to ask.   When he took our nature, he brought himself under the engagement of our duty.

5. Christ asketh what he knew would be given.   So John viii. 50, ' I seek not my own glory ; there is one that seeketh and judgeth.'   The Father was zealous for the Son's glory ; there was an oracle from heaven to assure him of it : John xii. 28, ' Father, glorify thy name. Then came there a voice from heaven, saying, I have both glorified it, and will glorify it again ; ' meaning, by strengthening him in the work of redemption.   And yet now again, ' Glorify thy Son, that he may glorify thee.'   Observe, providence doth not take away prayers.   We are to ask, though our heavenly Father knoweth we have need of these things, and we know God will give them to us : John xvi. 26, 27, ' At that day ye shall ask in my name ; I say not unto you, that I will pray the Father for you ; for the Father himself loveth you.'   The meaning is, though there be need of my great instance, and I need not tell you I will make intercession ; I pass by that now ; I only tell you of that free access you have to God, and his great affection to you ; yet still you must ask.   Assurance is a ground of the more earnest request. When Daniel understood by books the number of the years, then he was most earnest in prayer ; and when Elijah heard the sound of the rain, he prayed.   Prayer is to help on providences that are already in motion.

' That thy Son also may glorify thee.'—Here is another argument. It is usual in prayer to speak of ourselves in a third person ; so doth Christ here, ' That thy Son may glorify thee.'   This may be understood many ways ; partly as the glory of the Son is the glory of the Father ; partly by accomplishing God's work ; that I may destroy thy enemies, and save thy elect; partly by the preaching of the gospel in Christ's name, to the glory of God the Father.   He doth, as it were, say, I desire it for no other end but that I may bring honour to thee.

From this clause—

1. Observe, that God's glory is much advanced in Jesus Christ.   In the scriptures there is a draught of God ; as coin bears the image of Cæsar, but Cæsar's son is his lively resemblance.   Christ is the living Bible; we may read much of the glory of God in the face of Jesus Christ.   We shall study no other book when we come to heaven.   For the present, it is an advantage to study God in Jesus Christ.   The apostle hath an expression, 2 Cor. iv. 4, ' Lest the light of the glorious gospel of Christ, who is the image of God, should shine unto them.' Christ is the image of God, and the gospel is the picture of Christ, the picture which Christ himself hath presented to his bride.   There we see the majesty and excellency of his person ; and in Christ, of God. And ver. 6, the apostle saith, ' To give the light of the excellency of the knowledge of the glory of God, in the face of Jesus Christ.'   In Christ, we read God glorious ; in his word, miracles, personal excellencies, transfiguration, resurrection, we read much of God.   There we read his justice, that he would not forgive sins without a plenary satisfaction.   If Christ himself be the Redeemer, justice will not bate him one farthing.   His mercy ; he spared not his own Son.   What scanty low thoughts should we have of the divine mercy if we had not this

instance of Christ !   His truth in fulfilling of prophecies : Ps. xl. 7, 8, ' Then said I, Lo, I come ; in the volume of the book it is written of me, I delight to do thy will, O my God ; yea, thy law is within my heart.'   This was most difficult for God to grant, for us to believe ; yet rather than he would go back from his word, he would send his own Son to suffer death for a sinful world.   All things were to be accomplished, though it cost Christ his precious life.   God had never a greater gift, yet Christ came when he was promised : he will not stick at anything, that gave us his own Son.   His wisdom, in the wonderful contrivance of our salvation.   When we look to God's heaven, we see his wisdom ; but when we look on God's Son, we see the manifold wisdom of God, Eph. iii. 10.   The angels wonder at these dispensations to the church.   His power, in delivering Christ from death, and the glorious effects of his grace ; his majesty, in the transfiguration and ascension of Christ.   Oh ! then study Christ, that you may know God. There is the fairest transcript of the divine perfections ; the Father was never published to the world by anything so much as by the Son.

2. Observe, our respects to Christ must be so managed that the Father also may be glorified ; for upon these terms, and no other, will Christ be glorified : 2 Cor. i. 20, ' For all the promises in him are Yea, and in him Amen, to the glory of God by us ;'   Phil. ii. 10, 11, ' That at the name of Jesus every knee shall bow, and every tongue shall confess that Jesus Christ is Lord, to the glory of God the Father ;' John xiv. 13, ' Whatsoever ye shall ask in my name, that will I do, that the Father may be glorified in the Son.'   Look, as the Father will not be honoured without the Son : John v. 53, ' That all men should honour the Son, even as they honour the Father ; he that honoureth not the Son, honoureth not the Father that hath sent him ;' so neither will the Son be honoured without the Father.   It condemneth them who, out of a fond respect to Christ, neglect the Father.   As the former age carried all respect in the name of God Almighty, without any distinct reflection on God the Son, so many of late carry all things in the name of God the Son, that the adoration due to the other persons is forgotten.   The wind of error doth not always blow in one corner. When the heat of such a humour is spent, Christ will be as much vilified and debased.   Our hearts should not be frigidly and coldly affected to any of the divine persons.

3. Observe, it is the proper duty of sons to glorify their father : Mal. i. 6, ' If I be a father, where is mine honour ?'   Mat. v. 16, ' Let your light so shine before men, that others, seeing your good works, may glorify your Father which is in heaven.'

How must this be done ?

[1.] By reverent thoughts of his excellency, especially in worship ; then we honour him when we behave ourselves before him as before a great God ; this is to make him glorious in our own hearts, when we conceive of him as more excellent than all things.   Usually we have mean base thoughts, by which we straiten or pollute the divine excellency.

[2.] By serious acknowledgments give him glory : Rev. iv. 11, ' Thou art worthy, O Lord, to receive glory, and honour, and power ; for thou hast created all things, and for thy pleasure they are and were created.'

Now this is not in naked ascriptions of praise to him, prattling over words ; but when we confess all the glory we have above other men, in gifts or dignity, is given us of God, this is to make him the Father of glory : Eph. i. 17, 'That the God of our Lord Jesus Christ, the Father of glory, may give unto you the Spirit of wisdom and revelation, in the knowledge of him.'

[3.] When we make the advantage of his kingdom the end of all our actions : 1 Cor. x. 31, 'Whether ye eat or drink, or whatever you do, do all to the glory of God ;' Phil. i. 20, 'Christ shall be magnified in my body, whether it be by life or by death.' Christ had glorified him, yet he seeks now to do it more. Self will be mixing with our ends, but it must be beaten back. We differ little from beasts if we mind only our own conveniences.

[4.] By making this the aim of our prayers. We should desire glory and happiness upon no other terms : Eph. i. 6, 'To the praise of the glory of his grace, wherein he hath made us accepted in the beloved.' It is a mighty encouragement in prayer when we are sure to be heard : John xii. 28, 'Father, glorify thy name : then came there a voice from heaven, saying, I have both glorified it, and will glorify it again.' He begs that God would glorify his name in giving him the victory in this last combat. We ask of God for God : 'Those that honour me, I will honour them,' 1 Sam. ii. 30.

[5.] When we are content to be put to shame so God be honoured, to hazard all so we may glorify his name, though it be with the loss of life itself : Josh. vii. 19, 'My son, give, I pray thee, glory to the Lord God of Israel, and make confession unto him ;' Mal. ii. 2, 'If ye will not hear, and if ye will not lay it to heart, to give glory unto my name' (that is, by an ingenuous confession), 'I will even send a curse upon you.'

[6.] When you make others to glorify God : 2 Cor. ix. 13, 'They glorify God for your professed subjection unto the gospel of Christ.' Christians are to be holy, for Christ's honour lieth at stake.

[7.] When we can rejoice in God's glory, though advanced by others, be the instruments who they will ; as Paul did, Phil. i. 18, 'Notwithstanding every way, whether in pretence, or in truth, Christ is preached, and I herein do rejoice, yea, and will rejoice.'

[8.] When we are affected for God's dishonour, though done by others.

SERMON II.

As thou hast given him power over all flesh, that he should give eternal life to as many as thou hast given him.—JOHN XVII. 2.

HERE is the next reason of Christ's request ; the former was the glory of God, and here is another, the salvation of men. Unless the Father glorified him he could not accomplish the ends of his office, which was to glorify the Father in the salvation of man ; which could not be unless he were sustained in death, delivered out of death, and received into glory: 'If Christ be not risen, your faith is vain, and ye are yet in your sins,' 1 Cor. xv. 17. How should we know our discharge from sin, if our surety had not been let out of prison? Where should we have gotten an advocate to appear for us in the heavens, or a king to pour out the royal largess of gifts and graces to accompany the gospel, that it might be successful for our souls? From the context I shall observe two points :—

1. Observe, that, next to God's glory, Christ's aim was at our salvation. Christ doth not mention his own profit, but that 'thy Son may glorify thee,' and that he may give eternal life. These two were the scope of his sufferings and rising again to glory.

[1.] Of his sufferings: Dan. ix. 26, 'The Messias shall be cut off, but not for himself;' not for his own desert, nor his own profit; for no fault, no benefit of his own. So Rom. xv. 3, 'Christ pleased not himself; as it is written, The reproaches of them that reproached thee have fallen upon me.' The meaning is, he suffered the outrages of the wicked to promote the salvation of the elect; or the burden of our sins, by which God was dishonoured, fell on him. Christ sought not sweet things for himself; he had no respect to his own ease, but our happiness.

[2.] In his rising to glory he still eyed us; when he went to heaven he went thither on our errand, to seize upon it in our right, and to prepare it for our coming : John xiv. 3, 'I go to prepare a place for you.' Not so much to be glorified himself, as to get us thither : Heb. ix. 24, ἐμφανισθῆναι, 'There to appear in the presence of God for us.' Christ went to heaven that we might have a friend in court. He is entered into the heavens to appear for us; as if that were all the business of Christ in heaven, to remain there as our advocate.

Use 1. To show us the great love and condescension of Christ. The cross was sad work; all the wages was the salvation of our souls. In the eternal covenant he aimed at no other bargain : Isa. liii. 10, 'When thou shalt make his soul an offering for sin, he shall see his seed, he shall prolong his days, and the pleasure of the Lord shall prosper in his hands ;' that he might be effectual to save souls. They told David, 2 Sam. xviii. 3, 'Thou art worth ten thousand of us: if we flee away, they will not care for us ; neither if half of us die, will they care for us.' Public relation makes kings more valuable. Christ's soul was worth millions of ours ; and his life was more valuable than the life of men and angels; yet, to save ours, Christ layeth down his own, and he pleased not himself, that the pleasure of the Lord might prosper in our salvation.

Use 2. It teacheth us more self-denial, to do all for God's glory, and the good of the elect, both in life and death : Phil. ii. 17, 'Yea, and if I be offered up on the sacrifice and service of your faith, I joy and rejoice with you all.' A man that mindeth altogether his own things, liveth but a brutish life, beneath grace and reason. Reason will tell us that man was made sociable, and not only born for himself: grace raiseth actions to the highest self-denial. To deny ourselves is one of the first and most glorious precepts of christianity.

2. Observe, that the comfort and salvation of man doth much depend upon the glorification of Christ : 'Glorify me, that I may give eternal life.' The ends of his office are much furthered.

[1.] His glorification is a pledge of ours. God would do everything first in Christ ; elect him, adopt him, pour out the Spirit on him, raise him, glorify him, as the scripture everywhere manifests. Our nature is in heaven, as an earnest of our persons being there. He is called our forerunner, Heb. vi. 20, being gone before into heaven as a forerunner and harbinger, to take up room ; and 'the captain of our salvation,' Heb. ii. 11. When the head is in heaven, the members will follow. Whole Christ must be there ; he is not content with his heaven without us : John xiv. 3, 'If I go and prepare a place for you, I will come again and receive you unto myself, that where I am, there ye may be also ;' John xvii. 24, 'Father, I will that they also whom thou hast given me be with me where I am, that they may behold my glory that thou hast given me.'

[2.] His glorification is a pledge of his satisfaction. Our surety is let out of prison ; and when the surety is released, the debt is paid ; all the work is accomplished and effected : John xvi. 10, 'He will convince the world of righteousness, because I go to the Father.' There is enough done to bring souls to glory, for Christ is received to glory ; I am satisfied, I have found a ransom. So John xvii. 4, 5, 'I have glorified thee on the earth, I have finished the work thou hast given me to do. And now, O Father, glorify thou me with thine own self. Christ had never come out of the grave, never ascended, if anything else had remained to be done.

[3.] Christ glorified is a clearer ground of hope to the creature. When Christ was in the flesh he was poor, despised, crucified ; the apostle calleth it 'the weakness of God.' Many looked for a kingdom from him ; many believed in him when he was upon earth ; the thief owned him upon his cross : 'Remember me when thou comest to thy kingdom.' If the thief could spy his royalty under the ignominy of the cross, what may we expect from Christ in his glorified estate ? When David was hunted as a flea, or a partridge upon the mountains, there were six hundred clave to him, and had great hopes of his future exaltation ; they might look for more from David on the throne. Christ is now exalted, and hath a name above all names ; he still retaineth our nature, and that is an argument of love ; we go to one that is bone of our bone : and he is glorified in our nature ; that is an argument of his power.

[4.] Christ is really put into a greater capacity to do us good.

(1.) He hath seized on heaven in our right : John xiv. 3, 'I go to prepare a place for you.' God the Father prepared it by his decree ; but Christ, by his ascension, went to hold it in our name ; he took possession of it for himself, and his people, and ever since heaven's door hath stood open.

(2.) The advantage of his intercession : 1 John ii. 1, 'If any man sin, we have an advocate with the Father, Jesus Christ the righteous.' Christ is our advocate at God's right hand ; we have a friend at court. Offenders hope to be spared if they have interest in any that have the prince's ear. Jesus Christ is now in heaven at God's right hand, representing his merits. How can our prayers choose but be heard ? The Spirit is our notary to indite them, and Christ is our advocate to present them in court.

(3.) The mission of the Spirit. Christ carried up our flesh, and sent down his own Spirit ; as to fit heaven for us, Mat. xxv. 34, so to fit us for heaven: Rom. ix. 23, ' Vessels fitted for glory ; ' vessels of glory seasoned with grace. Now the Spirit is not given but by Christ's ascension: Eph. iv. 11, 12, ' When he ascended, he gave first apostles, then prophets, then evangelists, then pastors and teachers, for the perfecting of the saints, for the work of the ministry, for the edifying of the body of Christ.' This was his royal largess on the day of his coronation.

(4.) By his ascension all Christ's offices have a new qualification, and are exercised in another manner. Christ hath been mediator, king, priest, and prophet from the beginning of the world ; but the administration is different before his incarnation, in the days of his flesh, and after his ascension. Before his coming in the flesh, Christ was the great prophet of the church, foreshowing what was to come ; in his incarnation, pointing at what he did ; after his glorification, working faith, by representing what was past. So a priest ; before his incarnation, undertaking payment and satisfaction for our debts. In the days of his flesh, he made good his engagement ; after his ascension, he representeth his satisfaction made by his intercession, he appeareth as a righteous mediator, not by entreaty. Christ was a king by designation ; before he was incarnate, the old church had a taste of his kingly power ; when he lived upon earth, he was as a king fighting for the crown, a king in warfare ; after the resurrection, a king in triumph, solemnly inaugurated, he enters into his throne. Christ cometh into the Father's presence royally attended: Dan. vii. 13, 14, ' And I saw in the night visions, the Son of man with the clouds of heaven ; and he came to the ancient of days, and they brought him near before him ; and there was given him dominion, and glory, and all people, nations, and languages, that should serve him ; his dominion is an everlasting dominion, that shall not pass away.' After his resurrection, Christ is brought into God's presence, receiving all power in heaven and earth. Christ had this power from the beginning, but was not solemnly installed till then. As David had the power given him when anointed by Samuel, yet he endured banishment and tedious conflicts, and showed not himself till after the death of Saul, and till chosen by the tribes at Hebron ; so Christ was a Prince and Saviour before his ascension ; but it is said, Acts v. 31, ' Him hath God exalted by his right hand, to be a prince and a saviour.' He was prince by eternal right, and by gift and designation. In the midst of his abasement, Christ acknowledged himself king, John viii. 37. But after his ascension, he solemnly exercised it, and administered it for the good of the elect.

Well, then, let us meditate on these things, and draw water out of the wells of salvation with joy. It is better for us that Christ should be in heaven, than with us upon earth. A woman had rather have her husband live with her, than go to the Indies ; but yieldeth to his absence, when she considereth the profit of that traffic. We are all apt to wish for the apostles' days, to enjoy Christ with us in person ; but when we consider the fruit of his negotiation in heaven, we should be contented. It is better for us he should be there, to plead with the Father, and send his Spirit to us.

I come to the words.

'As.'—Some take this particle, συγκριτικῶς, comparatively; others αἰτιαλογικῶς, causally.   Comparatively; 'Glorify me,' i.e., as thou hast given me a power over all flesh, &c., give me a glory suitable to the authority; handle me according to the power and command which thou hast given me, as the plenipotentiary of heaven.   But it is rather taken causally, by way of argument.   It is not ὡς, but καθὼς, which may be rendered because.   Now the argument is double—(1.) It may be taken from a former grant of power, 'As thou hast given,' &c. Hitherto he had a right; now he pleadeth for possession, and a more full exercise of it; and (2.) From the end which that power is to be exercised for, the good of the elect, that he 'may give eternal life to as many as thou hast given him.'

1. I may observe something from that, 'As thou hast given him.' The memory of former benefits is an encouragement to ask anew. Experience begetteth confidence.   The heart is much confirmed when faith hath sense and experience on its side; and the belief of what is to come is facilitated by considering what is past.   We should believe God upon his bare word; yet it is an encouragement to have experience and trial.   By former mercies we have a double experience; we know that he will and can do for creatures.   Signal mercies are standing monuments of God's power: Isa. li. 9, 'Awake, awake, put on strength, O arm of the Lord; awake, as in the ancient days, in the generations of old.   Art not thou it that hath cut Rahab, and wounded the dragon?'   Rahab is Egypt, the dragon is Pharaoh; he that hath helped can and will.   We should not entertain jealousies without a cause: 1 Sam. xvii. 37, 'The Lord that delivered me out of the paw of the lion, and out of the paw of the bear, he will deliver me out of the hand of this Philistine.'   Former mercies are pledges of future. Deus donando debet—God by giving becometh our debtor: Mat. vi. 25, 'Is not the life more than meat, and the body more than raiment?' He enticeth hope by former mercies: Judges xiii. 23, 'If the Lord were pleased to kill us, he would not have received a burnt-offering and a meat-offering at our hands, neither would he have showed us all these things.'   God would not weary us altogether with expectation; something we have in hand, and therefore may expect more.   Well, then, when your hearts are apt to faint, take the cordial of experiences: Ps. lxxvii. 10, 'I said, This is mine infirmity; but I will remember the years of the right hand of the Most High.'   We are apt to indulge the peevishness of distrust after many deliverances: 1 Sam. xxvii. 1, 'I shall one day perish by the hand of Saul;' though God had put him twice into his hands: Rom. viii. 32, 'He that spared not his own son, &c., how will he not with him also freely give us all things?'   In common experiences, where we can have no absolute assurance, let us not baulk duty for danger: 2 Cor. i. 10, 'Who delivered us from so great a death, and doth deliver, in whom we trust that he will yet deliver us.'   Paul would finish his ministry notwithstanding danger.

2. Observe again from this, 'As thou hast given;' daturum te promisisti—thou hast promised to give.   God had promised to make over to him the plenary possession and administration of the kingdom; Christ pleadeth the grant and promise.   It is an excellent encourage-

ment in prayer when we can back our requests with promises: Ps. cxix. 49, 'Remember the word unto thy servant, upon which thou hast caused me to hope.' It is a modest challenge. God alloweth it, 'Put me in remembrance, let us plead together,' &c., Isa. xliii. 26. We may argue and dispute with God upon his own word; *chirographa tua injiciebat tibi, domine*—show him his own hand. Lord, thou hast said this and that, let it be fulfilled.

'Thou hast given him.'—As he was man and mediator; for as he was God, he had an eternal right, and an actual visible right by creation and providence; but Christ, as mediator, was to receive a crown. By 'gift: Ps. ii. 8, 'Ask of me, and I will give thee the heathen for thy inheritance.'

1. It noteth that Christ hath his kingdom by right, not by mere power. It is by the Father's grant he was solemnly invested and set upon the hill of Sion. They are rebels to God who do not acknowledge Christ to be King. There are several manners of possession. Satan is prince of the world, but he is a robber; he holdeth it not by grant from the Father, but by power; he hath actual possession of many nations, but no right.

2. It noteth what kind of right it is that Christ hath; it was by grant and donation. It is the great condescension of our Lord that he would hold all things by our tenure, by way of gift and grant from the Father. Free grace is no dishonourable tenure. Christ himself holdeth his kingdom by it. Why should proud creatures disdain this manner of holding? The lordship of the world was Christ's natural inheritance, yet he would hold all by grace.

'Power over all flesh.'—Flesh is chiefly put for men, though all creatures are under his dominion. We are sometimes expressed by our better, and sometimes by our baser part. By our better; every soul, that is, every man, Rom. ii. 9, and xiii. 1. Sometimes by the baser part: Isa. xl. 6, 'All flesh is grass;' Mat. xxiv. 22, 'No flesh would be saved;' and elsewhere. Here 'flesh' is fitly used; it is put for the nature of man in common, in opposition to those who are peculiarly Christ's by tradition and purchase. And by 'power over all flesh,' is meant a judiciary power to dispose of them according to pleasure; yea, of their everlasting estate. *Potestatem omnis hominis accepit, ut liberet quos voluerit, et damnet quos voluerit.* John v. 27, 'He hath given him authority to execute judgment also, because he is the Son of man.' It is the style of God himself; he is called, Num. xvi. 22, 'The God of the spirits of all flesh;' and more express to this purpose, Jer. xxxii. 27, 'Behold, I am the Lord, the God of all flesh: is there anything too hard for me?' So that it noteth not a naked authority, but an authority armed with a divine power. Now because God will not give his glory to another, we may hence observe:—

1. That Christ is true God, for otherwise he could not have such an absolute power. It is proper to his divine nature, though, as it is a gift, his whole person God-man be invested with it. He is called the only God, not excluding the Father, who subsisteth with him in the same essence, but including the Son: Isa. xlv. 22, 23, 'I am God, and there is none else: I have sworn by myself; the word is gone out in righteousness, and shall not return, that unto me every knee shall

bow, and every tongue shall swear ;' which is applied to Christ, Rom. xiv. 11, and Phil. ii. 9–11. He is called the great God; the supper of the Lamb is called 'the supper of the great God,' Rev. xix. 17; 'the true God,' 1 John v. 20. It should fortify christians against those abominable opinions wherein the godhead of Christ is questioned.

2. Observe that Christ as mediator hath power over all flesh. All kings and monarchs have certain bounds and limits, by which their empire is terminated; but God hath set Christ higher than the kings of the earth. He is the true catholic king; his government is unlimited: Ps. lxxxix. 27, 'Also I will make him, my first born, higher than the kings of the earth;' Mat. xxviii. 18, 'All power is given unto me, both in heaven and in earth;' and Dan. vii. 14, 'There was given him dominion, and glory, and a kingdom, that all people, nations, and languages should serve him: his dominion is an everlasting dominion, which shall not pass away; and his kingdom, that which shall not be destroyed.'] There is some difference about the extent of Christ's mediatory kingdom.

[1.] It is not only confined to the elect. We must distinguish between Christ's power and his charge. He hath a power given him over all; but there are some given to him by way of special charge, which is given for the elect, as to all spiritual ends, to rescue them from the power of Satan, as in this verse. As Joseph in Egypt; the power of all the land was made over to him, though his brethren had a special right in his affections. The kingdom of Christ, as merely spiritual and inward, is proper to the elect; that kingdom where Christ hath no other deputy and vicar but his Spirit; but for his judiciary kingdom, that is universal: Ps. ii. 8, 'I will give thee the heathen for thy inheritance, and the utmost parts of the earth for thy possession.' There is a reign over mankind, and those that do not subject themselves to Christ as a redeemer shall find him as a judge. Therefore, in Ps. ii., the judiciary acts of his power are only mentioned, 'breaking them with a rod of iron,' and 'vexing them in his hot displeasure.' He is lord over them in power and justice as God's lieutenant; they shall pay him homage and subjection as king of the world, or else they shall perish. He overruleth them as rebels, but he reigneth in the church as over voluntary subjects.

[2.] It is not confined to the church and things merely spiritual. This kingdom is as large as providence; and in the exercise of justice and equity magistrates are but his deputies. Christ is δεσπότης καὶ κύριος, 'the only Lord God, and our Lord Jesus Christ.' He is 'king of nations,' Jer. x. 7; 'king of saints,' Rev. xv. 3; 'head over all things to the church,' Eph. i. 22. Supreme and absolute in the world, but head to the church. He hath a rod of iron to rule the nations, and a golden sceptre to guide the church. In the world he ruleth by providence; in the church, by his testimonies: Ps. xciii., 'The Lord reigneth;' Ps. xxiv. 1, 'The earth is the Lord's.' And then, ver. 4, 'Who shall dwell in his holy hill?' I confess there is a question whether magistrates be under Christ as mediator? whether they hold their power from him? But I see no reason why we should doubt of it, since all things are put into Christ's hands; and that not only by an eternal right, but given to him; which noteth his right as mediator. Christ hath a right of merit, as lord of all creatures. He is 'lord both of the dead and living,' Rom. xiv. 9. The whole creature is delivered up to Christ, upon his undertaking the work of redemption; he hath a right of executing the dominion of God over every creature. Christ, the wisdom of the Father, saith, 'By me kings reign, and princes decree justice. By me princes rule, and nobles; even all the judges of the earth,' Prov. viii. 15, 16. And expressly he is said to be 'ruler of the kings of the earth.' Rev. i. 5.

Use 1. Comfort to God's children. All is put into the hands of Christ. A devil cannot stir further than he giveth leave; as the devils could not enter into the herd of swine without Christ's leave, Mark viii. When thou art in Satan's hands, the devil is in Christ's. Neither angels, nor principalities, nor powers can hurt. The reins of the world are in a wise hand: 'The Lord reigneth, though the waves roar,' Ps. xcix. 1. It was much comfort to Jacob and his children to hear that Joseph did all in Egypt. It should be so to us that Jesus doth all in heaven. He holdeth the chain of causes in his own hand. It will be much more for thy comfort at the last day. A client conceiveth great hope when one formerly his advocate is advanced to be judge of the court. Thy advocate is thy judge. He that died for thee will not destroy thee. Thy Christ hath power over all flesh, to damn whom he will, and save whom he will.

Use 2. An invitation to bring in men to Christ. Oh! who would not choose him to be Lord that, whether we will or no, is our master? He can hold thee by the chains of an invincible providence, that art not held with the bonds of duty. Oh! it is better to touch the golden sceptre than to be broken with the iron rod, and to feel the efficacy of his grace than the power of his anger. Christ is resolved creatures shall stoop. The apostle proveth the day of judgment: Rom. xiv. 10, 11, 'We shall all stand before the judgment-seat of Christ: for it is written, As I live, saith the Lord, every knee shall bow to me,' &c. Christ will bring the creatures on their knees; at the last day all faces shall gather blackness, and the stoutest hearts be appalled. Christ will have the better; it is better be his subjects than his captives.

Use 3. To magistrates, to own the mediator. You hold your power from Christ, and therefore must exercise it for him: Ps. ii. 10–12, 'Be wise now, therefore, O ye kings: be instructed, ye judges of the earth' (it is their duty chiefly to observe Jesus Christ); 'serve the Lord with fear, and rejoice with trembling. Kiss the Son, lest he be angry, and you perish from the way, when his wrath is kindled but a little.' Acknowledge Christ your Lord, or else he will blast your counsels; you shall perish in the midway: when you have carried on your designs a little while, you shall perish ere you are aware: Christ will call you to an account.

Two things Christ is tender of, his servants and his truth.

His servants are weak to appearance, but they have a great champion: what is done to them Christ counteth as done to himself: 'Saul, Saul, why persecutest thou me?' Acts ix. 4, when he raged against the saints: Isa. xlix. 23, 'Kings shall be thy nursing-fathers, and their queens thy nursing-mothers.' Christ hath little ones, that should be nursed and not oppressed.

But chiefly his truth. It is truth maketh saints: John xvii. 17, 'Sanctify them through thy truth; thy word is truth.' You should own your Lord and master, and not be indifferent to Christ or Satan. To tolerate errors, especially directly against Christ's person, nature, and mediatory offices, is but sorry thankfulness to your great master. He did not give you a commission to countenance rebels against himself. Whilst you maintain the power and purity of his ordinances, Christ will own you, and bear you out; but when, for secular ends, men hug his enemies, they are in danger to perish in the midway, in the course of their attempts.

'That he should give eternal life.'—*That* signifieth the end why Christ received so much power for the elect's sake, that he might be in a capacity to conduct them to glory; which otherwise could not be, if Christ's power were more limited and restrained. I might—

1. Observe, that Christ's power in the world is exercised for the church's good: Eph. i. 22, 'He is the head over all things to the church.' All dispensations are in the hand of a mediator for the elect's sake, to gain them from among others, to protect them against the assaults of others.

[1.] To gain them: 2 Peter iii. 9, 'He is not willing that any should perish, but that all should come to repentance.' If the elect were gathered, providence would be soon at an end. God's dispensations are guided by his decrees.

[2.] To protect them when they are gained. You must pluck Christ from the throne ere you can pluck a member from his body: John x. 28, 'I give unto them eternal life, and they shall never perish, neither shall any man pluck them out of my hand.' By his conduct and government we are secured against all dangers; they may pluck joint from joint, but they cannot pluck the soul from Christ that is once really implanted into him.

2. Observe that eternal life is Christ's gift. It is not the merit of our works, but the fruit of his grace: Rom. vi. 23, 'The wages of sin is death, but the gift of God is eternal life through Jesus Christ our Lord.' It is good to observe how the expression is diversified. Sin and death are suited like work and wages; but eternal life is a mere donative, not from the merit of the receiver, but the bounty of the giver. Works that need pardon can never deserve glory. Grace in us runneth as water in a muddy channel: the child hath more of the mother. It is true there is a concurrence of works, but not by way of causality, but order. God will first justify, then sanctify, then glorify. Justification is the cause and foundation of eternal life, and sanctification the beginning and introduction of it; and we have both by Christ. The first is obtained by Christ's blood, the second wrought by his Spirit. See Eph. ii. 8, 9, 'By grace ye are saved, through faith, and that not of yourselves; it is the gift of God: not of works, lest any man should boast.' The instrument of salvation is faith, which requireth a renouncing of works; and faith also is of grace. The Papists, to excuse the gross conceit of merit, say our works do not

merit but as they come from the grace of God, and are washed with the blood of Christ.   But neither salve will serve for this sore.

[1.] It is not enough to ascribe grace to God.   All justiciaries will do so.   The pharisee said, God, I thank thee I am so and so.   You confound the covenants when you think we may merit of God by his own grace.   God maketh us righteous by grace; and if by the exercise of it we deserve life, Adam under the covenant of works must then have been said to be saved by grace, because he could not persevere in the use of his free-will unless he had received it from God.

[2.] Nor as dyed in the blood of Christ, because faith disclaimeth all works as to the act of justification; and there is no merit if it be of grace.   Learn then to admire grace with comfort and hope.   Meritmongers are left to be confuted by experience.   Surely men that cry up works seldom look into their own consciences.   Let them use the same plea in their prayers they do in their disputes: give me not eternal life till I deserve it: Lord, let me have no mercy till I deserve it.   Or let them dispute thus, when they come to dispute with their own consciences in the agonies of death; then, *Optimum est inniti meritis Christi.*

3. Observe, the gifts that God is wont to give are not earthly riches, worldly power, transitory honours, but eternal life.   This was the great end for which he was ordained by the Father.   Many come to Christ as that man, Luke xii. 13, 'Master, speak to my brother, to divide the inheritance with me.'   He looked upon him as *aliquem magnum*, one furnished with great power, fit to serve his carnal ends.   Such fleshly requests are not acceptable to our mediator.   The Lord loveth to give blessings suitable to his own being.   He liveth for ever, and he giveth eternal life to the elect.   Learn, then, how to frame your requests.   Say, I will not be satisfied with these things: 'Remember me with the favour of thy people: O visit me with thy salvation; that I may see the good of thy chosen, that I may rejoice in the gladness of thy nation; that I may glory with thine inheritance,' Ps. cvi. 4, 5.

4. Observe, from the expression, 'eternal life.'   Our estate in heaven is expressed by life and eternal life.   This is a term frequently used to signify the glorified estate.   Now it doth imply not only our bare subsistence for ever, but also the tranquillity and happiness of that state.

[1.] It is life: 'Heirs together of the grace of life,' 1 Peter iii. 7.   Life is the most precious possession and heritage of the creature; there can be no happiness without it.   All our comforts begin and end with life.   Life is better than food: Mat. vi. 25, 'Is not the life more than meat, and the body than raiment?'   Poisons and cordials are all one to a dead man.   Creatures base, if they have life, are better than those which are most excellent: 'a living dog is better than a dead lion.'   All creatures desire to preserve life.   All the travail of men under the sun is for life, to prop up a tabernacle that is always falling: Job ii. 7, 'Skin for skin, and all that a man hath, will he give for his life.'   All our labour and care is for it; and when we have made provision for it, it is taken from us.   It is called 'the life of our hands,' Isa. lviii. 10.   We make hard shift to maintain it.   This life is a poor thing, it is no great matter to be heir to it: James iv. 14, 'What is your life? it is even a vapour, that appeareth for a little time, and then vanisheth away.'

[2.] It is life eternal; not like the earthly life, which is but as a vapour, a little warm breath, or warm smoke, turned in and out by the nostrils. Our present life is a lamp that may be soon quenched; it is in the power of every ruffian and assassinate. But this is life eternal. In heaven there is a fair estate; the tenure is for life; but we need not take thought for heirs; we and our happiness shall always live together. The blossoms of paradise are for ever fresh and green: therefore if we love life, why should we not love heaven? This is a life that is never spent, and we are never weary of living. This life is short, yet we soon grow weary of it. The shortest life is long enough to be encumbered with a thousand miseries. If you live till old age, age is a burden to itself: 'The days shall come in which they shall say, We have no pleasure,' Eccles. xii. 1. Life itself may become a burden, but you will never wish for an end of eternal life; that is a long date of days without misery and without weariness. Eternity is every day more lovely. Well might David say, 'The loving-kindness of God is better than life.' Men have cursed the day of their birth, but never the day of their new birth. Those that have once tasted the sweet and benefit of God's life never grow weary of it.

[3.] This life is begun, and carried on by degrees.

(1.) The foundation of it is laid in regeneration: then do we begin to live when Christ beginneth to live in us; and we may reckon from that day when, in the power of his life, we began to advance towards heaven; for then there was a seed laid of a life which cannot be destroyed. The life of nature may be extinguished, but not of grace: Rom. viii. 11, 'If the Spirit of him that raised up Jesus from the dead, dwell in you, he that raised up Christ from the dead shall also quicken your mortal bodies, by his Spirit that dwelleth in you.' The Spirit cannot leave his dwelling-place. It is said, John v. 24, 'He that heareth my word, and believeth on him that sent me, hath everlasting life, and shall not come into condemnation, but is passed from death unto life.' The change is wrought as soon as we begin to be acquainted with God in Christ.

(2.) Presently after death there is a further progress made. As soon as the soul is separated from the body, it begins to live gloriously. It is with Christ: Phil. i. 23, 'I desire to depart and to be with Christ;' it is in Christ here, but not so properly with him. And it is in paradise: Luke xxiii. 43, 'This day shalt thou be with me in paradise.' In Abraham's bosom: Luke xvi. 25, 'He seeth Abraham afar off, and Lazarus in his bosom.' And enjoyeth the fruit of good works: Rev. xiv. 13, 'Blessed are the dead which die in the Lord; from henceforth, yea, saith the Spirit, that they may rest from their labours, and their works do follow them.' There is not only a cessation from sin and misery, but an enjoyment of glory; and the body resteth without pain and labour till the resurrection, as in a bed: Isa. lvii. 2, 'He shall enter into peace: they shall rest in their beds, each one walking in his uprightness.'

(3.) After, at the resurrection of the body, there is a consummation of all joy. That is called 'the day of regeneration,' Mat. xix. 28. Body and soul shall be renewed perfectly, for immortality and glory. Then we live indeed. Therefore Christ saith, John xi. 25, 'I am the resurrection and the life.' All is consummate and full then; death hath some power till that day.

Use 1. To press us to labour after this holy life: John vi. 27, 'Labour not for the meat that perisheth, but for that meat that endureth unto everlasting life, which the Son of man shall give you.' Grace is the beginning and pledge of it. It is the beginning and seed of life; this is an immortal spark, that shall never be quenched: it is the pledge, 1 Tim. vi. 19; you may seize life as your right and inheritance. Oh! labour for it. This life is made bitter that thou mayest desire the other. Consider, all dependeth on thy state in this world; either thou art a child of wrath or an heir of life. Wicked men do die rather than live in the other world. It is better not to be than to be for ever miserable; to lie under the wrath of God, to be shut out of the presence of God for evermore.

Use 2. Bless the Lord Jesus Christ for opening a door of life for them that were dead in and by sin. The tree of life was fenced by a flaming sword: no creature could enter till Christ opened the way: 2 Tim. i. 10, 'By his appearing he hath abolished death, and hath brought life and immortality to light through the gospel.' Christ came from heaven on purpose to overcome death and take away the sting of it; and he is gone to heaven on purpose to make way for us. Our life cost Christ his death: John xvi. 5, 'Now I go away to him that sent me.'

'To as many as thou hast given him.'—Let us see the import of this phrase.

1. How we are said to be given to Christ.
2. Who are they that are given to Christ.
1. How we are said to be given to Christ.

[1.] By way of reward. There was an eternal bargain and compact: Isa. liii. 10, 'When thou shalt make his soul an offering for sin, he shall see his seed,' &c. We are members of his body, children of his family, subjects of his kingdom. This is a ground of certainty to the elect: 'The Lord knoweth those that are his,' 2 Tim. ii. 18. He made no blind bargain; he had leisure enough to cast up his account from all eternity.

[2.] By way of charge, to be redeemed, justified, sanctified, glorified: John vi. 37–40, 'All that the Father giveth me shall come to me; and he that cometh to me I will in no wise cast out. For I came down from heaven, not to do mine own will, but the will of him that sent me. And this is the Father's will which hath sent me, that of all which he hath given me I should lose nothing, but should raise it up again at the last day. And this is the will of him that sent me, that every one that seeth the Son, and believeth on him, may have everlasting life; and I will raise him up at the last day.' When the elect were made over to Christ, it was not by way of alienation, but oppignoration; they were laid to pledge in his hands, and God will call Christ to an account. None given to him by way of charge can miscarry. You trust Christ, and God trusted him with all the souls of the elect.

2. Who are they that are given to Christ? I answer—The elect are intended in this scripture, as is clear: ' He hath a power over all flesh,' but, ' to give eternal life to as many as are given to him.' So ver. 24, ' I will that all they whom thou hast given me may be with me.' None but the elect are saved. So ver. 10, ' All mine are thine, and thine are mine ;' where Christ's charge and the Father's election are made commensurable and of the same extent and latitude. They are opposed to the world: ver. 9, ' I pray for them ; I pray not for the world, but for them whom thou hast given me, for they are thine.' I confess it is sometimes used in a more restrained sense, of the apostles and believers of that age ; as ver. 6, ' Thine they were, and thou gavest them me, and they have kept thy word ;' and ver. 12, ' Those that thou gavest me I have kept, and none of them is lost but the son of perdition.' These were ἐκλεκτῶν ἐκλεκτότεροι, the elect of the elect. I confess sometimes the word is used in a larger sense, for Christ's universal power over all flesh : Ps. ii. 8, ' Ask of me, and I will give thee the heathen for thine inheritance, and the utmost parts of the earth for thy possession ;' not by way of charge, but by way of reward, they were given to him ; or rather, a power over them was given to him. There is a peculiar difficulty, ver. 12, concerning the son of perdition, how he was given to Christ. But I shall handle it when I come to that place. Christ, having spoken of the apostles keeping his word, taketh occasion to speak of Judas his apostasy.

Note hence :—

1. That there was, from all eternity, a solemn tradition and disposition of all that shall be saved into the hands of Christ. All God's flock are committed to his keeping. This giving souls to Christ was founded in an eternal treaty, Isa. liii. 10. Christ received them by way of grant and charge ; he hath a book where all their names are recorded and written : Rev. xiii. 8, ' All that dwell upon the earth shall worship him, whose names are not written in the book of life of the Lamb slain from the foundation of the world ;' Rev. xxi. 27, ' None shall enter in who are not written in the Lamb's book of life.' The book of life is there attributed to Christ, because he took this solemn charge upon himself, to conduct the heirs of salvation to glory. He is to see they come to him : John vi. 37, ' All that the Father giveth me shall come to me.' He knoweth them by head and poll : Isa. xlix. 12, ' Behold, these shall come from far ; and lo, these from the land of the north, and from the west, and these from the land of Sinim.' Man by man they are told out to him.

2. He is to keep them and look after them. Though there be many thousands, yet every single believer falleth under the care of Christ ; and accordingly he knoweth their names and their necessities : John x. 3, ' He calleth his own sheep by name, and leadeth them out.' He knoweth his sheep by name, John, Anna, Thomas. As the high priest carried the names of the tribes upon his bosom, so Christ knows the names of all the flock of God. There is not a poor servant or scullion (who are despicable creatures in the world) but Christ looks after him : Ps. xxxiv. 6, ' This poor man cried, and the Lord heard him, and saved him out of all his troubles.' Poor soul ! he is under such temptations, encumbered with such troubles, in such a task or

service. My Father gave me a charge of him, I must look to him. So many lambs as there are in the flock of Christ, there is not one forgotten.

3. Christ is to give an account of them unto God. He doth it by his constant intercession ; of which this prayer is a copy : 'They have kept thy word : I am glorified in them.' Christ is speaking good words of them to the Father ; he giveth you a good report behind your back. Satan is an accuser ; he loveth to report ill of believers ; but Christ telleth the Father how his lambs thrive. It is a grief to your advocate when he cannot speak well of you in heaven. But solemnly he will do it at the last day, when he is to present the elect to the tribunal of God : Heb. ii. 13, 'Behold I and the children which God hath given me.' Oh! it is a goodly sight to see Christ and all his little ones come together to the throne of grace. There is not one forgotten in the presence of Christ and all his angels. Christ will not be ashamed to own a poor despicable boy, a manservant, or a maid-servant, so they be faithful : Luke xii. 8, 'Whosoever shall confess me before men, him shall the Son of man also confess before the angels of God.' I died for this poor creature, and shed my blood for him. This is intended : 1 Cor. xv. 24, 'Then cometh the end, when he shall have delivered up the kingdom to God, even the Father.' A kingdom is sometimes put for the form of government, sometimes for subjects governed. The kingdom, that is the church, is solemnly presented as a prey snatched out of the teeth of lions : Eph. v. 27, $\ ν α\ π α ρ α σ τ ή σ η$, 'That he might present it to himself a glorious church, not having spot or wrinkle, or any such thing ; but that it should be holy and without blemish.' Christ will present his bride in triumph.

Use 1. Comfort to believers.

1. Concerning the safety of their eternal estate. Christ bargained for thee by name. That the Father and the Son should pitch upon such a forlorn and wretched piece of the creation as thou art, and they should talk together of thy heaven,[1] Son, this is one for whom thou must die! That thy name should be in the eternal register, written with the Lamb's blood in his own book of life. I must have a care of him. Ay! you will say, this were an excellent comfort, if I were sure I were one of them that is given to Christ. I answer—If he hath given Christ to you, he hath given you to Christ. God maketh an offer in the gospel. Are you willing to receive him for Lord and Saviour ? Then you put it out of question : 'To as many as received him, to them gave he power to become the children of God.' You are fellow-heirs with Christ. Christ is given to you in time.

2. In your particular straits Christ hath a care of you. Do you think he will break his engagement ? Christ hath plighted his truth to God the Father. Our groundless jealousies question the truth of Christ's word and solemn agreement. When we say, The Lord hath forgotten me, this is in effect to say, Christ is not faithful in his charge. The prophet chideth them : Isa. xl. 27, 'Why sayest thou, O Jacob, and speakest, O Israel, My way is hid from the Lord, and my judgment is passed over from my God ?' God doth not take notice of my case : such mistrust is a lie against the care of Christ.

Use 2. To press us, especially humble sinners, you that walk in

---

[1] Qu. "thee-in heaven"?—ED.

darkness, to come under these sweet hopes. God hath laid souls to pledge in the hand of Christ. Why should we be scrupulous? All the Father's acts are ratified in time by believers. He ordaineth, we consent; he chooseth Christ for lord and king: 'They shall appoint themselves one head,' Hosea i. 11. So he hath given souls to Christ, so should you.

1. Commit your souls to him by faith; this answereth to Christ's receiving the elect by way of charge: 1 Peter iv. 19, 'Let them that suffer according to the will of God commit the keeping of their souls to him in well-doing, as unto a faithful creator.' A man ventureth upon duty, and trusteth God with his soul: Ps. xxxi. 5, 'Into thy hands do I commit my spirit.' Paul knew Christ was an able and trusty friend: 2 Tim. i. 12, 'I know whom I have believed, and I am persuaded that he is able to keep that which I have committed to him against that day.' Committing the soul to God is a notion often used in the matter of faith, and doth most formally express the nature of trust and adherence. He is willing to receive your souls, and he is able to make good the trust. Therefore, in all times of distress and danger, when all things are dark to us, upon the warrant of the gospel, let us commit the soul to Christ, to be kept to salvation; refer yourselves to his care for pardon, defence, support, and glory.

2. Consecrate yourselves to Christ. Committing noteth trust; consecrating, obedience. You commit yourselves to his care, you resign and yield up yourselves to his discipline. Committing answereth the charge, but consecration the grant: Rom. xii. 1, 'I beseech you, therefore, brethren, by the mercies of God, that you present your bodies a living sacrifice, holy, acceptable unto God, which is your reasonable service.' By full consent a man embarketh with Christ, and is resolved no longer to be at his own keeping and disposal: Ps. cxix. 94, 'I am thine, save me, for I have sought thy precepts.' I am thine; Lord, I would not be my own, unless I be thine. As those who being denied protection by the Romans, offered up themselves and their whole estate to them. *Si nostra tueri non vultis, at vestra defendetis; quicquid passuri sumus, dedititii vestri patiantur,* &c.

SERMON III.

And this is life eternal, that they might know thee the only true God, and Jesus Christ, whom thou hast sent.—JOHN XVII. 3.

HERE our Lord declareth the way, means, and order how he would give eternal life to the elect; and so it is added as an amplification of the former argument. The words must be expounded by a metonymy. Such kind of predications are frequent in scripture: John iii. 19, 'This is the condemnation,' &c.; that is, the cause of it. Sometimes it signifies the outward means: John xii. 50, 'His commandment is life everlasting;' that is, his word is the most assured means of it. Sometimes the principal cause: 'Jesus Christ is the true God and eternal life,' 1 John v. 20; that is, the author of it.

'This is life eternal.'—Some understand these words formally, as if they were a description of eternal life, which consisteth in a sight of God. But I suppose it rather layeth down the way and means, and showeth rather what is the beginning and original of eternal life, than the formality and essence of it. It is not in this eternal life consisteth, but by this means it is gotten and obtained.

1. Partly because the word γινώσκειν, which is here used, is proper to the light of faith ; and so it is used ver. 7, 'They have known that all things whatsoever thou hast given me are of thee ;' and ver. 8, 'They have known surely that I came out from thee.' Vision is proper to the light of glory. It is more usually expressed by seeing than knowing : ver. 24, 'Father, I will that they also whom thou hast given me be with me where I am, ἵνα θεωρῶσι, that they may behold my glory.'

2. Christ is proving the reason, that unless he were glorified, he could not bestow eternal life; for there could be no knowledge without his ascension into heaven, and effusion of the gifts of the Holy Ghost, and so by consequence no eternal life. So that the words must be explained, 'This is life eternal ;' that is, this is the way to life eternal, or life eternal begun, and in the root and foundation.

'That they may know thee.'—That must be understood by way of apposition ; this is life eternal to know thee : and knowledge is here put for faith or saving knowledge. It is a known rule that words of knowledge do imply suitable affections ; as 1 Thes. v. 12, 'We beseech you to know them which labour among you ;' that is, reverence them. Or, more clearly to the present case : 1 John ii. 4, 'He that saith, I know him, and keepeth not his commandments, is a liar, and the truth is not in him. Our Saviour understandeth not naked and unactive speculations concerning God and Christ, or a naked map or model of divine truths. Bare knowledge cannot be sufficient to salvation, but a lively and effectual light. Faith is intended, as is clear by the mention of the double object—God and Christ. He that knoweth God in Christ knoweth him for his reconciled Father, and so leaneth on him. And affections and motions of grace are intended ; for it must be such a knowledge of God as discerneth him to be the chiefest good and only happiness. They know not God that do not choose him for their portion : 'They that know thy name will put their trust in thee,' Ps. ix. 10. Again, suitable practice and conversation is implied ; for surely St John knew Christ's meaning : 1 John ii. 3, 'Hereby we do know that we know him, if we keep his commandments.' So that in knowledge all the genuine effects of it are included—assent, affiance, practice, choice, necessary respect to God and Christ. Literal instruction is not enough to eternal life. A carnal man may know much of God and Christ, and yet be miserable. In point of the object, I know no difference between godly and carnal persons ; all the difference is in the force and efficacy ; as fair water and strong water differ not in colour, but only in strength and operation. I confess, in matters evangelical, nature is most blind ; but by reason of common gifts they may have a great proportion of knowledge, as to the letter, more than many of God's children. But of this elsewhere.

'The only true God :' τὸν μόνον ἀληθινὸν θεόν.—Much ado there hath been about this clause, I shall endeavour to bring all to a short decision. The doubt is, How can the Father be said to be the only true God, since the Spirit and the Son do also communicate in the divine essence?

1. Some to solve the matter, invert the order of the words thus, ' To know thee and Jesus Christ, whom thou hast sent, to be the only true God.' But if the construction would bear it, what provision is there then made for the godhead of the Holy Spirit, which is also a fundamental article?

2. Some say that the Father is not to be taken strictly and personally for the first person, but essentially for the whole godhead. But this seemeth not so plausible an answer, for then Christ must pray to himself. He prayeth here as God-man, and all along to the Father. For my part, I think the expression is used for a twofold reason— (1.) To exclude the idols and false gods ; (2.) To note the order and economy of salvation.

[1.] To exclude the idols of the Gentiles, foreign and false gods, such as are extra-essential to the Father ; and to note that that godhead is only true that is in the Father ; σὲ τὸν μόνον ἀληθινὸν θεὸν—' Thee the only, thee the true God.' The Son and the Holy Ghost are not excluded, who are of the same essence with the Father. Christ and the Spirit are true God, not without, but in the Father : John x. 30, ' I and my Father are one :' John xiv. 30, ' I am in the Father, and the Father in me ;' not divided in essence, though distinguished in personality. Such kind of expressions are usual in the scriptures, when any of the persons are spoken of singly ; as Rom. ix. 5, where Christ is said to be ' God over all, blessed for ever.' And more expressly, he is said to be θεὸς ἀληθινὸς, ' the only true God,' 1 John v. 20 ; by which neither the Father nor the Spirit are excluded from the godhead. Many such exclusive particles there are in scripture, which must be expounded by the analogy of faith ; as Mat. xi. 27, ' None knoweth the Son but the Father ; neither knoweth any man the Father, but the Son ;' where the Spirit is not excluded, ' who searcheth the depths of God,' 1 Cor. ii. 10. One person of the Trinity doth not exclude the rest. So see Isa. xliii. 11, ' I, even I, am the Lord ; and besides me there is no Saviour ;' which is applied to Christ : Acts iv. 12, ' Neither is there salvation in any other ; for there is no other name under heaven given among men whereby we must be saved ;' it only excludeth λεγομένους θεοὺς, those that are called gods, 1 Cor. viii. 5. There is no God but one. Many are called gods, ' but to us there is but one God, the Father.' As also it is the scope of Christ ; he would lay down the summary of christian doctrine ; the one member being opposed to the vanity of the Gentiles, the other to the blindness of the Jews.

[2.] To note the order and economy of salvation, in which the Father is represented as supreme, in whom the sovereign majesty of the deity resideth, and the Son sustaineth the office of mediator and servant : John xiv. 28, ' My Father is greater than I ;' not in respect of nature or essential glory, for therein they are both equal : Phil. ii. 6, ' Who, being in the form of God, thought it no robbery to be equal with God ;' but in the order of redemption, in which the Father is the principal party representing the whole deity, because he is the original and fountain of it. So 1 Cor. viii. 6, 'But to us there is but one God, the Father, of whom are all things, and we in him; and one Lord Jesus Christ, by whom are all things, and we by him.' God the Father is to be conceived as the supreme person, or ultimate object of worship, and the Son as lord and mediator.

'And Jesus Christ, whom thou hast sent;' that is, Jesus Christ, not as the second person in the Trinity, but as mediator.

Sent, implieth—

1. Christ's divine original: he came forth from God; he is *legatus a latere:* John xvi. 30, 'By this we know that thou camest forth from God.' He was a person truly existing before he was sent into the world, and a distinct person from the Father; for he that sendeth and he that is sent are distinguished.

2. His incarnation: Gal. iv. 4, 'When the fulness of time was come, God sent forth his Son made of a woman.'

3. It implieth his whole office of mediator and redeemer; wherefore he is called 'the apostle and high priest of our profession,' Heb. iii. 1. *Apostle* implieth one that was sent. Christ was the chief apostle and messenger of heaven; 'the high priest and apostle.' The high priest-hood was the highest calling in the Jewish church, and the apostleship the highest calling in the christian church; to note that the whole office of saving all the church, the elect of all ages, is originally in Christ. He is the great ambassador to treat with us from God, and the high priest to treat with God and appease his wrath for us.

The names of Christ are also of some use. Such scriptures are like gold, that may be beaten into thin leaves. In summaries and breviats every mark and letter is of use.

Jesus signifieth a saviour, as it is explained Mat. i. 21, 'Thou shalt call his name Jesus, for he shall save his people from their sins.' This is a part of our belief, to acknowledge Christ a saviour. Then *Christ* signifieth anointed.

We shall draw out the sum of all in a few points.

First, Observe, the beginning, increase, and perfection of eternal life lieth in knowledge.

[1.] The beginning of it is in knowledge. Knowledge is the first step to eternal life. In paradise Adam's two symbols were the tree of knowledge and the tree of life. As light was the first creature that God made, so it is in the new creation: Col. iii. 10, 'Put on the new man, who is renewed in knowledge after the image of him that created him.' By the enlightening of the Holy Ghost, the work of grace is begun, and the seed of glory is laid in the heart. The Holy Ghost representeth the pattern, and then conformeth us to it. Regeneration is nothing but a transforming light, or such an illumination as changes the heart: 2 Cor. iii. 18, 'We all with open face beholding as in a glass the glory of the Lord, are changed into the same image from glory to glory, even as by the Spirit of our God;' Eph. iv. 23, 'Be renewed in the spirit of your minds.' It maketh our notions of God and Christ to be active and effectual. The force of the new nature is first upon the mind; it taketh sin out of the throne. God, in the order of grace, followeth the order which he hath established in nature. Reason and judgment is to go before the will.

2. The increase of it is by knowledge: 2 Peter iii. 18, 'But grow in grace, and in the knowledge of our Lord and Saviour Jesus Christ.' The more thou growest in knowledge, the more thou growest in life. All the gradual progress and increase of the spiritual life is by the increase of light: 2 Peter i. 2, 'Grace be multiplied unto you by the knowledge of God and Jesus Christ our Lord.' Heat doth increase by light, as a room is warmer at high noon than in a chill morning. I confess through corruption and literary airy knowledge, men grow more carnal and careless, as new light quencheth old heat; but by the light of the Spirit the heart is more quickened and enlivened; and as the judgment is made solid, so the heart is more gracious.

3. The perfection of it is by knowledge: Ps. xvii. 15, 'When I awake, I shall be satisfied with thy likeness.' The heaven of heavens is to satisfy the understanding with the knowledge of God. One great end of our going to heaven is to better our notions and apprehensions. While the soul is prisoner in the body, we have but low and dark thoughts; but there we are illuminated on a sudden. One glimpse of God in glory will inform us more than the study of a thousand years.

Use 1. Is to show us the sad estate—

1. Of men without knowledge: Prov. xix. 2, ' Also that the soul be without knowledge, it is not good.' Fruit that hath but little sun can never be ripe. Men will say we are ignorant, but we hope we have a good heart. You can as well be without the sun in the world, as without knowledge and light in the heart. In all the communications of grace, God beginneth with the understanding; as strength to bear afflictions: Jer. xxxi. 19, ' After I was instructed, I smote on my thigh, and was ashamed, yea even confounded, because I did bear the reproach of my youth;' James i. 5, ' If any of you lack wisdom, let him ask it of God.' It is the perfection of the present life, and the foundation of the next. It is the perfection of the present life, the excellency of a man above the beasts; the more knowledge, the more a man; and the more ignorant, the more brutish: Ps. xlix. 20, ' Man that is in honour and understandeth not is like the beasts that perish;' Job xxv. 11, ' Who teacheth us more than the beasts of the earth, and maketh us wiser than the fowls of heaven.' If a man would glory in anything, it should be in the knowledge of God: Jer. ix. 24, ' Let him that glorieth glory in this, that he understandeth and knoweth me.'

2. Of those that have only a washy weak knowledge, not a living light and knowledge, that is rooted in their own hearts; they talk like parrots: like the moon, they are dark themselves, though from others they shine to others; like vintners that keep wine, not for use, but for sale: the cellar may be better stored, but it is for others: 2 Peter i. 8, ' For if these things be in you and abound, they make you that ye shall be neither barren nor unfruitful in the knowledge of our Lord Jesus Christ.' It is a disparagement to know Christ and never be the better for him. These are like the nobleman of Samaria, that saw the plenty of Samaria, but could not taste of it. Surely there are not greater atheists in the world than carnal scholars that have a great deal of light, but no grace. It is sad to hear of such a Christ and feel nothing: John xvii. 17, ' Sanctify them through thy truth; thy word is

truth.' They who are able to understand the word, but to no purpose, must needs doubt of the truth of it.

Use. 2. To press christians to grow in knowledge, that they may enter upon eternal life by degrees : Hos. vi. 3, ' Follow on to know the Lord.' There is a growth in knowledge as well as grace. It is not so sensible in the very increase and progress as that of grace is; because growth in grace is always *cum luctu*, with some strife, but the work upon the understanding is more still and silent. Draw away the 'curtain, and the light cometh in, and our ignorance vanisheth silently, and without such strife as goeth to the taming of lusts and vile affections ; yet afterwards it is sensible that we have grown: ' Ye were darkness, but now are ye light in the Lord,' Eph. v. 8 ; as a plant increaseth in length and stature, though we do not see the progress. We read of Jesus Christ that he grew in knowledge ; we do not read that he grew in grace : he received the Spirit without measure, and nothing could be added to the perfection of his innocence. Yet it is said, Luke ii. 40, ' The child grew ;' and ver. 52, ' Jesus increased in wisdom and in stature, and in favour with God and man.' The Godhead made out itself to him by degrees. Oh ! let us increase. It is notable that Moses his first request to God was ' Tell me thy name ; ' and afterward, ' Show me thy glory,' a more full manifestation of God. We should not always keep to our milk, our infant notions and apprehensions, but go on to a greater increase ; it much advanceth your spiritual life, and will be an advantage to your eternal life. They have the highest visions of God hereafter, that know most of him here upon earth. They are vessels of a larger capacity ; and though all be perfect, yet with a difference.

Now for means and directions, take these :—

1. Wait upon the preaching of the word. God appointed it, and hath given gifts to the church for this end and purpose. We should quicken one another: Isa. ii. 3, ' Come and let us go up to the house of the Lord, and he will teach us his ways.' God's grace is given in his own way. When men neglect and despise God's solemn institutions, they either grow brutish or fanatical, as we see by daily experience. Light as well as flame is kept in by the breath of preaching. By long attention you grow skilful in the word of righteousness. Men that despise the word may be more full of crotchets and curiosities, but that light is darkness. It is disputed which is the sense of learning, hearing or seeing. By the eye we see things, but must, by reason of innate ignorance, be taught how to judge of them.

2. You must read the word with diligence ; that is every man's work that hath a soul to be saved. They that busy themselves in other books will not have such lively impressions : Ps. i. 2, ' His delight is in the law of the Lord, and in his law doth he meditate day and night;' that must be our exercise, not play-books, stories, and idle sonnets. How many sacrilegious hours do many spend this way! *Castæ deliciæ meæ sunt scripturæ tuæ*—Augustine. Nay, good books should not keep from the scriptures. Luther in Gen. chap. xix. saith, *Ego odi libros meos, et sæpe opto eos interire, ne morentur lectores, et abducant a lectione ipsius scripturæ.* We should go to the fountain : 2 Tim. iii. 15, ' And that from a child thou hast known the holy scriptures, which are

able to make thee wise unto salvation.' We put a disparagement upon the word when we savour and relish human writings, though never so good and excellent, better than the word of God itself. This is the standing rule by which all doctrines must be confirmed; and you do not know what sweet, fresh, and savoury thoughts the Spirit of God may stir up in your own minds; for word-representations are not so taking as our own inward thoughts and discourses; these, like a draught of wine from the tap, are more fresh and lively. It is necessary, as I said before, to wait upon preaching, to hear what others can say out of the scriptures; but it is good to read too, that we may preach to ourselves. Every man is fittest to commune with his own heart; and that conviction which doth immediately arise out of the word is more prevalent. A man can be angry with any preacher but conscience. In another, when a matter is expressed to our case, we are apt to suspect the mixture of passion and private aims; but read thyself, and what thoughts are stirred up upon thy reading will be most advantageous to thee. Besides, those that are studious of the word have this sensible advantage, that they have the promises, the doctrines, the examples of the word more familiar and ready with them upon all cases. It is said of one, that he was a living bible and a walking library, βίβλος ἔμψυ-χος, καὶ μουσαίον περιπατοῦν; such a christian is a walking concord-ance. And whereas other christians are weak, unsettled in comfort or opinion, these have always scriptures ready. And let me tell you, in the whole work of grace you will find no weapon so effectual as the sword of the Spirit, as scriptures readily and seasonably urged. Therefore no diligence here is too much. If you would not be barren and sapless in discourse with others, if you would not be weak and comfortless in yourself, read the scriptures, that you may bring *sic scriptum est* upon every temptation, and urge the solid grounds of our comfort. I speak the more in so plain a point, because I would make men more conscionable, both in their closets and families, in this point, that they may not only have recourse to learned helps, and books of a human original, but to the word itself.

3. The scriptures must be read with prayer. We must plough with God's heifer if we would understand his riddle; we must beg the Spirit's help. The Spirit is the best interpreter: *bene orasse, est bene studuisse.* Every minister findeth prayer to be his best comment. So should you pray before and after reading the scriptures, as you do before and after you receive your bodily food. You do not know how prayer will clear up the eyes: Ps. cxix. 18, ' Open thou mine eyes, that I may behold wondrous things out of thy law.' There is some excellency in the letter of the scriptures; but this is nothing to what we see by the Spirit; it will make a man wonder at the excellency, efficacy, consonancy of these truths; a man seeth far more than ever he saw before. The Spirit is needful both to open the heart and to open the scriptures: Luke xxiv. 32, 'Did not our hearts burn when he opened to us the scriptures?' compared with ver. 45, 'Then opened he their understanding, that they might understand the scriptures.' To understand the truth, and to give us an active and certain persuasion of it; 'to open the heart,' Acts xvi. 14, inclining it to obedience, giving in light, that works a ready assent and firm persuasion, bringing forward the heart with power to obedience. In dark

places and difficult cases, when you have no certainty, you should 'cry for knowledge, and lift up your voice for understanding;' as the blind man that cried to Jesus, 'Lord! that I might receive my sight,' Mark x. 52.

4. Study the creatures. God is known out of his word, but his works give us a sensible demonstration of him. You have David's night and day meditation. His night meditation: Ps. viii. 3, 'When I consider thy heavens, the work of thy hands, the moon and the stars which thou hast ordained.' Not a word of the sun, the most noble creature: Ps. xix. 5, he speaks of the 'going forth of the sun like a bridegroom coming out of his chamber, and rejoicing as a strong man to run a race;' that is his morning meditation. When we walk out in the night or morning, we may think of God, view his stupendous works. The heathens had no other bible. Consider that the huge weight of the earth hangeth on nothing, like a ball in the air: Job xxiii. 7, 'He stretcheth out the north upon the empty place, and hangeth the earth upon nothing.' Consider the beauty of the heavens, with their ornaments; the bounding of the sea; the artifice in the frame of the smallest creatures, the excellent ministries, and subordination of the services of the creatures one to another, &c.

5. Spiritualise every outward advantage, so as to raise your hearts in the contemplation of God. As when we observe the wisdom of a father, or the bowels of a mother, let us take occasion to exalt the love and care of God. As from a mother's bowels: Isa. xlix. 15, 'Can a woman forget her sucking child, that she should not have compassion on the son of her womb? Yea, they may forget; yet will I not forget thee.' From the wisdom of a father: Mat. vii. 11, 'If ye then, being evil, know how to give good gifts unto your children, how much more shall your Father which is in heaven give good things to them that ask him?' *Tam pater nemo, tam pius nemo.* So the centurion mentions his own command and government when he desires Christ to put forth his power: Mat. viii. 8, 9, 'Speak the word only, and my servant shall be healed. For I am a man under authority, having soldiers under me; and I say to this man, Go, and he goeth; and to another, Come, and he cometh; and to my servant, Do this, and he doeth it.' As if he should say, All sicknesses are at thy beck, as well as these soldiers at mine. In your carriage to your children, and theirs to you, you may sublimate your thoughts to consider of that commerce between you and God. So in the work of your callings; a little is useful for bringing great matters to pass; think of providence. I press this, because it will be a double advantage; it will keep the heart heavenly, and you will serve faith out of common experiences, and so it will help us in our notions of God; for if limited creatures go thus far, how much more excellent is God!

6. Purge your heart more and more from carnal affections; these are the clouds of the mind, as in fenny countries the air is seldom clear: 'Blessed are the pure in heart, for they shall see God,' Mat. v. 8. We usually look upon God through the glass of our own humours. Carnal men fancy the eternal essence as one of their society, and misfigure God in their thoughts.

7. The last is, in the progress of knowledge, or search of truth, beware of novelism: 2 Tim. iii. 14, 'Continue thou in the things thou

hast learnt and been assured of, knowing from whom thou hast learned them.' There is as great care to keep what we have, as to gain more knowledge. The devil taketh advantage of our changes ; when we renounce old errors, he bringeth man to question truth ; as in public changes, when men shake off the ordinances of men, he stirreth up others to question the ordinances of God. And I have observed that some, out of a pretence of growing in knowledge, put themselves upon a flat scepticism and wary reservation, holding nothing certain for the present, but waiting for new light; such as these the apostle intendeth, 2 Tim. iii. 7, ' Ever learning, and never coming to the knowledge of the truth ;' they make profession of being studious in sacred things, but never come to any settlement, and are loath to hold to any principles, lest they should shut the door upon new light. New light is become a dangerous word, especially now in the latter times ; now we have a promise that ' knowledge shall be increased,' Dan. xii. 4. Aims at knowledge is the dangerous snare of these times, as the Gnostics pretended to more knowledge. This is a great snare. Satan promised more knowledge to our first parents: Gen. iii. 5, ' God doth know that in the day ye eat thereof then your eyes shall be opened, and ye shall be as gods, knowing good and evil;' which example the apostle setteth before our eyes, 2 Cor. xi. 3, ' But I fear lest by any means, as the serpent beguiled Eve through his subtlety, so your minds should be corrupted from the simplicity that is in Christ.' And he telleth us, ' Satan turneth himself into an angel of light,' ver. 13, 14.

Now for your direction know :—

1. Progress in knowledge is rather in degrees than parts ; not in new truths, but greater proportions of light. Light respecteth the medium, truth the object. I say, it is rather, not altogether. A man may walk in present practices which future light may disprove and retract ; but usually the increase of a christian is rather in the measure of knowledge than difference of objects. Our old principles are improved and perfected: Prov. iv. 18, ' The path of the just is as the shining light, that shineth more and more to the perfect day.' To know God more, and Christ more, to be more practically skilful in the word of righteousness: Heb. v. 14, ' Strong meat belongeth to them that are of full age, who by reason of use have their senses exercised to discern both good and evil.'

2. That fundamentals in the scripture are clear and certain. God hath not left us in the dark, but pointed out a clear way to heaven, of faith and good works: Eph. ii. 10, ' We are his workmanship, created in Christ Jesus unto good works, which God hath before ordained, that we should walk in them.' It is a disparagement to the word to make it an uncertain rule. The way to heaven is beaten, and we may observe the track and footprints of the flock. It is a good observation of Chrysostom, that the saints do not complain of the darkness of the scripture, but of their own hearts : ' Open thou mine eyes,' not, ' Make a new law.'

3. These necessary doctrines must be entertained without doubt and hesitancy. It is dangerous when foundation-stones lie loose. We are pressed ' to stand fast in the faith,' 1 Cor. xvi. 13, and to hold the profession of it without wavering, Heb. x. 23; not to inquire after the gods of the nations, Deut. xii. 30; and Gal. i. 8, ' Though an

angel from heaven should preach any other doctrine to you than that which ye have heard, let him be accursed.' The notion of new light chiefly aimeth at undermining the old doctrine of the scriptures. For the main of religion, a man should be settled above doubt and contradiction. Till we have certainty there cannot be grace. The soul is not brought under the power of truth; for things that are controversial have no efficacy and force. The great hindrance of saving knowledge is that natural atheism, and those habituated doubts which are found in the heart.

4. We must be zealous for lesser truths when we have received them upon certain grounds. Every piece and parcel of truth is precious; a little leaven of error is dangerous: Gal. v. 9, 'A little leaven leaveneth the whole lump.' Error fretteth like a gangrene, and grows still higher and higher. Men think it is enough to be careful of fundamentals; all other knowledge is but *scientia oblectans,* for delight, not safety. Oh! it is dangerous to stain the understanding, though you do not wound it. There are *maculæ* and *vulnera intellectus.* It is dangerous to be wanton in opinions that seem to be of smaller concernment. Men that play with truth leave themselves open to more dangerous errors. Some say, Fundamentals are few; believe them, and live well, and you are saved. This is as if a man in building should be only careful to lay a good foundation, no matter for roof, windows, or walls. If a man should untile your house, and tell you the foundation, the main buttresses are safe, you would not be pleased. Why should we be more careless in spiritual things?

5. Take up no practices nor principles but upon full conviction. This imposeth a necessity of often change, or at least of frequent doubting. Men do not search, but act out of blind obedience, and then they are liable to seduction: 1 Thes. v. 21, 'Prove all things, hold fast that which is good.' It is a pertinacy, not a constancy, when I have no clear warrant. A christian should be able to give 'an answer to every man that asketh him a reason of the hope that is in him, with meekness and fear,' 1 Peter iii. 15; otherwise we shall never be able to secure our practices and opinions against the objections in our own hearts, and answer the sophister in our own bosoms.

Secondly, Observe that no knowledge is sufficient to life eternal but the knowledge of God and Christ. I am to prove—(1.) No other knowledge is sufficient; (2.) How far this is enough for such an end and purpose.

The scripture asserts both, for the words are exclusive and assertive; there is no other knowledge, and this is sufficient.

1. No other knowledge is sufficient to life eternal. I shall prove it by two arguments:—

[1.] Out of Christ we cannot know God. The Gentiles had τὸ γνωστόν, something that was known of God, Rom. i. 19, 20, which served to leave them without excuse, but not to save their souls. The apostle instanceth in such attributes as are obvious, but more terrible than comfortable, as eternity, power, &c. They had some loose thoughts of his Godhead and power, but no distinct view of his essence; that is reserved for the scriptures. The scriptures are the picture of Christ, and Christ is the image of the Father: 2 Cor. iv. 4, 'Lest the light of the glorious gospel of Christ, who is the image of

God, should shine upon them.' God never made out himself to the world in that latitude and greatness as he hath done to the world in Christ. In Christ's person and kingdom the majesty of God is known; in the divine power of his operations, the strength of God; in the excellency of his benefits, the love of God. The wisest heathens, that hath no other glass than the book of the creatures whereby to dress up their apprehensions, could only see a first cause, a first mover, a being of beings, some great lord and governor of the order of the world, whom they mightily transformed and misfigured in their thoughts; they knew nothing distinctly of creation and providence, of the nature of worship, which is necessary; for whosoever is saved must not only know God's essence, but his will, for otherwise we shall but grope as the heathens did: Acts xvii. 27, 'That they should seek the Lord, if haply they should feel after him, and find him.' We cannot seek him to satisfaction.

[2.] Without Christ, no enjoying of God. It must be such a knowledge as bringeth God and the soul together. Now between us and him there is a great gulf; all gracious commerce is broken off between God and the fallen creature: John xiv. 6, 'No man cometh unto the Father but by me.' No free trade unto heaven but by Jacob's ladder: John i. 51, 'Hereafter you shall see heaven open, and the angels of God ascending and descending upon the Son of man.' There is no access but by Christ; and so no salvation but by him: Acts iv. 12, 'Neither is there salvation in any other, for there is none other name under heaven given among men, whereby we must be saved.' In the fallen state of man there is need of a mediator. In innocency we might immediately converse with God: God loved his own image. What could a just and holy man fear from a just and holy God? But now, that of God's creatures we are made his prisoners, we can expect nothing of mercy, because he is just. Guilty nature presageth nothing but evil: Rom. i. 32, 'Who knowing the judgment of God, that they which commit such things are worthy of death.' The great question of the world is, Wherewith shall I appease him, to give his justice content and satisfaction? Micah vi. 8. In all the inventions of men, they could never find out a sufficient ransom to expiate sin, to reconcile God, to sanctify human nature, that we might have commerce with heaven.

2. The sufficiency of this knowledge. For understanding of this, you must know that all breviates, where religion is reduced to a few heads, must be enlarged according to the just extent of the rule of faith; as in the commandments, where all moral duties are reduced to ten words; so in the summaries of the gospel, far more is intended than is expressed.

As for instance, there are two things in the text—the means and the object; the means, ' know;' the object, ' thee,' and ' Jesus Christ.'

1. The means, ' know.' It implieth acknowledgment, faith, fear, reverence, love, worship, and the glorifying God in our conversations. For it is easy to prove out of scripture the necessary concurrence of all these things in their order and place. For if I know God to be the only true God, I must fear, reverence, and obey him, or else I do not glorify him as God; as it is said of the heathens, Rom. i. 21,

' When they knew God, they glorified him not as God.' It is not a naked sight of his essence that will save a man: I must know him for a practical end, to choose him, and carry myself to him as an all-sufficient portion: I must honour him as the giver of all things; revere and worship him as the just governor of the world; and live purely, as he is pure; and worship him in a way suitable to the infiniteness, perfectness, and simplicity of his nature. A man is not saved by holding a right opinion of God. A man may be a christian in opinion and a pagan in life. So if I know Jesus Christ to be sent of God as mediator, I am to close with him, receive him as such by an active faith: Acts iv. 12, ' There is no salvation in any other;' not only *by* no other, but *in* him; it noteth union and close adherence, and not only that I should be of this opinion. As when a man is ready to perish in the floods, it is not enough to see land, but he must reach it, stand upon it, if he would be safe; so we must get into the ark; many saw it and scoffed, but all others were drowned in that general wrack that were not in it. There was no security for the manslayer till he got into the city of refuge: Phil. iii. 9, ' That I may be found in him.' It is not enough to cry, Lord, Lord; to have a naked opinion, or general and loose desires.

2. For the object, ' To know thee the only true God.' There are many articles comprised that are necessary to salvation; as that God is but one: Deut. vi. 4, ' Hear, O Israel, the Lord thy God is one Lord.' One in three persons: 1 John v. 7, ' There are three that bear record in heaven, the Father, the Word, and the Holy Ghost; and these three are one.' This God is a spirit: John iv. 24, ' God is a spirit, and they that worship him, must worship him in spirit and in truth.' He is holy, just, infinite, the creator of all things; that he upholdeth all things in his eternal decree, raising some to glory, leaving others, by their sins, to come to judgment: Rom. ix. 22, 23, ' What if God, willing to show his wrath, and to make his power known, endured with much long-suffering the vessels of wrath fitted to destruction; and that he might make known the riches of his glory on the vessels of mercy, which he had afore prepared unto glory?' All these articles concerning God. So concerning Christ, that he is the second person, incarnate, anointed to be a Saviour, ' to convince the world of sin, of righteousness, of judgment,' John xvi. 8. Of man's misery by nature, redemption by Christ, necessity of holiness, as a foundation of glory; all the articles of the practical catechism. It is a pestilent opinion to think that every man may be saved if he do in the general acknowledge Christ. It is said, Acts ii. 21, ' Whosoever shall call on the name of the Lord shall be saved;' not ' on the Lord,' but ' on the name of the Lord.' By the name of the Lord is meant all that which shall be revealed to us of the Lord Jesus in the scriptures. The meaning is, whosoever doth receive, acknowledge, and worship Christ, according to what the scriptures do reveal and testify of him, shall be saved. Many think the differences of christendom vain, and this general faith enough; but if a general acknowledgment were enough, why hath God revealed so many things, and given us such an ample rule, if with safety to salvation we may be ignorant whether he were true God and true man; whether he redeemed us by

satisfaction, or justified us by works, yea or no? They seem to tax the scriptures of redundances, and the apostles of rash zeal, for disputing with such earnestness for the faith of the saints, as Paul against Justiciaries, James against the Antinomists and Libertines, if a general profession of Christ was enough. So they tax the martyrs of folly, that would shed their blood for less-concerning articles. So all be resolved into Christ, men think it is enough: we need not inquire into the manner of the application of his righteousness, the efficacy and merit of his passion; as if it were enough to hold a few generals, and the more implicit our faith the better. Whereas the Lord would have us to abound in knowledge; and if we persist in any particular error against light, or do not search it out, our case is dangerous, if not damnable. I shall not take upon me to determine what articles are absolutely necessary to salvation; it will be hard to define, and we know not by what rule to proceed. In the general, it is exceeding dangerous to lessen the misery of man's nature, the merit and satisfaction of Christ, or the care of good works; these are contrary to that doctrine which the Spirit teacheth and urgeth in the church: John xvi. 8, 'When he is come, he will convince the world of sin, of righteousness, and of judgment.' All that can be certain is, that those opinions which are irreconcilable with the covenant of grace, or do overturn the pillar upon which it standeth, are irreconcilable with salvation.

Use 1. To confute them that say that every man shall be saved in his own religion, if he be devout therein, Turks, Jews, heathens; and among christians, Papists, Socinians, &c. You see this is life eternal; this, and nothing else—no religion but that which teacheth rightly to believe in Christ is a way of salvation. There is no salvation but by Christ: 1 Cor. iii. 11, 'For other foundation can no man lay than that is laid, which is Jesus Christ;' Acts iv. 12, 'Neither is there salvation in any other; for there is no other name under heaven given among men whereby we must be saved.' There is no salvation by Christ but by faith and knowledge. They cannot have benefit by him, as some say, if they live only according to the law and light of nature: Heb. xi. 6, 'Without faith it is impossible to please God;' and here it is said, 'This is life eternal, to know thee the only true God, and Jesus Christ, whom thou hast sent.' The heathens had many moral virtues, but unless God did reveal himself to them by extraordinary ways, which we cannot judge of, all their privilege was *ut mitius ardeant,* their works being but *splendida peccata.* If any now may be saved without Christ, Christ is dead in vain, and we may want the whole gospel and yet be safe; the philosophy of Aristotle and Seneca would be the way and power of God unto salvation, as well as the gospel. We must have a care lest, by going about to make them christians, we make ourselves heathens.

Use 2. Let us bless God for the gospel, that revealeth God and Christ. Many nations are spilt on the world without any knowledge of God and Christ, and are as sheep, whom no man taketh up. Blessed be God for our privileges. When we look to the hole of the pit from whence we were digged, we shall find ourselves as barbarous as others. *Portenta diabolica pene Ægyptiaca numina vincentia,* saith

Gildas of our idols. God threateneth Israel, Hosea ii. 3, 'I will strip her naked, and set her as in the day that she was born.' If we should despise the gospel, abuse the messengers of it, God will return us to our old barbarism; and we that were so shy of letting in popery, should usher in atheism. When the professors of the gospel were banished Cambridge, and Peter Martyr heard the sacring bell, he said, There is the gospel's passing bell. It would be sad if we should hear such a sound. The ministry (I may speak it without arrogancy) are the only visible party that uphold the life of religion in the land: the Lord knows what may be the sad fruits of their suppression, if either these lights should be extinguished by violence, or be starved for want of oil. Methinks our message should make our feet beautiful. We preach God and Christ. If we be a little earnest for the faith of the saints, remember it is for the good of your souls; it cannot be zeal for our interests, for this is the way to endanger them. Bear with us, it is in a case of salvation or damnation: 'If we be besides ourselves, it is for Christ,' 2 Cor. v. 13. If we seem to hazard all, many nations to whom God hath denied the mercy, would welcome it with all thanksgiving; when God hath opened a door of hope to the Indians, it may be it will be more precious.

Use 3. Study God in Jesus Christ. This is the most glorious subject of contemplation; there we may find him infinitely just and yet merciful, pardoning sinners yet salving the authority of this law; there we may see God and man in one person, and the beams of divine majesty allayed by the veil of human nature. In the godhead of Christ we may see his power, in his human nature his love and condescension. He is our Lord, and yet our brother; a man, and yet God's fellow and equal: Zech. xiii. 7, 'Awake, O sword, against my shepherd, and against the man that is my fellow, saith the Lord of hosts.' He would have a mother on earth, that we might have a Father in heaven; our relation and alliance to heaven groweth by him. In Christ only can we look upon God as a father: *Deum absolutum debent omnes fugere qui non volunt perire;* otherwise we shall perish, and be overwhelmed with despair. Again, *non solum periculosum est, sed etiam horribile, de Deo extra Christum cogitare.* In trials and temptations it is dangerous to think of God alone, to consider him out of Christ; but here infinite majesty condescendeth to converse with you. / The Indian gymnosophists would lie on their backs, and gaze on the sun all day. Oh! how should we, by the deliberate gaze of faith, reflect upon this μέγα μυστήριον, 1 Tim. iii. 16, this glorious mystery, fit for angels to look into! / Only get an interest in it, or else it will be more cold and comfortless; thy God and thy Christ, that is another thing when thou canst own God as thy father and Christ as thy brother. Luther saith, *Deus magis cognoscitur in prædicamento relationis quam in prædicamento substantiæ*—To know God in relation to us is far sweeter than to be able curiously to discourse of his essence: John xiv. 20, 'At that day ye shall know that I am in my Father, and you in me, and I in you.' When we know God in Christ, and Christ in us, this is to know him indeed; not only by hearsay, but acquaintance, to know him so as to love him, and enjoy him.

Use 4. To press us to seek salvation in no other but in God through Christ. Come to Christ; you are in need of salvation, and there is no other way: Acts iv. 12, 'Neither is there salvation in any other, for there is no other name under heaven given among men whereby we must be saved.' Christ is an all-sufficient Saviour, ' able to save unto the uttermost all that come unto God through him,' Heb. vii. 25; a plaster broad enough for every sore. Do you cast yourselves upon him; see if he will refuse you: John vi. 37, 'He that cometh unto me, I will in no wise cast off.'

Now I shall come to the particulars that are to be known concerning God and Christ.

First, Concerning God.

Doct. 1. That there is a God. This is the supreme truth, and first to be known: Heb. xi. 6, ' They that come to God must believe that he is.' The discussion is not needless. Though it be impossible to deface those impressions of the deity which are engraven upon our hearts, yet the drift of our desires and thoughts goeth this way, as if there were no God: Ps. x. 4, ' The wicked, through the pride of his countenance, will not seek after God; God is not in all his thoughts.' All his thoughts are, There is no God: Ps. xiv. 1, ' The fool hath said in his heart, There is no God.' Though he durst not speak it out, yet he saith it in his heart, he entertaineth some such suspicious thoughts and desires about this matter. Those that are guilty of treason would fain destroy the court-rolls; so carnal men would destroy all memorials of God. Yea, many of the children of God feel this temptation. Is there a God? It will not be lost labour to answer the inquiry. I shall pitch upon such arguments as are every man's money.

1. God is evidenced by his works:—

[1.] Of creation. The world is a great book and volume, the creatures are letters, the most excellent are capital letters. If you cannot read, the beasts will teach you: Job xii. 7, 8, ' Ask now the beasts, and they will teach thee; and the fowls of the air, and they shall tell thee. Or speak to the earth, and it shall teach thee; and the fishes of the sea shall declare unto thee. Who knoweth not in all these that the hand of the Lord hath wrought this?' The mute fishes, that can hardly make any sound, have voice enough to proclaim their creator. The apostle tells us, Rom. i. 20, ' The invisible things of him from the creation of the world are clearly seen, being understood by the things that are made, even his eternal power and godhead.' Like Phidias, who in his image carved his own name, there is God engraven upon every creature. But how doth the world show that there is a God? There must be some supreme and infinite cause, for nothing can be cause to itself; then it would be before it is. Aristotle acknowledged πρῶτον αἴτιον, a first cause. Every house must have a builder, and this curious fabric an infinitely wise architect. Thou that deniest God, or doubtest of his being, look upon the heavens: Ps. xix. 1, ' The heavens declare the glory of God, and the firmament showeth his handiwork.' His glory shineth in the sun, and sparkles in the stars. The sun is a representative of God in the brightness of his beams, extent of his influence, indefatigableness of his motion. All the motions of the creatures are so many pulses, by which we may feel after God.

[2.] By works of providence. The world is made up of things of different and destructive natures, and all that we now see would soon run into disorder and confusion were it not poised and tempered with a wise hand ; and when we are stupid, and do not mind these things, providence discovereth itself in judgments and unwonted operations : Ps. lviii. 11, 'So that a man shall say, Verily there is a reward for the righteous ; verily he is a God that judgeth in the earth.'

2. From the confession and common consent of all nations, even those that have been most rude and barbarous, there is none without some worship. The pagan mariners, Jonah i. 5, 'were afraid, and cried every man unto his god.' Those that were most estranged from human society, those that lived in the wilderness without law and government, have been touched with a sense of a deity and god-head ; which must arise from natural instinct. It cannot be any deceit, or imposition of fancy, by custom and tradition, falsehood usually not being so universal and long-lived. Men do what they can to blot out these notions and instincts of conscience. An invention so contrary to nature would have been long ere this worn out.

3. From our own consciences, that appal the stoutest sinner after the commitment of any gross evil. The heathens, that had but a little light, feared death : Rom. i. 32, 'They, knowing the judgment of God, that they that do such things are worthy of death,' &c. ; and 'they had thoughts excusing and accusing one another,' Rom. ii. 14, 15. As letters written with the juice of a lemon, hold them to the fire, they may be read. What terrors are in the hearts of wicked men after the commitment of sins against light, as incest, murder, promiscuous lusts, contemptuous speaking of God or his worship ! Though their sins were secret, hidden under a covert of darkness and secrecy, and not liable to any human cognisance, yet they still feared an avenging hand : their hearts have been upon them. Yea, atheists smitten with horror, what they deny in the day, they acknowledge in the darkness of the night, especially in distress. Diagoras, troubled with the strangury, acknowledged a deity. Or a little before death, their hearts are filled with trembling and horror.

4. From several experiences. The power of the word : 1 Cor. xiv. 25, 'Thus are the secrets of his heart made manifest ; and so falling down on his face, he will worship God, and report that God is in you of a truth.' There is some God guideth these men. There are devils, and they would undo all were they not bound up with the chains and restraints of an irresistible providence. God suffereth them now and then to discover their malice, that we may see by whose goodness we do subsist. So there are virtues, which must be by some institution, or by comformity to a supreme being, or a sense of his law. They cannot be out of any eternal reason, which is in the things themselves, nor by the appointment of man's will ; for then everything which man willeth would be good. Many arguments might be brought to this purpose, but I am shortly to handle this argument elsewhere.

By way of use.

1. Let us charge it upon our hearts, that we may check those private whispers and suspicions which are there against the being and glory of God. Many times we are apt to think that God is but a fancy,

religion a state curb, and the gospel but a quaint device to please fond and foolish men; and all is but talk to hold men in awe.   Oh! consider, in such truths as these we do not appeal to scripture, but nature.   You will never be able to recover your consciences out of this dread.   The devils are under the fear of a deity: James ii. 19, 'Thou believest that there is one God, thou doest well; the devils also believe and tremble.'   The devil can never be a flat atheist, because of the fear of the wrath of God tormenting him; he is not an atheist, because he cannot be one, it cannot stand with the state of a damned angel; there may be atheists in the church, but there are none in hell. Humble thyself for such atheistical thoughts and suggestions.   It is a sin irrational; all the creatures confute it: Ps. lxxiii. 22, 'So foolish was I and ignorant, I was as a beast before thee;' when he had an ill thought of providence.   When you go about to ungod God, you unman yourselves.   Common sense and reason would teach you otherwise.   Thoughts and desires that strike at the being of God are thoughts of a dangerous importance.   Oh! what a foul heart have I, that casteth up such mire and dirt!   Wrath came upon the Jews to the uttermost for killing Christ in his human nature; but these are thoughts that strike at God, and Christ, and all together.

2. It reproveth those that wish down, or live down this principle. Some wish it down: Ps. xiv. 1, 'The fool hath said in his heart, There is no God.'   It is his desire rather than his thoughts.   It is a pleasant thing for them to imagine that there is none to call them to an account.   Guilty men would fain destroy the righteous God, which is an argument of the worst hatred.   Some live it down: Titus i. 16, 'In works they deny him.'   It is the real language of their lives that there is no God.   There is no greater temptation to atheism than the life of a scandalous professor.   One surprised a christian in an act of filthiness, and cried out, *Christiane! Christiane! ubi Deus tuus?*— O christian! christian! where is thy God?   There are few atheists in opinion, more in affection, most in conversation of life.   You live in deceit and cozenage, and yet profess to believe an omniscient God; and your privy walkings are full of sin and excess.   There is blasphemy in your lives: Rev. ii. 9, 'I know the blasphemy of them which say they are Jews and are not, but are the synagogue of Satan.'   Mr Greenham tells of one who was executed at Norwich for an atheist; first he was a papist, then a protestant; then he fell off from all religion, and turned atheist.   How can you believe it is true that there is a God, when this truth hath so little power on the heart?

3. It presseth you to lay this principle up with care.   All Satan's malice is to bring you to a denial of this supreme truth; it is good to discern his wiles.   There are special seasons when you are most liable to atheism.   When providence is adverse, prayers are not heard, and those that worship God are in the worst case; the Lord doth not come in when we would have him.   The devil worketh upon our stomach and discontent; and when we are vexed that we have not our desires,· we complain, as Israel, Exod. xvii. 7, 'Is the Lord among us or no?' when they wanted water.   But still 'our God is in the heavens, and doth whatsoever he pleaseth.'   The saints in their expostulation still yield the principle: Ps. lxxiii. 1, 'Truly God is good to Israel;' how-

ever the state of things are, yet he is resolved to hold to principles. So
Jer. xii. 1, he layeth it down as an undoubted maxim, ' Righteous art
thou, O God.' God is God still. So when we meet with oppression,
men pervert judgment, others forswear themselves, our innocency doth
not prevail, the devil abuseth the rage of passions in such a case. As
Diagoras, a noted atheist among the heathens, became so upon this
occasion : he saw a man deeply forswearing himself, and yet was not
stricken with a thunderbolt. Consider, though this be a sure temptation, yet there is a God : Eccles, iii. 16, 17, ' I saw under the sun the
place of judgment, that wickedness was there ; and the place of righteousness, that iniquity was there.' What then ? ' I said in my heart,
God shall judge the righteous and the wicked ; for there is a time for
every purpose and for every work.' God will have a time to judge
this matter ere long. Still recover your supreme principle out of the
hands of the temptation. So in times of general oppression, when the
innocent party are left as a prey to their adversaries: Eccles. v. 8,
' When thou seest the violent perverting of judgment and justice in a
province, marvel not at the matter; for he that is higher than the
highest regardeth, and there be higher than they.' We may lose all
outward supports, but not our God. *Attamen vivit Christus, et
regnat.* So when second causes operate and accomplish their wonted
effects according to their fixed and stated course, ' All things continue
as they were,' 2 Peter iii. 4, they think the world is governed by chance
or nature ; so this proveth a snare. But you should see God at the
other end of causes ; he can change them as he pleaseth.

<hr>

SERMON IV.

*And this is life eternal, that they might know thee the only true God,
and Jesus Christ, whom thou hast sent.*—JOHN XVII. 3.

DOCT. 2. The next proposition is, that this God is but one, ' Thee the
only true God.' Deut. vi. 4, ' Hear, O Israel ; the Lord thy God is
one Lord.' The heathens multiplied gods according to their own fancies : they ' had lords many and gods many.' Austin in one of his
epistles speaketh of one Maximius, a heathen, who excuseth the poly-
theism of the gentiles, that they worshipped but one supreme essence,
though under divers names. *Ejus quasi quædam membra variis
supplicationibus prosequimur, ut totum colere valeamus*—that they
had several deities, that they might, as by so many several parcels,
adore the whole divine essence. The truth is, nature hath some sense
of it; for as it showeth there is a God, so it showeth there is but one
God. Socrates was a martyr to this truth. The Platonics worshipped
one supreme essence, whom they called ὁ βασιλεύς. The philosophers sometimes called God τὸ ὄν, that being; sometimes τὸ ἓν, that
one thing. Tertullian proveth that the soul was *naturaliter chris-
tiana*, as he speaketh, *O testimonium animæ naturaliter christianæ ;*
which he proveth from the forms of speech then in use. *Deus videt,*
&c.—what God shall award; God seeth ; let God determine of me,

and for me.   And in troubles they cried out, O God! and in straits they did not look to the Capitol, the imagined seat of such gods as the Romans worshipped, but to heaven, the seat of the living God.   Thus it is with the soul, saith he, when recovered out of a distemper.   The truth is, it was the dotage and darkness of their spirits to acknowledge many gods, as drunkards and madmen usually see things double, two suns for one.   But besides the consent of nations, to give you reasons: There is a God, and therefore but one God; there can be but one first cause, and one infinite, one best, one most perfect, one omnipotent.   If one can do all things, what need more gods?   If both be omnipotent, we must conceive them as agreeing or disagreeing; if disagreeing, all would be brought to nothing; if agreeing, one is superfluous.   God hath decided the controversy: Isa. xliv. 8, 'Is there a God besides me?   Yea, there is no God, I know not any.'   As if he said, If any have cause to know, I have, but I know none.

This point is useful, not only to exempt the soul from the anxious fear of a false deity, and to confute the Manichees, Marcion, Cerdo, and others, that held two sorts of gods, and those that parted the godhead into three essences, and the pagan fry.   But practically—

1. It checketh those that set up other gods besides him in their hearts.   If there be but one God, why do we make more, and give divine honour to creatures?   A worldling maketh his money his god, and a sensualist his belly his god.   Covetousness is called idolatry; and Phil. iii. 19, 'Whose god is their belly.'   How is covetousness idolatry? and how can any make their belly their god?   Who ever was seen praying to his pence, or worshipping his own belly?   I answer—Though it be not done corporally and grossly, yet it is done spiritually.   That which engrosseth our love, and confidence, and care, and choice, and delight, that is set up in the room and place of God; and this is to give divine honour to a creature.   Now this is in worldlings and sensualists.   For confidence, they trust in their riches for a supply, do not live on providence: 1 Tim. vi. 17, 'Charge them that are rich in this world, that they be not high-minded, nor trust in uncertain riches, but in the living God;' Prov. x. 15, 'A rich man's wealth is his strong city;' he is provided of a defence against all the chances and strokes of providence.   So for care; a man devoteth his time to his god, and the sensualist sacrificeth his estate, his health, his soul to his own gullet, many sacrilegious morsels to his own throat; every day he offereth a drink-offering, and meat-offering to appetite. O brethren! take heed of gods of man's making.   He is as much an idolater that preferreth his wealth to obedience, his pleasures before God's service, as he that falleth down to a stock.   It would be sad if on your death-beds God should turn you back, as he did the Israelites in their distress : Judges x. 14, 'Go and cry to the gods whom ye have chosen; let them deliver you in the time of your tribulation.' Go to your wealth, to your pleasures.

2. If God be but one, worship him with an entire heart.   The story goeth, that the senate, hearing of the miracles in Judea, decreed divine worship to Christ; but Tiberius the emperor crossed it, when he heard that he would be worshipped alone.   God is but one; our hearts should close with him as an all-sufficient portion : there is enough in one.   The

scripture speaks of 'believing with all the heart.' Other comforts and confidences must be disclaimed. Sometimes carnal persons set their hearts upon other comforts; Christ is not their whole delight: they would have Christ for their consciences, and the world for their hearts; Christ in an extremity, but their affections go out to other things. Sometimes they will have other confidences: they would trust Christ for their eternal salvation, to salve conscience; but the world engrosses their care, as if they were to shift for themselves in temporal things, and be masters of their own fortunes; as it appeareth when temporal supplies fail; when visible supplies are absent, then they despair. It is a mere mistake and folly to think it is easier to trust Christ for pardon of sins and eternal life, than for daily bread; as Christ said, Mark ii. 9, 'Whether is easier to say, Thy sins are forgiven thee; or to say, Arise, take up thy bed and walk?' The truth is, temporal wants are more pressing and urging than spiritual, and men are careless in the business of their souls.

Doct. 3. The next proposition is, that this God is one in three persons. This also is collected from the text. 'To know thee,' that is, the Father, with all the co-essential persons. They are undivided in essence, though distinguished in personality. Take a place of scripture: 1 John v. 7, 'There are three that bear record in heaven, the Father, the Word, and the Holy Ghost, and these three are one.' Let me a little open the doctrine of the Trinity by some short observations.

This is a mystery proper to the scriptures. Other truths are revealed in nature, but this is a treasure peculiar to the church. There are some passages in heathens that seem to look this way; as Plato speaketh of νοῦς, λόγος, πνεῦμα, mind, word, and spirit; and Trismegistus, πρῶτα θεὸς, &c. But these were either some general notions, received by tradition from the Jews, and by them misunderstood, for they dreamed of three distinct separate essences, or else passages foisted into their writings by the fraud and fallacy of some christians, who counted it a piece of their zeal to lie for God. It is not likely that God would give the heathens a more clear revelation of these mysteries than he did to his own people, the church of the Jews. We find it but sparingly revealed in the Old Testament, though I might bring many places where it is sufficiently hinted; but more distinctly in the New, after the visible and sensible discovery of the three persons at Christ's baptism: Mat. iii. 17, 'The Spirit of God descended like a dove, and lighted upon him, and lo, a voice from heaven, saying, This is my beloved Son, in whom I am well pleased.' *Voce Pater, Natus corpore, Numen ave.* The whole Trinity were present at that solemnity. Some darkness there is still upon the face of this deep; we shall have more perfect knowledge of it in the heavens: John xiv. 20, 'At that day ye shall know that I am in my Father, and you in me, and I in you.' Trinity in unity and unity in trinity still troubleth the present weakness of reason; but when we shall see God face to face, our knowledge shall be more satisfactory and complete. For the present, we must come to this truth with a sober mind, and adore it with a humble piety, lest we puzzle faith while we would satisfy and inform reason. There are many words which the church hath used in the explication

of this mystery, as unity, trinity, essence, person, consubstantial; which
though they be not all found in the scriptures, yet they are the best
that we can use in so deep a matter, and serve to prevent the errors
and mistakes of those who would either multiply the essence, or abolish
the persons. Some terms must be used, and these are the safest.
They be three, and yet one; and the most commodious way to solve it
to our understandings is, one in essence and three persons; for there
being three in the divine essence, the Father, the Word, and the Spirit,
each having the whole divine essence, and yet the essence undivided,
there must be some words to express the mystery. God, being one,
cannot be divided in nature and being; and there being three, every
one having the whole godhead in himself, distinguished by peculiar
relative properties, what term shall we use? Three ways of existence
there are in the nature of God, because of those three real relations—
paternity, filiation, and procession. One they are, and distinct they
are really. There is and must be a distinction, for the essence and
particular way of existence do differ. Whatever is said of the essence
is true of every person. God is infinite, eternal, incomprehensible; so
is the Father, Son, and Spirit. But now, whatever is said of the
existence, as existence, cannot be said of the essence; every one that is
God is not Father, Son, and Holy Ghost. I say, then, there being a
distinction between the nature and particular existences, there must be
some terms to express it. The Greek Church in the Nicene Council,
some three hundred and sixty years after Christ, worded it thus: The
occasion was this, some heretics said, If Christ be God, of the same
substance and being with the Father, then, when Christ was incarnate,
the Father was incarnate also. No, say the orthodox, though the οὐσία,
the substance or essence be the same, it is not the same ὑπόστασις, the
same subsistence in the godhead; and then began the public and received
distinction of οὐσία and ὑπόστασις: οὐσία signifying the nature or
substance; ὑπόστασις, the several manners of existence. And the
determination of the church was, that these were the fittest terms to
explicate this mystery. Not but that these words were used before in
this matter; as may appear out of divers authors that lived and wrote
before that famous Nicene Council, but they were not so accurately
distinguished, nor so publicly received. And indeed, though the word
οὐσία, essence, be not in scripture, yet ὑπόστασις is. There is ground
for οὐσία, for when the nature of God is expressed, it is expressed by
a word equivalent to essence, 'I Am that I Am,' Exod. iii. 14. So
ὁ ὢν, ὁ ἦν, καὶ ὁ ἐρχόμενος, 'He that was, and is, and is to come,' Rev.
i. 4. Then for ὑπόστασις, Christ is called, Heb. i. 3, χαρακτὴρ τῆς
ὑποστάσεως αὐτοῦ, 'The express image of his person.' It cannot be
rendered *essence*, but *subsistence;* for then Arius would have carried
the day, and Christ would be only ὁμοιούσιος. And the Father's
essence cannot properly be said to be impressed on the Son, since the
very same individual essence and substance was wholly in him, as
it was wholly in the Father; and the Son cannot be said to be like:
but now 'the express image of his subsistence;' or, as we now render
it, 'person,' doth provide for the consubstantiality of the Son; against
Arius; and for the distinction of the subsistences, against Sabellius.
Thus for a long time it was carried in the terms of *substance* and *sub-*

sistence. But how came the word *person* in use? I answer—The Latin Church expressed it by ' person,' upon these grounds : partly because they would have a word in their own language that might serve for common and vulgar use, and the right apprehension of this mystery ; partly because ὑπόστασις and *subsistence* were ambiguous, and of a doubtful signification, being both often in common acceptation put for the same thing ; and the Latin fathers, *timidius usi sunt eo vocabulo*, were shy in using that word ; partly because this word is very commodious, as being proper to particular, distinct, rational substances. Whatever is a person must be a substance, not an attribute or accident, as white or black ; a particular substance, not a general essence or nature. It must be living ; we do not call a book or a board a person. It must be rational ; we do not call a tree or a beast a person, though they have life ; but only man. And it must not be a part of a man, as the soul ; it must not be that which is sustained in another, but subsisteth of itself. So the humanity of Christ is not a person, because it hath no subsistence in itself, but is sustained by the godhead. Now a person in the godhead is an incommunicable subsistence in the divine essence, or the divine essence or nature distinguished by its incommunicable property ; or more plainly, a diverse and distinct subsistence in the godhead. And the word is not to be taken in the extreme rigour, to infer any separation or division in the godhead. Three persons among men make three separate essences, three men ; but not here three Gods ; for in the godhead the persons are not separate and divided, but only distinguished by their relative properties ; they are co-eternal, infinite, and may be in one another, the Father in the Son, the Son in the Father, both in the Spirit. We are material, and though we communicate in the same nature, yet we live separate. In short, the word *person* is used to show that they are not only three acts, offices, attributes, properties, qualities, operations, but distinct subsistences, distinguished from one another by their unchangeable order of first, second, and third— Father, Word, and Spirit—and their incommunicable properties of paternity, filiation, and procession, or unbegotten, begotten, and proceeding, and by their special and personal manner of operation, creating, redeeming, sanctifying. Creation is by the Father, redemption by the Son, sanctification by the Spirit. More may be said, but when shall we make an end?

Let us apply it.

Use. Let us bless God that we have such a complete object for our faith. We can want nothing that have Father, Son, and Spirit, the co-operation of all the persons for our salvation ; that we can consider the Father in heaven, the Son on the cross, and feel the Spirit in our hearts ; yea, that the whole Godhead should take up its abode, and come and converse with us: 2 Cor. xiii. 14, ' The grace of our Lord Jesus Christ, the love of God, and the communion of the Holy Ghost, be with you all. Amen.' Oh! what a treble privilege is this! Grace, love, and communion ; election, merit, and actual grace. This is a mystery, felt as well as believed. We have a God to love us, a Christ to redeem us, and a Spirit to apply all to the soul: 1 Peter ii. 3, ' If so be ye have tasted that the Lord is gracious.' Our spiritual estate standeth upon a sure bottom; the beginning is from God the Father, the dispensation from the Son, and the application from the Holy Ghost. The Father's electing love is engaged by the merit of Christ, and conveyed by the power of the Holy Ghost. There was a purpose by the Father, the accomplishment was by the Son, and exhibition is by the Spirit; it is free in the Father, sure in the Son, ours in the Spirit; the Father purposeth, the Son ratifieth, the Spirit giveth us the enjoyment of all. Oh! let us adore the mysterious Trinity; we are not thankful enough for this glorious discovery.

Doct. 4. That God, who is one in three persons, is the only true God, σὲ τὸν ἀληθινὸν θεὸν, 'Thee the only true God;' 1 Thes. i. 9, ' Ye turned to God from idols, to serve the living and true God.' All others are but idols and false gods; they are not able to avenge the contempt of them that wrong them, or to save those that trust in them: Gal. iv. 8, 'Then when ye knew not God, ye did service to them that by nature were no gods.' An idol is nothing but what it is in the valuation and esteem of men. Oh! then, let us not look upon religion as a mere fancy. God is, whether we acknowledge him or no. Usually, in great turns and changes, many turn atheists. Some turn short from gross idolatry to rest in superstition; others turn over, and lay aside religion itself, as if all were fancy and figment. Oh! consider, a God there is; who else made the world? And then, 'who is a god like unto the Lord our God?' Go, search abroad among the nations. It is some advantage sometimes to consider what a God we serve, above the gods of the Gentiles. God alloweth you the search for settlement and satisfaction: Jer. vi. 16, 'Thus saith the Lord, Stand ye in the ways, and see, and ask for the old paths, where is the good way, and walk therein, and ye shall find rest for your souls.' If you will make a serious comparison, see where you can anchor safer than in Christianity. Where can you have more comfortable representations of God than in the christian religion? And where can you have a purer representation of the christian religion than in the churches of the Protestants? All else is as unstable as water. Here God is represented as holy, yet gracious; and here you may meet with a strict rule of duty, and yet best for your choice. Let it confirm you in your choice; and bless God for the advantages of your birth and education. If you had been born among heathens, you had been liable to their darkness: ' The statutes of the Lord are right, rejoicing the heart,' Ps. xix. 10.

Secondly, Now we come to speak to the second head of christian doctrine, what is to be known concerning Jesus Christ? I shall not wander and digress from the circumstances of the text.

Here are three things offered to our consideration:—(1.) That he is sent; (2.) That he is Jesus, or a saviour; (3.) That he is Christ, or an anointed saviour.

First, That he is sent. I in part opened this in the explication; now I shall open it more fully. It implieth—

1. Christ's divine original; he was a person truly existing before he came into the world, as a man must be before he is sent; he came forth from God: Gal. iv. 4, 'When the fulness of time was come, God sent forth his Son, made of a woman, made under the law;'

ἐξαπέστειλεν, the word is a double compound, sent forth from God. Jesus Christ was in the Godhead; to note his intimacy and familiarity with God, he is said to be ἐν κόλπῳ πατρὸς, John i. 18, 'The only-begotten Son of God, which is in the bosom of the Father, he hath declared him.' He is not only *legatus a latere*, from the side of God, but from the bosom of God; so equals and dear friends are admitted into the bosom. Therefore he is said 'to come forth from God,' John xvi. 30. Not only to note the authority of his message, but the quality of his person, he came from out of the Godhead. No inferior mediator could serve the turn; such an errand required a God himself: nothing but an infinite good could remedy an infinite evil. Sin had bound us over to an eternal judgment, and nothing could counterpoise eternity but the infiniteness and excellency of Christ's person. He that came on such an errand must needs be God, both to satisfy God and to satisfy us. God could not be satisfied unless his sufferings had received a value from his person. To satisfy God offended there must be a God satisfying for the offence; therefore his blood is called 'the blood of God;' Acts xx. 28, 'Feed the church of God, which he hath purchased with his own blood.' The satisfaction must carry proportion with the merit of the offence. A debt of a thousand pounds is not discharged by two or three brass farthings. Creatures are finite, their acts are due, and their sufferings for one another, if they had been allowed, would have been of a limited influence. Merit is above the creature; no act of ours can lay an engagement upon God: 1 Sam. ii. 25, 'If a man sin against another, the judge shall judge him; but if he sin against God, who shall entreat for him?' The judge may accord a difference between man and man, and one man may make satisfaction to another; but to take up matters between us and God, a person must be sent out of the Godhead itself. So to satisfy us; he had need be able to grapple with divine wrath that would undertake our cause; he was not only to undergo it, but to overcome it. The creature would never have been satisfied if he had perished in the work; if our surety were kept in prison, and held under wrath and death, we should have had no assurance that the debt was paid: Acts xvii. 31, 'Whereof he hath given assurance to all men, in that he hath raised him from the dead.' Christ's resurrection is our acquittance and discharge: John xvi. 10, 'Of righteousness, because I go to my Father, and ye see me no more.' Well, then, we see the reasons why a person of the Godhead is employed in this work. You need not doubt but that it is accomplished to the full, since it is in the hands of such an able surety. Besides, it showeth the greatness of our sin and misery, that a person of the Godhead must be sent to rescue us. Sin fetched the Son of God from heaven, and if we subdue it not, it will sink us into hell.

2. It implieth his distinct subsistence, that Christ is a distinct person from the Father; for he that sendeth and he that is sent are distinguished. Mark, I say, it implieth distinction, but not inferiority, against the Arians. Persons equal by mutual consent may send one another, as we see among men; and Christ was equal with God: Phil. ii. 6, 'Who being in the form of God, thought it no robbery to be equal with God;' he might take that honour upon him without

usurpation. Now this sending is ascribed to the Father; as John x. 36, 'Say ye of him, whom the Father hath sanctified and sent into the world,' &c., and in other places. Partly because the Father in those places is not taken personally, but essentially; for the decree of the Father is the decree of the Son and Spirit; they are one in essence, and one in will, their actions are undivided. Partly because this peculiar personal operation is especially ascribed to the first person. The Father is said to send, and the Holy Ghost to qualify and fit him. It is ascribed to the Father, he sent the Spirit to accomplish it; to God the Son, who took human nature, and united it to his own godhead; to the Spirit of God, who formed, and sanctified, and furnished it with gifts without measure. In the economy of salvation, the original authority is made to reside in God the Father. So that here is a sensible argument to confirm the doctrine of the Trinity. Christ was sent, one of the persons took flesh by order and appointment of the whole Godhead. The distinction of the persons is by this discovered: Heb. i. 5, 6, 'For unto which of the angels said he at any time, Thou art my Son, this day have I begotten thee? And again, I will be to him a Father, and he shall be to me a Son? And again, when he bringeth in the first-begotten into the world, he saith, And let all the angels of God worship him.'

3. It implieth the incarnation of Christ: 'Sent into the world,' John x. 36. So Gal. iv. 4, 'God sent forth his own Son, made of a woman.' Christ's sending doth not imply change of place, but assumption of another nature. Now this was necessary, otherwise Christ neither ought to nor could suffer. Justice required that the same nature that sinned should be punished. If he had not been made of a woman he could not be under the law, the duty, or the penalty of it: Gal. iv. 4, 'He was made of a woman, made under the law.' Our sin was not to be punished in angels, or in any other creature that had not sinned, nor in man made out of nothing, or out of a piece of earth, or out of the dust, as Adam. God might have made Christ true man out of that matter, but he was made of a woman, one that was of our blood, of the same nature and essence with them that sinned. Our Saviour was not to be a sinner, but partaker of the same nature with them that sinned.

4. It implieth the quality of Christ's office; he is the messenger of heaven, and therefore called 'the angel of the covenant,' Mal. iii. 1. He is sent by God after lost sinners. He is called 'the apostle and high priest of our profession,' Heb. iii. 1. God sendeth out a messenger to bring sinners to himself, as wisdom sent out her maids; but Christ is the chief messenger and apostle. And mark, he is called there not only the apostle but high priest; partly to show that in all ages of the church Christ is the chief officer, therefore the highest calling, both in the Jewish and christian church is ascribed to him; but chiefly to show that Christ, as he is the ambassador to treat with us from God, so the high priest to treat with God and appease his wrath for us. Christ is the messenger that goeth from party to party; if he had not been sent to us we should neither know God nor enjoy him; he came from God to men that he might bring men to God. There was no knowing of the Father without him: Mat. xi. 27, 'No man knoweth

the Son but the Father; neither knoweth any man the Father save the Son, and he to whomsoever the Son shall reveal him.' There is no coming to the Father without him: John xiv. 6, 'I am the way, the truth, and the life; no man cometh to the Father but by me.' He came from heaven on purpose to show us the way and to remove all obstacles. This is Christ's office.

5. It implieth the authority of his office. Jesus Christ had a lawful call. He was designed in the council of the Trinity; his holiness, miracles, and divine power are his commission: 'Him hath God the Father sealed,' John vi. 27; as every ambassador hath letters of credence under the hand and seal of him from whom he is sent. Christ is the plenipotentiary of heaven; he hath his commission under the seal of heaven; all is valid that he doth in the Father's name; he hath authorised the Redeemer. Which is not only for the comfort of our faith; Christ entered upon his calling by authority, which I shall improve by and by; but for moral instruction, to look to our mission: Christ came not till he was sent. It is not good to cast ourselves upon offices and places without a lawful call and designation of God. In ordinary functions, education and abilities are call enough, and there we must keep. It is a tempting of providence to think God will bless us out of our way. A desire of change usually proceedeth from disdain, or distrust, or a thirst of gain, all which are sinful. But now, in higher callings, there must be a solemn mission: Rom. x. 15, 'How shall they preach except they be sent?' They must be authorised by God, the rules he hath left in the church. Our Lord Jesus Christ did not glorify himself by intrusion; he had a patent from the council of the Trinity, indited by the Father, accepted by himself, and sealed by the Holy Ghost.

Use. It showeth three things:—

1. The love of God. Here are many circumstances to heighten it in your thoughts; that he would not trust an angel with your salvation, but send his Son; he is to come in person: 1 John iv. 10, 'Herein is love; not that we loved God, but that he loved us, and sent his Son to be the propitiation for our sins.' He thought nothing too near and too dear for us. Usually man's love descendeth, and all his happiness is laid up in his children. Again, God had no reasons; he was moved by his own goodness; he had reasons to the contrary. We were enemies, but he sent his Son for enemies: Rom. v. 10, 'If when we were enemies, we were reconciled to God by the death of his Son,' &c. What was his Son sent for? Not to treat with us in majesty, but to take our nature, to be substituted into our room and place. Oh! praise the Father: Eph. i. 3, 'Blessed be the God and Father of our Lord Jesus Christ, who hath blessed us with all spiritual blessings in heavenly places in Christ;' 2 Cor. i. 3, 'Blessed be God, even the Father of our Lord Jesus Christ, the Father of mercies, and the God of all comfort.'

2. Christ's condescension. He submitteth to be sent: Ps. xl. 7, 8, 'Lo, I come; in the volume of the book it is written of me. I delight to do thy will, O my God; yea, thy law is within my heart.' We could never have asked so much as God hath given. He would not only borrow our tongue to speak to us, but our bowels to mourn for

us, and our bodies to die for us. He layeth aside his majesty, and taketh on himself the condition of a servant. It is irksome to us to go back ten degrees in pomp or pleasure upon just and convenient reasons. Oh! the wonderful self-denial of Christ! He laid aside the majesty of God, and submitted to the greatest abasement and suffering.

3. The value of souls and spiritual privileges. If we despise them, we put an affront upon the wisdom of heaven, and undervalue Christ's purchase. Freedom from sin, justification, holiness, they are the only things. Christ was sent from heaven to purchase them. Gold and silver would not buy them; money is not current in heaven, though it doth all things in the world: 1 Peter i. 18, ' We are not redeemed with corruptible things, as silver and gold, from our vain conversations, but with the precious blood of the Son of God, as of a lamb without spot and blemish.' Christ must come from heaven, and take a body, and shed his blood. Scourge your hearts with that question, Heb. ii. 3, ' How shall we escape if we neglect so great salvation?' Sure we should be more serious, and think that worthy of our best endeavours and greatest earnestness which Christ thought worthy a journey from heaven, and all the pains and shame he suffered.

Secondly, The next thing in the text is that he is Jesus: Mat. i. 21, ' Thou shalt call his name Jesus, for he shall save his people from their sins.' It is there interpreted to signify a saviour; an angel himself is the expositor. So here Christ is sent to be a saviour ; that is a principal object of faith, to look upon Christ as the Saviour of the world. A saviour properly is one that delivereth from evil. Now Christ doth not only deliver us from evil, from sin, the wrath of God, the accusations of the law, and eternal death, but positively he giveth us grace and righteousness and eternal life. He is a saviour to defend us, and a saviour to bless us: Ps. lxxxiv. 11, ' The Lord God is a sun and a shield; he will give grace and glory, and no good thing will he withhold from them that walk uprightly.' The mercies of the covenant are privative and positive. Many enter into a league that they will not hurt one another; but God is in covenant with us to bless us. If Christ had only procured some place for us, unacquainted with pain or pleasure, it had been much; but we have not only a ransom, but an inheritance ; instead of horrors and howlings, everlasting joys. Again, many are called saviours either because of their subordinate subserviency to Christ, instruments in inward and outward salvation; but these saviours needed a saviour. Christ is the true Jesus, who saveth as an author of grace, not as an instrument and means of conveyance. Now Christ is a saviour partly by merit, partly by efficacy and power; he doth something for us and something in us: ·for us, he prevaileth by the merit of his death; in us, by the efficacy of his Spirit; all his work is not done on the cross. Both are necessary, partly in regard of the difference of the enemies ; God and the law are in a distinct rank from sin and death, Satan and the world. God was an enemy ; he cannot be overcome, but must be reconciled; the law an enemy that could not be disannulled, but must be satisfied. Sin, the world, and Satan assault us out of malice, they make themselves our enemies; the law and God are made enemies out of our rebellion; therefore Christ must satisfy as well as overcome. To reconcile God, he shed his blood on the cross.   Justice must have a sacrifice and the law satisfaction; the curses of the law are not to fall to the ground; somebody must be made a curse to keep up the authority of the law; the law was an innocent enemy, and therefore not to be relaxed or repealed.   Partly in regard of the different fight of the other enemies, that are enemies out of malice.   Satan is not only a tempter but an accuser.   As a tempter, so Christ was to overcome him by his power; as an accuser, by his merit.   When Satan condemneth, Christ is to intercede and represent his own merit; the plaster must be as broad as the sore; so far as Satan is an enemy, so far must Christ be a saviour and redeemer, by his power against the temptations, by his merit against the accusations of Satan.   As the devil is an accuser, Christ is an advocate.   Partly because Satan hath a double power over a sinner—legal and usurped.   Legal, as God's executioner, by the ordination of God's justice: Heb. ii. 14, 'That through death he might destroy him that had the power of death, that is, the devil.' Christ is to die to put Satan out of office usurped, as the god of this world.   God made him an executioner, we a prince: John xii. 31, 'Now shall the prince of this world be cast out.'   Christ rescueth prisoners: Isa. xlix. 9, 'That thou mayest say to the prisoners, Go forth.'   He will rescue and recover the elect when by their own default they put themselves in Satan's hands.   Partly for our comfort.   By his own obedience and merit Christ giveth us a right and title, but by his efficacy and power he giveth us possession.   He is to buy our peace, grace, comfort, and then to see that we are possessed of it.

Well, then, own him as Jesus, as the only Saviour.   Acts iv. 17, the apostles were charged 'not to preach any more in the name of Jesus.'   Rest upon his merit, and wait for his power.

1. Rest upon his merit.   Troubled consciences, that think to help themselves by their own care and resolution, are like men that are like to perish in the waters, and when a boat is sent out to help them, think to swim to shore by their own strength.   You would be a saviour to yourselves, your own Jesus, and your own Christ.   God is very jealous of the creature's trust; and Christ saith, Isa. xlv. 5, 'I am the Lord, and there is none else; there is no saviour besides me.'   You would purchase your peace, conquer your own enemies, and then come to Christ.   No money of yours is current in heaven; the jewels of the covenant are not sold for any price but Christ's blood and Christ's obedience.   God saith, Isa. lv. 1, 'He that hath no money, let him come and buy wine and milk, without money and without price.'   He sold to Christ, but he giveth to you; he asketh nothing of you but acceptance.   Will you take it?   They that refuse Christ and refuse comfort till they be holy in themselves, they have a show of humility, they would wear their own garments, spend their own money; but the spirit is never more proud than when under a legal dejection; we scorn to put on Christ's robes, and are better contented with our own spotted garments; as in outward things we prefer a russet coat of our own before a velvet coat of another's.   This is peevish pride.

2. Wait for his power and efficacy in the use of means.   It is bestowed on us by virtue of his intercession: 'We are saved by his life,' Rom. v. 10; 'If when we were enemies, we were reconciled to God by

the death of his Son, much more, being reconciled, shall we be saved by his life.' We are reconciled by his merit, but saved by his life. He liveth in heaven, and procureth influences of his grace: ' Therefore he is' (said to be) ' able to save to the uttermost all that come unto God through him, seeing he ever liveth to make intercession for us,' Heb. vii. 25. In heaven he accomplisheth the other part of his priesthood. He doth not work out a part of man's salvation, and leave the rest to our free will : the sacrificing part is ended, and by his intercession we get the merit applied to us. But we must not be idle, we must come with supplications, and present the case to Christ, that Christ may present it to God. Our groans must answer to the earnestness of his intercession, and then we shall receive supplies. The word is called, ' The power of God to salvation,' Rom. i. 16. Those that conscionably use prayer, and wait for Christ in the word, will find him to be a saviour indeed. The word is the effectual means to save men, how foolish and despicable soever it seem in the world. God would work with us rationally. We cannot expect a brutish bent, &c.

Thirdly, The next thing is that he is Christ, an anointed saviour. This fitly followeth the former. *Jesus* signifies his divinity, and *Christ* his humanity. We are not only to know his person, but his office : John i. 41, ' We have found the Messias, which is, being interpreted, the Christ,' or anointed. This is often expressed in scripture : Ps. xlv. 8, 'He is anointed with the oil of gladness above his fellows;' Isa. lxi. 1, ' The Spirit of the Lord is upon me, because the Lord hath anointed me to preach good tidings unto the meek.' So Acts iv. 27, ' Against thy holy child Jesus, whom thou hast anointed, both Herod, and Pontius Pilate, with the Gentiles, and the people of Israel were gathered together.' So Acts x. 38, ' How God anointed Jesus of Nazareth with the Holy Ghost and with power.' Out of all which places we see that Christ's anointing is not to be understood properly, but by a trope ; the sign is put for the thing signified.

1. Who was anointed ? Among the Gentiles, the wrestlers were anointed. Which may be applied to Christ, who was now to wrestle and conflict with all the prejudices and difficulties of man's salvation. But it is rather taken from the customs of the ceremonial law. Three sorts of persons we find to be anointed among the Jews :—Kings ; as Saul, David, Solomon : 1 Sam. ix. 16, 'Thou shalt anoint him to be captain over my people Israel.' Therefore they were called, ' the Lord's anointed,' 1 Sam. xxvi. 11. Priests ; all the priests that ministered in the tabernacle or temple, chiefly the high priest, who was a special figure of Christ: Exod. xxix. 29, ' And the holy garments of Aaron shall be his sons' after him, to be anointed therein, and to be consecrated in them.' Prophets : 1 Kings xix. 16, 'Elisha the son of Shaphat shalt thou anoint to be prophet in thy room.' As oil strengtheneth and suppleth the joints, and maketh them agile and fit for exercise, so it noteth a designation and fitness for the functions to which they were appointed. So Christ, because he was not to be a typical priest, or prophet, or king, therefore he was not typically but spiritually anointed ; not with a sacramental, but real unction ; not of men, but of God immediately. Therefore we shall inquire how Christ was anointed. It implieth two things :—

[1.] The giving of power and authority: Heb. v. 5, 'Christ glorified not himself to be made an high priest; but he that said unto him, Thou art my Son; this day have I begotten thee.' Therefore though Christ be of the same power and authority with the Father, yet as mediator he must be appointed. Christ took not on him the honour of a mediator, but received it of his Father. God needeth not to appoint a mediator; it was his free grace. To save sinners is not *proprietas divinæ naturæ*, but *opus liberi consilii*. This counsel had its rise from the mercy and free grace of the Father; he might have required this punishment of ourselves. If any had interposed to mediate for us without God's will and calling, his mediation would have been of no value; a pledge whereof we have in Moses: Exod. xxxii. 32, 33, 'Yet now, if thou wilt, forgive their sins; and if not, blot me, I pray thee, out of the book of life. And the Lord said unto Moses, Whosoever hath sinned against me, him will I blot out of my book.' And besides, where should we have found a sufficient mediator, unless he should have given us one? Therefore there is much in the Father's anointing or appointment; therefore is the mediation of Christ so effectual; it is made by his own will: John viii. 42, 'I proceeded forth, and came from God; neither came I of myself, but he sent me;' John vi. 27, 'Him hath God the Father sealed;' as a magistrate hath the king's broad seal. Which is a great comfort; when we go to God, we may offer him Christ, as authorised by himself: Thou hast sent thy own Son to be a mediator for me. And we may plead it to ourselves in faith: God the supreme judge, the wronged party, hath appointed Christ to take up the controversy between him and me.

[2.] The bestowing on him the Holy Ghost, who might make the human nature fit for the work. So Acts x. 38, 'Him hath God anointed with the Holy Ghost and with power.' The human nature of Christ was fitted for the employment; for though it were exalted to great privileges, yet it could not act beyond its sphere; and sanctification is the personal operation of the third person. Now the work of the Holy Ghost was in the womb of the virgin, to preserve the human nature of Christ from the infection of sin. From a sinner nothing could be born but what was unclean and sinful; by this anointing Christ was made perfectly just, strengthened to all offices, especially to offer up himself: Heb. ix. 14, 'Who through the eternal Spirit offered himself without spot to God.' To overcome all difficulties and temptations: Isa. xlii. 1, 'Behold my servant whom I uphold, my elect in whom my soul delighteth; I have put my Spirit upon him.' The work of redemption was a weighty work: Christ had to do with God, devil, and man, to bear the wrath of God for the whole world.

2. To what was Christ anointed? To the office of a mediator in general; particularly to be king, priest, and prophet of the church. To be a prophet, to teach us by his word and Spirit: Mat. xvii. 5, 'This is my beloved Son, in whom I am well-pleased; hear ye him.' God bespeaketh audience. To be a priest, to intercede and die for us, To be a king, to rule us by his Spirit, and to give grace and glory to us.

Use 1. Let us receive Christ as an anointed saviour. Christ is set over us by authority; let us come to him as a prophet, denying our own reason and wisdom; as a priest, seeking all our acceptance with God through his merit. Let us plead, Lord, thou hast anointed Christ to offer himself a sacrifice for me. As a king, let us give up ourselves to the authority and discipline of his Spirit. God's anointing is the true reason and cause why we should come to Christ.

Use 2. Comfort; we are anointed too. Christ's ointment is shared amongst his fellows; he was anointed more than we, but we have our part: Ps. cxxxiii. 2, ' Like the precious ointment upon the head, that ran down upon the beard, even Aaron's beard, that went down to the skirts of his garment;' 1 John ii. 27, ' The anointing which ye have received of him abideth in you.' We are made prophets, priests, and kings; prophets meet to declare his praises, priests fit for holy ministering, kings to reign over our corruptions here, and with Christ for ever in glory, as the queen is crowned with the king.

<hr>

SERMON V.

I have glorified thee on the earth : I have finished the work which thou gavest me to do.—JOHN XVII. 4.

IN this verse there is another argument to inforce the main request of his being glorified; it is taken from the faithful discharge of his duty, and his integrity in it ; it was all finished, and finished to God's glory ; therefore it was not unjust that he should now desire to be glorified. When our work is ended, then we look to receive our wages. Now, saith Christ, ' I have finished the work ; ' and besides (which giveth weight to the argument), ' I have glorified thee.' The reason of Christ's request seems to be taken from the eternal covenant. Do your work, and you shall see your seed; and from those promises, 1 Sam. ii. 30, ' Them that honour me, I will honour ; ' Prov. iv. 8, ' Exalt her, and she shall promote thee ; she shall bring thee to honour, when thou dost embrace her.' Well, Christ showeth that his request is not unequal. Though this be the general relation of the context, yet it is good to note the particular dependence between this and the former verse. Christ said that it was eternal life to know him that was sent ; now he showeth he had discharged that work for which he was sent.

From Christ's suing for glory upon this argument, I might note, that we may plead promises. God saith, ' Put me in remembrance.' There is difference between a plea and a challenge ; hypocrites challenge God upon the merit of their works ; believers humbly urge him with his own promises. Not as if God did need excitement to make good his word ; but we need grounds of hope and confidence.

Again, because Christ asketh nothing but what God will give, I might observe, that when we have done our work we may expect our portion of glory. But I rather come to the particular discussion of the words.

The words may be considered in a mediatory or in a moral sense. In a mediatory sense ; so they are proper to Christ ; he prayed to the Father, ' That thy Son may glorify thee,' ver. 1. Now he saith, ' I have glorified thee;' meaning, in the days of his flesh. By a moral accommodation they may be applied to every christian; every christian should say, as Christ, 'I have glorified thee on the earth, I have finished the work which thou gavest me to do.'

First, and which is most proper, let us consider them in the mystical and mediatory sense. The first phrase is:—

'I have glorified thee.'—Christ glorified God many ways; by his person, as being 'the express image of his Father's glory,' Heb. i. 3. By his life and perfect obedience: John viii. 46, 'Which of you convinceth me of sin?' and ver. 49, 'I have not a devil, but I honour my Father.' By discovering his mercy: John i. 14, 'We beheld his glory, the glory as of the only-begotten of the Father, full of grace and truth.' By his miracles; when the sick of the palsy was cured, it is said, 'The multitude glorified God,' Mat. ix. 8; Mark xv. 31; at other miracles, 'They glorified the God of Israel,' Mark ii. 12. So his passion exceedingly glorified God's justice. In his doctrine, by discovering his glorious essence, and the purity of his worship. The system of divinity was much perfected and advanced by the coming of Christ.

Doct. That God was much glorified in Christ. God was much glorified in the creation of the world: Ps. xix. 1, 'The heavens declare the glory of the Lord, and the firmament showeth his handiwork.' The fabric of the whole world, especially of the heavens, declares his goodness, wisdom, and power. His goodness in communicating being to all creatures, life and motion to some; his wisdom, in making the creatures so various, and so excellent in their general kinds; his power, in educing all things out of the womb of mother nothing. God was glorified in his providences, especially in the great deliverances of the church from Egypt, and from the north; but mostly in Christ, redemption being the most noble work with which he was ever acquainted. It is notable that the Spirit of God in scripture often varieth the expression; at first it was, 'Blessed be God, that made heaven and earth;' then, 'I am the God that brought thee out of the land of Egypt;' then it is, Jer. xvi. 14, 15, 'It shall no more be said, The Lord liveth, that brought up the children of Israel out of the land of Egypt; but the Lord liveth, that brought up the children of Israel from the land of the north;' then it is, 'Blessed be the God and Father of our Lord Jesus Christ,' Eph. i. 3. In creation, the wisdom, goodness, and power of God appeared; there was no need of other attributes. In providence, the justice, mercy, and truth of God appears; but these in Christ in a more raised degree. In creation, the object was pure nothing; as there was no help, so no hindrance; but now in redemption, sin hinders; so that here is shown not only goodness, but mercy. In creation we deserve nothing; now we deserve the contrary. There was more wisdom seen in our redemption. The quarrel taken up between justice and mercy. Mercy would pity, and justice could not spare. In redemption there is more power; in creation, man is taken out of the earth; in redemption, out of hell. God's justice opposed redemption. Christ must be sent to satisfy justice, and the Spirit sent to take away unbelief. God made all with a word, he saved all with a plot of grace. In creation, man was made like God; in redemption, God is made like man. No deliverance like this ; Babylon was nothing to hell, and the brick-kilns of Egypt to the lake that burneth with fire and brimstone. When God delivered his people out of Babylon, he had to do with creatures; when he delivered them from the wrath to come, he had to do with himself. Justice put in high demands against the compassions of mercy ; his own Son must die with the wrath of God, and his own Spirit must be grieved in wrestling with the denials of men. Instead of our own obedience, we have the merit of Christ. Oh ! here are depths of mystery and wonder.

Use. God loseth no honour by Christ. God hath more glory, and we have larger demesnes of comfort and grace to live upon. All parties are satisfied; we have a better portion ; Adam had paradise, we have heaven ; God hath more glory ; the creatures are more acquainted with the infiniteness of mercy, power, and wisdom. Innocence continued had been a great benefit, but now it is more gracious and free ; and it is not the greatness of a benefit that worketh on gratitude so much as the graciousness and freeness of it. Our heaven costeth a greater price, and it is not given to God's friends, but those that were once his enemies.

' On earth.'—This phrase signifieth that Christ did not increase God's essential glory, for that is incapable of any addition ; his nature is infinite, and cannot be made more glorious and excellent ; but only that Christ manifested his glory more fully to the world.

Observe, Christ came down from heaven to make men glorify God. We had lesson enough before us in creation and providence, but men were stupid. Things to which we are accustomed do not work upon us ; in the gospel, God would set his praise to a new tune. God needeth us not, and our respects are due ; and yet at what cost is God to purchase the praise of the creature ! Blind and unthankful men, to dethrone the great God, and set up every paltry creature ! Therefore God sent his Son to revive the notions of the Godhead, and to give us further manifestations of his glory. That was Christ's errand, to glorify him on the earth.

' I have finished the work.'—Christ's work was to manifest the gospel, and to redeem sinners ; and how can he say, ' I have finished the work ; ' seeing the chief work of redemption was yet to come, the offering up himself to divine justice upon the cross ? I answer—He had determined to undergo death, and it was now at hand ; in the consent and full determination of his will it was done. So upon the cross, just before his death, he crieth, ' It is finished,' John xix. 30. It implieth—

1. The submission, faithfulness, and diligence of Christ ; he never left doing of his Father's work till he had brought it to some issue and period, and doth not sue out his own glory till our redemption was first finished: Phil. ii. **7**, ' He became obedient unto death, even the death of the cross,' the accursed death of the cross. Christ carried sinners in his heart to his dying day ; he never repented of his bargain : John xiii. 1, ' Having loved his own that were in the world, he loved them unto the end.' When he had most cause to loathe sinners, then he loved them ; in his bitter agonies, and the horrors of his cross,

Christ did not repent of his part. Plead the eternal covenant; you have God's oath that he will never repent of salvation this way: Ps. cx. 4, 'The Lord hath sworn, and will not repent: thou art a priest for ever, after the order of Melchisedeck.' Christ was not weary of suffering for sinners, and God will not be weary of pardoning them. Again, Christ was faithful in the days of his flesh; he hath lost nothing by going to heaven; he will finish what he hath begun: 1 Thes. v. 24, 'Faithful is he that hath called you, who also will do it.' This smoking flax will be blown up into a flame. These infant desires are buds of glory; this decay of sin will come to an utter extinction.

2. It noteth the completeness of our redemption: 'All is finished.' When he had set all things at rights, then he departed. Christ hath not left the work imperfect, to be supplied by the merit of our own actions; we are not half purchased: Heb. x. 14, 'By one offering he hath perfected for ever them that are sanctified.' Christ would not have died if the work had not been done; and if there were anything yet to do, he would die again. But Christ hath no more offering to make, nor suffering to endure, but only to behold the fruit of his suffering. He hath not purchased a possible salvation, whose efficacy dependeth on the will of the creature, nor the remission of some sins, and left others upon our score; nor made purchase of grace for a small time, but 'perfected for ever them that are sanctified.' Popish satisfaction, the loose, possible, pendulous salvation of Arminians, and the doctrine of the apostasy of the saints, are all doctrines prejudicial to the full merit of Christ. It is all finished; there is enough done to glorify God and save the creature; justice could demand no more for all engagements. Christ is not ashamed to plead his right at the bar of justice, and to avouch his work before the tribunal of God. This, 'it is finished,' is like Christ's seal to the charter of grace. Now take it, and much good may it do you! Oh! that we could rest satisfied with the merit of Christ, as divine justice is satisfied. What should trouble the creature when Christ hath entered his plea, 'Father, it is finished'? there is enough done. Christ hath no more to do but to sit at the right hand of God, and to rejoice in the welfare of the saints; there remaining nothing for us but to make our claim, and to live in joy and thankfulness. Christ did not compound, but pay the uttermost farthing: Rom. viii. 1, οὐδὲν κατάκριμα, 'There is no condemnation to them that are in Christ Jesus;' there is not one curse left. When Israel was brought out of Egypt, it is said, 'A dog shall not move his tongue against you,' Exod. xi. 7. Neither the law, nor wrath, nor conscience, nor Satan hath anything to do with you; the prison is broken up, the book cancelled, the bill nailed to Christ's cross, that it may never be put in suit again. The devil may trouble you for your exercise, but bear it with comfort and patience; you have an advocate as well as an accuser. Oh! that we had a faith suitable to the height of these mysteries, that we could behold the salvation of God in our serious thoughts, and echo to Christ's cry, 'It is finished, it is finished!' It is not a full-grown faith till we break out into some triumph; the child may now play upon the cockatrice's hole. I am much indebted to justice, but Christ hath paid all.

'Which thou hast given me to do,' δέδωκας; it is the same word

with that, ver. 2, 'Thou hast given him power over all flesh ;' and
now, 'the work which thou hast given me to do.' God, that gave him
his power, gave him his work.

Augustine interpreteth the word somewhat nicely, *non ait, jussisti,
sed dedisti; ibi commendatur evidens gratia; quid enim habuit quod
non accepit, etiam in unigenito, humana natura ?* If you allow this interpretation, as certainly this rigour of the word will bear it, then we may—

1. Observe that the privileges of the human nature of Christ are by
gift. Whatever the manhood of Christ was advanced to, by dwelling
with God in a personal union, it was by the mere grace of God. The
apostle referreth it to the Father's pleasure : Col. i. 19, ' It pleased the
Father that in him should all fulness dwell.' God would make free
grace appear in none so much as in our head, and set out Christ as the
example of his gracious election. Whatsoever honour the human
nature of Christ had, it had it by grace and gift, it was chosen to this
honour. Certainly we should ascribe all to grace, if Christ himself
did, if he accounted it a gift, that his human nature was taken into
the honour of the mediatory office.

2. We may observe, that work itself is a gift. Christ speaketh thus
of the work of the mediatory office, which was sad work, labouring in
the fire, in the fire of the divine wrath and displeasure. Elsewhere it
is said of our faith and suffering, Phil. i. 23, ' Unto you it is given, on
the behalf of Christ, not only to believe on him, but also to suffer for
his sake.' It is given of grace ; we should count duty an honour, and
service a privilege : Hosea viii. 12, ' I have written to him the great
things of my law ;' *honorabilia legis meœ.*

But I rather interpret it of giving in charge : Thou hast put this
office upon me of redeeming mankind, and this work I have done.

The note from hence is—

Observe that Christ had his work appointed him by God: Ps. xl.
7, 8, ' Lo, I come ; in the volume of the book it is written of me, I
delight to do thy will, O my God; yea, thy law is within my heart.'
It is a great condescension of Christ that he would come under a law,
and as a servant take work upon his own shoulders. The apostle saith
he came ' in the form of a servant,' Phil. ii. 7. He was a prince by birth,
yet he came as a servant of the divine decrees. He spake of commandments that he received from the Father. He wholly devoted himself
to his Father's will and man's benefit. Oh ! admire the proceedings
between the Father and the Son, by way of command and promise.
The transactions of heaven are put into a federal form, and as our
surety he is to receive a law.

Secondly, Let us consider the words in the moral sense and accommodation, and then in this plea which Christ maketh when he was
about to die we may observe these circumstances :—

1. What he says, *I have glorified thee.*

2. Where, *upon earth.*

3. How, *I have finished the work thou hast given me to do.*

Doct. They that would die comfortably should make this their
great care, to glorify God upon the earth, and finish the work which
he hath given them to do in their several stations and relations.

Here I shall show—(1.) What it is to glorify God upon the earth,

&c.; (2.) Why this should be our chief care; (3.) That when we come to die, this will be our comfort.

First, What it is to glorify God upon earth, &c.   Here—

1. *Quid?*   What it is to glorify God.
2. *Ubi?*   Upon the earth.
3. *Quomodo?*   By finishing the work which he hath given us to do.

First, *Quid?* 'I have glorified thee.' God is glorified actively and passively.

1. Passively, which noteth the event, which cometh to pass by the wisdom and overruling of God's providence; and so all things shall at length glorify God in the event: Ps. lxxvi. 10, 'Surely the wrath of man shall praise thee.' In the Septuagint it is ἑορτάσεται, shall keep holy day: the fierce endeavours of his enemies do but make his glory the more excellent. So our lie and unrighteousness may commend the truth and mercy of God, Rom. iii. 5, 7. Pharaoh was raised up for God's glory; as the valour of a king is discovered by the rebellion of his subjects, the skill of the physician by the desperateness of the disease. But this is no thanks to them, but to God's wise and powerful government; it will not lessen their fault and punishment. A wicked man may say in the end, I have been an occasion that God hath been glorified.

2. Actively we glorify God when we set ourselves to this work, and make this our end and scope, that we may be to the praise of his glorious grace. Some learn their school-fellows' lessons better than their own; they would have God glorified, but look to others rather than to themselves. We would have God glorified, but do not glorify him, are more careful of events than duties. We are ready to ask, 'Lord, what wilt thou do for thy great name?' but do not consider our own engagement, 'How shall I glorify God?'

But what is it thus actively to glorify God?

Ans. [1.] To acknowledge his excellency upon all occasions: Ps. l. 23, 'He that offereth praise glorifieth me.' Praising him for his excellencies, and declaring the glory of his attributes and works, is one way of glorifying him. God's glorifying of us is effective and creative, ours declarative and manifestive: 'He calleth the things that are not as though they were;' but we do no more but say things to be what they are, and that far below what they are. We declare God to be what he is, and are a kind of witnesses to his glory. He is the efficient and sole cause of all the good that we have and are, and bestows something upon us which was not before. This declaring the glory of God is expressed by two words, *praise* and *blessing*: Ps. cxlv. 10, 'All thy works shall praise thee, O Lord: thy saints shall bless thee.' Praise referreth to his excellency, blessing to his benefits; both must be done seriously and frequently, and with a deep impression of his goodness and excellency upon our hearts. Every address we make to God tendeth to this, that God may have his due praise understandingly and affectionately ascribed to him. Repentance and broken-hearted confession giveth him the praise of his justice; the exercise of faith, and running for refuge to the grace of the gospel, doth glorify his mercy; thanksgiving for benefits received, his benignity and goodness petitioning for grace, his holiness.

[2.] By a perfect subjection and resignation of our wills to his will. It is work glorifieth God more than words. Verbal praises, if destitute of these, they are but an empty prattle: Job xxxi. 20, ' If his loins have not blessed me, and if he were not warmed with the fleece of my sheep.' So 2 Thes. i. 11, 12, ' Wherefore also we pray always for you, that our God would count you worthy of this calling, and fulfil all the good pleasure of his goodness, and the work of faith with power ; that the name of our Lord Jesus Christ may be glorified in you, and you in him.' Many speak good words of God, but their hearts are not subject to him, as the devil carried Christ to the top of a high mountain, but with an intent to bid him throw himself down again. So many think to exalt God in their professions and praises, but they dishonour him in their lives. God is most glorified in the creatures' obedience, and submission to his laws or providence.

(1.) To his laws, when we study to please him in all things : Col. i. 10, ' That ye may walk worthy of the Lord unto all pleasing, being fruitful in every good work, and increasing in the knowledge of God.' It is a great honour to a master when his servants are so ready and willing to please him : ' I say to one, Go, and he goeth ; to another, Come, and he cometh ; to my servant, Do this, and he doeth it,' Mat. viii. 9. It is said of Abraham, God called him to his foot, Isa xli. 2. He went to and fro at his command. If God said, Go out of thy country, Abraham obeyed.

(2.) To his providence. It is an honour to him when we are contented to be what God will have us to be, and can prefer his glory before our own ease, his honour before our plenty. And so it was with Christ : John xii. 27, 28, ' Now is my soul troubled, and what shall I say ? Father, save me from this hour ; but for this cause came I to this hour. Father, glorify thy name ; ' that satisfied him, so God might be glorified. So Paul, Phil. i. 20, ' Christ shall be magnified in my body, whether it be by life or by death.' As a traveller takes the way as he findeth it, so it will lead him to his journey's end. We must be as a die in the hands of providence ; whether the cast prove high or low, we are still upon the square.

3. We glorify God rather by entertaining the impressions of his glory upon us than by communicating any kind of glory to him ; and so we glorify him when we grow most like him, when we show forth his virtues : 1 Peter ii. 9, ' Ye are a chosen generation, a royal priesthood, a holy nation, a peculiar people, that ye should show forth the praises of him who hath called you out of darkness into his marvellous light.' The children of God are a glass and image, wherein the perfections of God are visibly held forth ; his perfections are stamped upon us, that all that see us may see God in us. But alas ! most of us are but dim glasses, show forth little of God to the world. Thus the creatures glorify God objectively ; there is somewhat of the wisdom, goodness, and power of God stamped upon them, somewhat of God to be seen in every thing which he hath made. So man much more. There are *vestigia Dei*, the footsteps of God in the creatures ; but *similitudo et imago Dei*, the likeness and image of God in man, in his natural excellences, much more in the new creature, εἰς τὸ εἶναι, ' that we may be to his praise,' Eph. i. 12. There is more of God engraven

on us when a true spirit of wisdom, justice, holiness, truth, love prevaileth upon our hearts, and runneth through all our operations; when we live as such as converse with the great fountain of goodness and holiness. A christian's life is a hymn to God; his circumspect walking proclaimeth the wisdom of God; his awefulness and watchfulness against sin proclaimeth the majesty of God; his cheerful and ready obedience under the hardest sufferings proclaimeth the goodness of God; his purity and strictness, the holiness of God; the impression and stamp of all the letters of God's glorious name is imprinted upon his heart and life. A carnal christian polluteth his honour and profaneth his name: Ezek. xxxvi. 20, 'And when they entered unto the heathen, whither they went, they profaned my holy name, when they said to them, These are the people of the Lord, and are gone forth out of his land.' But how can God be polluted by us? As a man that lusteth after a woman hath committed adultery with her in his heart, while she is spotless and undefiled, Mat. v. 28. Carnal christians are a scandal to religion; they are called christians *in opprobrium Christi.* Men judge by what is visible and sensible, and think of God by his worshippers, by those who profess themselves to be a people near and dear to him.

4. By that which is an immediate consequence of the former, by an exemplary conversation, when we do those things which tend to the honour of God's name, and to bring him into request in the world: 1 Peter ii. 12, 'Having your conversation honest among the Gentiles, that whereas they speak against you, as of evil-doers, they may, by your good works which they shall behold, glorify God in the day of visitation;' Mat. v. 16, 'Let your light so shine before men, that they may see your good works, and glorify your Father which is in heaven.' Our holiness must be shown forth for edification, not for ostentation; not for our glory, but the glory of our heavenly Father. It is the fruitful christian bringeth most honour to God: John xv. 8, 'Herein is my Father glorified, that ye bear much fruit.' Glorifying God is not a few transient thoughts of God and his glory, or a few cold speeches of his excellences and benefits; this is not the great end for which we were made, and new made; but that we might be fruitful in all holiness, and show forth those impressions which God hath left upon us. In the impression we are passive; in showing it forth, active.

5. When we are active for his interest in the world. Our Lord took notice of it in his disciples: John xvii. 7, 'Now they have known that all things whatsoever thou hast given me are of thee.' If we are agents for his kingdom, he will be our advocate in heaven. This is the method of the Lord's prayer, 'Hallowed be thy name;' and then, 'Thy kingdom come.' This is the first means of promoting the great end. Jesus Christ himself telleth us this was the end of his coming into the world: John xviii. 37, 'To this end was I born, and for this cause came I into the world, that I should bear witness unto the truth.' It belonged to him in a more especial way, as the great prophet of the church; he came out of the bosom of God to reveal the secrets of God; and for the same end we all came into the world: Isa. xliii. 10, 'Ye are my witnesses, saith the Lord, and my servant whom

I have chosen, that ye may know and believe me, and understand that I am he.' They that felt the comfortable effects of his promises and his truth can best witness for him. A report of a report is little valued; we are all to witness to God, by entertaining it in our hearts and showing forth the fruit of it in our lives; this is a witness to an unbelieving and careless world: John iii. 33, 'He that hath received his testimony hath set to his seal that God is true;' Heb. xi. 7, 'By faith Noah, being warned of God of things not seen as yet, moved with fear, prepared an ark to the saving of his house, by which he condemned the world;' Phil. ii. 15, 'That ye may be blameless and harmless, the sons of God, without rebuke, in the midst of a crooked and perverse nation, among whom ye shine as lights in the world.' When you are diligent in holiness, patient and joyful under the cross, full of hope and comfort in great straits, meek, self-denying, mortified, you sanctify God in the eyes of others; you propagate the faith by an open profession: Mat. xi. 19, 'Wisdom is justified of her children.' When we suffer for it in times of great danger, and seal it with our blood, it is a great glory to God: John xxi. 19, 'This said he, signifying by what death he should glorify God.' It is an honour to God when, in the midst of temptations and discouragements, we are not ashamed of his ways.

6. By doing that work which he hath given us to do. But what is that work which he hath given us to do? *Ans.*—(1.) The duty of our relations; (2.) The duty of our vocations and callings.

[1.] The duty of our particular relations. They that are not good in their relations are nowhere good. This is a rule, that whatsoever we are, we must be that to God. A heathen could say, *Si essem luscinia, canerem ut luscinia,* &c.—If I were a lark, I would soar as a lark; if a nightingale, I would sing as a nightingale. As a man, I should praise God; as such a man, in such a relation, still I should glorify God in the condition in which he hath set me. If poor, I glorify God as a poor man, by my diligence, patience, innocence, contentedness; if rich, I glorify God by a humble mind; if well, I glorify God by my health; if sick, by meekness under his hand; if a magistrate, by my zeal, improving all advantages of service, Neh. i. 11. If a minister, by my watchfulness; if a tradesman, by my righteousness. From the king to the scullion, all are to work for God; every man is sent into the world to act that part in the world which the great Master of the scenes hath appointed to him: Titus ii. 10, 'That ye may adorn the doctrine of God our Saviour in all things.' As to husband and wife: Prov. xviii. 22, 'He that findeth a wife, findeth a good thing, and obtaineth favour of the Lord.' God expecteth that, in the catalogue of our mercies, we should bless God for our relations. Our relations are the sphere of our activity.

[2.] The duty of our vocation and calling. Every christian hath his way and place, some work which God gave him. But of this see more by and by.

7. When God is the great scope and end of our lives and actions; of all that we are, all that we do, all that we desire; God must be the ultimate end. In our ordinary actions: 1 Cor. x. 31, 'Whether ye

eat or drink, or whatever ye do, do all to the glory of God.' Not offer a meat-offering and drink-offering to appetite. The apostle instances in these things, partly because in these natural actions we are most apt to offend. Such is the unthankful nature of man, that we forget God when he remembers us most; when he is most present in the fruits of his bounty, then he is usually banished from our hearts. Corruptions are most stirring when we are warmed with the liberal use of the creatures. Job sacrificed when his children feasted: Job i. 5, 'And it was so, when the days of their feasting were gone about, that Job sent and sanctified them, and rose up early in the morning, and offered burnt-offerings according to the number of them all: for Job said, It may be that my sons have sinned, and cursed God in their hearts.' The devil bringeth his dish usually to our tables, disdain of the slenderness of our provision, quarrels, contentions, censures of the people of God, &c. Partly for greater emphasis. If in common actions we are to design God's glory as our end, much more in such actions as we make a business of. So in acts of grace; the creature cannot be the ultimate end, and God's goodness only a means thereunto. There is a great deal of learned folly and atheism vented, branding those as mystical divines that call upon men to mind things as God minded them, who aims at his own glory as his ultimate end, Eph. i. 6. They say man's ultimate end is his own happiness. Some cry up the principle of self-love. Then belike all the goodness of God is to be estimated by the felicity of man; this were to make man his own idol, and to measure all good and evil by his own interest. The fulfilling of God's will and promoting his glory should be the end of all obedience; otherwise we make not the creature for God, but God for the creature, and so make the creature better than God, as being the ultimate end of God himself, at least to us, as if the highest end of all his goodness were the felicity of the creature.

Secondly, *Ubi?* Where? On earth, 'I have glorified thee on earth.'

1. Where so few mind God's glory, where all seek their own things, their own honour, their own profit, their own personal contentment. A christian should walk in counter-motion to the generality of the world: Phil. iii. 20, 'But our conversation is in heaven;' Mal. iv. 1, 2, 'The day cometh that shall burn as an oven, and all the proud, yea and all that do wickedly, shall be stubble, &c. But unto you that fear the Lord,' &c. He is an exception from the common use and practice of mankind.

2. On earth, which is the place of our trial, where there are so many difficulties and temptations to divert us. We must glorify him on earth if we expect that he should glorify us in heaven. Many expect to glorify God in heaven, but take no care to glorify God here on earth. The saints in heaven glorify God, but without any difficulty, strife, and danger, it costs them no shame, no pain, no trouble, no loss of life or limb; but here where the danger is, there is the duty and trial: Mat. x. 32, 'Whosoever therefore shall confess me before men, him will I confess also before my Father which is in heaven.' Christ will remember them and their labour of love. When he cometh in his majesty, he is not ashamed of his poor clients and friends; these

owned me in my abasement, and I will own them in my exalted state. You cannot honour Christ so much as he will honour you : Mat. xix. 28, 'Ye which have followed me in the regeneration, when the Son of man shall sit in the throne of his glory, ye also shall sit upon twelve thrones, judging the twelve tribes of Israel.' Ye who are here exposed to sorrows and sufferings for his sake. It is fond to think of glorifying God in heaven, and singing hallelujahs to his praise, when thou dost not stand to his truth on earth. *Esse bonum facile est, ubi quid vetat est remotum.* The trial of duty is self-denial.

Thirdly, *Quomodo?* 'I have finished the work which thou hast given me to do.'

1. It is work that glorifieth God; it is not words and empty praises, but a holy conversation : Job xxxi. 20, 'If his loins have not blessed me, and if he were not warmed with the fleece of my sheep;' Mat. v. 16, 'Let your light so shine before men, that they may see your good works, and glorify your Father which is in heaven;' Ps. l. 23, 'Whoso offereth praise, glorifieth me; and to him that ordereth his conversation aright, will I show the salvation of God;' John xv. 8, 'Herein is my Father glorified, that ye bear much fruit, so shall ye be my disciples.' A godly fruitful life is the real honour, the other is but empty prattle. It is our work and actions, not our bare profession only; you may pollute God else, Ezek. xxxvi. 20, you may exalt him in profession, and pollute him in conversation. Many christians' lives are the scandal of their religion. Again, it is not wishes that glorify God, but practice. We would have God glorified, but do not glorify him. We would have him glorified passively, but do not glorify him actively, and are more careful of events than duties. We are troubled about God's name, and are more ready to ask, 'Lord, what wilt thou do for thy great name?' than, 'Lord, what wilt thou have me to do?' A christian should rather be troubled about what he should do, than about what he should suffer.

2. That every man hath his work. Life was given to us for somewhat; not merely that we might fill up the number of things in the world, as stones and rubbish : not to grow in stature; so life was given to the plants, that they might grow bulky and increase in stature : nor merely to taste pleasures; that is the happiness of the beasts, to enjoy pleasures without remorse. God gave men higher faculties of reason and conscience, to manage some work and business for the glory of God, and his own eternal happiness. The rule is general, that all Adam's sons are 'to eat their bread in the sweat of their brows,' to follow some honest labour and vocation. Adam's two sons were heirs-apparent of the world, the one employed in tillage, the other in pasturage. The world was never made to be a hive for drones and idle ones. It is true there is a difference between callings; some live by manual labours, others by more noble employments, as magistrates, ministers, who study for public good. Manual labour is not required of all, because it is a thing that is not required *propter se,* as simply good and necessary, but *propter aliud,* as for maintenance and support of life, to ease others, and to supply the uses of charity : Eph. iv. 28, 'Let him that stole, steal no more; but rather let him labour, working with his hands the thing that is good, that he may have to give to him that

needeth.' When the ends of labour cannot otherwise be obtained, then handy labour is required. All others are 'to serve their generation according to the will of God,' Acts xiii. 26. As instruments of providence to serve the common good, to promote the welfare of their family, neighbourhood, country. Those that spend their whole life in eating, drinking, sporting, and sleeping, are guilty of brutish idleness, one of Sodom's sins: Ezek. xvi. 49, 'Behold, this was the iniquity of thy sister Sodom; pride, fulness of bread, and abundance of idleness was in her and in her daughters.' And therefore those that are freed from service and handy labour are not freed from work and business. If any man must be allowed to be idle, then one member must be lost in the body politic. A man is born a member of some society, family, or city, and is to seek the good of it: he is ζῶον πολίτικον. We see in the body natural there is no member but hath its function and use, whereby it becometh serviceable to the whole. All have not the same office, that would make a confusion; but all have their use, either as an eye, or as a hand, or as a tooth. So in the body politic, no member may be useless, they must have one function or another wherein to employ themselves, otherwise they are unprofitable burdens of the earth. Again, every man is more or less intrusted with a gift, which he is to exercise and improve for the good of others, and at the day of judgment he is to give up his accounts; as you may learn from the parable of the talents, Mat. xxv. If he hath but one talent, it must not be hidden in a napkin. Well, then, if every man hath a gift, for which he is accountable to God, he must have a calling: 1 Cor. vii. 17, 'But as God hath distributed to every man, as the Lord hath called every man, so let him walk,' and choose his state of life. Besides, a calling is necessary to prevent the mischiefs of idleness, and those inconveniences that follow men not employed. Standing pools are apt to putrify, but running waters are sweetest. An idle man is a burden to himself, a prey to Satan, a grief to the Spirit of God, a mischief to others. He is a burden to himself, for he knoweth not what to do with his time; in the morning he says, Would God it were evening; and in the evening, Would God it were morning. The mind is like a mill; when it wanteth corn, it grindeth upon itself. He is a prey to Satan: 'The house is emptied, swept, and garnished; and then he goeth and taketh with himself seven other spirits more wicked than himself, and they enter in and dwell there,' Mat. xii. 44, 45. The devil findeth them at leisure. When David was idle on the terrace, he was tempted to adultery. Birds are seldom taken in their flight, but when they pitch and rest on the ground. He is a grief to God's Spirit: Eph. iv. 28, 'Let him that stole, steal no more; but rather let him labour, working with his hands, that he may have to give to him that needeth;' with ver. 30, 'And grieve not the Holy Spirit of God.' Idle men quench the vigor of their natural gifts, and lose those abilities that are bestowed on them. He is a mischief to others: 2 Thes. iii. 11, 'For we hear there are some that walk among you disorderly, μηδὲν ἐργαζομένους, ἀλλὰ περιεργαζομένους, working not at all, but are busybodies.' They that do nothing will do too much; no work maketh way for ill work, or for censure and busy inquisition into other men's actions, and so they prove the firebrands of contention and unneighbourly quarrels.   There must be a calling, and a work to do.

3. This work is given them by God.   He appointeth to every one his task, and will be glorified by no works but what are by himself assigned to them in their station :—(1.) By his word ; (2.) By his providence.

[1.] By his word.   There is no calling and course of service good but what is agreeable to the word of God : Ps. cxix. 105, ' Thy word is a light unto my feet and a lamp unto my paths.'   We must not settle in a sinful course of life.   Men may tolerate evil callings, but God never appointed them.   As for instance, if any calling and course of life be against piety, temperance, justice, it is against the word :. Titus ii. 12, ' Teaching us that, denying ungodliness and worldly lusts, we should live soberly, righteously, and godly in this present world.' Against piety ; as to be an idolatrous priest, or to make shrines for idols, which was Demetrius his calling in Ephesus ; and Tertullian, in his book *De Idololatria*, showeth this was the practice of many christians to get their livings by making statues and images and other ornaments to sell to heathen idolaters.   Against justice ; as piracy, usury, and other oppressive courses.   Against sobriety ; as such callings as merely tend to feed the luxury, pride, and vanity of men, so mountebanks, comedians, stage-players.   It were endless to instance in all.   In general, the calling must be good and lawful.

[2.] By his providence, which ruleth in everything that falleth out, even to the least matters ; especially hath the Lord a great hand in callings, and appointing to every one his estate and condition of life. In paradise, God set Adam his work to dress and prune the trees of the garden, Gen. ii. 15 ; and still he doth not only give abilities and special inclinations, but also disposeth of the education of the parent, and the passages of men's lives to bring them to such a calling : Isa. liv. 16, ' Behold, I have created the smith that bloweth the coals in the fire, and that bringeth forth an instrument for his work.'   Common trades and crafts are from the Lord.   The heathens had a several god for every several trade, as the Papists now have a tutelar saint ; but they rob God of his honour, he giveth the faculty and the blessing : Isa. xxviii, 26–29, ' His God doth instruct him to discretion, and doth teach him,' &c.   He giveth the state, and appointeth the work.   Your particular estate and condition of life doth not come by chance, or by the care, will, and pleasure of man, but the ordination of God, without whom a sparrow cannot fall to the ground.   In the higher callings of ministry and magistracy there is a greater solemnity.

But how should a man glorify God in his place and station wherein God hath set him ?

Ans. [1.] Be content with it, God is the master of the scenes, and appoints which part to act.   We must not prescribe to providence, at what rate we will be maintained, nor what we will do, but keep within the bounds of our place.   If you do anything that is not within the compass of your calling, you can have no warrant that it pleaseth God.   Christ would not intermeddle out of his calling : Luke xii. 14, ' Man, who made me a judge or a divider over you ? '   Uzzah's putting his hand to the ark cost him dear.   If troubles arise, we cannot suffer them comfortably, we are out of God's way. Most of our late mischiefs came from invading callings; as there are confusions in nature when elements are out of their places. God is glorified and served in a lower calling as well as in a higher; poor servants may 'adorn the gospel of God our Saviour in all things,' Titus ii. 10.

Ans. [2.] With patience digest the inconveniences of your calling. Affliction attendeth every state and condition of life, but we must go through cheerfully when in our way and place.

4. This work must be finished and perfected; we must be working till God call us off by death or irresistible providences. We must persist, hold out in God's way without defection: Rev. ii. 10, 'Be thou faithful unto the death; I will give thee a crown of life.' Get the gift of perseverance; happy are they that have passed such a tempestuous sea with safety. He was a foolish builder who laid the foundation of a stately fabric and was not able to finish it. Oh! when this is done, we may resign up ourselves to the mercy of God: 2 Tim. iv. 7, 8, 'I have fought a good fight, I have finished my course, I have kept the faith. Henceforth is laid up for me a crown of righteousness, which the Lord, the righteous judge, shall give me at that day; and not to me only, but unto them also that love his appearing.' It is an excellent thing, after such a dangerous voyage, to come safe to shore. How sweet is it to enjoy our past lives, and yield up our spirits to God, saying, Lord, I have made it my study to glorify thee: Isa. xxxviii. 3, 'Remember now, O Lord, I beseech thee, how I have walked before thee in truth, and with a perfect heart, and have done that which is good in thy sight.' Other souls are taken away, but yours are resigned.

Secondly, Why this should be our great care?

1. This is the end why all creatures were made: Rom. xi. 36, 'For of him, and through him, and to him, are all things.' When God did make the world, he did not throw it out of his hands, and leave it alone to subsist of itself, as a thing that had no further relation to him; but so guides it and governs it, that as the first production and continued subsistence of all things is from himself, so the ultimate resolution and tendency of all things might be to him. The whole world is a circle, and all the motions of the creatures are circular; they end where they began; as rivers run to the place whence they came. All that issueth out of the fountain of his goodness must fall again into the ocean of his glory, but man especially. If God had made us to live for ourselves, it were lawful; but Prov. xvi. 4, 'The Lord hath made all things for himself;' all things are made ultimately and terminatively for God, but man immediately. Creatures are made immediately for us, and submit to our dominion, or are created for our use.

2. From God's right and interest in us: Rom. xiv. 7, 8, 'For none of us liveth to himself, and no man dieth to himself. For whether we live, we live unto the Lord; and whether we die, we die unto the Lord; whether we live therefore, or die, we are the Lord's;' we are his, and therefore for him. All that you have is God's, and by giving it to you he did not divest himself of his own right. God scatters his benefits as the husbandman doth his seed, that he may receive a crop.

His glory is not due to another; he made us out of nothing, and bought us: 1 Cor. vi. 19, 20, 'Ye are not your own, ye are bought with a price; therefore glorify God in your body and in your spirit, which are God's.' If we had anything our own, we might use it for ourselves.

3. We shall be called to an account: Luke xix. 23, 'Wherefore then gavest not thou my money into the bank, that at my coming I might have required my own with usury?' We must give an account, what honour God hath had by us in our relations, as magistrates, ministers, masters of families, servants, husbands, wives, parents, children; what honour by our estates, relations, &c. We are obliged so deeply by preceding benefits, that if there were no account to be given, we should be careful to use all things for his glory. Oh! but much more when there will be so strict and severe an account: 'The Lord of those servants will reckon with them.' What we enjoy is not *donum*, a gift, but *talentum*, a talent, to be improved for our master's use. Beasts are liable to no account, because they have not reason and conscience, as man hath, and are merely ruled with a rod of iron: they are to glorify God passively; but we are left to our choice, and therefore must give an account.

4. Because of the great benefit that cometh to us by it. God noteth it, and rewards it. He noteth it: John xvii. 10, 'And all mine are thine, and thine are mine, and I am glorified in them.' Our Redeemer speaketh well of us behind our backs, and maketh a good report of us in heaven. And he rewards it in the day of his royalty. Christ will not be ashamed of his poor servants: Mat. xix. 28, 'Ye which have followed me in the regeneration, when the Son of man shall sit in the throne of his glory, ye also shall sit upon twelve thrones, judging the twelve tribes of Israel.'

5. The end ennobleth a man, and still the man is according to his end. Low spirits have low designs, and a base end is pursued by base actions: Mat. vi. 22, 23, 'The light of the body is the eye: if therefore thine eye be single, thy whole body shall be full of light; but if thine eye be evil, thy whole body shall be full of darkness.' Men are properly such as the end that they aim at; he that pursueth any worldly interest or earthly thing, as his end is earthly, he becometh himself earthly; the more the soul directeth itself to God, the more God-like; their inclinations are above the base things of this world: Ps. xvii. 14, 'From men of the world, which have their portion in this life, and whose belly thou fillest with thy hid treasures.' The noblest soul is for the noblest object; others do but provide for the flesh, they drive on no greater trade; they may talk of heaven, wish for it rather than hell, when they can live no longer, but their lives are only for feathering a nest, which will quickly be pulled down. To rule a kingdom is a nobler design than to play with children for pins or nuts. A man that designeth only to pamper his body, to live in all plenty, what a poor life doth he lead! A beast can eat, drink, sleep, as they do: Phil. iii. 19, 20, 'Whose end is destruction, whose god is their belly, and whose glory is in their shame, who mind earthly things; but our conversation is in heaven,' &c. They make a great pother in the world about a brutish life, which will soon have an end.

6. God will have his glory upon you, if not from you, for he is resolved not to be a loser by the creature: Prov. xvi. 4, 'The Lord hath made all things for himself, yea even the wicked for the day of evil;' Lev. x. 3, 'This is that which the Lord saith, I will be sanctified in them that come nigh me, and before all the people I will be glorified.' He will have the glory of his justice in the day of wrath and evil, if not the glory of his grace in the day of his patience and mercy. Therefore either he will be glorified by you, or upon you. Some give him glory in an active, some in a passive way. If he have not the glory of his command, which is our duty, he will have the glory of his providence in the event. And how sad that will be, judge ye, when you serve for no other use but to set forth the glory of his vindictive justice.

7. It must be our last end, which must fix men's mind, which otherwise will be tossed up and down with perpetual uncertainty, and distracted by a multiplicity of ends and objects, that it cannot continue in any composed and settled frame: Ps. lxxxvi. 11, 'Unite my heart to fear thy name;' James i. 8, 'A double-minded man is unstable in all his ways.' A divided mind causes an uncertain life, no one part of our lives will agree with another, the whole not being firmly knit by the power of some last end running through all.

Thirdly, That when we come to die, this will be our comfort, Christ hath left us a pattern here. And Hezekiah, Isa. xxxviii. 3, 'Remember now, O Lord, how I have walked before thee in truth, and with a perfect heart, and have done that which is good in thy sight.' Oh! the comfort of a well-spent life to a dying christian! 2 Tim. iv. 7, 8, 'I have fought a good fight, I have finished my course, I have kept the faith: henceforth there is laid up for me a crown of righteousness, which the Lord, the righteous judge, shall give me at that day; and not to me only, but to all them also that shall love his appearing.' Then a man can run over his life with comfort, when he hath been careful for the matter and end to glorify God.

Use. Oh! then, consider two things:—

1. The end why you were sent into the world. Why do I live here? Most men live like beasts, eat, drink, sleep, and die; never sit down, and in good earnest consider, Why was I born? why did I come into the world? and so their lives are but a mere lottery; the fancies they are governed by are jumbled together by chance; if they light of a good hit, it is a casual thing; they live at peradventure, and then no wonder they walk at random.

2. What we shall do when our lives are at an end, and we are to appear before God's tribunal. Oh! that you would consider this, now you are in your health and strength: Deut. xxxii. 29, 'Oh! that they were wise, that they understood this, that they would consider their latter end!' Much of wisdom lieth in considering the end of things. We are hastening apace into the other world, it is good to consider what we have to say when we come to die: Job xxxi. 14, 'What shall I then do, when God riseth up? and when he visiteth, what shall I answer him?' viz., at the latter end, when I am immediately to appear before God, when he summons us by sickness into his presence, and the devil is more busy at such a time to tempt and trouble us, and all

other comforts fail, and are as unsavoury as the white of an egg, then this will notably embolden our hearts: 2 Cor. i. 12, 'For our rejoicing is this, the testimony of our conscience, that in simplicity and godly sincerity, not with fleshly wisdom, but by the grace of God, we have had our conversation in the world.' Oh! will this comfort you, that you have sported and gamed away your precious time, that you have fared of the best, lived in pomp and honour? Oh! no; but this, I have made conscience of honouring and glorifying God, of being faithful in my place, in promoting the common good there, where God hath cast my lot. Oh! then, go on, your comfort will increase. If hitherto you have been pleasing the flesh, idling and wantoning away your precious time, say, 1 Peter iv. 3, 'For the time past of our life may suffice us to have wrought the will of the Gentiles, when we walked in lasciviousness, lusts, excess of wine, revellings, banquetings, and abominable idolatries.' You have too long walked contrary to the end of your creation, in dishonouring God, and destroying your own souls.

SERMON VI.

And now, O Father, glorify thou me with thine own self, with the glory which I had with thee before the world was.—JOHN XVII. 5.

JESUS CHRIST, as God-man, in this chapter, prayeth to God. His prayer is first for himself, and then for his members. In all things he is to have the pre-eminence, as being infinitely of more worth and desert than all. His prayer for himself is to be glorified, which he enforceth and explaineth. He enforceth it by sundry reasons; the last that he pleaded was, that he had done his work, and therefore, according to the covenant and agreement that was between them, he sueth out his wages. In the suit, he explaineth how he would be glorified: 'I have glorified thee on earth, and now, O Father, glorify thou me with thyself, with the glory which I had with thee before the world was.'

For the opening of this request, I shall propound several questions:—

1. According to what nature this is spoken?
2. What is this glory?
3. Why he seeketh of the Father, the first person? Could he not glorify himself?
4. Why is he so earnest for his own glory?

Quest. 1. According to what nature is this spoken, the divine or human? The reason of the doubt is, because to the divine nature nothing could be given, and the human nature cannot be said to have this glory which Christ had before the world was, for then it would remain no longer human.

I answer—The request is made in the person of the mediator. God-man is distinctly and separately to be applied to neither nature, but to the whole person. The person of Christ was hitherto beclouded during the time of his humiliation; now he desireth to be glorified, that is, that the divine majesty may shine forth in the person of the mediator; and that laying aside the form of a servant, he might return to the form of God, and that he might appear in his whole person, the human nature not excluded, as he was before the foundation of the world.

Quest. 2. The next question is, What is this glorifying ?

I answer—There is a twofold glorifying—(1.) *Per gloriæ manifestationem ;* (2.) *Per gloriæ collationem ;* by way of manifestation, and by way of gift and collation. Both are intended ; the manifestation concerneth both natures, and the collation or gift only the human nature. It must be understood according to the properties of each nature. *Quæ in tempore Christo dantur, secundum humanam naturam dantur.*

1. For the divine nature, Christ prayeth that it may be glorified by the clearer manifestation of his godhead, for that cannot receive any intrinsecal improvement or glory. It is ἀντάρκης καὶ ἀμετάθητος; but so far as it was humbled, so far it was glorified. Now Christ humbled himself, not by putting off his divine glory, but by suffering it to be overshadowed; as the light of a candle in a dark lanthorn, there is a light in it, but you cannot see it till the cover be taken away. Now Christ desireth that the cover and veil may be taken away. His glory was not lessened, but beclouded ; the divine essence that was hidden under the weakness of the flesh was now to be manifested and made known to all men. But you will say, it is παρὰ πατρὶ, not παρὰ ἀνθρώποις, he desireth the glory he had with him might be restored, not the glory with men. I answer—

[1.] The glory which he had with him may be more clearly manifested to the world ; he had it with the Father, yet beggeth it of the Father.

[2.] I answer again—There is somewhat more than manifestation in the world, for he saith, παρὰ σεαυτῷ, 'with thyself.' The Father was glorified by the Son, ἐπὶ τῆς γῆς, 'upon the earth ;' but now 'glorify thou me,' παρὰ σεαυτῷ, 'with thyself.' So John xiii. 32, 'If God be glorified in him, God shall also glorify him in himself,' or with himself. So that he beggeth a full use and exercise of the divine power, from which he had abstained in the time of his humiliation and abasement. Now that time being finished, he prayeth that it may be restored, that he may be exalted in the full manifestation and exercise of his divine power; that his whole person might be exalted again at the right hand of majesty.

2. For his human nature. The flesh was not yet glorified, and taken up to God's right hand, that is, exalted to the fruition of eternal glory, as afterwards it was above all creatures in heaven and earth. The human nature was to have as much glory as it is capable of, by being united to the divine person, immortality, power, clarity, knowledge, grace ; but not to have the properties of the divine nature really transfused, for then it would no longer be finite, nor remain a creature. It was to be raised to the full fruition of the glory of the divine nature, and freed from those infirmities to which, by the exigence of Christ's office upon earth, it was subjected. Thus what this glorifying is; but I shall speak more fully to it by and by.

Quest. 3. Why he seeketh it of the Father ? Could he not glorify himself, and exalt his own person and human nature ?

I answer—He could, but would not.

1. The Father is the fountain of the divinity; he is first in order, and so all such actions are ascribed to him. However, to show the unity of essence, Christ is said to do it as well as the Father: John v. 19, 'What things soever the Father doth, these doth the Son likewise.' The Father is said to 'sanctify the Son,' John x. 36, and the Son is said to 'sanctify himself.' The Father raiseth the Son from the dead. Eph. i. 10; and Christ saith, John ii. 19, 'Destroy this temple, and in three days I will raise it up again.' The Father placeth the Son at his right hand, Eph. i. 20; and the Son is said to 'sit down at the right hand of the Father.' However, because Christ came into the world to glorify the Father, and to show him to be the original and fountain of the divinity, therefore he saith, 'Father, glorify thou me with thyself.'

2. Because the Father is to be looked upon as judge and chief in the work of redemption. Man is the debtor, Christ the surety, and the Father the judge, before whose tribunal satisfaction is to be made. Therefore God the Father, after the price and ransom was paid, was to give Christ power and leave to rise from the dead, to ascend into heaven, and to govern and judge the world. And yet he raised himself by his own power. There is *potestas* and *potentia*, δύναμις and ἐξουσία, authority, leave, and power. Christ had power in himself, but he had leave from the Father: John x. 18, 'I have power to lay it down, and I have power to take it up again.' *Potentiam resurgendi Christus habet a seipso, sed potestatem a patre.* In this whole business, Christ is to be considered as the surety, that took our whole business upon himself, and rendered himself liable to the judgment of God so long, till the Father should declare himself to be satisfied, and so dismiss Christ from punishment. After full satisfaction, he was to raise him from the power of death, and to glorify him. As the Father delivered him for us, so the Father dismissed him, raised him again; he was not to break prison, but honourably to be brought out and rewarded by the judge.

Quest. 4. Why is he so earnest for his own glory?

I answer—All Christ's mediatory acts were for our sake, and so are his prayers.

1. To comfort his disciples against his sufferings; they were dejected, and therefore Christ in their hearing prayeth for divine glory: John xvii. 13, 'And these things I speak in the world, that they might have my joy fulfilled in themselves.' There is not a more excellent way of gaining upon others than to commend them to God in prayer for that which they desire.

2. To give the world an instruction, that suffering for God is the highway to glory: 2 Cor. iv. 17, 'Our light affliction, that is but for a moment, worketh for us a far more exceeding and eternal weight of glory,' as a necessary antecedent. We may suffer more for men than they are able to recompense, but there is nothing lost for God: 2 Peter i. 11, 'An entrance shall be ministered unto you abundantly into the kingdom of our Lord and Saviour Jesus Christ.' The whole scriptures witness the sufferings of Christ, and the glory that should follow; according to the measure of afflictions, there shall be a suit-

able weight of glory. There are notable passages in the story of Christ, to show the coupling of the cross and glory. The same disciples, Peter, James, and John, were the witnesses of his agonies, Mat. xxvi. 37, and of his transfiguration, Mat. xvii. 1. So where Christ began his passion there he began his ascension: Luke xxii. 39, ' He went out to the Mount of Olives, and his disciples followed him ; ' and Acts i. 12, he ascended from Mount Olivet.

3. For the advantage of his members. Christ knew it could not go well with the church unless it went well with himself; it was for our profit. The holy ointment was first poured on the head of the high priest, then on his members, Ps. cxxxiii. 3. His glory and grace is an argument of ours. He is endowed with the Spirit without measure, that we might have an unction from the Holy One. We are glorified with him, and are said to ascend with him: Eph. ii. 6, ' He hath raised us up together, and made us sit together in heavenly places in Christ Jesus.' Christ's glorification is a pledge of ours; he is gone thither as our forerunner, to seize on heaven in our right: Heb. vi. 20, ' Whither our forerunner is for us entered ;' and to ' prepare a place for us,' John xiv. 2. In heaven he is at God's right hand, and can procure it for us, and administereth and governeth the world for our good. He is in a greater capacity to do us good. He is our intercessor and the world's governor ; all things necessary to salvation can better be despatched by his intercession and power.

These things premised, the words will be easily opened.

' Father, glorify thou me with thine own self ;' that is, suffer me to return to the glory which I had in common with thee in the divine nature, by the resurrection of my body, ascension, and sitting down at thy right hand. Παρὰ σεαυτῷ, is opposed to ἐδόξασα σὲ ἐπὶ τῆς γῆς, it is with thy self : John xiii. 31, 32, ' Now is the Son of man glorified, and God is glorified in him. If God be glorified in him, God shall also glorify him in himself, and shall straightway glorify him.' God was glorified by Christ as a servant, with an extrinsic glory in the view of the world. And now Christ prays to be glorified in or with the Father himself, with his own proper essential glory, the Godhead being restored to its full use and exercise, and the humanity being raised to the full fruition of the comfort of it.

' Which I had with thee before the world was.'—Grotius and others say, *Non reali possessione, sed divina prædestinatione*, that is, by thy decree, in thy purpose and predestination. But that is not all, because he speaketh here of that infinite and essential glory, which is one and the same in all the persons, and so Christ had it as God blessed for ever ; and Christ having abstained from the use and exercise of it in a way proper to itself, now craveth a restitution.

The points are :—

Doct. 1. That Christ is God, true God, and hath an eternal co-equal glory with the Father before the world was. Before the world there was nothing but the eternal infinite essence, that was common to the Father, Son, and Holy Ghost. The Socinians seem to grant that he is of God, but not eternal God by nature; but here is a clear proof, ' Which I had with thee before the world was.'

Doct. 2. We may plead to God his own promises in deep and weighty cases: 'Put me in remembrance,' saith God, Isa. xliii. 26; as when death approacheth, or difficulties come upon us. Christ himself takes this course.

Doct. 3. The ground of all sound hope is what was done before all worlds. Christ had glory actually, and we have a grant of it: 2 Tim. i. 9, 'According to his own purpose and grace, which was given us in Christ Jesus, before the world began.' There was a grant of heaven and grace, and Christ received it for us. So Titus i. 2, 'In hope of eternal life, which God, that cannot lie, hath promised before the world began.' There was a solemn promise, which Christ received on our behalf. The frame of grace was ancient; God sealed up a large charter, and indented with Christ before ever there were any men in the world. Let us not look for our happiness in this world; our comforts do not depend upon the standing of it; when the world is no more, you may be happy.

Doct. 4. The chief point which I shall handle is, that Christ, in the economy or dispensation of grace, was reduced to such an exigence that he needeth to pray to be glorified: 'Father, glorify thou me with thyself, with the glory which I had with thee before the world was.' It is a matter of weighty consideration that Christ should pray his Father to bestow on him the glory which he wanted.

But how could Christ want glory, who was God-man in one person? To clear this, I shall a little state both his humiliation and his exaltation.

First, How far he humbled himself and wanted glory; what was, indeed, the utmost of his humiliation. Here I shall show—(1.) What glory he retained in the midst of it; (2.) What he wanted. Certainly though in his outward appearance he had no form and comeliness in him, yet inwardly he was the fairest of men; Isa. liii. 2, compared with Ps. xlv. 2.

1. What glory he was possessed of at the present. Christ had a double glory—the glory of his person, and the glory of his office.

[1.] The glory of his person. There was the union of the two natures; he did not lose his godhead though he took flesh; he was still the eternal Son of the Father, 'the brightness of his glory, and the express image of his person,' Heb. i. 3; John i. 14, 'The Word was made flesh, and dwelt among us,' ἐσκήνωσεν, he pitched his tent, 'and we beheld his glory, the glory as of the only-begotten of the Father.' He was still co-equal with his Father; the fulness of the Godhead dwelt in him; his flesh was taken into the fellowship of the divine nature as soon as it began to have a being in the womb of the virgin, the highest dignity a creature is capable of. The person of the Son was truly communicated to the nature of man, and the nature of man truly communicated to the person of the Son. He that was the Son of man was truly the Son of God, and he that was the Son of God was truly the Son of man; and by virtue of this union there was a communion higher than all other communions; the fulness of grace was subjectively and inherently in his human nature: 'He was anointed with the oil of gladness above his fellows,' Ps. xlv. 7. And he is said, John iii. 34, 'to receive the Spirit without measure,' both for the essence and virtue of it, to all effects and purposes, for himself and others; so that there needed nothing to be added to his full happiness. Christ was *comprehensor*; he perfectly knew upon earth what we shall know in heaven, and was perfectly holy and perfectly good.

[2.] The glory of his office was to be mediator between God and man; an office of so high a nature that it could be performed by none but him who was God and man in the same person; for he that would be mediator was to be prophet, priest, and king. As a prophet, he was to be *arbiter*, to take knowledge of the cause and quarrel depending between them; and as an *internuncius* and legate, to propound and expound the conditions of peace that are to be concluded upon. As he was a priest, he was to be an intercessor, to make interpellation for the party offending; and then to be a *fidejussor*, or surety, making satisfaction to the party offended for him. As he was a king, having all power both in heaven and earth, he was to keep and present the church of God so reconciled in the state of grace, and to tread down all enemies thereof. Here is a great deal of glory far above any creature.

2. What he wanted, that he should pray to be glorified. The glory of his person and office was yet but imperfect.

[1.] Of his person in both natures, it is said, Phil. ii. 7, ' He made himself of no reputation, and took upon him the form of a servant, and was made in the likeness of man,' ἐκένωσεν ἑαυτὸν; he made himself empty and void, not simply and absolutely, for then he would cease to be himself, and then he would cease to be God; but economically and dispensatively, veiling and covering his godhead under the cloud of his flesh, the beams of his divinity, as it were, wholly laid aside, only now and then it broke out in his works and speeches. Certainly he abstained from the full use and manifestation of it. He did not cease to be what he was, but laid aside the manifestation of it, and hid it in the form of a servant, as if he had none at all. The world could not discern him; to his own familiar friends he was now and then discovered, as occasion did require it. Otherwise in his whole course, his incarnation, nativity, obedience to the law of nature, to the law of Adam, law of sin, of Abraham, were a veil upon him. He suffered hunger, thirst, weariness, bitter agonies, shame of the cross, pain of death, ignominy of the grave; yea, he was not only in the form of a servant to God—' This commandment have I of my Father,' John vi. 38—but he was subject to worldly powers, ' a servant of rulers,' Isa. xlix. 7, wholly at their dispose. His human nature was subject to natural infirmities, hunger, thirst, fear, sorrow, anguish; he had not attained incorruption, impassibility, immortality, nor that glorious purity, strength, agility, clarity of body, which he expected, Phil. iii. 21, together with the fulness of inward joys and comforts in his soul. He lost, for a while, all sense and actual fruition of his Father's love: Mat. xxvi. 46, ' My God, my God, why hast thou forsaken me?' So that though he had the Spirit without measure in holiness, and righteousness, yet he was still humbled with unpleasing and afflictive evils.

[2.] For his office. It was managed as suited with his humiliation, and all his actions of prophet, priest, and king, could not be performed gloriously, but in a humble manner, as suited with his present state. He was an ordinary prophet, teaching in the world; as a priest, hanging on the cross; as a king, but he had but few subjects; therefore it is said, Acts v. 31, 'Him hath God exalted with his right hand to be a prince and a saviour,' as if he had not exercised any of his kingly office before, but he was but as a king anointed; he did not so evidently show forth the kingly office as afterward. Now he doth not overcome his enemies by force or by power. 1 Sam. xvi. 13: David was a king as soon as anointed, but for a long time he suffered exile and wandered in the wilderness before he was taken into the throne; so it was with Christ.

Secondly, His exaltation. What Christ prayed for might be known by the event. His exaltation begun at his resurrection, and received its accomplishment by his sitting at God's right hand. His exaltation answered his humiliation, his death was answered by his resurrection, his going into the grave by his ascending into heaven, his lying in the grave by his sitting at God's right hand, which is a privilege proper to Christ glorified. In the other we share with him, we rise, we ascend, but we do not sit at God's right hand. By his grave, though his body was freed from corruption, his human nature was discovered, but his body had not those glorious qualities as afterwards at his ascension.

Therefore, leaving his resurrection, let us speak of his ascension, and sitting on the right hand of God.

1. His ascension. Three things happened to Christ at his ascension.

[1.] The exaltation of his body and human nature; it was locally taken from the earth, and carried into heaven: Acts i. 9, 'While they beheld, he was taken up, and a cloud received him out of their sight,' into the same heaven into which we shall be translated. They err who say that Christ's ascension standeth in this, that Christ is invisibly present everywhere, which destroyeth the properties of a body. There was not only a change of state, but a change of place; it was a created nature, still finite.

[2.] The glorification of his person, which is the thing spoken of in this text; then all the thick mists and clouds which eclipsed his deity were removed. Not that there was any deposition or laying aside of his human nature; that is an essential part of his person, and shall continue so to all eternity; but only of all human infirmities. He laid aside his mortality at his resurrection, and necessity of meat and drink, but was not restored to his glory till his ascension; his body was so bright, that it shall pass though the air like lightning, clearer than the sun. Upon the earth he was ignorant of something of the day of judgment; now he hath all wisdom, not only in habit, but in act. Before he grew in wisdom, which he manifested by degrees; now the glory of his deity shineth forth powerfully.

[3.] A new qualification of his office. Christ hath exercised the mediatory office from the beginning of the world till now, before his coming in the flesh, when on earth, and after his ascension.

2. The next thing we are to speak of in the glorification of Christ is his sitting at God's right hand: Ps. cx. 1, 'The Lord said unto my Lord, Sit thou at my right hand, till I make thine enemies thy footstool.' It is Christ's welcome as soon as he came to heaven. The angels guarded and attended him, and they brought him near the ancient of days: Dan. vii. 13, 'I saw in the night visions, and behold, one like the Son of man came with the clouds of heaven, and came to

the ancient of days, and they brought him near before him.' They, that is, the angels did it, they are his ministers: Heb. i. 6, 7, 'When he bringeth in the first-begotten into the world, he saith, And let all the angels of God worship him. And of the angels he saith, Who maketh his angels spirits, and his ministers a flame of fire.' He cometh royally attended. Then the Father welcometh him with, 'Ask of me, and I will give thee the heathen for thy inheritance, and the utmost parts of the earth for thy possession,' Ps. ii. 8. As mediator, Christ was to have a grant of the kingdom by pleading his right, and then God seateth him on the throne, 'Sit thou on my right hand,' Ps. cx. 1. God doth, as it were, take his Son by the hand, and seat him on the throne.

This sitting on God's right hand implieth—

[1.] The giving of all power, or a restoration of him to the full use of the godhead. He had an eternal right, as the second person, but he was to receive a new grant: Mat. xxviii. 18, 'All power is given to me in heaven and in earth.' Christ, as God, hath all power, equal power with the Father by eternal generation; but as God incarnate, it is given to him. So Phil. ii. 9, 10, 'Wherefore God also hath highly exalted him, and given him a name above every name, that at the name of Jesus every knee shall bow, of things in heaven, and things in earth, and things under the earth;' to make all enemies stoop to him, that he might receive adoration from angels, men, and devils.

[2.] A grant of authority to rule according to pleasure. He is made prince of angels: Col. ii. 10, 'He is the head of all principality and power;' he is to be their sovereign Lord, and 'head of the church,' Eph. i. 22. Christ is to us the head of all vital influences, and judge of the world: Acts xvii. 39, 'He hath appointed a day, in which he will judge the world in righteousness by the man whom he hath ordained, whereof he hath given assurance to all men, in that he hath raised him from the dead.' This is the sum of Christ's glorification.

The uses of the whole.

Use 1. In that Christ prayeth for glory, it presseth us—

1. To take heed of dishonouring Christ, now he prayeth to be glorified. It was a great sin that the Jews crucified the Lord of glory; but they have some excuse, in that they knew not what they did: 1 Cor. ii. 8, 'Whom none of the princes of this world knew; for had they known it, they would not have crucified the Lord of glory.' His glory was not easily seen in his exinanition and abasement. But now we know more, and we cross his prayers, if we 'crucify him again afresh, and put him to open shame, Heb. vi. 6. We cannot indeed crucify Christ really, but we may draw the guilt of his enemies that crucified him upon us. By your scandalous lives, you do in effect, as to your intentions, deprive him of his glory, and approve the act of the Jews against him; you live as if no such thing had been done to Christ as his translation into heaven.

2. Since Christ so earnestly sued for his glorification, it is our duty, by all means, to procure and further his glory. We cannot do anything as his Father doth; we cannot bestow anything upon him but praise, and magnify him by a steadfast faith, and by a holy life. Mortified Christians are the glory of Christ.

3. It is comfort against the reproaches and oppositions of men as to the kingdom of Christ. Though the Jews scorn it, the Turks blaspheme it, heretics undermine it, yet Christ's prayers will do more than all their endeavours; still he will appear God manifest in the flesh. Christ's glory cannot be hindered, he hath prayed for it.

Use 2. In that Christ was glorified (for he cannot be denied whatever he demands), it is useful for our comfort, for our instruction.

1. For our comfort.

[1.] Christ's glorification is the pledge and earnest of ours. Had not he risen and ascended, and been received up into glory, neither we; the gates of death had been barred upon us, and the gates of heaven shut against us, and we should have been covered with eternal shame and ignominy. But now Christ, like another Samson, hath broken through the gates, and carried them away with him, our head is risen, and we in him, we receive of his fulness, glory for glory, as well as grace for grace. *Nobis dedit arrhabonem spiritus, et a nobis recepit arrhabonem carnis.* We have livery and seisin of the kingdom of heaven already in Christ. We are ascended with him: Eph. ii. 6, 'And hath raised us up together, and made us sit together in heavenly places in Christ Jesus.' In contracts, pledges are usually taken and given. Our head is crowned, and shall not the members? The human nature is already placed in the highest seat of glory.

[2.] It is a sign God hath received satisfaction. The Lord sent an angel to remove the stone, not to supply any power in Christ; but as a judge, when he is satisfied, sends an officer to open the prison doors. Our surety is delivered out of prison with glory and honour, God hath taken him up to himself. What is done to our surety concerneth us. Christ hath perfectly done his work, there is no more to be done by way of satisfaction. God was well pleased with him, or else he had not been at his right hand. Certainly all the work of his mediation was not accomplished on earth, he is now in exaltation, performing those other offices that remain to be fulfilled by him in heaven.

[3.] Hence we have confidence in his ability to do his people good. He is now restored to the full use and exercise of the godhead; he can give the Spirit, and perform all the legacies of the covenant. There were many repaired to Christ in the days of his flesh, when he was under poverty, crosses, death; the thief on the cross said, 'Lord, remember me when thou comest into thy kingdom.' What shall we not expect now he is entered into glory? Faithful servants follow their prince in banishment, but they have greater encouragement when he is on the throne. Those that adhered to David in the desert might look for much from him crowned at Hebron: Acts ii. 33, 'Therefore being by the right hand of God exalted, and having received of the Father the promise of the Holy Ghost, he hath shed forth this which ye now see and hear.' Not that then only he was endowed with the gifts of the Spirit; for whilst he was on earth, he was filled with the Spirit without measure; but then he received the accomplishment of the promise, of pouring out the Spirit upon us; for by promise is meant the accomplishment of the promise, for the promise was long before: Luke xxiv. 49, 'And behold, I send the promise of my Father upon you; but tarry ye in the city of Jerusalem till ye be endued with power from on high;' Acts i. 4, 'And being assembled together with them, commanded them that they should not depart from Jerusalem. but wait for the promise of the Father.' When he came to heaven, he received the fulfilling of this promise; for God did not bring Christ into heaven, as we are brought into heaven, merely to rest from labour, and to enjoy the reward of glory, but that he might sit in the throne of majesty and authority, to have power to send the Spirit, and gather the church, and condemn the world, and to apply to all the elect the privileges that he had purchased for them. There are effects of Christ crucified, and there are effects of Christ raised and exalted: Ps. lxviii. 18, 'Thou hast ascended on high, thou hast led captivity captive, thou hast received gifts for men ; yea, for the rebellious also, that the Lord God might dwell among them.' He gave gifts when he ascended, as kings do at their coronation. The humiliation of Christ hath its effects, in fulfilling the curses of the law, pacifying God's wrath and justice, the annihilation of the right which the devil had in elect sinners, purchasing a right of returning to God, and enjoying the grace of eternal life. The exaltation of Christ hath its effects, viz., the application of this righteousness, and to possess us of this right. When Christ was dead, it was lawful for those for whom he died to return to God, and enjoy his grace ; but it was not possible, for they were dead in sins. Therefore God raised up Christ, and gave him authority to pour out the Holy Ghost, that we should seek in grace, not only the force of satisfaction, but of regeneration ; that the effect of his abasement, this of his advancement. What a comfort this is, that Christ would not only die for us, but rise again, and pour out his Spirit, that his blood might not be without profit!

[4.] Here is comfort for the church ; while our head is so highly magnified, and made Lord of all, he will rule all for the best; certainly no good shall be wanting to them that are his: Ps. cx. 1, 'The Lord said unto my Lord, Sit thou at my right hand, until I make thine enemies thy footstool.' There shall come a time when the church shall have no enemies, so far shall it be from its being overcome by its enemies, that they shall curse themselves that ever they resisted the church.

[5.] Our sins shall not prejudice our happiness, seeing he sitteth at the right hand of God the Father to be our intercessor: 1 John ii. 1, 'If any man sin, we have an advocate with the Father, Jesus Christ the righteous.' We have a friend at court, a favourite in the court of heaven. If it were not for Christ's intercession, what should we do ? Those that know the majesty of God, their own unworthiness, the pollution of their prayers, what should they do ? The Spirit is our notary here: Rom. viii. 26, 'The Spirit helpeth our infirmities ; for we know not what to pray for as we ought; but the Spirit itself maketh intercession for us with groanings which cannot be uttered.' And Christ is our advocate in heaven : Rev. viii. 3, 'And another angel came and stood at the altar, having a golden censer, and there was given unto him much incense, that he should offer it with the prayers of all saints, upon the golden altar which was before the throne.' Our prayers have an ill savour as they come from us.

2. For our instruction. It teacheth us to seek heavenly things:

Col. iii. 1, 'If ye then be risen with Christ, seek the things that are above, where Christ sitteth at the right hand of God;' Phil. iii 20, 'Our conversation is in heaven, from whence also we look for the Saviour, our Lord Jesus Christ.' We should imitate Christ; whatever he did corporally, we must do spiritually. There is our treasure; if you are the children of God, he is your delight. There is our head; the inferior parts never do well when they are severed from the head. All that we expect cometh from thence, and therefore a natural desire of happiness carrieth the saints thither.

SERMON VII.

I have manifested thy name unto the men which thou gavest me out of the world: thine they were, and thou gavest them me; and they have kept thy word.—JOHN XVII. 6.

WE have now ended the first paragraph of this chapter, Christ's prayer for himself. Here he cometh to pray for others, the disciples of that age. When Jacob was about to die, he blesseth his sons; so doth Christ his disciples. Christ representeth their case with as much vehemency as he doth his own.

In this verse he useth three arguments—they were acquainted with his Father's name, belonged to his grace, and were obedient to his will. Or, if you will, you may observe—

1. The persons for whom he prayeth.

2. The reasons why he prayeth for them; which are three:—(1.) What Christ had done; (2.) What the Father himself had done; (3.) What they had done.

First, The persons for whom he prayeth, 'The men which thou hast given me out of the world.' Who are these? I answer—The disciples or believers of that age; not only the eleven apostles are intended, though chiefly; but it is not to be restrained to the apostles only.

1. Because the description is common to other believers; others were given him besides the eleven apostles. It is the usual description of the elect in this chapter, ver. 2, 'That he should give eternal life to as many as thou hast given him.' So ver. 9, 'I pray for them whom thou hast given me, for they are thine;' and ver. 24, 'Father, I will that they also whom thou hast given me be with me where I am;' and in other chapters of this Gospel.

2. Because Christ had made known the name of God to more than the apostles; many of the Jews and Samaritans had received the faith. Acts i. 15, there a hundred and twenty met together in a church assembly presently after Christ's death.

3. Otherwise they had been forgotten in Christ's prayer; for afterwards he prayeth only for future believers: ver. 20, 'Neither pray I for them only, but for those that shall believe on me through their word.' Mark, 'that *shall* believe.' But though the apostles are not only intended, yet they are chiefly intended, as appeareth by that expression, 'through their word.' We have seen who are the persons.

Now they are described to be 'the men which the Father hath given me out of the world.' *Men*, to note the greatness of the blessing; though they were frail, miserable men, corrupt by nature, as others are, yet by singular mercy they are made familiar friends of Christ, and some of them doctors of the world.[1] 'Which thou hast given me' by way of special charge. There is a double giving to Christ—by way of reward, by way of charge: these were given to him as a peculiar charge. 'Out of the world;' that is, out of the whole mass of mankind: when others were left and passed by, God singled them out, and gave them to Christ.

I shall open the phrase more fully in the next clause.

The points of doctrine are these :—

1. Observe, in the business of salvation Christ would deal with us not by angels, but by men given him out of the world, that is the description of the apostles and doctors of the church in the text. 'To us he hath committed the word of reconciliation.' God could teach us without pastors, and manifest himself unto us by inward and secret illapses into the heart; but he useth the ministry of men, and that not out of indigence, but indulgence; not for any efficacy in the preacher, but for congruence to the hearer, as a means most agreeable to our frail state. There is mercy in this appointment.

[1.] It is most for the glory of God. God's honour cometh freely from us when the instruments are vile and despicable. We are apt to sacrifice to the next hand. Acts xiv., they brought oxen and garlands to sacrifice to Paul and Barnabas. 2 Cor. iv. 7, 'We have this treasure in earthen vessels, that the excellency of the power may be of God, and not of us.' These are most apt to rival God, as children thank the tailor.

[2.] It trieth our obedience. We look for extraordinary miracles and ways of revelation; God would see if we can love truth for truth's sake, rather than for the teacher's sake, and take it from the meanest hand. It is not *who*, but *what* is delivered. Foolish man would give laws to God. Christ impersonateth our thoughts: Luke xvi. 30, 'If one went to them from the dead, they will believe.' Had Christ come in person, spake to us in an audible voice, or sent an angel, they would believe.' Foolish thoughts! God trieth you by Moses and the prophets. It is a deceit to think if we had more glorious means it would be otherwise with us. Christ came in disguise: John i. 11, 'He came unto his own, and his own received him not;' and the word is brought to us in earthen vessels. It is merited by God-man, it is dispensed by the power of God by man.

[3.] It is the most rational way. He doth not rule us with a rod of iron, by mere power and majesty, but draweth us by the cords of a man, by counsels and exhortations. He dealeth with us by those with whom we have ordinary converse, 'as a man with his friend,' Exod. xxxiii. 11. What should sinners do if God should come and thunder to them in majesty and glory? Exod. xx. 19, 'Let not the Lord speak to us.' He veileth it under the cloud of human weakness. There is no conversing with the terribleness of majesty but by intermediate persons. Men speak to us that have a feeling of our infirmi-

---

[1] Qu. "word"?—ED.

ties. Prophets are ὁμοιοπαθεῖς, 'Men of like passions with ourselves,' James v. 17. If angels should teach us, we would think the precepts too strict for men. Men know how to speak to us by speaking from the heart to the heart: Prov. xxvii. 19, 'As face answereth face in a glass, so doth the heart of man to man.' There may be lesser differences in regard of complexion and constitution, but they know the general nature of man.

[4.] It is the surest way. If men deceive us, they deceive themselves; we have experience of their fidelity in other things, and they confirm it by their own practice. They are subjected to the law of the same duties and necessities, sometimes seal the truth with their blood.

[5.] It is a comfortable way. Paul, a great sinner before conversion, Peter, a great instance of the infirmities and falls of the saints, yet, from their own experience of the power and comfort of the gospel, preach it to us. Well, then, scorn not God's institution, but admire the wisdom of it. We are bound to submit, though we could see nothing but folly: 1 Cor. i. 21, 'It pleased God by the foolishness of preaching to save them that believe.'

2. Observe, again, it is a special privilege to be chosen to privileges of grace when others are passed by: 'Given me out of the world.'

[1.] There is a world of others, and they are left to themselves. Christ hath not the tithe of mankind: Jer. iii. 14, 'One of a city, and two of a tribe.' Christ doth not take them by dozens or hundreds, but by ones and twos. Grace falls on few. Christ seeketh out the elect, if but one in a town.

[2.] They were as eligible as we, only we were singled out by mere grace. The lot might have fallen upon them as well as upon you; thousands in the world were as eligible: Ezek. xviii. 4, 'Behold all souls are mine; as the soul of the father, so also the soul of the son is mine.' All were made by the same God out of the same mass of nothing: he is equally judge of all; all had sinned. Thy soul was as polluted as theirs, as liable to God's judgment, as deep in the same condemnation; yet such was his good-will and pleasure, to single us out. This is the glory of his grace, *miserabor cujus misertus fuero*: Mal. i. 2, 3, 'Was not Esau Jacob's brother? saith the Lord, yet I loved Jacob, and I hated Esau.' Though all men be equal in themselves, yet mercy can make a distinction. The best reason is God's good pleasure. Well, then, apply this.

(1.) Look to the distinction. How many steps of election may we walk up? That we were not toads and serpents, but men, the same nothing was as pliable; not men only, but christians, within the pale of the church; not christians at large, but born there, where the mists and fogs of popery were dispelled; nor Protestants at large, but called to a stricter profession; still in every degree multitudes were cut off. That I was not a christian, but a minister, an officer in the church: 1 Tim. i. 12, 'He counted me faithful, putting me into the ministry.' Plato gave thanks for three things—that he was a man, not a woman; a Grecian, not a barbarian; not an ordinary Greek, but a philosopher. A christian may much more give thanks.

(2.) To the reason of this distinction: John xiv. 22, τί γέγονεν,

'How is it that thou wilt manifest thyself to us, and not unto the world?' Luke i. 43, 'And whence is this to me, that the mother of my Lord should come unto me?' When you have searched all you can, you must rest in Christ's reason: Mat. xi. 26, 'Even so, Father, for so it seemed good in thy sight.' God's supremacy over all things in heaven and in earth maketh him free to choose or refuse whom he pleaseth. It is not because you were better disposed than others; many of a better temper were passed by: God raised up a habitation to the Spirit out of crabbed knotty pieces. A man in a wood leaveth the crooked timber for fuel. The young man that went away sad was of such a sweet natural temper, that it is said, Christ loved him.

Secondly, Let us now come to the reasons why he prayeth for them.

First, What he did: 'I have manifested thy name to them;' in which Christ intimateth his own faithfulness and their future usefulness. His own faithfulness; for this was one way of Christ's glorifying his Father on earth, by communicating the tenor of the christian doctrine to the disciples; so that some of them by the light received were to be special instruments of converting the world. Ἐφανέρωσα, 'I have manifested;' by outward teaching, and inward illumination. Outward teaching was necessary; the mystery of the gospel was but sparingly revealed by former prophets; but Christ, who was in the bosom of the Father, knew the depth and bottom of it.' John i. 18, 'No man hath seen God at any time; the only-begotten Son, who is in the bosom of the Father, he hath declared him;' and accordingly he revealed it to the disciples. And besides, by an inward light he gave them to understand it; for Christ preached publicly, but all did not understand him, but those to whom 'it was given to know the mysteries of the kingdom of God,' Mat. xiii. 11. So much is intimated in the word ἐφανέρωσα. And herein Christ fulfilled that prophecy, Ps. xxii. 22, 'I will declare thy name unto my brethren.' The disciples of Christ, especially the apostles, are adopted into the privileges of co-heirs with Christ, and therefore to them he declared his Father's name, than which there could not be a greater privilege. Now by the name of God, some understand one thing, some another, according to the different acceptations of the word *name.* Largely, and more generally, we may understand, whatever is necessary to be known and believed to salvation concerning God's will and essence; that is his name; all by which the Father might be known, as men are known and distinguished by their names. The meaning is, that he had made known to them the whole doctrine concerning God's will and essence, teaching them that in one essence of God there are three distinct persons, Father, Son, and Holy Ghost; that the Father begot the Son, his substantial image, by eternal generation, and sent him in time, that he might take a true human nature on him, that so he might become a mediator between God and us, by whom alone we have access to God, that we may obtain grace and life eternal. Now this he manifested in his doctrine, in the course of his life, and by the light of the Spirit, freeing them from all prejudices, contracted by their own darkness, or the obscure doctrine that was then taught in the church.

1. Observe Christ's faithfulness to his own charge. He opened all the mysteries of God's name, that is, of the true religion to them.

We that are ministers, and you that are masters of families, should learn of him. It is our duty to teach the flock committed to our charge: Acts xx. 20, 'I kept back nothing that was profitable to you, teaching you publicly, and from house to house.' We are to draw out all the truths necessary to salvation. It is not enough that ministers live honestly and unblamably, that they are hospitable and kind, but they must teach the people to read God's name. If you hire a man to prune the vineyard and he diggeth in the field, to fight in the battle and he watcheth the stuff, it is not the work you set him about. So to you that are masters of families; the apostles were Christ's own family; God expecteth it from you: Gen. xviii. 19, 'I know him, that he will command his children, and his household after him, and they shall keep the way of the Lord.' Do not disappoint the Lord; he reckoneth upon it; your family should be a little flock, a little church. Families are the fountains of church and commonwealth. Oh! how sweet will it be when we come to die, if we could say, as Christ, we concerning our flock, you concerning your families, ' I have manifested thy name to them that thou gavest me out of the world; thine they were, and thou gavest them me, and they have kept thy word.'

2. Observe the earnest desire Christ had to glorify his Father, by living, teaching, dying;—thy name, thy word. Oh! that we would learn of our Lord to glorify our Father which is in heaven; to be contented to do anything, to be anything, so we might be to the glory of God!

3. Observe the excellency of the doctrine of the gospel; its certainty, its clearness.

[1.] Its certainty. It is not a doctrine forged in the brain of men, but brought out of the bosom of God into the breasts of the apostles, and from them conveyed to us. In this word you have the Father's heart; Christ told it the apostles: ' I have manifested thy name to them,' &c. Christ is the original author: Heb. i. 2, ' In these last times he hath spoken to us by his Son.' The Son of God is the first man in the roll of the New Testament prophets; the first was not an angel, but God's own Son, the messenger of the covenant, the apostle of our confession. Though Christ doth not speak to us immediately in person, yet he spake to us by the apostles; they have their light from Christ. Therefore he that readeth the word should seem to hear Christ speak. This was that which he whispered to the apostles in secret.

[2.] The clearness of the scriptures. Christ knew all the counsels of God, and he hath manifested his name to the apostles. There is a light shining; if we see it not, it is a sign we are lost: 2 Cor. iv. 3, 4, ' If our gospel be hid, it is hid to them that are lost; in whom the god of this world hath blinded the minds of them which believe not, lest the light of the glorious gospel of Christ, who is the image of God, should shine unto them.' What an advantage have we above the Gentiles and above the Jews!

(1.) Above the Gentiles. The doctrine of the essence and will of God cannot be known by the light of nature. Somewhat of his glory shineth in the creatures: Rom. i. 20, ' For the invisible things of him from the creation of the world are clearly seen, being understood by the things that are made, even his eternal power and godhead.' Some characters there are in conscience, though horribly defaced; but alas! the furthest reach of nature cometh short of salvation. Nature is blind as well as lame in things supernatural; there are some few remains of light to keep the law of nature alive in the soul, for the advantage of civil society and moral business. When nature putteth on the spectacles of art, still she is blind. There are many inventions to polish reason; to sharpen discourse, there is logic; for language, rhetoric; for government and equity, laws; for health, physic; for manners, ethics; for societies of men, politics; for families, economics; but for worship, nothing; their piercing wits were there blunt. Man is naturally wise for everything but to maintain a respect between him and God. They knew there was a God, and that this God ought to be worshipped; but what he was, and how he should be worshipped, they knew not; their knowledge was rather a mist than a light. His works told them that he was wise, powerful, and good; but they were unhappy in their determination of his worship; they sat abrood, and proved but fools: 'They professed themselves to be wise, but became fools,' Rom. i. 22. While they intended him honour, they carved to him the greatest contempt; whilst they would express him in the image of the creatures, they dishonoured him. Natural light is but small in itself, and corruption maketh it less. They knew nothing of the misery of man and the remedy by Christ; our fall in Adam, original sin, and the work of redemption were mysteries to them; they could not dream of these things; when they were revealed they counted them foolishness. They spoke of virtue as a moral perfection; of vice, as a stain of nature; but nothing of righteousness and sin, as relative to the covenant of God. God used the heathen as instruments to put nature to the highest extent. How may we pity them that they could go no further, and admire God's mercy to us that we, being weaker than they in natural gifts, are yet stronger in grace; that a boy out of a catechism should know more than they! Their misery was great in abusing the light of nature; our misery will be greater, and damnation double, if we abuse the light of nature and grace.

(2.) Above the Jews, whom God acquainted with his statutes above all other nations. They knew little of the name of God in comparison of what we know. Therefore Moses desires to know God's name, Exod. iii. 13; and it is said, Judges xiii. 18, 'Why askest thou after my name, seeing it is secret?' The divine glory was hidden and under a veil. In those appearances of Christ little was known in respect of what was known at his incarnation. It is spoken in reference to the present dispensation. Some notice they had of this mystery. God acquainted them with his name by degrees: as Exod. vi. 3, 'I appeared unto Abraham, unto Isaac, and unto Jacob, by the name of God Almighty; but by my name JEHOVAH was I not known to them.' God had made himself known by other names; to the fathers by the name of God Almighty; the name Jehovah, that should be an appellation among his gathered people, giving a being to his people, and making good his promises. Afterwards, 'I am the God of Abraham, the God of Isaac, the God of Jacob,' as more relating to the covenant. Afterwards, Jer. xxiii. 5, 6, 'I will raise up to David a righteous branch, this is the name whereby he shall be called, THE LORD OUR RIGHTEOUSNESS.' Then God will be known by his grace, justifying his people, and accepting them for Christ's sake. But in the New Testament all is open and clear; he is called 'the God and Father of our Lord Jesus Christ,' Eph. i. 5. Then God the Father and the mediator were clearly made known. Alas! the Jewish church knew little of the doctrine of the Trinity, the distinction of the persons, the quality of the mediator, the way of salvation. What they knew was obscured, and the doctrine of the Messiah horribly depraved.

Use. Let us bless God for the word, and take heed unto it, as to a light shining in a dark place. What would be our condition if we had not the scriptures among us? We should be no better than savages in the wilderness, or as the body without the soul, the earth without the sun. God might immediately have revealed himself to man; he that made the heart can enstamp it with the knowledge of his will; but he would state his doctrine into a settled course, that we might not coin oracles to ourselves, or obtrude fancies on others: 'We have λόγον βεβαιότερον, a more sure word of prophecy, whereunto ye do well that ye take heed, as to a light that shineth in a dark place,' 2 Peter i. 19. He knoweth to what liberty we incline in preaching divine things. No more πολυμερῶς καὶ πολυτρόπως of 'those divers ways and manners, wherewith God spake in times past to our fathers by the prophets,' Heb. i. 1. After the closing of a perfect canon there needed nothing but ordinary revelation. This is sufficient to salvation, if there were no book else; if the world were full of books, and this only were wanting, there were no certain way nor rule to heaven. Here is God's heart discovered to us, and our hearts to ourselves; it is a ray of the face of God in Christ: John i. 18, 'No man hath seen God at any time; the only-begotten Son of God, that lay in the bosom of the Father, he hath declared him.' Satan hath been ever maligning this light, that he might more securely domineer in the world. Christ undertook he would declare God's name to his brethren, and here he hath done it. Oh! let it come with divine authority upon your hearts, in all the precepts, promises, threatenings of it, that you may come to a nearer sight of God and yourselves.

4. Observe the necessity of a divine light before we can understand the things of God: 'I have manifested thy name,' &c.

[1.] There must not only be an outward sure rule of doctrine, but an inward light. We can have no savoury apprehensions of the things of God till Christ himself become our teacher; the Son of God must always be the interpreter of his Father's will; he is the Word that speaketh to the heart. All men by nature are ignorant of the name of God, without any saving knowledge: Eph. v. 8, 'Ye were sometimes darkness;' not only in the dark, but darkness itself; 'but now ye are light in the Lord;' that is, enlightened by his Spirit. This is proper to the elect, those who are given to him. The church is Christ's open school, the scriptures our book, the ministers are the ushers, and Christ is the inward teacher. Some are only taught by the ministers, others are taken aside and taught by Christ himself in private. His public lectures are read to all hearers, but the elect are taught of God: John vi. 68, 'Lord, to whom shall we go? thou hast the words of eternal life.' Others may hear the word, but they perish in their own blindness and unbelief. Some play the truants in Christ's school; they will not hear, they pass judgment on themselves: Acts xiii. 48, 'As many as were ordained to eternal life believed.' The whole city was met to hear, but none believed but the elect; and the apostle doth not say, 'As many as believed were ordained to eternal life,' but 'as many as were ordained believed.' It is not given to all: Mat. xiii. 11, 'It is given to you to know the mysteries of the kingdom of heaven, but to them it is not given.' All the difference is in the will of God; so that the scholars in this kind are 'the called according to his purpose.' Christ's teaching is of no larger extent than his Father's election. Some schoolmasters, besides their common care, do teach such children apart as they love most, they take them and point with the finger; so doth Christ manifest himself to those that are given him out of the world by the inward work of his grace. Moral suasion is common to all, but he taketh some aside and worketh on their hearts.

[2.] For the manner of this teaching; it is accompanied with force and power. There is always an operation that goeth along with this teaching: John vi. 44, 45, 'No man can come to me except the Father that hath sent me draw him. It is written in the prophets, They shall be all taught of God.' There is teaching and drawing; the inspiration and the impression go together. He is an incomparable teacher; he giveth the lesson, and a heart to learn it; with information he reformeth, and with the knowledge of our duty he giveth a will and power to do it. He teacheth the promise so as to make us believe it; the commandment so as to make us obey it. The soul is God's echo: Ps. xxvii. 8, 'When thou sayest, Seek ye my face, my heart said unto thee, thy face, Lord, will I seek.' He reformeth by his light, and exciteth by the power of his grace. In short, it is a powerful teaching, joined with an inward working. His scholars are sure of proficiency, for he hath their hearts in his hands, and can move them according to his own pleasure. There is not only an illumination of the mind, but a bowing of the will. Corrupt nature in man is strong enough to resist anything of man, as he is man.

[3.] The necessity of this inward light; without it the word will not work. Many hear outwardly that are never the better: John vi. 44, 'No man can come to me except the Father which hath sent me draw him.' There must be an inward light, an inward operation on the soul, or the word is without effect; the heart must be opened as well as the scriptures. As all the multitude that thronged on Christ did not touch him as the diseased woman did, who touched the hem of his garment: 'Who touched me?' saith Christ, 'knowing that virtue had gone out of him,' Mark v. 30. Many may come to an ordinance, but virtue passeth out to few. The outward minister can but speak to the ear; it is Christ works grace in the heart: unless the Holy Ghost come down, and open the mouths of preachers to speak, and the hearts of people to hear, all is to no purpose.

Use. Well, then, every time you come to the opening of the scriptures, look for this inward light to shine into your hearts, that you may have a saving knowledge of God in Christ. Remember you come to hear that doctrine which Christ hath brought down from the bosom of the Father, and he must bring it into your bosoms.   There are two sorts of hearers:—

1. Some are careless, that come hither, but scarce hear the minister; their bodies are in the sanctuary, but their spirits are in the corners of the earth.   Their coming is made fruitless by the wandering of their hearts; they have experience of the power of Satan, not of Christ.   The devil presenteth to their fancy such objects as carry their spirits from God and his work: Ezek. xxxiii. 31, 'They come unto thee as the people cometh, and they sit before thee as my people, and they hear thy words, but they will not do them; for with their mouth they show much love, but their heart goeth after their covetousness.'   Carcases without a spirit are but carrion; clothes stuffed with straw, that were a mocking; so is a body present at hearing the word without a soul. What is the difference between an absent body and a wandering spirit? God knocketh at the heart, but there is none within to hear him.

2. Some hear the minister, but do not wait for the illumination of Christ, which sometimes God grants to us in the hearing of the word: Acts xi. 15, 'As I began to speak, the Holy Ghost fell on them;' this is to draw us to attention: Acts xvi. 14, 'Whose heart the Lord opened, that she attended to those things that were spoken by Paul.' When God disposeth us to hear his word attentively, he approacheth to us in mercy.

SERMON VIII.

I have manifested thy name unto the men which thou gavest me out of the world : thine they were, and thou gavest them me, and they have kept thy word.—JOHN XVII. 6.

THE next argument is what the Father had done in and about believers; he disposed them into the hands of Christ: 'Thine they were, and thou gavest them me.'   Where is—(1.) His interest in believers; (2.) His act about believers.

First, His interest in believers: 'Thine they were.'   How is this to be understood?   Divers have framed divers senses; thine by creation, thine by election, thine by sanctification.   The Father being first in order of the persons, all original works are proper to him; so creation is ascribed to him; so the Lord saith, Ezek. xviii. 4, 'All souls are mine,' all created by him.   But this sense is not so proper to this place, because those for whom Christ prayed not might plead this interest; so Satan is God's, the wicked and all creatures are God's.   By election; thine by free election, mine by special donation: 1 Peter ii. 9, 'Ye are a chosen generation, a peculiar people.'   The first and highest act of grace is ascribed to him; they are his chosen and peculiar ones.   These were eternally his, and by the continuation of the same purpose of grace they are always his.   This is proper to this place; only sanctification may be included, which is, as it were, an actual election.   As by original election the heirs of salvation are distinguished from others in God's purpose and counsel, so by actual election they are visibly distinguished and set apart from others; so 'Thine they were,' by an excitement of thy Spirit and grace stirred up to follow me, and chose me in this special way of service. Sanctification is also ascribed to the Father: John vi. 44, 'No man can come unto me except the Father that hath sent me draw him;' and Jude 1, 'To them that are sanctified by God the Father.' The first effect of saving grace is ascribed to him, as the first rise of grace is from his love. I prefer the middle sense, and do only take in the latter as the effect: 'Thine they were;' they were chosen by the purposes of thy grace, and called, which is the effect of that grace passing upon their hearts.

From hence—

1. Observe that Christ pleadeth interest as an argument in prayer. It is meet, when we come to pray to God, that we can say, We are his. This way would Christ endear his own disciples to the Father's respect and grace: Ps. cxix. 44, 'I am thine; save me.' The great work of christians should be to discern their interest, that they may come to God with some confidence. Though you cannot say, I am thine, with respect to the purposes of his grace; yet at least you should say, I am thine, in your own dedication and choice. *Si nostra tueri non vultis, et tamen vestra defendetis.* Many a trembling christian dareth not say, He is mine; but he is resolved to say, I am his; that is the fitter argument with God. With our own souls, in our own straits, plead, He is mine: Ps. xlii. 11, 'Why art thou cast down, O my soul? and why art thou disquieted within me? Hope thou in God, for I shall yet praise him, who is the health of my countenance, and my God.' But in prayer plead, I am his; though you cannot plead his choice, plead your own resignation. Consider, it is a forcible argument. Every one will provide for his own: 'He is worse than an infidel who will not provide for his own, especially those of his own household.' It is a comfortable argument. When we cannot speak of our works, we may speak of our interest: Lord, I am a sinner; but I am thine: I am a poor wretch; but I am one that would not be his own, unless I am thine. Oh! but says the poor soul, if I could say that I am thine, one that belongeth to the purposes of thy grace, there were some comfort. *Ans.* It is sweet, when we can say mutually, 'I am my beloved's, and my beloved is mine.' But are you not willing to choose him, though you cannot say he hath chosen you? The choice of our portion discovereth our interest. Canst thou in truth of heart say? Lord, 'I have none in heaven but thee, none upon earth that I desire in comparison of thee,' Ps. lxxiii. 25. If you can, in the sincerity of your hearts, call God to witness this, it is sweet. Though thou canst not apply Christ, canst thou resign thyself? Then we have the fruit of election, though we have not the sense of it. God certainly hath chosen us when, by the work of his grace, he maketh us choose him. Fallen man is not dainty in his choice, till a work of grace passeth upon him; he turneth from the creator to the creature; he saith to the world, Would to God thou wert mine! to riches, honours, pomp, Would thou wert mine! 'Happy is the people that are in such a case.' It is grace turneth us from the creature back again to God; God is our portion, because we are his; God cannot refuse that heart which he hath thus drawn to himself.

2. Observe again, that none are given to Christ but those that were first the Father's: 'Thine they were;' he had chosen them in the purposes of his grace, and disposed them into Christ's hands. Thine by election, mine by special donation. The acts of the three persons are commensurable, of the same sphere and latitude; those whom the Father chooseth, the Son redeemeth, and the Spirit sanctifieth. The Father loveth none but those that are given to Christ, and Christ taketh charge of none but those that are loved of the Father. Your election will be known by your interest in Christ, and your interest in Christ by the sanctification of the Spirit. All God's flock are put into Christ's hands, and Christ leaveth them to the care of the Spirit, that they may be enlightened and sanctified. In looking after the comfort of election, you must first look inward to the work of the Spirit on your hearts, then outward to the work of Christ on the cross, then upward to the heart of the Father in heaven: 1 Peter i. 2, 'Elect according to the foreknowledge of God the Father, through sanctification of the Spirit, unto obedience, and sprinkling of the blood of Jesus Christ.' There is a chain of salvation; the beginning is from the Father, the dispensation through the Son, the application by the Spirit; all cometh from God, and is conveyed to us through Christ, by the Spirit.

Secondly, The Father's act about believers: 'Thou gavest me them.'

How are they given to Christ? Things are given to Christ two ways—by way of reward, or by way of charge.

1. By way of reward. So all nations are given to him by way of reward: Ps. ii. 8, 'Ask of me, and I will give thee the heathen for thy inheritance, and the uttermost parts of the earth for thy possession.' He is Lord of all, Acts x. 36, even of the devils. All flesh are thus given to him, to be ruled by him. This donation is very large, and compriseth elect and reprobates. All nations are Christ's heritage in this sense, as well as the church. All power in heaven and in earth is given to him, to dispose of elect and reprobates according to his own pleasure. Only in this giving by way of reward there is a difference; some are given to Christ at large, to be disposed of according to his pleasure; others are given to him for some special ministry and service, as hypocrites in the church; and so Judas was given to him, as Christ saith, ver. 9, 'Of them which thou hast given me, I have lost none but the son of perdition.' Again, others are given to him by way of special and peculiar interest, to be members of his body, subjects of his kingdom, &c. So only the elect are given to Christ; the great bargain that Christ drove with his Father was an interest in souls; therefore it is said, Isa. liii. 10, 11, 'When thou shalt make his soul an offering for sin, he shall see his seed, he shall prolong his days, and the pleasure of the Lord shall prosper in his hand. He shall see of the travail of his soul, and be satisfied.' This was all the gain that Christ reckoned of.

2. By way of charge. This again is proper to the elect, who are redeemed, justified, sanctified, glorified. The elect are made over to Christ, not by way of alienation, but oppignoration; none of them who are given to Christ by way of charge can miscarry: John vi. 37, 'All that the Father giveth me, shall come to me; and he that cometh to

me, I will in no wise cast out;' and ver. 39, 'This is the will of him that sent me, that of all which he hath given me, I should lose none, but should raise it up again at the last day;' and John x. 28, 29, 'I give unto them eternal life, and they shall never perish, neither shall any man pluck them out of my hand. My Father, which gave them me, is greater than all; and no man is able to pluck them out of my Father's hand.' There is Christ's faithfulness and the Father's power engaged, therefore this must needs be proper to the elect.

Now, because both these ways are proper to the elect, that I observe is, that the Father's elect are given and committed to the Son, as his purchase and charge.

First, They are given to him by way of reward. Christ, by virtue of his purchase, hath many relations to believers: they are given to him as subjects of his kingdom, as scholars of his school, as children of his family, as the spouse of his bosom, as the members of his body. All these relations I shall insist upon; for this was the honour that was granted to Christ upon his obedience. It was much that Christ would be our king, more that he would be our master, more that he would be our father, more that he would be our husband, and yet further that he would be our head: he counted it an honour, and bought it at a dear rate.

1. We are given to him to be subjects of his kingdom. Christ is Lord of all the world, but he prizeth no title like that of king of saints, Rev. xv. 3, to rule as Lord in the church; no throne like the conscience of a humbled sinner. The heart is Christ's best presence-chamber; he loveth to have his chair of state set there. He had an eternal right together with the Father and the Holy Ghost, but he would come and suffer and be crowned with a crown of thorns that he might have a new right as mediator, and have the crown of glory put upon his head in the church: Acts v. 31, 'Him hath God exalted with his right hand to be a prince and a saviour.' The Father promised it long before upon bargain and contract. There is never a subject that Christ hath but is bought, and with the dearest price, his sovereign's own blood: Mat. xx. 28, 'He gave himself, λύτρον ἀντὶ πολλῶν, a ransom for many.' Many subjects die in other kingdoms that the prince may be seated in the throne; but here the prince dieth for the subjects, that he may govern his spiritual realm with more peace and quietness. As the price was great, so the Father hath made him a large grant.

[1.] Christ's empire is universal, and spread throughout the world. He properly is the catholic king; there are no bounds and limits of his empire: Isa. liii. 12, 'Therefore will I divide him a portion with the great, and he shall divide the spoil with the strong.' Some of all nations are given to him: Isa. xlix. 12, 'Behold, these shall come from far; and lo, these from the north, and from the west, and these from the land of Sinim,' north, west, south, Jews and Gentiles. The Jews, that are now his enemies, shall appoint to themselves a head; as the tribes flocked to Hebron to crown David: Hosea i. 11, 'Then shall the children of Judah and the children of Israel be gathered together, and appoint themselves one head, and they shall come up out of the land.' There is no king like Christ for largeness of command

and territory. All monarchs have certain bounds and limits by which their empire is terminated; Christ's empire runneth throughout the whole circuit of nature; he hath a multitude of subjects.

[2.] Christ's empire is eternal: 'Of the increase of his government there shall be no end,' Isa. ix. 7. Kings must die, and then their favourites may be counted offenders. So Bathsheba said to David (who yet was a type of the reign of Christ), 1 Kings i. 21, 'When my lord the king shall sleep with his fathers, I and my son Solomon shall be counted offenders.' But Christ liveth and reigneth for evermore. But you will say, Christ doth not reign for ever, but 'till he hath put all enemies under his feet, when he shall resign up the kingdom to the Father,' 1 Cor. xv. 24. I answer—In kingly dignity there are two things, *regia cura* and *regius honor*—kingly care and kingly honour. Kingly care, by which he ordereth and defendeth his subjects; and kingly honour, which he receiveth from his subjects. Certainly Christ shall be king for ever and ever: Luke i. 33, 'And he shall reign over the house of Jacob for ever, and of his kingdom there shall be no end;' because he shall always be honoured and adored as king and mediator. He shall resign the kingdom, that is, that way of administration; for when the elect are fully converted and sanctified, and their enemies destroyed, there will be no need of this care. Now thus we are given to Christ, that he might be a king universally and eternally. He ruleth us by a sweet covenant, he might rule us by power. Other kings find subjects, he maketh them. He might rule us, for he bought us, he hath an absolute right over us. As there was a covenant between the Father and Christ, so between Christ and the church. He propoundeth no less than a kingdom: Isa. x. 8, 'Are not my princes altogether kings?' Christ's title is by purchase, conquest, and consent. All Christ's subjects were vessels of wrath, vessels of hell, in their natural estate; he recovered us from the devil by power and conquest, he bought us out of his Father's hands by merit and price.

In short, concerning this kingdom, which belongeth to the second person, the Father appoints it, the Son merits it, the Holy Ghost as Christ's viceroy governs it. The Father chooseth a certain number of men, giveth them to Christ; the Son dieth for these men, ransometh them from the grave and hell, and committeth them to be ruled and governed to the Spirit, as Christ's vicar; the Spirit useth the ministry of men, we are the Holy Ghost's overseers, ·Acts xx. 28, by which grace is wrought, and so we are united to Christ. Our work by the power of the Spirit is to bring them to Christ, and Christ bringeth us to God the Father by his intercession and by final tradition, which is the last act of Christ's mediatory kingdom: 1 Cor. xv. 24, 'Then shall he deliver up the kingdom to the Father.' God giveth us to Christ, Christ to the Spirit, the Spirit uniteth us to Christ, and Christ bringeth us to God. So that if we would enter into this kingdom, we must go to God the Father, confess thou art a traitor and rebel, desire him not to enter into judgment with thee, but seek to be reconciled. If thou thus comest to the Father, he will send thee to the Son; as Job xlii. 8, God biddeth the friends of Job to seek his intercession: I will not be pleased with you but in Christ: 'If I did not regard the presence of Jehoshaphat, I would not look to thee, nor see thee,' 2 Kings iii. 14. Go to the Son, reflect upon Christ's merit and intercession; say, Lord, appear for us before thy Father; were it not for thee he would not regard my face. The Son will send you to the Spirit: I cannot bring you to God in your impurity and rebellion; go to the Spirit of my Father, that he may wash you, and purge you. Plead the promise of the Spirit: John xvi. 13, 14, 'Howbeit, when he that is the Spirit of truth shall come, he will guide you into all truth; for he shall not speak of himself: but whatsoever he shall hear, that shall he speak, and he will show you things to come. He shall glorify me, for he shall receive of mine, and shall show it to you.' When we come to the Spirit, he will send us to Moses and the prophets; hear them. The word is 'the rod of his strength.' By the word we are gained, by the sacraments we take an oath of allegiance, in prayer we perform our homages, in alms and acts of charity we pay him tribute; praise and honour are the revenues of this crown.

Thus I have showed the title, the largeness of the grant, and the manner of administration.

2. We are given to Christ as scholars in his school. He is the great prophet, and doctor of the church. Certainly Christ loveth the honour of this chair; he counteth it an honour to be our prophet. It is his title, Acts iii. 22, 'A prophet shall the Lord your God raise up to you from among your brethren.' Christ he came out of the bosom of God, to show his mind and heart; he is called 'the apostle and high priest of our profession,' Heb. iii. 1. Christ taketh the titles of his own officers. Though he be Lord of the church, yet he is an apostle. He counteth it an honour to be a preacher of the gospel, God's legate à latere, the Son of God is first on the roll of gospel preachers. He laid the foundation of the gospel when on earth; he teacheth now he is in heaven; others teach for him. Christ counts it his liberty to teach; he is to be a light to the Gentiles. He doth not teach the ear, but the heart; he is still to nurture us, and bring us up. He is an excellent teacher; he doth not only set us our lesson, but giveth us a heart to learn. The scripture is our book, but Christ is our master, and we shall see wondrous things if he doth but open our eyes.

3. We are to be children of his family. A master is not so careful as a parent. This was the thing propounded to allure Christ to the work of redemption: Isa. liii. 10, 'He shall see his seed;' he shall have a numberless issue and progeny. Though all are Benonis, sons of sorrow, and Christ died in the birth, yet this was his privilege, 'He shall see his seed.' Jesus Christ hath a great family, take it altogether: Rev. vii. 9, 'A great company which none could number, redeemed out of all nations, and kindreds, and people, and tongues.' Christ is wonderfully pleased with the fruitfulness of his death. It is his great triumph at the last day, Heb. ii. 13, 'Behold I and the children which God hath given me.' It is a goodly sight when Christ shall rejoice in the midst of them, and go with this glorious train to the throne of the Father. Jesus Christ is our brother and our father: by regeneration and the merit of the cross, our father; but in the possession of heaven, our brother. We are co-heirs with him.

4. We are given to him as the wife of his bosom. As a father giveth the daughter whom he hath begot to another for a spouse and wife, so doth God give his elect to Christ. Indeed, Christ hath bought her at his Father's hands; other wives bring a dowry, but Christ was to buy his spouse. As Saul gave his daughter to David, but first he was to kill Goliath, and to bring the foreskins of a hundred Philistines, 1 Sam. xvii. 25, and xviii. 25; so God gave Christ the church for a spouse, to be redeemed by his blood; the infernal Goliath was to be slain. Eve was taken from Adam when he lay asleep; so when Christ was a-dying, the church was, as it were, taken out of his side. He was willing to die that his spouse might live. Christ left his Father at his incarnation, his mother at his passion, to make the church his spouse, as a man leaveth father and mother, and cleaveth to his wife. This honour Christ getteth by the power of his Spirit; it costs him long wooing. David had bought Michal with the danger of his life, yet he was fain to take her away from Phaltiel, 2 Sam. iii. 13, &c. The devil hath gotten Christ's spouse into his hands; Christ by his Spirit is to rescue her, and oblige her to loyalty. Hereafter is the great day of espousals, the bride's, and the Lamb's hope. Christ's honour as well as our comfort is but incomplete now:· 'Then he shall present the church to himself, a glorious church, not having spot or wrinkle, or any such thing, but that it should be holy, and without blemish,' Eph. v. 27. Christ is now decking her against that time. We are to accomplish the months of our purification; odours and garments are to be brought out of the king's treasury, Esther ii. 12.

5. We are to be members of his body. Next to that of the Son of God, there cannot be a greater title than Head of the church. Poor creatures!·that Christ will take us into his own mystical body, to quicken us, enliven us, and guide us by his grace! If he were a head to all things, that had been somewhat: Col. ii. 11, 'He is the head of all principality and power.' But he is their head for the church's sake: 'And gave him to be the head over all things to the church,' Eph. i. 22, over them to us; He counteth himself not perfect without us, 'Which is his body, the fulness of him that filleth all in all;' that we should be called the fulness of Christ! He esteemeth himself as maimed and imperfect without us. He treateth his mystical body with the same respect as his natural; that was raised, ascended, glorified; so shall we. For the present he is grieved in our miseries, as well as we exalted in his glory, and so he communicates to us and with us.

Use 1. Admire the love of God in this donation.

1. Of God the Father, that he should bestow us upon his own Son. As Christ pleadeth it to the Father, so should we plead it to ourselves: we were God's, and he gave us to Christ. Electing love is the sweetest; others were his as well as you: Ps. xxxvi. 7, 'How excellent is thy loving-kindness, O God!' That God should cast a look on you!

2. Of God the Son, that he should take us as a gift from the Father, and as a reward of all his services. Nothing could be more welcome than the tender of souls. Consider, nothing could be added to the greatness of him who was equal with the Father; the privileges

of the incarnation were but as so many milder humiliations ; but his main reason was to gain an interest in souls : nothing else could bring Christ out of heaven into the manger, the wilderness, the cross, the grave. What was his reward for all his expense of blood and sweat ? He came from heaven, took our nature, shed his blood ; Christ is very thirsty of an interest in souls: Isa. liii. 11, 'He shall see of the travail of his soul, and shall be satisfied.' This is enough ; I do not begrudge my pains, my temptations, my agonies. A woman safely delivered after sore and sharp labour, forgetteth all her past sorrow for joy of the birth. Christ longed till his incarnation, feasted himself with the thoughts of his free grace : Prov. viii. 31, 'Rejoicing in the habitable parts of his earth, and my delights were with the sons of men.' Afterwards he longed for his passion : Luke xii. 50, 'I have a baptism to be baptized with, and $\pi\hat{\omega}\varsigma$ $\sigma\upsilon\nu\acute{\epsilon}\chi\omicron\mu\alpha\iota$, how am I straitened till it be accomplished !' His delight was with the sons of men.

3. Bless the Spirit for his attesting, witnessing, working the comfort of all this in all our souls. We have the Father in heaven, the Son on the cross, the Spirit in our hearts. We are given to Christ, but Christ is given to us by the Spirit ; our interest is wrought and applied by the Holy Ghost. It is the Spirit of the Father, the Spirit of the Lord Jesus Christ, who is his executor ; he is to see Christ's will accomplished ; he is Christ's vicar in his kingly and prophetical office.

Use 2. Let us consecrate and give up ourselves to Christ. Walk as his : 1 Cor. iii. 23, 'Ye are Christ's, and Christ is God's !' Look for all from him, by dependence on him ; be whatever you are to him, to his glory. You are given up to him, you are not at your own dispose ; neither tongue, nor heart, nor estate is thine ; God gave it, and if thou art a christian, thou hast given up thyself to him.

SERMON IX.

I have manifested thy name unto the men which thou gavest me out of the world : thine they were, and thou gavest them me, and they have kept thy word.—JOHN XVII. 6.

SECONDLY, They are committed to him by way of charge
     In opening this I shall inquire—
     1. Who are the persons that are thus given to Christ ?
     I answer—The elect, and no other. They are given to him out of the world, a selected company ; as in the text, 'Those whom thou hast given me ;' such as shall surely and infallibly be brought to grace, and conducted to glory : John vi. 37, 'All that the Father giveth me, shall come to me ;' and ver. 39, 40, 'This is the Father's will which hath sent me, that of all which he hath given me, I should lose nothing, but should raise it up again at the last day. And this is the will of him that sent me, that every one which seeth the Son, and believeth on him, may have everlasting life, and I will raise him up at the last day.' And can the Father's will be disappointed ? (I wonder what can men object against so plain a scripture !) And when they are come

they cannot miscarry : 'This is the will of him that sent me, that of all that he hath given me, I should lose nothing;' not a leg, not a piece of an ear. Christ hath received a special charge.

But you will say, It is said, John xvii. 12, 'Those which thou hast given me I have kept, and none of them is lost but the son of perdition.' So it seemeth some may be lost which are given to Christ.

[1.] I answer—The word *given* is there used indefinitely, for those given to Christ by way of reward, as well as those given to him by way of charge. Hypocrites, because of their external vocation, are said to be given to Christ by way of ministry and service, but not by way of special charge. That is notable which Christ saith, John xiii. 18, 'I speak not of you all, I know whom I have chosen: but that the scripture may be fulfilled, He that eateth with me hath lift up his heel against me.' Where he showeth plainly that one of them was not of the number of the elect, and should not receive the privileges of his especial charge ; though he was chosen to the calling of an apostle, yet not to eternal life. Christ knoweth the number of the heirs of salvation, and who only are given him by way of ministry and service of the church.

[2.] I may answer by interpreting the phrase ϵi $\mu \grave{\eta}$ $\acute{o}$ $\upsilon \grave{i} \grave{o} s$ $\tau \hat{\eta} s$ $\grave{\alpha} \pi o \lambda \epsilon \acute{i} a s$. The words are not exceptive, but adversative ; none of them is lost, but the son of perdition is lost ; the words are not rendered 'except the son of perdition,' but, 'but the son of perdition ;' it is not *nisi*, but *sed*. There is no exception made of Judas, as if he had been given to Christ, and afterward had fallen away. It is not *nemo nisi filius perditionis*, but when he had mentioned their keeping, he would adversatively put the losing of Judas. This phrase or manner of speech is often used in scripture ; so Rev. xxi. 27, ' And there shall in nowise enter into it anything that defileth, neither whatsoever worketh abomination, or maketh a lie ; but they which are written in the Lamb's book of life ;' ϵi $\mu \grave{\eta}$, where the words are not exceptive ; for then it would follow that some which work abomination should enter into the kingdom of heaven ; but adversative, these shall not enter, but others shall enter. So Mat. xii. 4, ' It was not lawful for him to eat, neither for those which were with him, but only for the priests ;' ϵi $\mu \grave{\eta}$, it is not exceptive, as if the priests were of David's company.

2. What was this charge ? It will be opened by considering what the Father proposed concerning the elect, and what the Son undertook.

[1.] What the Father proposed. The words of Heaven are $\check{\alpha} \rho \rho \eta \tau a$ $\rho \acute{\eta} \mu a \tau a$, ' unutterable words, which it is not lawful for a man to utter, 2 Cor. xii. 4. Those secret ways of discourse and communication between the Father and the Son are to be adored with reverence and deep silence, were it not that the Spirit of God hath put them into such forms as are suitable to those transactions and intercourses which are between man and man. It is usual in scripture to put the passages between God and Christ into speeches : Ps. xl. 6–8, ' Sacrifice and offering thou didst not desire ; mine ears hast thou opened : burnt-offering and sin-offering hast thou not required. Then said I, Lo, I come ; in the volume of the book it is written of me, I delight to do thy will, O my God: yea, thy law is within my heart;' Ps. ii. 8, 'Ask of me, and I will give thee the heathen for thy inheritance, and the utmost parts of the earth for thy possession;' Ps. cx. 1, 'The Lord said unto my Lord, Sit thou at my right hand, until I make thine enemies thy footstool.' The Father came to Christ, and did, as it were, say to him, Son, I am loath that all mankind should be lost, and left under condemnation; there are some whom I have chosen to be vessels and receptacles of my mercy and goodness; and because I am resolved that my justice shall be no loser, you must take a body and die for them, and afterward you must see that they be converted to grace, justified, sanctified, guided to glory, and that not one of them should miscarry; for I will take an account of you at the last day. It is easy to prove all these things out of scripture. That there are a certain definite number, see 2 Tim. ii. 19, 'The foundation of the Lord standeth sure, having this seal, The Lord knoweth those that are his.' There is no lottery nor uncertainty in the divine decrees; the number is stated, sealed; none can add to it, or detract any one person that Christ received a command to lay down his life for: John x. 18, 'This commandment have I received of my Father;' for them only I lay down my life, viz., for my sheep. That Christ is to see them converted to grace: John vi. 37, 'All that the Father giveth me shall come to me; and him that cometh to me I will in no wise cast out.' And without miscarrying, guided to glory: John x. 28, 29, 'I give unto them eternal life, and they shall never perish, neither shall any pluck them out of my hand. My Father, which gave them me, is greater than all; and none is able to pluck them out of my Father's hand.' That Christ is to give an account of bodies and souls: John vi. 39, 'And this is the Father's will that hath sent me, that of all which he hath given me, I should lose nothing, but should raise it up again at the last day.' Which accordingly he doth: Heb. ii. 13, 'Behold, I and the children which God hath given me.'

[2.] What Christ undertook. The whole proposal of the Father: Ps. xl. 8, 'Lo, I come to do thy will, O God.' Christ consented to all the articles of the eternal covenant; not only to take a body to die, but to take a particular charge of all the elect; as Judah interposed for Benjamin, so doth Christ for the souls committed to him: Gen. xliii. 9, 'I will be surety for him; of my hand shalt thou require him: if I bring him not to thee, and set him safe in thy presence, let me bear the blame for ever.' So doth Christ say concerning all the persons that fall under his charge. If I do not see them converted, justified, sanctified, conducted to glory, count me an unfaithful undertaker, and let me bear the blame for ever.

3. The ground of this charge, why the Father doth not save them by his own power, but committed them to the Son? I answer—

[1.] Partly in majesty; God would not pass out grace but by a mediator; and therefore, when he was resolved that he would not lose the whole race of mankind, but repair his image in some of them, and had selected whom he pleased out of the mass, yet in majesty he would not immediately communicate grace to them but by Christ. There is a difference between man in innocency and man fallen. Man in innocency had immediate communion with God; God was present with his image: but now man fallen needeth a mediator; our approaches to God are unhallowed, his presence to us is dreadful: 1 Cor. i. 30, 'Of him are ye in Christ Jesus, who of God is made to us wisdom, righteousness, sanctification, and redemption.' The heathens were sensible of the necessity of intermediate powers (it is strange, you will say), or else what shall we make of that, 1 Cor. viii. 5, 6, 'For though there be that are called gods, whether in heaven or in earth (as there be gods many, and lords many): but unto us there is but one God, the Father, of whom are all things, and we in him; and one Lord Jesus Christ, by whom are all things, and we by him.'

[2.] In justice. Though God were resolved to show mercy to the fallen creature, yet he would carry on his act of grace in such a way that justice might be satisfied for sin: Rom. iii. 25, 26, 'Whom God hath set forth to be a propitiation, through faith in his blood, to declare his righteousness for the remission of sins that are past, through the forbearance of God. To declare, I say, at this time his righteousness; that he might be just, and the justifier of him which believeth in Jesus.' Therefore, for satisfaction of his justice, he sent his Son into the world, that, taking our nature on him, he might therein suffer for our offences, and mediate a peace between God and fallen man; and that not by bare entreaty, but by satisfaction; therefore we are given to Christ. I confess it is hard to say that God by any necessity of nature required this satisfaction; the exercise of his justice is free, and falleth under no laws; but it was most convenient to preserve a due sense and apprehension of the Godhead.

[3.] In love and mercy. God was resolved that the heirs of salvation should infallibly be conducted to everlasting life; he would not be defeated of his purpose, and therefore would have them quickened by virtue of that power and life that was given to Christ. God would now deal with us upon sure terms, and take order sufficient for attaining his end, and therefore he would not trust us with any but his own eternal Son, that nothing might be wanting. There is not only a command laid upon us, but a command and a charge laid upon Christ. Christ is a good depository; of such care and faithfulness, that he will not neglect his Father's pledge; of such strength and ability, that nothing is able to wrest it out of his hands; of such love, that no work can be more willing to him; he loveth us far better than we do ourselves, or else he had never come from heaven for our sakes; of such watchfulness and care, that 'his eyes do always run to and fro throughout the earth, that he may show himself strong in the behalf of them that trust in him.' Providence is full of eyes, as well as strong of hand. Were we our own keepers we should soon perish; but Christ is charged, who is a loving, faithful, able keeper, who is resolved to preserve us safe, till he doth at the last day present us to the Father.

Use. 1. It informeth us of two things:—

1. Of the certainty of the elect's salvation. If the elect should not be saved, Christ should neither do his work nor receive his wages. How can they miscarry that are Christ's own charge? He hath such power that 'none can pluck them out of his hands,' John x. 28. He had need of a stronger arm than Christ that must do it. When you can pluck him out of the throne then he may lose his flock. He hath

grace enough to convert them: John x. 10, 'I am come that they might have life, and that they might have it more abundantly;' and he hath power enough to keep them; John x. 28, 'I give unto them eternal life, and they shall never perish, neither shall any pluck them out of my hand.' Shall we say that the Son, though he hath power, wants will? This is blasphemy. He came down from heaven with this resolution: John vi. 38, 'I came down from heaven, not to do my own will, but the will of him that sent me.' Now, this is the Father's will, that they should come, and that they should not be lost; and it is meat to Christ to accomplish it: John iv. 34, 'My meat is to do the will of him that sent me, and to finish his work.' Now it is a rule, *Qui potest et vult, facit.* He that can do, and will do, doth it undoubtedly.

2. It informeth us of Christ's distinct and explicit notice of the elect.

[1.] Of their persons, he knoweth the definite number, all their names; he lieth in the Father's bosom, knoweth his secrets: 'He is worthy to open the book,' Rev. v. 4, 5; and he hath a register of his own, wherein their names are recorded: Rev. xiii. 8, 'Whose names are not written in the Lamb's book of life.' Man by man, name by name, they are all written there; as the high priest carried their names in his breast, so doth Christ; thy name is engraven on his heart: John x. 3, 'He calleth his own sheep by name, and leadeth them out.' 'Clement also, with other my fellow-labourers, whose names are in the book of life,' Phil. iv. 3. John, Anna, Thomas, Clement, they are recorded; and Christ takes such special notice of them as if there were none other in the world.

[2.] Their condition and necessities, how obscure and poor soever they be in the account and reckoning of the world: Ps. xxxiv. 6, 'This poor man cried, and the Lord heard him!' Poor soul! he is liable to such temptations, overwhelmed with such troubles, he crieth to me to help him. It was the theology of the Gentiles, *dii magna curant, parva negligunt*—that the divine powers did only take care of the great and weighty concernments of the world, but neglected the lesser: Isa. xl. 27, 'Why sayest thou, O Jacob, and speakest, O Israel, My way is hid from the Lord, and my judgment is passed over from my God?'

Use 2. It persuadeth us wholly and absolutely to resign up ourselves into Christ's hands. The Father is wiser than we; he knoweth well enough what he did, when he commendeth us to his Son. Let us give up bodies and souls to Christ, all that we have. Faith is often expressed by committing ourselves to Christ; it answereth the trust the Father reposed in him: 1 Peter iv. 19, 'Wherefore, let them that suffer according to the will of God commit the keeping of their souls to him in well-doing, as unto a faithful creator.' The apostle knew what he did when he trusted Christ with his soul: 2 Tim. i. 12, 'I know whom I have believed, and I am persuaded that he is able to keep that which I have committed unto him against that day.' Is thy soul laid a pledge in Christ's hands? It is no easy work. That we may know what it is, let me open it a little.

[1.] You must chiefly commit your souls to him. Most men lose their souls to keep the body.   That which a man chiefly looketh after is his jewels and precious things, in a dangerous time, to commit them to the custody of a friend.   So a christian, whatever becometh of him in the world, he is careful to lay up his soul in Christ's hands, that it may be kept from sin and the consequents of sin.   Alas! while we have it in our own keeping it will soon miscarry.   Now concerning this committing the soul to Christ, let me observe:—

(1.) That this act is most sensible in time of deep troubles and death, when we carry our lives in our hands, trust Christ with your souls: Ps. xxxi. 5, 'Into thy hands I commit my spirit: thou hast redeemed me, O Lord God of truth.'   So Christ: Luke xxiii. 46, 'Father, into thy hands I commend my spirit.'   Can we trust Christ, upon the warrant of the gospel, when troubles are nigh and fears of death?   Lord, take my spirit; as Stephen, Acts vii. 59, 'Lord Jesus, receive my spirit.'   We must do it in our life, especially as often as we renew covenant; but then most sensibly when we come to die.   Jesus Christ is always the depository of souls; but when we come to die, or are in special troubles, then we are chiefly solicitous about our souls; as when a house is a-burning we are not careful about our lumber, but run to fetch our jewels to put them in a safe hand.

(2.) Whenever we do it, it must be an advised act.   A man must be sensible of the danger he is in, of the many temptations to which he is exposed, what a sorry keeper he is of his own heart (Satan could fetch a prey out of paradise, Judas out of Christ's company), what abilities Christ hath: 2 Tim. i. 12, 'I know whom I have believed, and I am persuaded that he is able to keep that which I have committed to him against that day.'   Presumption is a child of darkness; it cometh from ignorance and incogitancy.   Faith is deliberate and advised; a christian can venture his soul upon Christ's grace notwithstanding infirmities, upon Christ's power notwithstanding temptations; this precious thing is daily in danger, yet I can trust it in Christ's hands; he that made it can best keep it, and guide us by his grace, and direct us in this dangerous passage.

(3.) It must still be accompanied with some confidence.   We must be quieted: 'I am persuaded he is able to keep that which I have committed to him.'   We should not distrust when we have resigned ourselves to the care and tuition of his Spirit.   Christ's charge will be safe from danger.   It is our weakness to be full of doubts and fears.   We may be assaulted, but we are safe in the Father's purpose and the Son's protection.   Too much confidence in sanctification, and too little in justification, will unsettle us.

(4.) There must be a care of obedience: 'Lord Jesus, receive my spirit.'   'Commit your souls to him in well-doing,' 1 Peter iv. 19.   Sins will weaken trust; an impure soul cannot be committed to Christ's custody.   Would we commit dung to a friend to keep?   There must be a giving up ourselves to him in love, as well as committing ourselves to him in faith: John xii. 26, 'If any man serve me, let him follow me; and where I am, there shall also my servant be.'

(5.) It must arise from a chief care of your souls.   Most men are negligent herein; they watch over their goods, but neglect their souls, and lose their souls to keep these trifles.   What account can they make to God at the last day? These live as if they had no souls, and can they be said to commit their souls to God?

2. We must give up our bodies to him, and the conveniences of the body, to let him dispose of us according to his pleasure. We shall have a body at the last day, and that body will have glory enough; that falleth under Christ's charge: John vi. 39, 'This is the Father's will that hath sent me, that of all which he hath given me I should lose nothing, but should raise it up again at the last day.' He that cannot do the lesser, it is impossible he should do the greater; he that will not trust God with his earthly substance, credit, estate, how will he trust God with his soul for eternal salvation? 'Which is easier to say, Thy sins are forgiven thee, or to say, Arise, and walk?' Mark ii. 9. It is more difficult to believe for salvation, but bodily inconveniences are more pressing and sensible. The welfare of the body must not be committed to wealth or wit, but to Christ. A christian is not troubled what shall become of him; he leaveth himself to Christ's disposal, which is the way to allay his cares and fears.

Thirdly, The third argument is what they had done, in the next clause, 'They have kept thy word.' Here is another reason, their obedience. He had mentioned what the Father had done, now what they had done. His ministry with them was not without success and fruit. This phrase, 'kept thy word,' is very significant; it implieth not only outward hearing, but knowledge: Mat. xiii. 23, 'He that receiveth the seed into good ground, is he that heareth the word and understandeth it,' &c. Nay, not only knowledge, but assent and believing, embracing the promises of the gospel: Luke viii. 15, 'Having heard the word, keep it, and bring forth fruit with patience.' Not only assent, but the fruits of love and obedience: 1 John ii. 4, 'He that saith, I know him, and keepeth not his commandments, is a liar, and the truth is not in him.' Not only single obedience, but constant profession and perseverance: Prov. xvi. 20, 'My son, keep thy father's commandments, and forsake not the law of thy mother.' They have not failed as Judas. Now there is a twofold keeping of the word—a legal keeping and evangelical. The legal keeping is absolute and perfect obedience; if there be but the least failing, Moses accuseth and condemneth you. The evangelical keeping is filial and sincere obedience. Those imperfections Christ pardoneth, when he looketh back and seeth many errors and defects in life, as long as we bewail sin, seek remission, strive to attain perfection. All the commandments are accounted kept when that which is not done is pardoned.

'Thy word.'—He doth not say *my* word, but *thine*. He elsewhere referreth his doctrine to the Father: John vii. 16, 'My doctrine is not mine, but his that sent me.' So here he mentioneth the divine authority of his doctrine.

1. Observe, Christ speaketh good of his people to his Father.' Satan is an accuser, he loveth to speak ill of believers; but Christ telleth his Father how his lambs thrive. It is a grief to your advocate when he cannot speak well of you in heaven, and say, 'They have kept thy word, I am glorified in them.' How grievous is it when your very advocate is forced to be an accuser! Isa. xlix. 4, 'I have laboured in vain, and spent my strength for nought.' I have sent my gospel,

and it doth no good.   It is Christ's complaint against the obstinacy of the Jews.   Again, whom will you imitate, Christ or Satan ?   To slander and accuse is the devil's property; we should be more tender in divulging the infirmities of the saints; it is the devil's work. Christ, when he prayeth for his enemies, he mollifieth their crime, and softeneth it with a gentle interpretation : Luke xxiii. 34, 'Father, forgive them; they know not what they do.'   Christ excuseth, Satan accuseth.

2. Observe again, 'They have kept thy word.'   Christ speaketh good of them, though they had many failings.   The disciples often miscarried, were of weak faith, passionate when they met with disrespect: Luke ix. 54, 'Lord, wilt thou that we command fire to come down from heaven and consume them?'   But Christ returneth this general issue, 'They have kept thy word;' so James v. 11, 'Ye have heard of the patience of Job;' yea, and of his impatience too, when he cursed the day of his birth; but the Spirit of God putteth a finger on the scar.   It is a ground of hope, notwithstanding many weaknesses and failings, Christ loveth not to upbraid us with infirmities. We commend with exceptions, and when we seem to praise we come in with a *but*, like a stab under the fifth rib; yea, we blast much good with a little evil, as flies only go to a sore place.

3. Observe, it is the duty of God's people to keep his word.   It is the greatest commendation Christ could give his disciples, 'They have kept thy word.'   Mark, christians, it is not your duty to hear the word only, but to keep it; not to know the word only, but to keep it. Rickets cause great heads and weak feet.   We are not only to dispute of the word, and talk of it, but to keep it.   We must neither be all ear, nor all head, nor all tongue, but the feet must be exercised.   Now, what is it to keep the word ?   We are said to keep it when we watch over it, that it be not lost by ourselves, nor taken away by others.   It noteth three things—that it must be impressed on our hearts, expressed in our lives, retained in our conversations.

[1.] To keep the word is to feel the force of it in our hearts, that our hearts may be more bent and set towards God, for else the word is lost to ourselves.   A man may better his knowledge by the word, but yet he doth not keep it, nor feel the virtue and force of it.   The brains may be warmed when the heart is not, and we may keep the notion when the motion is gone and lost.   Oh! consider, we know God as we love him, we know him aright when we know him as we are known ; he knoweth us to love us, to choose us, to gain us to himself and to Christ.   So should we know him for our portion, to have no rest till we have an interest in Christ.

[2.] It must be expressed in our life : Luke xi. 28, 'Blessed are they that hear the word of God, and keep it.'   To keep the law is to live according to the prescript of it.

[3.] There must be a perseverance to retain it in our conversations : Rev. iii. 18, 'Thou hast kept my word, and hast not denied my name.' Do we thus keep the word ?   All dependeth on it: John xiv. 15, 'If ye love me, keep my commandments.'   Christ conjureth us by all the love we bear to him, ver. 23, 'If any man love me, he will keep my words ; and my Father will love him, and we will come unto him, and make our abode with him.' If there be any faith in the heart, by which we esteem Christ, we must not only keep it in memory, but keep it in faith. Do you honour him in your lives. Can we venture anything to keep the word when the world would take our crown from us?

Use. We may know when Christ will speak good of us; not when we hear, and when we are taught, but when we keep the word : yet this we must do, understand and keep his word, not customs, not traditions of ancestors, nor fancies; we must receive his word as his word: 1 Thes. ii. 13, 'For this cause thank we God without ceasing, because when ye received the word of God, which ye heard of us, ye received it not as the word of men, but (as it is in truth) the word of God, which effectually worketh also in you that believe.'

SERMON X.

Now they have known that all things, whatsoever thou hast given me,
are of thee.—JOHN XVII. 7.

IN this verse there is another argument why he should be heard for the apostles, which may be taken either from the towardliness of the disciples, or the fidelity of Christ. The one is implied in the other ; the towardliness of the apostles in discerning the divine nature and mission of Christ ; the fidelity of Christ in referring all to his Father ; 'they know it,' and 'I have taught it them ;' for he urgeth not only their proficiency, 'they have known,' but his own faithfulness, he had glorified his Father in his doctrine. Both which are arguments ; they that have made such progresses are to be respected ; and I that have been faithful have deserved it in their behalf.

I shall first open the words.

'Now.'—Heretofore they were ignorant, but now I can say this for them, 'they have known,' &c.; as a schoolmaster, when he hath taught a child, looketh for his reward when the work is done.

'They have known.'—Things above reason are known by faith and revelation ; by my teaching and illumination they are brought to conceive and acknowledge it ; for he saith before, 'I have manifested thy name to the men that thou gavest me out of the world.'

'That all things whatsoever thou hast given me.'—It doth not refer to what he had received from God by eternal generation as the only-begotten Son of God, but to what he had in commission as mediator ; and he saith, 'all things whatsoever,' as implying his authority over the world: ver. 2, 'Thou hast given him power over all flesh.' His interest in the elect, 'Thine they were, thou gavest them me,' ver. 6. His doctrine; it was given him in charge by the Father ; Christ taught no other doctrine but what he received from his Father : John vii. 16, 'My doctrine is not mine, but his that sent me.' It was not of his invention, but delivered according to the instruction received from his Father. His power to work miracles, that it was not by magical imposture, or the help of the devil, but by the power of God.

The pharisees would not believe it: Luke xi. 20, 'If I by the finger of God cast out devils, no doubt the kingdom of God is come upon you :' Mat. xii. 28, ' If I cast out devils by the Spirit of God, then the kingdom of God is come unto you.' The imposition of the mediatory office : John vi. 69, 'We believe, and are sure, that thou art that Christ, the Son of the living God ; ' John i. 41, 'We have found the Messias, which is, being interpreted, the Christ.' The union of the two natures : 'That I came out from thee, and was sent from thee,' ver. 8. And the apostles knew this: Mat. xvi. 16, 'Simon Peter answered and said, Thou art Christ, the Son of the living God.' The apostles knew Christ to be very God and very man in one person ; the veil of his human nature and natural infirmities did not hinder their eyes from seeing him.

'Are of thee ; ' that is, ratified by thee as the supreme judge ; invented or found out by thee as the supreme author ; all is from thy sovereign favour and gracious decree, flowing from thee as the supreme cause and power. Of thee as an author, of thee as a cause, of thee as a judge.

Observations.

1. Observe Christ's faithfulness to his Father, in two things—in revealing his mind ; in referring all things to his glory. In revealing his mind, he acted according to his instructions : ' The doctrine is not mine, but his that sent me,' John xii. 50 ; 'Whatsoever I speak, even as the Father said unto me, so I speak.' In referring all things to his glory : John vii. 18, 'He that speaketh of himself, seeketh his own glory : but he that seeketh his glory that sent him, the same is true, and no unrighteousness is in him.' Now, if we would glorify God, we should learn of our Lord and master, not speak from our own fancy, nor to our own ends ; either way we may be false prophets, when we speak false doctrine, or for wrong ends ; the one leads the people into error, the other into formality, or a dead powerless course ; though usually both are coupled together: Acts xx. 28, ' There shall arise from among you men speaking perverse things, to draw disciples after them.' Perverse doctrine and a perverse aim are seldom severed ; as a bow that is warped can hardly shoot right.

Use 1. Be persuaded of the truth of what you deliver, and look to your aims ; the best of us know but in part, and are apt to err ; and we are renewed but in part, and are apt to warp, and to look asquint on our own interests. Little do you know what strugglings we have to satisfy our own souls, and then regulate and guide our aims.

2. It is useful also to hearers. If you would glorify God, you must learn of Christ ; not live according to your own wills, nor for your own interests. The end falleth under a rule as well as the action. You are not to be led by fancy, but scripture ; not to aim at your own profit, but God's glory. It is hard to say which is worst, to baulk the rule or pervert the end. He that doth evil with a good aim maketh the devil serve God, though ignorantly and sinfully ; but he that doth good with an evil aim maketh God serve the devil ; ' you make me to serve with your iniquities.' It is sad to wrong God, as the highest sovereign, by breaking a law upon any pretence whatsoever ; and it is worse to wrong God as the utmost end : the one is the effect of

ignorance, the other of disobedience. Natural light showeth that the supreme cause must be the utmost end. A man may err in a positive law; but this is the standing law of nature and reason, that all our endeavours should be to God.

2. Observe, the proficiency of the apostles in Christ's school; they knew that all things whatsoever was given him, was of God. At first they were rude and ignorant; and Christ saith, 'Now they know;' and they had many disadvantages; they were conscious to all the natural weaknesses which Christ discovered in his conversation, his hunger, thirst, weariness; and yet 'they have known,' &c. How did they come to know this? I answer—Partly by the internal light of the Holy Ghost: Mat. xvi. 16, 'Thou art Christ, the Son of the living God;' ver. 17, 'And Jesus answered, Blessed art thou, Simon Barjona; for flesh and blood hath not revealed it unto thee, but my Father which is in heaven.' The saving knowledge of Christ's person and offices cannot be gotten but by special revelation from God; we must see God as we see the sun, by his own beam and light. Partly by the consideration of his miracles, in which some beams of the Godhead did shine forth, and by which his human nature was, as it were, counterbalanced: John iii. 2, 'Rabbi, we know that thou art a teacher come from God; for no man can do these miracles that thou dost except God be with him.' Partly by special observation of the singularity and excellency that was in Christ's person, his conversation, miracles, doctrine, which made his testimony more valuable, and in a rational way served to beget respect to him, and a human belief that he was a person of great holiness and strict innocence, without partiality: Mark xii. 14, 'Master, we know that thou art true, and carest for no man; for thou regardest not the person of men, but teachest the way of God in truth.' With such fidelity as to God; he came not in his own name: John v. 42, 'I am come in my Father's name.' With such grace and authority: Mat. vii. 29, 'The people were astonished at his doctrine; for he taught them as one having authority, and not as the scribes.' All he did was with heavenly majesty and authority; a sovereign majesty was to be seen in Christ's teaching, proper to himself. Besides his faithfulness as a minister, with such clearness, evidence, and demonstration, there was sufficient declaration to the world, at his baptism: Mat. iii. 17, 'Lo, a voice from heaven, saying, This is my beloved Son, in whom I am well pleased;' agreeing with the prophecy of him, Isa. xlii. 1, 'Behold my servant, whom I uphold; my elect, in whom my soul delighteth.' At his transfiguration before three persons, that for the holiness of their lives were of great credit, Mat. xvii. 5. Before all his disciples, John xii. 28, 'Father, glorify thy name: then came there a voice from heaven, saying, I have both glorified it, and will glorify it again.' To the world, at his resurrection, Acts xvii. 31, 'Whereof he hath given assurance unto all men, in that he hath raised him from the dead.' To which resurrection the Jews were conscious. Those that reported it wrought miracles; these men sought not themselves, had no advantage, but visible hazards; their witness was agreeable to the writings of the prophets; the doctrine built on it very satisfactory; there is in it what every religion pretendeth to, though in a higher way. Though miracles are now ceased, yet it is

confirmed by the truth of the word ; God continually confirmeth it by the seal of the Spirit, and there is an inward certioration, whereby believers are satisfied : John xviii. 37, ' For this cause came I into the world, that I should bear witness unto the truth : every one that is of the truth, heareth my voice ;' that is, enlightened by the Holy Ghost, receiveth and believeth it ; but those that have a mind to wrangle, God will not satisfy. And then for his miracles, they were not miracles of pomp and ostentation, not destructive miracles, but actions of relief. When the pharisees said, ' He casteth out devils by Beelzebub, the prince of devils,' Mat. xii. 24, he proveth that his main aim was to cast out Satan : ver. 26, ' If Satan cast out Satan, he is divided against himself.' Would Satan consent that his kingdom should fall ? He would not go to dispossess himself. All his aim was to promote holiness and the kingdom of God.

I note this :—

[1.] That you may know that the apostles had sufficient means to convince the world of the certainty of the christian doctrine. The inward testimony of the Spirit, the apostles would not allege it ; by miracles and rational probabilities they were fitted to deal with the world, and to appear as witnesses for him, when they were to give an account : Acts v. 32, ' And we are witnesses of these things, and so is the Holy Ghost, whom God hath given to them that obey him.' This inward witness is proper to believers ; the other may be alleged to infidels. By the Spirit is meant there a power to work miracles.

[2.] That you may know the way of God's working with men, usually all these three concur to the working of faith—there is the light of the Spirit, external confirmation, and the use of fit instruments.

(1.) The light of the Spirit, without which there can be no grace nor faith : 1 John v. 6, ' It is the Spirit that beareth witness, because the Spirit is true ;' that is, that word which the Spirit himself hath revealed is truth, for he is not only the author and inditer of the word, but the witness ; he worketh in the hearts of the faithful, so that he persuadeth them of the truth of the word.

(2.) There is external confirmation. Though miracles cease, yet we have the testimony and consent of the church, who by undoubted and authentic rolls hath communicated her experience to us, which is visibly confirmed by the providence of God, not suffering the truth to be oppressed.

(3.) There is the use of fit instruments, specially gifted for this purpose. Though the effect of the word doth mainly depend on the Spirit, yet there is a ministerial efficacy in the messengers : Acts xiv. 1, ' They so spake, that a multitude both of the Jews and also of the Greeks believed.' Not that the faith of the hearers doth merely depend upon the excellency of the preacher ; yet certain it is that one way of preaching may be more fit to convert than another, both in regard of matter and form. Pure doctrine, for the matter, is more apt to convert than that which is mixed with falsehood : as pure water cleanseth better than foul, and good food nourisheth better than that which is in part tainted. He that can divide the word aright, and prudently apply it, is more powerful to work than he that seeth by an half light, or presseth truth loosely, and not with judgment and solidity.   Not as if they could infallibly convert, but they are more likely; they do not carry the grace of conversion in their mouths. Then for the form, with more plainness, clearness, strength of argument.   God hath given to some gifts above others, not to bind himself to them, but in the way of instruments they are more powerful, though the weakest gifts are not to be despised.   And in the quality of the persons, holy persons are more polished shafts in God's quiver.

[3.] I observe it to press you to regard all these things—

(1.) The power of the Spirit, if you would profit in Christ's school. The watering-pot will do nothing without the sun, nor the word without his testimony : 1 Cor. iii. 7, 'So then, neither is he that planteth anything, neither he that watereth, but God that giveth the increase.' The Spirit is to confirm truth to you by way of witness and argument.   By way of witness : 1 John v. 7.   'For there are three that bear record in heaven, the Father, the Word, and the Holy Ghost.'   There is a secret persuasion, especially when you are reading and hearing, that insinuateth itself with your thoughts; doubtless this is the word of God : Acts xvi. 14, 'Whose heart the Lord opened, that she attended to those things that were spoken by Paul.'   By way of argument; working such things, from whence you may conclude it is God's word : John viii. 32, 'Ye shall know the truth, and the truth shall make you free.'   When ye are freed from the bondage of sin, then ye are enlightened to see the truth of the gospel; by experience ye shall know the truth.

(2.) Take in the advantage of external confirmation.   By miracles Christ's testimony was made valuable to the apostles.   You have not only authentic records, wherein these miracles are recorded, which as a history may be believed, but the testimony of the church, which hath experience of the truth and power of the gospel for many ages; the lives of the godly, who are called God's witnesses, 1 Cor. xiv. 26; the providences of God in delivering his church, in their miraculous preservations : Ps. lviii. 11, 'Verily there is a God that judgeth in the earth.'   Answers of prayer grounded on the word. Upon all these grounds practise upon this truth, that Christ came out from God.

(3.) Choose out to yourselves faithful teachers, such as Christ was, delivering the word with authority and faithfulness to God and men ; such as do not seek their own things, fear no man's face, and come with the powerful evidence and demonstration of the Spirit.   And indeed ministers should be careful to manifest themselves to the consciences of those with whom they deal, that they may have 'a testimony of Christ speaking in them,' 1 Cor. xv. 3, that he teacheth in and by them ; they should be assured of their doctrine, that Christ brought it out of his Father's heart, not speaking by rote like parrots: 1 John i. 1, 'That which was from the beginning, which we have heard, which we have seen with our eyes, which we have looked upon, and our hands have handled of the word of life ;' that which our hearts have felt, that which we have not by rote, not by guess, but by experience : 1 Tim. vi. 13, 'Jesus Christ, witnessed before Pontius Pilate a good confession.'

3. Observe Christ's gentleness in bearing with their failings : 'Now they have known.'   It was a long time ere they could be gained to a

sense of his divine power, therefore he chargeth them with hardness of heart, 'Mark vi. 52, 'They considered not the miracle of the loaves, for their hearts were hardened.' So Mark viii. 17, 'Perceive ye not yet, neither understand? Have ye your hearts yet hardened?' And now, in his intercession to his Father, he mentioneth not their hardness, nor the obstinacy of their prejudices, nor their present weakness, but their knowledge: 'Now they know;' they have been obstinate, but he covereth that, at least doth but imply it. How willing is Christ to spread a garment on our nakedness! Past sins shall not hurt us when they do not please us. When a man turneth from grace to sin, then all his righteousness is forgotten: Ezek. xviii. 24, 'All his righteousness that he hath done shall not be mentioned.' So he that turneth from sin to grace, or from grace to grace: ver. 22, 'All his trangressions that he hath committed they shall not be mentioned unto him;' it is all undone by repentance and reformation. How do men differ from Christ! We upbraid men with past failings, when they are repented of. It is hard to put off the reproach of youth; when God maketh them vessels of mercy, they will not suffer them to be vessels of honour; *Hi homines invident mihi gratiam divinam.* As the elder brother upbraideth the reformed prodigal: Luke xv. 30, 'As soon as this thy son was come, which hath devoured thy living with harlots, thou hast killed for him the fatted calf.' This is an envious disposition, and cross to God; you go about to take off the robes of honour which God hath put upon them, and to despoil them as the spouse was of her ornaments.

4. Observe what is the chief object of faith; to believe the divine authority and commission of Christ, and that his power to dispense salvation to the creatures was given him from his Father. There is a world of comfort in this. The Father, being first in order of the persons, is to be looked upon as the offended party, and as the highest judge.

[1.] He is to be looked upon as the offended party. All sin is against God: Ps. li. 4, 'Against thee, thee only, have I sinned, and done this evil in thy sight.' He had offended Uriah, abused Bathsheba; the injury was against them, but the sin against God: 'against thee, thee only.' This may be referred to all the persons, but it chiefly concerneth the first person, to whom we direct our prayers, and who is the maker of the law. Christ, the second person, satisfied for the breach of it: 'It is against thee, thee only.' Now this is our comfort, that our guilt and sin was not cast on Christ's person without the Father, without his privity and consent; nay, it is his own plot and design; it was the Father's counsel, rather than the creature's desire. So that we may quiet our consciences by that promise, Isa. xliii. 25, 'I, even I, am he that blotteth out thy transgressions for my own name's sake.' God the Father would have you look to him as one that hath only to do in this matter. Sin is a grief to the Spirit, it is a crucifying of Christ; but in the last result of it, it is an offence to God the Father, because it is a breach of his law. God is the fountain of the divinity; yea, all that is done to the other persons redoundeth to the Father, as our Saviour reasoneth: 'He that despiseth me despiseth him that sent me.'

[2.] The Father is the highest judge. All the persons of the Godhead are co-essential, and co-equal in glory and honour; only in economy or dispensation of salvation, the Father is to be looked upon as judge and chief. Man is the debtor, Christ the surety, and the Father the judge before whose tribunal the satisfaction is to be made; therefore Christ saith, 'My Father is greater than I.' And in the whole work of our redemption he is to be considered as a superior; therefore all the addresses, not only of the creatures, but of the Son of God himself, are to his Father for pardon, as if it were not in his own single power: Luke xxiii. 34, 'Father, forgive them; they know not what they do.' If it passeth with God the Father, then the business is ended. So 1 John ii. 1, Christ is said to be 'an advocate with the Father,' as supreme in court, as the advocate is beneath the judge. So John xiv. 16, 'I will pray the Father, and he shall give you the Comforter:' pardon, comfort, and grace cometh from the Father. It is true, it is said, Mat. ix. 6, 'that the Son of man hath power on earth to forgive sins;' but it is by commission from the Father, as we shall see anon. Well, then, the Father is the supreme judge: whatever passeth in his name is valid and authoritative. Now it is he that committed the work of redemption to Christ; he is the supreme judge. Eli saith, 1 Sam. ii. 25, 'If one man sinneth against another, the judge shall judge him; but if a man sin against the Lord, who shall entreat for him?' The meaning is, if one man hath trespassed against another, the magistrate may take up the controversy, by executing justice, and causing the delinquent to make satisfaction to the party offended; but who shall state the offence, and compose the difference between God and us? The sin is committed against the judge himself, the highest judge, from whom there is no appeal; no satisfaction can be made by mortal men, and no person is fit to arbitrate the difference. Therefore God himself is pleased to find out a remedy; and in all that the Son did, he hath a great hand and stroke in it. The Father's act is authoritative and above contradiction. If he had not given us a mediator out of his own bosom, we had for ever lain under the guilt and burden of our sins. This had its rise from the grace and mercy of the Father.

But let us see what the Father doth in the business of our redemption, that we may with comfort look upon Christ as a constituted authorised mediator by the decree and counsel of heaven.

(1.) As the supreme author, it was the Father's contrivance and motion to Christ to regard the case of sinners: I look, and there is no intercessor; I see there is none fit to go between fallen man and me. Son, you shall take their case in hand. And therefore he is said to give Christ: John iii. 16, 'God so loved the world that he gave his only-begotten Son.' In the purpose of his thoughts to send Christ: Gal. iv. 4, 'When the fulness of the time was come, God sent forth his Son, made of a woman.' I shall open it in the next verse. To sanctify him: John x. 36, 'Say ye of him whom the Father hath sanctified and sent into the world?' &c. To consecrate him for the great work of redemption; as when a thing is set apart for divine uses and purposes, it is said to be sanctified; so was Christ sanctified when he was set apart for the work of redemption. Nay, to seal him:

John vi. 37, 'Him hath God the Father sealed;' a metaphor taken from those who give commissions under hand and seal. Christ is a mediator confirmed and allowed under the broad seal of heaven. So Heb. x. 5, 'A body hast thou prepared for me;' and ver. 7, 'Lo, I come; in the volume of the book it is written of me, to·do thy will, O God;' as if God had set down in a book a draft and model of his designs, and then showed it to Christ.

(2.) As the supreme cause, in whom divine power was eternally resident, he assisteth Christ in the accomplishment of this work, and qualifieth him for his office, with power and mercy. Christ in his own person would show us the fountain from whence all mercies do arise: Ps. xlv. 7, 'He was anointed with the oil of gladness above his fellows.' The Father is not only said to beget him, but to anoint him. His compassionate spirit he received from the Holy Ghost: Luke iv. 18, 'The Spirit of the Lord is upon me, because the Lord hath anointed me to preach the gospel,' &c. God gave him tenderness and bowels to poor broken-hearted sinners. So for power and strength: John v. 19, 'The Son of man can do nothing of himself,' as separate and distinct from the Father; not out of any weakness, but because of the unity of the essence, as God, and on the federal agreement, as mediator.

(3.) As supreme judge, he appointeth his sufferings, and the measure of the satisfaction he was to make: Acts iv. 28, 'To do whatsoever thy hand and thy counsel determined before to be done.' Whatever men did to him, it was by his hand and counsel. We must look to a higher court, from God's providence to God's decree. If it had been done without his knowledge and consent, nothing would have been done for our salvation: 'Him being delivered, ἔκδοτος, by the determinate counsel of God, ye have taken,' Acts ii. 23; a word taken from alms to beggars. We wanted a price for our redemption, and God gave it out of his own treasury: Rom. iv. 25, 'He was delivered for our offences;' a metaphor taken from a judge who delivereth up the malefactor into the hands of the executioner. Christ was delivered by God as our surety, one that by his decree was to be responsible to his justice for man's sin. The Father was to reward him for this by raising him from the dead, and to give him leave to return to his own glory; therefore he asketh leave to return to heaven, ver. 5, 'And now, O Father, glorify thou me with thine own self, with the glory which I had with thee before the world was.' After the price and ransom was paid, the Father was to give Christ a power to rise from the dead, and to go into heaven. There is *potestas* and *potentia*, δύναμις, ἐξουσία. Christ had power in himself, and leave from the Father; till the Father should declare himself to be satisfied, Christ was not to be dismissed from punishment. Our surety was not to break prison, but honourably to be brought out by the judge, for this was the assurance God would give the world: Acts xvii. 31, 'He will judge the world in righteousness, by the man whom he hath ordained; whereof he hath given assurance unto all men, in that he hath raised him from the dead.' It is not only an effect of the divine power, but an act of divine justice. And being raised up, he is to be crowned with glory and honour, as having abundantly done his work for the salvation of creatures: Heb. ii. 9, 'We see Jesus, for the suffering of death, crowned with glory and honour.' The Father's heart was so taken with it, that he honoureth Christ for this reason. And again, he giveth power and authority to save sinners: Acts v. 31, 'Him hath God exalted to be a prince and a saviour, to give repentance to Israel, and forgiveness of sins.' He hath raised him up to be a prince of salvation. Here is the end of all, that Christ as mediator might be in a capacity to bring souls to heaven. And in this work there is a constant co-operation of the divine power; 1 Cor. i. 30, 'Of God he is made to us wisdom, and righteousness, and sanctification, and redemption.' All the emanations of grace come originally from the Father, in and through Christ, to all his members.

Use 1. Comfort. What would have become of us, if the Father himself had not found out such a remedy? God had power to punish sins in our own person, he needed no mediator. To save sinners is not *proprietas divinæ naturæ*, but *opus liberi consilii*; it dependeth on God's appointment; and if Christ had been a mediator only by the vote of the creature, he might have been refused: Exod. xxxii. 33, 'Whosoever hath sinned against me, him will I blot out of my book.' There is much in the Father's act. Now God hath given Christ a faculty to this purpose; when we go to God, we may offer a mediator authorised by himself: Thou hast sent thy blessed Son to be a mediator for me: 2 John 9, 'He that abideth in the doctrine of Christ, he hath the Father and the Son.' You may urge it upon your fears and suggestions of Satan. God is not only the wronged party, but supreme judge; it is no matter what Satan saith, or your own hearts say, if the Lord hath said he will accept sinners in Christ: Rom. viii. 33, 34, 'Who shall lay anything to the charge of God's elect? It is God that justifieth; who is he that condemneth? It is Christ that died.' Who can condemn? Satan may say, I can; and conscience, I can. God, whose act is sovereign, doth acquit. God hath so great an interest in Christ, that he can deny him nothing: John xiv. 31, 'That the world may know that I love the Father.' He will be the sinner's surety for his Father's sake.

Use 2. Glorify God the Father; it is the end of the whole dispensation of grace. Glorify him in your expectations; the Father himself loveth you. Glorify him in your enjoyments, all is 'from the Father of lights,' James i. 17. There is no defect in Christ: John xvii. 23, 'I in them, and thou in me, that they may be made perfect in one, and that the world may know that thou hast sent me, and that thou hast loved them, as thou hast loved me.' God hath loved him, not only as his own Son, but our saviour: John x. 17, 'Therefore doth my Father love me, because I lay down my life, that I might take it again.'

SERMON XI.

For I have given unto them the words which thou gavest me; and they have received them, and have known surely that I came out from thee, and they have believed that thou didst send me.—JOHN XVII. 8.

CHRIST in this verse further explaineth the argument that was urged before, which was taken from their proficiency in his school, and that they had a right sense of and faith in the dignity and quality of his person. This faith is set forth by all the requisites of it.

First, The means by which it is wrought; that is, the word, the doctrine given to him by his Father, and by him to his apostles: *for I have given unto them the words which thou gavest me.*

Secondly, The nature of faith, which consisteth in knowledge and acceptation: *they have known surely, and they have believed them.* Λῆ-ψις and γνῶσις are the two acts of faith.

Thirdly, The object of faith, the mission of Christ, and his coming out from the Father : *that I came out from thee, and they have believed that thou hast sent me.*

First, I begin with the means of faith: 'For I have given unto them the words which thou gavest me.' The only difficulty is how the word was given unto Christ. Some think it is meant of the divine and infinite knowledge and wisdom which was communicated to Christ by eternal generation; but that is very improper, *quæcunque Christo dantur, secundum humanitatem dantur.* It is meant of that giving which Christ had as mediator, as the ambassador hath his instructions according to which he is to act. Now saith Christ, I have taught them according to the instructions which I received as mediator. These are said to be given, to be infused and revealed to his human soul.

1. Observe, the word is the proper means to work faith. We see here the apostles had no other means of salvation than Christ's word; when Christ giveth an account of their faith, he doth not mention his miracles, but his doctrine. Again, he doth not speak only of the internal manifestation of the Spirit, ' I have manifested thy name ;' but also of the outward revelation, ' I have given to them the words which thou gavest me.' We have a general saying, Rom. x. 17, ' Faith cometh by hearing, and hearing by the word of God.' This is the usual method and way of grace's working ; God will insinuate the efficacy of his Spirit by outward counsel and instruction, and by the ear transmit his grace to the heart, that he might work *fortiter, suaviter.*

Use 1. It reproveth the folly of two sorts of men ; there are some that think the word cannot work unless it be accompanied with miracles, and others that think the Spirit will work without the word.

1. Those that think the word will not work without miracles, and therefore expect a reviving of miracles, to authorise that ministry which they mean to receive. Vain thoughts ! In the primitive times, when miracles were in force, we read of some converted by the word without miracles, but of none converted by miracles without the word: Acts xi. 20, 21, 'Some of Cyprus and Cyrene, when they were come to Antioch, spake unto the Grecians, preaching the Lord Jesus. And the hand of the Lord was with them ; and a great number believed, and turned to the Lord.' They wrought no signs, only preached the Lord Jesus. There is not one instance in the whole word of any one converted by a single miracle. It is natural to us to idolise visible helps and confirmations. Those mentioned Acts xi. were not apostles, but private brethren, who in that extraordinary time used their gifts, and were successful.

2. Those that expect the illapses of the Spirit, without waiting upon the word. It is true God can work immediately, but the question is about

his will. God is not tied to means, but we are bound and tied. God may use his liberty, but this doth not dissolve our duty and obligation; we are to lie at the pool, if we expect the stirring of the waters. There is a great deal of difference between the want of means and the contempt of them. I should always suspect that grace that is wrought in us in the neglect of the means. The regular way of faith is by the word; it hath pleased God to consecrate it. God could have converted the eunuch without Philip, but we are to submit to his will. Paul that received his consternation miraculously, had his confirmation from Ananias; Christ had preached him into terror from heaven, but he sendeth him to Ananias for comfort.

Use 2. It stirreth us up to attend upon the word; it is God's instrument: Rom. i. 16, 'I am not ashamed of the gospel of Christ; for it is the power of God to salvation, to every one that believeth;' the meaning is, it is a powerful instrument to work faith; as the first sermon that ever was preached, after the pouring out of the Spirit, converted three thousand souls. An angel could slay a hundred and eighty-five thousand men in a night by his own natural strength; but it is easier to kill so many men than to convert one soul. All the angels in heaven, if they should join all their forces together, they could not convert one soul to God; but yet this power will God discover in the ministry and co-operation of weak men. Those that do not delight to hear the word have no mind to see the miracles of grace. The power is of God, yet it is wonderfully joined with the word; it is not enclosed in it, but sent out together with it when God pleaseth. It is God's ordinance, and under the blessing of an institution.

2. Observe, again, the certainty of christian doctrine. The word delivered to the apostles was received from the Father by Christ. It was no invention of his own, but brought out of the bosom of the Father: John vii. 16, 'My doctrine is not mine, but his that sent me.' So John xiv. 10, 'The words that I speak, I speak not of myself;' that is, not as mediator. It was prophesied of Christ, who was the great prophet of the church: Deut. xviii. 18, 'I will raise them up a prophet from among their brethren, like unto thee, and will put my words in his mouth, and he shall speak unto them all that I shall command him.' Christ said, 'his Father gave it him.' Christ was consecrated prophet of the church by the Trinity: Mat. iii. 17, 'This is my beloved Son, in whom I am well pleased.' There was the Father's voice, the Holy Ghost as a dove, and the Son was there in person.

Use. Which should stablish us the more in the truth, and is a pattern to ministers. It is excellent when we can say, 'My doctrine is not mine, but his that sent me;' or, as Paul, 'That which I received of the Lord I have delivered to you,' 1 Cor. xi. 23.

3. Observe, among the things which the Father gave to the Son, one of the chiefest is the doctrine of the gospel. Let us look upon it as a gift; the Father gave it, the Son gave it. Here is a double gift; it was a gift from the Father to Christ, and from Christ to the apostles: 'I have given them the word which thou gavest me.' Next to Christ the gospel is the greatest benefit which God hath given to men. He that despiseth the gospel, despiseth the very bounty of God, and men cannot endure to have their love and bounty despised. As when David

sent a courteous message to Nabal, and he was refused, he threatened to 'cut off from Nabal every one that pisseth against the wall.' Take heed you despise not God's special gifts. The preaching of the word, it was Christ's largest in the day of his royalty: Eph. iv. 8, 11, 'When he ascended up on high, he gave some, apostles; and some, prophets; and some, evangelists; and some, pastors and teachers;' as princes, when crowned, have their royal donatives. Those that grudge at the ministry, and count it a burden, they do in effect upbraid Christ with his gift, as if it were not worth the giving. Those that labour in the ministry, are his especial gift to us. They are but sottish swine that trample such pearls under feet. We should think of them as the special favours of Christ. I do not speak of the persons, but the calling. This disposition showeth no love to Christ.

Secondly, The next thing is the nature of faith. There are two things spoken of in the text—γνῶσις and λῆψις, 'they have received them, and have known surely.'

First, I begin with the latter, in order of words, as first in order of nature, ἔγνωσαν ἀληθῶς, 'they have known surely.' The word ἀληθῶς, which signifieth truly, surely, is used to exclude that literal historical knowledge which may be in carnal men.

1. Observe, faith cannot be without knowledge. It is not a blind assent: Rom. x. 14, 'How shall they believe in him of whom they have not heard?' We must know what Christ is before we can trust him with our souls: 1 Tim. i. 12, 'I know whom I have believed.' We must see the stay and prop before we lean upon it, otherwise we shall neither be satisfied in ourselves, nor be able to plead with Satan, nor answer doubts of conscience. He that is impleaded in court, and doth not know the privileges of the law, how shall he be able to purge himself? Fears are in the dark. The blind man spoke reason in that conference between Christ and him, when Christ asked him, 'Dost thou believe on the Son of God? He answered and said, Who is he, Lord, that I might believe on him?' John ix. 35, 36. We must know what God is. Till we have a distinct knowledge of the nature of God, and the tenor of the covenant, we shall be full of scruples. Well then—

Use 1. It discovereth the wretched condition of ignorant persons. We are not so sensible of the danger of ignorance as we should be. God will render vengeance 'to them that know not God, and that obey not the gospel,' 2 Thes. i. 8. Poor wretches! they live sinfully and die sottishly; they live sinfully, they are under no awe of conscience, because they have no knowledge; and when they come to die, they die sottishly; like men that leap over a deep gulf blindfold, they know not where their feet shall light. In their lifetime, at best they live but by guess and some devout aims; and when they come to die, they die by guess, in a doubtful, uncertain way.

Use 2. To press christians to gain more distinct knowledge, if you would settle your souls in a certainty of salvation. God may lay trouble of conscience upon a knowing person; but usually persons ignorant are full of scruples, which vanish before the light as mists do before the sun.

2. Observe, they know surely. In the knowledge of faith there is an undoubted certain light. It dependeth upon two things that cannot

deceive us—the revelation of the word, and the illumination of the Spirit. The knowledge of faith is less than the light of glory for clearness, but equal for certainty; it hath as much assurance from God's word, though not so much evidence as ariseth from enjoyment.

3. Observe, they know ἀληθῶς, truly, indeed. Every kind of knowledge is not enough for faith, but a true, sound knowledge. There is a form of knowledge as well as a form of godliness; Rom. ii. 20, compared with 2 Tim. iii. 5. A form of knowledge is nothing else but an artificial speculation, a naked model of truth in the brain, which, like a winter sun, shineth, but warmeth not.

But let us a little state the differences.

[1.] The light of faith is serious and considerate. Faith is a spiritual prudence, it is opposed to folly as well as ignorance: Luke xxiv. 25, 'O fools, and slow of heart to believe all that the prophets have said!' Faith always draweth to use and practice. It is a knowledge with consideration: Eph. i. 17, 'That the God of our Lord Jesus Christ, the Father of glory, would give unto you the spirit of wisdom and revelation in the knowledge of him.' Many have parts, but they have not wisdom to make the best choice for their souls. There is a great deal of difference between knowledge and prudence; it is excellent when both are joined together: 'I, wisdom, dwell with prudence,' Prov. viii. 12. Wisdom is the knowledge of principles, prudence is an ability to use them to our comfort. Knowledge is settled in the brain, not the heart. When wisdom 'entereth into thy heart,' Prov. ii. 10, it stirreth up esteem, affiance, love. A carnal man may have a model of truth, a traditional disciplinary knowledge, such as lieth in generals, not particulars, and is rather for discourse than life. A vintner's cellar may be better stored than a nobleman's; he hath wines, not to taste, but sell; a carnal man hath a great deal of knowledge for discourse, not to warm his own heart.

[2.] The light of faith is a realising light, ἔλεγχος οὐ βλεπομένων, 'Faith is in the evidence of things not seen,' Heb. xi. 1; it maketh absent things present to the soul. But the light of parts is a naked, abstract speculation, it is without feeling, there is no sense and feeling of the things apprehended. True knowledge is expressed by tasting; 1 Peter ii. 5, 'If so be that ye have tasted that the Lord is gracious.' Tasting implieth more than seeing; there is not only apprehension, but experience: Phil. i. 9, 'I pray God that your love may abound more and more in knowledge and in all judgment, ἐν πάσῃ αἰσθήσει, in all sense. To others it is but an empty barren, notion: Phil. iii. 10, 'That I may know him, and the power of his resurrection,' that is, experimentally. Carnal men have no feeling of the force of the truths they apprehend, only now and then some fleeting joys; it is not realising and affective. Strong water and running water differ not in colour, but in taste and virtue. They may know the same truths, but it differeth in relish; they know the things of God only as things in conceit, not in being.

[3.] The light of faith is wrought by the Spirit, this but a hearsay, knowledge gathered out of books and sermons; they shine with a borrowed light, as the moon that is dark in itself, and hath no light rooted in its own body. These shine with other men's light: John

iv. 42, 'Now we believe, not for thy saying, but we have heard him ourselves, and know that this is indeed the Christ, the Saviour of the world.' Men talk of things by rote after others, and are rather said to rehearse than understand; it is not written in their hearts, but only reported to their ears: Heb. viii. 10, 'I will write my law in their hearts.' Truth is written there by the finger of the Spirit, to others it is but traditional, learned as other arts by man. Now there is a great deal of difference between seeing God in the light of the Spirit, and seeing God and the things of God by the reports of men, as between seeing countries in a map, or book of geography, and knowing them by travel and experience.

[4.] It is a transforming light: 2 Cor. iii. 18, 'We all as in a glass beholding the glory of the Lord, are changed into the same image, from glory to glory, even as by the Spirit of the Lord.' Looking upon the image of Christ, we are changed into the same image and likeness, from glory to glory; as Moses his face shone. Conversing with Christ, it altereth and changeth the soul, which is hereby 'renewed in knowledge after the image of him that created him,' Col. iii. 10. That is no true light and knowledge of God that doth not bridle lusts and purify the heart; a wicked man's knowledge, it is light without fire, directive, not persuasive: 1 John ii. 3, 4, 'Hereby we know that we know him, if we keep his commandments. He that saith, I know him, and keepeth not his commandments, is a liar, and the truth is not in him;' it is a lie and pretence; unactive light is but darkness. In paradise there was a tree of life and a tree of knowledge; many taste of the tree of knowledge that never taste of the tree of life.

[5.] The light of faith is an undoubted certain light, but in wicked men it is always mingled with doubting, ignorance, error, and unbelief. It is not convictive, but a loose, wavering opinion, not a settled, grounded persuasion; they have not 'the riches of the assurance of understanding,' Col. ii. 2; that dependeth on experience, and inward sense of the truth, and is wrought by the Holy Ghost. And therefore the apostle speaketh of the evidence and demonstration of the Spirit: 1 Cor. ii. 4, ἐν ἀποδείξει τοῦ πνεύματος καὶ δυνάμεως, 'in the demonstration of the Spirit, and of power.' Ἀποδείξις is a clear, convincing argument, by which the judgment is settled; it cometh in upon the soul with evident confirmation.

Secondly, The next thing in the nature of faith is λῆψις: 'I have given them the words which thou gavest me, and they have received them.' There is a receiving Christ and a receiving the word. Sometimes the act of faith is terminated on the person of Christ; as John i. 12, 'To as many as received him, to them gave he power to become the sons of God, even to as many as believe on his name.' Sometimes on the promises; to show that as there is no closing with Christ without the promise, so there is no closing with the promise without Christ; first we receive the word of Christ, and then Christ himself, and in Christ life and salvation; that is the progress of faith: Acts x. 42, 'Through his name, whosoever believeth in him shall receive remission of sins.'

Observe that faith is a receiving the word of Christ. The notion is elsewhere used: Acts ii. 41, 'Then they that gladly received the word were baptized.' Unbelief, it is a rejecting the counsel of the word, and faith a receiving it. Unbelief is thus described: Acts xiii. 46, 'Since ye put away the word of God from you.' So Luke vii. 30, 'But the pharisees and lawyers rejected the counsel of God against themselves;' that is, refused the counsel of God, to their own loss and ruin. On the contrary, when Cornelius was converted, it is said, Acts xi. 1, 'The apostles heard that the Gentiles also had received the word of God.' So that we may describe faith with reference to this act, a motion in the heart of man, stirred up by the Spirit of God, to receive the whole word of God.

Let me open it a little.

1. Receiving is a relative word, and supposeth an offer. God offereth on his part, and we receive on ours. As in all contracts and covenants between party and party, one party offereth such an advantage or commodity upon such conditions, the other receiveth the offer, consenteth to the conditions, and expecteth that the covenant should be made good; so in the covenant of grace, Christ offereth remission of sins, and the whole blessings of the gospel, under the condition of faith and repentance. We are said to receive this word, or this gospel, when we consent to the conditions, and wait for the accomplishment of the blessing; we are willing to come to trust him for the grace of the covenant, and to come under the bond of the duty of it.

2. In this receiving, the soul must be convinced that it is the word of God, and that he will deal with creatures upon such a covenant. For in this covenant it is not as it is in other contracts; the party contracting doth not appear in person, but dealeth with us by officers and substitutes. God tendereth his covenant by the ministry of man. Now, whosoever would receive it in God's name, must be undoubtedly persuaded that they are commissioned and authorised by God to tender such a covenant to us. Therefore the apostle saith, 1 Thes. ii. 13, 'When ye received the word which ye have heard of us, ye received it not as the word of man, but (as it is indeed) the word of God, which effectually worketh also in you that believe.' A man that would profit by the ministry must settle himself in this persuasion, that the doctrines delivered in scripture have God for their author. We come in God's stead, to strike up a bargain with you for your souls; this bindeth the ear to attention, the mind to faith, the heart to reverence, the will and conscience to obedience. We are to entertain all the doctrines of the word, without any suspense of judgment and contradiction. We are to put to our seal to Christ's testimony: John iii. 33, 'He that hath received his testimony, hath set to his seal that God is true.' Usually there is some privy atheism in us; we look upon the gospel as a golden dream, and well-devised fable. This is properly assent, and should be soundly laid. Lord, thou wilt not fail thy poor creatures, if they venture their souls on thy word.

3. The whole word must be received. In every covenant there is a precept as well as a promise. We mar the very form of it when we reflect on the promise, and neglect the precept. It is great error in them that think that receiving of the word is done when we apply the promises, as if nothing were needful to salvation but to say, I trust that my sins are forgiven me in Christ. The gospel hath not only

promises, but commands, conditions, and articles of the covenant, which are no less to be received than the promises. First, receive the commandment concerning repentance and conversion, with a resolution to cast thyself on Christ; and then be of good confidence, thy sins shall be forgiven thee. There is in faith not only an assent, but consent; assent to the truth of God, consent to the articles of the covenant; assent to the truth of the contract, consent to the terms, and affiance or confident waiting for the promise; all these are in faith. Hypocrites are said ' to receive the word with joy,' Luke viii. 13 ; but they received only the word of promise with joy. It is pleasing to the conscience to hear of pardon of sins. Men may have vanishing fleeting joys. A carnal man would have God's grace, but he would have none of his counsel.

4. This must be received with all the heart. The work of faith is not confined to the acts of the understanding ; there are some motions of the heart. Philip puts the eunuch to this trial, Acts viii. 37, ' Believest thou with all thy heart? and he said, I believe that Jesus Christ is the Son of God.' God is as careful of the duty of the gospel as of the duty of the law ; he that required that we should love him with all our hearts hath also required that we should believe in him with all our hearts ; he required the whole heart in love, and he expecteth the whole heart in faith.

Now, because this is the critical difference between true faith and counterfeit, I shall apply this receiving to both the objects of faith, the word and the person of Christ, because the doctrine concerning both is of near affinity, and the one is opened by the other. In receiving the person of Christ, there is the same method of the acts of faith as there is in receiving the word of God. (1.) There is an offer. Faith receiving, presupposeth an offering ; we do not snatch at Christ, but receive him. Sinners snatch at Christ sometimes, when God's hand is not open to give him. (2.) We must look at this offering as made by God himself. Faith taketh Christ out of his Father's hands. (3.) We must take whole Christ, as Lord and Saviour ; and (4.) We must take him with our whole hearts.

Therefore I shall explain this receiving with the whole heart in reference to both objects, the word and Christ.

First, What is it to receive the word with our whole hearts ? There is nothing so difficult as to draw the acts of faith into a method.

1. It implieth an act of the will ; there must not only be knowledge and acknowledgment that the doctrine is true, but an actual choice and a willing acceptation. Faith apprehendeth the covenant made in Christ, not only as true, but good ; and so answerably there is not only a believing with the mind, but a believing with the heart : Rom. x. 10, ' With the heart man believeth.' The faculty answereth the object : 1 Tim. i. 15, ' This is a faithful saying,' πιστὸς ὁ λόγος, and then, πάσης ἀποδοχῆς ἄξιος, ' worthy of all acceptation,' &c. So that there is required some motion of the heart, besides intellectual assent.

2. This act of the will is accompanied with some sensible affection : Heb. xi. 13, ἀσπασάμενοι τὰς ἐπαγγελίας, ' they embraced the promises ;' they hugged and clasped about, and embraced the promises. All acts of faith do necessarily imply answerable affections. The

children of God embrace the promises with delight, receive the threatenings with trembling and reverence, and the commandments with all cheerfulness: Acts ii. 41, 'Then they that received the word gladly,' ἀσμένως, not as a people that are overcome receive laws from the conqueror, or as Zipporah circumcised her child, with grudging and discontent, but with hearty and cheerful consent. I confess there is, and ever will be, an opposition of the flesh: a man doth not receive the whole word as a thirsty man receiveth sweet drink, but as a sick man, or one that is thirsty after health receiveth physic, or a bitter potion, with an earnest serious desire, though his appetite loatheth it. There is a hearty consent to God's terms, because they know it will be for their welfare; as Laban, when he heard Jacob's proposals, 'What shall I give thee? the speckled and spotted among the flocks.' Gen. xxx. 34. Laban said, 'Behold, I would it might be according to thy word.' Oh! would to God that this were my share, that God would take up the quarrel between himself and me!

3. This affection is accompanied with a pursuit, or serious making after those hopes. There is a care and anxiousness of obedience, or taking the next course to speed, that we may find him, and feel him in our consciences: 'They received the word gladly, and were baptized,' Acts ii. 41. In every contract where the parties are agreed there is a signing and sealing; so 'they received the word,' and 'were baptized;' that was the next course to come under these hopes. A contract lieth void and dead if there be consent yet no performance. So 'faith without works is dead.' Faith is a consent to God's covenant, yet because there is no answerable obedience, this consent is void, and to no effect. Now this is the utmost extension of the will, in motions and addresses towards Christ. Faith is expressed by coming to Christ, *qui se dat in viam.* A man putteth himself into the way of salvation, upon a search and inquiry after Christ. We know not what will come of it, but we will continue seeking: 'I will go to my father.'

4. These endeavours are supported by affiance, or a resolution to wait upon God till the blessings of the covenant be accomplished and made good. Though they meet with difficulties, they keep wrestling with God: Gen. xxxii. 26, 'I will not let thee go unless thou bless me.' There is an obstinate purpose: Job xiii. 15, 'Though he slay me, yet will I trust in him.' So they will have Christ, whatever it cost them: Phil. iii. 8, 9, 'I count all things but loss for the excellency of the knowledge of Christ Jesus my Lord, for whom I have suffered the loss of all things, and do count them but dung, that I may win Christ, and be found in him, not having mine own righteousness, which is after the law, but that which is through the faith of Christ, the righteousness which is of God by faith.' Faith may be shaken, but it will not lose its hold; as a tree groweth though it be bended with the wind. Thus you see what it is to receive the word with our whole heart: not only to acknowledge the truth of it, but to choose and accept it as our direction, with all cheerfulness, and accordingly make out after the hopes of christianity, resolving not to be discouraged, whatever entertainment we meet with from God and the world.

Secondly, There is a receiving Christ with the whole heart. Art thou willing to take Christ upon these terms? Yes, saith the soul, with all my heart. This answer were enough, if it were simple and genuine. But because we profane and prostitute these words to every slight matter, the deceit is not so easily discovered. We are wont to say of every trifle, I love such a thing with all my heart ; I will do it with all my heart ; whereas these words are of a sacred sound and importance : and did not we adulterate them so often as we do, but keep them consecrate to God, to whom alone they are proper, the very pronouncing of them would awaken conscience ; we could not give such an answer but conscience would give us the lie. Let us then inquire into the thing, and see a little in the nature of the thing (for there is no trust in the expression), what this believing in Christ with all the heart, or receiving Christ with all the heart, doth imply. I answer—

1. It implieth that your whole and sole dependence must be entirely carried out to him. God will have no rivals in the trust and confidence of the creature. A king in his progress, that takes up an inn, will have it wholly to himself, much less will he have any to share with him in his own bedchamber. So here, you must trust Christ alone with your welfare. We believe with our whole heart when we have such a persuasion of his sufficiency that we durst venture all in his hands ; in matter of remission of sin we mind no confidence but in his grace : Heb. x. 22, ‘ Let us draw near with a true heart, in full assurance of faith,’ ἀληθινῇ καρδίᾳ, a heart that doth not secretly run out to other props and confidences. Truth and sincerity in believing is there intended, not in obedience. Faith is a simple single trust in God’s mercy ; the heart is very deceitful. Christ beareth the name, but the confidence is secretly built on our own merits ; as those women in Isaiah, chap. iv. 1, ‘ We will eat our own bread, and wear our own apparel, only let us be called by thy name.’ People will say they trust in Christ alone, and yet secretly rest on their own innocency and good meanings. But most sensibly this perverseness of trust is discovered in matters of providence ; those that put half their trust in Christ, and half in the world, do not believe with their whole hearts. They pretend they can trust Christ for pardon, grace, and glory, and yet cannot trust him for a morsel of bread ; they find no difficulty in believing in Christ for salvation and remission of sins, and yet cannot believe that he will give them daily bread. What should be the reason ? Heaven and pardon of sins are greater mercies, and, if conscience were opened, we should see the difficulty to obtain them to be greater. There are more natural prejudices, but bodily wants are more pressing to a conscience not sufficiently convinced. And here faith is presently to be exercised with difficulties. In matters of grace, men are more slight and inconsiderate, and content themselves with some general cold persuasions, and therefore do not believe with their whole hearts. Alas ! temporal salvation is more easy. Can you look for heaven, who cannot trust him for a crust of bread ? Do you know what it is to venture your souls in Christ’s hands, notwithstanding sins, notwithstanding death, and yet soon despond in time of danger, and when outward means of preservation fail ?

2. To receive Christ with the whole heart is to receive him as an all-sufficient saviour, when every faculty seeketh contentment in Christ.

We ought not only to acknowledge him to be the true mediator, but to choose and receive him for our all-sufficient portion. Worldly men look to Christ as fit for their consciences, but look to the world as an object for their affections. Now Christ should not only pacify the conscience, but satisfy the heart. We should come to him, not only as a physician to heal our wounds, but as a husband to satisfy and content our love, as a meet object for our affections. The whole soul is to clasp about him. He is not only good in a way of profit, but amiable in a way of excellency ; therefore the whole heart is to be given him. The things of the world are good but for one thing ; food is good to satisfy the appetite, yet we must have clothes to warm the back. But Christ is good for all things ; he is not only the physician of the soul, but the beloved : Ps. lxxiii. 25, 'Whom have I in heaven but thee ? and there is none on earth that I desire besides thee ;' since there is none so fit to match and wed their affections.

3. To receive him with the whole heart is to make after him with the earnest motions and lively affections of the soul, as desire and delight. Carnal men have a naked imaginary persuasion, but no lively affections to Christ, unless it be for a very small while. They never felt the bitterness of sin, and so have not such vehement and strong motions of heart towards Christ. Conviction of conscience differeth much from literal assent. Carnal men have a literal assent, and a speculative delight in contemplation, but not such labour and travail of soul to get an interest in Christ. Swimming is for life and death ; it is not a work proper for him that standeth on firm land, but for those that are ready to be swallowed up of the waves. Nor have they such delight ; a stomach always full knoweth not the sweetness of bread. Christ relisheth only with troubled consciences.

SERMON XII.

*I pray for them : I pray not for the world, but for them which thou
hast given me ; for they are thine.*—JOHN XVII. 9.

CHRIST, having urged several arguments on the behalf of the disciples,
cometh now to limit his prayers to them, which is a new argument :
‘ I pray for none but those which thou hast given me ;’ not for obstinate persecutors and perverse rebels, but for thine own, thy charge
put into my hands.   If I had prayed for any which belong not to the
purpose of thy grace, thou mightest deny me ; but ‘ I pray not for the
world, but for thine,’ therefore hear me.

In the words you have :—

1. The object of Christ’s prayer.

2. The object limited, *I pray for them ;* which is amplified negatively by a refusal to pray for others, *I pray not for the world.*

3. The reasons, *thou hast given them me,* and *they are thine ;* mine
by oppignoration, not alienation, thy charge put into mine hands.   I
have a charge over them, and thou hast a right in them.   Christ was
tender of his charge, and the Father still loved and owned them.
Thy right and propriety is not lost by thy donation, but confirmed,
for they are thine.   It is not only a reason of the donation, but an
argument that Christ useth in prayer.

First, The great matter, that needeth not so much to be cleared as
to be vindicated, is Christ’s refusal to pray for the world.   It needeth
not to be cleared, because Christ doth expressly limit the persons, ‘ I
pray for them ;’ he doth not only explain it, whom he meaneth by
them, ‘ those which thou hast given me ;’ which explication, if nothing else had been added, would have been exclusive, and would
have amounted to them, and only them ; but he doth himself exclude
the world from having any share in his prayers.   By the *world,* he
meaneth the reprobate world, not only the unregenerate elect, who are
sometimes called the world, but *reprobos amatores sæculi,* as the Car-
thusian, the reprobate perverse world.

But some object, and it is fit they should be heard :—

1. That the apostles only are here intended, and that there is not a
distinction between the elect and reprobate, but between the apostles
and others ; for afterwards Christ prayeth for others ‘ that shall believe through their word,’ ver. 20.   I answer—

[1.] The apostles are chiefly intended, but not only ; elsewhere doth
he pray for the disciples and believers of that age ; there were more
than the eleven apostles, and if they be excluded, they have no name
in Christ’s prayer.

[2.] All others besides the apostles could not be reckoned to be in
the world ; now here is a perfect distribution of men into two ranks
—those that were given him, and the world.

2. Others say that the words are not to be taken as utterly exclusive, but only that he prayed not for the world in this place ; the requests of fatherly protection, the gift of the Spirit, love and concord,
being only proper to them that did actually believe : elsewhere, they

say, they find Christ praying for the world. They bring that place for one, Luke xxiii. 24, ' Father, forgive them ; for they know not what they do ;' where he prayed for his persecutors, some of which never were converted. I answer—

[1.] We must distinguish the prayers of Christ as a holy man, and the prayers of Christ as mediator. So *Camero. Owen*, p. 44, &c. ; *Gomarus in locum*, and *Rainoldus de Intercessione*, &c. As he was a holy man, he was to lay aside all show of revenge. This was not a prayer by virtue of his office as mediator, but in answer to his duty, as he was subject to the law, and a private person. Those things which he did in obedience to the law as a private person were not acts of mediation ; they were acts of the mediator, but not as mediator. He taught us to pray for enemies : Mat. v. 44, ' Love your enemies, bless them that curse you, do good to them that hate you, and pray for them that despitefully use you, and persecute you.' Revenge is forbidden, and pardon and prayer enjoined.

[2.] Christ did not pray for all his persecutors, and every one of them, but only for those that sinned out of ignorance, as the words imply ; chiefly for the standers-by, rather than the priests and pharisees, many of which came rather out of curiosity than despite. Yea, this supplication was effectual and successful to all the elect intended. This prayer brought in three thousand, Acts ii. 41, who are charged with Christ's death, ver. 23 and 36, and again five thousand, Acts iv. 4, who are charged with ignorance in this matter : Acts iii. 15, ' And killed the prince of life ; ' ver. 17, ' I wot that through ignorance ye did it, as did also your rulers.'

3. Again, they urge, ver. 21, ' That the world may believe that thou hast sent me.' Some say that by the *world* is meant the unregenerate elect. This, though it blunteth the force of the objection, yet I think it not so full an answer.

[1.] Because it is not directly made for them. Mark, it is not a prayer, but a reason of prayer ; Christ would have prayed more directly for the unregenerate elect.

[2.] He would have prayed for a more effectual means of conversion than the beholding the unity and concord of his church : ' That they may be one, as thou, Father, art in me, and I in thee ; that they also may be one in us, that the world may know that thou hast sent me.'

[3.] The word *world*, in this whole chapter, is taken for the reprobate world, or those which are opposed to them which are committed to him by his Father.

[4.] The substance of that prayer is for the elect not yet converted, for Christ prayeth for ' all that shall believe through their word,' ver. 20. And then, ' that they may be all one,' &c., ' that the world may believe that thou hast sent me ; ' so that the unregenerate elect are not intended. Well, but then doth Christ pray for the reprobate world, that they may believe ? I answer—No ; faith or believing is there taken for a more full conviction, that they may be convinced and rendered more inexcusable. It is not taken in a strict sense, for a saving comprehension and receiving of Christ, but for a conviction and acknowledgment. Divisions in the church usually breed atheism in the world ; all is false when so many ways and differences. So think they Christ is an impostor, the word a fable. Now this kind of conviction is not only termed believing in scripture, but explained, ver. 23, 'That the world may know that thou hast sent me.' Nay, let us grant that faith is taken in the highest and strictest sense; yet there is a difference between praying for such a thing as may be a likely means of working faith, and praying that they may believe. Christ only prayeth 'that his people may be one,' that the world may not plead prejudice; at most, he doth but obliquely reflect upon the world in that prayer, that they may have means of conviction, but not grace. Christ denieth that the world either hath, or ever shall have, the grace of faith : ver. 25, 'O righteous Father, the world hath not known thee; but I have known thee, and these have known that thou hast sent me.' And the special reason why the elect have known, though the world have not known, is rendered, ver. 26, 'I have declared unto them thy name, and will declare it;' by which is meant the special manifestation of his grace given to believers of all ages, which was given to the disciples of that present age, and will be given to all future believers. A serious consideration of the context will refute all these sophisms. Thus I have taken off the objections.

Let me handle one doubt more. But if they were absolutely predestinated, why doth Christ pray for them ?

I answer—Predestination includeth all things that are necessary to the salvation of the predestinated; and so the prayers of Christ must be taken in as well as other means.

Take an argument or two why Christ did not, could not, doth not pray for the reprobate world. This prayer must either argue :—

1. A nescience of his Father's decrees, which cannot stand with the unity of his person, especially as now in glory. While upon earth he knew it, and approved it, that God by an immutable decree had left some to be justly hardened to their own ruin : Mat. xi. 25, 26, 'I thank thee, O Father, Lord of heaven and earth, because thou hast hid these things from the wise and prudent, and hast revealed them unto babes. Even so, Father, for so it seemed good in thy sight.' Or—

2. A contradiction to his will and express decree. It is true we do not sin by asking a thing contrary to God's decree; as when I ask a parent's life, whom God hath determined to cut off by such a sickness, which I know not; but if I did, it is no rule to me. But now God's decree was a rule to Christ in his mediatory actions, as the moral law was a rule to his moral actions; and therefore when the decree of God called for one thing, and the moral law for another, Christ was both to show his moral affections and mediatory obedience: 'Father, let this cup pass; nevertheless not as I will, but as thou wilt,' Mat. xxvi. 39. There was an innocent desire of nature, but an express submission to his Father's will.

3. Because all Christ's prayers were to be grounded on a promise. There was an indenture drawn up between him and his Father; he had the assurance to be heard in whatsoever he asked : Ps. ii. 8, 'Ask of me, and I will give thee the heathen for thine inheritance, and the uttermost parts of the earth for thy possession;' John xi. 42, 'I knew that thou hearest me always.' Therefore he must needs exclude the reprobate world out of his prayers.

Observations.

First, Let us look upon it as a mediatory action.

1. Observe, here was the first solemn offer of Christ's mediation between God and man, and therefore upon this place we may ground the doctrine of his intercession, 'I pray for them.'

Here I shall speak of—(1.) The person who is the intercessor; (2.) The nature of the intercession; (3.) The privileges and fruits of it.

1. The intercessor, 'I pray.' The Syriac twice repeateth the pronoun; I, even I, pray for them; it is not an ordinary high priest, but I; I that am thy beloved and only-begotten Son, co-eternal, and consubstantial with thyself; I that have glorified thee upon earth, and done thy work; I that am holy and harmless; I whose prayers thou hast promised to hear; I who am an authorised mediator, sent into the world for this purpose. There are all these advantages in the intercession of Christ, let us go over them a little briefly. I shall refer them to these heads—the dignity and dearness of his person, the sublimity of his office, the value of his satisfaction, the articles of the covenant, or the promise of being heard.

[1.] The person of Christ; and there you have—

(1.) His dignity, he is God-man, and so fit for this office: Job ix. 33, 'Neither is there any daysman between us, that might lay his hand upon us both.' He communicates with God in the same nature, and we with him; he is our brother, and God's fellow. Our kinsman is in the court of heaven, pleading for us; he appeareth there in our nature, to set on our salvation. We need not be ashamed to go to him, nor he to go to God. He is of near alliance to us, and to God himself, God's own natural Son; which doth not only give him a power to prevail with God, but a sufficiency to do us good. None but Christ could serve our turn in this matter. Who can know all our needs, all our sins, all our thoughts, all our desires, all our prayers, all our purposes, and wait upon our business with God night and day, that no wrath break out upon us, but Jesus Christ, who hath his constant residence in heaven at his Father's right hand? There is an all-sufficiency required to intercession, as well as oblation.

(2.) The dearness of his person, called, 'his dear Son,' Col. i. 13, the Son of his love, one with him. God bids him ask what he will: Ps. ii. 8, 'Ask of me, and I will give thee the heathen for thy inheritance, and the uttermost parts of the earth for thy possession.' When Christ came first into heaven, he was to make his demand. He proclaimed it on earth when Christ was baptized, consecrated to God for the priesthood: Mat. iii. 17, 'Lo, a voice from heaven, saying, This is my beloved Son, in whom I am well-pleased.' There was such perfect love and consent of mind between God and Christ, that if he had never died, God could not have denied him anything.

[2.] The value of his satisfaction. Christ is an intercessor not by entreaty, but by merit: John xvii. 4, 'I have glorified thy name on earth, I have finished the work that thou gavest me to do.' The greatest work that ever could be done, if you respect the importance of it. The creating of a thousand worlds would not bring in such a revenue to heaven as this one work of redemption; or the difficulty of it, the Son of God to be made flesh, sin, a curse, states most abhorrent from the felicity of the divine nature ; or his willingness to undertake it, ' Lo, I come to do thy will.'   He longed to be at it ; though he had infinite complacency in the bosom of the Father, yet as soon as God had made a habitable world, Prov. viii. 30, 31, ' There I was by him, as one brought up with him ; and I was daily his delight, rejoicing always before him, rejoicing in the habitable part of his earth, and my delights were with the sons of men.'   He longed for that time when he might leave the company of angels and dwell among us, and feasted himself with the thoughts of his own grace.   And with so much faithfulness : I not only finished the work, but glorified thee ; all he did was for his Father's glory.   This could Christ plead as the ground of his requests ; he hath paid for all that he asketh, not only made satisfaction for sin, but given a price for glory.   He cannot out-ask his own merit ; his blood speaketh if Christ should hold his peace : Heb. xii. 24, ' And to the blood of sprinkling, that speaketh better things than that of Abel's.'   As clamorous as Abel's blood for vengeance.   It doth not speak against us, though we have made him to serve with our iniquities, but speaks the more for us, to pacify his wrath, to pardon us, and to do us good.

[3.] The sublimity of his office.   It is an authoritative act.   God hath always refused such mediation as is not authorised by himself. When Moses interposed for the children of Israel, said God, Exod. xxxii. 10, ' Let me alone, that my wrath may wax hot against them ;' because he would reserve this honour for him who alone hath this office under the broad seal of heaven.   So it is very notable that Christ refused all mediation to him in the days of his flesh.   As of his apostles: Mat. xv. 23, ' His disciples came and besought him, saying, Send her away, for she crieth after us,' &c.   But Christ would show that he was solicitous enough for the welfare of sinners, he needed no inter-cessors.   So his own mother, when she interposed for the honour of the wedding : John ii. 4, ' Woman,' saith he, ' what have I to do with thee ?'   As if he had said, Cannot I do it without your intermeddling ? In these answers, Christ would show that he would have sinners come of themselves, without any mediation of their fellow-creatures, they being no authorised mediators.   God alloweth no other mediator of redemption but Christ, and Christ no other mediator of intercession but himself.   It is sacrilege in the Papists to set up others ; none is worthy to appear before God but Christ ; and how unworthy soever we are, Christ will have us to come to himself.   God hath set him up for this purpose, and no copartners are allowed.   As it was said to Uzziah, 2 Chron. xxvi. 18, ' It pertaineth not to thee to burn incense, but to the priests, the sons of Aaron, that are consecrated to burn incense.'   Incense could be offered by no other but a priest, and our prayers by none but by Christ : Heb. vii. 28, ' The law maketh men priests which have infirmity ; but the word of the oath, which was since the law, maketh the Son, who is consecrated for evermore.' Christ is consecrated by an oath to abide overmore in the office, which oath is renewed and confirmed upon his return to heaven : Ps. cx. 4, ' The Lord hath sworn, and will not repent, Thou art a priest for ever, after the order of Melchisedeck ;' compared with ver. 1.   God will never repent of dispensing grace in and through him to sinners; as long as Christ's consecration lasteth, none must meddle with his office.

[4.] The articles of the covenant, or the promise of being heard. Therefore Christ speaketh with such confidence: John xi. 42, 'I know that thou hearest me always;' and Ps. ii. 8, 'Ask of me, and I will give thee the heathen for thine inheritance,' &c. There was a covenant drawn up between God and Christ; the Lord promised him, as the fruit of his labours and sufferings, that he should obtain all manner of grace for his people. All these things show us the advantages of having such a mediator and intercessor.

2. The nature of Christ's intercession. It is a part of his priestly office, of which there were two acts—oblation and intercession. Oblation was made once on the altar of the cross, and intercession is the continuation of his sacrifice, or the presenting it in heaven. It must be explained by analogy to the priests of the law. The sacrifice was slain without the camp, and then the priests were to enter with the blood within the veil, into the holy of holies, with sweet incense, and so to cause a cloud to arise over the mercy-seat. 'But Christ being come, an high priest of good things to come, by a greater and more perfect tabernacle, not made with hands; that is to say, not of this building; neither by the blood of goats and calves, but by his own blood, he entered in once into the holy place, having obtained eternal redemption for us,' Heb. ix. 11, 12. Jesus Christ having offered up himself upon the cross, where he was both priest and sacrifice, he is gone within the veil, 'Not into the holy places made with hands, which are the figures of the true, but into heaven itself, now to appear before the presence of God for us,' Heb. ix. 24. It is not a vocal, but a real intercession. Christ is gone into heaven, and there presents his person, both in our nature and his own, together with his merits, lifting up desires which are as a cloud of incense before the mercy-seat, for our comfort and salvation: Rev. viii. 3, 'And another angel came and stood at the altar, having a golden censer, and there was given unto him much incense, that he should offer it with the prayers of all saints upon the golden altar, which was before the throne.' The high priest entered not for himself, but for the people, having the names of the twelve tribes upon his breast and shoulders; so Christ is entered on the behalf of us all, bearing the particular memorial of every saint graven upon his heart. The high priest staid within the sanctuary for a short time, and so came out to bless the people; Christ entered within the veil at his ascension, and we must wait till his coming out to bless us, which will be at the day of judgment. All this while he hath his residence in heaven, and then he will open to us and give us entrance. So that Christ's intercession is 'A constant representation of his merit for the pardon of our sins, and for our acceptance; together with strong desires conceived in the human nature for the good of the creature, for all their exigencies and employments, that so his whole purchase may be applied to us, and we may receive grace to help in time of need.' It is a representing of his own merit, the worthiness of his person. As God-man, he is the Son of God, yet the creature's advocate; and the merit of his obedience and passion: 'I have glorified thee upon the earth;' as one that was to plead for his life showed *cubitum sine manu,*

his hand lost in the service of the state. All this is to the Father, who being appeased, all the rest of the persons are appeased; for they are one, and agree in one. He pleads with God for the application of good things procured by his oblation, especially in deep exigencies and conflicts. Christ hath knowledge at other times, but then he hath a fellow-feeling: Heb. iv. 15, 'We have not an high priest that cannot be touched with the feeling of our infirmities, but was in all points tempted like as we are, yet without sin.' His heart is entendered by his own experience.

3. The fruits and benefits of this intercession. They are many; I shall name the chiefest.

[1.] This secures our justification and the pardon of our sins. Christ watcheth against what objections justice makes, and against Satan's wiles, and that we ourselves, by our daily breaches, may not cast ourselves out of the favour of God. He justifieth us against the accusations of enemies, covereth our sins from the sight of God: Rom. viii. 34, 'Who is he that condemneth? It is Christ that died, yea, rather that is risen again, who is even at the right hand of God, who also maketh intercession for us.' So Zech. iii. 1, 2, there is our advocate and accuser : 'He showed me Joshua, the high priest, standing before the angel of the Lord, and Satan standing at his right hand to resist him. And the Lord said unto Satan, The Lord rebuke thee, O Satan, even the Lord that hath chosen Jerusalem, rebuke thee.' When we are summoned by the justice of God to defend ourselves against the exceptions and complaints which are preferred against us, our attorney appeareth in our name and behalf ; so when Satan accuseth us day and night, he makes up all the breaches that fall out between God and us: 1 John ii. 1, 'If any man sin, we have an advocate with the Father, even Jesus Christ the righteous.' When we have mudded the stream, Christ maketh all clear again.

[2.] The acceptation of all our persons, works, and services: 1 Peter ii. 5, 'We are made an holy priesthood, to offer up spiritual sacrifices, acceptable to God by Jesus Christ.' We communicate with Christ in all his offices ; we are spiritual priests, consecrated to him by baptism. The ordinary priests were first consecrated in the great laver before they were to offer sacrifices ; so we are purified and cleansed in the laver of regeneration, and then offer to God these sacrifices. As Christ was temple, priest, and sacrifice, so are we. God dwelleth in us as in a temple: 2 Cor. vi. 16, 'Ye are the temple of the living God ;' 'As the godhead dwelt in Christ bodily,' Col. ii. 9. We are consecrated to be priests to God, being sanctified by him, cleansed in the laver of his blood, our persons received into favour. And then we offer ourselves, bodies, services to God ; and so we perform duties acceptable to him ; because when we act the priest, Christ acteth it over again, presents our services to God in his censer : Rev. viii. 3, 'Another angel came and stood at the altar, having a golden censer, and there was given unto him much incense, that he should offer it with the prayers of all saints upon the golden altar which was before the throne.' He puts no filth nor dross into his golden censer. As the priests under the law were to examine the sacrifice before it was offered to the Lord, so doth Christ examine our services, not to reject them, but to better them in his own oblation; and so by his intercession our duties and all the good works of our lives are recommended to God.

[3.] It encourageth us to come to the throne of grace with boldness. God would have prayer in heaven to encourage us to prayer on earth; Christ is always with God to set on every request. This is the copy of Christ's intercession. Besides, you have the groans of the Spirit in your hearts: Rom. viii. 26, 'The Spirit itself maketh intercession in us, with groanings that cannot be uttered.' Christ is our advocate, the Spirit our notary, we the solicitors: Isa. lxii. 6, 7, 'Ye that make mention of the Lord keep not silence, and give him no rest,' &c. We may know what Christ is doing for us in heaven by the work upon our hearts. Oh! then, let us never rest till we have an interest in his intercession. This is the great prop of our faith and confidence, to know that we are comprehended in Christ's prayers. You have a friend in court, he hath liberty of immediate access, he is a favourite, the Father loveth him, and you for his sake. Our friend prayeth to our dear Father for his own children. When Joab saw the thing was pleasing to David, he interceded for Absalom, 2 Sam. xiv. 1. God can deny him nothing; if you have ten thousand accusers it is no matter, your advocate will answer all their accusations. Never leave till you get it evidenced that it is your privilege; choose him, go to God by him, ratify God's appointment by your own choice. Faith is a consent; wait for the Spirit's intercession; those groans will end in joys. It is the great comfort of the church that we have such a mediator, who will effectually plead our cause with the Father.

We may look upon it as a moral, as well as a mediatory act, an act of Christ's love to his own disciples, chiefly the apostles, who were, as it were, his family and special charge.

Out of this example of Christ let us learn to pray one for another; it is a spiritual act of love. You may discern the hypocrisy and sincerity of your love to others by your carelessness or seriousness in prayer for them; for if we desire a thing, we will pray for it with importunity. By this the saints have communion with one another at a distance.

Chiefly this concerneth ministers for their charge; they should be of Samuel's temper; though he had received affronts from Israel, 'God forbid that I should sin against the Lord, in ceasing to pray for you,' 1 Sam. xii. 23. Their sin doth not exempt you from the duty you owe to them for God's sake; they look to a higher obligation than civil respects and an interchange of kindness. But especially are we bound to pray for them if, as the apostles here, they are gained to any degree of faith, knowledge, and obedience: 2 Thes. i. 11, 'We pray always for you, that God would count you worthy of this calling, and fulfil all the good pleasure of his goodness, and the work of faith with power.' What encouragement hath a minister to go to God for such, not only when you send for him in times of sickness, but always, as the apostle saith, 'in every address to God.' It is sweet to give an account of the thriving lambs, and to desire the Lord to perfect his work. And it argueth in the minister sincerity to take pleasure in their gracious estate, and to account it, as it were, his own benefit that God hath any way blessed them with grace, which moveth him again to commend their case to God.   Certainly if we have but any portion of the unity of the Spirit, or any share in the communion of saints, or any respect to God's glory, thus it would be.

Again, it concerneth masters of families.   Your family is your charge, given you of God; pray for them in the bowels of love.   You are to make an errand to the throne of grace, not only for yourselves, but your children and servants; as the centurion came to Christ for his servant, Mat. viii. 6.   If we did not want hearts, we could never want an occasion of recourse to God.   By virtue of our relation we are to espouse the interests of our family, and to plead with God on their behalf, as we would on our own.   Job is an excellent pattern: Job i. 5, he 'rose early, day by day, and offered burnt-offerings for his children,' in the time of their feasting.   His great care was to keep his children in the favour of God; he knew no hurt in their feasting, had heard none by information; yet because miscarriages are usual in the heat and license of feasts, the family should not be without a daily sacrifice: 'For Job said, It may be that my sons have sinned, and cursed God in their hearts.'   Up then betimes, as Job did, and milk out a blessing for your families; not only in general, as men will put up cursory prayers, out of custom and use, for their families; they pray God to bless their families; but bring them forth by head and poll, and set them before the Lord, as 'Job offered sacrifices according to the number of his children;' or as Christ here, 'I pray for these,' pointing to the apostles; Lord! for these, and every one of them.   The occasion of Job's prayer is not manifest.   If you do but suspect that a child hath such a disease, you will go to a physician.   Should we have less care of their souls?   Christ says they live in an evil world, ver. 11, therefore he prays for them.

Again, look on this prayer of Christ not only as an act of love to his charge and familiars, but as an act of prudence as to the apostles, who were to bring others to believe by their word: 'I pray for them; I pray not for the world,' &c.   These that are designed for the great work of the gospel, chiefly for them: they had to do with obstinate Jews and idolatrous Gentiles, and they had need take the blessing of Christ's prayers along with them.   Ministers and dispensers of the mysteries of salvation above all men need the help of your prayers. How affectionately doth Paul call for this everywhere! 1 Thes. v. 25, 'Brethren, pray for us.'   It is a duty you owe, and it may be not only of great comfort to us, but of great profit to yourselves.   God would have all orders and estates in the church to be obliged to one another; you for our instructions, we for your prayers: 'The head cannot say to the foot, I have no need of thee,' 1 Cor. xii. 21.   Our calling is encumbered with the more difficulties, and that we may be acquainted with all sorts of Satan's enterprises, our persons may be exposed to more temptations than yours.   The many things requisite to make our ministry useful call for your prayers; abilities, the right use of them; fruit and success, that we may be able pastors, faithful, successful; that we may have abilities, which are a common gain; whatever gifts are bestowed on ministers, are for the people's profit; that out of love of ease, or love of the world, or error, we may not mislead you, nor be disheartened for lack of success.   Instead of praying for ministers, many now pray against them; the calling is repined at, as if it were some heavy plague and judgment sent upon the world.   But therefore you have need to pray the more: 2 Thes. iii. 2, 'That we may be delivered from unreasonable and wicked men; for all men have not faith.'   Pray that the lights of the church be not eclipsed; pray for our standing amidst the assaults of Satan.   It is not enough to give us love and maintenance, but we must have your prayers.

So much for the object of Christ's prayer.

Secondly, Now for the limitation of that object: 'I pray not for the world, but for them that thou hast given me.'   Many things may be inferred out of this limitation.

1. Universal redemption is disproved; for those for whom Christ prayed not, for them he died not.   These two offices of the priesthood must not be severed.   Christ doth not only profess to pray for these, but denieth to pray for the world.   His intercession is of the same latitude with his redemption; they are acts of the same office, and of the same extent and latitude.   All men were not intended in his passion and intercession.   See sermon on 2 Cor. v. 16.

2. The weakness of the world, notwithstanding all their outward props and supports; although they be strong, and have many on their side, yet they have not Christ on their side.   He hath left the world out of his prayers; he will not so much as take their names into his lips.   Therefore, Rom. viii. 31, 'If God be for us, who shall be against us?'   What will that party do that have God against them?   Against how many will you set me? said Antigonus.   You may shake your spear, and bid defiance against all the powers of darkness; they have not Christ among them, he will not speak one good word for them; they may have riches, honours, friends, countenance in the world, but God will never take their part.

3. The dangerous and sad condition of worldly men.   Oh! it is a sad thing not have a name in Christ's prayer.   There is a great number left out; and if you will know who they are, they are called 'the world.'   It presseth us to come out of that state·where we are in this danger.   Men that are now worldly may be in the roll of God's election, but it is no comfort to them.   'I pray not for the world;' so it is expressed; and as long as thou art worldly, thou canst take no comfort in Christ's intercession.   Certainly this should be an effectual consideration with the people of God, to cause them 'to keep themselves unspotted from the world,' James i. 24.   These have the benefit of Christ's prayers.   A christian should never be quiet till he be clearly out of that number which is excepted.   Christ hath a constant enmity and antipathy against mammon; there must be a separation from the world, and a contempt of earthly·things, before we can have an interest in him.   The world maketh a sport of these things; but what can be more terrible than to be shut out of Christ's prayers?   He curseth those for whom he doth not pray; and that is the reason why men that are besotted with the world do always wax worse and worse.

SERMON XIII.

And all mine are thine, and thine are mine ; and I am glorified in them.—JOHN XVII. 10.

WE have, in the former verse, the first solemn offer of Christ's intercession or mediation between God and man ; and therein he doth professedly refuse to pray for the world. His reason was, he would pray for none but those that were dear to his Father and to himself. Now of the elect he might say, They are not only mine, but thine. They are given him by the Father, not by way of alienation, but oppignoration ; the Father lost no right by his grant and donation. The gift of the Father to Christ differeth from all the gifts of men. When men give, they alter the property of the thing given, or certainly are not so careful about it. When you give your son to be a servant or an apprentice to another, or when a scholar is put out to school, you lessen your care towards him ; or, to instance in a relation less mercenary and servile, when you give your daughter in marriage, you think there is a child bestowed, your fatherly title and propriety is not abolished, but your care is lessened. But now, though God hath put believers into Christ's hands, yet he hath not put himself out of possession, but hath still reserved his own right and care ; for the establishment of the creature's comfort, Christ is taken in with himself. Christ hath a title proper to his distinct and personal operation to involve him in the care : Christ hath a title by purchase and redemption, and the Father hath a title proper to his personal operation by election : ' I pray for them which thou hast given me, for they are thine.' The joint possession and care of the Father, together with Christ, is proved by a general assertion, built on that perfect communion that was between them : ' All mine are thine, and thine are mine,' &c.

The sentence is applicable to things and persons :—

1. To things : *Τὰ ἐμὰ πάντα σὰ ἐστι, καὶ σὰ ἐμὰ,* the original will bear it ; so the fathers generally understood it of the concreated [1] and infinite riches of the Godhead, which all the persons had in communion. Epiphanius confuting the Sabellians, moveth this question : *Τὶ δὲ ἐστὶν τὰ τοῦ πατρὸς ?* and answereth, *Θεὸς ὁ πατήρ ; θεὸς ἐγω εἰμι : ζωὴ ὁ πατήρ ; ζωὴ ἐγὼ εἰμι.* The parallel place seems to countenance this exposition : John xvi. 15, ' All things whatsoever the Father hath are mine ; therefore, said I, that he shall take of mine, and shall show it unto you.' Christ had spoken of his departure, his absence was to be supplied by the Spirit ; now lest this should seem to derogate from himself, he saith, ' He shall take of mine ;' he shall enrich the church with the treasures purchased by me ; I bought them with a dear price, and in the way of grace will distribute them. Now lest this should derogate from the Father, he addeth, ' All things whatsoever the Father hath are mine ;' the same fulness of the Godhead, majesty, perfection, essence, blessedness. It is the Father's Spirit and mine. Christ came in as an heir to the Father, and the Spirit as executor to Christ of his last will and testament. I cannot utterly exclude this sense, yet I think it is not the formal intent of this place.

[1] Qu. ' uncreated ' ?—ED.

From hence we may gather the unity, and yet the distinction of the divine persons, they have their distinct right and title, and yet they all communicate in the same essence, dignity, and privileges.

2. To persons; and so it implieth not the uncreated riches of the Godhead, but their created goods and possessions. Believers are the created treasure of the divinity, and every person hath a distinct right. Christ saith to the Father, 'They are thine,' and again, 'They are mine;' and the Spirit is not to be excluded, though he be not mentioned, as appeareth in the parallel place but now quoted. They are God's children, Christ's members, and the Spirit's temples.

But to come more closely to the words: 'All mine are thine, and thine are mine.' How are believers Christ's? how the Father's? The first title Christ hath to us is the same that he hath to all things else; all things are God's and Christ's by creation and preservation. So the whole Godhead saith, Ezek. xviii. 4, 'All souls are mine.' God is the maker and judge of all. But that sense is too large for this place. Christ useth it as a special argument why he prayed for his own and not for the world. Another sort of creatures must be understood; by creation the beasts are theirs as well as men: Ps. l. 10, 'For every beast of the forest is mine, and the cattle upon a thousand hills.' But there is a peculiar heritage in which they delight, of which it is said, 2 Tim. ii. 19, 'The foundation of the Lord standeth sure, having this seal; the Lord knows those that are his.' There is a number of men whose names are written and sealed; now these are the Father's, the Son's the Spirit's. The text speaketh only of the two first persons, and so I shall mainly carry on the discourse. The distinct possession must be understood according to the personal propriety of each person; thine by election, mine by redemption. All that I am to redeem, to make intercession for, that are to have benefit by me, are God's elect; and all God's elect are to have benefit by me.

The point which I shall handle is, the commensurableness of the distinct propriety of all the persons in believers; election, redemption, and sanctification are of the same sphere and latitude. They are one joint possessor, Lord and maker: 'All mine are thine, and thine are mine.' All that the Father electeth the Son redeemeth; and I may add (because he communicateth in the same unity of essence) the Spirit sanctifieth. So the apostle, 1 Peter i. 2, 'Elect, according to the foreknowledge of God the Father, through sanctification of the Spirit unto obedience, and the sprinkling of the blood of Jesus Christ,' the same persons are interested in these personal operations of the same Godhead. Election is ascribed to God the Father, sanctification to the Spirit, and reconciliation to Jesus Christ. The beginning is from God the Father, the dispensation through his Son Jesus Christ, and the application through the Holy Ghost. This is the chain of salvation, and never a link of this chain must be broken. The Son cannot die for them whom the Father never elected, and the Spirit will never sanctify them whom the Father hath not elected nor the Son redeemed.

Reason 1. From the unity of essence. They are one; and if any person be interested in them, all must; otherwise men might be beholden to Christ that were never beholden to the Father nor the Spirit. They are ὁμοούσιοι and ὁμότιμοι, of one essence and of equal dignity; none shall be beholden to one that are not beholden to the other. It is very notable that when Christ speaketh of his own flock, and the certainty of their conversion and the sureness of their estate, he saith, John x. 27–30, 'My sheep hear my voice, and I know them, and they follow me; and I give unto them eternal life, and they shall never perish, neither shall any man pluck them out of my hand. My Father which gave them me is greater than all, and no man is able to pluck them out of my Father's hand: I and my Father are one. He is greater than me as redeemer. If I acknowledge them for mine, they must have grace, and cannot miscarry. We are two persons, but one God; he is a joint-cause working together with me, one in power, one in counsel.

Reason 2. From the unity and agreement in will and design. They are one, and agree in one; the persons are resolved to glorify one another. In man's salvation the Father will have the honour of electing, that the Son may have the honour of purchasing, and the Spirit the honour of sanctifying. It is said of the Spirit, John xvi. 14, 'He shall glorify me, for he shall receive of mine, and shall show it unto you:' and Christ saith, John xiv. 13, 'Whatsoever ye shall ask in my name, that will I do, that the Father may be glorified in the Son.' The Son came into the world to make good the purposes of the Father: John viii. 50, 'I seek not my own glory;' and the Son sendeth the Spirit. God sendeth the Son, and the Spirit anointeth Christ: Acts x. 38, 'God anointeth Jesus of Nazareth with the Holy Ghost and with power.' There is a perfect agreement, mutual missions between them.

Use 1. To condemn them which put asunder those operations which God hath joined together, the Arminians in doctrine, the common people in practice.

1. The Arminians in doctrine, by dividing Christ from election, or election from Christ; as if Christ were to die for those that were never elected and chosen to life, equally as for those that were; or as if he expected glory from and designed salvation unto all alike. These trouble the links of the chain of salvation. How can it be said, 'All thine are mine, and mine are thine,' when God would never own them, and the Spirit would never sanctify them?

2. The common people, that sever the election of God and redemption of Christ from the sanctification of the Spirit. They say Christ died for them, when there is no evidence of it; or that God loveth them, when there are no fruits of his love. The fruit of the Father's love is sending of the Spirit, and 'he that hath not the Spirit of Christ is none of his,' Rom. viii. 9. If God had chosen thee, thou wouldst be sanctified. Sanctification it is as it were an actual election; John xv. 19, 'Because I have chosen you out of the world, therefore the world hateth you.' As by election we are distinguished from others in the counsel of God, so by sanctification we are actually set apart. If Christ had died for thee, thou wouldst have the whole fruit of his purchase: Eph. v. 25, 'Christ loved the church, and gave himself for it, that he might sanctify and cleanse it with the washing of water by the word.'

Use 2. Information how believers come to be possessed of such excellent privileges. All that are God's are Christ's, and all things

that are Christ's are ours by faith.   There is the same communion
between us and Christ as there is between Christ and God: 1 Cor. iii.
23, 'All are yours, for you are Christ's, and Christ is God's.'   We
have it from the Father's love by the Son's purchase.   Christ was
God's natural heir ; he made a purchase that he might adopt heirs,
and take them in with himself : by faith we are taken in.   We may
say between us and Christ, ' All mine are thine, and thine are mine ;'
' I am my beloved's, and he is mine ;' Cant. ii. 16.

Use 3. To show us the comfort of the faithful.   God and Christ
have an equal interest in them: the Father loveth them as Christ's, as
his own ; Christ careth for them as the Father's, as his own : 1 John
i. 3, ' Our fellowship is with the Father, and with his Son Jesus
Christ.'   God made the elect members of Christ's body, that he might
redeem them.   Christ made them children of his family, that he might
love them.   The Father saith, ' They are mine ;' the Son saith, ' They
are mine.'   The power of God issueth through Christ for their salvation : 2 John 9, ' He that abideth in the doctrine of Christ, he hath
the Father and the Son.'   We may expect the fruits of elective love
and the fruits of Christ's purchase.   Two are better than one; we have
the Father to love us, the Son to redeem us, the Spirit to sanctify us,
and bring us to God ; it is a great advantage : John xvi. 27, ' The
Father himself loveth you.'   When Joab saw the thing was pleasing
to David, he interceded for Absalom : 2 Sam. xiv. 1, ' The king's
heart was towards Absalom.'   We have more confidence to speed in
our prayers : he loveth us for his own sake, and for Christ's.   Christ
hath satisfied the justice of God, and God is reconciled ; we have more
boldness of access to him ; we need not fear his justice, we have a
double claim, and may lay hold with both hands.

1. We have God on our side, who is the supreme judge, the offended
party, the first cause and fountain of blessing.

2. By Christ we have a near relation to God : we are Christ's more
than angels ; they are ministering spirits, not the spouse of Christ's
bosom, nor members of his body.   God hath given us to him, as he
brought Eve to Adam ; we are near to God : John xiv. 20, ' I am in
my Father, and you in me, and I in you ;' as a woman married to the
king's son by the king's consent.   The whole blessings of Christ's purchase are ours ; we have God in our nature working righteousness,
making atonement, meriting blessedness, sending the Spirit as purchased by him.

' And I am glorified in them.'—So we render it, that it may lie
indifferent to any sense, though the word properly signifieth, I have
been glorified in them.   It relateth not only to their past, present, but
future endeavours for Christ's glory.

But how was Christ glorified by his disciples ?

Ans. 1. Passively, as he glorifieth himself in them, by comforting,
refreshing their hearts, doing good to persons so despicable and unworthy, and manifesting the riches of his glory in them.

2. Actively, by their faith, by their ministry, by their life and
conversation.

[1.] By their faith. To glorify any one, is to have a good esteem
of him.   Those that did not believe did as it were obscure the dignity

of his person, rejecting him as a contemptible man. Now the apostles do everywhere express their faith in his godhead, and their sense of the dignity of his person and office, as I cleared in opening the 7th and 8th verses.

[2.] By their ministry. Christ was by them made known, and was yet to be further manifested. After the resurrection they were his heralds, to proclaim his triumphs for him over death and hell; and his ambassadors, to go out into the world and gather subjects for his kingdom.

[3.] By their life, and so by the constancy of their profession, when others shrink in the wetting: John vi. 66–68, 'From that time many of his disciples went back, and walked no more with him. Then said Jesus unto the twelve, Will ye also go away? Then Simon Peter answered him, Lord, to whom shall we go? thou hast the words of eternal life.' By their self-denial: Mat. xix. 27, 'Behold, we have forsaken all, and followed thee;' fathers, mothers, nets, trades, &c. So by their holiness and fruitfulness of conversation, they were such a company of which Christ was not ashamed.

This is a new argument that Christ urgeth for their respect with the Father; whence I observe :—

Doct. That the more we desire to glorify Christ, the more confidence we may have of his intercession for us.

1. It is the evidence of our interest in the Father, and the Son, and Spirit. Interest is the ground of audience; none can hope to speed with the Father but his own, those that are God's and Christ's.

[1.] It is an evidence that we have an interest in the Father; he acknowledges them for his that glorify his Son, them and no other: John xvi. 27, 'The Father himself loveth you, because ye have loved me, and have believed that I came out from God.' God's love can have no cause but itself; our love to Christ is a certain sign of God's love to us. It is not the principal reason why he loved them, but the argument whereby Christ would prove that his Father loved them. So that this is the evidence, if we would have any confidence of our interest in God, and speeding at the throne of grace. Do you glorify Christ by love and faith? Christ is his beloved, and he loves all them that love Christ. So again, John v. 23, 'That all men should honour the Son, as they honour the Father: he that honoureth not the Son, honoureth not the Father which hath sent him.' Every man naturally is touched with a reverence towards the Godhead. Now God the Father commandeth we should yield a like reverence to the Son, who is his living and perfect image. He that doth not worship Christ and honour Christ doth but worship and serve an idol; for he doth not honour God in that way wherein he will be honoured, and hath revealed himself, because they are in the unity of the Godhead, neither of them can be worshipped without the other.

There is a noted story of Amphilochius, bishop of Iconium; when the Arians, who denied the godhead of Christ, had freedom of their meetings and lectures and disputes, under Theodosius the Great, to the great disturbance of the church, and the emperor could by no means be drawn to suppress them, Amphilochius, after he had tried all other means without effect, found out a way worthy of record, saith

Theodoret, whereby to make the emperor sensible of the evil of his toleration. One day as he came into the palace, and the emperor and his son Arcadius were standing together, whom he had lately made joint-emperor with himself, Amphilochius saluteth the father with accustomed reverence and humility; but when he cometh to the son, he speaketh to him as to a private child, and stroking his head, saith, How dost thou, my child? without other expression of civil honour and reverence. The emperor was exceeding angry at the contempt, and that he had not given his son equal honour with himself, and therefore, after many rebukes, causeth him to be dragged out of the palace with disgrace; and as they were pulling and haling him, he, turning to the emperor, said, O emperor! after this manner, and infinitely more, is God the Father angry with those that do not honour his Son equal with the Father, but make him less in nature and dignity. By this sensible conviction the emperor was touched in conscience, and with tears embraceth the good old man, and presently maketh a law against the Arians, in which, under a great penalty, he forbiddeth their public meetings and lectures against the godhead of Christ, and by the blessing of God was confirmed in the true religion, in which before he staggered and wavered.

All this is brought to show that God will not own us unless we honour Christ, and glorify him as we glorify the Father.

[2.] It is the evidence of our interest in the Son. Those that mind Christ's glory, he mindeth their salvation. He is interceding for you in heaven when you are glorifying him on earth; he is doing your business in heaven when you are doing his business in the world; he is your advocate, and you are his bailiffs and factors: Mat. x. 32, 'Whosoever shall confess me before men, him will I confess also before my Father which is in heaven.' When you own Christ in the world, and avow his name and truth in the world, you shall lose nothing. When you come to pray, Christ will own you: Father, hear him, this is one of mine. You cannot honour Christ so much as he will honour you. When carnal men come to pray, Christ saith, 'I know them not.' Oh! it is sad to be disowned in the court of heaven, when Christ disclaimeth any interest or intendment in his purchase for us, they are nothing akin to me, are none of mine. When we do all things for by-ends, we disclaim God for a paymaster, and therefore must look for our reward elsewhere.

[3.] It is a sign of your interest in the Spirit: John xvi. 14, 'He shall glorify me, for he shall receive of mine, and shall show it unto you;' that enlightening, quickening comfort and refreshing which we have, when it is used to the glory of Christ, it is a sign the Spirit dwelleth in us.

2. Because the glorifying of God in Christ is the great condition of the covenant of grace. God hath made a bargain with believers to give them grace, and by way of return he expecteth glory. All the privileges of the covenant are leased out to the heirs of the promise, and this is the rent and acknowledgment which God hath reserved to himself. See the form of this contract, Ps. l. 15, 'Call upon me in the day of trouble, I will deliver thee, and thou shalt glorify me.' In all experiences of grace God will be glorified. Glory and praise are the

revenues of the crown of heaven, and all the persons of the Godhead are joint-possessors; the Father will be glorified, the Son and the Spirit will be glorified too. Well, then, they that expect all comfort, and do not regard duty, they mistake the tenor of the covenant. God must needs be angry when we deny him his rent and acknowledgment; you forfeit your lease and charter, and how will you do to pray with confidence? It is notable in the covenant of grace, what God doth to us in a way of mercy, the creatures return to God again in a way of duty. God justifieth, sanctifieth, glorifieth the creature, these are the great blessings of the covenant; and in our way we are to do it again to God to justify, sanctify, and glorify God. To justify God: Luke vii. 29, 'And all the people that heard him, and the publicans, justified God, being baptized with the baptism of John.' To sanctify God: Isa. viii. 13, 'Sanctify the Lord of hosts in your hearts;' and here, 'I am glorified in them.' We are to justify God, his ways against the cavils of the world, the riches of grace against the prejudices of our own hearts; to sanctify God, to set him aloof in point of fear and trust, above all the powers and excellences in the world, as to sanctify is to set apart from common use; and then we glorify him when we advance him in our thoughts, and faith, and esteem. Our best thoughts are but a disgrace to the Godhead; he is advanced far above all blessing and praise; yet God counteth he hath another throne when he is exalted in thy heart.

3. Because we gratify the aim of God. God's great end in all his dispensations is to glorify his Son, and in his Son himself; God seeketh his own glory by glorifying Christ in our nature. We had neither had . word, nor gospel, nor Christ, nor grace, but for his glory. It is said, Prov. xvi. 4, 'The Lord hath made all things for himself;' that is, for the manifestation of his glory; for God, being so perfect as he is, can no other ways be advanced; it must be, therefore, to make himself known. He made the world that he might be glorified, and for the same reason he made us in Christ: Eph. i. 12, 'That we should be to the praise of his glory,' εἰς τὸ εἶναι; all that we are in religion is for this end. We had need respect God's glory, for we owe all that we have to it; God is set upon it: 1 Sam. ii. 30, 'They that honour me, I will honour.'

Use 1. Information. We lose nothing by glorifying Christ; it is a pledge of our interest in his intercession. We shall have this honour and comfort, that Christ will be our advocate. In the world we are like those six hundred that were David's companions in the wilderness, they had hard service and little wages; but when David was crowned in Hebron, they were all advanced to offices and places of power and trust. In the world, if we glorify Christ indeed, we shall meet with hard entertainment, but you will not repent of it when Christ appeareth in the day of his royalty. Nay, for the present you will lose nothing; worldly losses are made up in spiritual comforts, and that is a good exchange. Do but observe Peter's question and Christ's answer: Mat. xix. 27, 28, 'Peter said, Behold we have forsaken all, and followed thee, what shall we have therefore?' In Peter's question we may observe, that albeit we suffer little for Christ, we think much of it. Peter's case was poor and slender. Alas! what did he leave? A poor cottage, a net, a fishing-boat; he had no lands nor heritage: from a fisherman he was made a disciple. The loss is little; but we think it a great matter if we part with our superfluities, with the tenth part of a child's portion for Christ's cause, and owning Christ's interest, or the propagation of religion. Nay, if we suffer but a disgraceful word, or discountenance, or a small inconvenience in our name, or estates, we are apt to say with Peter, 'What shall we have therefore?' Thoughts of merit are natural, and we put a high price upon our petty services; what shall we be the better? But observe Christ's answer: 'And Jesus said unto them, Verily I say unto you, that ye which have followed me, in the regeneration, when the Son of man shall sit in the throne of his glory, ye also shall sit upon twelve thrones, judging the twelve tribes of Israel.' Pray mark, Christ pardoneth the infirmity of the demand, there was somewhat of pride in it, and somewhat of fleshiness, in having respect to a carnal reward; the dreamed-of earthly honours, that Christ would share and divide among them; but Christ passeth it over, and gives a gracious answer. Nay, mark, Christ promiseth a greater reward than Peter could expect, 'a kingdom to each of them in the regeneration.' I shall not examine that expression, that doth not so suit with my purpose; but I observe, that though the things we do and suffer for Christ be not worthy to be spoken of, yet the least thing, if done in sincerity, will be highly esteemed and richly rewarded; Christ will intercede for thee, and plead for thee with his Father, and if once he openeth his mouth, thou canst never miscarry. The apostle saith, Heb. vii. 25, 'He is able to save to the utmost all that come unto God by him, seeing he ever liveth to make intercession for them.' Christ, when he hath begun to intercede, doth not give over till thou hast honour enough for honouring him; 'He will save thee to the utmost.' Oh! why should we be prejudiced against the service of Christ? Certainly we shall be no losers in the end. Christ will not be behind hand with you; he is making way for your everlasting glory by his constant intercession. Now therefore be not troubled; you need not seek another paymaster than Christ; we have something in hand, there is present comfort, besides what we have in hope.

Use 2. Exhortation; to press us to glorify Christ. Order your lives so that Christ may plead, 'Father, I am glorified in them.' I do not press you now to glorify God in general, but to glorify Christ as mediator.

But what is it to glorify Christ? I answer—

1. You will glorify him by faith. Christ is glorified, when you acknowledge his person and office, as revealed to you in the word, and accordingly build your hopes and comfort on him. Now faith hath a double office—it accepts Christ from God, and presents Christ to God; it accepts Christ in the word, and maketh use of him in prayer.

Let us speak of both these.

[1.] It accepts Christ. When men slight the offers of Christ which God maketh to them, they dishonour him exceedingly; it is a contempt cast upon the Son of God, as if he were not worth the taking: Acts iv. 11, 'This is the stone which was set at nought of you builders, which is become the head of the corner.' God made him a glorious foundation of hope and comfort, and you pass him by as nothing worth; it is a high scorn put upon the choice of God, and the excellency of Christ. You look upon him as rubbish, not worth the regarding, and God sets him out as a precious stone: Mat. xxii. 5, ' But they made light of it, and went their ways; one to his farm, another to his merchandise,' ἀμελήσαντες; they would not take it into their care and thoughts. A careless disregard of the offers of the gospel offendeth God exceedingly; you slight the wisdom of the Father and the love of Christ. God employed all his wisdom in the contrivance of grace; the gospel is the masterpiece of heaven. The Father discovereth the riches of his wisdom, and Christ paying a ransom, obeying and dying, discovered the riches of his love and grace; and when this is offered to you, you will not take it into your care and thoughts; it is the greatest dishonour you can cast upon him. But now, ' To them that believe, Christ is precious,' 1 Peter ii. 7. τιμή; they can see nothing so worthy their study, and time, and care, and thoughts. This is the sum of their desires, that they may take Christ as God offereth him; all other things are but σκύβαλα, dung and dog's-meat in comparison of the excellency of him, ' that I may be found in him,' Phil. iii. 9. By this esteem and care Christ is exceedingly glorified.

[2.] It presents Christ. In all our endeavours to God we must build our acceptance on the merits of Christ: John xiv. 1, ' Ye believe in the Father, believe also in me.' There is a belief in God and a belief in Christ, in his merits. We should never go to God but we should take Christ along with us; in all your addresses make use of him. Whenever you have to do with God, you must go to him in Christ; and you must go to him with a confidence that you shall speed the better for his sake: Eph. iii. 12, ' In whom we have boldness, and access with confidence, by the faith of him.' A man may use some liberty and freedom with God when he hath Christ on his side, and offer up his prayers to God in the mediation of his beloved Son. Out of Christ we can see nothing but majesty armed with wrath and power; but now, when you make use of Christ as a mediator, you may take hold of God with both hands; justice and mercy are on your side, you have merits to urge as well as requests. But, alas! how little do we glorify Christ in our addresses to God. We come with little hopes, with little confidence, our best is but guess and conjecture. Thus by faith should we glorify Christ. Low and base apprehensions that men have of Christ dishonour him.

2. By the holiness of your conversations. Every christian should walk so as remembering that Christ's honour lieth at stake. It is not a moral life that I persuade you to, but a christian life, such a life wherein Christ may be specially honoured.

[1.] For the manner; your practice should be elevated according to the height of your privileges in Christ. A christian should do more than a man: 1 Cor. iii, 3, ' Are ye not carnal, and walk as men?' We expect that he should go faster that rides on horseback than he that goeth on foot. In christianity, duties are elevated to a greater proportion; the laws are the same, but we have higher engagements. Wherein do ye differ from others? There should be a singularity of holy life. There should be something more in your lives than if ye

came out of the school of a philosopher, or Jews, or Turks, or moral
heathens, that know not Christ.

[2.] For the principle; Christ must be honoured.   You must make
him the principle of your obedience to God.   You must make use of
Christ not only in point of acceptance but assistance: Phil. iv. 13, 'I
can do all things through Christ, that strengtheneth me;' Gal. ii. 20,
'Nevertheless I live, yet not I, but Christ liveth in me, and the life
which I live in the flesh, I live by the faith of the Son of God, who
loved me, and gave himself for me.'   He will be honoured by dependence, as the cause of all our spiritual being.   Whatever we have, life,
sense, and motion, it is derived from him our head, to us his members.
You rob him of his chief glory if you do not depend upon him, and
make him the principle and head of every vital influence.

[3.] For the end; you must make his interest the great end of your
lives: Phil. i. 21, 'Ἐμοὶ τὸ ζῆν, Χριστὸς, 'For me to live is Christ.'
He would not have life for any other end but to advance Christ; all
is done with a pure eye to him: Rom. xiv. 7, 8, 'For no man liveth
to himself, and no man dieth to himself: for whether we live, we live
unto the Lord; or whether we die, we die unto the Lord; whether
therefore we live or die, we are the Lord's.'   A regenerate man must not
live as his own man, but as the Lord's, as one that is wholly given up to
Christ, not wedded to his own interest, but altogether for Christ's glory.

[4.] The motive must be gratitude to Christ; all must be done for
Christ's sake: 2 Cor. v. 14, 'For the love of Christ constraineth me.'
God's love in Christ should be the great swaying motive.   Shall I not
do something for him that died for me?   Christ is exceedingly honoured when there are such kind of arguings and workings in the heart.

3. We must glorify Christ in our enjoyments.   When we think of
our title to anything, think, This I have by gift, be it justification,
sanctification, glorification, comfort of the creatures.   Whatever privilege we look upon as ours, we must see Christ in it: 1 Cor. iii. 22, 23,
'All are yours, and ye are Christ's, and Christ is God's.'   All mercies
swim to us in his blood; he purchased them of God, and conveyed
them to us, that we might be sensible that we have all in and by
Christ.   He did not only purchase them, but began to us in every
privilege: Christ first had them and then we; he was elected, justified, sanctified, rose again by covenant, ascended, and was glorified;
in all these things, Christ would show himself to be the heir of all
things.   He was the elder brother, and had the pre-eminence as the
heir; he would possess, and then make the testament.   It is true, in
the comforts of the world, Christ possessed little, but he had a right
and title, which he hath made over to us.   To declare his right, the
creatures, one time or another, did him homage; the angels ministered
to him, the devils confessed him, the winds and seas were at his beck,
a fish paid him tribute.   Well, then, look upon Christ in every enjoyment; he was the purchaser, and he was the first heir and possessor.

4. We glorify Christ by doing and suffering for the advancement of
his interest and kingdom.   Never were there such a zealous parcel
of men as in the first days of the gospel; they seemed to some as if
they were even mad for Christ: 2 Cor. v. 13, 'For whether we be besides ourselves, it is to God;' much in spirit, much in labours, much

in afflictions. Primitive zeal is much decayed. Many are like the carbuncle; if you look upon it afar off, you would think it all on fire; but touch it, and it is key-cold. Religion is turned into a mere prattle and talk; few mind the interest of Christ. A christian should be always devising how he may lay forth himself for Christ, for the advancement of his ordinances, enlargement of his kingdom; and to this end we should neither spare body nor estate, nor life itself. You should honour him with your substance: Prov. iii. 9, ' Honour the Lord with thy substance, and with the first-fruits of all thy. increase;' it is but a tribute to the King of the church. Now miracles are ceased, God will propagate the gospel by the bounty of those that have tasted the sweetness of it; if the Lord hath need of it, why should we stick at anything? Honour him with your relation. As a magistrate; magistrates must improve the interest of Christ by discountenancing error; they who reign by Christ must reign for him; see if God doth not reckon with Gallios. As a merchant, honour him with thy traffic, to promote religion by trade: Deut. xxxiii. 18, 19, ' And of Zebulun he said, Rejoice, Zebulun, in thy going out; and Issachar in thy tents. They shall call the people unto the mountain, there shall they offer sacrifices of righteousness: for they shall suck of the abundance of the seas, and of treasure hid in the land.' Every affair should be cast into the mould of religion, or we do not act as christians. Jesuits and papists will rise up in judgment against us. So in your private sphere, do something for Jesus Christ in your families. A christian should not have any relation but he should make some advantage of it for the honour of Christ. So for suffering, Christ is glorified in the courage of those that bear forth his name to the world. Let it not be grievous to us; it is much to be active for God, but it is more to be passive. Let glory to Christ be written, though it be with our blood; only with these cautions:—

[1.] We must think ourselves to be honoured by this service, how grievous, disgraceful, and troublesome soever it be: 2 Cor. v. 9, φιλο-τιμούμεθα, 'Therefore we labour, that whether present or absent, we may be accepted of him.' We labour; that is, we strive after this honour, to labour with ambition. The meanest service about princes is honourable, if it be a groom, or any other inferior employment. A servant of the Lord is a higher honour than the prince of the power of the air; Satan's title is windy and lofty. To do for Christ, saith Ignatius, is a greater honour than to be a monarch of all the world. Christ is such an excellent person, that anything that is done in and about him reflecteth an honour upon the person that doeth it. The second temple exceeded Solomon's because of Christ's presence: Hag. ii. 9, ' The glory of the latter house shall be greater than of the former, saith the Lord of hosts; and in this place will I give peace, saith the Lord of hosts.' Bethlehem was ' little among the thousands of Judah,' Micah viii. 2, yet there Christ was born. So hardship with Christ, brown bread with Christ, shame and disgrace with Christ, is honour-able: Acts v. 41, ' They went away from the presence of the council, rejoicing, ὅτι κατηξιώθησαν ἀτιμασθῆναι, that they were counted worthy to suffer shame for the sake of Jesus Christ;' it is, that they were honoured to suffer dishonour for Christ. Service is an honour, suffering a privilege: Phil. i. 29, 'To you it is given in the behalf of Christ, not only to believe in him, but also to suffer for his sake.' Unless you have this mind, it is but a factious obstinacy, not a religious suffering and doing for Christ.

[2.] There must be a sense of your unworthiness: Luke xvii. 10, 'When you have done all, say, We are unprofitable servants; we have done that which was our duty to do.' A poor unworthy creature. Alas! what have we done? Christ is doubly honoured—by a direct aim and tendency of the endeavour, and by your humble profession. David prepared for the temple with all his might: 1 Chron. xxii. 14, 'Now behold, in my trouble I have prepared for the house of the Lord an hundred thousand talents of gold, and an hundred thousand talents of silver,' &c.; a poor gift for the great God! We are apt to over-value our services and endeavours, therefore it is very good to retain a humble modest sense of them. Poor creatures! what do we do, that have received, not only life and breath, but grace and glory, and all things from Christ? It is good to be humble for what we do, and to acknowledge it to be a thing wholly unworthy of God.

[3.] You must ascribe all to Christ's glory; as Joab, when he had conquered Rabbah, sent for David to take the honour; so must we do for Christ. This is still doubling of honour and glory: 1 Cor. xv. 10, 'By the grace of God I am what I am; and his grace which was bestowed upon me was not in vain; for I laboured more abundantly than they all; yet not I, but the grace of God which was with me.' The pen doth not deserve praise if the writer draweth a fair letter: Gal. ii. 20, 'I live, yet not I, but Christ liveth in me; and the life which I live in the flesh, I live by the faith of the Son of God.' The stars disappear when the sun shineth in its strength. The work is enough, let God take the honour: 1 Chron. xxix. 14, 'But who am I, and what is my people, that we should be able to offer so willingly after this sort? for all things come of thee, and of thine own have we given thee.' David never speaketh in that strain, but on the occasion of a singular mercy. David ascribeth all to God, the ability, the will, the goods, the mind. So in all our engagements for Christ, he must have the praise; as one man in a press or crowd lifteth up another, and he only is seen, when the other is lost in the throng.

5. By being zealous for his institutions; then you honour Christ, by giving the wisdom and power of a lawgiver to him. The highest power of a prince is legislative. When you keep to Christ's laws, you count him faithful in his house, and acknowledge him king in his church. But now, when we set up our threshold by God's threshold, Christ is dishonoured, as if he were not faithful in his house: Mat. xv. 6, 'Thus have ye made the commandments of God of none effect by your traditions.' By the traditions of men ye make void the law of God, ἠκυρώσατε, ye unlord the law, so the word signifieth.

6. By taking some solemn time to meditate of and admire the excellency of his person and the fulness of his redemption. In heaven this will be our great work, there they praise the Lamb for evermore: Rev. iv. 10, 11, 'The four-and-twenty elders fall down before him that sat on the throne, and worship him that liveth for ever and ever, and cast their crowns before the throne, saying, Thou art worthy, O Lord, to

receive honour, and glory, and power; for thou hast created all things, and for thy pleasure they are and were created.' They do not slight their glorious work. All the glory they have is God's mere bounty; they hold it by grace, and magnify it by grace. So Rev. v. 8, 'The four beasts and four-and-twenty elders fell down before the lamb, having every one of them harps, and golden vials full of odours, which are the prayers of the saints.' There is the employment of the church militant and triumphant. Harps, which are instruments of praise, belong to souls already glorified; as vials full of odours belong to believers on earth. The earth is the true place of prayer, as in heaven we shall be employed in eternal thanksgivings. All the church is yielding homage to Christ; it is the study of saints: Eph. i. 16, 'I cease not to give thanks for you.' It was Paul's constant practice, he breathed nothing but Christ: 1 Cor. ii. 2, 'I determined to know nothing among you, save Jesus Christ, and him crucified.' Our thoughts of Christ should be sweet to us; we should have ravishing apprehensions of him from day to day, ravishing thy heart with the excellency of Christ.

Use 3. Is consolation to them that desire to glorify Christ. It is a singular prop in your prayers, in every address you have an interest in Father and Son : ' They are mine,' saith the Lord; I loved them with an everlasting love. ' They are mine,' saith Christ; I redeemed them with an everlasting redemption. And will not God provide for his own, and Christ for his own? Can he that hath the Father and Son miscarry and doubt of audience ? You have the Father, who is the original fountain of blessing; and you have Christ, who is the golden pipe and conveyance. But especially in your last address, when you lie on your deathbed; you know Christ's own plea, John xvii. 4, 5, ' Father, I have glorified thee upon earth, I have finished the work that thou hast given me to do. And now, Father, glorify thou me with thyself, with the glory that I had with thee before the world was.' It is a sweet evidence. What doth God look for from the creature but glory ?

Object. 1. But you will say, I cannot glorify Christ in my addresses to God, and cannot come with an assurance becoming his purchase. I answer—

1. When we cannot apply, let us disclaim: Lord! we come not in our own names, our own worth and desert, which is none at all; we come in the merits of Christ; we know 'there is no other name under heaven;' Hosea xiv. 3, 'In thee the fatherless findeth mercy;' that is, every person that wanteth a guide, relief, and support. Though we cannot say, Father, yet we can say, we are fatherless, we have none to help us.

2. If we cannot speak of the love that he beareth to us for Christ's sake, yet let us plead the love that he beareth to him. Christ's name is very dear and precious in heaven, being God's beloved Son: Lord, for the love that thou bearest to Christ. We are his clients, though we cannot say we are his members. Though I cannot say, Thou art mine, yet I may say, He is thine, a mediator of thy setting up. God might have refused us, if Christ had not letters-patents from heaven, and his commission under the broad seal of God: John vi. 27

'Him hath God the Father sealed.'   Lord, he is thy own authorised mediator.   Moses was refused, that interposed of his own accord, Exod. xxxii. 32, 33.   I have nothing to bring thee but a mediator of thine own.   It is a prevailing argument.

Object. 2.   Alas! there is little that I do for God; my, station is private: those in the magistracy and ministry, that are in an eminent sphere of activity, they may glorify Christ, they do his work upon earth; but what do I do?   I answer—

1. God will be glorified by every man in his way and place: John xvii. 4, 'Father, I have glorified thee upon earth, I have finished the work that thou hast given me to do.'   We must not speak of our rank, Christ is glorified by thy diligence and faithfulness in thy private place, a man-servant, or a maid-servant: 1 Cor. vii. 22, 'He that is called in the Lord, being a servant, is the Lord's free man;' being redeemed from the thraldom of Satan, and servitude of sin, he doth glorify Christ: Titus ii. 9, 10, 'Exhort servants to be obedient unto their own masters, and to please them well in all things, not answering again, not purloining, but showing all good fidelity, that they may adorn the doctrine of God our Saviour in all things.'   Godly servants, what an ornament are they to the gospel!   By the first inlets of religion into a family, it is made beautiful and lovely in the eyes of carnal men, who esteem the doctrine by the life and practice of the professors of it. Servants in those days were bought and sold like beasts.   The Lord doth not esteem men by the places they hold, but by their carriage in them.

2. There is no station so private but thou mayest do something for Christ, to bring up thy children in the nurture of the Lord, to instruct thy servants, thy neighbours, thy fellow-servants.   Zeal is like fire or like leaven, it will spread and diffuse itself.

Object. 3.   I have laboured, but to little purpose.

Ans. Success is not thy work, but God's.   We must mind our duty, and leave the success to God; we shall not be responsible for lack of success, but want of endeavours: Isa. xlix. 4, 'Then I said, I have laboured in vain, I have spent my strength for nought, and in vain; yet surely my judgment is with the Lord, and my work with my God.' It was a complaint of Christ himself; his ministry was without fruit, yet not without reward.   We may have the crown of faithfulness, if not the fruit.   A minister is like a fountain that always runneth, 'whether they will hear, or whether they will forbear.'   So you must act in your families.

Object. 4.   I was never called to martyrdom.   I doubt I shall not glorify him.

Ans. 1.   Wish not for troubles, but leave them to God; and when they come, take up his cross.   Simon of Cyrene was compelled; we must not choose our cross, but bear it.   Christ himself did not carry his cross till it was laid upon him; we must not seek it, but take it up; not brew our cup, but drink it.   When a cross meeteth us in our way, which we cannot escape without sin or breach of conscience, we must bear it.

2. There is seldom a time when religion is not difficult, and doth not put us on some inconvenience, if not upon the displeasure of a magistrate, yet of carnal friends; if not for some main truths of chris-

tianity, yet for some of Christ's lesser institutions; present truths usually go cross to interests.

3. The less trouble abroad, the more at home; if you do not conflict with a naughty world, yet with a naughty heart. There are doubts in point of comfort, difficulties in point of obedience. A christian, in good earnest, never meeteth with a sleepy lazy time, all calm and rest. It is good to be jealous of ourselves; it doth not weaken our confidence in Christ, but our fleshly security.

Object. 5. But I have many self-ends, and do what I can, they will be interposing; and I can do nothing for Christ, but am ready to be biassed by some carnal aims.

Ans. It is impossible to think to be without failings, as to our ends and principles, as well as the manner of duty; but a christian is judged by his main scope and purpose of his life. If this be the main thing, Christ will own you, and intercede with God for you.

SERMON XIV.

And now I am no more in the world, but these are in the world, and I come to thee. Holy Father, keep through thine own name those whom thou hast given me, that they may be one, as we are.—JOHN XVII. 11.

HITHERTO Christ had argued with the Father, and showed many reasons why he would pray for the disciples. Now he cometh from arguments to requests. Here the prayer itself beginneth. His first request is, that God would have a care of them when he was gone from them; as a father, when he is about to die, commendeth his children to the care and tutelage of a near friend; so doth Christ commend his disciples to God: 'And now I am no more in the world,' &c.

The circumstances notable in the verse are these—

1. The occasion of the prayer, wherein there is a new cause and reason why he commendeth them to the Father, 'And now I am no more in the world, but these are in the world, and I come to thee.'

2. The compellation of the party to whom the prayer is made, 'Holy Father.' Titles are suited to requests: Rom. xv. 13, 'Now the God of hope fill you with all joy and peace in believing.'

3. The matter of the prayer, for perseverance in grace, 'Keep through thine own name.'

4. The parties prayed for, 'Those which thou hast given me;' an argument often urged before.

5. The end of the prayer, or of the blessing asked in prayer, 'That they may be one;' which is amplified by the exemplary pattern, 'as we are one.' Or rather, the whole is a new request; two matters are prayed for—conservation from evil, and perfection in good. Christ prayed for *conservationem a malo, et perfectionem in bono.*

In this verse there is a large field of matter. Let me explain the words, and then raise some practical observations.

First, I begin with the occasion.

'I am no more in the world;' that is, by and by I shall be no more. Christ was yet in the world; for he saith, ver. 13, 'These things I speak in the world;' still subject to the miseries of it; his passion was not over, his sorest combat was at last, and that was nigh at hand; but Christ went to it with such a resolved mind, that he seemed already to be exempted from a worldly condition. But how 'no more in the world,' since he saith, 'I am with you to the end of the world'? He is spiritually still with us, but he was about to withdraw his corporal presence.

'But these are in the world.'—I am almost on shore, but these are still to remain at sea, floating upon the waves; out of the duty of their calling, they are to stay behind, and must expect tempests, labours, dangers, and persecutions, infirmities within, and temptations without. The world is a step-mother to the saints; Christ pitieth their case that they are to stay in the world, as those that are in the haven pity their fellows that are left behind at sea in the midst of the storm.

'And I come unto thee.'—An explication of what he said before, 'I am no more in the world;' only it addeth something more. 'I am no more in the world,' implieth only his death; but 'I come to thee,' his ascension. It is expressed before: John xvi. 5, 'I go my way to him that sent me: I go to the Father,' ver. 10. I am about to enter into the glory of the Father. It doth not signify, as Lyranus would have it, I come to thee in prayer, by way of address and supplication; but, I come to be with thee in glory. Mark, there was a great deal of time yet to pass, forty days after the resurrection. Faith presents things future as present; in this sense we enter heaven before our time.

In this clause, the occasion, I observe three things:—

1. Christ's ascension, *Father, I come to thee.*

2. The necessary ceasing of his corporal presence by virtue of that ascension, *I am no more in the world.*

3. Christ's care to make up that defect to his people; it is the occasion of the present address to God.

Of these in their order.

First, Of Christ's ascension, 'I come to thee.' Here is—(1.) The history; (2.) The reasons; (3.) The benefits; (4.) The use that we may make of it.

1. The history of Christ's ascension. There are many circumstances; I shall touch upon them briefly.

[1.] The time when he had finished his work, not only of doing and suffering, but giving sufficient instructions to the apostles about his kingdom: Acts i. 3, 'He was seen of them forty days, speaking of the things pertaining to the kingdom of God.' As Hezekiah was to 'set his house in order before he died,' Isa. xxxviii. 1, so Christ would not ascend into heaven till he had set all at rights upon earth. Christ would have his house well governed after his death, and therefore stayeth forty days to give instructions.

[2.] The place from whence he ascended; from the Mount of Olives, Acts i. 12. A mount, a high and eminent place, to ascertain them of the truth of his ascension; he did not withdraw himself secretly, as at other times, but in open view. The place is yet again notable: the

Mount of Olives was the place from whence he went to be crucified; the same mountain yielded him a passage to his cross and his crown; there his pains and torments began, in the garden of that mount, and thence he ascended. How often doth the Lord make that place that hath been the scene of our sorrows to be the first steps to our rising and advancement! Wherever the saints die, they have their Olivet, in the prison, on the scaffold, their sick beds, where they have been racked with tormenting pains. As sometimes with wicked men, the place of sin is the place of vengeance. So Ahab's dogs licked up his blood in the same place where he shed the blood of Naboth.

[3.] The place to which, the third heaven. The tabernacle figured the church, the temple heaven. In the temple were three partitions; the court, where was the altar of burnt-offerings; the holy place, where was the table, candlestick, shew-bread, and the altar of burnt-incense; then the holy of holies, where the high priest came once a year. So in that vast space which the scriptures call heaven, there are, as it were, three storeys—the etherial heaven, the starry heaven, and the heaven of heavens; into this Christ, as our high priest, is entered. There was not only a change of his presence, but a translation of his body into the high and holy place.

[4.] The witnesses, the eleven apostles; these were his choice witnesses, not the whole company of believers.

[5.] Another circumstance was his last action a little before his ascension: Luke xxiv. 50, 'He blessed his disciples;' nay, it is added again, to put the greater emphasis upon it, ver. 51, 'And while he blessed them, he was parted from them, and carried up into heaven.' It is the fashion of good men to die blessing; Jacob and Moses, when they were to take their leaves of the world, they blessed the tribes. Christ, before he would go, would first leave his blessing; nay, the last act with which he would close up his life was an act of blessing, to show that now the curse was removed, and he was going to heaven to convey the blessing to all the heirs of salvation: Acts iii. 26, 'Unto you first, God having raised up his son Jesus, sent him to bless you, in turning away every one of you from his iniquities;' as God blessed Adam and Eve, when his work was done.

[6.] The manner: Acts i. 9, 'When he had spoken these things, while they beheld, he was taken up, and a cloud received him out of their sight.' The cloud answered to God's appearance in the tabernacle. When we look on the clouds, this was Christ's chariot; he will come again in like manner.

[7.] In his ascension he went to heaven as a conqueror, he triumphed over his enemies, and gave gifts to his friends: Eph. iv. 8, 'When he ascended up on high, he led captivity captive, and gave gifts unto men.' As glorious conquerors lead their chief enemies fettered in iron chains. So Col. ii. 15, 'Having spoiled principalities and powers, he made a show of them openly, triumphing over them in it,' *ἐν αὐτῷ, non sudore et sanguine aliorum, ut quondam imperatores solebant.* There is some difficulty about the exposition of that place; those seem too literally to interpret it that think there was some open pomp and show. The Papists say he went to the *limbus patrum,* and took Abraham, Isaac, Jacob, and other holy men of the Old Testament, along with him in triumph to heaven; but then he should have taken the devils. Zanchy thinks there was some real visible triumph, visible not to all, but to God, angels, and men, leading the devils through the air. Still it seemeth too gross, and to be asserted without warrant. But this must be interpreted suitably to the other acts of his office; this triumph must be referred to his ascension. Christ fought for heaven, and struck the last stroke on the cross, seized on the spoil at his resurrection, led them in triumph at his ascension, and by his quiet sitting on the throne his subjects enjoy the benefit.

[8.] Christ's entertainment by the angels. Some were left to comfort the apostles: Acts i. 10, 'While they looked steadfastly towards heaven, two men stood by in white apparel.' These two men were two angels in the shape of men. When the husband is to go a long journey, he writeth to the wife from the next stage, whilst her grief is fresh and running, and giveth an account of his welfare. Christ despatcheth two messengers out of his glorious train, which message being done, they accompany him with other angels into heaven: Dan. vii. 13, 'I saw one like the Son of man, with the clouds of heaven, and they brought him near before him.' They, that is, the angels; the Son of man, that is, Christ, as appeareth by the next verse, they wait upon him, and guard him into the presence of God. Certainly if the angels came so cheerfully to proclaim his incarnation when born, what triumph is there by that blessed company in heaven at his ascension! Still the angels are in Christ's company; when he cometh to judgment, the angels shall come with him. Christ coming into the presence of the Father, is royally attended; his entrance into heaven is glorious, with glorious applauses and acclamations: Ps. xxiv. 11, 'Lift up your heads, O ye gates, and be ye lift up, ye everlasting doors, and the king of glory shall come in;' viz., at the coming of his humanity; so Justin Martyr, Basil, Euthymius. But clearly there is an allusion to the bringing the ark into the place prepared by David for it; a figure of Christ's entrance into heaven. They applaud him as mighty in battle, as newly returned from the spoils of his enemies. The entrance of a victorious and triumphant captain is there described, and so it is proper to Christ. Once more, the blessed saints have the like applause. Isaiah describes it, Isa. lxiii. 1–3, 'Who is this that cometh from Edom, with dyed garments from Bozrah? this that is glorious in his apparel, travelling in the greatness of his strength? I that speak in righteousness, mighty to save. Wherefore art thou red in thine apparel, and thy garments like him that treadeth in the wine-fat? I have trodden the wine-press alone, and of the people there was none with me,' &c. There is a dialogue, as before, to express the saints' acclamations to Christ; the church is brought in there wondering at Christ's glorious triumph over all his enemies, as returning victorious from some bloody fight, like a great commander in goodly rich robes, besprinkled with the blood of his enemies.

[9.] The last thing is his welcome from God: Ps. ii. 8, 'I will give thee the heathen for thine inheritance,' &c.; Ps. cx. 1, 'The Lord said unto my Lord, Sit thou at my right hand, until I make thine enemies thy footstool;' compared with Mat. xxii. 44. In the day of his inauguration God will say, Welcome, Son; sit at my right hand; all the kingdoms of the earth are thine. Christ doth not only enter as a conqueror, but as a favourite : Son, thy work is well done ; sit at my right hand ; that is God's first word to him ; and then, Ask what thou wilt, it is thine. It is a fashion among great princes, when they would show great affection or extraordinary liking to any, they bid them ask what they would ; as Herod to Herodias's daughter : Mat. xiv. 6, 7, ' When Herod's birthday was kept, the daughter of Herodias danced before them, and pleased Herod : whereupon he promised with an oath to give her whatsoever she would ask.'   And Ahasuerus to Esther : Esth. v. 3, ' What wilt thou, queen Esther, and what is thy request ? it shall be even given thee, to the half of the kingdom.'

2. The reasons why.   Christ would not have gone, if it had not been expedient : John xvi. 7, ' Nevertheless, I tell you the truth, it is expedient for you that I go away.'   A woman had rather have her husband live at home than go to the Indies, but when she considereth that it is to do her good, to enrich the family by traffic, she yieldeth her consent, it is a profitable voyage.   So it is expedient that Christ should go to heaven.   In the infancy of the church Christ was present as a nurse, but he would not have them always hang on the teat.   The reasons of Christ's ascension are these :—

[1.] He is gone that we may look upon him as in a greater capacity to do us good.   All weakness is now removed from him, his human nature glorified, and placed in heaven, his majesty restored ; we may now reflect upon the glory of his person with comfort ; he is now a king on the throne, a king in his palace, and a place of royal residence.   David was king as soon as anointed by Samuel, but when he was crowned in Hebron then did he actually administer the kingdom.   Christ had his followers in the days of his flesh, as David had his four hundred companions in the desert.   The thief owned Christ upon the cross, and Christ tells him, ' This day shalt thou be with me in paradise,' Luke xxiii. 43.   What may we not expect from Christ now in heaven !   Every office is royally exercised ; as a prophet he sendeth out his Spirit ; as a king, he ruineth his adversaries ; as a priest, he intercedeth with God.

[2.] To prepare a place for us : John xiv. 2, ' I go to prepare a place for you.'   It is good to consider how Christ prepareth heaven for us by his ascension.   It was prepared before the world began, by the decree of God the Father : Mat. xxv. 34, ' Come, ye blessed of my Father, inherit a kingdom prepared for you from the foundation of the world.' This was an inheritance intended for the heirs of promise ; by a free choice he designed the persons, and their particular portion and degree of glory.   But because we are to hold heaven, not only by gift, but by purchase, Christ came from heaven to prepare it, and went to heaven again to prepare ; yet further to open the door that was before shut up ; as our head, he went to seize upon it in our right ; as our legal head, he possesseth heaven in our names ; as a guardian taketh up lands for the heir, Christ holdeth heaven in our right ; till we be ready for it, he keepeth possession.   And as our mystical head and author of grace, he dispenseth the Spirit, and maketh us fit for that place, making intercession for us, that our sins be no impediment.   He is called our forerunner : Heb. vi. 20, ' Whither the forerunner is for us entered, even Jesus, made an high priest for ever after the order of Melchisedec.' His going is to make way for us ; as our harbinger, to take up rooms and lodgings for us.   As the captain of our salvation, he hath taken up quarters for himself and all his company : Heb. ii. 10, ' It became him for whom are all things, and by whom are all things, in bringing many sons to glory, to make the captain of our salvation perfect through sufferings.'   Christ hath opened heaven's door that was shut up ; there was a guard set upon paradise, but Christ hath removed it.   He is gone to fit all things for our entertainment, as Joseph was sent into Egypt to prepare for Jacob.   Die when we will, our place is ready ; there is nothing to keep us out.   The church is tossed with waves, but Christ is gone ashore, and hath secured for us a landing-place ; and his ascension is a pledge of ours, as he rose as the firstfruits of them that slept.   It is the meritorious, exemplary, efficient cause of our ascension.

[3.] To represent his satisfaction.   The Levitical priest was to enter into the sanctuary with blood, so doth Christ into heaven, to show that he had done his work.   The apostle hath an expression which needeth opening : Heb. viii. 4, ' If he were on earth, he should not be a priest.' What is the meaning ?   Was not Christ a priest when he was on earth ?   I answer—Yes.   Why then doth the apostle say that ' if he were on earth he should not be a priest ?' that is, he could not discharge the whole office of the priesthood ; for the high priest once a year carried the sacrifice through the court before the sanctuary, and there killed it, and there took the blood thereof into the holiest of all, and presented himself before the Lord to intercede for the people : so Christ carried his sacrifice out of the city, offered it up to God, and then entered into the heavenly sanctuary, where he liveth for ever to intercede for us, and his blood always runneth fresh ; and therefore, if he were on earth he could not discharge the whole office of a priest. So Heb. ix. 24, ' For Christ is not entered into the holy places made with hands, which are the figures of the true, but into heaven itself, now to appear in the presence of God for us,' ἐμφανισθῆναι.   As the high priest entered on the behalf of the people, with the names of the twelve tribes on his breast and shoulders, so Christ is entered on the behalf of us all, bearing the memorial of every saint on his heart. Mark, the apostle saith, ' Now to appear,' not only once.   The high priest stayed not within the sanctuary, but Christ is our constant lieger in heaven, all the time from his ascension unto this day, constantly, still, while it is called *now*.

[4.] To pour out the Spirit ; John vii. 39, ' The Holy Ghost was not yet given, for Christ was not yet glorified.'   When the husband is wanting, then he sendeth tokens ; so when Christ is glorified, then he giveth out the Spirit ; as Elijah, when he ascended, let fall his mantle. Proper acts have their proper fruits.   Christ in earth established our right, and in heaven he puts us in actual possession ; the purchase was by Christ's exinanition, the application by his advancement.   It was not meet Christ should use a royal act till his advancement, and till he went to the Father ; he ascended then, that his blood might not be spilt in vain, but that he might be in a capacity to execute his own testament ; unless Christ had ascended, we needed not this supply.

3. The fruits and benefits of his ascension.

[1.] It is a sign God hath received satisfaction. His resurrection was a pledge of it, then our surety was let out of prison, the Lord sent an angel to remove the stone ; not to supply any power in Christ, but as a judge when the law is satisfied, sendeth an officer to open the prison doors with power and authority: Heb. xiii. 20, 'The God of peace, that brought again from the dead our Lord Jesus.' Christ was not to break prison. While the surety lieth in prison, the debtor can have no discharge. But now Christ's ascension gives a further degree of assurance. Christ is not only taken out of prison, but taken up to God with glory and honour. God hath taken up our surety to himself, and rewarded him. Christ hath perfectly done his work, or else he had never been taken out of the grave, much less taken up to God. God is well pleased with him ; he hath not only a discharge, but a reward. Christ is said not only to ascend, but to be received into glory, 1 Tim. iii. 16, ἀνέβη, ἀνελήφθη, an active, and a passive word ; the one noteth the power of his godhead, the other noteth the grant of the Father. Christ took upon him the quality of our surety, and he must pay every farthing ere he can go to his Father. It is a sufficient pledge : John xvi. 10, ' Of righteousness, because I go to the Father, and ye see me no more.' Thus there was an everlasting righteousness established ; he was never to see God's face more if he had not perfectly done his work : Gen. xliii. 5, 'Ye shall not see my face, except your brother be with you.' He is God's favourite.

[2.] It is a pledge of our ascension: John iii. 13, 'No man hath ascended up to heaven, but he that came down from heaven, even the Son of man that is in heaven.' *Ascendit solus, sed non totus.* Head and members must be together ; our head being there before, the members must follow after. Christ speaketh as if he were not content with his own heaven without us : ver. 24, 'Father, I will that they also whom thou hast given me be with me where I am, that they may behold my glory which thou hast given me.' Christ took our flesh to heaven, and left his Spirit, which is an earnest of our glory : 2 Cor. v. 5, 'He hath given unto us the earnest of the Spirit.' God never taketh anything from his children, but he sendeth them a better thing in the room of it.

[3.] We have an intercessor at God's right hand, a favourite in the court of heaven : 1 John ii. 1, 'If any man sin, we have an advocate with the Father, even Jesus Christ the righteous ;' as when offenders have a favourite in court. We need a mediator in heaven ; he is gone to disannul all Satan's accusation. The sacrificing part is done and ended, and his intercession now taketh place. We have these two great advantages in prayer—Christ is our advocate, and the Spirit our notary.

Use 1. Information.

1. It informeth us of the privileges of God's children. When a child of God dieth, he doth but go to his Father. Christ and we have the same relation : John xx. 17, 'I ascend unto my Father and your Father, to my God and your God.' He is no more in the world, but still he is. He doth not say, 'I am no more,' but 'I am no more in the world ;' they do not leave life, but the world. As Christ was the Son of God by nature, they are the sons of God by grace, and when they die, they go to their heavenly Father, to a sweet rest, to the bosom

of God. The same entertainment Christ had, we shall have, a joyful entertainment, a sweet welcome when we come to heaven, and the conduct of angels thither: Luke xvi. 22, 'The beggar died, and was carried by the angels into Abraham's bosom.' God will take us as it were by the hand, with a 'Well done, good and faithful servant; thou hast been faithful over a few things, I will make thee ruler over many things, enter thou into the joy of thy Lord,' Mat. xxv. 21.

2. It informeth us that all that Christ did was for a believer's use and comfort; if he cometh into the world, it is to merit; if he ascendeth into heaven, it is to apply. He descended from heaven for the redemption of man; after that work is accomplished, he ascendeth thither again to bestow it on us; and at the last day he will come again and fetch his bride; as when all things are ready, the heir cometh in person to fetch the bride into his father's house. Going, coming, staying, still Christ is ours. He was born for us, he lived for us, he rose again and ascended for us: it is for our good that he went away; whatever he did, in his abasement and exaltation, it was for our good.

3. It informeth us that the greatest comforts may be supplied, Christ's corporal presence by the presence of the Spirit: 2 Cor. i. 5, 'That as our sufferings in Christ Jesus have abounded, so our consolation also hath abounded through Christ.' They should lose nothing by his departure: John xiv. 16, 'I will pray the Father, and he shall give you another comforter, that he may abide with you for ever.' He would not leave them orphans. We cannot be made unhappy by the want of any outward comfort; we have the more of God, the less we have of these outward helps. If the corporal presence of Christ can be recompensed by the presence of the Spirit, certainly lesser supports of life will be recompensed.

Use 2. Exhortation.

1. To all sorts of persons to get an interest in Christ, and to clear it up to their souls. How sweet would it be if when we are no more to be in this world, we could say, 'Holy Father, I come to thee!' We all affect this, 'Let my latter end be like his,' as Balaam spake. *At oportuit sic vixisse.* An evidence of this is, if you ascend with Christ: Eph. ii. 6, 'He hath raised us up together, and made us sit together in heavenly places in Christ Jesus.' Head and heart ought to be together. Your head is in heaven; if your heart be there too, you are members of his mystical body. How shall a man know that he is ascended with Christ?—

[1.] If the things of the world seem small; as when we are in a high place, men seem as ants. Worldly glory will appear to be small, and worldly profits small. But when we are upon earth, heavenly things seem small, as stars appear but as spangles.

[2.] If you behave yourselves to him as to a glorified person. Do you serve him? John xii. 26, 'If any man serve me, let him follow me, and where I am, there shall my servant be. If any man serve me, him will my Father honour.' Carnal men crucify him again.

[3.] If you keep yourselves 'unspotted from the world,' James i. 26. No unclean thing shall enter into heaven. The world is a defiling thing; that filth that cleaveth to our fingers in telling of money is an emblem of the filthiness of the world. A man that looketh to be like Christ in glory certainly would not defile himself in the world. If a prince marry a mean woman, would he endure to see her live like a scullion? Christ hath married our nature. A man that loveth the world, and would always live here, is like a scullion that lieth among the pots. Would you yourselves hug nastiness, and embrace the dunghill?

2. To press God's children to be holy and heavenly in their minds, to wean their affections from the world. We should be where Christ is: Phil. iii. 20, 'Our conversation is in heaven, whence we look for the Saviour, the Lord Jesus Christ;' Col. iii. 1, 'If ye then be risen with Christ, seek those things which are above, where Christ sits at the right hand of God.' Who would not desire to be in heaven now Christ is there? As the loadstone draws iron to it, let us be present in heaven, as Christ is present on the earth by the Spirit. Though our bodies are tied with the fetters of the flesh, yet let our souls ascend, let our minds be there, our wishes, our desires there; by these means we walk in heaven before our time. A stone, though it breaks to pieces by the fall, will move to its centre; though we naturally abhor death, we should desire it to be with Christ. It is a shame that a stone should be carried with greater force to its centre than we to Christ.

Use 3. Comfort. We have Christ for us in the heavens: Heb. iv. 14, 'Seeing therefore that we have a great high priest that is passed into the heavens, Jesus the Son of God.' We have Christ always for us in heaven; he hath a part of his office to perform there. His absence doth not hinder us from having a right to him, or a spiritual possession of him. He is ours, and he hath his residence in heaven, and hath power to open it to us and give us entrance. His high honour doth not hinder him from the discharge of his office to do us good. He is at God's right hand, and yet 'a minister of the sanctuary.' Christ hath a ministry, and part of his service to perform in heaven; is our faithful agent: Heb. viii. 1, 2, 'We have such a high priest who is set on the right hand of the throne of the Majesty in the heavens, a minister of the sanctuary.' For all his glory, Christ is called τῶν ἁγίων λειτουργὸς, a minister of holy things; he taketh care of all holy things which we present to God, and to convey holy and spiritual things to us. Christ is not stately: many forget their poor friends when advanced; Christ regardeth his poor church as much as ever. The butler, when he was advanced, forgot Joseph: but he remembereth us; he disdaineth not to look after every poor christian: Heb. iv. 15, 'We have not a high priest which cannot be touched with the feeling of our infirmities.' His heart is not changed by his honour, but he in a greater capacity to do us good. Having such a friend in heaven, we need not fear a foe upon earth. Heaven is open for us: Heb. x. 19, 20, 'Having boldness to enter into the holiest by the blood of Jesus, by a new and living way which he hath consecrated for us, through the vail, that is to say, his flesh.'

Use 4. Direction in the sacrament. If we have anything to do with Christ, we know where to seek him: 'Blessed are they that believe, and have not seen,' John xx. 19. Those that are far from court never saw the king. God hath removed Christ out of sight that we might behold him by faith. Let us look for him in the sacrament, not for his bodily presence.   How can he be there bodily, when he is received into glory?   But for his spiritual presence, the influences of his grace, and a derivation of virtue from his person.

Secondly.   The next point is the necessary ceasing of his corporal presence upon his ascension : 'I am no more in the world, but these are in the world.'   Let us see the reason why he will be no more with us.   Now the reasons why Christ would withdraw his bodily presence from us are these :—

1. That he might try the world, and yet in a way suitable to his glorious estate.   Christ, when he came to try the Jews, he came in disguise, not as the Son of God, in majesty and glory : John i. 11, ' He came unto his own, and his own received him not.'   Still to try men's obedience there must be some veil.   If he should be present in the world, in a glorious way becoming his majesty and empire, there would be no trial ; and therefore in a manner he still cometh in disguise, his glory is veiled under the ministry of men, and carried on in a spiritual manner.   If he should appear in glory and power, sinners durst not quack, and so the wickedness of man would not be discovered, nor would the faith of his people be exercised with such praise and honour if he were personally and gloriously present.   This is the commendation and praise of christianity, that they can 'walk by faith' when they cannot 'walk by sight;' 2 Cor. v. 7, 'We walk by faith, not by sight.'   They see not Christ, because he is absent in body ; yet they believe in him, and love him, and send their hearts after him.   So 1 Peter i. 8, 'Whom having not seen ye love; in whom, though now ye see him not, yet believing, ye rejoice with joy unspeakable and full of glory.'   Faith is eagle-eyed, and can look above the clouds.   The absence of Christ did not prejudice their comfort and hope.   Faith contenteth itself with an intellectual sight and certainty. This is a trial of christians, when they can believe in Christ, and rejoice in Christ as if they did see him with their bodily eyes, and hear him with their bodily ears.   *Ibi figunt desiderium, quo nequeunt inferre conspectum*, saith Leo—They fasten their hearts upon him, though they cannot fasten their eyes.   Faith is sight enough.   Thus would Christ try the world ; but yet, as I said, in a way suitable to his glorious estate. If he should still have continued his body among us in that state of weakness wherein he conversed in the world, his holy body would still be subject to abuse, and the injuries and scorn of wicked men, which would not agree with his glorification ; and therefore, after his resurrection, he only showed his body to some few chosen witnesses, and so departed into heaven, that it might be no more seen, till he cometh to the last judgment with glory and power.   So Christ himself saith, Mat. xxiii. 39, ' Ye shall not see me henceforth till ye shall say, Blessed is he that cometh in the name of the Lord ;' that is, till ye be compelled to say so, though now ye are angry at the children that welcomed me in this manner : Mat. xxvi. 64, 'Hereafter shall ye see the Son of man sitting on the right hand of power, and coming in the clouds of heaven.' Never till then, after I am taken down from the cross and buried.

2. That way might be made for his spiritual presence.   Some presence of Christ there must be for our comfort and safety : ' I will not leave you comfortless, ὀρφάνους, but will come unto you,' John xiv. 18.

That Christ is still spiritually present with the church is clear by those promises to the apostles and to believers. To the apostles and their successors: Mat. xxviii. 20, 'I am with you always, to the end of the world.' Into whatsoever place and time of the world our lot is cast, we may have an assurance of Christ's presence, that is, of his assistance and blessing, as much as if he were actually and corporally present with us. To ministers: now if they improve their interest, they might have Christ in their company, as the apostles had; they are taken into the same patent and charter. So also to all believers: Mat. xviii. 20, 'Wherever two or three are met together in my name, I am present in the midst of them.' Whenever we are met together in any religious work and business, Christ's gracious presence is with us; in this sense he will never depart from believers. Now this gracious presence was not vouchsafed till his corporal presence was removed. Partly because Christ will do nothing unnecessarily. When he was personally present, to solve their doubts, to instruct them in all cases, the Spirit was not poured out in such abundance; as it is usual still with God to make up to us in spiritual supplies what we want in outward helps. Partly because his disciples had carnal thoughts of his bodily presence, and rested in it, which was to be confuted by his absence. Partly to make way for his unlimited universal influence; his bodily presence could only be in some places; but now he is ascended, 'he filleth all things,' Eph. iv. 10. As the sun, if it should come down and shine on one particular field, it could not diffuse its beams far and near; but now it is fixed in the firmament, nothing is hidden from its light. So Christ exalted, scattereth his beams and influences everywhere, into all parts and corners of the world. Partly because it was meet that Christ should enter into his glory and kingdom, before he declared his efficacy to men by the more plentiful pouring out the Spirit; as princes use at their coronation to give gifts and send abroad ambassadors. So when Christ was in his royal palace, 'he gave gifts unto men, and he gave some, apostles; and some, prophets; and some, evangelists; and some, pastors and teachers,' Eph. iv. 8–11.

Use 1. For confutation of the Lutherans, who, to establish their doctrine of consubstantiation, make Christ's ascension to be, not a local remove, but only a change of the manner of his presence; they say he is still corporally present, but not visibly; as if the human nature of Christ were made invisibly omnipresent, and not locally removed and carried into heaven. This is a doctrine contrary to scriptures; for it is expressly said, Acts i. 11, that 'he was taken up into heaven.' And by virtue of this taking up he is no more in the world, no more in the earth, nor in any place thereof; for it is said, Acts iii. 21, 'That the heavens must contain him till the time of the restitution of all things;' there is his personal presence fixed. And therefore 'if any say, Lo here, or Lo there, believe him not.' It is flatly contradictory to scripture that Christ should be corporally present on earth till he cometh to judgment; and it is contrary to the truth of Christ's body; though it be glorified, it is not deified; a body cannot be omnipresent and without quantity, for then it is no more a body. And it is a doctrine barren, and of no use; the presence of Christ's body is not so absolutely necessary to the comfort of a christian : John vi. 63, ' It is the Spirit that quickeneth, the flesh profiteth nothing.' Nearness or distance of place doth not help or hinder his presence with us or efficacy upon us. The degree of his gracious operation doth not depend upon the degree of his personal presence ; as if Christ were like the sun, shining more or less hot according to the difference of his posture and situation. Christ doth not work like a natural agent, by contact, but according to his free pleasure, and the wise dispensation of his own will ; and our communion with him is wholly spiritual and mystical, not gross and carnal : ' The flesh profiteth nothing.' Yea, it is against our comfort. Christ hath business to do for us in heaven, and it is our advantage that he is no more in the world. If he were not in heaven, he were not a priest : Heb. viii. 4, ' If he were on earth, he could not be a priest.' And again, Heb. vii. 26, we had need of a priest ' who is made higher than the heavens ; ' that is, that is ascended into the third heaven, those ἀχειροποίητα ἅγια, ' those holy places not made with hands, now to appear in the presence of God for us,' Heb. ix. 24. But to leave this.

Use 2. To press christians to look for the spiritual presence of Christ, though they do not enjoy his bodily. You may make use of Christ, now he is in heaven, as the disciples did on earth, to ask him questions, to seek his counsel, to commend your prayers and persons to God. It is no disadvantage to faith that Christ is removed out of sight, but only an occasion given whereby it may discover itself with more praise. Therefore let us believe in Christ, though we see him not ; we shall one day see him in the heavens to our comfort, and to the terror of the wicked ; in the meantime, let faith serve instead of vision. It will be your commendation, ' whom having not seen, ye love,' 1 Peter i. 8. God hath removed Christ out of sight, to make way for the exercise of faith and love ; and it is much better by faith to converse with him in heaven, than by sight to see him upon earth : John xx. 29, ' Blessed are they that have not seen, and yet believe.' Thomas would make his senses the judge ; he must feel the wounds, and put his finger in the print of the nails, and thrust his hand into his side ; which discovered the weakness of his faith. Faith is not grounded on sense, but testimony. Be not discouraged, though you never saw him in the flesh, you shall one day see him in heaven ; though you could not hear his gracious words, yet you have whispers and counsels from his Spirit. You saw him not hanging on the cross, yet ' he is crucified before your eyes,' Gal. iii. 1. In the word and sacraments he is notably and plainly laid forth to faith. The gospel is a magical glass, as it were, wherein God will have the soul look, that we may see our absent friend, *sic oculos, sic ille manus, sic ora ferebat ;* there are the very postures of Christ. Therefore let us make use of our present advantages ; you may expect as powerful influences from him as if present in person ; as the sun doth not come down from heaven, but only his influence. There is a derivation of virtue from his person ; yea, Christ is not like the sun ; the farther absent from us in body, the more powerful is his influence : Eph. iv. 10, ' When he ascended up on high, he filled all things.' Briefly then, if you have anything to do with Christ, you know where to seek him. Those

that live far from court, never saw their king, yet they enjoy the benefit
of his government, and are bound to allegiance.   Christ is as meek, as
gentle, as easy to be entreated as ever.

Use 3. For the conviction of them that please themselves in fond
wishes and excuses; they think that if they had lived in the days of
Christ's flesh, and had heard his words, full of grace and wisdom, it
could not have been but they should have believed in him; they would
never have crucified him, as the carnal Jews, and never have rejected
his person and doctrine.   Thus they bind the efficacy and virtue of
Christ to his corporal presence; as if it would have been a greater
advantage to them than his spiritual.   A great deceit of the heart!
This plea proceedeth upon a false supposal, as if Christ's virtue
depended upon the nearness and distance of place.   If there be any
difference, now in heaven he is most apt to work, because he is entered
upon his royalty, and the actual exercise of his kingdom.   The apostles
themselves, when they had Christ's presence, were more gross, dull,
and carnal; but afterwards they savoured nothing but heaven and
life eternal.   And again, it is usual for men to dislike present dispensations, and betray their duties by their wishes.   Alas! if Christ were
now present in the form of a servant, what sorry entertainment would
most give him!   We think we should not have done what the Jews
did; in probability we would have done worse: you grieve his Spirit
as much as they did affront his person; the malice of the Jews was
more gross, but ours is as inexcusable.   Besides, there is a natural
reverence that even hypocrites will bear to their godly ancestors:
Mat. xxiii. 29, 30, 'Woe unto you scribes and pharisees, hypocrites;
because ye build the tombs of the prophets, and garnish the sepulchres
of the righteous, and say, If we had been in the days of our fathers,
we would not have been partakers with them in the blood of the
prophets.'   Dead things and persons do not exasperate and cross
present interests; the prophets, that lived in their ancestors' days,
were out of sight, no eyesore to present practices, their speeches were
not personally directed to them.   The worst men usually honour the
dead, but are injurious to the living.   As much as we detest the
memory of Annas and Caiphas, so do they of Korah, Dathan, and
Abiram.   The name of Judas is not more odious to us than Ahab to
them; therefore our detestation of the Jews, or longing for the person
of Christ, is no argument of great devotion to him.

SERMON XV.

And now I am no more in the world, but these are in the world, and
I come to thee   Holy Father, keep through thine own name
those whom thou hast given me, that they may be one, as we
are.—JOHN XVII. 11.

THIRDLY, The next point is taken from that clause, 'But these are
in the world.'   Christ's apprehensiveness of the danger of believers in
their worldly state.

In managing this argument—(1.) I will open the danger; (2.) Why God permitteth it; (1.) Christ's apprehensiveness of it.

1. To open the danger. There is danger from within and from without; within are lusts, and without are temptations; they are subject to many infirmities, and exposed to infinite dangers and temptations.

[1.] From within. If we could live as fish in the salt sea, fresh, without any taint of saltness, without receiving a savour from things without, the danger would not be so great.: 2 Peter i. 4, 'Having escaped the corruption that is in the world through lust;' the root of the matter is within us. The world without would do no harm were it not for the world in our own hearts. Pleasures, honours, profits are dangerous snares, but not to an angel. When John reckoneth up the contents of the world, he doth not reckon up the objects, but the lusts: 1 John ii. 16, ' The lust of the flesh, the lust of the eye, and the pride of life.' Satan is our enemy, the world is the bait, but our heart is the traitor. Baalam could not hurt Israel till he corrupted them by whoredoms. The worst enemy is within us; we carry the danger in our own bosoms. We must look for blows in the world, but inward ulcers are worse than wounds, because the evil is inward, and the constitution of the body helpeth it. Sins are more dangerous than troubles, because they are aided by nature.

[2.] From without. The world is an evil place, both in regard of sin and misery; we are sure to be vexed or defiled, to be corrupted by the favours or discouraged by the frowns of it. In the world we have a great many enemies; there is the god of the world, and the powers of the world, and the men of the world, and the things of the world.

(1.) There is the god of this world. This country in which we dwell, it is the kingdom of Satan, Christ's bitter enemy. He is called ' the prince of the world,' John xii. 31, not by right, but the world hath made him so. Can God's children live long in peace in the kingdom of Satan? He cannot endure to lose one corner of his empire, therefore frowns and flatters, and seeks to corrupt or discourage the saints: 2 Cor. iv. 4, ' The god of this world hath blinded the eyes of them that believe not.' Titles are suited to the matter in hand. Satan blindeth most, as the god of this world; the creature is but suborned, Satan is at the back of it, and lieth in ambush to surprise our souls; ' Is not the hand of Joab in all this?' The devil is in the snare. The world is Satan's chessboard; we can hardly move back or forth but the devil sets out one creature or another to attack us, either by fear, causing us to draw back, or by the love of some worldly creatures alluring us out of the lists wherein we should walk.

(2.) The powers of the world; usually they are set against Christ, and therefore at the latter end of the world they shall be broken and dashed to pieces. The world is a country wherein the church is a stranger; every man fearing God is like a strange plant brought from a far country, hath much ado to grow. The wicked are like nettles and thistles, that grow without ploughing or watering, because they grow in their own place; but the soil and air of the world doth not suit with the saints; one time or other they are nipped, here is no kindly weather for them. A christian is not only a stranger, but an unconformist to the world : Rom. xii. 2, 'And be ye not conformed to this world, but be ye transformed in the renewing of your minds.' In every age there is something or other started up for his trouble and exercise. In his Father's house he is taught to do otherwise, and this putteth him upon trouble. If God giveth the church a little rest, it is but like a well day out of the fit of an ague, to recover strength for the next trial; a mortified saint, that is drawn up to heaven, and would live by the laws of his Father's house, must look for frowns : 'Yea, and all those that will live godly in Christ Jesus must suffer persecution,' 2 Tim. iii. 12. Christ's grapes must expect the winepress; all their care should be to yield good liquor. It is a statute, like the laws of the Medes and Persians : Acts xiv. 22, 'That through many tribulations we must enter into the kingdom of God.' Neither doth experience cross that rule; the apostle saith, Rom. viii. 35, 36, 'Who shall separate us from the love of God? shall tribulation, or distress, or persecution, or famine, or nakedness, or peril, or sword? As it is written, For thy sake we are killed all the day long, we are accounted as sheep for the slaughter.' The world is the slaughter-house and shambles of the saints ; here Christ was slain, all his witnesses butchered. Christ's lambs must look to have their throats cut. There is an old enmity between the seed of the woman and the seed of the serpent; it lasteth from Abel till the day of judgment. Jacob's and Esau's quarrel began from the day of their birth : Ps. cxxix. 1, 'Many a time have they afflicted me from my youth, may Israel now say;' from my youth upward, ever since Christ had a seed in the world. The world would not be the world, nor you christians, if the world did not hate you. Satan cannot change his nature, and the world waxeth worse and worse. Instead of marvelling to see the children of God afflicted and persecuted, we should marvel to see it otherwise. If one should tell you that your way lieth through a stony country, full of bushes and briars, you would think yourselves out of the way if you should meet with nothing but green and pleasant plains. The roadway to heaven is through a howling wilderness; if you have a foot of good land, it is God's blessing.

(3.) The men of the world. A man cannot hold any communion with them, but he shall be the worse for them : 1 John v. 19, 'We know we are of God, and the whole world lieth in wickedness.' The men of the world are sooty dirty creatures; we cannot,converse with them, but they leave their filthiness upon us. It is hard to touch pitch and not be defiled : Acts ii. 40, 'Save yourselves from this untoward generation.' We grow in a wilderness, and there are many crooked trees that are like to twine about us, and to hinder our growth towards heaven. To disentangle ourselves, there must be a great deal of care. So 2 Tim. ii. 21, 'If a man, therefore, purge himself from these, he shall be a vessel unto honour.' 'From these;' from what? In a great house, there are vessels of gold and vessels of earth, some to honour, and some to dishonour. There are carnal seducers that are apt to pervert us by their enticement and example, as black pots leave their soil upon those that touch them ; so base persons and carnal heretics infect us with their sinful pollutions. By converse we are tainted unawares; as antinomian doctrines make the children of God less strict; though they do not pervert their judgment, yet they weaken their care and strictness. Nature is more susceptible of evil than of good. We easily catch a sickness, but we do not get health from one another. Ears of corn do not catch and hang upon men, but thorns do: Phil. ii. 15, 'We live in the midst of a crooked and perverse generation,' that are as briars and thorns, very catching.

(4.) The things of this world. The world is the valley of snares, and so to the children of God it often proveth the valley of sorrows. Frequency of converse maketh the snare more easily to insinuate. It is hard to be much conversant in any matter, and not to receive some tincture from it. These things, honours, pleasures, profits, they are accustomed objects, they are bred up with us; we must of necessity be conversant with meats and drinks and worldly substance, and insensibly they leave a taint upon the soul, especially where we have them at full. Worldly prosperity is a great snare to the saints; and things are better preserved in brine than honey. How soon is the soul corrupted. The warm sunshine maketh the weeds grow as well as the flowers. I observe great alterations in David's spirit; in adversity he spared his enemy, when he found Saul in the cave; in prosperity, he killed his servant, when he plotted Uriah's death; when he threatened Nabal in affliction, he bore with Shimei. God's children have a better country when they have the world's best advantages. Some fruits are not natural in England; though the weather be good, they do not agree with the soil.

2. Why God permitteth them to be in the world; he might have taken them to himself, and glorify them as soon as sanctify them, or else have gathered them into some island, some obscure angle and corner of the world, out of harm's way. But I answer—That doth not suit with God's dispensations: John xvii. 15, 'I pray not that thou wouldst take them out of the world, but that thou shouldst keep them from the evil.' The Lord hath some ends to be accomplished. He can at first conversion make us perfect and glorified saints; it is his wisdom to take a time; as Absalom was not to see the king's face presently, so we must wait our time.

[1.] For his own glory. The sweetness and power of grace is more discovered in this worldly estate. It is more wonder to maintain a candle in a bucket of water than in a lanthorn, or a spark in the midst of the sea: 'God's power is made perfect in weakness,' 2 Cor. xii. 9; that is, it is more gloriously discovered. Excellent things suffer a kind of imperfection till there be an occasion to discover them; therefore the apostle would glory in infirmities, as they occasioned a greater exercise of the divine grace. In this worldly estate, grace is discovered not only by its operation, but by conquest and victory; not only as it worketh, but as it fighteth: 1 John iv. 4, 5, 'Ye are of God, little children, and have overcome them, because greater is he that is in you than he that is in the world: they are of the world, therefore speak they of the world, and the world heareth them.' There is a spirit that worketh in the saints, and a spirit that worketh in the world; these two are conflicting; the world is the lists and place of battle, but Satan is beaten in his own territory: 'Stronger is he that is in you than he that is in the world.' The saints may be molested, but not overcome. Still God hath his elect, and Christ his members, though Satan hath so many factors and agents for his kingdom. Look, as Israel was sent into Egypt that God's power might be made known—'For this cause have I raised thee up, for to show in thee my power, and that my name may be declared throughout all the earth,' saith God to Pharaoh, Exod. ix. 16—so we are in the world that his power may be known. We had missed many wonderful passages of providence if Israel had not been in Egypt. God will have us take many experiences of the sweetness and power of grace along with us to heaven. As travellers at night talk of the foul way and the dangers of the journey, so in heaven we shall discourse of the praises of our Redeemer, and his wise and powerful conduct. God would have us take these frequent experiences of grace along with us.

[2.] To try us. Were it not for the worldly state, there would be no place for temptation, nor room for the exercise of grace. He will not glorify us as soon as convert us; neither can we expect to go singing to heaven, and without blows: Heb. vi. 12, 'Be ye followers of them who through faith and patience have inherited the promises.' Never any went to heaven, but there was a time to exercise both his faith and patience; we are to run and fight, this is common to all the saints. In the way to heaven many things will befall us, that will make it seem unlikely that we shall ever come thither; so we have need of faith; and troubles must have their turn ere heaven be possessed, so we have need of patience. Why should we look for a peculiar privilege? 1 Peter v. 9, 'The same afflictions are accomplished in your brethren that are in the world.' All the saints are troubled with a busy devil, a naughty world, and a corrupt heart. Name but one saint of God that hath been excused, that went to heaven without trials and temptations. That quiet estate which you dream of is without precedent. The cross is the badge of this society; as Elijah said, 'Am I better than my fathers?' You are not better than all the saints, than your other brethren that are in the world. You should be ashamed to be alone, and never called out to exercise. There is a measure of sufferings appointed, and every member must take his share. It is distributed by a wise hand, so much for the head, so much for the shoulders, so much for hands and feet: Col. i. 24, 'Who now rejoice in my sufferings for you, and fill up that which is behind of the afflictions of Christ in my flesh.' Would we only be irregular, and refuse to take our burden? Briefly, there would be no temptation, no trial, were it not for the worldly estate, but here we must look for it. The skill of a mariner is known in a storm, and so is our fortitude and other graces tried and discovered. I have read in the lives of the fathers of a devout man that being one year without any trial, cried out, *Domine, reliquisti me, quia non me visitasti hoc anno*—Lord! thou hast forgotten me, and for a whole year hast not put me upon any exercise. Those whom God will make most perfect, he putteth them upon the greatest trials. Abraham had never been represented as the father of the faithful if he had not been exercised so much, with so many hazards and temptations.

[3.] To convince the world by their example, their strictness, patience, fortitude. They are in the world, but not of the world. If a christian were not a member of the world, he would never be the wonder of the world. They have flesh and blood as others have, and have not divested themselves of the affections and interests of nature; the same bodies, the same interests; yet they can deny all, and upon the convenient reasons of religion abhor the pleasures and dear contentments of this life, and become weaned, mortified, strict, holy; and this raiseth the world's wonder: 1 Peter iv. 4, 'They think it strange that you run not with them to all excess of riot, speaking evil of you.' They are so bewitched with these things that they wonder how any can resist the temptation. Godly men are to walk up and down the world as God's witnesses: 'Ye are my witnesses, saith the Lord,' Isa. xliii. 11. They testify that there is a reality in religion, and how it worketh, by the strictness and mortification of their lives. They are to be examples to the world: 2 Cor. iii. 3, 'Ye are the epistle of Christ, ministered by us, written not with ink, but with the spirit of the living God, not in tables of stone, but in fleshly tables of the heart.' By your lives God writeth his mind to the world; you are a living rule, a walking Bible.

[4.] To fit them for glory. We do not commence *per saltum*. Vessels of honour must be seasoned: Col. i. 12, 'Who hath made us meet to be partakers of the inheritance of the saints in light.' What should an unmortified man do in heaven? Heaven would be a prison to him, the company of God and the communion of saints a burden. We do not come into God's presence hot and reeking from our lusts; we are first set in the garden of the church before we are transplanted to the upper paradise; they grow a while in the land of grace, that they may take kindly with the soil.

(1.) Partly to weaken our desires to the world. The stones were to be hewed and squared before they were to be set in the temple; there was no noise of axe or hammer heard there. So during our worldly state we are humbled with many afflictions, that we may be weaned by degrees from the world and worldly objects: Gal. vi. 14, 'God forbid that I should glory, save in the cross of Jesus Christ, by whom the world is crucified to me, and I unto the world.' The world doth not suit with the saints, as children are weaned from the teat by wormwood: when men are pleased in the world they forget their country. We stir liquors and syrups that are over the fire, that they may not stick and burn to. As Esther, when she was chosen for Ahasuerus's bride, was 'to accomplish the months of her purification' before she was presented to him, Esther ii. 12; so some days are to be spent in our purifying and sanctifying before we are presented to God.

(2.) Partly to make us long for glory. Our worldly estate is cumbersome; here are sins and afflictions, that we may long for a better estate: Ps. cxx. 5, 'Woe is me that I sojourn in Mesech, that I dwell in the tents of Kedar!' As the Israelites' task was doubled, that they might long for Canaan and cry out for the land of rest. The inconveniences of our pilgrimage make the everlasting estate more sweet; troubles without us, diseases upon us, and sins within us, and all to make us long for home. Notwithstanding all the hard usage and entertainment in the world, how difficultly are we weaned!

3. Christ's apprehensiveness of this danger. You shall see it is a circumstance often mentioned: a little before his death, at his death, now in heaven.

[1.] A little before his death. We have two instances—one when he was about to wash his disciples' feet and institute the supper: John xiii. 1, 'Jesus having loved his own that were in the world, he loved them unto the end.' Christ was then thinking that he should shortly depart; his thoughts were not on his own glory so much as our danger. If Christ would have thought of his own, he might have thought of the angels and glorified saints. Cyril and Chrysostom observe that he did not think of angels and glorified saints, but of his own in the world, those that were left to the miseries and temptations of an evil and unquiet world. No question it was sweet to Christ to think of the glorified saints and angels; but they were safe, and now was a time to show pity rather than delight. The other instance we have in his prayers in this place, from the 11th to the 17th verse. I might mention many passages in his sermons. Christ, when he was about to leave us, he had the affection of a father to his children, or of a dying husband to his wife; he was careful of our estate after his departure.

[2.] So at his death. A great thing that was in the eye of Christ was victory over the world: Gal. i. 4, 'He gave himself for us, to redeem us from the present evil world.' Certainly Christ is willing to help you, when he suffered so much that he might help you. When you love the world, you cross the end of Christ's death; his whole life was but a renouncing the world. The poverty of Christ upbraideth our aspiring projects and pursuits of worldly greatness. We seek to join house to house and field to field, and 'he had not a place whereon to lay his head.' But in his death he would make all sure. One thing that he purchased of the Father is grace to subdue the world. When he was to die, he said, Lo I give myself, upon condition thou wilt give them grace; let them be freed from the bondage of carnal fears and carnal desires. There is not a thing more answerable to the design and aim of his death than this is.

[3.] After his death and ascension into heaven, he is tenderly affected toward believers in the world; he still retaineth his human nature and his human affections, the same heart and the same pity: Heb. iv. 15, 'We have not a high priest that cannot be touched with the feeling of our infirmities.' Christ, though he be exalted, is tenderly affected towards those that are left behind; he is still tenderly affected towards you in all your straits and troubles and infirmities. Christ's exaltation hath made no change in his bowels; he carried his love with him, not only into the grave, but into heaven; he is our Lord, but still our brother: as God, he knoweth our infirmities; and as man, he feeleth them; his love is most at work when you are in danger. Oh! what a comfort is this in all your temptations! There is one in heaven that seeth and feeleth all this; let us bear it the better, and ride out the storm. If a man were persuaded that his friends on shore knew what tempests he endured at sea, and were praying for him, it would be a great comfort to him in his distress. Christ's heart worketh towards thee; he who is always heard is now praying for thee in heaven; he is touched with a feeling of thy infirmities. How should this comfort us! They have many snares and many enemies; Lord, help them!

The reasons of this apprehensiveness and tender feeling are his interest, love, charge, and experience: they are his own: John xiii. 1, 'Having loved his own that were in the world, he loved them to the end.'

(1.) His interest. Christ hath a share going in every believer. As when there are ships at sea in which you have a share, you pray for their safe return, and are tenderly affected when you hear they are in danger. Christ is loath to lose his share; he had but now pleaded his interest with the Father: ver. 10, 'All thine are mine, and mine are thine.' We are a part of his goods; the world would weaken the estate of Christ. Believers are his treasure, and they are in danger of rocks and pirates; and therefore he prayeth to the Father. Now Christ hath an interest in them, not only by the Father's grant, but their own dedication; they are his, and all that they suffer is for his sake: ver. 14, 'I have given them thy word, and therefore the world hateth them.' Let a man go on in a wicked, carnal, ungodly way, and the world will not vex him. Let a man once be zealous for Christ, and then he must expect trouble enough. They endure all this for me, and shall I not be sensible? If a child should inadvertently break his leg or arm, you would pity him; but if he should break his leg or arm in your service or defence, to rescue his father, you would pity him more.

(2.) His love: John xiii. 1, 'Jesus having loved his own which were in the world, he loved them to the end.' Those whom we love, we are troubled about their welfare. A careless father may die, and never be troubled what shall become of his children; but love is very solicitous. Alas! poor orphans, they are without a guide and guardian, left to snares and temptations, and shall it not pity them? Hugo crieth out, *O charitas, quam magnum est vinculum tuum! Deum in terram traxisti, cruci affixisti, sepulchro clausisti!* &c.—O love, how great is thy power! it was love that brought Christ from heaven, that nailed him to the cross, that laid him in the grave, that carried him again to do our business with God. Had it not been for love he had never come from heaven, and left the bosom of the Father for the lap of the virgin, the form of God for the veil of flesh, the glory of heaven for the darkness of the grave. Had it not been for love, he had never died to deliver us from this present evil world, he had never been sensible of our state and condition. Love is jealous and sensible of all the dangers of the party beloved; the same love of Christ that exposeth us to troubles and hazards for Christ's sake, the same love maketh Christ compassionate of our miseries and sorrows. We are jealous of his honour, and he is jealous of our safety.

(3.) His charge. Christ hath taken an office upon him, to defend, pity, and guide the elect through all temptations to salvation. Now Christ cannot be unfaithful in his office: Heb. iv. 15, 'We have not a high priest that cannot be touched with the feeling of our infirmities.' He that is passed into the heavens is still our high priest. Give me leave to admire that expression, Heb. viii. 2, λειτουργὸς τῶν ἁγίων, 'a minister of the sanctuary.' When he was upon earth he came in the form of a servant, and now he is in heaven he is still a servant. We may speak what Christ hath spoken for us, he is our officer and minister even in heaven, not only in the state of his abasement, but in the state of his exaltation. Our Lord would be ours, not only in love but duty, that so we might have the greater assurance. Till all the saints come to heaven, Christ looks upon himself as bound in point of office, they are his charge; he cannot be loving to the church, nor faithful to the Father, if he should do otherwise.

(4.) His experience: Heb. iv. 15, 'He is touched with the feeling of our infirmities, was in all points tempted as we are, yet without sin.' Pray mark, 'in all points.' Christ hath had experience of all trials whereinto any of his servants can fall, poverty, forsaking of friends, exile, imprisonment, hunger, nakedness, watching, weariness, pain of body, heaviness of heart, desertion as to sense, wrath and curse of God. Christ hath carried his feeling with him into heaven; he knew what poverty meaneth, what trouble of conscience, what heaviness of spirit meaneth. Christ could not so experimentally pity us, so feelingly pity us, if he were not like us in all things; his heart was entendered by experience, as a man that hath felt the gout and felt the stone. Israel knew the heart of a stranger; Christ knew the heart of a man that is left to the world's frowns and snares. He took a communion of our nature and miseries, as a pawn and pledge that he will pity us and help us: Heb. ii. 10, 'The captain of our salvation was made perfect through sufferings.' Christ, though he was perfect, he received the Spirit without measure, yet he lacked one thing which his office required, to be a perfect mediator, till he had an experimental feeling. So Heb. ii. 18, 'In that he himself hath suffered, being tempted, he is able to succour them that are tempted.' Christ was able as soon as he came from heaven. As God, what could he not do? But there is an ability of sufficiency, and of idoneity, an experimental ability. Christ had experience, though not of sin, yet of temptation to sin; he is not only able, but willing; he knoweth what it is. Christ would borrow our nature to make experiments.

Use 1. To teach us to walk with caution, and in a continual dependence upon God. We are continually assaulted, and live in the midst of snares. A man that cometh into the world, saith Luther, is like a traveller that cometh into an inn where there dwell none but thieves. Now he that carrieth jewels about him had need to take heed; the diversity, the frequency, the continuation of temptations should make us wary. The diversity; there are baits for every temper, honours for the ambitious, wealth for the covetous, and pleasures for the sensual. The devil hath a diet to feed every distemper; some are sullen, not bent to pleasures, but Satan is not at a loss to fit them with a temptation, there are profits for them; others are facile and more easy, they have pleasures; others would be great, they have honours; and when Satan knoweth the lust, he suiteth the bait; he is an old sophister, well skilled in the tempers of men. Therefore, seeing that in every business, in every bit of meat, in every recreation, there are snares, we we had need feed with fear and trade with fear. When there is an enemy in the country, we keep constant watch and ward. Then, for the frequency and continuance of temptations, they are always about us.

Long suits prevail at last.   From the first use of reason till the hour of death, as long as God continueth our abode in the world, we are in danger.   There are many baits ; Satan is crafty, and the world is spiteful, and our hearts are naught.   We are now upon our trial, the great work of religion is to walk in a constant watchfulness and dependence. Alas ! many are as if they were in the haven already ; so negligent, so careless, as if they were in the midst of paradise, out of temptations.

Use 2. To press us to grow weary of the world ; it is a place full of snares ; here we have many snares and many enemies.   If we have a mind to sin no longer, why should we desire to live in the world ?   The world is a step-mother to the saints ; why should we desire to hang upon the dug?   He that would always live here is like a scullion that loveth to lie among the pots.   In heaven we have pure company, and are out of the reach and danger of temptations.   The devil, when he was not fit for heaven, was cast out into the world, a fit place for misery, sin, and torment ; it is Satan's walk and circuit.   Here is antichrist, the devil's eldest son ; here are *terriculamenta et irritamenta*, fears and snares.   It is a dirty odd corner of the universe ; we can hardly walk up and down but we shall defile our garments.   Here are briars to hitch us, snares and baits to entice us.   There is a more excellent country above, where we shall have the company of God and the fellowship of the saints, saints without corruption, other manner of saints than here. There is no tempter there, there should be your country.   In a pet we long for heaven, but it should be out of a resolved judgment.   Men fight in the world as long as they are able, and then make heaven their refuge.   It should not be a melancholy wish ; we should desire heaven, not as weary of work and service, but as weary of temptation.

Use 3. Examination.   What kind of temper have we ?   There are ' children of this world,' Luke xvi. 8.   The world is their own mother, they love to lie hanging on the dugs and teats.   And there is a spirit called ' the spirit of the world,' 1 Cor. ii. 12, a genius that suiteth with present conveniences ; there is ' their portion,' Ps. xvii. 14 ; ' Their names are written in the earth,' Jer. xvii. 13 ; that is their happiness. The nature of the world's sons is all for the lusts of the flesh, the lusts of the eye, and the pride of life ; to go fine, to feed high, to shine in worldly pomp, affect honours and great places.   Too many christians are baptized into this spirit.   There is a use of the things of this world, but we should use them with fear ; they cannot smell the rose of the field, Christ hath no scent or savour.   Oh ! it is a sad character to be a child of this world ; one that hath the nature of the mother in them, one of the world's breed.   A child of God is a pilgrim and stranger : Ps. cxix. 19, ' I am a stranger in the earth.'   Abraham purchased but a sepulchre ; that is all the faithful can lay claim to on earth.   He looketh on himself as born and bred in another land ; his mother is a princess, the bride, the Lamb's wife ; and his Father is in heaven ; he is in the world, but not of the world.

Use 4. Comfort.   Christ is apprehensive of your danger.   All trials you meet with do either better your hearts or hasten your glory. Christians must expect danger, but need not fear it.   *Formido sublata est, non pugna.*   You are not absolutely freed from molestations of the world, but you have a sanctified use of them : John xvi. 33, ' These things have I spoken unto you, that in me ye might have peace; in the world ye shall have tribulation: but be of good comfort, I have overcome the world.' The victory consisteth not in not suffering and not fighting, but keeping what we fight for: 2 Tim. iv. 18, 'The Lord shall deliver me from every evil work;' not from the lion, but sin.

Use 5. The example of Christ. When we die, let us be mindful of the danger of our relations that we leave behind us, our families, church, ministry; commend them to God. Dying christians should be best at the last; dying Moses left a song. Do not leave the world without a testimony of your love and zeal: 2 Peter i. 14, 15, 'Knowing that shortly I must put off this my tabernacle, even as our Lord Jesus Christ hath showed me. Moreover, I will endeavour that you may be able after my decease to have these things always in remembrance.'

SERMON XVI.

And now I am no more in the world, but these are in the world, and I come to thee. Holy Father, keep through thine own name those whom thou hast given me, that they may be one, as we are.—JOHN XVII. 11.

SECONDLY, I come to the compellation of the party to whom the prayer is made, 'Holy Father.' This compellation is to be observed. Titles of God in scripture are suited to the requests made to him; as 2 Thes. iii. 16, 'The God of peace give you peace always by all means.' So Rom. xv. 5, 'The God of patience and consolation grant you to be like-minded one towards another.' He prays for brotherly forbearance and sweetness.

In the several paragraphs of this chapter, Christ speaketh to his Father in a different style, according to the nature of the address. Ver. 1, 5, it is 'Father' only; in ver. 28, it is 'righteous Father,' because of the truth and equity which he observeth in his gracious dispensations; and here it is 'holy Father.' When he beggeth things suitable to his commutative justice, then it is 'righteous Father;' but when he asketh things suitable to his holiness, it is 'holy Father.' Certainly it is a great relief to faith in prayer to pitch upon such a name and title in God as suiteth with the nature of the request; it begetteth a confidence that he both can and will do us good. When we call a man by his name, he will look about upon us; and when we ask things according to his nature, he will pity us.

But why doth Christ use this title at this time?

I answer—Some take *holiness* more largely, for the general goodness and perfection of the divine essence; a branch of which is his veracity or truth in keeping promises; and conceive the argument thus: the holy God cannot break his word, nor be stained with any unfaithfulness; therefore unless God should deny himself, he will 'keep them through his own name.' But I rather think it is specially put for his purity. Christ goeth to his Father as a pure fountain of grace, for sanctification for his disciples. Holiness, it is the object of God's approbation, the effect of his operation ; he worketh holiness, and he delighteth in it. 'Holy Father,' that art holy in thy essence, holy in thy influences, holy in thy dispensations, 'sanctify them by the truth ;' thou that abhorrest all that is evil, workest all that is good, 'keep them from the evil.' God hateth sin as much as we do, and infinitely more ; and therefore it is some hope that he will help us against it.

Doct. When we deal with God in prayer, especially for grace and sanctification, we must look upon him as a holy Father.

1. I will open the holiness of God. Holiness implieth a freedom from sin and defilement ; ἄγιος, from the privative particle *à* and γῆ, *terra* in whom there is no earth, no pollution, but all heavenly purity. When God speaketh to us he crieth out, Jer. xxii. 29, 'O earth, earth, earth, hear the word of the Lord.' We are earth in our understandings, in our affections, in our practices. But when the seraphims speak to God, they cry, 'Holy, holy, holy ;' as if it were said, 'Without earth, without earth, without earth.' Briefly, God's holiness is an attribute by which we understand his essence to be most perfectly just and pure ; at the utmost distance from sin and weakness ; loving and liking himself above all, and the creatures, as they do more or less partake of his glory. Now God is called, 'The holy one ;' not *an* holy one, but *the* holy one : 1 Sam. ii. 2, 'There is none holy as the Lord.' He doth not say, There is none holy but the Lord, but there is none holy *as* the Lord. Therefore let us see the difference between the holiness of God and the holiness of the creatures. This is an argument fit for a seraphim ; it becometh an angel's mouth rather than man's ; the angels, that come nearer to God in essence, can best proclaim his holiness. But our ear hath received a little thereof. 'None is holy as the Lord ;' because God is essentially holy, infinitely holy, and originally holy.

[1.] He is essentially holy. God is not only holy, but holiness itself, goodness itself ; it is his very essence. The creatures, when they are holy, they are holy according to the law ; the holiness of angels or men is a conformity to the law of their creation ; as we say he is holy whose heart and life doth exactly agree with God's law. But God's will is his rule, his essence is his law, and therefore all his actions are necessarily holy. The divine *esse* and being, as it is the beginning of all beings, so it is the rule of all moral perfections. All created holiness is but a resemblance of God's, either a conformity to God's nature, or a conformity to God's will. Habitual holiness is a conformity to God's nature, actual holiness is a conformity to God's will ; his will is the rule, his nature is the pattern. But now God is a rule to himself ; there are no eternal reasons of good and evil beyond God. Things are not first holy, and then God doeth them ; but God doeth them, and therefore they are holy ; he himself is his own rule. Any one may err that hath not the rule of righteousness in himself ; God's act is his rule, therefore he cannot sin. The hand of the artificer faileth often in cutting, because his hand is not the rule by which he worketh ; there is a rule or line without him ; sometimes he striketh right, sometimes wrong. If the hand of a man were the rule, it were impossible he should work amiss. There is a rule prescribed to angels and men ; their will is one thing, their rule another, for no creature is holy by its own essence. This notion is of practical use; there is holiness in all that cometh from God; when he afflicteth us, and our friends, or suffereth us to be unjustly afflicted by men; when he spareth our enemies, multiplieth our sorrows, his act is his rule; God's will is the supreme reason of all things. Again, holiness in us is an accessary quality, a superadded gift; our essence may remain when holiness is gone. Now holiness in God is not a quality, but his essence. The angelical essence continueth when holiness is lost, as in the devils. So the man remaineth when the saint is fled; but in God, his essence and his holiness are the same. This is of practical use to humble the creature. Sin is contrary to the very nature of God; it is not only contrary to our interests, but to God's nature. A man hateth that exceedingly which is contrary to his nature. Now in our corrupt natures there is a direct contrariety to the nature of God. Actual sins are but a blow and away. Original sin is a standing contrariety; there is a settled enmity between God and us. Similitude is the ground of likeness;[1] the aversation of a man from a trade, and other antipathies are but a faint resemblance of this.

[2.] God is infinitely holy, *super-purissimus*. The faithful in this life are holy, but imperfectly; but 'God is light, and in him is no darkness at all,' 1 John i. 5. Of all creatures, light is the most pure and defecate; therefore it is put to resemble God's holiness. Our life is a chequerwork of light and darkness. Adam, in his innocency, though he had no corruption, yet was mutably holy; he might commit evil; though he were not *peccator*, a sinner, yet he was *peccabilis*, one that might sin. But God is at the greatest distance and elongation from sin and weakness: James i. 13, 'God cannot be tempted with evil, ἀπείραστος κακῶ, neither tempteth he any one.' Once more, the blessed spirits and angels, though they are perfectly holy in their kind, yet finitely and derivatively; they do not love God as much as he might be loved. God loveth himself as much as he can be loved; there is as much purity in his love as there is perfection in his essence. The creatures' holiness is limited; we cannot love God so much as he is to be loved. God loveth the lowest saint with a higher love than the highest angel can love God. The good angels, though they have been God's constant menial servants, without the least spot or taint of sin in nature or life; and though they be confirmed in their happy estate, either by the merit of Christ, or their many years' experience and communion with God, yet there is folly in them in comparison of God, because of that essential mutability that is in any creature: Job iv. 18, 'He chargeth his angels with folly.' It is spoken of good angels, who are opposed to dwellers in houses of clay. It were too easy a charge for the apostate spirits, to charge them with folly; the angelical nature, though it be pure, yet because it is mutable, hath some kind of folly in it, it was once liable to rash attempts against the dignity and empire of God. Briefly, the holiness of God cannot be lessened nor increased, being always infinitely perfect. The regenerate creature must still be increasing to further degrees, till it come to the measure of the stature in Christ; the blessed spirits, though separated from all defilement, yet infinitely come short of that glorious holiness which agreeth to the nature of God, and God is still raising it higher

---

[1] Qu. 'liking?'—Ed.

and higher in the saints on earth. Their holiness riseth and groweth like Ezekiel's waters; but God is always equal in holiness, because in infiniteness there are no degrees.

SERMON XVII.

And now I am no more in the world, but these are in the world, and I come to thee. Holy Father, keep through thine own name those whom thou hast given me, that they may be one, as we are.— JOHN XVII. 11.

THIRDLY, The matter of the prayer, for perseverance in grace.

'Keep through thine own name.'—'Ἐν τῷ ὀνόματί σου τήρησον αὐτούς; it may be rendered 'in thy name,' or 'by thy name,' or 'for thy name's sake;' ἐν, as ב among the Hebrews, may be thus rendered, 'by thy name,' Heb. xi. 2. 'Ἐν ταύτῃ, 'by which the elders obtained a good report.' 'For thy name,' Eph. iv. 32, 'As God for Christ's sake hath forgiven you;' Θεὸς ἐν Χριστῷ. So Rom. xvi. 2, 'Receive her in the Lord,' ἐν κυρίῳ; that is, for the Lord's sake. (1.) If it be 'in thy name,' then the meaning is, in the knowledge of thy truth; for by the name of God is meant anything by which he is made known. The doctrine of the gospel in this chapter is called, 'his name,' ver. 6; 'I have manifested thy name to them;' meaning the whole doctrine of godliness. So Christ prayeth, 'Keep them in thy name;' that is, in the constant profession of the truth; let them not be cheated out of it by Satan, nor affrighted out of it by persecutions; but let them constantly hold it forth, defend and propagate it to the world. (2.) 'By thy name;' so God's name is himself, and himself is his name. So Exod. xxiii. 21, 'My name is in him;' that is, he is of the same essence and glory with me. So 'by thy name,' is by thy self, thy power, mercy, goodness, truth, διὰ τῆς σῆς βοηθείας—Chrysostom; by thy gracious assistance. (3.) 'For thy name's sake,' to show forth thy mercy, truth, faithfulness. These expositions may be compounded— Keep them in thy truth, or the worship and profession of thy name, by thy power, for thy name's sake, to discover thy mercy and truth; thy mercy, in taking them into a state of grace; thy truth, in preserving them in the state of grace. The points are two :—

1. That the perseverance of the saints, or their conservation in the state of grace, is sure and certain.

2. That we are kept in the state of grace by God's name, by his power, for his glory.

Doct. 1. That the perseverance of the saints, or their conservation in a state of grace, is sure and certain.

1. I shall show how I build the certainty of perseverance on this place.

2. I shall handle the doctrine, confirming it by other grounds.

First, How this doctrine of the certainty of the saints' perseverance is built on this place. Christ hath begged it, and he beggeth it for all the saints. Christ hath begged it, and the prayers of Christ, who is God's beloved Son, cannot possibly return in vain, there being such an absolute conformity and consent between the will of God the Father and the Son: John xi. 42, 'I know that thou hearest me always.' Christ cannot be denied audience and acceptance in the court of heaven, especially in a request upon which his heart is set. His people are so wonderfully dear to him, that he would not lose one of them; and then Christ is so wonderfully dear to God, that he must needs speed in all his requests. Therefore if Christ hath mediated for the conservation of the saints, the Father will grant what he asketh. Yea, the Father himself loveth the saints; the thing is pleasing to him. It is notable that when Christ had spoken of the perseverance of the saints, he adds, John x. 30, 'I and my Father are one;' as noting not only the unity of essence, but the consent of will, that was between them in this work. Well, then, look, as Christ redeemeth us because the Father required it, the Father will love us and preserve us because the Son asketh it. If Christ bear any respect to the Father's command, or the Father to Christ's prayers, the elect are sure to be saved. Christ hath engaged God's name to keep us. What can be objected against this? They say that Christ prayed conditionally, Keep them if they will. But here is no condition expressed. Christ absolutely prayeth, Keep them; and such a condition would make the gift of God to depend upon man's will; and so to persevere would rather be man's act than God's gift, the determination being on man's part. Nay, the main thing which is to be kept is our will, and so the condition would destroy the very nature of the request. They say, Christ prayeth only for the apostles. I answer—It cannot be restrained to the apostles; it is the common privilege of all the saints: 'Those which thou hast given me.' Christ explaineth himself, and extendeth it to believers of all ages: ver. 20, 'Neither pray I for these alone, but for those which shall believe in me through their word.' Christ's prayer is every way as good as a promise.

Secondly, Let me handle the doctrine itself. The doctrine of perseverance is much impugned, but the earth is never the more unsettled because to giddy brains it seemeth to run round. Let me state, and then confirm it.

First, State it.

1. Seeming grace may be lost: Mat. xxv. 29, 'From him that hath not shall be taken away even that which he hath;' compared with Luke xviii. 18, 'Whosoever hath not, from him shall be taken away even that which he seemeth to have.' Blazing comets and meteors are soon spent, and may fall from heaven like lightning, while stars keep their orb and station; sandy building will totter. The hypocrites 'shall be discovered before the congregation,' Prov. xxvi. 26.

2. Initial or preparative grace may fail: Heb. vi. 4, 5, 'They who were once enlightened, and have tasted of the heavenly gift, and were made partakers of the Holy Ghost, and have tasted the good word of God, and the powers of the world to come, may fall away;' such as illumination, external reformation, temporary faith, some good beginnings. Some die in the pangs of the new birth, and are still-born. **Plenty of blossoms doth not always foretell store of fruit.**

3. True grace may suffer a shrewd decay, but not an utter loss.   In temptations it may be sorely shaken; the heel may be bruised as Christ's was, but 'his seed remaineth in him,' 1 John iii. 9; as Peter denied Christ, though he did not fall from grace: Luke xxii. 32, 'I have prayed for thee, that thy faith fail not.'   The leaves may fade when the root liveth.   Chrysostom saith concerning Christ's prayer for Peter, οὐκ ἔρει ἱνὰ μή ἀρνήσῃ, ἀλλὰ ὥστε μὴ ἐκλείπειν τὴν πιστὶν—He doth not say, that he might not deny him, but that his faith might not fail and altogether vanish.

4. Such grace as serves to our well-being in Christ may be taken away, joy, peace, cheerfulness.   A man may be living though he be not lively; a man may have a being when his well-being is lost; he is a man, though a bankrupt.   So a christian, the operations of grace may be obstructed for a great while; a fit of swooning is not a state of death; there may be no acts, and yet the seed may remain, this may last; for a long time David did not recover himself, it was near a year after his sin: 1 Sam. xii. 14, 'The child that is born of thee shall surely die;' compared with Ps. li., title, 'A psalm of David when Nathan the prophet came unto him, after he had gone in to Bathsheba.'

5. Grace indeed, if left to us, would be soon lost; we showed that in innocency.   But it is our advantage that our security lieth in God's promises, not our own strength, that we are not our own keepers.   God would not trust this jewel but in safe hands.   Perseverance is God's gift, not man's act; he is engaged in Christ to maintain it: John x. 28, 29, 'I give to them eternal life, and they shall never perish, neither shall any man pluck them out of my hands.   My Father that gave them me, is greater than I; and no man is able to pluck them out of my Father's hands;' they neither shall nor can be taken out of God's hands.   God and Christ is engaged in the keeping of them; Christ by God's command, as mediator, God by Christ's merit; and therefore he that separateth us from God must tug with Jesus Christ himself, and be too hard for him also, or else he can never pluck them out of his hands.   If they should question Christ's power, because of the ignominy of the cross, the Father's hands are also engaged for our greater assurance: 'None is able to pluck them out of my Father's hands.'   God never made a creature that should be too hard for himself.

6. We do not plead for any wild assurance and certainty of perseverance.   We do not say that he that neglects means, and grieves the Spirit, do what he will, yet he is sure he shall not miscarry; that is against the nature of God's dispensation, and the nature of this assurance, and therefore but a vain cavil.

[1.] It is against the nature of God's dispensation; for whom he maketh to persevere, he maketh them persevere in the use of means. Hezekiah had assurance of life for fifteen years, yet he takes a lump of figs, and applies it as a plaster to the boil, Isa. xxxviii. 5, compared with ver. 21.   Or more clearly, Acts xxvii. 22, 'There shall be no loss of any man's life among you, but only of the ship.'   But yet, ver. 31, 'Except the shipmen abide in the ship, ye cannot be saved.'   We are bound to get food and raiment, if we would live.   It is the devil's divinity, Thou art sure not to fall, therefore neglect means; it was Satan's cavil against God's protection over Christ: Mat. iv. 6, 'If thou be the Son of God, cast thyself down; for it is written, He shall give his angels charge concerning thee, and in their hands they shall bear thee up, lest at any time thou dash thy foot against a stone.' Thou learnest this doctrine from the devil—Thou mayest do what thou wilt, thou art sure to be saved.

[2.] It is against the nature of assurance; he that hath tasted God's love in God's way cannot reason so. He that hath a good father, that will not see him perish, shall he waste and embezzle his estate, he cares not how? A wicked child may presume thus of his father, though it be very disingenuous, because of his natural interest and relation to his father; the kindness which he expecteth is not built on moral choice, but nature. But a child of God cannot, because he cannot grow up to this certainty but in the exercise of grace; this certainty is begotten and nourished by godly exercises. And the thing itself implieth a contradiction; this were to fall away, because we cannot fall away; you may as soon say that the fire should make a man freeze with cold, as that certainty of perseverance in grace should make a man do actions contrary to grace.

7. Again, we do not say a believer is so sure of his conservation in a state of grace as that he needeth not be wary and jealous of himself: 1 Cor. x. 12, ' Let him that thinketh he standeth take heed lest he fall.' There is a fear of caution that is warrantable. There is a difference between the weakening of the security of the flesh, and of our confidence in Christ. None more apt to suspect themselves than they that are most sure in God, lest by improvidence and unwatchfulness they should yield to corruption. Christ had prayed that Peter's faith might not fail; yet, together with the other apostles, he biddeth him watch, Luke xxii. 40, 46. The fear of God is a preserving grace, and taken into the covenant: Jer. xxxii. 40, ' I will never depart from them to do them good,' and ' I will put my fear into their hearts, and they shall not depart from me.' God's love will not let him depart from us, and fear will not let us depart from God. This is a fear that will stand with faith and certainty; it is a fruit of the same Spirit, and doth not hinder assurance, but guard it; this is a fear that maketh us watchful against all occasions to sin and spiritual distempers, that we may not give offence to God; as an ingenuous man, that hath an inheritance passed over to him by his friend in court, is careful not to offend him; there is a cautelous and distrustful fear.

8. Again, this certainty of our standing in grace doth not exclude prayer: Luke xxii. 46, ' Watch and pray, that ye enter not into temptation.' Perseverance is God's gift, and it must be sought out in God's way, by Christ's intercession, to preserve the majesty of God, and by our prayer, that we constantly profess our dependence upon God, and renew our acquaintance with him. Besides, by asking blessings in prayer we are the more warned of our duty; it is a means to keep us gracious and holy. As those that speak often to kings had need be decently clad, and go neat in their apparel, so he that speaketh often to God is bound to be more holy, that he may be acceptable to him.

9. Once more, and I have done with the state of the question. It is not a discontinued, but a constant perseverance that we plead for. Not as if a child of God could be quite driven out of the state of grace;

though he be saved at length, he cannot fall *totus, a toto, in totum*, from all grace and godliness, in the whole man, with full consent; he may sin, but not fall totally, no more than finally. There is something remaineth; a seed: 1 John iii. 9, 'Whosoever is born of God doth not commit sin, for his seed remaineth in him;' an unction: 1 John ii. 27, 'But the anointing which ye have received of him abideth in you.' There is a root in a dry ground, that will bud and scent again.

Well, then, this we hold, that true grace shall never utterly be lost, though it be much weakened, but by the use of means shall constantly be preserved to eternal life.

Secondly, Having stated the point, let me now confirm it. The grounds of perseverance are these:—

1. On the Father's part, there is an everlasting love and all-sufficient power. His everlasting love; God doth not love for a fit, but for ever: Ps. ciii. 17, 'The mercy of the Lord is from everlasting to everlasting upon them that fear him;' before the world was, and when the world is no more. There can be no change in God's counsels, because they are accompanied with infinite wisdom and power. God never repented in time of what he purposed to do before time: Rom. xi. 29, 'The gifts and calling of God are without repentance.' By *gifts* are meant gifts proper to the elect, remission of sins, grace and glory, and by *calling* is meant effectual calling, such as is κατὰ πρόθσειν, 'according to his purpose,' Rom. viii. 28. God never repented of it; he is never ashamed of nor sorry for his choice; though men be unworthy, it is the reason why he brought them under the grace of the covenant. His all-sufficient power and almightiness is engaged in the preservation of grace: John x. 29, 'My Father, which gave them me, is greater than all, and no man is able to pluck them out of my Father's hands.' As long as God hath power we are safe; and this power is engaged by his love and will.

2. Then on Christ's part there is his everlasting merit and constant intercession.

[1.] For his merit: Heb. ix. 12, 'By his own blood he entered in once into the holy place, having obtained eternal redemption for us.' Legal expiations did but last from year to year, but Christ's is for ever and ever. The Levitical priest, once every year entered into the holy place, but Christ is once gotten into heaven, his redemption is eternal; not only as it is of use for all ages of the church, but in respect of every particular saint. Those who are once redeemed by Christ, they are eternally redeemed; not for a time, to fall away again, but to be saved for ever. So Heb. x. 14, 'By one offering he hath perfected for ever them that are sanctified.' He hath not only purchased a possibility of salvation, but hath perfected them, hath made purchase of all that we need to our full perfection; it is not for a certain time, as if afterwards they could be taken out of his hands, and so perish, but for ever; and this for all those that are sanctified, separated by God's purpose and decree, and afterwards renewed and sanctified in time, set apart to be vessels of honour to God.

[2.] Then for his constant intercession, a copy of which we have in this place. It is said, Heb. vii. 25, 'Wherefore he is able to save unto

the uttermost all that come unto God through him, seeing he liveth
for ever to make intercession for us.' He is interceding with God, that
the merit of his death may be applied to us, and that is salvation to
the uttermost. The heirs of salvation need not to fear miscarrying;
Jesus Christ, who is the testator, who by will and testament made
over the heritage to them, he liveth for ever to see his own will executed. Though he died once to make the testament, yet he liveth for
ever to see it made good. Christ is risen from the dead, and dieth no
more, and therefore a believer cannot miscarry.

3. On the Spirit's part, there is a continued influence, so as to maintain the essence and seed of grace. The Father's love is continued by
the merit of Christ, that he will not depart from us, and we are preserved by the Spirit of Christ, that we may not depart from him. He
doth not only put into our hearts faith and fear, and other graces at
first, but he maintaineth and keepeth them, that the fire may never go
out. Our hearts are his temples, and he will not leave his dwelling-
place. There is a continued influence. Now this he doth to preserve
the honour of Christ and the comfort of believers; he glorifieth Christ,
and is our comforter. It is to preserve the glory of Christ. Christ
hath received a charge from the Father: John vi. 39, 'This is the
Father's will which hath sent me, that of all which he hath given me
I should lose nothing, but should raise it up again at the last day;'
nothing, neither body nor soul. In point of honour, and that he may
be true to his trust, he sendeth his Spirit as his deputy or executor,
that his merit may be fully applied; therefore, for the honour of
Christ, wherever the work is begun it is continued. . Christ is called,
Heb. xii. 2, 'The author and finisher of our faith.' Wherever the
Spirit is an author he is also a finisher; when the good work is begun,
he will also perfect it, and continue his grace to the end. It was said
of the foolish builder, ' He began, and was not able to make an end.'
This dishonour cannot be cast upon Christ, because of the power and
faithfulness of the Spirit; he doth κατεργάζεσθαι, go through with the
work which he hath begun: Phil. i. 6, ' Being confident of this, that
he that hath begun a good work in you will perform it unto the day
of Christ.' The Spirit is to fit vessels for glory; he doth not use to
leave them half carved, but finish them for the honour of Christ. The
Spirit is faithful to Christ, as Christ is to the Father. The Father
chooseth the vessels, Christ buyeth them, and the Spirit carveth and
fitteth them, that they may be vessels of praise and honour. He is
our comforter; working grace, he puts us into an expectation of comfort and glory; and therefore, to make it good, he carrieth on the work
without failing: Rom. viii. 23, ' And not only they, but ourselves also,
who have the first-fruits of the Spirit; even we ourselves groan within
ourselves, waiting for the adoption, to wit, the redemption of our body;'
2 Cor. i. 22, ' Who hath sealed us, and given the earnest of the Spirit
in our hearts.' We have the taste and the pledge of it; it is good, it
is sure. The first degree of grace is conferred as a pledge of eternal
life; he giveth it as an earnest or pledge, assuring us of a more perfect
enjoyment of him. It is a pledge of the whole crop; as an earnest,
hereby God assureth us that he will pay the whole sum. An earnest
is a pledge whereby we confirm a bargain; it is a piece of money

whereby we are assured he will pay the whole. Grace, it is the livery and seisin of glory; as soon as a real change is wrought in us, we have a right that is indefeasible; it is engaged by promise. Therefore, that the Spirit may be faithful, when he hath given us the first-fruits, the earnest, shall he not give us the inheritance?

Use 1. It exhorteth us to persevere with the more care: 1 John ii. 26–28, 'These things have I written unto you concerning them that seduce you. But the anointing which you have received of him abideth in you, and ye need not that any man teach you; but as the same anointing teacheth you of all things, and is truth, and is no lie, and even as it hath taught you, you shall abide in him. And now, little children, abide in him, that when he shall appear, ye may have confidence, and not be ashamed before him at his coming.' Since we have so many advantages of standing, let us not fall from him. Oh! how great will your sin be if you should fall and dishonour God! We pity a child that falleth when it is not looked after; but when a froward child wresteth and forceth itself out of the arms of the nurse, we are angry with it. You have more ground to stand than others, being brought into an unchangeable estate of grace, being held in the arms of Christ; so that God will be very angry with your slips and fallings. Mercy holdeth you fast, and you seek to wrest yourselves out of mercy's arms. Never any can sin as you do; there is much frowardness in your sins. You disparage the Spirit's custody, the merit of Christ, and the mercy of the Father: Heb. iv. 1, 'Let us therefore fear, lest a promise being left us of entering into his rest, any of you should seem to come short of it.' Some seem to stand, and do not; and some seem to fall utterly, and do not. A child of God indeed cannot come short, but he should not seem, nor give any appearance of coming short. Our course in religion is often interrupted, though it be not broken off; this is a seeming to come short of it. Hereby you bring a scandal upon the love of Christ, as if it were changeable; upon the merit of Christ, as if it were not a perfect merit. Though we do not fall so as to break our necks, yet we may fall so as to break our bones.

Use 2. If you fall, be not utterly discouraged. As the spinster leaveth a lock of wool to draw on the next thread, there is somewhat left when you are departed from God; you have more holdfast in him than an unregenerate sinner. A child, though a prodigal, will go to him, and say, Father: Ps. cxix. 176, 'I have gone astray like a lost sheep; seek thy servant, for I do not forget thy commandments.' Through natural weakness I have gone astray like a sheep, but I seek thy commandments; there is some grace left yet: Isa. lxiv. 8, 'But now, O Lord, thou art our Father; we are the clay, and thou art the potter; we are all the work of thine hand.' The church pleadeth thus: nay, God is angry when we do not plead so: Jer. iii. 4, 'Wilt thou not from this time cry, My Father, thou art the guide of my youth?' You have an interest in God yet. Thus do, and your fall will be like them that go back to fetch their leap more commodiously.

Use 3. When you stand, let it incite you to love and thankfulness. Nothing maketh the saints more love God than his unchangeableness. His mercy made you come to him, and his truth will not suffer you to depart from him. Mercy and truth are like Jachin and Boaz: Micah

vii. 20, 'Thou wilt perform the truth to Jacob, and the mercy to Abraham, which thou hast sworn unto our fathers, from the days of old.' The covenant was made with Abraham, and made good to Jacob. You may rejoice notwithstanding your weakness and Satan's daily assaults; as Daniel in the lions' den, to see the lions ramping and roaring about him, yet their mouths muzzled: 2 Sam. ii. 9, 'By strength shall no man prevail;' that is, by his own. That any of us have stood hitherto, let us ascribe it wholly to God: we might have been vile and scandalous, even as others. Many of better gifts may fall away, and thou keepest thy standing. What is the reason? We have done enough a thousand times to cause God to depart from us: Deut. xxiii. 14, 'If he see any unclean thing among thee, he will turn away from thee.' And is it not strange that the Spirit of grace should yet abide with us hitherto, when there is so much uncleanness in every one of us? The great argument of the saints why they love and praise him is the constancy and unchangeableness of his love: Ps. cxxxvi., 'For his mercy endureth for ever;' and Ps. cvi. 1, 'Praise the Lord, O give thanks unto the Lord; for he is good, for his mercy endureth for ever.' No form more frequent in the mouths of his saints.

Use 4. If any fall often, constantly, frequently, and easily, they have no interest in grace: 1 John iii. 9, 'Whosoever is born of God doth not commit sin;' οὐ ποιεῖ ἁμαρτίαν, he maketh not a trade of sin, that is the force of that phrase. God's children slip often, but not with such a frequent constant readiness, into the same sin. Therefore he that liveth in a course of profaneness, worldliness, drunkenness, 'his spot is not the spot of God's children,' Deut. xxxii. 5. You are tried by your constant course: Rom. viii. 1, 'That walk not after the flesh, but after the Spirit.' What is your road and walk? I except only those sins which are of usual incidence, and sudden surreption, as anger, vanity of thoughts; and yet for them a man should be more humble. If it be not felt, nor striven against, nor mourned for, it is a bad sign. What is your course and walk? There is a uniformity in a christian's course. It is nothing to have some fits and good moods and motions.

Use 5. It provoketh us to get an interest in such a sure condition. Be not contented with outward happiness; things are worthy according to their duration. Nature hath such a sense of God's eternity that the more lasting things are, it accounteth them the better. The immortal soul must have an eternal good. Now all things in the world are frail and passing away, therefore they are called 'uncertain riches,' 1 Tim. vi. 17, compared with Prov. viii. 18, 'Riches and honour are with me, yea, durable riches and righteousness.' The flower of these things perisheth, their grace passeth away; in the midst of their pride and beauty, like Herod in his royalty, they vanish and are blasted. The better part is not taken away: Luke x. 42, 'Mary hath chosen the better part, which cannot be taken away from her.' A man may outlive his happiness, be stripped of the flower of all. Worldly glory is sure to end with life, that is transitory; and still they are uncertain riches, uncertain whether we shall get them, uncertain whether we shall keep them. By a care of the better part, we may have these **things with a blessing:** Mat. vi. 33, 'Seek ye first the kingdom of

God, and the righteousness thereof, and all these things shall be added to you.' Gifts, they are for the body, rather than the person that hath them. Men may be carnal, and yet come behind in no gifts. Judas could cast out devils, and yet afterwards was cast out among devils: 1 Cor. xii. 31, the apostle had discoursed largely of gifts, but saith he, 'Yet I show you a more excellent way,' and that is grace, that abideth. Many that have great abilities to pray, preach, discourse, yet fall away; according to the place which they sustain in the body, so they have great gifts of knowledge, utterance, to comfort, direct, instruct others, to answer their doubts, to reason in holy discourse, and yet may fall foully: Heb. vi. 4, 5, 'They may be once enlightened, and have tasted of the heavenly gift, and were made partakers of the Holy Ghost, and have tasted the good word of God, and the powers of the world to come.' They may have a great share of church gifts. Nay, gifts themselves wither and vanish when the bodily vigour is spent: 1 Peter i. 24, 'All flesh is grass, and all the glory of man as the flower of grass; the grass withereth, and the flower thereof falleth away.' Whatever excellency we have by nature, wit, knowledge, strength of natural parts, nothing but what the Spirit of God worketh in us will last for ever. So for seeming, unsound grace, as false faith, such as beginneth in joy, will end in trouble; it easeth you for the present, but you shall lie down in sorrow. General probabilities, loose hopes, uncertain conjectures, vanishing apprehensions of comfort, all fail. The planting of true faith is troublesome at first, but it leadeth to true joy; you may look upon the gospel with some kind of delectation. Thorns may blaze under the pot, though they cannot keep in the fire. Do not rest in 'tasting the good word of God,' Heb. vi. 5, in some slight and transitory comfort. Hymeneus and Alexander are said to 'make shipwreck of faith,' 1 Tim. i. 19, 20; that is, of a false faith. So for a formal profession, men may begin in the Spirit and end in the flesh: Gal. iii. 3, 'Are ye so foolish, having begun in the Spirit, are ye now made perfect by the flesh?' A man may seem to himself, and to the church of God, to have true grace; nay, he may be enlightened, find some comfort in the word, escape the pollutions of the world, foul gross sins; yea, these good things may be the works and the effects of the Spirit of God, not of nature only, not professed out of a carnal aim; but there is no settled root, and therefore it is but of short continuance. But certainly that form that is taken up out of private aims will surely fail. God delighteth to take off the mask and disguise of hypocrites, by letting them fall into some scandalous sins. Paint is soon washed off. Therefore rest not in these things, till solid and substantial grace be wrought in your hearts.

Use 6. Is comfort to God's children. Grace is sure, and the privileges of it sure. Grace is sure; through your folly it may be nigh unto death, but it cannot die. This is the advantage of spiritual comforts, that they do not only satisfy our desires, but secure us against our fears: Isa. xxxv. 10, 'The ransomed of the Lord shall return, and come to Zion with songs, and everlasting joy upon their heads: they shall obtain joy and gladness, and sorrow and sighing shall flee away.' Once in Christ, and you shall be for ever preserved. The leaven and the dough can never be severed when kneaded together, so neither can you from Christ. Grace would be little better than temporal things if it did yield but temporary refreshment. You are sure that nothing shall cut you off from enjoying God, for nothing shall altogether cause you to cease to love God. The children of God would be troubled, though their grace should not fail, if their privileges should be cut off; but you are sure of both. God will maintain a spark, and the seed remaineth, and the privileges of grace are sure too. This was figured under the law. An Israelite could never wholly alienate his title to the land: Lev. xxv. 23, ' The land shall not be sold for ever; for the land is mine, for ye were strangers and sojourners with me.' His title to the land shall not be quite cut off, ' it shall not be sold for ever;' which was a type of our spiritual inheritance in Christ, which cannot be alienated from us. He might for a while alienate and pass away his inheritance, yet the property remained; he knew it would return again. So here, God's children are never disinherited. By regeneration we are made co-heirs with Christ; we have an interest in the whole patrimony of the gospel. Now God will not cut off the entail, nor take the advantage of every offence which his children commit. To insure us, he hath not only put the entail into our hands, by giving us his promise, but he hath given us earnest and seisin in part, and he hath chosen a feoffee in trust to keep the estate for us; our heavenly patrimony is kept safe in his hands. It is true we forfeit it by the merit of our actions, but the trust standeth still enrolled in the court of heaven, and is not cancelled. Christ is to look to that, and it being conveyed in and by him as the first heir, he is to interpose his merit; as under the law, if the person were not able to redeem the inheritance, the kinsman was to redeem it. Christ is our kinsman after the flesh, he is our *Goel*, and maketh all firm and sure between God and us. It is true we lose the evidences that are in our keeping, peace of conscience, joy in the Holy Ghost; but the estate is indefeasible, and cannot be made away from us. Well, then, you see that grace is kept, and the privileges of grace are kept. Oh, what a sweet comfort is this!

But now, because comforts are never prized but in their season, men that have not been exercised in spiritual comforts nauseate these sweet truths; they know not what it is to be left to uncertainty, when troubles come like waves, one upon the neck of another. Let us see when these truths will be sweet and seasonable.

1. In great troubles, when God seemeth to hide his face, oh! how sweet it is to hear God say, Gen. xxviii. 15, ' Behold I am with thee, and will keep thee in all places whither thou goest, and will bring thee again into this land; for I will not leave thee until I have done that which I have spoken to thee of.' All this shall better thy heart or hasten thy glory. We are apt to think that God will cast us off, and will never look after us any more, though formerly we have had real experience of his grace. What a foolish creature is-man, to weaken his assurance when he should come to use it, to unravel all his hopes and experiences! Times of trouble are a fit season to make use of this comfort.

2. In the hour of temptation, and hard conflicts with doubts and corruptions, when you find their power growing upon you, you are

ready to say, as David did after all his experiences, 'I shall one day perish by the hand of Saul,' 1 Sam. xxvii. 1; and many times out of distrust ye give over the combat; then say, 'Who shall separate us from the love of God?' One came to a pious woman, when she had been exercised with a long and tedious conflict, and read to her the latter part of the 8th of the Romans; she broke forth in triumph, 'Nay in all these things we are more than conquerors through him that loved us.' Sin or death cannot divide you from Christ; Christ will treat Satan under your feet, and weaken the malignant influence of the world.

3. In times of great danger and defection, through terror and persecution; as Sanders trembled to think of the fire; especially when others fall fearfully that were before us in privileges and profession of zeal and piety, when the first become last, when eminent luminaries are eclipsed, and leave their orb and station; as the martyrs were troubled to hear of the revolt of some great scholars that had appeared for the gospel. When Hymeneus and Philetus, two eminent professors, fell, it was a great shaking: 2 Tim. ii. 18, 19, 'Who concerning the truth have erred, saying, That the resurrection is past already, and overthrow the faith of some. Nevertheless, the foundation of the Lord standeth sure, having this seal, The Lord knoweth them that are his.'

4. In times of disheartening, because of the difficulties of religion, and the use of means groweth troublesome. To quicken us in our christian course, think of the unchangeableness of God's love. All grace riseth according to the proportion and measure of faith; loose hopes weaken endeavours: 1 Cor. ix. 26, 'I therefore so run, not as uncertainly; so fight I, not as one that beateth the air.' As those that run at all give over when one hath overreached them, they are discouraged; when hope is broken, the edge of endeavours is blunted. Go on with confidence, ye are assured of the issue; by these endeavours God will bless you and keep you; there is a sure recompense.

5. In the hour of death, when all things fail you, God will not fail you; this is the last branch: Do but wait, I will not forsake you; notwithstanding all that I have done, all that I have promised, there is more behind than ever you have enjoyed; death shall not separate. Olevian comforted himself with that, Isa. liv. 10, 'For the mountains shall depart, and the hills be removed; but my kindness shall not depart from thee, neither shall the covenant of my peace be removed, saith the Lord, that hath mercy on thee.' In the pains of death, sight is gone, speech and hearing is departing, feeling almost gone, but the loving-kindness of God will never depart. Oh! the Lord give us such a confidence in that day, that we may fix this comfort in our thoughts.

Doct. 2. That we are kept in the state of grace by God's name, by his power, for his glory.

God's attributes are called his name, because by them he is known, as a man by his name. I shall inquire—

1. What of the name of God is engaged in the preservation of the saints.

[1.] His truth, in opposition to our fickleness and falseness: 1 Cor.

x. 13, 'God is faithful, who will not suffer you to be tempted above what ye are able to bear, but will with every temptation make a way for you to escape, that ye may be able to bear it.' God cannot deny himself; his faithfulness is laid at pledge with the creatures. When difficulties and troubles are too hard for you, call him by his name: Lord, thou art faithful. When Judah was about to pass a hard sentence upon Tamar, she showed him his token, his bracelets, ring, and staff, 'Whose are these?' So may God's promises be showed to him.

[2.] His mercy, in opposition to oui unworthiness; mercy to pardon and pity and help us. Poor creatures! they will surely miscarry if I do not go down and help them: Heb. iv. 16, 'Let us come boldly to the throne of grace, that we may obtain grace, and find mercy to help us in time of need.' God is not upon his tribunal of justice, but his throne of grace. When you are in spiritual straits, be not discouraged; the time of need is a time for God to show himself. God hath mercy to pardon, and grace to pity and help; mercy for the recovery of every sinner, grace as a remedy for every misery. Do but observe thy heart, what thou wouldst have, and tell God every day.

[3.] His power, against our weakness: 2 Peter i. 5; 'We are kept by the power of God, through faith unto salvation.' This is our garrison; we cannot stand a moment longer than God upholdeth us by his power; as a staff in the hand of a man, take away the hand, and the staff falleth to the ground; or rather, as a little infant in the nurse's hand, which is God's own comparison: Hosea xi. 3, 'I taught Ephraim also to go, taking them by their arms.' If God should but let loose his hand, as he doth sometimes to make us sensible of our weakness, we should soon miscarry; as if God should let loose his hand of providence, all the creatures would fall into nothing.

[4.] I might mention his holiness, against our sinfulness. He is not only 'the Holy One,' but 'the Holy One of Israel,' the church's sanctifier; as the pipe would be dry if the fountain cease to run. But this is enough. *Deus, quantus est!* His whole name is engaged by Christ to do his people good.

2. Why we are only kept by God.

[1.] Nothing else could keep us but God's name. We should surely miscarry if our standing did depend upon the frailty of our will. We are weak, and the enemies and difficulties of our salvation are very great, corruptions within, and temptations without us; created grace could never hold out. One of the fathers bringeth in the flesh saying, *Ego deficiam;* the world, *Ego decipiam;* and Satan, *Ego eripiam.* But God saith, *Ego custodiam,* I will keep them, never fail them, nor forsake them; and there lieth our security. The world is a slippery place; it is strange that any hold their footing. We are carnal, and carnal persons are about us. It were strange for a man to keep his health in a town where every person, every house, and the air itself is infected with the plague; this is our condition. Then for the malice of Satan, he is a restless enemy, watcheth all advantages, as a dog that standeth waving his tail: it is Chrysostom's comparison. His envy and malice are bent against them that have most grace. There were two Adams, and both were tempted. In our hearts there is great deal of variableness; in the best of God's saints many ups and downs in points of grace. Our hearts are rebellious: Jer. v. 23, 'This people have a revolting and rebellious heart, they are revolted and gone;' Jer. xiv. 10, 'My people have loved to wander.' It is natural to the creature to be fickle and inconstant, especially in point of grace. It is a miracle that we, having such naughty hearts, where there is so much pride, love of pleasures, worldly cares, brutish lusts, any of us should hold out to the end. Would not we wonder to see a herb that we prize grow in the midst of weeds, a candle to burn in the water.

[2.] It is meet none else should. God will have this honour from all saints, and he will put this honour upon the saints, that he will be their guardian and keeper; not only angels, who are 'ministering spirits, sent forth to minister to them that are the heirs of salvation,' Heb. i. 14; they have a great deal of employment about God's children; but God himself will keep them: 1 Peter i. 5, 'Ye are kept by the power of God through faith unto salvation.' If your protection were visible, all the princes of the world would come short of your guard and attendance. God will be your watchman, your keeper, to foresee the danger and defend you from it: this honour he will have. He that is the maker of the world is the preserver of it; the keeping of the world could be trusted in no other hands but his that made it. So he is the preserver of the saints, as well as their maker: 1 Sam. ii. 9, 'By strength shall no man prevail;' he keepeth the feet of his saints; you rob God of the honour of your salvation by other confidences.

Use. It exhorteth us—

1. To a continual dependence on the name of God. All creatures have their refuges, the heirs of salvation are described to be those 'that fly for refuge to lay hold upon the hope that is set before them,' Heb. vi. 18. Now what is their refuge? Prov. xviii. 10, 'The name of the Lord is a strong tower; the righteous runneth into it, and is safe.' At Babel, to secure themselves, they would 'build a high and strong tower,' Gen. xi. 3, 4. We have a strong tower built to our hands. We that are at continual war should have a place of retreat; here is a sure one, you have it without cost; you need in the hour of temptation to make speed to it. What is this running, but pleading his faithfulness, looking up to his power, magnifying his grace in your dependence? Those that go forth in the strength of their own resolutions are sure to miscarry, as Peter was a sad instance.

2. To confidence. We may boast of his name: Ps. cxviii. 10–12, 'All nations compassed me about: but in the name of the Lord will I destroy them. They compassed me about, yea, they compassed me about: but in the name of the Lord I will destroy them. They compassed me about like bees; they are quenched as the fire of thorns: for in the name of the Lord I will destroy them.' Thrice it is, 'in the name of the Lord I will destroy them.' When we have such a keeper as is omnipotent, why should we fear? Though thou hast so many infirmities, allurements, discouragements, corrupt inclinations, thou standest not by thine own strength. Christ hath engaged God's name to keep thee: Ps. xvi. 8, 'I have set the Lord always before me; because he is at my right hand, I shall not be moved.' It is well that we have so good a second: a christian is a soldier that may triumph

before the victory.   It was a proverb, ' Let not him that putteth on his armour boast as he that putteth it off.'

3. To thankfulness.   Did we believe the power of corruption, we should be more thankful: 2 Cor. i. 21, ' Now he which stablisheth us with you in Christ, and hath anointed us, is God.'   He doth all, and being engaged with Christ, by virtue of your interest in him you shall stand. None should be proud of their standing in the state of grace; God must have all the glory: 1 Peter iv. 11, ' If any man speak, let him speak as the oracles of God: if any man minister, let him do it as of the ability that God giveth, that God in all things may be glorified through Jesus Christ, to whom be praise and dominion for ever and ever.   Amen.'

SERMON XVIII.

And now I am no more in the world, but these are in the world, and I come to thee.   Holy Father, keep through thine own name those whom thou hast given me, that they may be one, as we are.—
JOHN XVII. 11.

FOURTHLY, We are now come to the fourth circumstance, the persons for whom he prayeth, ' Those which thou hast given me.'   Some ancient copies read, ὃ δέδωκας μοῖ, ' thy name which thou hast given me ; ' but I will not trouble you with that.   Most read as we do, ὃυς, ' those which thou hast given me.'   But who are they ? and what is meant by God's giving us to Christ ? and why is it mentioned here ?   The phrase is often repeated, and used in many verses of this chapter.

I shall now explain it once for all.

1. Who are the persons that were given to Christ ?

I answer—Generally the elect, particularly the apostles.   The elect are and may be comprised within the expression ; for, ver. 9, it is put in contradistinction to the reprobate world, for whom Christ will not pray : ' I pray for them ; I pray not for the world, but for them that thou hast given me, for they are thine.'   But in the principal scope of this verse, the disciples of that age are intended, and among them chiefly the apostles, who are ἐκλέκτων ἐκλεκτότεροι, the elect of the elect ; for he doth principally pray for others afterward : ver. 20, ' Neither pray I for these alone, but for those which shall believe on me through their word.'   But after that again, both the disciples and all others that belong to the purposes of God's grace are folded or bound together up in this one expression : ver. 24, ' Father, I will that they also whom thou hast given me be with me where I am, that they may behold my glory.'   All which showeth that this expression, ' those which are given to Christ,' is a character proper and peculiar to the elect, and so Christ meaneth it in this place.   Nothing can be objected against this, but that in the verse next my text, ver. 12, ' Those that thou gavest me, I have kept, and none of them is lost but the son of perdition.'   So that either we must take this giving in a larger sense, or allow that some of those given to Christ may be lost.   I answer—

I might take the word in a larger sense indeed, as it is sometimes used in scripture, for those given to Christ only by way of reward, though not by way of charge, as I shall distinguish by and by. Hypocrites, because of their external vocation, are said to be given to Christ by way of ministry and service, but not by way of special charge. And it is notable what Christ saith of Judas, John xiii. 18, 'I speak not of you all, I know whom I have chosen: but that the scripture might be fulfilled, He that eateth bread with me hath lift up his heel against me;' where he showeth plainly that one of them was not of the number of the elect, and should not receive the privileges of his special charge; though he was chosen to the calling of an apostle, yet not to eternal life, but only given by way of ministry and service. But this would seem to cross the constant use of the phrase in this chapter. I answer therefore by interpreting the phrase, ϵi $\mu \grave{\eta}$ $\acute{o}$ $vi\grave{o}s$ $\tau \hat{\eta}s$ $\grave{a}\pi o\lambda \epsilon ias$, 'but the son of perdition;' the words are not exceptive, but adversative, and must be thus construed, 'None of them which thou hast given me is lost, but the son of perdition is lost.' And mark it, we do not render it *except* the son of perdition, but *but* the son of perdition; it is not *nisi*, but *sed;* there is no exception made of Judas, as if he had been given to Christ, and afterward had fallen away; but when he had mentioned their keeping, he would adversatively put the losing of Judas. This phrase or manner of speech is often used in scripture. So Rev. xxi. 27, 'There shall in nowise enter into it anything that defileth, neither whatsoever worketh abomination, or maketh a lie; but they that are written in the Lamb's book of life,' ϵi $\mu \grave{\eta}$; where the words are not exceptive, for then it would follow that some that work abomination were in the Lamb's book; but adversative— They shall not enter, but others shall enter. So Mat. xii. 4, 'David entered into the house of God, and did eat the shew-bread, which was not lawful for him to eat, neither for them which were with him, but only for the priests,' ϵi $\mu \grave{\eta}$; it is not exceptive, as if they were of David's company, but adversative—It was not lawful for them to eat, but it was lawful for the priests.

2. How are they said to be given to Christ? Persons are given to Christ two ways—by way of reward, or by way of charge.

[1.] By way of reward, and so more largely all nations are given to him: Ps. ii. 8, 'Ask of me, and I will give thee the heathen for thy inheritance, and the uttermost parts of the earth for thy possession;' and John xvii. 2, 'As thou hast given him power over all flesh.' This donation taketh in elect and reprobate. Nations are his heritage, as well as the church; only in this giving by way of reward, there is a difference; some are given to Christ at large, to be disposed of according to his pleasure; others are given to him for some special ministry and service, as hypocrites in the church; and thus Judas, amongst the rest, was given to Christ, though 'a son of perdition.' And again, others are given to him by way of special and peculiar interest, to be members of his body, subjects of his kingdom, children of his family. So only the elect are given to him: John xvii. 6, 'Thine they were, and thou gavest them me, and they have kept thy word.' The great bargain that Christ made for his Father was only[1] an interest in souls.

[2.] By way of charge. This again is only proper and peculiar to

---

[1] Qu. 'with his Father was only for'?—ED.

the elect; they were given to Christ by way of charge, to be redeemed, justified, sanctified, glorified; given, not by way of alienation, but oppignoration, laid at pledge in his hands, so that none of them can miscarry. I shall name some places to prove this way of giving: John vi. 37–39, ' All that the Father giveth me shall come to me,' &c.; where you see they shall surely and infallibly be brought to grace, and as infallibly be conducted to glory; and when they come, they cannot miscarry: ' This is the Father's will that hath sent me, that of all that he hath given me I should lose nothing.' Christ hath received a charge, he is to look to all God's flock, not to lose a leg, or a piece of an ear. So John x. 28, 29, ' I give unto them eternal life, and they shall never perish, neither shall any man pluck them out of my hands. My Father which gave them me is greater than all; and no man shall pluck them out of my Father's hands.' Where see Christ's power and faithfulness is engaged by the Father's gift for the preservation of the saints. So that we see what it is to be given to Christ, to become his reward, his charge.

3. A third question yet remaineth. Why is it mentioned here? The phrase, as I said, is often used in many verses of this chapter; but the repetition is not needless: it is not an empty tautology, but repeated for the more ample consolation and instruction of the apostles, that in the midst of their troubles they might look upon themselves as given to Christ, and so the more interested in a sure preservation; for God is bound to make good his grant, and Christ his trust. Christ pleadeth his own faithfulness: ver. 12, ' While I was with them in the world, I kept them in thy name: those which thou gavest me I have kept.' He made good his trust, and therefore now pleadeth with the Father that he would make good his grant: ' I am no more in the world, do thou keep them;' and he useth the same argument, ' Those which thou hast given me;' that swayed with him to keep them, and he knew the Father would take care of them for the same reason.

Well, now, having laid this foundation, let me—

Observe that this is a ground of solid consolation and establishment to the elect, that they are by the grant of God the Father given and committed to God the Son as his purchase and charge. The point is genuine, for this giving is by way of gift and charge; and this giving is proper to the elect, as we have proved; and it is here urged as a ground of establishment and consolation. Christ expresseth the elect by such a character, ' Those which thou hast given me,' not only to specify the persons, but to declare the ground of audience—Keep them, because they are those which thou hast given me.

Therefore, in following of it, I shall use this method :—

1. I shall more largely explain the manner of God's grant and donation to Christ.

2. I shall show you how it is a ground of establishment and consolation.

3. I shall enforce all by application.

First, To open the nature of the grant, let us again resume the distinction of giving by way of reward and charge. These two answer to one another, as work and wages. Christ taketh upon himself a charge of souls, and all his reward is that he may have an interest in them. Let us begin with the charge, the work first, and then the wages.

1. They are given to him by way of charge.   What his charge was will be opened by considering what the Father proposed concerning the elect, and how the Son undertook it.

[1.] What the Father proposed.   The words of heaven are ἄρρητα ῥήματα, 2 Cor. xii. 4, ' Words which it is not lawful for a man to utter.' Those secret ways of discourse and communication between the Father and the Son are to be adored with reverence and deep silence, were it not that the Spirit of God hath put them into such forms as are suitable to the transactions and intercourse which pass between man and man.   It is usual in scripture to put the passages which concern God and Christ into speeches: Ps. xl. 6–8, ' Sacrifice and offering thou didst not desire, mine ears hast thou opened : burnt-offering and sin-offering hast thou not required.   Then I said, Lo, I come : in the volume of the book it is written of me, I delight to do thy will, O my God ; yea, thy law is within my heart ;'. Ps, ii. 8, ' Ask of me, and I will give thee the heathen for thine inheritance, and the uttermost parts of the earth for thy possession ;' Ps. cx. 1, ' The Lord said unto my Lord, Sit thou at my right hand, until I make thine enemies thy footstool.'   The Father came to Christ, and did, as it were, say to him, Son, I am loath that all mankind should be lost, and left under condemnation ; there are some whom I have chosen to be vessels and receptacles of my mercy and goodness ; and because I am resolved that my justice shall be no loser, you must take a body and die for them ; and afterwards you must see that they be converted to grace, justified, sanctified, guided to glory, and that not one of them doth miscarry ; for I will take an account from you of them.   It were easy to prove all these things out of scripture, to wit, that there are a certain definite number whom God chooseth to be vessels of mercy : 2 Tim. ii. 19, ' The foundation of the Lord standeth sure, having this seal, The Lord knoweth those that are his.'   There is no lottery nor uncertainty in the divine decrees ; the number is stated and sealed, none can add to it, nor detract or take away any one person.   And that Christ received a command to lay down his life for them, and for them only : John x. 15, ' I lay down my life for my sheep ;' and ver. 18, ' This commandment have I received of my Father.'   The description is a limitation ; it is for his sheep.   God would have none of Christ's blood to run waste.   That he is to do this, that the honour of justice may be salved, and so mercy have the freer course : Rom. iii. 25, 26, ' Whom God hath set forth to be a pro-pitiation through faith in his blood, to declare his righteousness for the remission of sins that are past, through the forbearance of God.   To declare, I say, his righteousness ; that he may be just, and the jus-tifier of him which believeth in Jesus.'   The Son was not only to use entreaty, but to make satisfaction ; not that God by any necessity of nature required it ; the exercise of justice is free, and falleth under no laws ; but it was most convenient to preserve a due sense and appre-hension of the Godhead.   That Christ was to see them converted, it was the express will of God : John vi. 38, 39, ' For I came down from heaven, not to do mine own will, but the will of him that sent me.   And this is the Father's will that hath sent me, that of all which he hath given me, I should lose nothing, but should raise them up again at the last day ;' and by conversion, to be possessed of all the privileges of the gospel; and without miscarrying to be guided unto glory: John x. 28, 29, 'I give unto them eternal life, and they shall never perish, neither shall any man pluck them out of my hand. My Father that gave them me is greater than all; and no man is able to pluck them out of my Father's hand.' They are one, and act by joint power and joint consent. And after all this, he is to give an account of bodies and souls: John vi. 39, 'That of all which he hath given me, I should lose nothing, but should raise them up again at the last day.' Which accordingly he doth when he presents the kingdom to the Father, and appeareth before him with all his little ones, as a prey snatched out of the teeth of lions: Heb. ii. 13, 'Behold, I and the children which God hath given me.'

[2.] What Christ undertook; the whole proposal of the Father was accepted: Ps. xl. 7, 8, 'Lo, I come; in the volume of the book it is written of me, I delight to do thy will, O my God; yea, thy law is within my heart.' Christ consented to all the articles of the treaty and eternal covenant, not only to take a body to die, but to take a particular charge of all the elect. As Judah interposed for Benjamin, so doth Christ for all the souls committed to him: Gen. xliii. 9, 'I will be surety for him, of my hand shalt thou require him; if I bring him not to thee, and set him safe in thy presence, let me bear the blame for ever.' So doth Christ say concerning all the persons that fall under his charge. If I do not see them converted, justified, sanctified, saved, count me an unfaithful undertaker, and let me bear the blame for ever.

2. By way of reward. As in a covenant there is not only a duty incumbent, but a benefit accruing to the party that contracteth; so Christ in this eternal treaty dealt with God by way of bargain and purchase; his aim was to get a special interest in, and relation to believers, as mediator. This was all the gain he reckoned of: Isa. liii. 10, 'When thou shalt make his soul an offering for sin, he shall see his seed, he shall prolong his days, and the pleasure of the Lord shall prosper in his hand.' And therefore by virtue of this purchase he hath many relations to them; they are given to him as subjects of his kingdom, as scholars of his school, as children of his family, as the spouse of his bosom, as the members of his body. All these relations I shall insist upon; for this was the honour granted to Christ upon his obedience; I mean, he counted it an honour, and bought it at a dear rate, and yet was contented with the purchase. Alas! nothing could be added to the greatness of his person, who was equal with the Father in glory and power; the privileges of the incarnation were but as so many milder humiliations; but he was so tender of souls that he was pleased to take it as a gift from his Father, and a reward of all his services. Mark it, nothing else could bring Christ out of heaven into the manger, the wilderness, the cross, the grave, but to get an interest in your souls: Isa. liii. 11, 'He shall see of the travail of his soul, and shall be satisfied.' What did he gain by all his expense of blood and sweat, his temptations, agonies, taking our nature, bearing our burden, but to see you safe in the arms of mercy, that he might be your king, your prophet, your priest, your head? Next to the title of the Son of God, Christ valueth that of being head of the church. And see how

the relations are diversified, that he might come nearer and closer to
us: a king is a more large relation, a master hath a more particular
inspection; a master may be faithful and careful, but he hath not the
bowels of a father; a father is very tender, but the greatest intimacy
is between husband and wife, we are the wife of his bosom; if husband
be a relation too remote, because the union is civil, he comes nearer to
us yet, he will be our head, we his members, where the union is natural.
Let us go over these severally.

[1.] We are given to him to be subjects of his kingdom.   Christ is
lord of all the world, but he prizeth no title like that of king of saints,
Rev. xv. 3.   No throne to him like the conscience of a humble sinner;
the heart is his best presence-chamber, there is his throne of state set.
He had an eternal right, together with the Father and Holy Ghost,
but he would come and suffer, and be crowned with a crown of thorns,
that he might have a new right as mediator, and have the crown of
glory put upon his head in the church.   Therefore it is said, Acts v.
31, that upon his resurrection, 'God hath exalted him to be a prince
and a saviour, to give repentance unto Israel, and forgiveness of sins.'
The grant was made long before, when he first contracted with Christ
about the salvation of the world; but when the price was paid, then it
was made good.   There is never a subject Christ hath, but he is bought,
and with the dearest price, his sovereign's own blood: Mat. xx. 28,
'The Son of man gave his life a ransom for many,' λυτρόν ἀντὶ
πολλῶν.   In other kingdoms many subjects die, that the prince may
be seated in the throne; but here the prince dieth for the subjects'
sakes, that he may govern his spiritual realm with peace and quietness.   And as the price was great, so the Father hath made him a
large grant.   Christ's empire is universal; properly he is the catholic
king, there are no bounds and limits of his kingdom; first or last, in
all the habitable parts of the earth there are or shall be some that
acknowledge his sceptre: Isa. xlix. 12, 'Behold, these shall come from
far; and lo, these from the north, and from the west, and these from
the land of Sinim.'   From the east, west, north, south, Jews, Gentiles;
the Jews that are now his enemies shall acknowledge his sovereignty:
Hosea i. 11, 'Then shall the children of Judah, and the children of
Israel be gathered together, and appoint themselves one head, and they
shall come up out of the land.'   As the tribes flocked to Hebron to
crown David, so shall these to crown Christ; and this royal garland
shall Christ wear to all eternity.   It is true it is said, 1 Cor. xv. 29,
'He shall resign up the kingdom to the Father.'   I answer—In kingly
dignity there are two things—*regia cura* and *regius honor*—kingly
care, by which he ordereth and defendeth his subjects against enemies,
that shall cease; but the kingly honour which he receiveth from his
subjects shall be for ever and ever; he shall always be honoured as
king and mediator of the church.   He shall resign the kingdom; that
is, that way of administration by which he now governeth; for when
the elect are fully converted and sanctified, and enemies destroyed,
there will be no need of this care.   Now after he hath bought us out
of his Father's hands by his merit and purchase, he is forced to recover
us from the devil by his power and conquest.   The word is the rod of
his strength, the sacraments are our oath of allegiance; in prayer we

perform our homages, by alms and acts of charity we pay him tribute, and praise and obedience are the constant revenues of his crown. This is the first grant.

[2.] We are given to Christ as scholars of his school. He is the great prophet and doctor of his church; certainly Christ loveth the honour of this chair. He hath also obtained this title, Acts iii. 22, ' A prophet shall the Lord your God raise up to you from among your brethren; him shall ye hear.' Christ came out from the bosom of God to show us his heart and mind. So he is called, Heb. iii. 1, ' The apostle of our profession.' Christ doth so love a relation to his church, that you see he taketh the titles of own officers; though he is Lord of the church, yet he is ' the apostle of our profession;' he counteth it an honour to be a preacher of the gospel. The Son of God is first in the roll of gospel preachers; he is God's legate *à latere*, an apostle: he laid the foundation of the gospel when he was upon the earth, and he teacheth us now he is in heaven: he doth not teach the ear, but the heart; he doth not only set us our lesson, but giveth us a heart to learn it; the scripture is our book, and Christ our great master; and when he openeth our eyes, we shall see wondrous things in his law. Other teachers teach for hire, but he bought this liberty of God, that he might open his school, and become a light to Jew and Gentile.

[3.] We are given to him to be children of his family. The only thing propounded to allure Christ to the work of redemption was, Isa. liii. 10, ' He shall see his seed,' that he might have a numerous issue and progeny. He delighteth in us, though we are all Benonis, sons of sorrow. Though he died in the birth, yet he is wonderfully pleased with the fruitfulness of his death; as a woman delivered after sharp and sore sorrow, forgetteth all her past sorrow for joy of the birth. At the last day this will be Christ's rejoicing and crown, to see the multitude of his little ones all brought together: Heb. ii. 13, ' Behold, I and the children which thou hast given me.' It is a goodly sight, when Christ shall rejoice in the midst of them, and go with them, as a glorious train, to the throne of God the Father. Jesus Christ is our brother and our father; by regeneration and the merit of the cross he is our father; but in the possession of heaven he is our brother, for we are co-heirs with him.

[4.] We are given to him as the spouse of his bosom. This is another of Christ's honours, to be the church's bridegroom. The epithalamium is in Canticles and Ps. xlv. There the nuptials are celebrated. Ministers, they are, as John Baptist was called, ' Friends of the bridegroom.' Look, as a father giveth her whom he hath begotten to another for a spouse and wife, so doth God give his elect to Christ. Indeed Christ hath bought the church at his Father's hands; other wives bring a dowry, but Christ was to buy. As Saul gave his daughter to David, but first he was to kill Goliath, and to bring the foreskins of a hundred Philistines, 1 Sam. xvii. 25, and xviii. 25; so God gave Christ the church for a spouse, but Christ was to redeem her with his blood, the infernal Goliath was to be slain. Yea, ere Christ did obtain this honour, he gaineth our consent by the power of his Spirit, working with the entreaties of the word: Hosea ii. 14, ' I will allure her, and bring her into the wilderness, and speak comfortably unto her;' and ver. 19, 20, 'I will betroth thee unto me for ever; yea, I will betroth thee unto me in righteousness, and in judgment, and in loving-kindness, and in mercies; I will even betroth thee unto me in faithfulness, and thou shalt know the Lord.' First I will allure, then betroth; as David, after he had bought Michal with the danger of his life, yet was fain to take her away from Phaltiel, 2 Sam. iii. 13. The devil hath gotten Christ's spouse in his own arms; he is fain to rescue her, and oblige her to loyalty by the entreaties of his Spirit. Hereafter is the day of espousals; now the church is called the bride, then the Lamb's wife. Christ's honour, as well as our consent, is incomplete; then he cometh to fetch her, and present her to God, Eph. v. 27, and bring her into his Father's house. Christ is decking her against that time; we are to accomplish the months of our purification, and to have odours and garments out of the king's wardrobe, Esther i. 12.

[5.] We are given to him to be members of his body. Here is the nearest relation, and that which Christ most prizeth, next to the title of the Son of God, to be head of the church. Oh! what an honour is this to poor creatures, that Christ will take us into his own mystical body, to quicken us and enliven us, and guide us by his grace! To angels he is a head in point of sovereignty and power: Col. ii. 10, 'And ye are complete in him, which is the head of all principality and power.' But to the church he is a head by virtue of mystical union. Angels are his ministering spirits, but we his spouse; they are not called his bride, nor the spouse of his bosom, nor the members of his body. In the Ephesians, the church is called 'his body,' the 'fulness of him that filleth all in all,' Eph. i. 23. Poor creatures are πλήρωμα Χριστοῦ; he doth not count himself perfect without us, as if he were a maimed, imperfect Christ till all the church be where he is. He treateth his mystical body with the same respect that he doth his natural; it is raised, ascended, glorified, so shall we. For the present there is some communion between us; he is grieved in our miseries, and we are exalted in his glory. As there is a mutual passage of spirits between the head and the body, so there is a communion between Christ and us by donatives and duties.

Secondly, How this is a ground of establishment and consolation.

1. By this gift we have an interest both in God and Christ: 1 John i. 3, 'That which we have seen and heard declare we unto you, that ye also may have fellowship with us; and truly our fellowship is with the Father, and with his Son Jesus Christ;' 2 John 9, 'He that abideth in the doctrine of Christ, he hath both the Father and the Son.' God will make good his gift, and Christ his trust. God bestowed us upon his Son, to oblige Christ to the greater respect; and Christ hath bought us of his Father, that the gift might be sure and certain. The Son loveth us, because the Father required it; the Father loveth us, because the Son merited it. If Christ be faithful to his Father, or the Father be loving and respectful to Christ, we cannot miscarry. We have an interest in the Father, who is the fountain of mercy; in the Son, who is the golden pipe and conveyance. God made the elect to be members of Christ's body, that he might redeem them; and Christ made them children of God's family, that he might

love them and bless them. Electing love and Christ's purchase are the two fountains of salvation. God, who is the supreme judge, offended party, first cause and fountain of blessing, he requireth the Son to die for us ; and Christ hath undertaken it, and made good his word.

2. God hath put the business of our salvation into safe hands. He would not be defeated of his purpose, therefore he hath given the elect to Christ, that they may be quickened by virtue of that power and life which was given to him. He would deal with us upon sure terms, and therefore took order sufficient to attain his end ; he would not trust us with any but his own eternal Son. There is a charge laid on Christ, who is a good depositary, of such care and faithfulness, that he will not neglect his Father's pledge ; of such strength and ability, that nothing can wrest us out of his hands ; for he that doeth it had need of a stronger arm than Christ's, John x. 28, 29. Of such love, that no work can be more pleasing to him ; he loveth us far better than we do ourselves, or else he would never have come from heaven for our sakes. Of such watchfulness and care, that his eyes do always run to and fro throughout the earth. Providence is full of eyes, as well as strong of hand. As the high priest bore the names of the tribes upon his breast and shoulders, so doth Christ the memorial of every saint ; he knoweth their names and their necessities ; though many thousands in the world, yet every single believer falleth under the care of Christ, as if none besides him ; he knoweth them by head and poll, their wants, necessities. They are written in the ' Lamb's book of life,' Rev. xiii. 8. Christ keeps a register of them. There is not only God's book of remembrance, but the Lamb's book of life. He knoweth every distinct sheep by name, and constantly giveth an account of them to God: ' I am glorified in them.' It is grievous to our advocate when he is forced to be an accuser. He taketh a distinct and implicit notice of them: Isa. xl. 27, ' Why sayest thou, O Jacob, and speakest, O Israel, My way is hid from the Lord, and my judgment is passed over from my God?' Ps. xxxiv. 6, ' This poor man cried, and the Lord heard him, and delivered him out of all his troubles.' If it were not for this our keeper, we should surely perish ; but Christ is our keeper, who is faithful, loving, able, watchful. *Qui potest et vult, facit.* Christ's own charge cannot miscarry. If the elect should not be saved, Christ would neither do his work, nor receive his wages.

Use. To press us to come under these sweet hopes. There is nothing wanting but the clearing up of our interest, that you may be of the number of those that are given to Christ. You will know it by God's act towards you, and by your act towards God.

1. By God's act towards you. If we be given to Christ, Christ is given to us. We are given to Christ before all time, and in time Christ is given to us; by converting grace he and we are brought together. God makes an offer in the gospel; are we willing to receive him for Lord and Saviour? Then you put it out of question. Are you moved by the Spirit to receive him upon God's offer. Conversion, it is as it were an actual election. By original election the heirs of salvation are distinguished from others in God's purpose ; so by conversion, or actual election, they are visibly distinguished. What

excitements of grace can you speak of that urge you to come to Christ? All that are given to him come to him.

2. By your act towards Christ. All the Father's acts are ratified in time by believers; he ordaineth, we consent; he chooseth Christ for Lord and king, and 'they shall appoint themselves one head.' So God's giving of souls to Christ is ratified by the believers' act. As there is a double giving on his part, by way of charge and by way of reward, so there is a double act on our part, committing, and consecrating ourselves to Christ.

[1.] Committing ourselves to Christ. Can we wholly and absolutely resign up our souls into his hands? The Father is wiser than we; he knew well enough what he did when he commended us to his Son. Faith is often expressed by 'committing ourselves to Christ;' it answereth the trust the Father reposed in him: 2 Tim. i. 12, 'I know whom I have believed, and I am persuaded that he is able to keep, παραθήκην μου, that which I have committed unto him against that day.' This is not an easy matter, it argueth a sense of danger, a solicitous care about the soul, and an advised confidence. What care hast thou ever taken to lay thy soul safe? What confidence hast thou of Christ's ability? Didst thou think thou couldst be safe without him? Thou wouldst be an unfaithful guardian. Knowingly canst thou venture eternity on thy present state?

[2.] Consecrating ourselves to him: Rom. xii. 1, 'I beseech you by the mercies of God, that ye present your bodies a living sacrifice, holy, acceptable to God, which is your reasonable service.' Then walk as his, it is dangerous to alienate things once consecrated: 1 Cor. iii. 23, 'Ye are Christ's.' Whatever you have, you must give up to him for his glory. You have nothing at your own dispose, neither tongue, nor heart, nor estate; as long as a man reserves to himself an interest, he will miscarry. Nabal called what he had, 'My bread, and my water, and my flesh,' 1 Sam. xxv. 11. Did you ever make a serious resignation of yourselves to God? Ps. cxix. 94, 'I am thine, save me; for I have sought thy precepts.'

SERMON XIX.

And now I am no more in the world, but these are in the world, and I come to thee. Holy Father, keep through thine own name those whom thou hast given me, that they may be one, as we are. —JOHN XVII. 11.

FIFTHLY, The last circumstance, 'That they may be one, as we are,' is the aim of Christ's request, which is unity and consent among the apostles. It is illustrated by the pattern or exemplar of it, 'As we are one.'

The explicatory questions are two:—

1. What kind of unity this is that is prayed for.
2. Under what respect it is prayed for in this place.

First, What this unity is? How one? One in judgment, or one

in heart, or one body knit together with the same spirit? I answer—
All these; for consider for whom Christ prayeth, for the disciples of
that age, and principally for the college of the apostles; now saith he,
'Let them be one.' There is a double unity—mystical and moral.

1. Mystical union is the union of believers with Christ the head,
and with one another; with Christ the head by faith, and with one
another by love; *ἵνα ὦσιν ἕν,* understand *ἓν σῶμα;* so it agreeth with
the letter of this place, nay, with the meaning. This union of believers in the same body is often compared with the mystery of the
Trinity; and it is elsewhere expressed by one body, as Col. ii. 19, ' And
not holding the head, from which all the body by joints and bands
having nourishment ministered, and knit together, increaseth with the
increase of God;' a place full to this purpose, where all believers, in
regard of their union with the head, and with one another, are set
forth as one body, governed under one head, by one spirit, by which
they increase and grow up, till they come to such a kind of unity as
is among the divine persons. I cannot exclude this, because where
Christ's prayers are indefinite, it is good to interpret them in their full
latitude, and according to the extent of his purchase. And yet I think
this is not principally intended, because, as I said, Christ chiefly
prayeth for the apostles and disciples of that age, not for the church
catholic or universal.

2. There is a moral union, and that is twofold—(1.) Consent in
doctrine; (2.) Mutual agreement and concord of affection. As it is
said of the church, Acts iv. 32, ' The multitude of them that believed
were of one heart and one mind.' One heart, that noteth agreement
in affection; and one mind, agreement in judgment: for both these
doth Christ pray.

[1.] Let them be one in doctrine and judgment. Christ had
intrusted them with the weightiest affair the sons of men are capable
of, with the promulgation of the gospel; a doctrine which Christ
brought out of the bosom of the Father, and gave it to the apostles,
and they to the church; and Christ obtained that which he prayed
for. There is such an exact consent and harmony between the doctrine of the apostles, that is a sufficient foundation for the faith and
unity of the church. For the faith of the church : 1 Cor. xv. 10, 11,
' I laboured more abundantly than they all ; yet not I, but the grace
of God which was with me: therefore whether it were I, or they, so
we preach, and so ye believed.' We have no cause to stumble and
take offence at the doctrine delivered by the apostles; though. God
used several instruments, of different gifts and opportunities of service,
yet all were conducted by an infallible Spirit : ' So we preached, all
of us,' &c. So for unity and concord in the church: Eph. iv. 3–5,
' Endeavouring to keep the unity of the Spirit in the bond of peace.
There is one body, and one Spirit, even as ye are called in one hope
of your calling; one Lord, one faith, one baptism,' &c.

[2.] Let them be one in heart, and with joint consent carry on this
great charge that is committed to them. So did the apostles, by
unanimous consent, divide their labours for the edification of the world,
and kept a fellowship among themselves: Gal. ii. 9, ' They gave to me
and Barnabas the right hand of fellowship, that we should go unto

the heathen, and they to the circumcision ;' with such concord and agreement was this great work managed between them ; for all this did Christ pray.   And this suiteth with the pattern in the text, ' As we are one.'   As between the Father and the Son there was a mutual agreement in the carrying on the work of redemption, so between the apostles in carrying on the doctrine of redemption.

Secondly, In what manner doth Christ pray for it ?   Here some take this only as a new petition, different from the former ; he had prayed for preservation, now for unity.   But there is a causal particle, ἵνα, and therefore some connection : ἵνα may be taken *specificativè*, keep them, by making them one ; the safety of the church dependeth much upon the unity of it.   Or *terminativè*, keep them, that they may be one.

I had intended, because of the necessity of the matter, to have spoken of the union of the church with Christ, and then with one another But because he chiefly prayeth for the apostles (though others are not excluded), and because the union of the church, as one body, animated with the same Spirit, will fall under discussion in ver. 21 and 23, I shall adjourn it to that place.

Only now I shall observe—

1. How much Christ's heart is set upon the unity and oneness of his members.   Here he prayeth for the apostles ; in ver. 21 he prayeth the same for all believers.   Upon this occasion let us see how much it was in the aim of Christ.

[1.] Therefore was he incarnate.   He united the divine and human nature in his own person, that he might unite us to God by himself, and with one another.   God and man had never been one in covenant if they had not first been one in person.   The hypostatical union maketh way for the mystical.   It was the main end of Christ's coming into the world, Eph. i. 10, ' That in the fulness of time he might gather together in one all things in Christ.'   The angels and blessed spirits, and the saints in all nations, have communion with us in Christ under the same head.   He would gather the elect rational creatures into a body, one with God in Christ, saints and angels.   As all the heads of a discourse are summed up in the conclusion, so Christ would draw all into one body.   He took a natural body that he might have a mystical body.   Christ would not only leave us the relation of friends and brethren, but fellow-members.   He would gather together all into one ; not only into one family, but into one body.   Brothers that have issued from the same womb, that have been nursed with the same milk, have been divided in interests and affections, and defaced all feelings of nature ; Cain and Abel, Jacob and Esau, are sad instances.   But this mischief is not found in members of the same body ; there is no contestation and disagreement. . Who would use one hand to cut off another ? or divide those parts, which preserve the mutual correspondence and welfare of all ? Again, brothers, if they do not hurt one another, they do not care for one another ; each liveth to himself a distinct life apart, and studieth his own advantage.   But it is not so in the body ; each member liveth in the whole, and the whole in all the members ; and they all exercise their several functions for the common good ; 1 Cor. xii. 25, ' The members should have the same care one of another.' We are not friends and brethren, but members.

[2.] No one thing is so much inculcated in his sermons : John xv. 17, 'These things I command you, that ye love one another.' Will you take a charge from a dying man? This was the great charge that Christ left at his death; it was a legacy as well as a precept. Speeches of dying men are wont to be received with much veneration and reverence, especially the charge of dying friends. The brethren of Joseph, fearing lest he should remember the injuries done to him in seeking his life, selling him into Egypt, they use this plea, Gen. l. 16, 17, 'Thy father commanded us before he died, saying, So shall ye say unto Joseph, Forgive, I pray thee now, the trespass of thy brethren, and their sin; for they did thee evil: and now we pray thee, forgive the trespass of the servants of the God of thy father.' We count it a piece of natural honesty to fulfil the will of the dead. When Christ took his leave of the disciples, this was the charge that he left upon them. Therefore when thy heart beginneth to be exulcerated, consider, What love do I bear Christ, since I do not respect his last commandment? Again, as it was Christ's last commandment, so it was his new commandment: John xiii. 34, 'A new commandment I give unto you, That you love one another; as I have loved you, that ye also love one another.' It was his solemn charge; a new commandment! How new, since it was as old as the moral law or law of nature? New because excellent, 'as a new song ;' or new because solemnly and expressly renewed by him and commended to their care; as new things and new laws are much esteemed and prized; Christ would have this commandment always new and fresh ; or new because enforced by a new argument : 'As I have loved you, so should ye love one another.' When we see how much Christ hath loved us, even to the death of the cross, we may learn to love with a new kind of love: *Experti amorem meum tam novum et inauditum.* This was a new kind of love indeed, to enkindle love in our souls. Christ gave us such a new kind of love as was never seen nor heard of. Christ came from heaven to propound us a pattern of charity ; as to repair and preserve the notions of the Godhead by the greatness of his sufferings, so to show us a pattern of charity, and to elevate duty between man and man : Eph. v. 2, 'Walk in love, as Christ also hath loved us, and hath given himself for us, an offering and a sacrifice to God of a sweet-smelling savour.' In Christ's example we see the highest pattern of love: John xv. 9, 'As the Father hath loved me, so have I loved you.' His Father loved him with an infinite love, yet parted with him for the salvation of men ; and Christ parted with himself, and all to raise our love to God and men the higher. But I digress.

[3.] In his prayers, that which he reinforced again and again is unity and love. When he was about to die he foresaw the divisions of the church, and that Satan would by all means endeavour to sow strife ; corrupt nature putteth us on discords. He left some apostles, others believers, but all men ; wherefore he prays for the apostles, 'Let them be one ;' for believers, 'Let them be one.' Christ, that left unity as a charge in his last sermons, he would leave it as a legacy in his last prayers. But why was Christ so earnest in his prayers?

(1.) Because it is such an excellent blessing. Christ would not have been so earnest for it if it had not been so excellent. I would not digress into a commendation of concord and love: *pax ab omnibus laudatur, a paucis servatur;* all commend it, though few observe it; yet a little will not be unnecessary. This is the strength and safety of the church: Col. iii. 14, 'And above all things put on charity, which is σύνδεσμος τῆς τελειότητος, the bond of perfectness,' or a perfect bond, the cement of the church. The church is but one temple, where stones squared by grace are cemented with love, and inhabited by the same Spirit; this keepeth them fast in the building. This is the beauty and safety of the church, the joining that runneth through all the squared stones. As the health of the outward body dependeth on the symmetry and proportion of the members, and the harmony and disposition of all the parts, so doth the welfare of the church upon the bond of love. Next to truth, there is not a greater blessing; and Christ prayeth for the apostles, that they might be kept in the truth for this end, that they might be one in love. And as nothing is more profitable to the church, so nothing is more acceptable to God; it pleaseth God exceedingly to see all that call him Father to love as brethren. Certainly there is not a greater grief to his spirit than to see us divided in opinion and affection, in our prayers and supplications. Certainly there is much in concord in praying, when all God's children do besiege heaven with uniform and joint supplications. Things stick in the birth, because we are not agreed what to ask. As reformation sticketh towards men, because we are not agreed what to hold forth to the world, so it sticketh as to God, because we are not agreed what to ask. When the Israelites would have God's help, it is said they came all as one man to ask his counsel: Judges xx. 1, 'Then all the children of Israel went out, and the congregation was gathered together as one man, from Dan even to Beersheba, with the land of Gilead, unto the Lord in Mizpeh.' Oh! when shall it be so amongst us? There is not only altar set up against altar, but prayer against prayer. We are first divided in practices and opinions, and then in prayers; God's dear children and servants are divided in language; we cannot in charity but judge them to be acted with the same spirit, inspired with the same breath, yet they yield a different sound. It is said of the primitive believers that 'they continued, ὁμοθύμαδον, with one accord, in prayer and supplication,' Acts i. 14; and 'they were with one accord in one place' when the Holy Spirit descended on them, Acts ii. 1. And yet how seldom doth any public congregation meet with one mind in the same place! as in an organ, when some pipes do make a sound, others keep silence: Mat. xviii. 19, 'If two of you shall agree on earth, as touching anything that they shall ask, it shall be done for them of my Father which is in heaven. God looks for an agreement and harmony in our requests, if we would speed with him.

(2.) Because Christ foresaw how much the church would need this blessing. Divisions will arise, an evil most unsuitable to christianity, and yet the evil genius that hath attended it; partly through Satan's malice; he cannot else hold the empire and title to the world; he is not only prince of the power of the air, but the God of this world. God permitteth him in his righteous judgment not only to have a great power over the elements, but to rule in the hearts of men. Now he could not keep his own, nor prevail against the church, were it not for divisions. As Cyrus in Herodotus, going to fight against Scythia, coming to a broad river, and not being able to pass over it, cut and divided it into divers arms and sluices, and so made it passable for all his army ; this is the devil's policy, he laboureth to divide us, and separate us into divers sects and factions, and so easily overcometh us. Christ knew that the envious man would sow tares. Partly through weakness and imperfection of knowledge, divers men may agree in one aim, and yet not in one way. The apostle saith (which indeed is the great canon and rule of charity, when it is rightly understood and applied), Phil. iii. 15, 16, ' Let us therefore, as many as be perfect, be thus minded ; and if in anything ye be otherwise minded, God shall reveal even this unto you : nevertheless whereto we have already attained, let us walk by the same rule, let us mind the same thing.' I observe there, that among the godly, because of difference of light, especially in times of reformation, there will be difference of judgment, though they agree in the same aim. As when divers physicians are sent for to a sick person, some think that the best way to cure the sick person is to take away all the corrupt blood at once, others think it best to take it away by little and little ; here is a difference in judgment, but yet the aim is the same, all intend the good of the sick party : so it is in curing a sick church ; some are for taking away all, and beginning upon a new foundation, others for a regular reformation, to try all ways and all means of recovery ; this is a difference. Or rather thus : when a house is on fire, some are for pulling it down, others are for quenching it, and letting the building stand ; it requireth a present remedy, and in this hurlyburly the master's voice is not always heard. So it is in reformation of inveterate errors and customs that have crept into the church ; there is a difference of judgment about the cure, and God's voice in the confusion is not always heard. Partly through vile affections ; man's nature is very prone to discords, out of pride, worldly interests, desire of precedency, envy of one another's reputes, irregular zeal ; all these make us touchy. Some are of a. salt and fiery humour, like flax and gunpowder, the least spark catcheth, and setteth them into a flame. Much experience hereof we have in these dogdays of the church, wherein every one is barking and biting at one another, whereby Christ is exceedingly dishonoured, and the cause of religion much disadvantaged. Therefore that there might be some sparks of love kept alive in the church, is Christ so earnest with the Father, ' Let them be one.'

(3.) That we might know that unity among believers is a possible blessing. It seemeth many times past hope, and that it were as good to speak to the winds to be still as to men's prejudices and boisterous affections. Ay ! but there is hope ; Christ hath prayed for it, and his prayers are as good as so many promises : John xi. 42, ' I know that thou hearest me always.' This is a fountain of comfort and hope.

(4.) To encourage us to pray for it. Endeavours with men are without fruit and success ; but let us ply the throne of grace more, and learn of Christ to go to our heavenly Father, and wrestle with him in supplications. In one place it is said, Rom. xii. 18, ' If it be possible, as much as in you lies, live peaceably with all men.' *Fac quod tuum est.* We must do whatever is possible; but we are not in the place of God: 2 Thes. iii. 16, 'The God of peace give you peace always by all means.' It seems as if a small matter would set all right, but we have it not in our power; a little light, a little love; a little light to make the prejudices vanish, a little love to conquer animosities. But God alone must do the work; he can bow men's rugged and crooked spirits: Isa. xi. 6, 7, 'The wolf also shall dwell with the lamb, and the leopard shall lie down with the kid, and the calf, and the young lion, and the suckling together, and a little child shall lead them; and the cow and the bear shall feed, their young ones shall lie down together; and the lion shall eat straw like the ox.' It is an allusion to the beasts in the ark, where all enmity was taken away; they were all tame. So the gospel can meeken the heart. Not that so disagreeing tempers shall remain in the christian church, which (though the ravenous disposition of some did cease) would make a motley company, and (as the prophet speaks) like a speckled bird; but besides the extinction of noxious qualities, all shall be governed by the same Spirit of truth and holiness.

[4.] Christ died for this end: Eph. ii. 14–16, 'He is our peace, who hath made both one, and hath broken down the middle wall of partition between us; having abolished in his flesh the enmity, even the law of commandments contained in ordinances; for to make in himself of twain one new man, so making peace; and that he might reconcile both unto God in one body by the cross, having slain the enmity thereby.' He died, not only to reconcile us to God, but to one another, to make of twain one body, and destroy the enmity in his flesh. Other sacrifices are a sign of separation, therefore he would be a sacrifice of union. The flesh of bulls and goats were a wall of partition between Jews and Gentiles; but he would destroy the enmity in his flesh, to make of twain one. So Caiaphas prophesied, John xi. 52, that Christ should die to 'gather together in one the children of God that were scattered abroad.' Christ died to enlarge the pale, that all nations, though of different rites, customs, and interests, might become one.

[5.] This he aimed at in his ascension, and the pouring out of the Spirit. We read of the unity of the Spirit: 'Keeping the unity of the Spirit in the bond of peace,' Eph. iv. 3. It is called the unity of the Spirit, not because the union is spiritual and mystical, but because the Spirit is the author of it. Therefore it is said, 1 Cor. xii. 4, 'There are diversities of gifts, but the same Spirit.' Christ would have but one spirit to run through all his members, that as they are united to one head, so they may be animated by one spirit. Christ is the head of the church, and the Spirit is the soul of the church. There is a spirit of communion. Look, as it is said, Ezek. i. 21, 'When the beasts went, the wheels went; and when those stood, these stood; and when those were lifted up from the earth, the wheels were lifted up over against them;' the reason is, because 'the spirit of the living creature was in the wheels.' So because the same spirit is in one christian that is in another, therefore they have the like affections, to procure the good of one another as much as may be. Christ giveth us the Spirit to make us one. But of this spirit of communion more hereafter.

[6.] This is the end of his gracious dispensations, he giveth us grace and assurance of glory to this end: John xvii. 22, 'And the glory which thou gavest me I have given them, that they may be one, even as we are one.' Understand it of the privilege of filiation; we are made sons that we may live as brethren; or of the gift of grace, the glorious image of God is impressed on all the saints, that likeness may beget love; or of an interest in glory, that those that expect to live in the same heaven may not fall out by the way, and disagree on earth.

[7.] It is the end of his ordinances and appointments in the church. Baptism and the Lord's supper are to keep the saints together. It is sad indeed that the world maketh them apples of strife, when Christ made them bonds of love : 'We are all baptized by one Spirit into one body, and have been all made to drink into one spirit,' 1 Cor. xii. 13. It notes our union with Christ and one with another. And 1 Cor. x. 17, 'We being many, are one bread and one body; for we are all partakers of that one bread.' The sacraments are banners, under which we do encamp, and profess our union and brotherhood in the army of Christ.

Use 1. How contrary are they to Christ that love strife and sow discord among brethren; they are the devil's factors, agents for the kingdom of darkness; they wholly frustrate the design and undertaking of Jesus Christ. He was incarnate, preached, prayed, died, &c., that his people may be one. Yea, they do not only what in them lieth to frustrate Christ, and make void his aim, but do also disparage him before the world; he holdeth out to all the world that his people are one body, one family, one house, and yet they are crumbled into factions. Divisions in the church beget atheism in the world. Oh! let it not seem a small thing to rend the unity of the church. But where shall this be charged? Every one will excuse himself from the guilt of the present breaches. Certainly we have all cause to reflect upon our own hearts, and not make application for others. It is usual with us to do as Judas; when Christ told his disciples somewhat that concerned him, he looked round about upon the disciples. So we look about upon others, when we should smite upon our own thigh. One of the bellows of strife is crimination and recrimination; therefore let us see a little who is guilty. The unity is twofold—one in mind, one in heart; one in judgment, one in affection. Now what hast thou done contrary to either of these unions?

1. If thou hast been a stickler in novel opinions, whereby division hath been caused in the church, thou hast dis-served the aim of Christ. Christians are bound to be of one mind: 1 Peter iii. 8, 'Finally, be ye all of one mind,' &c.; Phil. ii. 2, 'Fulfil ye my joy, that ye be likeminded, having the same love, being of one accord, of one mind;' 1 Cor. xiii. 2, 'Though I have all faith, so as I can remove mountains, and have no charity, I am nothing.' But you will reply, Will you enforce judgment or impose belief, and make me an hypocrite and yourself a usurper? And what are novel opinions? You condemn others, and they you; you preach against them, and they against you. Yea, but yet christians should strive, as much as is possible, to be all of a mind; and it should trouble thee if forced to differ from the general judgment of the church. In doubtful matters, take not up an

opinion which will offend : 'Beware of doubtful disputations.' He that dissents had need have plain evidence, and that the truth should be brought with much demonstration to the conscience, arguments had need be express and clear, and he had need pray much, and consult and confer with others. But when singularity and diversity of opinions is affected, *homini congenitum est magis nova quam magna mirari*, and without any fear and jealousy, men let loose their hearts to novelties, this is blameworthy. When we have the consent of the church, a less light will serve the turn than for a dissent.

2. Hast thou done anything to hinder the church from being of one heart?

[1.] By professing principles of separation; certainly it is a crime. It is against love, as error is against faith ; it cuts asunder the bands and sinews of Christ's mystical body. In these times, the charge of this sin is so frequent, that the sin is little regarded. Every modest dissent and unconformity is branded with the name of schism, that men think schism no such matter, or no such crime : Jude 19, 'These be they who separate themselves,' ἀποδιορίζοντες. Now it is dangerous to separate, and hard to discern when it is lawful. The question of separation lieth in the dark, but the enforcements of love are plain and open. Divers allow but three grounds of separation—intolerable persecution, damnable heresy, and gross idolatry. We should hold communion as long as Christ will. Scandal is a ground of mourning, but not a ground of separation, and whenever it is done, it must be with grief.

[2.] They that prosecute controversies in such a way as will not stand with love, viz., with passion, bitterness of spirit, damning all opposites, suppressing them by the power of the sword. Wrath, exulceration, and bitterness of spirit, are opposite to love. Michael durst not bring a railing accusation. The worst adversaries are overcome with soft words and hard arguments. Railing and reviling makes men deaf to the tenders of reconciliation : Ps. cxx. 7, 'I am for peace ; but when I speak, they are for war.' So is damning all opposites, casting them out of Christ, urging things beyond the weight and consequence of the opinion, censuring others as not spiritual, 1 Cor. xiv. 37. Interest makes men passionately and irregularly zealous : 1 Cor. i. 2, 'To all that in every place call on the name of Jesus Christ our Lord, both theirs and ours;' not as a party impropriating Christ, 'I am of Christ.' So is domineering over men's consciences, and obtruding opinions by force ; these are said 'to go in the way of Cain,' Jude 11.

Use 2. Let us be as earnest for unity as Christ; let us think of charity more than we have done, how to preserve peace, as well as truth. Certainly we that have one Father, are born of one mother, acknowledge one elder brother, even Christ, by whom we are adopted, hope for one patrimony, we should be more careful 'to keep the unity of the Spirit in the bond of peace.' We have a great many contentions now for one holy contention : Heb. x. 24, 'Let us consider one another, to provoke to love and to good works.' What arguments shall I use ? The danger of the Papists on one hand, of sects on the other. Of Papists; if ever the beast were likely to recover of his wounds, now it is. Our divisions make us first a laughing-stock to the enemy, and then a prey; first we are had in contempt, then they use violence. And it may be just with God to suffer it; when piety decreaseth, charity is exiled; and bitterness, partialities, strife, suspicions are only left to reign and flourish. Certainly, if once a peace were settled in the Reformed churches, the prophecies concerning antichrist would soon be accomplished; those relicts of God's election, which do as yet remain in spiritual Babylon, would soon come out from amongst them, who are now scandalised at our divisions: as when a boat is to take in passengers, when all the passengers are in the boat, they launch out, and hoist up sail. They are weary of the idolatry and superstitions of the Romish church, and would soon break the cords wherewith they are now held; truth would have a greater power: Acts iv. 32, 33, 'And the multitude of them that believed were of one heart and of one soul; neither said any of them that aught of the things which he possessed was his own, but they had all things common. And with great power gave the apostles witness of the resurrection of the Lord Jesus, and grace was upon them all.' As to sects on the other side, libertines daily increase, by means of the divisions amongst them that fear God, and grow formidable in the variety of their combinations and endeavours: Jude 11, 'Woe unto them, for they have gone in the way of Cain, and run greedily after the error of Baalam for reward, and perished in the gainsaying of Core.' There would be an end of this itch if all that fear God would join together as one man in the defence of the gospel. Alas! we have striven long enough, hindered the common salvation long enough; scandals enough have been given: it is high time to renounce all fruits of revenge and ambition, and think of peace and unity.

But you will say, What would you have us to do?

I answer—Something with God, something as to men. Something with God; pray and mourn, lay to heart the divisions that are among God's people. I speak for Sion's sake; we should be very earnest with God for Sion: Isa. lxii. 1, 'For Sion's sake I will not hold my peace, and for Jerusalem's sake I will not rest, until the righteousness thereof go forth as brightness, and the salvation thereof as a lamp that burneth.' A great house is smitten with breaches, and a little house with clefts; not only kingdoms, but particular families are destroyed, when the members of them are divided in opinions and affections: Ps. cxxii. 6, 'Pray for the peace of Jerusalem; they shall prosper that love thee.' Let this be your constant request to God; be not acted with a private factious spirit.

Something is to be done with men. I do not speak now how to keep peace; it is past that; but how to restore it now it is lost. What shall we do? The apostle telleth you, Phil. iii. 15, 16, 'Let us therefore, as many as be perfect, be thus minded: and if in anything ye be otherwise minded, God shall reveal even this unto you. Nevertheless whereto ye have already attained, let us walk by the same rule, let us mind the same thing.' There is no remedy now left but brotherly forbearance towards those that hold the foundation. It were to be wished that we could agree, not only in fundamentals, but in all other the accessaries of christian doctrine. But this cannot be hoped for. What then? Shall the rent go further and further without any remedy? No; let therefore all parties that, in the judgment of a regular charity, may be presumed to have owned Christ, walk together as far as they have attained. And how is that? I can only propound my wishes and desires; let them, reserving their private differences to themselves, come under some common rule, or solemn acknowledgment of the foundations of religion. What if there were a form drawn up to that purpose, to which both should stand? I think to state fundamentals is a matter of great difficulty. God would make us cautious of every truth; therefore the canon of the scripture is very large. But there are some things propounded in the scriptures as absolutely necessary, without which salvation cannot be had. If we were mutually engaged to the profession of these, patiently bearing with one another in other things undecided, mutually abstaining from magisterial decisions and enforcements, and obtruding opinions upon one another by violence, and all rash condemnations, castings out of Christ, limiting religion to our own party, saying, Here is Christ, and there is Christ; as if Christ were divided; commending one another's prosperity to God by mutual prayers, this were a healing course. Let us perform all mutual offices of love and spiritual counsel to one another, strengthening one another in solid piety, holding forth light in the lesser differences, with all modesty and candour; and in civil matters standing as one man against the common enemy, and using endeavours to promote the kingdom of Christ, without any reflections on our private honour, profit, and interests. If this were once done, I doubt not but the fog would vanish, and we should find ourselves nearer to one another than we do imagine. I am not altogether out of hope that this will be done, because of the promises. It is done already in the kingdom of Poland, between the Lutherans and the Calvinists.

Use 3. To persuade the ministers of the gospel to a greater concord and amity in the joint discharge of their work. Christ prayeth here for the apostles, ' that they may be one.' How should we agree together in pressing duty, reprehending sin! This would be an effectual and potent means, not only to the peace of the church, but success of the gospel. Schism in the church of Corinth arose from the emulation of ministers among themselves, one striving to excel the other in eloquence and favour among the people, and contemning Paul and others, that followed the simplicity of the gospel. So the apostle noteth it elsewhere: Phil. i. 15, ' Some preach Christ out of envy and strife, and some also of good-will.' It is usual that one carpeth at another's gifts, one standing in the way of another's honour and profit; like men in a boat, jostling at one another till the boat itself be sunk. One faileth, and yieldeth to the promises and threatenings of the world, another standeth stoutly; and from their different practices there proceed different interests and opinions. We should with a combined strength promote the gospel.

2. Observe the pattern; he doth not only pray, ' Let them be one,' but shows what kind of oneness he meaneth, ' as we are one.' Some think that by *we* is meant the Father and Christ as mediator, between whom there was an agreement in the work of redemption; this is true: but unity of essence, I suppose, is here intended, there being a plain intimation in the context of the περιχώρησις, peculiar to the Trinity

(viz., ver. 21). But what then shall we say to the Arians? I answer—In this καθώς is implied, not ἰσότης, but ὁμοιότης; not an exact equality, but some resemblance; not the same unity, but a like.

Doct. The union of believers with Christ the head, and with one another, hath some resemblance to the unity that is between the divine persons themselves.

1. It is a spiritual union, not natural or civil, but divine and spiritual.

2. It is a close union. Between the Father and the Son there is not only consent, but unity of essence; there cannot be a greater unity. So there is a close unity between the members of the mystical body, by love, and peace, and concord, and delighting in one another. It is *unitas pluralis, et pluralitas unita*, saith Bernard.

3. It is a constant and inseparable union. The divine essence may be distinguished, but not divided. They that are united to Christ cannot be separated from him, and should not from one another. Take heed of straggling. What becomes of the member that is cut off from the body, the branch from the root? It is dangerous to run from the shepherds' tents.

4. It is a holy union. There is no unity but what standeth with purity: Mark ix. 56, 'Have salt in yourselves, and peace one with another.' The heart must be kept pure and holy. Loose zeal, it is not unity, but compliance. Peace with men is bought upon hard terms when we must go to war with God; it is better still to be a man of contention. An agreement in evil is like that of Herod and Pilate, who shook hands against Christ: Heb. xii. 14, 'Follow peace with all men, and holiness, without which no man shall see God.' A man may see God without peace, but he cannot see God without holiness.

5. It is a unity which consisteth with order and distinction. There is in the church a subordination of callings, by which its beauty and strength is maintained; and if we would keep this unity, we must yield honour to one another's gifts and places. In the body natural, the eye meddleth not with hearing, nor the ear with seeing; the foot talketh not; the office of the hand is to dress the body, that of the foot to support the body. The soul giveth life to all the parts, there is ground of unity; but the parts have several offices, and there is ground of order and comeliness. The soul enlivens the feet, as well as the hands and breast. It is comfortable to see all conscionably in their way joining together for the common good.

Use. Let us study to imitate the Trinity; as in the case now before us, there is a little resemblance of the mystery of the Trinity. Men cry for a union, and yet make no conscience of separation. They would have an unholy mixture, a carnal compliance and consent, for carnal ends, out of worldly policy; as ice amasseth into a body iron, water, wood, sticks, and stones. We have one unity, but observe not due distinction therein. Is there not a horrible invasion of callings, and thence comes confusion and disorders? Ministers turn soldiers, and soldiers turn ministers? Oh! but remember, Christ commendeth this pattern to us, Walk as those that are one, as Christ and the Father are one, seeking one another's welfare, rejoicing in one another's graces, as if they were our own; contributing counsel, sympathy, spiritual assistance, and prayers for the common good. When the finger is hurt, there is pain through the whole body. We should live as if we had but one essence and interest. It is almost in vain to hope for the public at present, but in your particular societies, faithfully yet regularly use your gifts for the common good, so as that you may neither dishonour the head nor dissolve the union between the members.

3. I observe that Christ seeketh it of God; he beggeth perseverance, 'that they may be one.'

Doct. It is God that keepeth the saints together. Nature is prone to discord; if God should leave us, we should soon discover what is in our hearts. God doth it sometimes by his providence, letting loose the common enemy, as a dog let loose makes the sheep run together; or by inflicting great distress, as two ends of wax are joined together in the fire; or he can take off contention, as a judge. Sometimes by his Spirit, and the constant influences of his grace, of light and love. God made Esau a friend to Jacob. Let spirits be never so rough, he can meeken them.

Use. Acknowledge God in this matter. He will be known as the Lord of hosts, and as the God of peace. Acknowledge him in this matter, in prayer and praise. In prayer, before division is broken out; if God did but leave men to their own sway, they would never be at peace. After divisions are broken out, prayer is the best means to settle the church. It is God's prerogative to speak peace; when men have wearied themselves in the pursuit of it, it is God must give it. Acknowledge him in praise in days of peace and tranquillity; when there is a happy union among the people of God, give thanks to his name for it, for it is God alone, who is the 'God of the spirits of all flesh,' that unites the spirits of men to one another.

SERMON XX.

While I was with them in the world, I kept them in thy name : those that thou gavest me I have kept, and none of them is lost, but the son of perdition; that the scripture might be fulfilled.—JOHN XVII. 12.

IN this verse Christ declareth how he had performed his duty to the apostles when corporally present with them, which help was now to be removed. He had said before, 'I am no more in the world;' and he saith now, 'Whilst I was with them in the world, I kept them,' &c.

The argument is taken from the necessity of the request, and the equity of it.

1. The necessity. He could no longer keep them as he had kept them, by his visible presence, outward ministry, and familiar conversation; therefore he beggeth the Father to keep them. Christ is careful to remedy every defect; when the visible external custody was to have an end, then he beggeth the spiritual.

2. The equity. When thou commendedst them to me, I kept them;

now I commend them to thee, do thou keep them. Which is not
to be so understood as if Christ did totally resign his charge unto the
Father, or as if the Father and Son kept us by turns. No; as the
Father is not hitherto excluded, so not the Son for the future. But he
speaketh of his visible familiar presence and care, which was now to
cease ; and in lieu of it he beggeth his Father's custody and tutelage ;
and that upon this ground, because of his faithfulness during his
corporal presence.

In the words, you may observe—

First, Christ's care.

Secondly, The fruit of it—(1.) As to the elect ; (2) As to the son of
perdition. Which, that it might not be scandalous to his custody,
or manner of keeping, is mollified by a prediction or prophecy of
scripture.

' While I was with them in the world ; ' corporally, visibly present,
familiarly conversant. He speaketh as if he were already gone, because
the time of his departure was at hand.

' I kept them in thy name.'—Christ kept them, as man, instru-
mentally, by teaching, conversing, warning, by daily precepts and
examples ; as God, as the principal agent, by inward influxes and
operations of grace; as it is presently added, ' in thy name,' by thy
authority and power, for thy glory.

' Those that thou gavest me I have kept, and none of them are lost.'
—I shall only open the different manner of keeping and losing, spiritually and corporally ; none were lost by death or defection. Spiritually,
Christ kept them against the world, the flesh, and the devil. Satan
had a spite at them : Luke xxii. 31, ' Simon, Simon, behold Satan hath
desired to have you, that he may sift you as wheat.' Their own hearts
are weak and apt to stagger : John vi. 66, ' Many of his disciples went
back, and walked no more with him. Then said Jesus unto the twelve,
Will ye go away also ? ' The world is a dangerous place. He had
kept them corporally from death and danger ; they were neither killed,
nor drowned, as they were in danger : Mat. viii. 25, ' Master, save us ;
we perish.' That Christ kept both ways, is clear by this evangelist's
own exposition, John xviii. 9, ' That that saying might be fulfilled,
which he spake, Of those which thou gavest me, have I lost none.'
Christ is there capitulating for his disciples ; that place showeth he
had an exact care of their bodies as well as their souls.

' But the son of perdition.'—Let us clear this a little. May any of
those that are given to Christ miscarry ? Certainly no ; his charge
was, John vi. 36, ' That of all which the Father had given him, he
should lose nothing.' His prayer is, John xvii. 24, ' Father, I will that
they also whom thou hast given me be with me where I am.' But what
shall we make of this place ? I will not trouble you with the several
answers, but give you that which I conceive most proper. Here pray
mark, it is not *except*, but *but*, and it must be supplied ; only Judas
was lost, who is not excepted, but opposed : not excepted as one of the
former ; εἰ μή is not put exceptively, but adversatively, as in the curt
forms of scripture it is taken elsewhere. I say, there is no exception
made of Judas, as if he had been given to Christ, and afterwards fallen
away ; but when he had mentioned their keeping, he would **oppositely**

put the losing of Judas. This phrase, εἰ μὴ, is thus used, Rev. xxi. 27, 'There shall in nowise enter into it anything that defileth, neither whatsoever worketh abomination and maketh a lie, but, εἰ μὴ, they which are written in the Lamb's book of life;' Mat. xii. 4, 'It was not lawful for him to eat (namely, of the shew-bread), neither for them which were with him, but, εἰ μὴ, only for the priests.' And yet more clearly, 2 Kings v. 17, 'Thy servant will henceforth offer neither burnt-offering nor sacrifice unto other gods, but unto the Lord;' Acts xxvii. 22, 'There shall be no loss of any man's life, but of the ship.'

By the 'son of perdition,' is certainly meant Judas. Christ had before said, 'One of you is a devil,' John vi. 70; John xiii. 18, 'I speak not of you all, I know whom I have chosen; but that the scripture should be fulfilled, He that eateth bread with me hath lift up his heel against me;' and ver. 21, 'Verily, verily I say unto you, that one of you shall betray me.' It is a Hebraism, as τέκνα ὀργῆς, 'Children of wrath,' Eph. ii. 3, so a child of hell. Judas did not only merit perdition, but was destined to it, as a son of death; 'for he shall surely die,' 1 Sam. xx. 31. So because Judas did not only deserve destruction, but was appointed to it, therefore he is called the 'son of perdition;' though the treason was not fully accomplished, yet he was about to execute it. Nonnus rendereth it, 'a son of the destroyer,' as referring to Satan.

'That the scripture might be fulfilled.'—*That* is many times put for *then*. It was not therefore foretold, that it might be done; this would put the sin on God; but this was the event, then the scripture was fulfilled. But what scripture? Our Lord hath not respect to one place, but to many, that speak of Judas's treason and punishment: Ps. xli. 9, 'Yea, my own familiar friend, in whom I trusted, which did eat of my bread, hath lift up his heel against me.' Which is applied to Judas, John xiii. 18, 'He which eateth bread with me hath lift up his heel against me.' So Ps. lxix. from ver. 21 onwards, 'They gave me also gall for my meat, and in my thirst they gave me vinegar to drink,' &c. The 26th verse is applied to Judas. Acts i. 20, 'For it is written in the book of Psalms, Let his habitation be desolate, and let no man dwell therein.' So Ps. cix. 8, which is also quoted in that place, 'His bishopric let another take.'

Why is this passage mentioned?

1. To comfort the disciples, that they might not stagger in their faith.

2. To avoid the scandal, as if Christ could not discern a hypocrite.

3. To show God's hand and counsel in all this, as by and by more fully.

Because this text mainly concerneth a matter past, and there is no commonplace but what hath been handled in the former verse, I shall despatch all in brief hints.

First, I begin with Christ's care: 'Whilst I was with them in the world, I kept them in thy name.'

1. Observe, we cannot withstand danger by our own strength. It is Jerome's observation. Christ saith, 'I kept them;' he doth not say, I gave them free-will to keep themselves. And it is confirmed by another scripture, 1 Sam. ii. 9, 'He keepeth the feet of his saints.'

The feet are put for all kind of actions, courses, and endeavours; 'For by strength shall no man prevail;' that is, by his own strength. God will have this honour, as to be the author of grace, so the preserver of it; as the making of the world and keeping of the world is put into the same hands. You rob God of his honour when you look elsewhere. Take heed then of going forth in the strength of your own resolutions. The devil doth not fear us, but the guard that is about us. Peter was a sad instance: 'Though all men do deny thee, yet will not I deny thee.' At first he outbraveth a whole troop, and afterwards falleth by the accusation of one damsel. A bold resolution doth not carry out a man so far as a humble dependence; a silly wench discourageth this stout champion. Every small temptation is sufficient to overturn a man puffed up with the confidence of his own strength, the weak blast of a damsel's question. What poor creatures are we when God leaveth us! We cannot be without these providences. *Audeo dicere*, saith Austin, *utile esse superbis cadere in aliquod manifestum apertum peccatum, ut salubrius sibi displiceant.* The saints fall so often that they may stand the firmer. Nay, if you do not fall foully, you will meet with a great deal of uncomfortableness and weariness in the ways of God; our strength will soon tire. Learn this, the best of you, you that seem to have most reason to stand. Peter had been with Christ on the mount, Mat. xvii. 1, in the garden, Mat. xxvi. 37, assured of his glory, armed against his sufferings, and yet now denieth him.

2. Observe how loyal, faithful, and tender Christ is over his charge. He is loyal to God: 'I have kept them in thy name;' faithful to his flock, he omitted no point of the duty of a good shepherd; he was tender of them: 'Whilst I was with them in the world, I kept them;' and now he surrendereth his charge into God's hands. Judas was lost, not out of any impotency and carelessness in Christ, he was not in his commission; but through his own malignity. Christ is faithful, for he giveth an account to God; none of them is lost; just as he will at the last day; it is but a type of what he will do then. He will present all the faithful to God: Heb. ii. 13, 'Behold, I and the children which God hath given me.' And he will disclaim hypocrites, as he doth Judas.

Use 1. Let us learn how safe it is to be in Christ's hands and keeping. Christ was a faithful shepherd when he was upon the earth; and though his corporal presence be removed, yet it is supplied by the Spirit; he hath still a care of his flock; the lambs, those that are most tender, he carrieth them in his bosom; he hath a particular care of every single believer, though there be so many thousands in the world: John x. 3, 'I know my sheep by name.' John, Anna, Thomas, however called and distinguished in the world. He is careful to provide good large pasture, to supply your defects. His conduct is gentle and tender, as the little ones are able to bear, and to guide you with dispensations suitable to your work, and temptations are proportioned to your growth and experience. Paul was not buffeted till his rapture: 'After ye were illuminated, ye endured a great fight of afflictions,' Heb. x. 32. The castle is victualled before it is besieged. He is constantly watchful over you, taketh notice of decays of grace and spiritual languishments, to reclaim and reduce his people when gone astray: Isa. xxx. 21, 'Thine ears shall hear a voice behind thee, saying, This is the way, walk in it, when ye turn to the right hand, and when ye turn to the left.' You may be confident of his keeping, if you will but choose him for a shepherd, and put your souls as a pledge in his hands: Ps. xxiii. 1, 'The Lord is my shepherd, I shall not want.' Walk on in a course of obedience, referring yourselves to Christ's care.

Use 2. We should learn of Christ to be faithful to our charge. We that are ministers should keep those that are committed to us in God's name, that when we die, or by providence are called away from our people, we may plead our faithfulness: 'Father, I have kept them in thy name.' If we give not warning to the sinner, 'his blood will God require at our hands,' Ezek. iii. 20. As under the law, if an ox or sheep were laid to pledge, and it did miscarry, the party was to make it good; so Heb. xiii. 17, 'They watch for your souls as they that must give an account, that they may do it with joy, and not with grief.' It is a heavy charge and a great trust; the account of lost souls will be craved at your hands. So also you that are called to a family, you have a charge; you are not only to provide for them corporally, but spiritually, that when you die, you may commend them to God upon these terms: 'Whilst I was with them, I kept them in thy name.'

3. Observe, God hath many ways of keeping, mediate and immediate. Immediate, by his own Spirit, this Christ beggeth for them; mediate, by Christ's corporal presence: 'I have kept them;' by the guides of the church; by angels, they are a part of our guard: Heb. i. 14, 'Are they not all ministering spirits, sent forth to minister to them that are heirs of salvation?' They have a great deal of employment about God's children: Ps. xci. 11, 'He shall give his angels charge over thee, to keep thee in all thy ways.' Against bodily dangers the angels watch over us, God against spiritual dangers. So by grace in the heart: Prov. iv. 5, 'Get wisdom, and she shall keep thee.' These are the inward means of preservation.

Use 1. Admire the providence of God about such a creature as man is. It is counted a matter of great state to have at our heels a long train of followers; these mighty peers of heaven are our attendants. How many guards hath he set upon us! His Spirit, his angels, glorious angels, they behold God's face, and watch over our feet; his ministers, the outward supplies of providence, and grace in the heart. If our protection were visible, all the princes in the world would come short of it; a guard full of state and strength. Even little ones have their angels stand by their cradles.

Use 2. Learn to wait upon God, though you want an outward guard and veil of safety. Christ's corporal presence was removed, and supplied by the Spirit; and if God can make us amends for Christ's company, certainly for an outward comfort and blessing. Do not limit God to one way of keeping; he hangeth the earth upon nothing, how doth he keep the earth? A feather will not stay in the air: 'Man liveth not by bread alone, but by every word that proceedeth out of the mouth of God,' Mat. iv. 4. Not only by the outward supply, but the promise and the sustentation of providence. God can bring water out of the rock as well as out of the fountain. When we have outward supplies, we are many times worst. Our well-being doth not lie in these things, but in God's care, which may be expressed in several ways. Christ may put that question to us that he did to the apostles: Luke xxii. 35, 'And he said unto them, When I sent you without purse, and scrip, and shoes, lacked ye anything? And they said, Nothing.' God sendeth abroad his servants many times to make experiments of the care of his providence ; they are helpless and shiftless, but did ye lack anything? The Lord can wonderfully incline the hearts of men, and dispose of the creatures for the supply of his people; he cometh in by wonderful and unexpected ways of supply. It were easy to give instances, if my intended brevity would permit. Merlin was hid in a hay-mow in the massacre of Paris, and a hen came constantly and laid an egg every day for a fortnight.

4. Observe, that Christ's keeping extendeth to corporal safety. So it is quoted, John xviii. 8, 9, 'If ye seek me, let these go their way, that the saying might be fulfilled which he spake, Of those which thou gavest me, have I lost none.' God is in covenant with both body and soul, and he looketh after both ; for the body, as far as it is necessary for his service, and for our profit and salvation, as well as for the soul ; therefore it is but reason we should depend upon him for both. It is a pretty question, Which is more difficult, to believe in Christ for temporals or spirituals ? The reason of doubting is because promises for temporals are not so express, and so exactly accomplished in the letter, as they are in spirituals. But certainly heaven and pardon of sins are greater mercies ; and if conscience were opened and the heart serious, we should see the difficulty to obtain them to be greater. There are greater and more plausible prejudices against pardon of sins than against daily bread. God feedeth all his creatures, even the young ravens; but he pardoneth but a few, and blesseth them with all spiritual blessings. But here is the mistake : bodily wants are more pressing, and here faith is presently to be exercised with difficulties ; and men are careless of their souls, and so content themselves with some general desires and loose hopes of ease and eternal welfare, which hopes import their security and presumption, not their gospel faith. But certainly, he that durst venture his estate into Christ's hands by a genuine act of faith, doth a less thing than he that by a genuine act of faith ventures his soul. They say they find no difficulty in believing in Christ for salvation and pardon of sins, and yet cannot trust him for daily bread, for maintenance, which God giveth to the ravens, and bestowed upon them when they were children of wrath. Well, then, trust Christ for these common mercies. You shall have temporal safety as long as God hath a mind to employ you in his service, and as much as is necessary to glorify him and keep your hearts good. In other things we must moderate our desires ; God is a better judge than we are ourselves ; and then by an undisturbed faith, without doubts and carkings, wait upon him. When you cark, and run to unlawful means, you take Christ's work out of his hands, and put it into your own ; yea, you put yourselves out of Christ's keeping, and put your safety into the devil's hands. Oh! the children of God should consider this. Do you expect God should give you spiritual and eternal safety,

and not temporal? Shall he give the greater, aud not the less? Martha was of this temper: John xi. 23, 24, 'Jesus saith to her, Thy brother shall rise again.' Oh! saith she, 'I know he shall rise again at the last day;' as if it were an easier matter to raise him up after so many years, than after four days. If you put your souls, which are the more excellent part, into Christ's hands, will you not put your bodies? Will you not trust him with all that you have? You should make experiments this way. How are you temporally kept? It is good to be acquainted with God by little and little; to trust him with smaller matters, and then with greater. And what is this trust? Leave all to God's disposal, having served providence in the use of means. It is a shame to see christians prole and shift, as if they had no Father in heaven, no Mediator to take care of them.

Secondly, Now I come to the success and fruit of Christ's care.

1. As to the elect.

2. As to Judas.

1. As to the elect: 'I have kept those whom thou hast given to me, and none of them is lost.' None of the elect can be lost; God's election cannot be weakened by the falling of hypocrites. Christ may lose members, as he is head of a visible church, but not as he is head of a mystical body: 'One of you shall betray me, but I know whom I have chosen,' John xiii. 18. As if he had said, This will not defeat my purposes of grace. So Rom. xi. 7, 'The election hath obtained it, and the rest were blinded.' God's election worketh through all prejudices, wicked parents, bad education, a dumb ministry; and others are hardened, notwithstanding all advantages, as Judas, though of the seed of Abraham, though an apostle, though under Christ's inspection. The fathers compared Paul and Judas, Paul an open enemy, Judas a seeming friend: 1 Tim. ii. 18, 19, 'Who concerning the truth have erred, saying that the resurrection is past already, and overthrow the faith of some. Nevertheless, the foundation of God standeth sure, having this seal, The Lord knoweth them that are his.' As those that build a palace are wont to lay a firm foundation, so God in building a heavenly city, he hath laid a foundation, by which is meant God's election, which is the great groundwork of salvation; whoever fall, God's elect stand sure.

Use. Let us not be troubled at the defection of hypocrites, let it not shake our belief of the doctrine of perseverance; be not offended, as if the salvation of the elect were not sure. Though glorious luminaries are quenched, and those that seemed to be stars leave their orb and station, God's election standeth sure. When a tree is shaken, rotten and unsound fruit comes clattering down. The devil never had such a season to set men on work to broach the doctrine of the apostasy of the saints, because of the general defection and miscarriage of eminent professors. In this case let us run to the scriptures. The defection of one from the college of the apostles was a great scandal; but Christ saith, 'That it might be fulfilled which was written.' So when any scandal falleth out, thus should we run unto the scriptures.

2. As to Judas, who is here called 'the son of perdition.'

1. Observe, in the general, there are some persons that are so wilfully set to destroy and damn themselves, that they may be called sons of

perdition; as here is one that perisheth in Christ's own company, a prey taken out of his hands, one that was never the better for all the care of Christ, for seeing his holy life, and for the excellent discourses that he heard from him, for all the kindness he had showed to him in taking him into a near office and service about himself, for bestowing on him the gift of miracles, for trusting him with the bag. Christ had lately washed his feet, as well as of the rest of the apostles; yet he obstinately goeth on in ways of self-perdition, and his purpose of betraying his Lord and master, yea, contrary to many warnings given him.

Use. Oh! take heed of a wilful obstinacy, and wresting yourselves out of the arms of mercy! of being of such a disposition that nothing will reclaim you, for that is to be a son of perdition. Wilful sins have a greater mark upon them than other sins; as when you go—

1. Against an express commandment: Prov. xiii. 13, 'Whoso despiseth the word shall be destroyed, but he that feareth a commandment shall be rewarded.' If a commandment stand in your way, it should be more than if a band of armed men stood to hinder you. Many make nothing of a commandment; they fear a judgment from God, or a punishment from men, but never stand upon the word of God.

2. Against express warnings of those that wish well to your souls: Deut. i. 43, 'So I spake unto you, and you would not hear, but rebelled against the commandment of the Lord, and went presumptuously up into the hill.' When men are wedded to their own inclinations, outfacing all challenges in God's name, they will do what they are set upon: Ps. xii. 4, 'With our tongues will we prevail, our lips are our own: who is lord over us?' This is not far from a judgment: 2 Chron. xxxvi. 15, 16, 'And the Lord God of their fathers sent to them by his messengers, rising up betimes and sending, because he had compassion on his people, and on his dwelling-place. But they mocked the messengers of God, and despised his words, and misused his prophets, until the wrath of the Lord rose against his people, till there was no remedy.' This contempt will draw down wrath, no means to appease God.

3. Against checks of conscience, and motions of God's Spirit in our hearts: Acts vii. 51, 'Ye stiff-necked and uncircumcised in heart and ears, ye do always resist the Holy Ghost.' Conscience telleth them ye ought not to yield to this sin, whatever the profit and pleasure be; yet men kick against the pricks, and do that which their own hearts disallow: Rom. xiv. 22, 'Happy is he that condemneth not himself in the thing that he alloweth.' And in spite of these good motions they will go forward to perfect the sin which they have in chase; then God lets them alone, lets them go on, till they perish.

4. Against restraints of providence, when God hath hedged up their way with thorns, or they have found much inconvenience in that course: 2 Chron. xxviii. 22, 'In the time of his distress he trespassed yet more and more: this is that King Ahaz;' the scripture sets a brand upon him. As Baalam would go on, 2 Peter ii. 16, 'But was rebuked for his iniquity: the dumb ass, speaking with man's voice, forbad the madness of the prophet;' when men go on over the belly

of more than ordinary opposition, till they perish.   A miracle will
not stop a sinner in the violent pursuit of his lusts.   Providence
hath a language that biddeth us stop, but the sway of lusts is great,
and breaks through all restraints.   Oh! take heed then of being self-
willed, stout-hearted in a sensual course, wedded to our own inclinations,
of being a slave to sensual appetite, and being led by it more than by
holy reasons.   Take heed of love to some unmortified lust, especially
to covetousness; this is the cause of extreme violence in sin: Jer.
xliv. 16, 17, 'As for the word that thou hast spoken to us in the name
of the Lord, we will not hearken unto thee.   But we will certainly do
whatsoever thing goeth forth out of our own mouth, to burn incense
unto the queen of heaven, and to pour out drink-offerings unto her.'

2. Observe from his character, 'The son of perdition.'   The same
name is given to antichrist, 2 Thess. ii. 3, 'That man of sin be revealed,
the son of perdition.'   Judas was a type of antichrist; as they said of
the blind man, John ix. 9, 'Some said, This is he; others said, He is
like him.'   The pope boasteth that his seat is apostolical, and that
he is the successor of an apostle.   If we grant it, and he will needs be
a successor of an apostle, there is an error in the person; it is not
Peter, but Judas.   Let us see the parallel.

[1.] Judas was not a stranger, but a pretended friend and an
apostle: Acts i. 17, 'He was numbered with us, and obtained part of
this ministry.'   So the pope obtained part of this ministry.   Turks
and infidels are enemies to Christ.   Antichrist must be one that
seeketh to undermine Christ under a pretence of friendship, ἀντι-
χριστὸς, for and against Christ; he 'maketh war with the horns of the
Lamb,' Rev. xiii. 11.   If he were a professed adversary, what mystery
were there in it?   Now it is 'a mystery of iniquity,' 2 Thes. ii. 7;
'a false prophet,' Rev. xvi. 13.   It is wisdom to discern him: Rev.
xiii. 18, 'Here is wisdom: let him that hath understanding count the
number of the beast.'

[2.] Judas sold Christ for a small matter; so *omnia Romœ venalia*,
—pardons, indulgences, freedom from purgatory, all to be bought at
Rome.   The antichristian state maketh a market of religion; truth
is made to yield to interest and profit.

[3.] Judas betrayed Christ with a kiss.   Antichrist is a true adversary of Christ, and yet pretendeth to adore him.   He pretendeth to be
his servant and vicar, and is his enemy; not an enemy without the
church, but within the church, that betrayeth Christ under a colour of
adoration.

[4.] Judas was a guide to them that came to take Jesus.   Christ is
in heaven, death hath no more dominion over him.   His natural body
is above abuse, but in his mystical body he still suffereth: Acts ix. 4,
'Saul, Saul, why persecutest thou me?'   The pope is the head of
the persecuting state; others are his emissaries and agents, to persecute Christ in his members.   It is a politic religion, carried on with
cruelty.

[5.] Judas was υἱὸς ἀπωλείας, 'the son of perdition,' as destroying
himself, and involving others in the same condemnation.   So is antichrist called in the Revelations, ἀπολλύων, Rev. ix. 11, and ἀπολ-
λυόμενος, the destroyer of souls, of himself and others.

Use. Let all these things open our eyes, that we may behold the man of sin. One egg is not more like another than Judas and antichrist.

3. Observe, that carnal practices will end in perdition. Because Judas is called the 'son of perdition,' let us see what course he took to undo himself. Let us look upon his sin and punishment.

[1.] For his sin. In the story of Judas, four sins are most remarkable—his covetousness, his hypocrisy, his treason, and his despair.

(1.) His covetousness. This was the root of all, as indeed it is 'the root of all evil,' 1 Tim. vi. 10. Christ had made him his treasurer; and carrying the bag is a shrewd temptation to a carnal heart: John xii. 6, 'This spake he, not that he cared for the poor, but because he was a thief, and had the bag, and bare what was put therein.' He was a bad keeper of the stock, appropriating it to his own use, to make himself a store and a subsistence; having a mind to forsake Christ, because he had so often heard him speak of his sufferings, and the persecution of the apostles. And mark, he pretends piety and religion to disguise his covetousness, when it was his own private interest: 'There was a woman that took a pound of ointment of spikenard, very costly, and anointed the feet of Jesus;' ver. 3, 'And Judas said, Why was not this ointment sold for three hundred pence, and given to the poor? But this he said, not that he cared for the poor, but was a thief, and had the bag.' At length love of money, joined together with spleen, prevailed on him so far that he sold his own master. He that loveth the world hateth God; he that is greedy of gain will sell his soul, and heaven, and Christ for money; there is nothing so vile but he will yield to it. There was somewhat of envy and revenge in it: Mat. xxvi. 14, 15, 'Then one of the twelve, called Judas Iscariot, went unto the chief priests, and said unto them, What will ye give me, and I will deliver him unto you? And they covenanted with him for thirty pieces of silver.' 'Then;' when was it? When Christ had checked him for rebuking the woman, he stomached the disappointment, as carnal men will storm when their hypocrisy is discovered, and their carnal ends disappointed. Christ by commending the woman enraged him.

(2.) His hypocrisy. He continued the profession of an apostle, preached against sin, seemed to be zealous for the poor. Nay, his hypocrisy was augmented by the constant means he had to convince him, he was hardened in it the more. Jesus Christ was a constant preacher of repentance; and all those sermons and discourses Judas heard securely. Christ often admonished him of his sin: John vi. 70, 'Have I not chosen you twelve, and one of you is a devil?' John xiii. 18, 'I speak not of you all, I know whom I have chosen; but that the scripture may be fulfilled, He that eateth bread with me hath lift up his heel against me.' He was threatened that it had been better for him that he had never been born: Mat. xxvi. 24, 'The Son of man goeth as it is written of him; but woe unto that man by whom the Son of man is betrayed; it had been good for that man if he had not been born.' But all this would not do, it did not rouse his conscience, and make him bethink himself, and to consider that he was not hidden in his disguise. When Christ spoke it more pressingly: Mat. xxvi.

SERMON XXI.

*And now I come to thee; and these things I speak in the world, that
they might have my joy fulfilled in themselves.*—JOHN XVII. 13.

OUR Lord is still amplifying that argument of his own departure, and
the disciples' danger in the world, and so justifieth his earnestness in
prayer for them.   I come to thee, and must leave their company, and
therefore I have need to make some provision for them.   In the argument of this text, Christ showeth what was his special aim in the
whole prayer.   He is so earnest, not to blemish the Father, as if he
were backward and wanted mercy, but for their comfort, that they
might know what prayers were laid up in store for them, and to give
them a taste of his own care.   He prayeth with them, that they might
know how he prayed for them.   Christ would have something left
upon record, as a pledge of his affections to the church: ' These things
I speak in the world,' &c.

In the words, not to speak of the occasion, *I come to thee;* which
signifieth not his address in prayer, but his ascension to God, as was
cleared before, ver. 11.   In the rest of the words we have Christ's
action, and Christ's aim, the comfort of the disciples; where we have
the author, *my joy;* the manner how received for quantity, *fulfilled;*
the quality, *in themselves.*

' And these things I speak in the world;' that is, make this prayer
in their hearing; λαλῶ, ' I speak,' it signifieth prayer with an audible
voice; elsewhere he useth the word ἐρωτῶ and θήλω.   And here a
record and pattern is left for the use of the church in all ages.

' That they may have my joy.'—What is the meaning of that?

1. Because he rejoiceth in our good.   *My joy,* and *your joy* are distinguished: John xv. 11, ' These things have I spoken to you, that
my joy should be fulfilled in you, and that your joy might be full.'
There is nothing maketh the heart of Christ so glad as to see his
members thrive in peace and grace.   So the apostle Paul: Phil. ii. 2,
' Fulfil ye my joy.'   Nothing could be more comfortable to Paul than
to see the Philippians thrive in grace.   Thus some interpret it actively
of the joy which Christ hath in the good of his members.   But I suppose it is rather to be taken passively, ἐν ἑαυτοῖς, ' in themselves.'

2. Others think that by *my joy* is meant a joy like mine; when they
feel the same desires kindled in their hearts, they may be comforted
with the workings of the same spirit of prayer in them; that is, feel
such a joy as I feel in uttering these requests.   But this doth not run
so smoothly.

3. ' My joy,' because he is the author of it.   *Gaudium ex me.*   Joy
which I work as mediator and redeemer.   Of ourselves we have nothing
but despair and trouble: Isa. lvii. 19, ' I create the fruit of the lips;
peace, peace to him that is afar off, and to him that is near, and I will
heal him.'   We possess it, but it is Christ's joy; he worketh it, and
causeth it by his Spirit; elsewhere it is called, ' joy in the Holy Ghost,'
1 Thes. i. 6.

4. ' My joy,' because he is the object of it.   *Gaudium de me.*   That

that joy which they have conceived from my presence with them, or care of them, may not be lessened, but increased, that this spiritual joy may be fulfilled. These two latter are of chief regard.

'May be fulfilled;' not only accomplished, but be abundant; as chap. xv. 11, 'That your joy may be full.' The filling up of joy is a phrase proper to St John: chap. iii. 29, 'This my joy therefore is fulfilled,' saith John the Baptist, because he heard the bridegroom's voice. So 1 John i. 4, 'These things we write unto you, that your joy may be full.' And 2 Epist. ver. 12, 'I trust to come unto you, and speak face to face, that our joy may be full.' Possibly this joy is called a full joy, not with respect to itself, but with respect to other joys. In itself it is always a-growing, and receiveth a daily increase, till it be perfected in heaven. Here we have but some forerunning beams of the noon of glory, the first-fruits of the harvest. The joy of the world is a lank empty joy.

'In themselves;' that is, in their hearts, by their own feeling and experience; they have need of something within, for they have nothing without: John xvi. 33, 'In the world ye shall have tribulation; but be of good comfort, I have overcome the world.'

To draw all to some doctrinal head and issue. Of Christ's coming to God I have spoken already. I might observe the force of the word to comfort the heart, 'These things I speak, that my joy may be fulfilled.' But I shall content myself with two observations.

1. Observe, that this prayer of Christ's is a fountain of consolation. This joy ariseth from the things he now spoke in the world, partly because here we have a taste of Christ's heart, how zealously he is affected for our good. When he took his leave of us, he took his leave of us with blessings and supplications. Partly because here we have a copy, model, or counterpart of his intercession. Here you may know what he is now doing for you in heaven. Christ is their advocate and intercessor, he pleadeth their right, and sueth for blessings; he prayed for their preservation, unity, and glory. There are two ways to know Christ's intercession—by this record, and his intercession in our hearts: Rom. viii. 26, 'The Spirit itself maketh intercession in us, with groanings that cannot be uttered.' The Spirit testifieth to our hearts the quality of that intercession Christ maketh for us in heaven; it is the echo of it; the inward interpellation of the soul is the echo of Christ's intercession. Now that the word and Spirit must go together, the form of it is left upon record. Here is a public record to look upon in all discomforts and troubles of the church; and this breedeth a full joy. Partly because Christ's prayers are so many promises; he prayeth for excellent blessings, and is sure of audience. Well, then, remember these prayers of Christ for your comfort; when we are pressed down with any evils in the world, let us run to Christ's prayers. As Luther said, Let us sing the 46th psalm; so say I, Let us meditate on John xvii.; here is a remedy for all the afflictions of the church.

2. Observe Christ's care to leave his people joyful; and careful he is, very solicitous about it before his departure.

First, I shall inquire what this joy is that Christ would establish.

1. For the kind of it, 'My joy;' not a worldly joy, but heavenly; not corporal, but spiritual. It ill beseemeth christians to set their hearts

on earthly things, or suffer the world to intercept their joy : Phil. iv. **4**, ' Rejoice in the Lord always; and again I say, Rejoice.' The apostle was in prison when he wrote it, he had nothing else to rejoice in at that time; but what he had felt the sweetness of himself he imparts to others. What can a man desire more than joy? You are at liberty to rejoice, as he speaketh elsewhere of marriage : ' You are at liberty to marry, ἀλλὰ μονὸν ἐν κυρίῳ, but only in the Lord;' such a joy you may have as Christ works, *ex me, de me*, of which I am the object and the author. You need not fear; that which Christ would establish is a cheerful piety, not a profane joy : ' Christ's delights are with the sons of men,' Prov. viii. 31. He feasteth himself with the thoughts of his grace; it is, as it were, the Lord's recreation; therefore certainly the sons of men should have their delights with God. If the Lord, that sitteth upon the throne of majesty and glory, if he delights in us, should not we delight in a God that is so excellent and worthy?

2. In what manner he would have it received, πεπληρωμένην, 'fulfilled in them.' The joy is full because the object is infinite; we can desire nothing beyond him. .Desire answereth to motion, joy to rest; when we can go no further, there we rest. What can we desire beyond God? Acts xiii. 52, ' The disciples were filled with joy, and with the Holy Ghost;' their hearts could hold no more. Narrow vessels are soon filled with the ocean. It is a full joy, not in itself, but with respect to worldly joy. Worldly joy is scanty, unstable, and vanishing; it cannot satisfy nor secure the heart. Take away the creatures from the worldling and you take away his joy; the object lieth without him. But, John xvi. 22, ' Your joy shall no man take from you;' they cannot plunder you of peace of conscience and joy in the Holy Ghost. This ravisheth the heart: 1 Peter i. 8, ' Ye rejoice with joy unspeakable and full of glory;' Phil. iv. 7, ' The peace of God, that passeth all understanding, keep your hearts and minds through Jesus Christ.' It is better felt than expressed; a creature worketh it not, but a divine operation. Paul heard in heaven, ἄῤῥητα ῥήματα, ' unspeakable words.' So this, being a foretaste of heaven, cannot be conceived and expressed; you cannot imagine how sweet it is, and still it increaseth till we come to heaven, and lose ourselves in these eternal ravishments.

3. It is inward for the quality of it, ἐν ἑαυτοῖς, it is wrought in the midst of afflictions; there is sweetness within when bitterness round about us; like the wood that was thrown in at Marah, it maketh bitter waters sweet, Exod. xv. 25. Saints are fed with hidden manna, Rev. ii. 17. Their life is hid and their joy is hidden: 1 Peter i. 6, ' Wherein ye greatly rejoice; though now for a season, if need be, ye are in heaviness through manifold temptations.' Without there are persecutions, temptations, afflictions from Satan and the world, and within joy; they have meat and drink which the world knoweth not of; the world seeth it not, and therefore the world will not believe it.

Secondly, How much Christ's heart is set upon it. It appears by the provision he made for them; when he departed he left the Comforter: John xiv. 19, ' I will not leave you comfortless; I will come unto you;' John xv. 11, ' These things have I spoken to you, that my joy might remain in you, and that your joy may be full.' He doth not say, that my authority may remain over you, but my joy; and if we would make Christ's heart glad, or our own, we must obey his commandments; for when he enjoineth obedience to his disciples, it is that he may rejoice in our comfort. In his instructions he teacheth them how to pray: John xvi. 24, ' Ask, and ye shall receive, that your joy may be full;' and now he prayeth himself, ' That they have my joy fulfilled in themselves.'   Christ maketh this to be his main work and aim, that in this life we might have peace of conscience and joy in the Holy Ghost, and in the life to come joy for evermore.   Now lest ye should think this was only for the twelve apostles, you shall see it was the end of the whole word. The scriptures were written, Rom. xv. 4, ' That we through patience and comfort of them might have hope.' The whole ministry of the church serveth to the fulfilling of this joy.

Thirdly, Reasons why Christ was so solicitous about this matter.

1. Because of the great use of it in the spiritual life, to make us to do and to suffer: Neh. viii. 10, ' The joy of the Lord is your strength.' This is as oil to the wheels.   It is a question which is most useful, godly joy or godly sorrow: sorrow maketh us serious, joy active. But why should I divide what God hath joined ? *Gaudium ineffabile cum suspiriis enarrabilibus.*   Both are wrought by the same Spirit; he is a comforter, and he descended in the form of a mourning dove.   But certainly joy doth more quicken us in well-doing; it rendereth the functions of body and mind free and vigorous, that we may walk with alacrity and good conscience.   The joy that we press you to is not a wantonness by which we cast away all care and labour, and give ourselves up to ease and lusts, as those do that make their life to be nothing else but a recreation; but such a joy as maketh us go about our duties and callings with comfort.   This is sweet, when a man, out of the refreshings of the Spirit, can go about the business which God hath given him to do with delight: Acts xx. 24, ' Neither count I my life dear to me, so I might finish my course with joy, and the ministry which I have received of the Lord Jesus, to testify the gospel of the grace of God.'   As the eunuch ' went his way rejoicing,' Acts viii. 39. Not like slow asses that go by compulsion, but like generous horses, that delight in their strength and swiftness; to take pleasure in praying, in hearing, in suffering, in doing good, in following the duties of our calling.   Most men count sorrow to be a virtue, and joy to be an indecent presumption.   When men are sluggish, carnal, careless, that they may flow in worldly delights, this is naught.

2. To mar the taste of carnal pleasures.   The soul cannot remain without some oblectation; it delighteth either in earthly or in heavenly things.   Love will not remain idle in the soul.   Now God will give us a taste of spiritual joy, of pleasantness in wisdom's paths, that we might disdain carnal pleasures.   It is not a wonder for a clown, that hath not been acquainted with dainties, to love garlic and onions; but for a prince, that hath been acquainted with better diet, to leave the dainties of his father's table for those things, that were strange.   I do not wonder at carnal men, that they are delighted with carnal objects; they never knew better; but for a child of God, that hath tasted how gracious and sweet God in Christ is, to find sap and savour in coarser fare, this is wonderful.

3. It is for his honour. Nothing bringeth reproach upon the ways of God so much as the sadness of those that profess them. *Spiritus Calvinianus est spiritus melancholicus,* was a Lutheran proverb, because the Calvinists were against wakes and dancings and revels. You darken the ways of God by your melancholy conversation. Religion should be cheerful, though not wanton and dissolute. We are to invite others: Ps. xxxiv. 2, 'My soul shall make her boast in the Lord; the humble shall hear thereof, and be glad.' Otherwise thou art as one of the spies that discouraged the children of Israel, by bringing up an evil report upon the land of Canaan.

4. Because he delighteth to see us cheerful: ' He delighteth in the prosperity of his saints.' Certainly the Lord doth not delight in a sad devotion, and that the finger should always be in the wound. As a man delighteth that his fields should prosper, and laugh with fatness, so doth Christ in the saints. They are his charge: John xv. 11, ' These things have I spoken unto you, that my joy might remain in you, and that your joy might be full.' Would you make Christ's heart glad, keep your own cheerful.

Fourthly, I shall give you some observations concerning joy.

1. God's providence to all the creatures doth aim at their joy and welfare. In inanimate creatures there is a cessation and rest, in the beasts a sensitive delectation, in a man joy. All actions that tend to the preservation of life, have their pleasure mixed with them; and therefore certainly he hath provided some christian joy for a christian. All actions of godliness have a delight mixed with them.

2. Spiritual joy ariseth more from hope than possession: Rom. xii. 12, 'Rejoicing in hope;' Heb. iii. 6, 'If we hold fast the confidence, and the rejoicing of the hope firm unto the end ;' Rom. v. 2, ' We rejoice in hope of the glory of God.' It is an affection proper to the next life; but some birds sing in winter. Though we have not an actual possession of glory, yet there is a certainty of possession.

3. This joy is more felt in adversity than prosperity: 1 Peter i. 6, ' Wherein ye greatly rejoice; though now for a season, if need be, ye are in heaviness through manifold temptations;' Rom. v. 3, ' We glory in tribulation.' Partly from God himself ; he proportioneth his comforts to our sorrows, and then sheddeth abroad his love most plentifully : 2 Cor. i. 5, ' As the sufferings of Christ abound in us, so our consolation also aboundeth by Christ.' Partly from the saints ; they rejoice most in afflictions, because they taste in them what evil they are freed from in Christ. If we never had afflictions, we should not know what it is to be freed from eternal horrors and pains ; but when we feel them then we say, If I have much ado to bear these temporal sorrows, what should I have done if I had been still liable to eternal! O blessed be God for my deliverance in Christ ! Partly because of sweet experiences. We are kept from perishing with the world; a servant and stranger is turned out of doors, but a son is corrected. If it serveth for nothing else, yet for a spite to Satan, to confound him, when he thinketh he hath most advantage against us now, to overwhelm us with grief; as when one seeketh to wrest a staff out of our hands, we hold it the faster.

4. Those have the highest feeling of joy that have tasted the bitter-

ness of sorrow : Isa. lvii. 18, ' I have seen his ways, and will heal him :
I will lead him also, and restore comforts, unto him, and to his
mourners ;' Jer. xxxi. 18, ' I have surely heard Ephraim bemoaning
himself thus, Thou hast chastised me, and I was chastised,' &c.; ver.
20, ' Is Ephraim my dear son ? is he a pleasant child ? for since I
spake against him, I do earnestly remember him still,' &c.   Unutterable groans make way for ineffable joys ; they feel the most lively
elevation of joy as a recompense for the pangs of the new birth.   God
permits sorrows, that we may find the fuller comfort.   Bernard thinks
that the joy of the saints is greater than the joy of angels, because
they who have been kept, and not restored, had never experience of
any other condition ; however, his reason is notable : *Placet sanctis
securitas, sed ei magis qui timuit ; jucunda omnibus lux, sed liberato de
potestate tenebrarum jucundior ; transisse de morte ad vitam, gratiam
duplicat.*

5. The feelings of this joy are up and down, yet when the joy is
gone, the right remaineth, and this joy will be fulfilled : John xvi. 22,
' Ye now have sorrow, but I will see you again, and your heart shall
rejoice, and your joy no man taketh from you.'   If we lose it ourselves,
it is not utterly lost.   The sun is always moving, but it doth not
always shine, and display his rays with a merry countenance ; so a
christian meeteth with many rubs, but still he holdeth on his course to
heaven ; and therefore, where sense faileth, faith should make supply.

6. The nature of man is more acquainted with sorrows than with
pleasures.   Men naturally are more susceptible of sorrow than of joy.
Partly because of the presages of a guilty conscience : Heb. ii. 14,
' Through fear of death, they were all their lifetime subject to bondage.'
Men are more ingenious and inventive to torment themselves than
they are to find out arguments of joy.   Partly out of ingratitude :
Mal. i. 2, ' I have loved you, saith the Lord ; yet ye say, Wherein hast
thou loved us ? '   We grieve more for a mean affliction than we rejoice
in many great blessings.   As if the humours of the body be out of
order, or one joint break, this is enough to make us sink, and ill at
ease ; so one light affliction sinks us.   Partly because God hath laid
this burden of sorrow upon us to make us long for heaven : ' Few and
evil are the days of the years of my life.'

Use 1. To show us the goodness of God, who hath made our wages
a great part of our work, and our reward our service.   The Lord doth
not require of us to lance and gash ourselves ; his ways are not sour
ways ; he hath made it a part of our duty and homage to rejoice in
him.   Oh ! that he should deal so bountifully with us in this life !
The world might be a Bochim, and it is a Beracha.   It is indeed a
vale of tears ; but yet the sun shineth sometimes when it raineth.   Oh !
how should this make us in love with the service of God !   They are
happy that minister in his presence.   It is a request, Ps. xc. 14, ' Oh !
satisfy us early with thy mercy, that we may rejoice and be glad all
our days.'   Certainly God alloweth us to come with such requests, for
he commandeth us to rejoice : 1 Thes. v. 16, ' Rejoice evermore.'   We
might weep evermore, yet he saith, ' Rejoice evermore.'

Use 2. To take off the slander brought on the ways of God, as
if they were dark and uncomfortable, as if we should abandon and

renounce all delight.　Oh! that wicked men would but make experience! God doth not require that you should renounce delight, but change the course of it.　Joy is not abrogated, but preferred.　Do not think the practice of religion is full of sadness and heaviness.　Will you believe the spies, that have been in the land of promise? The righteous are only fit to give testimony to the comfort of a converted estate; a stranger intermeddleth not with their joys.　If any of God's children be uncomfortable, it is because they have not tasted deep enough of the promises, the Comforter suffereth some contradiction from their hearts and lusts: but what is this to your estate? The souls of wicked men are still under bondage; in the midst of their greatest joys, their pleasures are mixed with fear; as Belshazzar was soon put out of his mirth.

Use 3. Let us despise the dreggy delights of the world.　We are empty by nature, and worldly joy filleth not but with wind.　Since Christ hath made such provision for our consolation, why should we seek it elsewhere? God hath forbid no joy but what is hurtful.　Outward mercies bring in some joy, but not a full joy.　Godliness doth not unman us, and hinder the course of any true natural affection. But no outward thing should be our chief joy; a light touch is best: 1 Cor. vii. 30, 'They that rejoice should be as if they rejoiced not.' First we have an interest, then a comfortable use of the creatures. Hast thou wealth, power, greatness? Do not bind up thy heart with these things, they will be gone, and then thy joy will be gone too. When they take up too much of our affections, they are curses, and will prove our sorrow: Eccles. vii. 6, 'As the crackling of thorns under a pot, so is the laughter of the fool: this also is vanity;' a slight superficial thing.　Vain men are catched with every light pleasure, as a fire soon taketh in thorns.　Thorns burning under a pot make a great noise, and so carnal mirth maketh much noise.　Worldly men promise themselves a great deal of pleasure and contentment, but this fire is soon out, so worldly joy is soon gone.　Let us not delight in fleshly liberty; the pleasures of sin are short-lived, and carnal pleasures leave bitterness and remorse behind them: Prov. xiv. 13, 'Even in laughter the heart is sorrowful; and the end of that mirth is heaviness.'　As laughter, through dilatation of the spirits, maketh us sad afterwards.　The fuel of carnal pleasures is gross, burdensome, oppressive to reason, it hindereth the free contemplation of the mind, and lasteth but for a little while; we need to be refreshed with other pleasures.　But God in Christ is full and fresh to all eternity; angels are not weary of him.　Besides, carnal mirth is but madness; Eccles. ii. 2, 'I have said of laughter, It is mad; and of mirth, What doeth it?'　It is good for no serious purpose.　Solomon challengeth the masters of mirth; what doth it but displace reason, and give way to vanity and lightness? I know there is a lawful use of inoffensive mirth; but when we take pleasures, they should not take us: Eph. v. 4, 'Neither filthiness, nor foolish talking, nor jesting, which are not convenient; but rather giving of thanks;' ver. 19, 'Speaking to yourselves in psalms, and hymns, and spiritual songs; singing, and making melody in your hearts to the Lord.'　There is a mirth becoming the gravity of a christian.

Use 4. Reproof to two sorts:—

1. To those that are always sad.   Christians do not live up to that care and provision which Christ hath made for them.   In scripture it is, 'Rejoice evermore,' 1 Thes. v. 16.   And they live as if God had said, Weep evermore.   It is verily a fault, however disguised; in some it deserveth pity; in others chiding and rebuke.   In some pity, that are under penal disturbance; when God putteth any into the stocks of conscience, they cannot come out at pleasure; these are irresistible chains; a poor creature lieth bound till God saith, Go forth.   Those chains of darkness in which the devils are held are their own everlasting horrors.   It is God's prerogative, 'to create the fruit of the lips, peace, peace,' Isa. lvii. 19.   Joy is his immediate dispensation.   We wonder, considering the comforts of the gospel, that there should be any such thing as trouble of conscience, because we know not what it is to lie under God's mighty hand, to be cast into the prison, shall I say, or the hell of our consciences.   Alas! poor creatures!   We cannot break prison when we will.   It is easy for those that stand upon the shore to say to those that are tossed upon the waves, Sail thus. They are tugging for life, the cause is beyond our direction and their choice.   But these persons are to be pitied, yet counselled.   Besides God's power, we mingle much of our own obstinacy and peevishness, as Rachel would not be comforted, Jer. xxxi. 15.   We are to invite them to Christ, and they are bound to hearken.   Their present duty is to come for ease : Mat. xi. 28, 'Come unto me, all ye that are weary and heavy laden, and ye shall find rest for your souls.'   That is the only gracious issue of soul-troubles; as Christ cried, 'My God,' on the cross, they are not exempted from believing.   But others are to be chidden.   It is a sad thing that christians should not have the wisdom to make use of their own felicity.   We often hug a distemper instead of a duty, as if God were better pleased with dolorous impressions : Lam. iii. 33, 'He doth not afflict willingly, nor grieve the children of men.'   Not with his heart, so it is in the Hebrew.   It argueth ill thoughts of God.   Baal's priests gashed themselves to please their idols ; but God delighteth in the prosperity of his saints.   Men think there is more of merit and satisfaction in what is afflictive ; it is a kind of revenge they take upon themselves.   God hath required sorrow to mortify sin, but not to satisfy justice; he would have us triumph in Christ whilst we groan under the body of death.   Oh! consider, sourness is a dishonour to God, a discredit to your profession, a disadvantage to yourselves, a grief to the Spirit, because you resist his work as a comforter.   Besides, there is much of ingratitude in it; complaints and murmurings deface the beauty of his mercies.   As a snail leaveth a frothy slaver upon the fairest flowers, so do unthankful christians leave their own slaver upon the rich mercies of God vouchsafed to them in Christ; when they are always complaining, and never rejoicing in God, they leave the slaver of their murmurings upon them, as if all were nothing.   If a king advance a man, and he always is sad before him, he is angry : Neh. ii. 3, 'Why is thy countenance sad, seeing thou art not sick ?   This is nothing else but sorrow of heart.   Then I was sore afraid.'   Because men are prejudiced against godly joy, let me tell you it is a fruit of the Spirit : Gal. v. 22, 'The fruit of the

Spirit is love, joy,' &c.   In the garden of Christ there groweth other fruit besides crabs.   It is a great privilege of Christ's spiritual kingdom : Rom. xiv. 17, ' The kingdom of God is righteousness, and peace, and joy in the Holy Ghost.'   It is a help in the spiritual life : Neh. viii. 10, ' The joy of the Lord is your strength.'   It is as wings to the bird, that makes you fly higher ; a sad christian hath lost his wings.

Well, then, consider these things.   Besides your unfitness hereby for your duty, the uncheerfulness of professors darkeneth the ways of God, and brings a scandal upon Christ's spiritual kingdom.   What cause have you to be always sad ?   It must be either your afflictions or your sins.   For afflictions, if your eyes were opened, and earthly affections mortified, you would see no cause of grief.   It can never be so ill with a christian but he hath matter of rejoicing.   Nothing can deprive you of God, of your interest in Christ : Job xv. 11, ' Are the consolations of God small,' that they cannot counterbalance worldly afflictions ? Your discontent cannot be greater than your grounds of comfort.   It is true nature will work ; afflictions are bitter in the root, but the fruit is sweet to a spiritual palate : Heb. xii. 11, ' No chastening for the present seemeth to be joyous, but grievous ;' it doth but *seem* bitter, carnal sense is not a fit judge.   But then for your sins.   I confess, joy is proper to God's children, behaving themselves as children ; but what shall we do when we have sinned ?   I answer—There is a time to mourn, and this is the season of it : ' If her father had spit in her face, should she not be ashamed seven days ? ' Num. xii. 14.   It is good to be sensible of the displeasure of a father.   Ay ! but in this heaviness there should be a mixture of joy.   Though there be a time to mourn, yet ' Rejoice evermore.'   Great heaviness, without a mixture of joy, is sinful.   In this sense we should not mourn without hope. We have to do with a God that is not implacable ; he mixeth love with his frowns : ' In the midst of judgment he remembereth mercy ;' and therefore we should mix joy with our sorrows : Jer. iii. 14, ' Turn, O backsliding Israel, for I am married to you.'   God doth not forget his relation to us, and so should not we.   Come again, and I will make up all breaches between you and me.   A believer may fall grievously, but not finally.   He doth not fall so but that God takes hold of him ; and we should learn to take hold of God.   Labour to recover your former condition, that you may freely rejoice again ; by this means love is renewed and strengthened.

2. The other sort are those that would rejoice, but do not provide matter of joy.   Christ saith, ' That my joy may be fulfilled in themselves.'   But in whom ?   He had pleaded their interest, ' They are thine ;' he had spoken well of them to the Father, ' I am glorified in them.'   Alas ! the joys of others are but ' stolen waters, and bread eaten in secret,' frisks of mirth, when conscience is asleep.   A man cannot rejoice in God till he hath some interest in him : 1 Sam. xxx. 6, ' David encouraged himself in the Lord his God,' when all was lost at Ziklag ; pray mark, ' his God.'   *Tolle meum et tolle Deum*—take away *mine*, and take away *God*.   God is better known *in prædicamento relationis, quam in prædicamento substantiæ*.   God in his nature is terrible ; God in covenant is sweet : Hab. iii. 18, ' Yet will I rejoice in the Lord, I will joy in the God of my salvation.'   When all things

fail, a child of God runneth to his interest.   The object of joy is good, but not good in common, but *my* good.   Excellency and propriety are the two conditions of the object of joy.   Therefore holy joy is not every one's duty, but theirs that have an interest in God.   There are some duties proper to the saints, that suppose such a state and interest. Prayer and hearing are common duties, the obligation lieth on all the creatures, it is the homage they owe to God ; but now they are not immediately bidden to rejoice.   All are bound to provide matter for joy, but not all to rejoice.   Carnal men are for the present under wrath, liable to hell, bondage is their portion ; therefore clear up your interest, if you would rejoice in God.   Men delight in their children because they are their own.

Use 5. To raise your minds to the exercise of this joy.   We should be more careful than we are to maintain our peace and joy.

To help you, I shall show—

1. What reason a christian hath to rejoice.

2. By what means he may get, keep, and maintain it.

First, What reasons a christian hath to rejoice.   The causes of joy may be referred to his past estate, his present interest, his future hopes.

1. The remembrance of his past estate.   A christian may stand wondering at the change which God hath made in his soul: 1 Peter ii. 9, ' That ye should show forth the praises of him who hath called you out of darkness into his marvellous light.'   The light is the more marvellous because of the foregoing darkness.   Past miseries are sweet in the remembrance.   It will be a part of our happiness in heaven to look back ; as travellers in the inn discourse of the dangers and dirtiness of the way.   It is matter of renewed joy to see how the weeds of sin are rooted out, how the buds of grace begin to grow in the garden of our hearts.   No man looketh on the sea with more comfort than he that hath escaped the dangers of a shipwreck ; as the Israelites, when they saw the Egyptians dead on the shore, sung a song of triumph ; so doth a christian rejoice when he considereth his change, what he was, what he is.

2. His present interest, sense, and feeling.   We have mercies in hand as well as mercies in hope, something exhibited as well as promised ; God's eternal love, with all the blessings that issue thence, of justification, sanctification, &c.   Paul triumphs in this : Rom. viii. 37, ' Nay, in all these things we are more than conquerors, through him that loved us.'   God hath adopted them to be children, heirs of his heavenly kingdom ; if the world maketh war against them, they have peace with God, they are in a reconciled estate ; in frame of heart they are regenerate, they have the first-fruits of the Spirit, sweet experience of grace ; not only the wine of Canaan, but the clusters of Canaan ; they have communion with God, though banished from men.   It is the nature of the mind to delight itself in the possession of any solid good. No good can satisfy but the supreme ; this we are in part possessed of as soon as grace is wrought in the heart.

3. His future hopes: Heb. iii. 6, ' If we hold fast the confidence and the rejoicing of hope firm unto the end.'   We are heirs-apparent to the crown of heaven.   We may rejoice in what we possess, we may glory in what we hope for.   This ravisheth the heart to think of it ; we shall

have what infinite mercy will bestow, infinite merit purchase, and the ample promises of the reward[1] hath revealed. The body of sin will be destroyed, and we shall be out of the reach of temptations.

Secondly, By what means it is maintained. God hath appointed graces and ordinances for this end.

1. Graces ; faith, hope, and obedience.

[1.] Faith ; it is a help to joy ; it representeth the excellency, truth, and reality of spiritual things. That which we rejoice in must be good, true, present. All joy ariseth from the presence of some good, either in actual possession or firm expectation. Thus doth faith : Heb. x. 34, ‘ Knowing in yourselves that in heaven ye have a better and an enduring substance.’ Faith is not an opinion or wild guess ; heaven is a pleasing fancy to a carnal man, but it is a reality, a substance, an enduring substance to a believer. The world is a fashion, perishing, moveable. It is the nature of faith to make things absent, present ; it giveth a being to hope, it sets up a stage in the heart of a believer, where God is represented acting whatever he hath promised ; and this not by a naked fiction or empty speculation, as a man may frame ideas of things that never shall be, as in the dream of dotage of a distempered fancy they make a soul as if seen with bodily eyes. Faith gives to its object not only a naked representation, but an actual presence.

[2.] Hope ; this dependeth much on faith ; it is an earnest elevation of the mind to look for what faith counteth real. Now hope ravisheth the soul, as if it had its head above the clouds : ‘ Rejoicing in hope,’ Rom. xii. 12. Joy is proper to enjoyment, but hope serves instead of enjoyment ; they feast and entertain their souls with their glorious hopes.

[3.] Obedience ; faith giveth the title, hope the sight, obedience the evidence, therefore it is necessary to the establishing of joy. Nay, it hath an effective influence ; it is God’s method. First he poureth in the oil of grace before the oil of gladness : Heb. vii. 2, ‘ First being by interpretation King of righteousness, and after that also King of Salem, that is, King of peace ;’ Rom. xiv. 17, ‘ The kingdom of God is not meat and drink, but righteousness, and peace, and joy in the Holy Ghost.’ Sin taketh away joy and peace ; the whole strength of men and angels cannot make the conscience of a sinner to rejoice. Yea, the children of God must take heed that they do not violate peace of conscience by allowing the least sin. You are to walk so that you may be in a condition capable of joy ; none walk sweetly but they that walk strictly : Acts ix. 31, ‘ They walked in the fear of the Lord, and in the comfort of the Holy Ghost ;’ that is a sweet couple.

2. Ordinances. I shall name them.

[1.] The word. The joy that hypocrites have is from the word : Heb. vi. 5, ‘ They have tasted the good word of God.’ A temporary faith findeth joy in the word ; all the fault is, it is but a taste, some slight experience, which they do not continue and maintain. Here is represented fuel for faith and hope, God’s infinite mercy, Christ’s infinite merits, the glory of the next world. Joy is, as it were, the blaze of the soul. Love keepeth the fire burning ; but now, if we would have it blaze and flame up, we must come to the word, this is the bellows.

---

[1] Qu. ‘word’ ?—Ed.

When the angel preached the gospel, he said, Luke ii. 10, 'Behold, I bring you glad tidings of great joy, which shall be to all people.' We come to hear good news from heaven; though an angel be not the messenger, yet the message is the same; God openeth his heart to us.

[2.] Prayer; wherein we open our hearts to God; it hath a pacative virtue. Many psalms begun with anguish end with triumph, as if he had received good news that his affairs were altered. Hannah when she had prayed, 'her countenance was no more sad,' 1 Sam. i. 18. God is 'the Father of mercies, the God of consolations,' 2 Cor. i. 4; the nearer to him, the nearer to the fountain of joy. There are joys felt in prayer, by retiring into God's presence: Ps. xvi. 11, 'In thy presence there is fulness of joy; at thy right hand there are pleasures for evermore.' Heaven is a place of joy, because of the constant communion we have with God there. God doth not love to send us away sad.

[3.] Sacraments; because of sweeter experiences: Cant. i. 4, 'We will be glad, and rejoice in thee: we will remember thy love more than wine.' They are sealing ordinances: Heb. vi. 18, we have 'strong consolation;' Mat. xxvi. 30, 'When they had sung an hymn, they went out into the Mount of Olives,' though it were a sad time. The eunuch went away rejoicing as soon as he was baptized, because he was made sure of the grace of God, Acts viii. 39. It is as when a man hath a good lease confirmed to him. It is not the bread and wine rejoiceth the heart, but the renewing of the covenant.

[4.] Meditation; it refresheth the soul, and feeds joy. It is the proper natural use of reason. The speculation even of terrible things is grateful. It was the comfort God himself took in his works; he made them, he saw them. It is a refreshing to the soul to think of creation and providence; as a son taketh pleasure in a history wherein are recorded his father's valiant acts. It is a pure recreation. But oh! the sweetness of redemption, the excellency of glory! The thoughts are sent as spies into the land of promise; hereby we have a Pisgah-sight; it giveth us a foretaste of heaven, and filleth our souls with joy and blessedness.

SERMON XXII.

I have given them thy word; and the world hath hated them, because they are not of the world, even as I am not of the world.—JOHN XVII. 14.

CHRIST had urged several arguments on the behalf the apostles, their interest, his own departure, their danger in the world; this is the argument he now presseth. Their danger, because of the world's hatred, is set forth by the occasion of it; their office, 'I have given them thy word;' the cause of it, 'They are not of the world;' which is amplified by their conformity to the pattern and example of Christ, 'Even as I am not of the world.' So that we have here the condition of the saints in the world, and then their constitution and temper.

' I have given them thy word.'—Partly by external revelation in his ministry during life, partly by inward illumination he had given them the knowledge of it: John xvi. 27, ' Ye have loved me, and have believed that I came out from God;' John xvii. 6, ' I have manifested thy name to the men which thou gavest me out of the world.' Partly by tradition or commission; he had left the word with them, not only that they might profess it, but preach it to others. There is an emphasis in 'thy word;' Christ grounded his plea with the Father upon it. Men are wont to respect those that suffer for their sake and cause.

' And the world hath hated them.'—By the *world* is meant that party which is contrary to Christ's kingdom; they are sometimes called ' the kingdom of darkness,' because the devil is their head and chief; sometimes ' the world,' because that is their aim; they are guided by the malicious spirit of Satan, and acted by their own ends and interests. Briefly, they are called ' the world,' either because the greatest, the most flourishing part of mankind are obstinate against the gospel; or because their whole bent, their way, their savour, is of the world, they relish nothing but the world, the wicked, unbelieving, obstinate part of the world. And it is said, ' hath hated them.' Hitherto in their profession they have had but sad experience of the world, and in the course of their future ministry they can expect no better.

' Because they are not of the world.'—' Of the world;' that is, of that strain and sort of men; as *of the devil,* is to be swayed by him: John viii. 44, ' Ye are of your father the devil; and the lusts of your father ye will do.' They are different from the world in spirit, in worship, in conversation.

In spirit, or in the frame of their hearts: 1 Cor. ii. 12, ' Now we have received, not the spirit of the world, but the spirit that is of God.' There is a particular genius that runneth out that way; they have other manner of affections and dispositions.

In worship, they are to root out inveterate superstitions, both among Jews and Gentiles. Now men are tender of their old customs and traditions. Unconformity doth exasperate them, much more zealous opposition against traditions received from their fathers.

In conversation, they are come out from among them, they are heteroclites: 1 Peter iv. 4, ' They think it strange that you run not with them to all excess of riot, speaking evil of you.' Their course is a countermotion to the fashions of the world; they have renounced worldly desires and practices.

' Even as I am not of the world,' most estranged from the customs and fashions of it: John viii. 23, ' Ye are from beneath, I am from above; ye are of this world, I am not of this world.' He tasted of the world's hatred: John xv. 18, 19, ' If the world hateth you, you know it hated me before it hated you. If ye were of the world, the world would love its own; but because ye are not of the world, but I have called you out of the world, therefore the world hateth you.' This is added for the consolation of the disciples, that it may not be grievous to them to suffer what their master suffered before them. When the king is wounded in battle, should the soldier shrink? They have my spirit, and are to inherit my office ; and they that have Christ's spirit must look for Christ's entertainment.   Only when it is said, ' Even as I am not of this world,' it noteth not an exact equality, but some conformity.   Christ never was of the world : Heb. vii. 26.   He was ' holy, harmless, undefiled, separate from sinners ;' that is, he never was of their number.   After the fall, all men are of the world ; but by regeneration they are so no more ; therefore it is said, John xv. 19, Ye are not of the world, but I have chosen you out of the world.'   Ye are separated by God's fan, the wheat from the chaff, and cut off from your old root by the sword of the word.

1. Observe, that christians, especially ministers, to whom Christ hath given his word, must expect the world's hatred.   I apply it to both, because Christ hath given the word to both ; to ordinary christians by regeneration, to ministers by special commission.   Ordinary christians are cut off from the world by the sword of the word, and conformity is the ground of love, as difformity and dissonancy of practice is of hatred and aversation.   And ministers have a special commission to preach it.   And then both hold forth the word : ministers clearly, they manage the fan ; and of private christians it is said, Phil. ii. 15, 16, ' That ye be blameless and harmless, the sons of God, without rebuke, in the midst of a crooked and perverse nation, among whom ye shine as lights in the world, holding forth the word of life.' They copy out the word in their lives ; they are a living sermon, a walking rule ; they preach by their lives : the truth is held forth in a minister's mouth, but in a believer's conversation.

[1.] Christians, that do not let fall the strictness and majesty of their conversations, if they keep the word that Christ hath given to them, that is, keep close to it, they must expect troubles.   Christ's subjects are the world's rebels, and if they will not forfeit their allegiance to Christ, the world will fall upon them.   You must not expect friends in the world ; your great friend and patron is in heaven : John xvi. 33, ' In me ye shall have peace, in the world ye shall have tribulation.' He propoundeth it disjunctively ; we have seldom both together. Christ leaveth his subjects in Satan's territories and dominions, that he might try their allegiance : 2 Tim. iii. 12, ' All that will live godly in Christ Jesus shall suffer persecution ;' he doth not say, that profess Christ, but that will live godly in Christ, that are strict, holy, true to their principles.   And it is not an observation proper to that age.   As long as the enmity lasts between the two seeds, opposition will continue.   Satan never wanted a party to support his empire.   The persecution of the church began in Abel, and will not be finished till the day of judgment ; and it is a wonder to see an Abel without a Cain. Afterwards, in Abraham's family, Gal. iv. 25, ' As then, he that was born after the flesh persecuted him that was born after the spirit, so it is now ;' and still we may say, ' So it is now.'   So it hath been, and so it will be.   So afterward Jacob and Esau struggled together in the belly, and the quarrel began before the birth.   And so it is in all ages ; Satan hath not changed his nature, nor the world left its wont. Emperors and kings have become christian, but Satan never yet became christian ; and there never wanteth a strong faction in the world to abet him against the church.   In our times we had great hopes, but still the spirit of enmity continueth, though under other forms and appearances. We see there is a quick conversion from a malignant to a sectary; the term is changed, but not the person. I would not be mistaken. By a malignant, I mean that which the scripture meaneth, not one that dissents from others in civil matters, but one that is an enemy to the power of godliness. And by a sectary, I mean one that is so in the scripture notion, a party-maker in the church, a carnal man under a plausible form, opposing the holy and strict ways of God. I tell you, this conversion is easy. A piece of soft wax, that was but now stamped with the shape of the devil, may be easily stamped again with the seal that is carved into the shape of an angel; the wax is the same, but the impression is different. It is no new thing for the saints of God to be in peril of false brethren, as well as of open enemies; nay, rather than sit out, the devil can make use of one saint to persecute another; as Asa, a good prince, put the prophet in the stocks, and Christ calleth Peter, Satan. The devil may abuse their zeal, and this is strange, that a lamb should act the wolf's part. Usually indeed he maketh use of the world; it is the providence of God that the wicked hate Christ and his messengers. Christ doth usually reveal his ways to the world by the quality of the men that rise against them; it must needs be good what such men hate; their very respect would be a suspicion, and their approbation a contumely and disgrace; a man would have some cause to suspect himself if he had their favour. Thus you see christians, though in a private sphere, that would live godly in Christ, must expect their share in the world's hatred. Now the Lord permits it, εἰς μαρτύριον, 'for a testimony;' for a testimony to his servants, for a testimony against his adversaries, for a testimony to the ways of God; all these will be gathered out of the same expression, as it is recited by several evangelists: Mark xiii. 9, 'They shall deliver ye up to councils, and in the synagogues ye shall be beaten; and ye shall be brought before kings and rulers for my sake, for a testimony against them,' εἰς μαρτύριον αὐτοῖς, that by your zealous defence they may have a sufficient knowledge of the ways of God, and so be convinced or confounded by them: Luke xxi. 13, 'It shall turn to you for a testimony,' ἀποβήσεται δὲ ὑμῖν εἰς μαρτύριον, that is, a proof of your loyalty; and Mat. xxiv. 14, it is only εἰς μαρτύριον, 'The gospel of the kingdom shall be preached in all the world for a witness;' implying, to the truth. God chooseth his eminent servants to be his champions, that the world may know that there is somewhat excellent in their principles, worth the suffering for. God will not have his servants to go to heaven without a testimony; nor his enemies to go to hell without a testimony, and a sting in their consciences; nor any age to pass away without a testimony.

[2.] Ministers; this is usually their portion; few of the apostles and prophets came to a natural death. As their calling is eminent, so are their sufferings: James v. 10, 'Take, my brethren, the prophets, who have suffered in the name of the Lord, for an example of suffering affliction, and of patience.' He doth not say, Take them for an example of holiness, but of suffering and patience. They were the worthies of God, eminent for holiness, yet chiefly for sufferings. The prophets, that were God's own mouth, sheltered under the buckler of their special commission, and the singular innocency and holiness of their lives, and yet they suffered; what recompense did they receive for all their pains, but saws and swords and dungeons? Now the ministers of all ages are mustered and enrolled for the same war with the prophets and apostles; we maintain the same cause, though with less vigour and strength, and we expect the same crown; why should we grudge to drink of the same cup? In these latter times, God hath reserved the ministry for all the contempt and scorn that villany and outrage can heap upon their persons. But why should we look for better entertainment? You would think the world should hate false teachers; surely they have most cause: but if they slight us, and neglect to provide for us, remember it is a wonder that they do not persecute us. But this falleth out partly by the malice of men, partly by the providence of God.

(1.) By the malice of men. To preach is to bait the world. *Prædicare nihil aliud est quam derivare in se furorem mundi.* We are to cross carnal interests, to wrestle with vile affections, to pull the beast out of men's hearts; and we are like to be bruised in the conflict: 1 Cor. xv. 32, 'I have fought with beasts at Ephesus;' most probably the rude multitude, that were ready to tear him in pieces when he cried down the worship of Diana. Carnal interests are very touchy, worse than vile affections. The doctrine of the gospel cannot be preached in power, but it draweth hatred upon the person that preacheth it: John vii. 7, 'The world cannot hate you, but me it hateth, because I testify of it that the works thereof are evil.' We are to contest with public miscarriages; interests and powers stir up the malice and rage of men; sore eyes cannot endure the light, nor a guilty conscience the word: John iii. 20, 'For every one that doeth evil hateth the light, neither cometh he to the light, lest his deeds should be reproved.' The Ethiopians curse the sun: Rev. xi. 10, 'The two witnesses tormented them that dwell on the earth.' This drowsy world would fain take a nap and sleep, were it not for some bawling preachers. Proud, covetous, carnal men, men wedded to their interests, will hate us, if we preach in good earnest; as a good thresher maketh the straw to fly about his ears. Nay, and errors are more touchy than sins; a drunkard is more patient of conviction than a seducer. Errors take away the light of reason, and leave nothing but the pride of reason. A drunkard standeth upon lower ground; his practices cannot endure the test of the light of nature; but every erroneous person thinketh he standeth upon the upper ground, because of the height of his pride and the plausibleness of his notions.

(2.) By the providence of God. Preachers are like Gideon's lamps in earthen pitchers. Possibly the apostle may allude to it when he saith, 'We carry this treasure in earthen vessels,' 2 Cor. iv. 7. Now, as when the pitcher is dashed to pieces, the lamp breaketh out to the amazement of the adversaries, so the sufferings of ministers are a great confirmation to their doctrine.

Use 1. Advice to us—(1.) To prepare for sufferings; (2.) When they come, do not count it strange.

First, To prepare for sufferings. It will do us no hurt to be prepared for sufferings. It hath ever been the lot of God's people to be obnoxious to the world's hatred, and we ourselves cannot look for any exemption. I shall lay down several probabilities, to show when God is about to bring trouble on the church.

1. Observe, that after God hath laid in many spiritual comforts, there comes a time to lay them out again; and after great receipts, we are put upon great expenses. The disciples first enjoyed Christ's presence and ministry, and then were exposed to a dreadful persecution. John xi., Christ biddeth them 'make use of light, because darkness was coming upon them.' Never was the gospel powerfully preached but trials came : 1 Thes. i. 5, 'For our gospel came not unto you in word only, but also in power, and in the Holy Ghost, and in much assurance.' And it follows, ver. 6, 'Ye received the word with much affliction.' God will try how we can live upon the comforts of the gospel. Castles are first victualled, and then besieged: Heb. x. 32, 'After ye were illuminated, ye endured a great fight of afflictions.' The churches of Asia had horrible desolations after a powerful ministry. The Germans, after a sufficient promulgation of the gospel, suffered many sad years.

2. Observe, after trials and reformations there come trials and probations, that after we have submitted to the ways of God, we may honour them with sufferings. The ten persecutions were after Christ had set up the ordinances of the gospel. The Marian and bloody days were after King Edward's reformation. God will have every truth honoured in its season. When the witnesses had finished the testimony of their prophecy, after a short time they were slain, Rev. xi.

3. Observe, when reformations stick in the birth, God will promote them by troubles; he taketh his own fan into his hand : Mat. iii. 12, 'Whose fan is in his hand, and he will thoroughly purge his floor.' When men cannot or will not effect it, God will purge his floor, and cleanse the church from profane mixtures. Christ came with his whip to cleanse the temple, John ii. 15. Grosthead prophesied that the church should not be reformed, but *ore gladii cruentandi.* God usually tendereth a reformation to the world with a judgment in his hand; and if the reformation be obstructed, the judgment will proceed : Ezek. xxiv. 12, 13, 'She hath wearied herself with lies, and her great scum went not forth out of her; her scum shall be in the fire. In thy filthiness is lewdness; because I have purged thee, and thou wast not purged, thou shalt not be purged from thy filthiness any more, till I have caused my fury to rest upon thee.' When the pot is put over the fire, if the scum remaineth still, he overturneth all.

4. Observe, when there are great differences among God's own people, the end is bitter. We warp in the sunshine. The dog is let loose that the sheep may run together. A piece of wax, when it is broken, put it together never so often, it will not close; but put it into the candle, and the ends stick close together. Ridley and Hooper could agree in a prison. A little before Dioclesian's persecution, the church was rent and torn by intestine broils, pastor against pastor, and people against people. Ease begets pride and wantonness, and that maketh way for contention. God may solder you in your own blood, and effect union by making you objects of the same hatred and persecution. Nazianzen was wont to call the enemies of the church,

κονοὺς [1] διαλλάκτας. The turbulent enemies many times prove the best reconcilers, and the wolves bring the sheep together.

5. Observe, libertines and fanatical persons, when they increase in power and numbers, become cruel : Jude 11, 'Woe unto them, for they have gone in the way of Cain.' The Donatists are of detestable and accursed memory, because of their insolent cruelties : Hosea v. 5, 'The revolters are profound to make slaughter.' Men that have cast off the holy faith, after some profession, the Lord keep us from their tender mercies! The Arians grew bloody. Want of truth is usually made up by a supply of rage. Lees and dregs are usually very tart and sour.

6. Observe, when religion hath received wounds in the house of her friends, and occasion is given to the world by scandals to think evil of the ways of God, God taketh his scourge in his hand, and the devil hath an advantage, he stirreth the malignant world against the children of God ; as a sect of monsters, the gnostics, by their impure and libidinous courses, made christianity odious, and then the heathens rose up against them as pests of mankind. Satan is a liar, but never his lies carry more pretence.

7. Observe, when there is a decay of the power of godliness and formality and contempt of the word take place, which are the usual effects of prosperity. As soon as we come out of miseries, we run into disorders ; therefore God is wont to return us into our old chains and captivity, that we may wanton it no more : Hosea v. 15, 'I will go and return to my place, till they acknowledge their offence, and seek my face : in their affliction they will seek me early.' I will try them by adversity, I will try what my rod will do to better my people. As also to discover hypocrites. When the ways of God are in fashion, many pretend for him ; and so religion is turned into a fashion and empty pretence. Salvian observeth that the church, like a river, loseth in depth what it gaineth in breadth ; as a woman that hath borne many children is with every birth the weaker ; as a large body is less active. Carnal men coming under a profession of religion weaken the power of it.

8. Observe, when professors grow worldly, this awakeneth the world's rage and God's rod. The men of the world take mammon for their God, and the conveniences of this life for their portion. Now when the children of God put in for a share, and are all for worldly hopes and worldly interests, it stirreth up their sleepy enmity ; they cannot endure to be discountenanced : Luke xvi. 8, 'The children of this world are in their generation wiser than the children of light.' This is their generation and sphere ; as a people take it ill to be beaten and foiled in their own land : They are active to recover their interest, and are full of watchful malice. God is very jealous of mammon ; and when the world gets into the church, God's rod whippeth it out again. By the world God will show us the vanity of our aspiring projects. When vessels grow musty, they are not fit for use. I find the spirit of the world breathing in most christians, who are proling for worldly greatness, as if they served the god of this world. Some transform their christian hopes into a worldly hope, and look for a sudden coming of Christ in carnal pomp, and dream of greatness and dominion.

---

[1] Qu. 'κοινοὺς'?—ED.

I shall say no more, but that it is a doctrine fit for a worldly age. The disciples had such a dream, and Christ cureth it by those threatenings, Mat. xxiv. But because that was not a sufficient cure, but after Christ's resurrection they ask, Acts i. 6, 'Lord, wilt thou at this time restore the kingdom unto Israel?' therefore there were many persecutions in the primitive times. If ever God should send a scourge, men would complain of their affecting worldly greatness, and aspiring to raise their families.

Secondly, When sufferings come, do not think them strange: 1 John iii. 13, 'Marvel not, my brethren, if the world hate you.' Wonder is for things unusual. We do not wonder at the darkness of the night, as we do at the darkness of an eclipse. Therefore if any thing were a marvel, this were, that ever it should be otherwise, that you ever see the church of God to have any ease and peace. We may stand wondering at the bounty of God, that we have so much peace as we have. The church must have a time of learning and training up, and must be in the school of afflictions and persecutions: 1 Peter iv. 12, 13, 'Beloved, think it not strange concerning the fiery trial which is to try you, as though some strange thing happened unto you. But rejoice, inasmuch as ye are partakers of Christ's sufferings.' Alas! why should it now seem strange? Christ had foretold it, the constant experience of the church ratifies it. The disposition of the world is the same; Satan never did, nor ever will turn christian; and the world will never leave its old wont. Why should we wonder at these things? When ministers are put to hardships, it may be their revenues straitened, scanted, why should we think it strange? The apostles had not so much. Paul was put to a hard shift for his living, to make tents. Obadiah fed the prophets, by fifty and fifty in a cave, with bread and water. Your means are short and straitened by the malice of men, the apostles had no standing revenues, and were put to hard shifts for a livelihood. Therefore do not think it strange; it is the bounty of God that it is no worse.

Use 2. Of caution.

1. Before you choose any way, do not judge of things by the world's hatred or applause. Why? 'I have given them thy word, therefore the world hateth them.' A philosopher could say, *Nunquam tam bene agitur cum rebus humanis, ut meliora placeant pluribus*—It was never so well with the world that the best things could please the most; therefore the world may appear against the ways of God. Be not swayed by their opinion in taking up the course of thy profession.

2. If thou art convinced, do not defer profession till the times are more quiet. This is the deceit of men's hearts. Alas! when will the ways of God be exempted from persecution? You may expect it a long time. Will Satan ever be at an agreement with God? Do you ever think to hear of a Jesus without a cross? As the husbandman stands expecting till the river be drawn dry, and still it runs with a constant stream, so you may expect till the times be more quiet, and the ways of God exempted from trouble; but the children of God must constantly expect trouble in the world. The devil hath a potent and powerful faction in the world.

3. If thou dost profess the ways of God, take heed of giving Christ

a short allowance; but first sit down and count the charges; come what will come, here I will stick: Luke xiv. 26, 27, 'If any man come to me, and hate not his father and mother, and wife and children, and brethren and sisters, yea, and his own life also, he cannot be my disciple. And whosoever doth not bear his cross, and come after me, cannot be my disciple. For which of you intending to build a tower, sitteth not down first and counteth the cost, whether he have sufficient to finish it?' &c. Thus should you resolve upon sufficient evidence and demonstration. When a man hath set apart such a sum of money for building, he spends willingly and freely while that lasts; but after that is gone, every penny goes from him with grudging. So sit down and count the charges, and give Christ a large allowance.

4. If thou dost profess, do not allay the world's hatred by any carnal means, by abating one jot of your zeal, or by any fond compliance; for honour or dishonour, for esteem or disesteem, put it into the hands of God: Prov. xvi. 7, 'When a man's ways please the Lord, he maketh his enemies to be at peace with him;' as he made Jacob find favour with Esau, the three children in Babylon in the eyes of the prince. God hath the key of every man's heart and respect; we must not break open the door by carnal compliance. God hath a golden key, and he can open it; you must not force conscience, that your interest may be favoured.

5. When you are actually burdened with the world's hatred in the course of your profession, be not dismayed. Whenever this is thy case, thou art an object of Christ's prayers. When Christ was to go to heaven, he remembers all that are hated for his sake. Christ maketh the world's hatred an argument, and we may conceive thence a ground of hope; it is a singular consolation, a sign you belong to God, and have an interest in his care. If their hatred be for righteousness' sake, and your being zealous in the ways of God, then you may know God will keep you; for that is the main request, 'Keep them through thine own name.' And why? 'Because I have given them thy word, therefore the world hates them.' The more they are our enemies for God's sake, the greater help will God afford us. Men use to send relief there where the battle is sharp and hottest; so when the battle is sharpest and hottest, thou hast an interest in God's protection.

Second point. 'The world hateth them, because they are not of the world;' because of their strictness and holiness, they live contrary to their interests and lusts; this is the very cause.

Observe, there is such a sin as antipathy against the power of godliness, or hatred of others because of their strictness in the service of God and diligence in heavenly things.

Here—

1. I shall give you instances of this from the word of God.

2. Discoveries of this κακία, or malignity.

3. Reasons of it; and then come to apply it.

First, Instances of it from the scripture. The world's hatred is disguised under other pretences, but this is the proper cause of it. The word is the best judge of that, which is a searcher of the thoughts and intents of the heart. God and his word have the same properties: Heb. iv. 12, 'The word of God is quick and powerful, and sharper than any two-edged sword, piercing even to the dividing asunder of soul and spirit, and of the joints and marrow, and is a discerner of the thoughts and intents of the heart.' Now what doth the word say? The word of God doth tell us doctrinally that it is so, and giveth instances and examples of it.

1. Doctrinally, that it is so. Let us begin with that place which describeth the first rise of it: Gen. iii. 15, 'And I will put enmity between thee and the woman, and between thy seed and her seed.' There is a natural enmity between the two seeds, as there is between a toad and a man, a wolf and a lamb, a raven and a dove; so there is between the seed of the woman and the seed of the serpent; that is, between Christ and his upright followers, and so many of mankind as fall to the devil's share; an enmity that will never be laid aside while the world is the world, and till the devil turn christian and be converted, which will never be. The next place is, Prov. xxix, 27, 'An unjust man is an abomination to the just, and he that is upright in the way is an abomination to the wicked.' There is a mutual enmity between the good and the bad, so as they can never piece in a firm friendship; only there is a difference between the prosecution of this hatred: the just hate not *virum*, but *vitium;* sin is to be hated, not the person; as we are not to love the sin for the person's sake, so we are not to hate the person for the sin's sake. A good man abhorreth that which is evil; he loatheth it in others, but chiefly in himself. Or, as the schools distinguish, there is *odium abominationis et offensionis*, and *odium inimicitiæ.* The godly are offended with the evil deeds of others, though they do not hate their persons; but the wicked hate the godly, *odio inimicitiæ*, they have an inbred enmity against them, and seek their destruction, they hate them despitefully, because of the old hatred. The next place is, John xv. 19, 'If ye were of the world, the world would love its own; but because ye are not of the world, but I have chosen you out of the world, therefore the world hateth you.' You see men are divided into two ranks, some are of the world, and some are not of the world. Some there are whose hopes and hearts and conversations are wholly here; their manners, the temper of their spirits, and the course of their worship, is wholly calculated for the world. Others there are that neither conform to the world in judgment, affections, nor practice, but wholly savour things past this life, are fitted for another world, breathe after it, and labour for it. Now let us see what different entertainment both these meet with. Some are dandled on the world's knees, suck freely of the breasts of her consolation; others are troubled, and molested, and exercised with all manner of displeasures. And why? Because they are chosen out of the world, and called to the love and enjoyment of better things. It is true there may be contentions and emulations among the men of the world, as their lusts and interests interfere and cross one with another; but because they differ not in contrary general principles and ends, the hatred which they have towards their own is nothing so violent and extreme as that which they have against the godly; and they do not so hate one another but that they can easily agree in this common enmity against those who are upright with God; as Herod and Pontius Pilate did, and the Herodians and pharisees against

Christ, and Gebal, and Ammon, and Amalek against Israel. Thus you see doctrinally the scripture speaketh of such a thing.

2. By way of instance and example. Let us see how this spirit of enmity hath been working, and how the holy men of God have had bitter experience of it. Abel was slain by Cain. Let us begin with Cain, the patriarch of unbelievers. Now the Holy Ghost giveth us a comment on that action: 1 John iii. 12, 'Not as Cain, who was of that wicked one, and slew his brother. And wherefore slew he him ? Because his own works were evil, and his brother's righteous.' The one was the seed of the woman, the other of the serpent; the one worshipped God after the right order, and brought the first, the fat, the tenth, to the Lord: the other was slight and careless in worship. The Targum of Jerusalem mentioneth a dispute that happened between them concerning the providence of God, and the last judgment, and the world to come, and those wholesome doctrines by which godliness is maintained. *Non est judicium, nec judex, nec sœculum aliud, nec munus pro justis, nec pœna pro impiis.* However, this we are sure, it was for his godliness that this outrage was committed upon him. Let us go a little lower; in the story of the patriarchs, we shall find Isaac scoffed at by Ishmael, Gen. xxi. 9 ; upon which practice of his, the apostle glosseth thus : Gal. iv. 29, 'As he that was born after the flesh persecuted him that was born after the Spirit, so it is now.' Scoffing and mocking is a kind of persecution; ever so it was, and ever so it will be, while there are two seeds in the world. Whatever civility the men of the world have, they are all opposite to grace and godliness ; and do not only refuse and resist it in themselves, but hate it and persecute it in others. I say, they that have not the image of God in themselves, they cannot endure the lustre of it in others. And therefore it is the ordinary lot of God's children to suffer hard things from the men of the world. If you go a little further, Jacob, because of the blessing and birthright, was pursued to the death by Esau, and driven out of his father's house, Gen. xxvii. xxviii., and there was matter of godliness and profaneness in this : Heb. xii. 15, 'Not as profane Esau, who for one morsel of bread sold his birthright.' Instances are endless, but by these brought you see the point fully made good. And over and above what was to be proved, you may collect that no bonds of duty can allay it ; for in these instances given you may observe that Cain and Abel, Isaac and Ishmael, Jacob and Esau, were all brothers, members of the same church and family, tied to one another by the nearest and strictest bonds of kindred and acquaintance; yet because the one was holy and the other wicked, did they hate one another.

Secondly, Discoveries that this hatred that is commenced against the people of God ariseth from an antipathy to godliness. This part of the discourse is necessary, because wicked men will not own that they hate others for their goodness; they disguise it with other pretences, as the Jews did excuse their hatred to Christ, when he told them, John x. 32, 'Many good words have I showed you from my Father ; for which of these works do you stone me ? ' They could have no quarrel against him unless they would quarrel at a good turn, and reward evil for good. But ver. 33, 'The Jews answered, For a good work we stone thee not, but for blasphemy, because thou, being a man, makest thyself equal with God.' So will carnal men say, it is not for their holiness that they hate them, but for their pride, covetousness, censoriousness, and hypocrisy. But when they neither hate, nor abhor, nor avoid these sins in themselves, or other men, yea, do wink at fouler and grosser evils, even against the light of nature, which themselves live in, or else tolerate and make nothing of them in their friends, they do clearly convince themselves, if they would attend to it, that the pretended causes of their hatred are but cloaks of their malice, which is truly raised in them by the contrariety of their nature to that which is good. Shall a leper loathe another because of a few pimples in his skin? or shall he that is tumbled into the ocean in drink vaunt against another who, on slippery ground, is fallen into a ditch? Besides, these allegations are usually false; for it is the fashion of evil men first to caluminate Christ and his followers, and then to hate them : as they would clothe the primitive christians with the skins of bears and of wild beasts, and then worry them and bait them with dogs, as if they were bears. From the beginning, Satan hath been both a liar and a murderer, John viii. 44 ; first a liar, then a murderer with the more pretence.

But to take off all cavils, let us see how it appeareth that this hatred is the effect of their abhorrence of that which is good and holy.

1. This is some discovery of it ; because the servants of God have been hated most, and troubled by the worst men ; which is a shrewd presumption that the proper reason of this hatred is because they are so evil and the other so good. So David concludeth from the ill conditions of his enemies, their bad nature, violence, and ingratitude : Ps. xxxviii. 20, ' They also that render evil for good are mine enemies, because I follow the thing that good is.' In Nero's time, about the 70th year of Christ, Nero made a law, *Quisquis christianum se profitetur, tanquam generis humani convictus hostis, sine ulteriori sui defectione capite plectetur.* Traján moderated it, *Id genus hominum non inquiri, repertos autem puniri oportere.* So usually it falleth out that the worst and most virulent enemies to religious men are the vicious and debauched ; those that are infamous for other crimes, atheists, whoremongers, and pot-companions ; these have the greatest pique against them, because they cannot endure the brightness of God's image in them.

2. Because the best of men, who have the least alloy of corruptions, and are most eminent for strict and exemplary conversation, are most hated and maligned : Ps. lxiv. 5, ' They shoot their arrows at the perfect ;' 2 Tim. iii. 12, ' All that will live godly in Christ Jesus must suffer persecution.' Morality doth not exasperate ; it shineth with a faint beam, and is not so troublesome to the sore eyes of the world ; and they that have but the form and outward skin of godliness escape better than they that have the life and power of it. A wolf doth not worry a painted sheep. But when any are holy indeed, and of a strict innocency, they are hated, and contradicted, and spoken against.

3. Because when religion is accompanied with other things that a man would think should assuage malice and allay the heat and rage of men against them, yet it escapeth not. As for instance, godly

meek men, that are guilty of nothing but worshipping God in sincerity, and desiring to go to heaven with all their hearts, are persecuted. If this hatred did only light upon busy intermeddlers, that did trouble men's lusts and interests, it were another matter. *Oditur in hominibus innocuis nomen innocuum.* The primitive christians were quiet and harmless, their weapons were prayers and tears; and they prayed for the health of their emperors, though they could not drink their healths. *Cajus Sejus vir bonus, nisi quod christianus :* yet he was hated for being a christian. John the disciple of love, was banished into Patmos. Moses, the meekest upon earth, had those that spoke against him. Chrysostom observeth of those holy men, Heb. xi. 38, 'They wandered about in deserts and mountains, and caves and dens of the earth,' ἀλλὰ καὶ ἔκει ὄντες ἔφευγον, they would not allow them the recess and retirement of a cave, or den, and obscure grot, where they were far enough from troubling the world; but they were hunted up and down like a partridge upon the mountains; and they were driven out of their obscure refuges, where they desired to worship God in silence. Though there are many excellences which are wont to deserve respect; as nobility of birth; there were many noble martyrs; Isaiah, of the blood royal, yet sawed asunder, as they report: eloquence and learning; the men of Lystra called Paul Mercurius, Acts xiv. 12, the god of eloquence, yet stoned him, ver. 19: philosophy and other learning, as Justin that is called Martyr, a learned man, and yet suffered. Mere christianity and godliness is the mark and butt of spite and rage.

4. It appeareth by their invention of lies and ridiculous crimes to palliate their hatred; as against the primitive christians their worshipping of an ass's head, their drinking the blood of a child in their meetings. These are a testimony to their consciences that they could find nothing against them 'but in the matter of their God,' Dan. vi. 5. They have no real matter against them, and therefore feign and suppose these crimes to justify their opposition, for they devise crimes because they find none.

5. Because, if a man be strict and conscientious, mortified, sober of life and behaviour, the world is apt to judge him one of such a hated party. As if any named the name of God with reverence, they suspected them for heretics if they said, If the Lord will. And we read in the story of the French martyrs, when Sanpanlius reproved a man for swearing, he was presently suspected to be a Huguenot, and so condemned. As if it were said, in the language of the damsel to Peter, 'Thou art one of them, for thy speech bewrayeth thee.' If any were humble, mortified, serious, the world suspecteth them.

6. The consciences of wicked men are as a thousand witnesses. *Non amo te Sabedi,* &c. Ask conscience what is the matter; they cannot look upon them without fear and shame. Their heart riseth against them; and what is the reason? All regular affection may be justified; the cause is bad, and men are loath to render it.

7. It appears by the joy wicked men take when they have anything offered to justify their opposition; as suppose by the scandals of any that profess the ways of God, as the heathens took an advantage from the impurity of the gnostics to defame all christians. Regular

zeal is accompanied with compassion, and flieth not from the persons
to the cause, from the faulty to the innocent, to the whole generation
of the just.   It is hatred, πρὸς τὰ γένη, as Haman thought scorn to
lay hands upon Mordecai alone, but sought to root out the whole seed
of the Jews, Esther iii. 6.

SERMON XXIII.

*I have given them thy word ; and the world hath hated them, be-
cause they are not of the world, even as I am not of the world.*
—JOHN XVII. 14.

THIRDLY, Having given the instances and discovery of the world's
hatred to the people of God, I now come to the reasons thereof.

1. Difference and estrangement in course of life is a provoking thing.   Therefore men that live in any sinful course are loath that
any should part company with them : 1 Peter iv. 4, ' Wherein they
think it strange that ye run not with them to all excess, speaking evil
of you.'   Therefore they hate them, because of the difference in the
course of life.   Now this suitableness and oneness of course can never
be between the serious worshippers of God and others.   There is a
contrariety in their dispositions : the one have the spirit of the world,
the other have a heavenly spirit, 1 Cor. ii. 12.   They are employed in
the service of contrary masters, Christ and mammon, Mat. vi. 24,
Christ and Belial, 2 Cor. vi. 15.   They are guided by contrary rules,
the law of sin and the law of righteousness, the customs of the
world, and the will of God ; and they are carried in all their ways and
actions to contrary ends, the one living for earthly, the other for
heavenly things ; whence it must necessarily follow that they must
continually cross one another in the course of their conversation.

2. This is not all : it is not only a difference, but a difference about
religion ; and usually hatreds that arise from difference in religion are
very deadly; that which is for the restraint of passion is made the
fuel of it, and instead of a judge a party.   The Samaritans and Jews
could not endure one another.   The nearer they agree the strife is the
greater, when they are outstripped in that form.   *Proximorum odia
sunt acerrima.*   A Turk hateth a Jew more than a christian, a Jew
hateth a christian more than others.   So in the other subdivision,
the nearer and more conjoined in a common profession, the greater the
particular breach, and the hatred more fierce.

3. It is not only a difference about religion, but between the true
religion and false.   False worships, though never so different, may
better agree together than the false with the true ; as darkness and
darkness will better suit than light and darkness, and one error will
give better quarter to another than either will to the right worship
of God.   The heathens tolerated the Epicureans, that denied providence, and took away all respect and care about divine matters ; and
yet persecuted christians.   The strict profession of the name of the
true God enrageth more than to say, ' There is no God.'   The

Romans, when they had captivated any nation, worshipped the gods of it, except it were Jehovah, the God of the Jews; yea, afterward, though the Jews were equally against the idolatries of the Gentiles as the christians, yet they were not so generally hated and persecuted. So that hatred and persecution is the church's lot, and the evil genius that followeth the gospel wherever it goeth. Other religions, though much different among themselves, can agree well enough and live together in peace, when the malignity of the world is turned upon that which is true. Under Rome antichristian the Jews were tolerated, but not Protestants.

But why is there such a spite and enmity at the sincere and serious profession of the true religion? It is needful to speak to this, that we may search this sore to the bottom. Holiness is lovely, and there is a natural veneration of what is strict, and godliness in the power of it tendeth to love and meekness, and teacheth men patience in wrongs, and readiness to give and to forgive, to do good to all, to pass by injuries, and to render good for evil. Why should such an amiable thing be hated? I answer—

1. The devil's instigation is one great cause; he hath great wrath against the saints; their increase presageth his ruin: Rev. xii. 12, 'The devil is come down unto you, having great wrath, because he knoweth he hath but a little time.' And he hath great power over wicked men: Eph. ii. 2, 'The prince of the power of the air, the spirit that now worketh in the children of disobedience.' As he worketh other sins in them, so this sin of hatred and trouble to the saints: John viii. 44, 'Ye are of your father the devil, and the lusts of your father ye will do; he was a murderer from the beginning.' And Cain is said to be 'of that wicked one,' 1 John iii. 12. They are his seed, and there is an old enmity between the seeds. The original cause is malignity against God: Rom. i. 30, 'Haters of God.' It is a part of original sin; they hate God, and hate his saints. God should speed no better than his saints, if he were in their power. But the actual cause is—

2. On man's part; and there seemeth to be a double reason—pride and envy. Pride is impatient of reproof, and envy looketh with an evil eye upon their privileges and advantages in Christ.

[1.] Pride, which is impatient of reproof. Strictness is an object reviving guilt: Heb. xi. 7, 'Noah, moved with fear, prepared an ark to the saving of his family, whereby he condemned the world.' Your life is a reproof, that maketh them ashamed: John vii. 7, 'The world hateth me, because I testify of it, that the works thereof are evil.' Every wicked man loveth another, *velut fautorem, adjutatorem, et excusatorem sui criminis.* One wicked man doth not put another to the blush. It is no shame to be black in a country of negroes, where all are black. Their conversation is a living reproof. Thy guilt is upbraided by their righteous works; their conversation upbraideth thy conscience; the sense of thy guilt and negligence is revived by their righteous works, and serious diligence in heaven's way. We are impatient of a verbal reproof, much more of a real. Their holy lives beget a fear and awe: Mark vi. 20, 'Herod feared John, knowing that he was a just man and holy, and observed him.' Christ saith here not only, 'I have given them thy word,' but, 'They are not of the world.' They do not only teach things contrary to the world, but live contrary to the world. Many a strict preacher may be a carnal man, and the world and he may agree well enough. They look upon sermons as words spoken of course; it is the holy conversation that enrageth most, as elephants are enraged with gorgeous apparel. They have no veil and cloak for their sins. Thieves rob in the night; they would fain extinguish the light. The world cannot endure to be condemned by that light that shineth from the godly, as the sun is burdensome to the owl and other night-birds: John iii. 19, 20, 'This is the condemnation, that light is come into the world, and men loved darkness rather than light, because their deeds were evil. For every one that doeth evil hateth the light, neither cometh he to the light, lest his deeds should be reproved.'

[2.] Envy at God's favours bestowed on them: John xv. 19, 'If ye were of the world, the world would love its own; but because ye are not of the world, but I have chosen you out of the world, therefore the world hateth you.' Cain was not only upbraided by Abel's better sacrifice, but envied God's acceptance of him, Gen. iv. 4, 5. Joseph's parti-coloured coat and his father's favour stirred up envy in his brethren. This is the difference between envy and emulation: envy is accompanied with laziness, as emulation with industry. There is between the good, ἀγαθὴ ἔρις, a good contention, Heb. x. 24, who shall be most forward. Emulation is good, if separated from carnal aims; but envy, which is accompanied with sloth, maketh a man malign that good which is in others. Envy hath an evil eye, it cannot look upon goodness without grief. When others are at the top of the hill, and they lie lazily at the bottom, they fret at those which are at the top; they will not put in for the privileges of christianity, and therefore are troubled with those that do so. Divine grace hath made a distinction, and those whom God blesseth to be objects of his love, the world chooseth to be objects of hatred.

Use 1. If the children of God hath the world's respect at any time, they have need to look to their consciences. Do not you symbolise with them in carnal practices? Luke vi. 26, 'Cursed are you when all men speak well of you, for so they did to the false prophets.' Phocion, upon a general applause, went home, and said, *Quid mali feci?*—Do not you at least let fall the majesty of your conversation? A child of God may find external favour, as the three children did in Babylon, by God's overruling power on men's spirits: Prov. xvi. 7, 'When a man's ways please the Lord, he maketh his enemies to be at peace with him.' The world may do it in design; as Hannibal abstained from Fabius his fields, to render him suspected; or else to oblige by courtesies, and gain them to their faction and party. However you have cause to look to yourselves; it is ill to be solicited, as a chaste matron is troubled to be solicited to lust. Have not you given them some advantage? Do not you share with them in their wickedness? When the world's respects run out so fairly and smoothly towards you, you have cause to suspect yourselves. At least, take the more heed that you do not seek to make your conversation more pleasing, by suiting yourself to the customs and sinful courses of carnal men.

Use 2. To press all to avoid this sin and snare of death, especially in these times of dissension.   Oh ! take heed, whatever you do, whatever differences you cherish, or whatever party you stick to, that you be not guilty of hatred against the power of godliness.   Let not the saints act the wicked's part.   The spirit of enmity seeketh other pretences.   Hold not communion with the wicked world in their malignity and spite against God's children.

1. It is a mark of a child of the devil, the express image of Satan. Thereby our Saviour convinced the Jews to be of their father the devil, because they hated him that came from God : John viii. 40, 41, ' But now ye seek to kill me, a man that have told you the truth, which I have heard of God : this did not Abraham.   Ye do the deeds of your father ;' and ver. 44, ' Ye are of your father the devil, and the lusts of your father ye will do : he was a murderer from the beginning, and abode not in the truth, because there is no truth in him ;' and 1 John iii. 10, ' In this the children of God are manifest, and the children of the devil : whosoever doeth not righteousness is not of God, neither he that loveth not his brother.'   This manifests men to be the children of Satan, because they love not their brethren, as Cain loved not Abel.   You express the image of Satan to the life, when this is the ground of your hatred.

2. It is a very provoking sin ; and it is the more provoking, because we enjoy so many benefits by them.   It is sad to hate men for their godliness, for Christ's name's sake.   Look, as it is a commendation of kindness on the one side, so it is an aggravation of injury on the other : Mat. x. 42, ' Whosoever shall give to drink unto one of these little ones a cup of cold water only, in the name of a disciple, verily I say unto you, he shall in nowise lose his reward.'   The height of this sin is the sin against the Holy Ghost, the wilful persecuting of the known truth ; therefore take heed that you be not guilty of any spice and degree of it.

3. It is possible for them that profess religion to hate one another for their strictness in that religion.   Pseudo-christians may be hot and violent ; the beast pusheth with the Lamb's horns, Rev. xiii. ; Isa. lxvi. 5, ' Your brethren that hated you, that cast you out for my name's sake, said, Let the Lord be glorified.'   Men that are brethren, that have great pretences of zeal, hate you for my name's sake.   Nay, the people of God may have a spice of carnal envy, and be guilty of some unkindness, if not hatred to their godly brethren.   Job was deeply censured by his godly friends, and Paul by his own hearers : 1 Cor. iv. 10, ' We are fools for Christ's sake ;' that is, in their account.   Though there be not in them that desperate hatred against the power of godliness, yet there is offence too often taken, and carried on with too great heat and animosity : some godly men are too favourable to their own interests.

4. When there is a secret rising of heart against the purity and strictness of others, natural malignity beginneth to work, you had need suppress it betimes ; exulcerated lusts will grow more tumultuous. One godly man may reprove another that is less godly, reprove his conscience by his life, they cannot look upon them without shame. Let it be a holy emulation, not a carnal envy.

5. In opposing those that are godly, we had need be tender : ' Take

care what thou doest, for this man is a Roman,' Acts xxii. 26.   A man
that meddleth with any that profess religion in strictness had need go
upon sure grounds: Mat. xviii. 6, 'Whoso shall offend one of these
little ones which believe in me, it were better for him that a millstone
were hanged about his neck, and he were drowned in the depth of the
sea.'   Men that know the danger will not easily kick against the pricks.
At least, do not join with the opposite, eat and drink with the drunken,
and smite your fellow-servants; for 'the lord of that servant shall come
and cut him asunder, and appoint him his portion with the hypocrites,'
Mat. xxiv. 49–51.   When you cry up a confederacy with wicked men,
to prosecute your private differences with more advantage, there is
much of the hatred of godliness in it.

6. If you be glad when you find any blemish whereby to eclipse the
lustre and glory of their innocency, there is a secret hatred.   You
should be affected with the scandal brought upon the common cause:
Phil. iii. 18, 'For many walk, of whom I have told you often, and now
tell you even weeping, that they are the enemies of the cross of Christ;'
not real christians, but professors only.   The Hams of the world laugh
to see a Noah drunk.   It is a sign you hate them because they are
holy, when you are glad of any blemish wherewith to stain them, especially when the miscarriages of a few are cast upon all.

7. To be at a great distance from this, take heed of the hatred of
any man.   We should love all men with the love of good-will, though
' our delight should be in the excellent ones of the earth,' the saints
of God.   There is φιλαδελφία and ἀγάπη: 2 Peter i. 7, 'Add to
brotherly kindness charity.'   Live in enmity and malice with none,
though you take just offence at their sins, as Lot's righteous soul was
vexed from day to day: 2 Peter ii. 8, 'For that righteous man dwelling among them, in seeing and hearing vexed his righteous soul from
day to day with their unlawful deeds.'   It troubled him to see them.
They are an abomination, by way of caution for ourselves, and just
abhorrence of their impurities, but we must not hate them with a mis-
chievous hatred, *odio inimicitiæ.*

Use 3. Advice to the people of God.

1. Be not amazed at it if you meet with trouble and opposition from
wicked men, even for goodness' sake: 1 John iii. 13, 'Marvel not, my
brethren, if the world hate you.'   So it hath ever been, and so it will
be.   We are surprised and perplexed at it, as men use to be at something that is strange.   The wonder is on the other side; if there be
any remission of this enmity, it were a shrewd suspicion that we were
of their stamp, or complied too much with their humours, and did
symbolise with them in carnal practices: Luke vi. 26, 'Cursed are you
when all men speak well of you; for so they did to the false prophets.'

2. To walk holily and watchfully, so to live that their religion may
be their only crime, and to keep up the repute of godliness, that they
may not be hated as evil-doers, but as saints: 1 Peter iv. 15, 'Let
none of you suffer as a murderer, or as a thief, or as an evil-doer, or
as a busybody in other men's matters.'   It is a sad thing to be a
martyr to passion, interest, vainglory, and private conceits and opinions,
to suffer for your own shame.   The world doth but watch for such an
advantage: their conscience telleth them you do not deserve their

hatred, and therefore they seek other pretences. Do not suffer for pride, indiscreet zeal, and unnecessary intermeddling. It is the glory of the christian religion always to have holy martyrs and infamous persecutors; that they should have nothing against them but in the matter of their God.

3. Let not this discourage you; the power of godliness, as it is a provoking, so it is a daunting thing. The wicked hate you and fear you: Mark vi. 20, 'Herod feared John, knowing that he was a just man, and an holy, and observed him; and when he heard him, he did many things, and heard him gladly.' He feared him, not only as a zealous preacher, but as a strict man. A man would think that John had more cause to fear Herod. And God will respect it; it is his quarrel, though you have the management of it; you have good company; Christ suffereth with you: 1 Peter iv. 13, 'Rejoice inasmuch as ye are partakers of Christ's sufferings.' You do not only suffer for him, but with him; in such a case ye are not only looked upon as his, but him. They cannot hate you as much as they do Christ; you are the world's eyesore, but God's delight; you have glorious assistance, glorious hopes, 'The Spirit of God and of glory resteth upon you,' 1 Peter iv. 14.

4. 'Walk wisely towards them that are without,' Col. iv. 5. How is that? Not to swerve from the course of a godly life, or neglect our service to God, or to cool and slack in our zeal for his glory, or to conform ourselves to any of their wicked practices; but to forbear to provoke them without cause, 'To live peaceably with all men as much as is possible,' Rom. xii. 18; 'To overcome evil with good,' ver. 21. This was that which Christ hath prescribed: Mat. v. 44, 'Love your enemies, bless them that curse you, do good to them that hate you, and pray for them that despitefully use you, and persecute you.'

Third point. A christian should live in the world as one that is not of the world. There is not a total separation from the men of the world. Live in the world he doth; here is his corporal presence and conversation, but not his heart. And live in the world he must; here is his station and place of service: 1 Cor. v. 10, 'Yet not altogether with the fornicators of this world, or with the covetous, or extortioners, or with idolaters; for then must we needs go out of the world.' As the soul is in the body, but not of the body. Ὁικει μὲν ἐν τῷ σώματι ἡ ψύχη, οὐκ ἐστὶ δὲ τοῦ σώματος—Just. Mart. So a christian is in the world, but not of the world. Use the world we may without offence; when a christian is sanctified he is not glorified, and doth not divest himself of the innocent interests and concernments of flesh and blood; they have bodies as others have, and must eat, drink, sleep, and put on apparel as others do: 1 Cor. vii. 31, 'And those that use the world as not abusing it.' The use is allowed, the abuse only is forbidden. We may use the world as a means to sweeten our pilgrimage, but not to weaken our hopes. A man may use the comforts of this life to draw good out of them, to employ them for God, as encouragements to piety, and instruments of mercy and bounty.

But how then positively are they not to be of this world? Not of the world's gang and faction, nor acted by the same principles, to the same ends.

1. There is a difference in the inward principles—the spirit of the

world and the Spirit of God. Christians are acted by the Spirit of God, not by the spirit of the world: 1 Cor. ii. 12, 'Now we have received, not the spirit of the world, but the Spirit which is of God.' There is a particular genius that suiteth with worldly affairs, and fits men to turn and wind in outward employments, as the ostrich's wings serve her only to run, not to fly; their hearts and affections wholly run out this way. It is the character of some: John iii. 31, 'He that is of the earth is earthly, and speaketh of the earth.' They mind nothing, affect nothing, speak of nothing, but the earth.

2. They are under different rulers. Christ is head of the church, and he professeth 'that his kingdom is not of this world,' John xviii. 36. But now the devil is called 'the god of this world,' 2 Cor. iv. 4, the head of the worldly state.

3. There is a difference in their course and conversation. The children of God, $\tau\hat{\omega}$ $\kappa\alpha\nu\acute{o}\nu\iota$ $\sigma\tauο\iota\chi\acute{\eta}\sigma\upsilon\sigma\iota\nu$, Gal. vi. 16, 'Walk according to the rule of the word.' The men of the world, $\kappa\alpha\tau'$ $\alpha\iota\hat{\omega}\nu\alpha$ $\tau\upsilon\hat{\upsilon}$ $\kappa\acute{o}\sigma\mu\upsilon$ $\tau\upsilon\acute{\upsilon}\tau\upsilon$, Eph. ii. 2, 'According to the course of the world,' as fishes swim with the stream. A christian is the world's nonconformist: Rom. xii. 2, 'Be ye not conformed to the world;' he is estranged from the pursuits and aspiring projects of worldly men, and can deny the interests and concernments of the flesh for God's sake.

4. There is a difference in their aims. A christian liveth to glorify God: 1 Cor. x. 31, 'Whether ye eat or drink, or whatever you do, do all to the glory of God.' And a child of the world is all for aspiring projects, how to compass the conveniences of the present life, and advance his secular interests: Phil. ii. 19, 'They mind earthly things.'

5. Their ends are different. A christian is hastening to his country, his way is upward; first he gets his heart in heaven, and then his soul, and then his body. But a carnal man is grovelling and tending downward, first to the earth, and then to hell. So that you see there is a perfect difference and counter-motion; they are not of the world, nor of that faction, communion, or fellowship.

But if you ask me why?

[1.] Because of Christ's example. We do not worship the god of this world, nor mammon, but Christ. Worldly men had need seek another god, Jesus Christ is not for their turn, 'I am not of this world;' he is not a worldly Christ. We are to imitate our great master, to be unlike the world, and like Christ; to be led, not by the course of the world, but by Christ's example. Christ, by his own example, hath put a disgrace upon worldly greatness: he chose a mean estate, to teach us to be contented with a little, and his eye was 'to the glory set before him,' Heb. xii. 2. Christ's poverty was not out of necessity, but choice; his were the cattle upon a thousand hills. At his birth, he was born in an inn; to show that he came into the world as a stranger and passenger. In the course of his life we find that he had a bag that was filled with alms, but no annual rent, or constant possessions: Mat. viii. 20, 'Foxes have holes, and the birds of the air have nests; but the Son of man hath not where to lay his head.' Christ was no landed man, he had no tenement of his own. Christ speaketh it when a young man came to him and professed to follow him; he had no certain place of residence, neither house, nor furniture, nor household stuff; certainly he was little beholden to the world, it would hardly afford him house-room and lodging: 'The earth is the Lord's, and the fulness thereof,' yet Christ, his own Son, had but little of it. He begged a draught of water of a stranger when he was weary, John iv., and every way lived as a poor man, not out of necessity but choice. He refused a crown when proffered him: John vi. 15, 'When Jesus perceived that they would come and take him by force, and make him a king, he departed again into a mountain himself alone.' He had no heart to these things, no relish in crowns and worldly glory. When he died, he was not master of a cup of cold water to quench his thirst; his coat was all his legacy, and he lodged in a borrowed grave. This was the captain of our salvation, whose steps we are to follow. You see what a disgrace he put upon crowns, and honours, and pleasures, and the glory which we doat upon. Christ came from heaven on purpose to cast contempt upon the world by his own choice and course of life.

[2.] Because of their new birth. Man's heart naturally is addicted to the world, and runneth thither, whither the world carrieth it, even to forsaking God; but by grace it is turned the quite contrary way: 'We have forsaken all, and followed thee,' Mat. xix. 27; and Ps. xlv. 10, 'Forget also thine own people, and thy father's house.' It is the proper work of grace to alter the course of nature, to take us off from the world, and bring us to God by degrees, first in heart, and then in soul, and then in body. It is everywhere made an effect of the new birth: 1 John v. 4, 'He that is born of God overcometh the world.' The children of God have somewhat of the Father in them. Grace of all things cometh nearest the nature of God. Now God is our heavenly Father, therefore the children that are born of him cannot be worldly. See another place: 2 Peter i. 4, 'That by these ye might be made partakers of the divine nature, having escaped the corruption that is in the world through lust.' There is something divine in a christian, therefore he cannot live as other men. When we press men to strictness, they will say, We are saints, and not angels. Yea, but saints have a new nature, over and above that nature which they received from Adam, and therefore should live a heavenly life. They have a higher life which overruleth the other, the Spirit that governeth the motions of the soul. Look, as the planets have a motion of their own, by which they walk in their own path and course; and besides, there is a rapid motion, by which they are carried about in twenty-four hours: so christians have an old nature, and an overruling nature, that carrieth them on contrary to their own motion and tendency. The soul we received from Adam looketh after the conveniency of the outward life, the decent state of the body: naturally men use their souls only as a purveyor for the body, for outward comforts and outward supports; but when there is a new nature from Christ, the regenerate part must have its operation. In the new birth, principles of more raised and elevated nature are brought into the soul.

[3.] Because of their great and glorious hopes. They are chosen out of this world: 2 Peter i. 4, 'Whereby are given unto us exceeding great and precious promises, that by these ye might be made partakers of a divine nature, having escaped the corruptions that are in the world through lust.' There is an estate that dependeth upon the new birth. God's children cannot complain for want of a child's portion; they have promises as so many leases, a right to the inheritance in light. Now a christian, that hopeth for another world, should not live according to the fashions of this world: Rom. xii. 2, 'And be not conformed to this world, but be ye transformed in the renewing of your mind.' This is an unworthy base world; you are acquainted with a better. If a man were in a strange country, where he saw none but rude savages, that had not shame enough to cover their nakedness, would he conform himself to the guise of this country? We, that have other hopes, should have other lives: 1 Thes. ii. 12, 'That ye would walk worthy of God, who hath called you unto his kingdom and glory.' There is a description of a christian's life. It beseemeth worldly men to look after worldly things. Leave things that perish to men that perish. *Incolæ cœli estis, non hujus seculi.* If you must not die as they die, do not live as they live, lest you are in their case at the point of death, 'who have their portion in this life,' Ps. xvii. 14. Wicked men have their whole portion in this life, because they look for no more; no wrong is done to them, it is but their own choice. But a believer will not give God an acquittance nor discharge, having such great promises.

Use 1. To show us what to judge of persons that live so as if they were of the world. You may know it by these three notes—when they do nothing worthy of their new nature, their glorious hopes, and the example of Jesus Christ.

1. Nothing worthy of the new nature. What difference is there between you and others? The christian should be like Saul, so much higher by the head than other men. Wherein do you differ? 1 Cor. iii. 3, 'Are ye not carnal, and walk as men?' κατ᾽ ἄνθρωπον. Men of an ordinary nature, destitute of the Spirit, would do the same. Christ maketh it to be the ground of hatred, 'because they are not of the world.' The world will soon scent out him that is regenerate, he walketh so as to convince the world; they 'declare plainly that they seek a country,' Heb. xi. 14; their hopes are discovered in their conversation. They reprove the world: Heb. xi. 7, 'By faith Noah, being warned of God of things not seen as yet, moved with fear, prepared an ark to the saving of his house, by which he condemned the world.' A carnal man justifieth the world, as Israel justified Sodom. Carnal men are called the children of this world; the spirit of the mother is in them, the spirit of the world inclineth them, they are all for lusts of the flesh, lusts of the eye, and pride of life, to go fine, to feed high, to shine in worldly pomp, affect honour and great places. Too many christians are baptized into this kind of spirit; they live as if they were born and bred here, and then they justify the carnal practices of men. Therefore what difference should there be between a christian and the world! 1 Peter iv. 4, 'They think it strange that you run not with them to all excess of riot, speaking evil of you.' Mortifying pleasures, denying interests upon religious reasons, this maketh the world wonder what kind of nature have these men. This showeth that there is something divine in you.

2. Nothing worthy of their hopes, and of that eternity which they expect. When men waste their strength and time in worldly projects

and pursuits, they live as if their portion were only in this world. A traveller, that is to stay but half an hour in a room, or for a night in an inn, would he adorn it with hangings?   They that are so much in this world, they show they do not look for a better: Prov. xv. 24, ' The way of the wise is above ; ' their heart is fixed on heaven, and the face of their conversation is turned that way.   Your lives do not bear proportion with your hopes.   Well, then, what do you make the scope of your lives?   A christian is satisfied with nothing but eternity : 2 Cor. iv. 18, $\mu\dot{\eta}\ \sigma\kappa\omega\pi o\acute{v}\nu\tau\omega\nu\ \dot{\eta}\mu\hat{\omega}\nu$, ' While we look not at the things that are seen, but at the things that are not seen ; for the things that are seen are temporal, but the things that are not seen are eternal.'   A christian useth the world, and followeth his business, but he doth not make it his scope ; his heart is within the veil.   There is an eternal principle in the heart of every godly man, and therefore they cannot be satisfied with the things of the world ; he mindeth other things in a subordination to eternity, mercies and duties of his calling, with respect to his usefulness and service ; and therefore spendeth his time and estate so that his main work is to provide for eternity : 1 Tim. vi. 19, ' Laying up in store for themselves a good foundation against the time to come, that they may lay hold of eternal life.'   But now men think they can never have enough in the world, and make but slight provision for the life to come ; they make all things sure in the world, and any slight assurance serveth the turn for eternity ; they live as if their hopes were altogether in the world, they do not make eternity their scope.

3. Nothing worthy of Christ's example.   In Christ's example we may take notice of two things—the heavenliness of it, and the courage of it.

[1.] The heavenliness.   Christ despised the world ; the great encouragement of his human soul was ' the glory set before him,' Heb. xii. 3.   He came from heaven on purpose to set us this example.   But now, when a christian followeth the world, when he is of this temper that he could wish to live always that he might enjoy the world always, ' they have their reward,' $\dot{a}\pi\acute{e}\chi ov\sigma\iota$, Mat. vi. 2.   They discharge God of all his promises, and look for no more.   A thousand worlds will not satisfy a craving heart ; but a child of God is content with the least mercies, but not satisfied.   Contentment respects God's allowance ; but this is not their portion : they do not murmur, but yet they desire more ; a reprobate's portion will not serve the turn.   Nothing is more acceptable to a carnal heart in conceit, than to live here for ever, and to delight themselves in meat and drink, and the sports and glory of the world.   Now this is quite contrary to the example of Christ, a disposition that seeketh to make the life and death of Christ of none effect.   Christ came from heaven to earth to fetch us to heaven ; if thou cleavest to the world, Christ's coming is vain ; he lived in a poor estate, to teach us to despise the world ; his life was a sermon of mortification ; he died to deliver us from the present world ; he ascended that we might follow him with our hearts while we live here.

[2.] The courage of Christ's example.   He was not for the humour of that age : John viii. 23, ' Ye are from beneath, I am from above ; ye are of this world, I am not of this world.'   He speaketh to the carnal Jews, that looked for a pompous Messiah, that should maintain their worship and state, and deliver them from the Roman yoke and servitude. Christ was not a Messiah for their turn; if Christ had complied with their humours, he had been more generally received. So a christian's courage is a counter-motion to the fashions and humours of the age. We must not be afraid to be singular in holiness. So was Christ: Acts ii. 40, 'Save yourselves from this untoward generation;' not only in purpose and thought of heart, but externally in course of life. When men are afraid to estrange themselves from the corrupt and carnal courses of the world that are in fashion, they do not write after Christ's copy. What father would endure his son should be intimate with his enemies, and symbolise with them in practice and conversation? Therefore you must look to this; you are in danger. Christ's example is only left upon record, and the world's example is before your eyes; living examples work much, and taint insensibly. The prophet complained, Isa. vi. 5, 'Woe is me, for I am undone, because I am a man of unclean lips, and I dwell in the midst of a people of unclean lips.' An estrangement in the course of life will draw trouble upon you; but persecution is not as bad as hell, nor is man's wrath to be feared as much as God's judgments. Carnal men may make great profession of the name of Christ, but they humour the world: 1 John iv. 5, 'They are of the world, therefore speak they of the world, and the world heareth them;' they comply to humour the carnal world in their inveterate customs and superstitions.

Use 2. To press christians not to conform to the world. It is Paul's exhortation, Rom. xii. 2, μὴ συσχηματίζεσθε, 'Be not conformed to the world.' It is a sad thing when christians are cast into the world's stamp and mould, to symbolise with them in practices and affections.

Two things you should take heed of—the world's spirit, and the world's courses and practices.

First, The world's spirit. A man is good or evil according to the disposition of his heart: Phil. iii. 19, 'They mind earthly things.' The apostle doth not describe carnal men there by any notorious scandalous sin, but by the inward frame of the spirit. This is most odious in the eyes of God; the carnal conversation is an effect of a carnal frame of spirit. First men mind earthly things, and then in time they come to hate the gospel, and to symbolise with the world in practices: 2 Tim. iv. 10, 'Demas hath forsaken us, having loved this present world;' James iv. 4, 'Ye adulterers, and adulteresses, know ye not that the friendship of the world is enmity with God? Whosoever therefore will be a friend of the world, is the enemy of God.'

Now the frame of the heart may be known—

1. By the working of the thoughts, counsels, and deliberations. Therefore we should observe what we think of and meditate most upon. Inventions serve affection. As the heart is, so are the thoughts and counsels. A worldly man is always thinking of the world, and framing endless projects how to grow great and high. Therefore it is said, 2 Peter ii. 14, 'They have an heart exercised with covetous practices;' that is, always plotting how to bring the world into their net. As the apostle would have Timothy to 'exercise himself unto godliness,' 1 Tim. iv. 7, that is, to be much in consulting and contriving how to carry on

the holy life with most advantage; so 'their hearts are exercised with covetous practices,' that is, with worldly purposes and thoughts. All sins do more or less discover themselves by the thoughts; for a man will deliberate to accomplish that which he aimeth at; and chiefly worldliness occupieth the thoughts, for it is a serious madness, full of carking and caring and vain projects. When our Saviour would represent a worldling, he bringeth him in musing, Luke xii. 17, 18, 'And he thought with himself, saying, I will do thus and thus,' καὶ διελογί-ζετο. *Verbum mire appositum*, saith Beza; for a worldly man is always framing dialogues within himself, between his reason and his carnal desires. Distractions in worship are chiefly ascribed to covetousness: Ezek. xxxiii. 31, 'With their mouth they show much love, but their heart goeth after their covetousness.' The prophet instances in that sin, though other lusts withdraw the heart and distract in hearing, as unclean glances, vainglory, &c. Words are but thoughts expressed; there is a quick intercourse between the mind and the tongue. Now it is said, John iii. 31, 'He that is of the earth is earthly, and speaketh of the earth.' There is nothing of heaven in their thoughts, nothing in their language and communication, a heavy clod cannot move upward of itself. Observe the drift of your thoughts, your first and last thoughts morning and evening, what guest haunteth you in duties. When the heart is deeply engaged, the mind cannot be taken off from thinking.

2. By your esteem. When a man prizeth worldly things, when you overrate them, have too greatening thoughts of the world, the devil is at your elbow, and the spirit of the world is set a-work: 'Happy is the people that is in such a case,' Ps. cxliv. 15. What is the treasure of the soul? Carnal men have no savour of Christ. God's people sometimes may be taken with a glittering show of worldly things, but their solid esteem is in Christ, he is their treasure; the soul feasts itself with the riches of grace. To a carnal heart, heavenly things are but a notion, it worketh no more than a dream; to a gracious heart, the substance of the world is but a fancy: John xiv. 17, 'Whom the world cannot receive, because it seeth him not, neither knoweth him.' The world cannot see things that are not of great profit and benefit.

3. By the bent and resolution of the will: 1 Tim. vi. 9, 'They that will be rich,' &c.; not *is*, but *will be;* James iv. 4, 'Whosoever will be a friend of the world, is the enemy of God.' Grace is known by the full purpose of the heart: Acts xi. 23, 'He exhorted them all that, with full purpose of heart, they would cleave unto the Lord;' what he fixeth upon as his end and scope.

4. By a special sagacity and dexterity in the matters of the world, and a dulness in the things of God: Luke xvi. 8, 'The children of this world are in their generation wiser than the children of light.' They have ostrich's wings, not to fly, but to run. It is strange to hear how sottishly worldly-wise men will speak of religion and the ways of God; they are dull and blockish in religion, though otherwise of great ability: Rom. xvi. 19, 'I would have you wise unto that which is good, and simple concerning evil.'

5. By the stream of your desires. Desires are the pulses of the soul. You may know the temper of your souls by the beating of the pulses,

by the current and-drift of your desires, as physicians judge by appetite. The saints plead their affections: Isa. xxvi. 8, 'The desire of our soul is to thy name, and to the remembrance of thee.' They cannot justify their innocency, yet they plead their integrity, the vigorous bent of their souls. So the spirit of the world is known by an unsatisfied thirst, and the ravenousness of the desires, which rise with enjoyment, for still men crave more. Such a dropsy argueth a distempered soul; the soul is transported beyond all bounds of modesty and contentment: Isa. v. 8, 'Woe unto them that join house to house, and field to field, till there be no place, that they may be placed alone in the midst of the earth.' The inordinate inclination still increaseth, and men never have enough.

6. By your grief at worldly losses and disappointments. Men lose with grief what they possess with love; the affliction riseth according to the degree of the affection. They that 'rejoice as though they rejoiced not, weep as if they wept not,' 1 Cor. vii. 30. Earnest affection will not brook disappointment: 1 Tim. vi. 10, 'For the love of money is the root of all evil; which while some coveted after, they have erred from the faith, and pierced themselves through with many sorrows.' The sorrow will be answerable to the desire. You grieve more for the loss of wealth than for the loss of God's countenance. The bridegroom is gone, and you never mourn; but upon every worldly loss the heart is dejected. What slight thoughts have men of God! Thou art sad if thou hast lost but a ring of value, the offals of thy estate; but God's accesses and recesses are never noted. Grief followeth love. When Jesus wept for Lazarus, the Jews said, 'Behold how he loved him!' John xi. 35.

7. Fear of want, or an extraordinary solicitousness about outward provisions, that is a sure note of a worldly heart. Christ was disputing against worldliness, and among other precepts, he saith, Luke xii. 29, 'Seek not ye what ye shall eat, nor what ye shall drink, neither be ye of doubtful mind;' μὴ μετεωρίζεσθε; be not hovering between doubts and fears. This is to take God's work out of his hand. Suspicious fears argue too much of the spirit of the world. God would have us look no further than the present day: 'Sufficient for each day is the evil thereof,' Mat. vi. 34. God is very careful of our good. He hath made carking a sin; he might have left it as a punishment.

8. By excessive delight in worldly comforts. A man may be worldly that is not carking and ravenous. Esau saith, 'I have enough, my brother,' Gen. xxxiii. 9. Your too much complacency is a great sin. When men are satisfied with the present portion, it is as great, if not a greater sin than to desire more: Luke xii. 19, 'Soul, thou hast much goods laid up for many years; take thine ease, eat, drink, and be merry.' He took too great delight in his portion; they bless themselves in their worldly enjoyments, as if they had happiness enough: Ps. lxii. 10, 'Trust not in oppression, become not vain in robbery: if riches increase, set not your heart upon them;' not in point of delight and trust; your delight should not be terminated on the creature.

9. By envying the worldly happiness that others enjoy. This is a great fault in the children of God; you are not of this world. Though you have not such costly furniture, rare accommodations as others

have, though you are not the world's fondlings, dandled on the world's knees, you have a better portion in Christ: Ps. iv. 7, 'Thou hast put gladness in my heart, more than the time when their corn and their wine increased.' It is a disparagement to your privileges and hopes: Ps. xvii. 14, 'From men which are thy hand, O Lord, from men of the world, which have their portion in this life, and whose belly thou fillest with hid treasures: they are full of children, and leave the rest of their substance to their babes.' It is your time to be princes in disguise. The less splendour in the world, the more lustre in grace. Grace would not be so eminent, if worldly glory were greater. Who that is owner of a palace would envy another a dunghill?

Secondly, A worldly conversation; which is seen in two things—

1. Immoderate endeavours for the world, to the neglect of God: Luke xii. 24, 'So is he that layeth up treasure for himself, and is not rich towards God.' All things must be looked after in subordination to God. When Sarah saw Ishmael scoffing at Isaac, she thrust him out of doors. When Mammon upbraideth God, and worldly things encroach, and allow God no room but in the conscience, then we are immoderate.

2. Carnal compliance. The worldling serveth the times, cozeneth, lieth, cheateth, hateth Christ; so must not you: 1 John v. 19, 'And we know that we are of God, and the whole world lieth in wickedness,' as a carrion in a sink.

[1.] Consider your condition; you are strangers. The fathers of old dwelt in tents; we never read that Abraham made any purchase but of a grave. Cain built cities. David was a king, yet a stranger: Ps. xxxix. 12, 'For I am a stranger with thee, and a sojourner, as all my fathers were.' The world is not our country. The fathers of the Old Testament, for the most part, lived a wandering life: Heb. xi. 14, 'For they that say such things declare plainly that they seek a country.' Jacob passed over Jordan with a staff, Gen. xxxii. 10. It is a most unbeseeming thing as can be for one that professeth himself a christian to take up with the things of this world.

[2.] Consider it is a dishonour to God, and a scandal to religion, to be of a worldly conversation, to profess an interest in Christ, and yet run after such low things.

SERMON XXIV.

I pray not that thou shouldest take them out of the world, but that thou shouldest keep them from the evil.—JOHN XVII. 15.

CHRIST having enforced his request, explaineth it; not to inform God, but to comfort the disciples, as explications in prayer are for our benefit. Our heavenly Father can interpret our sighs and breathings, but formed and explicit words have a greater force and efficacy upon our hearts. This explication is delivered, κατὰ ἄρσιν καὶ κατὰ θέσιν.

1. Κατὰ ἄρσιν, 'not that thou shouldest take them out of the world;' that is, presently glorify them, either by an ordinary death, or

by an extraordinary translation, as Elijah and Enoch were translated. Christ was not ignorant of their danger, yet he would have them ride out the storm; he would not carry his disciples to heaven with him, nor doth he pray his Father to do it, though he loved their company, and they his, that they could be content to die with him; as John xi. 16, 'Let us also go, that we may die with him;' yet, 'I pray not that thou wouldst take them out of the world.'

2. *Κατὰ θέσιν*, 'but that thou shouldest keep them from the evil;' ἐκ τοῦ πονηροῦ, it may be rendered from the evil one, or from the evil thing, as referring to a person or thing. To a person; the evil one is often put for the devil: Mat. xiii. 19, 'When any one heareth the word of the kingdom, and understandeth it not, then cometh the wicked one, ὁ πονηρὸς, and taketh away that which he heard;' 1 John ii. 13, 'I write unto you, young men, because ye have overcome, τὸν πονηρὸν, the wicked one;' 1 John iii. 12, 'Not as Cain, who was ἐκ τοῦ πονηροῦ, of that wicked one, and slew his brother.' Or else to the evil thing: Mat. vi. 13, ῥῦσαι ἡμᾶς ἀπὸ τοῦ πονεροῦ, 'deliver us from evil;' Mat. v. 37, 'Whatever is more than this, cometh of evil,' ἐκ τοῦ πονηροῦ; 1 John v. 19, 'The whole world lieth, ἐν τῷ πονηρῷ, in wickedness.' Which shall we prefer? I answer—Since the words lie so indifferently for either sense, we may interpret them of both; keep them from the author of evil, and from evil itself; from sin, from the power and snares of the devil, from destruction, till their ministry be accomplished. Satan he is the author; the world is the bait. Sin is the hook. Keep them from the devil, that they may not come under his power; from the world, that they may not be deceived by its allurements. Briefly, this keeping may be referred to their life or to their souls; keep them alive as long as they have work to do; keep their souls, that they may neither, by the world or by the devil, be drawn to do anything unseemly and unbecoming their profession: 2 Cor. xiii. 7, 'I pray God that ye do no evil, but that ye should do that which is honest;' and Rev. iii. 10, 'I will keep them from the hour of temptation, which shall come upon all the earth, to try them that dwell upon the earth.' It is meant of a preservation in the time of a bloody persecution under Trajan. Christ prays for temporal and spiritual safety; temporal safety, so far as is necessary to carry on the duty of their calling.

Points.

1. Observe that it standeth with the wisdom and goodness of God to continue us in the world, notwithstanding the dangers of it. Christ loved his disciples, and knew they were exposed to the world's hatred; yet, 'I pray not that thou shouldst take them out of the world.' In evil times sometimes God taketh his children out of the world, and sometimes he continueth them in the world; both dispensations stand with his wisdom and goodness. There are reasons on both sides.

[1.] For taking them away in evil times. It standeth with his goodness, that they may not feel the smart of them: Isa. lvii. 1, 'The righteous perisheth, and no man layeth it to heart, yea, the merciful man is taken away, none considering that the righteous is taken away from the evil to come.' When corn is gathered in, then the beasts are turned into the field. God valueth his saints so that he doth not count the world worthy of them : Heb. xi. 38, ‘Of whom the world was not worthy.’ He showeth his jewels, and then shutteth them up into the casket. And with his wisdom, that they may not be corrupted. The wisdom of providence concurreth to our preservation, as well as the power of grace. Enoch was translated and taken out of the world in a wicked age : 1 Cor. xi. 32, ‘But when we are judged, we are chastened of the Lord, that we might not be condemned with the world.’ What judging and chastening was it ? Not only by sickness, but by death : ‘Many are sick, and many weak, and many fallen asleep.’

[2.] Christ continueth them in the world, as the disciples here ; partly because he hath need of them, as the disciples were to preach the gospel ; partly that they might have more experience, and a more grown faith : they might try God, and God might try them ; they might have experience of his faithfulness, and he of their loyalty. The world must have a time of trial, and so must we. Nay, he dealeth thus with believers ; they are continued in evil times, either because God hath more work for them to do, or that they may carry more experience with them to heaven.

Use. To refer it to the wisdom and goodness of God, either to go or tarry. Christ knew there was service for them to do, therefore he was express, ‘I pray not that they may be taken out of the world.’ We that know not the counsels of God must refer ourselves to his pleasure.

2. Observe, that as long as we have a ministry and service to accomplish, we should be willing to continue in the world. Paul was at a strait : Phil. i. 21–23, the cause was service ; ‘For me to live is Christ, and to die is gain. For if I live in the flesh, this is the fruit of my labour,’ viz., bringing honour to Christ ; ‘yet what I shall choose, I wot not : for I am in a strait betwixt two, having a desire to depart, and to be with Christ, which is far better.’ He is ravished with the thoughts of it ; but then he considereth the profit of the church : ver. 24, ‘Nevertheless, to abide in the flesh is more needful for you ;’ and service casts the scale. Paul’s case is the case many times of mortified christians ; after long experience of God, and weanedness from the world, they are in such a strait. Natural motion is swifter in the end ; the nearer they draw to the end the more vehemently do they long for Christ’s company. Some make it a question which is hardest, to bear affliction or to wait for glory, the work of patience or the delay of hope ? Desire is a more restless affection than sorrow, yet I should think the depth of sorrow is more burdensome than the strength of desire. Many of God’s children are tempted to make away themselves ; but I never heard of any that were tempted to make away themselves in the height of assurance, or out of the vehemency of spiritual desire, though the present life be accompanied with many vexations and afflictions. Despair maketh men to lay violent hands on themselves, but not assurance ; as Saul fell upon his sword, and Achitophel went home and hanged himself, and Judas was his own executioner. But assurance, though it desireth God’s presence, yet it tarrieth God’s leisure. Waiting is a fruit of faith, as well as confidence. Spiritual desires are always conceived with submission and obedience ; if God hath more work, they can brook the

delay of the reward, and tarry for their wages. I remember a passage of a heathen, of Tully, in his *Somnium Scipionis*, when Scipio had said, 'If true life be only in heaven, why stay I then upon earth? why haste I not to come to you?' 'No,' saith his father; 'unless God free thee from the fetters of thy body, thou canst not come hither. Men are born and bred upon this condition, that they should promote the good of the world. You must not fly from the duty assigned by God; the soul is to be kept in the custody of the body till it be commanded thence by God that gave it at first.' This was his saying; and indeed it is wonderful. Christians, learn to wait God's leisure; it is bettter to be with Christ, but you must not look for your wages till you have done your work. When a sentinel is set upon the watch, he must not come off without the commander's leave, and till he is discharged by authority. God hath set us in a watch, and we must not leave our ground till we have done all that is enjoined us, till we receive a fair discharge.

This point will serve to open two cases:—

Case 1. Whether men confessing Christ may make away themselves to avoid the cruel torments of their persecutors, and they know not certainly what their strength may be able to sustain? This was a great case in the primitive times, and it may be still of use. Eusebius telleth us, lib. viii. cap. 24, that in the time of Dioclesian's persecution, which was very bloody and cruel, there were divers that procured death to themselves by leaping down from lofts and high places, or else thrust themselves through with knives or swords.

I answer—This is sinful. Christ prayeth not that his disciples 'might be taken out of the world,' but 'kept from the evil.'

The sinfulness appeareth—

1. Because this is an act of disobedience, contrary to the law of God: 'Thou shalt not kill.' Now the more unnatural any act is, the greater is the crime. A man is not lord of life and death.

2. It is an act of distrust: 1 Cor. x. 13, 'There hath no temptation taken you but such as is common to men: but God is faithful, who who will not suffer you to be tempted above that ye are able; but will with the temptation also make a way to escape, that ye may be able to bear it.' God will either temper the affliction to our strength, or raise our strength to the degree of the affliction. Christ hath laid in this prayer for our encouragement in this case, 'Keep them from the evil;' it is a making haste, as if God would not be faithful, but require brick where he giveth no straw.

3. It is a disparagement and dishonour to the cause which we maintain. It robbeth God of a great deal of glory, when he calleth us out to show our love to him, to take our lives out of God's hands, when he claimeth them: Rom. xiv. 7, 8, 'For none of us liveth to himself, and no man dieth to himself: for whether we live, we live unto the Lord, and whether we die, we die unto the Lord; whether we live therefore, or die, we are the Lord's.' Providence hath singled you out to be witnesses; God by his providence challengeth his due; it is a retracting of your vows. And therefore, though God may be merciful to the soul, yet the act is unnatural and sinful and base, when God hath drawn you out to be his champions and witnesses to the world.

Case 2 is about wishing for death. You know the law doth not only forbid acts, but thoughts and desires; therefore, is it lawful to long for death and dissolution? We find instances on both hands in the scriptures. The murmuring Israelites are taxed: Exod. xvi. 3, ' Would to God we had died by the hand of the Lord in the land of Egypt.' And it is usual for men in a pet to wish themselves dead, to curse the day of their birth, and long for the day of their death. On the other side, Paul, out of a spiritual affection, desireth to be dissolved, and to be with Christ: Phil. i. 23, ' I have a desire to depart, and to be with Christ.' What shall we say in this case?

I answer in several propositions:—

1. There is a great deal of difference between serious desires and passionate expressions. The desires of the children of God are deliberate and resolved, conceived upon good grounds, and after much struggling with flesh and blood to bring their hearts to it. Carnal men are loath that God should take them at their word; as he in the fable that called for death, and when he came, desired him to help him up with his burden. Alas! they do not consider what it is to be in the state of the dead, and to come unprovided and unfurnished into God's presence. We often wish ourselves in our graves; but if God should take us at our word, we would make many pauses and exceptions. Men that in their miseries call for death, when sickness cometh will run to the physician. Many gifts are promised if life could be restored. None more unwilling to die than those that in a passion wish for death.

2. We must carefully look to the grounds of these wishes and desires. Carnal wishes for death arise, either—

[1.] Out of violent anger, and a pet against providence; as Jonah, chap. iv. 3, ' Therefore now, O Lord, take, I beseech thee, my life from me, for it is better for me to die than to live;' and ver. 8, ' He fainted and wished in himself to die, and said, It is better for me to die than to live.' The murmuring Israelites, when they felt the famine of the wilderness, wished they ' had died in the land of Egypt.' When men are vexed with the world, they look upon death as a release, to take vengeance upon God, to deprive him of a servant.

[2.] In deep sorrow; as Job iii. 11, ' Why died I not from the womb? why did I not give up the ghost when I came out of the belly?' and Job vi. 8, 9, ' Oh that I might have my request, and that God would grant me the thing that I long for! even that it would please God to destroy me, that he would let loose his hand, and cut me off.' Elisha: 1 Kings xix. 4, He sat down under a juniper-tree; and he requested for himself that he might die, and said, It is enough; now, O Lord, take away my life, for I am not better than my fathers.'

[3.] From the peevishness of fond and doting love: 2 Sam. xviii. 33, ' O my son Absalom, my son, my son Absalom, would God I had died for thee! O Absalom, my son, my son!' As the wives of the barbarians, that burn themselves to attend the ghosts of their dead husbands.

[4.] From distrust and despair; the evil is too hard for them, they are at their wits' end: Job vii. 15, ' My soul chooseth strangling, and death rather than life.' In all these cases it is but a shameful retreat from the conflict and burden of the present life, from carnal irksomeness under the labours and burdens of the present life, or a distrust of God's help.   There may be murder in a rash wish, if it proceed from a vexed heart.   These are but froward thoughts, not a sanctified resolution.

3. Such desires of death and dissolution as are lawful, and must' be cherished, come from a good ground; a heart deadened to the world, they are crucified to it, their hearts are mortified, ' set on things above,' Col. iii. 1.   Some competent assurance : Rom. viii. 23, ' We groan, waiting for the adoption, viz., the redemption of our body.'   They have tasted the clusters of Canaan ; as Simeon : Luke ii. 28, 29, ' Lord, now lettest thou thy servant depart in peace, for mine eyes have seen thy salvation;' the eyes of his faith, as well as of his body.   Now, Lord, I do but wait for my departure hence, as a merchantman richly laden desires to be at his port.

4. You must look to the end.   Men have a blind notion of heaven ; they expect a carnal heaven, as the Jews looked for a carnal Messiah, to enjoy a Turkish paradise, full of ease and pleasure.   The people of God desire heaven to have a perfect union and communion with him whom their souls love : Phil. i..23, ' I desire to depart, and be with Christ;' Phil. iii. 20, ' Our conversation is in heaven, whence we look for a Saviour;' they long to see him, to be where he is.   Heart and head should be together.   And so also to be freed from sin : Rom. vii. 24, ' O wretched man that I am ! who shall deliver me from this body of death ?'   They would be in heaven that they may sin no more.   Men look upon heaven as a kind of reserve, if the world do not hold.   We should desire heaven, not to be freed from trouble, but to be freed from sin, and to be with Christ ; there must be a holy desire of a better life.

5. The manner must be regarded ; it must be with submission : Phil. i. 24, ' Nevertheless to abide in the flesh is more needful for you;' otherwise we encroach upon God's right, and would deprive him of a servant without his leave.   A christian will die and live as the Lord will ; while others want submission to live in trouble, he is satisfied ; or to die if he be not in trouble ; if it be the Lord's pleasure, a believer is satisfied with long life, Ps. xci. 16 ; he is willing to live and die as God liketh ; he will wait till his change comes, when God will give him a discharge by his own immediate hand, or by enemies.   *Gratias agimus, quod a molestis Dominis liberamur.*   God knoweth how to choose the fittest time, otherwise we know not what we ask.

3. Observe, that a spiritual victory over evil is to be preferred before a total exemption from it.   Christ doth not pray for an absolute immunity and deliverance, but a preservation from the evil of the world. Christ prayeth thus, and so he teacheth us to pray, Mat. vi. 13, ' Lead us not into temptation, but deliver us from evil.'   When we say, ' Lead us not into temptation,' he doth not mean that we should pray for an absolute exemption from temptation ; that is the lot of all the saints ; but that we may not fall under the weight of a temptation, that is, εἰσενέγκῃς, and it is explained, that he would not as a judge, by a spiritual excommunication, put us into the hands of Satan, to be crushed by him, as it is explained in the next verse, ' But deliver us from evil.'

Use 1. It teacheth us how to pray to God.   Our prayers should be to be delivered not from the world so much as from the evil of the world, from sins rather than afflictions.   The saints seek grace rather than deliverance in their afflictions, direction as well as protection, that they may do nothing unseemly while they suffer: Ps. cxli. 3, 4, 'Set a watch, O Lord, before my mouth, keep the door of my lips. Incline not my heart to any evil thing, to practise wicked works with them that work iniquity ; and let me not eat of their dainties.'   And they desire improvement rather than a discharge ; for the saints do not conceive prayers out of interest, but from a principle of the new nature.   To a gracious eye, sustentation under the cross is better than absolute deliverance ; the deliverance is a common mercy, the sustentation is a special mercy.   Carnal men may be without affliction, but carnal men have no experience of grace ; and bare deliverance is no sign of special love, but improvement is : 'My grace is sufficient for thee.'   It is divinity preached from heaven makes the saints to rejoice in infirmities.   Paul before was earnest to be freed from the trouble.

Use 2. How to wait and hope for the blessings of Christ's purchase. Absolute immunity is not to be looked for, but victory and conservation : 2 Tim. iv. 18, 'The Lord shall deliver me from every evil work, and will preserve me unto his heavenly kingdom.'   A christian placeth his hope chiefly on that.   Paul could not look for such a deliverance again from the lion, but from an unworthy carriage.   The blessings which Christ hath obtained of his Father are rather spiritual and celestial than temporal ; therefore he is more solicitous to free us from sin than from trouble : Mat. i. 21, 'Thou shalt call his name Jesus ; for he shall save his people from their sins ;' not from their troubles, their sorrows, but their sins.   We would be delivered from sickness, trouble, danger ; but Christ is a spiritual saviour ; the great deliverance is to be freed from sin.

Use 3. To teach us to suffer with patience.   Let us endure the evil of punishment, that we may escape the evil of sin.   Moral evil is worse than natural ; it is better to be miserable than to be sinful.   Of all evil sin is the greatest : to be carnal, a swearer, a drunkard, an unclean person, this is a greater evil than poverty, sickness, blindness, lameness; this doth not separate from God.

4. Observe the danger of the worldly estate.   It appears in two things :—

First, The multiplicity of snares.   The whole world is full of snares, and we can walk nowhere but we are like to be defiled.   It is a vale of tears, and a place of snares ; and therefore a vale of tears because a place of snares, which make the saints go up and down groaning : Rom. vii. 24, 'O wretched man that I am ! who shall deliver me from this body of death ?'   All conditions of life may become a snare, prosperity, adversity : Prov. xxx. 8, 9, 'Give me neither poverty nor riches ; feed me with food convenient for me ; lest I be full, and deny thee, and say, Who is the Lord ? or lest I be poor, and steal, and take the name of God in vain.'   Mark, either condition hath its snares, but prosperity hath most.   As a garment too short will not cover our nakedness, and too long proveth *lacinia præpendens*, ready to trip up our heels.   Many that carry themselves well in one condition quite miscarry in another ; as it is observed of Joab : 1 Kings ii. 28, 'That he turned after Adonijah, though he turned not after Absalom.' 'Ephraim is a cake not turned,' Hosea vii. 8. The young prophet that withstood the king is overcome with the insinuations of the old prophet, 1 Kings xiii. 16, 17. Some miscarry in adversity, others in prosperity, but more there; as diseases that grow of fulness are more dangerous than diseases that grow of want. The taking God's name in vain is not so bad as denying God: 'Lest I be full and deny thee; lest I be poor, and take thy name in vain.' They that are full live as if there were no God at all; there is the snare; and in adversity we are impatient, as in prosperity we are forgetful of God. Paul 'learned of Christ how to be abased and how to abound,' Phil. iii. 12. We must do both. But there is a greater snare in prosperity; the more of the world the worse; as fat and fertile grounds are most rank of weeds, and produce most thorns and thistles: Rom. viii. 39, 'Nor height, nor depth, shall separate us from the love of God that is in Christ Jesus our Lord.' The depth of misery is a snare, and the height of happiness too; there the snare is greater. Misery is often made an occasion to bring us to Christ, but never fulness, ease, and plenty. The moon is never eclipsed but when at full; God's children have most miscarried then. David was not soiled with lust whilst he wandered in the wilderness, but whilst he walked on the terrace of his palace; then men discover themselves, as a leaky vessel is known when it is filled with water. Adversity makes men more reserved and serious; when the vessel is empty, its hollowness and unsoundness is least discovered. Thus every condition may prove a snare. So every calling and course of life. In ordinary callings, a long familiarity breedeth a liking, and the soul receiveth taints from objects to which we are accustomed. Men that have much to do in the world had need take heed of a worldly spirit; continual presence of the object secretly linketh the affections; long suits prevail at length, and green wood kindleth by long lying on the fire. When the course of your callings and employments put you much upon worldly business, the heart is drawn away from God insensibly, and you will find less savour in holy things. Yea, in that calling which immediately respects the service of God there wants not snares: 1 Tim. iii. 6, 'Not a novice, lest being puffed up with pride, he falleth into the condemnation of the devil.' Holy things are often abused by a perverse aim. Those that are set on the pinnacles of the temple are in danger; the devil carried Christ thither with an intent to tempt him. Christ prayeth here principally for the college of the apostles; ministers are in danger as well as others; we have our temptations as well as you. Nay, in all actions and employments, worship, feeding, trading, sporting, all these may become a snare; and temptations are like the wind, that bloweth from every corner, east, west, north, and south. So there are temptations in worship to pride, self-confidence, carnal distractions. Satan stealeth away our hearts from under Christ's own arm: 'When the sons of God met together, Satan was amongst them,' Job i. 6. Not only our table may be turned into a snare, but duties into dung. In recreations, eating, drinking, bodily refreshments, there is a snare. Job i. 5, Job sacrificed while his children were a-banqueting. At a feast there are more guests than are invited; evil spirits haunt such meetings; and usually men let loose themselves to a carnal liberty at such a time. Satan, to be sure to be welcome, bringeth his dish with him, a bait for every humour : 1 Tim. iv. 5, 'The creatures must be sanctified by the word of God and by prayer.' We must not only ask God's leave, but his blessing. So pleasures, if not sanctified, bring a brawn and deadness upon the heart : 1 Tim. v. 6, 'She that liveth in pleasure is dead while she liveth.' So also in all places; in company, and when we are alone, we are still in danger. In company, we are in danger to be provoked to wrath or tempted to sin ; though open excesses manifest their own odiousness, yet secretly we learn of one another to be cold, careless, less mortified. In good company, nature is very susceptible of evil, and we imitate their weaknesses sooner than their graces : Gal. ii. 13, 'Barnabas was carried away with their dissimulations.' So in privacy, when we are alone, the devil often abuseth our solitude; Christ was tempted in the wilderness, Mat. iv. 1. In the vast world there is no corner where a man can be privileged from temptations ; how hard a matter is it to be alone when we are alone, or to have none with us but God and our own souls ! It is good to be alone with God, but not with Satan : John xvi. 32, 'Ye shall leave me alone, and yet I am not alone, for the Father is with me.' Now few can say so. Alas ! we have cause to say, Here I am alone, but I am not alone, for Satan is with me. So also there is danger from the men of the world, and the things of the world. The men of the world are apt to ensnare us by their counsels or threatenings. Sin is as earnest to propagate itself as grace. Wicked men would have the whole world to be all of a piece ; they are panders and bawds to wickedness, to draw others into the same snare with which they are held themselves ; they are the devil's factors, and when they cannot prevail, then they rage, and slander, and persecute : 'They think strange that you do not run with them into the same excess of riot, speaking evil of you,' 1 Peter iv. 4. The wills of men are ranked with the lusts of the flesh ; ver. 2, 3, 'That he no longer should live the rest of his time in the flesh, to the lusts of men, but to the will of God. For the time past of our life may suffice us to have wrought the will of the Gentiles, when we lived in lasciviousness, lusts, excess of wine,' &c. Then the things of the world. There are several baits for every temper, pleasures, honours, profits. Satan is well skilled in tempers ; he dresseth the temptation in that livery which suiteth with every man's humour and complexion, and plieth that object which suiteth with the distemper. He knoweth every distemper loveth the diet that feedeth it ; hath honours for the ambitious, wealth for the covetous, pleasures for the sensual ; and God by a righteous dispensation permitteth it: Jer. vi. 21, 'Therefore thus saith the Lord, Behold, I will lay stumbling-blocks before this people, and the fathers and the sons together shall fall upon them.' As when we suspect a servant to be given to filching, we leave loose money about the house to try if he will steal it ; so God, to try us, may suffer Satan to ply us with a diet suitable to our distemper.

Secondly, The next reason is our own weakness. There are not only snares and temptations in the world, but there is a flexibleness in the party tempted : James i. 14, 'Every man is tempted, when he is drawn away of his own lust, and enticed.' The fire burneth in our own hearts; Satan doth but blow up the flame. There is bad liquor in the vessel; Satan giveth it vent, and sets it abroach with violence: Mat. v. 28, 'He that looketh on a woman to lust after her, hath committed adultery with her already in his heart.' There is an intrinsical flexibleness in the heart, a treacherous party within. The evils of the world were tolerable, if there were not lust in the heart: 2 Peter i. 4, 'Having escaped the corruption that is in the world through lust.' We carry the worst enemy in our own bosom; Satan could not prevail against us were it not for our own lusts; as the Philistines could not prevail against Samson if Delilah had not lulled him to sleep, or as Balaam first corrupted Israel before he could curse them. Nay, when there is grace wrought, still there is a treacherous party within: Mat. xxvi. 41, 'The spirit is willing, but the flesh is weak.' The will hath a proneness still, and in your affections there is a suitableness to carnal baits. It is as with a garrison besieged; though the treacherous party be weakest in the town, yet they may do much hurt; so there is still corruption enough to open the door to Satan.

Use. 1. Caution. Take heed; the world is a dangerous place, even to a disciple of Christ; and therefore you have need 'to use it as if you used it not.' The heart is soon tainted, and that insensibly. There are two remedies that you should constantly use—watching and prayer; they are prescribed by our Saviour: Mat. xxvi. 41, 'Watch and pray, that ye enter not into temptation.' These must always go together. We watch that we may not be careless; we pray that we may not be self-confident. These two duties help one another; the heart is best kept when it is commended to God. We watch only to discover the approaches of the enemy; and we cry for God's help against the temptation. As watching helps prayer, danger descried giveth quickness, fervency, and earnestness in supplication; so also prayer helpeth watching. We can best maintain our station when we call in God's help.

1. Watch, and that especially against two things—the occasions of sin, and the privy distempers of the heart.

[1.] The occasions of sin. Do not put yourselves upon danger; it is a sign of a naughty heart to dally with occasions; as ravens, when they are driven away from the carrion, will stand within the scent. It is not good to be within the scent of sin. Lot and his wife were not to look back upon Sodom: Gen. xix. 26, 'Lot's wife looked back from behind him, and she became a pillar of salt.' The act in itself was not sinful, but it was forbidden to them as an occasion of sin. You shall see, ver. 29, Abraham looked towards Sodom and Gomorrah, and he is commended; but it was forbidden to Lot: ver. 17, 'Escape for thy life, look not behind thee;' because it was likely to work relentings. He was loath to leave that pleasant vale; the sight was more like to work on Lot's heart and his wife's than Abraham's, and prove a snare to them. Therefore Lot's wife is turned into a pillar of salt. Pray mark it; Ananias and Sapphira were stricken dead for a sin, and Lot's wife for putting herself upon a temptation to sin. God hath declared his displeasure against hankering after corruption as well as closing with it; and in these days sin is not grown less dangerous, nor

God less angry with it. A wanton look, putting ourselves upon the presence of a temptation without a call, 'beholding the wine while it sparkleth in the glass,' these are temptations, and we have no need to tempt the tempter. Satan is waiting for such advantages; he can interpret the silent language of a blush, a smile, a frown, a look, the glance of a lustful eye; he is watchful, and is an excellent naturalist, skilled in the external gestures and motions of the spirits.

[2.] Against privy distempers. We are not only to watch against actual sins, but the secret growing of evil habits, especially against deadness, drowsiness, and those distempers that insensibly creep upon the heart. Conversing with worldly pleasures and worldly objects breedeth a deadness, and withdraweth the heart ere we are aware. Natural conscience is kept waking against foul lusts and corruptions; they are in a dead sleep that can, as Jonah did, sleep in a storm, that fall into brutish practices without remorse. But the great end of spiritual watching is to keep the heart in frame, to prevent the sly encroachments of the world. But how shall we know when the world doth encroach? I answer—When your care is lessened towards heavenly things, and your delight is lessened in them.

(1.) When your care is lessened towards heavenly things, you are not so serious, so frequent in communion with God. This is Martha's fault; she 'was cumbered about much serving, while Mary sat at Jesus his feet, and heard his words,' Luke x. When you begin to lessen your course of duty, though the same abilities, opportunities, and necessities continue, and only out of respect to the world, it is a carnal distemper, especially when the world beginneth to upbraid conscience. If I hear as much, and pray as much, and meditate as much as I was wont, it will engross my time and hinder my worldly pursuits. As Sarah thrust Ishmael out of doors when he began to scoff at Isaac, it is good to thrust the world out of the heart when it encroacheth too much. Be it the world of carnal delight, or of carnal profit, when it would defraud God, or the soul, or the family of its due allowance, it is sad.

(2.) When your delight is lessened, and you have lost your savour of the word or the ordinances, or sabbath, and prize communion with God less, God is defrauded: 1 John ii. 15, 'Love not the world, nor the things of the world; for if any man love the world, the love of the Father is not in him.' The love of the world hath made you weary of God. When the affections are scattered to other objects, it is adultery; the wife of the bosom is defrauded of her right. So it is spiritual adultery when the world hath intercepted your delight, and you go a-whoring after it. It is idolatry to divert our trust, and adultery to divert our delight. Worldliness is expressed by both terms—adultery and idolatry: Ps. lxxiii. 27, 28, 'Thou hast destroyed all them that go a-whoring from thee; but it is good for me to draw near to God.' Estrangement of affection from God is called there, 'going a-whoring from God,' and opposed to delight in communion with God. And it is spiritual idolatry: Col. iii. 5, 'Mortify your earthly members; fornication, &c., and covetousness, that is idolatry.' And Eph. v. 5, 'No covetous person, that is an idolater, shall inherit the kingdom of Christ and of God.' Therefore though we do not run into gross sins, we must watch against these distempers, lessening of our care of and delight in heavenly things.

2. Pray. God is the best guardian and keeper ; he must watch over our watching : Ps. cxli. 3, 'Set a watch, O Lord, before my lips, and keep the door of my mouth.' Our security lieth in the restraints of his grace and the conduct of his Spirit : 2 Tim. i. 12, 'I know whom I have believed, and I am persuaded that he is able to keep that which I have committed to him against that day.' Give your souls to Christ to keep ; it is our best jewel, it is fit it should be in safe hands. In every prayer we do anew charge Christ with our souls ; the heart is best kept when commended to Christ. To quicken you, consider how weak the highest saints have been, when God hath loosed his hand and left them to themselves. David was a holy man, a grown man, a saint of long standing, of many experiences, yet he was overcome by his eyes. Joseph was a youth, a servant, had a fair opportunity, which David wanted ; he did not tempt, but was tempted, yet he resisted : Gen. xxxix. 9, 'How shall I do this wickedness, and sin against God ?' Who would have thought that Lot, that was kept righteous in Sodom, should have miscarried in the mountain, where there was none but his own family ?. God sometimes will show us such instances, that we may learn to wait and depend on him.

5. Observe the necessity of God's keeping. Christ would never make a prayer to his Father for it if it had been in their own power to keep themselves. It is God must keep us ; if he doth but leave us to grapple with a temptation in our own strength, we are soon gone : 'Keep them from evil.' This point hath been of often recourse in this prayer, therefore I shall be the briefer in it :—(1.) How God keepeth us ; (2.) Why God keepeth us.

First, How God keepeth us ? God hath many ways of keeping us, but they may be reduced to two—either by his Spirit or providence.

1. All the inward work is despatched by the Spirit, by the power of which he suppresseth inclinations to sin, and layeth on restraints of grace : Gen. xx. 6, 'I withheld thee from sinning against me.' So in his people he weakeneth the power of sin, prevents us by the counsels of his grace from giving consent, leaves the awe of grace upon the soul to weaken the power of sin : Jer. xxxii. 40, 'I will put my fear into their hearts, that they shall not depart from me ;' and giveth actual strength when tempted : 2 Cor. xii. 9, 'My grace is sufficient for thee ;' and when we fall God raiseth us, that we perish not. Sometimes God lets us fall ; as a father, when the child is busy about the fire, puts his finger to a coal, that he may be afraid of it. It is one of his methods to bring us to heaven, to make us taste of sin's bitterness. David prayeth, ' Restore unto me the joy of thy salvation, and uphold me by thy free Spirit,' Ps. li. 12.

2. By his providence.

[1.] He removeth the provoking occasions and objects of sin : Ps. cxxv. 3, 'The rod of the wicked shall not rest upon the lot of the righteous, lest they put forth their hand to do iniquity' We need this outward help ; if we had oftener occasions, we should be more angry, more voluptuous, more worldly.

[2.] Violent temptations are not permitted where he seeth we are most weak. As Jacob drove as the little ones were able to bear, 1 Cor. x. 13, 'God will not suffer us to be tempted above what we are able, but with the temptation will make a way to escape, that we may be able to bear it.' He doth not give us into the enemies' hands, and leave us to the malice of Satan or the violence of men; all is guided with wisdom and care.

[3.] By withholding occasions and opportunities, when temptation hath prevailed: Job xxxiii. 17, 'That he may withdraw man from his purpose, and hide pride from man.' When we have conceived a purpose, God hindereth the execution; such disappointments are a great mercy.

Secondly, Why God alone must keep us.

1. From the nature of God. He is able: 2 Tim. i. 12, 'I know that he is able to keep that which I have committed to him;' 1 Peter i. 5, 'Who are kept by the power of God;' Jude 24, 'To him that is able to keep you from falling.' He is wise: 2 Peter ii. 9, 'The Lord knows how to deliver the godly out of temptation.' God is skilful and well versed in this work. God is faithful, and will not fail: 2 Thes. iii. 3, 'The Lord is faithful, who will stablish you, and keep you from evil.' Our establishment and preservation from damning sins is among the blessings of the covenant; his faithfulness lieth at stake.

2. From our weakness. We cannot keep ourselves. We are so weak, we are apt to consent to lusts, or to faint under afflictions. We can no more stand against Satan than a lamb can against a wolf. The world hath a treacherous party in our own hearts. The best things are most dependent—a sheep, not a wolf; a vine, not a bramble; a saint, he is always depending.

Use 1. Do not forfeit God's keeping. This may be done; therefore we pray, Mat. vi. 13, 'Lead us not into temptation.' God, as a judge, puts us for our exercise under Satan's hands; as a malefactor is put into the serjeant's hands, if he will not be ruled; this is a spiritual excommunication. Partly to cure us of self-confidence, or resting in our own strength. We use to try men that boast with a heavy burden; so doth the Lord: Judges x. 14, 'Go and cry unto the gods whom ye hath chosen; let them deliver you in the time of your tribulation.' Partly to cure us of neglect and unthankfulness, when we do not take notice of God's keeping, when God hath lent us his grace, and we think we are not beholden to him; as if a man is weary, and another should lend him his staff to go by, and thereupon he should begin to slight him. He taketh no notice of his preservation that doth not walk answerably to it; dependence should beget observance: Phil. ii. 12, 13, 'Work out your salvation with fear and trembling; for it is God that worketh in you, to will and to do according to his good pleasure.' When we do not thrive under his custody it is scandalous. God will take away the hedge, let the boar of the forest come in and eat them down.

Use 2. To press the children of God to two duties—dependence, confidence.

1. Dependence: 1 Chron. xx. 12, 'We have no might against this great company, neither know we what to do, but our eyes are up to thee.' We must profess that we do not stand by our own strength,

but are as a staff in the hand of a man, or a child in the hand of the father: Ps. lxx. 5, 'I am poor and needy, make haste unto me, O God: thou art my help, and my deliverer, make no tarrying, O my God.' God is honoured when we acknowledge him for our guardian.

2. Confidence that he will preserve us in that grace to which he hath called us in Christ. There will be shakings and wanderings, as a tree fastened at the root is driven to and fro with violent blasts. There may be an interruption of the acts of grace; as a man in a swoon, or as stunned by a great blow, but he is alive: so there may be particular falls, but we shall not fall constantly, readily, easily. As in a land flood the meadows may be overflown, but the marshes are drowned every tide. Preservation from damning sins is sure and certain; Christ hath asked it. God is able to keep us. Happy are they that have an interest in Christ's prayers, and that have God for a guardian. Therefore wait upon God with hope in the midst of temptations.

6. I observe from the last words, 'the evil,' from the evil one, or evil thing; it lieth indifferently.

[1.] From the evil one. Observe, Satan hath a great hand in the evils that befall us in the world, both afflictions and sin. He instigateth our enemies, and inflameth our lusts.

(1.) He instigateth our enemies. Christ said, Luke xxii. 53, 'This is your hour, and the power of darkness;' Rev. xii. 12, 'The devil is come down unto you, having great wrath, because he knoweth that he hath but a short time.' If you could behold with bodily eyes this evil spirit hanging on the ears of the great men of the world and of the common people, to animate them against the saints, you would more admire the work of God that you do subsist.

(2.) He inflameth our sins and lusts: 1 Cor. vii. 3, 'Lest Satan tempt you for your incontinency.' The sin is ours, but Satan joins with it and makes it more violent; as in storms and tempests, when matter is prepared, the devil maketh them more formidable.

Use 1. Let persecutors take heed; the devil is near, and they are guided by him, though they see him not: Rev. xvi. 14, 'They are the spirits of devils working miracles, which go forth to the kings of the earth.'

Use 2. Here is advice to the people of God. (1.) To beware of sins, that you gratify not Satan with the displeasure of God. Do you think Peter would ever have given such advice to Christ as he did, if he knew Satan had been in it? Would carnal men ever lie if they knew the devil filled their hearts? Acts v. 3, 'Why hath Satan filled thine heart, to lie to the Holy Ghost?' Would men sin so freely if they knew the hand of Satan was in all? And if the Lord should give you over to his power, if he should give Satan charge over you, how far might he hurry and carry you! (2.) Let this teach you dependence upon God so much the more: Eph. vi. 12, 'For we wrestle not against flesh and blood, but against principalities, against powers, against the rulers of the darkness of this world, against spiritual wickedness in high places.' We have to do with the devil as well as men, and therefore have need to look up to God. And this is thy comfort, O christian, that God is stronger than Satan.

[2.] From the evil thing, that is, the evil of persecution; keep them from being destroyed till they have accomplished their ministry.   Observe, God keepeth his saints temporally, till their work is ended, by a special providence.   He delivers them from diseases and from the fury of men, as long as he hath any service for them in the world. Therefore, whenever you have escaped any visible and sensible danger, when you are come out of a terrible disease, or kept from the fury of men, improve it accordingly ; it is for service.

But rather it may be understood of the evil of sin ; keep them from the evil.   And so the note is, that sin is the greatest evil.   Christ doth not say, Keep them from trouble.   No ; let them ride out the storm ; but keep them from the evil of sin.

<hr>

SERMON XXV

They are not of the world, even as I am not of the world.—
JOHN XVII. 16.

IN this verse Christ repeateth the argument used in the 14th verse. This repetition is not idle and of no use; it is Christ that speaketh. The reason of the repetition may be conceived either with respect to the disciples, the persons for whom and in whose hearing he prayed, and so it is to inculcate their duty ; or with respect to God, the person to whom he prayed, and so he urgeth their danger.   For in the 14th verse he showed this was the cause why the world hated them ; now he maketh it the reason why he prayeth for them, that they may be kept : ' Keep them from the evil : they are not of the world, even as I am not of the world.'

In the general observe, that repetitions of the same point are sometimes necessary : Phil. iii. 1, ' To write the same things to you, to me it is not grievous, but for you it is safe.'   Repetition of the same things is tedious and irksome to nature, but profitable to grace.   It is tedious to nature, partly out of an itch of novelty.   Most men have but an adulterous love to truth ; they love it while it is new and fresh ; there is a satiety that groweth by acquaintedness ; the Israelites grew weary of manna, though angels' food.   Partly out of the impatiency of guilt ; sores cannot endure to be rubbed again and again ; frequency of reproof and admonition is like the rubbing of a sore, grievous to a galled conscience : John xxi. 17, Peter was grieved that he should say to him the third time, ' Lovest thou me ? ' as reviving his apostasy, bringing to remembrace his threefold denying of Christ, questioning his fidelity.   Sinners do not love to be suspected or urged much ; it reviveth guilt, and maketh it fly in the face of conscience.   None are weary but they that cannot endure to be remembered of their duty. But it is profitable to grace—(1.) To cure weakness; (2.) To further duties.

First, To cure weakness.   Our knowledge is little, our affections changeable, our memories weak, our attention slight.

1. Our knowledge is little.   Narrow-mouthed vessels take in liquor by drops, so do we divine truths, and therefore you have need to hear

the same things often, that your understandings may grow familiar and acquainted with these notions : Isa. xxviii. 10, 'For precept must be upon precept, precept upon precept, line upon line, line upon line, here a little and there a little.' They must be taught as little children are wont to be taught when they learn to read and write, to know letter after letter, and to draw line after line ; we must go over it again and again, that you may understand it more. Frequent inculcation maketh us to observe every part and point ; you take it in by degrees.

2. Our attention is small. We do consider it when we understand it. Since the fall, we have lost our settled and solemn thoughts ; the roving vanity of our minds needeth this outward cure. When truth is again brought into the view of the understanding, the mind is set a-work ; first we learn, and then we meditate. If christians would observe their hearts, they would find it hard to go along with the preacher at first hearing ; but when they go over it in their thoughts, then it worketh spiritually, and they consider it with affection upon a review. Mary 'kept all these sayings in her heart,' Luke ii. 51. We mind things but slightly, there must be apprehension before musing ; study findeth out a truth, meditation improveth it.

3. Our memories are weak. We have a short memory in the best things. A man needeth no remembrancer to put him in mind of worldly gain, and to revenge injuries ; but as to good things, our memories are as a bag with holes, or as a grate or sink, that retaineth the mud, and lets the running water go : Heb. ii. 1, 'Therefore we ought to give the more earnest heed to the things which we have heard, lest at any time we should let them slip.' We are as sandy ground or leaky vessels ; we have much lost the practical memory, have few actual thoughts of truths in the season of them. Men forget what we have told them of God's justice, his omnipresence, the day of judgment. When we are about to faint under afflictions, Heb. xii. 5, 'Have ye forgotten the exhortation that speaketh unto you as unto children ? ' ' My son, despise not thou the chastening of the Lord, neither faint when thou art rebuked by him.' It is a main office of the Spirit to remember us of truths in their season : John xiv. 26, 'The Comforter, which is the Holy Ghost, whom the Father will send in my name, he will teach you all things, and bring all things to your remembrance, whatsoever I have said unto you.' It is one thing to know, another thing to remember ; seasonable thoughts are a great relief in temptation : 2 Tim. iv. 2, 'Preach the word, be instant in season, out of season,' εὐκαίρως, ἀκαίρως. We may press truths when there is no such express need of them, in season press them again ; it is a great advantage.

4. Our wills are slow and averse. It is not enough for a slow and dull servant to hear the commands of his master, but they must be often told him. We must be urged again and again, as Christ doth Peter. The heart is averse and deceitful ; we give a slight answer to the first demand, Will you do this for God ? 2 Peter i. 12, 13, 'Wherefore I will not be negligent to put you always in remembrance of these things, though ye know them, and be stablished in the present truth. Yea, I think it meet, as long as I am in this tabernacle, to stir you up, by putting you in remembrance.' Most men love to hear, as being greedy of novelty and speculation, expecting things that are rare

and less known.   It is our duty to press things that are more known, to urge the will: 1 John ii. 21, 'I have not written to you, because ye know not the truth, but because ye know it, and that no lie is of the truth;' not to acquaint them with new doctrine, but to urge them to steadfastness.   All preaching is not to enlighten the understanding, but to gain the will, to stir you up again.   Our affections are changeable; heated water groweth cold again: we have need of the same truths to revive our frame.   Our affections soon flag, as a bird cannot always keep upon the wing, and remembrance worketh not so much as present excitement.   It were an excellent work to put you into the same frame again.   Our corruptions and temptations daily arise; we lose what we have wrought, we had need be quickened anew, put in mind again, that we may be kept in a good frame : 2 Peter iii. 1, 'This second epistle I now write unto you, in both which I stir up your pure mind by way of remembrance.'

Secondly, It helpeth duties.

1. Meditation.   The mind worketh freely upon such objects to which it is accustomed; in things rare and seldom heard of there is more need of study than meditation, to search them out.

2. It helpeth application.   We hear to do and practise, not only to know.   We do not hear to store the head with notions, but that the life and heart might be bettered.

Use 1. Let it not be grievous to you to hear the same things pressed. Common truths are not too plain for our mouths, nor too stale for your ears.   If you should hear the same sermon preached again, observe God's providence: 'A sparrow doth not fall to the earth without our heavenly Father.'   Have I considered of this, meditated of it?   Doth not my heart need it again?   Sure there is somewhat in it that God directeth the minister to it again.   Usually we come to hear sermons with an unmortified ear, and bewray an itch of novelty, as the Athenians, who loved to hear of new things.   And this puts preachers upon ungrounded subtleties and quintessential extracts, and so the gravity and sobriety of religion is lost.   Or else there is pride in it, as if they were above these common helps; the most learned need a remembrancer.   Some will say, This I knew before; they can teach me no more than I know already : 1 Cor. viii. 2, 3, 'If any man think that he knoweth anything, he knoweth nothing yet as he ought to know: but if any man love God, the same is known of him.'   Dost thou practise what thou knowest?   This is a new hint from God to humble thee, to quicken thee.   God seeth that I do not live up to my knowledge, and therefore the same truth is returned.   Preachers should hear sermons, as prophets studied their own prophecies, as godly, as prophets; there is difference between the man and the prophet.   Or else for want of affection.   In music, if a man hear an excellent lesson, he would hear it again; the second hearing is sweetest to a gracious heart. If it be grievous to any, it is to us that do more deeply consider it, and weigh it before it is brought.   If it be not grievous to us, it is safe to you.   It is a great wantonness and gluttony when men cannot endure to eat twice of one dish.

Use 2. It serveth to encourage you in your private exercises of rehearsing and meditation ; this is chewing the cud : Ps. lxii. 11, 'God hath spoken once, twice have I heard this, that power belongeth to God;' it was often revolved in the mind. The meat is taken into the mouth, and digestion is afterward. Repetition is the outward help, meditation the inward; conscience preacheth over the sermon again to the heart.

Use 3. To ministers, not only to study new things, but to inculcate those that are of a common use: Jude 5, 'I will therefore put you in remembrance, though ye once knew this.' We are not to content your curiosity, but to provide for your benefit; not to please the Athenian, but to profit the christian. We are not cooks, but physicians. People do not remember half we preach, or they lose their affections. Christ often repeateth the same sentences, so do the apostles. You may repeat the same things, only with these cautions:—

1. That it be in matters mainly necessary. There are some standing dishes at Christ's table.

2. That it be with variety of enforcement, to avoid tediousness, κοίνα καινῶς. There are several notions to help us; every time we should have new thoughts, *adoro plenitudinem sacræ scripturæ*, that all be subjected to profit, not a cover to laziness. There is much of God's providence to be observed in inclining the heart; not only the efficacy of the Spirit in quickening gifts is to be regarded, but the power of his providence in determining the thoughts. Much of God is to be seen in the choice of the subject.

But let us look upon the words more particularly; the reasons of this repetition, with respect to the disciples, or to God.

First, With respect to the disciples. It is repeated in their ears for their comfort and instruction: 'They are not of the world, even as I am not of the world.' It either noteth their outward condition, or their inward temper and constitution, or both; they have little of the world's respect, and the world hath little of theirs: Gal. vi. 14, 'The world is crucified to me, and I unto the world.' A dead man hanging on the cross is a miserable and ignominious spectacle. I despise the world, and the world despiseth me, as a crucified man is made an object of shame and scorn. Paul sought not after the world, nor did the world seek after him. All the honours, pomps, delights, which the world doteth upon, were as a crucified man in whom there is no form and comeliness why he should desire them; thus they are to a gracious eye. Both senses are taken, and the pattern will agree to both—Christ's Spirit, Christ's life.

Take it for their constitution and temper of mind: 'They are not of the world, as I am not of the world.' Christ repeateth it again in the hearing of the disciples.

Observe, that we can never enough be cautioned against the world. We had need to be pressed often and often in this matter.

1. Because of our proneness to it. The love of the world is natural to us. We need it in part, and we love it more than we need it. There are several reasons; partly because worldliness is a part of original sin; it is a disease we are born with. The commandment that forbiddeth the original sin saith, 'Thou shalt not covet.' It is hard for any to say they are not tempted to covetousness; it is their nature. Partly by custom; we are daily conversant about the things of the

world ; our affections receive taint from the objects with which we usually converse ; long converse is a bewitching thing. Partly because it is of a present enjoyment ; we have the world in hand and heaven in hope, and think heaven a fancy, a notion, and the world substance : Prov. viii. 17, ' Riches and honours are with me ; yea, durable riches and righteousness.' The judgment of men is different from the judgment of the word : we have a sensible experience of the profit of the world. Partly because it is a serious sin, applauded by men : Ps. x. 3, ' The wicked boasteth of his heart's desire, and blesseth the covetous, whom the Lord abhorreth.' Men think well of it, and stroke it with a gentle censure ; it is not so foul an act. A drunkard is more liable to reproach than a worldling. It is consistent with the gravity and strictness of profession. Religion is a serious thing, and of all corruptions it is most incident to them that profess religion ; the dissoluteness of luxury will not stand with the external gravity and strictness of profession ; licentious persons do procure shame, and are publicly odious. Partly because it is a cloaked sin : 1 Thes. ii. 5, ' Neither at any time used we flattering words, nor a cloak of covetousness ; God is witness.' It is hard to discover it and find it out, there are so many evasions, of necessity, providence, and provision. It is a great part of religion to ' keep ourselves unspotted from the world,' James i. 27.

2. Because of the heinousness and danger of it. It is called adultery : James iv. 4, ' Ye adulterers and adulteresses, know ye not that the friendship of the world is enmity with God ? Whosoever therefore will be a friend of the world is the enemy of God.' It is most unsuitable to the matrimonial contract between God and the soul, wherein God propoundeth himself as God all-sufficient. Now, as if we had not enough in God, men go a-whoring to the creatures. It is idolatry : Col. iii. 5, ' And covetousness, which is idolatry.' So Eph. v. 5, ' No covetous person, who is an idolater, hath any inheritance in the kingdom of Christ and of God.' It diverteth our trust, robbeth God of the fairest flower in his crown, of his sovereignty, the trust and dependence of the creature. It is ' enmity with God,' James iv. 4. The world is the greatest encroacher upon God and grace ; it robbeth God and destroyeth grace. The comforts of christianity relish not with them that love the world. It is impossible at the same time to look with one eye to heaven and another to the earth.

3. Because of the unsuitableness of it to the divine nature. It is most unsuitable to the new nature : 1 John v. 4, ' Whatsoever is born of God overcometh the world.' It is unsuitable to our hopes. God hath provided heaven on purpose to draw us off from the world. God is most liberal in this world to the worst ; as Judas had the bag. These are gifts for worldly men, not for God's favourites : Gen. xxv. 6, ' Unto the sons of the concubines which Abraham had, Abraham gave gifts, and sent them away from Isaac his son.' Isaac had the inheritance. It is contrary to the aim of Christ ; his whole aim in coming and going was to bring us to heaven : Heb. xi. 16, ' Now they desire a better country, that is an heavenly ; wherefore God is not ashamed to be called their God, for he hath prepared for them a country.'

Use. To press us to beware the more of worldliness. Christ doth once and again say, ' They are not of the world.' 2 Kings v. 26, ' Is it a time to receive money, and to receive garments, and olive-yards, and vineyards, and sheep, and oxen, and men-servants, and maid-servants?' Especially in these times, in which so many miscarry by worldly practices, and when God hath declared so much of his displeasure against worldly greatness. To this end—

1. Consider your condition ; you are strangers and pilgrims. David was a king, yet not at home in the world: Ps. xxxix. 12, 'I am a stranger, and a sojourner with thee, as all my fathers were.' We never read that Abraham made any purchase but of a grave ; Cain built a city. We are gone hence to-morrow, and who would hang a room in an inn ?

2. We are called to better things : 1 Thes. ii. 11, 12, 'As ye know how we exhorted, and comforted, and charged every one of you, as a father doth his children, that ye would walk worthy of God, who hath called you unto his kingdom and glory.' It is not for princes to embrace the dunghill. Who would believe that a man raking in a dung-hill or nasty ditch were heir to a crown ? You show yourselves hereby to be unworthy of heaven.

3. Take the apostle's argument : 1 Tim. vi. 7, 'We brought nothing with us into the world, and it is certain that we can carry nothing out.' The millwheel turneth round all day, but at night it is in the same place. So at death, we are in the same estate as at our birth. A man's wealth doth not follow him, but his works do. Your iniquity will find you out. You did not come rich into the world, and you were born to die. In our birth we were contented with a little cradle, at death with a little grave ; but here we join house to house, as if the whole world would not contain us.

4. Consider how hard it is to have Christ and the world, to have heaven and the world: Mat. xvi. 26, 'What shall it profit a man to gain the whole world, and lose his own soul? or what shall a man give in exchange for his soul?' You are put to your choice ; who would lose a crown to be owner of a dunghill? It is a vain design to think to reconcile Christ and mammon.

5. Thou art as thy love is. If thou lovest this world thou art worldly ; if thou lovest God thou art godly. A man is not as his opinion is, but as his affection is ; a bad man may be of a good opinion, but a bad man can never have good affections. The soul is as wax, it receiveth an impression from the object. Take a glass, put it towards heaven, there you shall see the figure of heaven ; put it towards the earth, and you see the figure of the earth, trees, meadows, fruits : thou receivest a figure from the objects to which thou appliest thy heart, earthly things or heavenly.

But you will say, What would you have us do? Is it a fault to enjoy the world? No ; but to have a worldly spirit.

(1.) Be not of a worldly spirit when thou wantest the things of this world. Be not over-careful for the things of this life ; use the means God hath ordained, trust God with the issue and event of all. Carking implies not only distrust, but discontent with God's allowance ; and both imply worldliness, distrust, and fear : Luke xii. 22, 'Take no thought for your life, what ye shall eat ; neither for the body, what ye shall put on.' I am sure discontent doth. Be contented with a mean condition; if these things were good for us, God would never deny them to us, never have bidden us to contemn them. Saints are never more illustrious than when they have least of the world; the less splendour they have in the world the more bright and glorious are they; had the saints a worldly glory, their grace would not appear with such advantage.

(2.) Be not of a worldly spirit when thou hast the world. A godly man may be a rich man; but take heed of trust, immoderate delight, and pride in them. Do not trust in them, for they are vain; nor delight in them, for they are snares; nor be proud of them, they do not make us better; we do not value a horse by the trappings, but by his spirit and courage. We may accept the allowance of providence; it is not having wealth, but setting the heart upon it, nor the enjoyment, but trust in it, that is condemned: Ps. lxii. 11, 'Trust not in oppression, become not vain in robbery; if riches increase, set not your heart upon them.' You will be apt to do it; but divert your heart, draw it off into another country: 1 Tim. vi. 17, 'Charge them that are rich in this world, that they be not high-minded, nor trust in uncertain riches;' and ver. 19, 'Laying up in store for themselves a good foundation against the time to come, that they may lay hold on eternal life.' Get a bank in heaven, make an advantage of it for religion, to confirm your title to heaven by more evidences. Our wealth follows us not into another world, but our works do. A man that loveth his money is willing to part with it, to assure his title to an earthly inheritance.

(3.) Be not dejected and over-sorrowful when thou losest them; thou art but delivered of a burden, a charge, and a snare; riches are a clog to thee. We are sure to give an account.

Take the words as they denote the outward condition of the disciples: 'They are not of the world;' that is, not respected by it, as if they were of their number and faction, left out of the world's tale and count.

1. Observe, it is a hard thing to digest the world's neglect and disrespect. We had need be urged again and again; partly because every one would be somebody in the world, and have some interest here, τὶς μέγας; and when we miss our aims, sorrow is obstinate, sufferings harsh and irksome to flesh and blood, because we admire things below, and have too good an opinion of them.

Use. This should be regarded by us in these times. When some grasp the world, and use all kind of means to get it into their hands, others are apt to envy at them; when they see others have all, and themselves poor, men think themselves wronged.

1. Let them alone; look after better things: Ps. xvii. 14, 'From men of the world, who have their portion in this life, and whose belly thou fillest with thy good things.' If they grow fat upon common mercies, we have no reason to pine and murmur. You have not such large estates, costly furniture, fine clothes, but you have a better heart; it is enough. Let the world's fondlings be dandled on the world's knees; you have a better portion, full breasts to suck on, purer consolations. When a river is troubled the mud will come on top. In troubles, sin would be uppermost. You have no reason to change conditions.

2. Remember by whose providence it falleth out. You think God is not wise enough; you will teach him whom to advance and whom not. Princes have their *arcana imperii.* Shall our servants know all our counsels? Many times God raiseth bad men to high places, not because they deserve it, but because the age deserveth no better : Phil. ii. 14, 15, 'Do all things without murmurings and disputings, that ye may be blameless and harmless, the sons of God.'

3. If you are favoured by God, why should you trouble yourselves about the world's respects? In choosing heirs to salvation, God doth not ask their counsel. Thou hast the testimony of God's Spirit, and many now in hell have had much of the world's respects. Their disrespect cannot hurt thee; it may profit thee, if thou art not wanting to thyself. If God should take counsel of the world, whether he should assume thee to glory or cast thee into hell, then their respects were to be sought after; but God will deal with thee alone, not ask their opinion, but refer it to thine own conscience. If all the world should respect thee, what is this to God, who will judge thee by another rule? They had need of steady heads that walk on high places. When men study to preserve the world's good opinion they lose it. God is master of their respects. If men did not study to please the world, they would not only have more quiet, but more success.

2. Observe again, an excellent means to digest the world's neglect is to consider the example of Christ. It is our duty, it will be for our comfort, and it turneth to our profit.

1. It is our duty. In his example we have a taste of his Spirit : 'I am not of the world,' saith Christ; and we should 'imitate Christ as dear children,' Eph. v. 1. They that love to live in delight and pleasures are but christians in name. If we had no other reason to contemn the vanity of the world than the life of Christ, this were enough. Who was wisest, Christ or you? Who can make the better choice, Christ or you? Who is in error, Christ or you? Christ chose a poor life, and you affect greatness.

2. It will be your comfort. It is a sweet comfort in all conditions to remember the similitude of condition between Christ and us : 'Shall the disciple be above the lord?' What more honourable than to carry the cross after Jesus Christ? Christ hath worn this garment : Col. i. 24, 'Who now rejoice in my sufferings for you, and fill up that which is behind of the afflictions of Christ in my flesh.' Christ was exposed to the envy of Satan and his agents. Art thou better than Christ? He suffereth with us, because we should suffer with him : Mat. xxv. 45, 'Verily I say unto you, inasmuch as ye did it not to one of the least of these, ye did it not to me;' Acts ix. 4, 'Saul, Saul, why persecutest thou me?' Man and wife, if they love one another, had rather live together in the meanest estate than in the greatest glory and abundance asunder. Christ and a christian are fellow-sufferers; we are conformed to his sufferings, and he hath a feeling of ours.

3. It will be for our profit. The issue will be glorious; we must first suffer, then enter into glory; winter is before the spring : Rom. viii. 17, 'If so be that we suffer with him, that we may be also glorified together;' 2 Cor. iv. 10, 'Always bearing about in my body the dying of the Lord Jesus, that the life also of Jesus might be made manifest

in our mortal flesh;' 2 Tim. ii. 11, 12, 'It is a faithful saying, for if we be dead with him, we shall also live with him : if we suffer, we shall also reign with him.' If we would be like Christ in glory, we must be like him in suffering.

Use. Meditate on this. God had but one Son, he came into the world without sin, but he could not get out without a cross. Art thou poor? so was Christ. Hast thou enemies? so had he. Art thou disdained? Christ went this way to glory, and so must thou. He was charged maliciously, blackened with slanders, accused falsely, &c., the like usage you must expect.

Secondly, With respect to God. How solicitous is Christ about those who are not of the world! Compare ver. 14 with this. His Father's choice must be made good; his own delight is in those that are like him. Christ loveth himself, and his own reflection in the saints. Christ is at perfect antipathy with the world; and a christian loveth what he loves and hateth what he hates. If you have the world's hatred against you, remember you have Christ's prayers.

SERMON XXVI.

Sanctify them through thy truth : thy word is truth.—John XVII. 17.

Here is Christ's second request for his disciples. Where—

1. The request itself, *sanctify them.*
2. The manner how it is to be accomplished, *through thy truth.*
3. The reason why it is to be so accomplished, *thy word is truth.*

The main points are the influence of truth upon sanctification, and that the word is the public record and register of this truth.

Now I shall make some entrance upon the verse.

First, The request; and here—(1.) What he prayeth for; (2.) To whom ; (3.) For whom.

First, What he prayeth for, sanctification.

1. Observe, Our chief aim in prayer for ourselves and others should be to be sanctified. Christ prayeth for sanctification.

[1.] What it is to be sanctified. To sanctify is—(1.) To consecrate or set apart for some holy use; (2.) To cleanse or purify; (3.) To adorn with gifts of grace.

Some prefer the first acceptation, and apply it particularly to the apostolical calling. 'Sanctify them,' that is, separate them, and set them apart for the work of an apostle. So Christ was sanctified, that is, set apart for the work of redemption. But it is not sanctify them *for* thy truth, but *in* or *by* thy truth, ἐν τῇ ἀληθείᾳ ; and therefore this scripture hath a more general respect and signification. However, in the work of holiness, all the senses may be taken in ; for whoever are sanctified are set apart, cleansed, and adorned with grace.

(1.) Set apart by God and by themselves. By God, both in time and before time. Before time they are set apart by God's decree, to be a holy seed to himself in and by Christ; separated from the perishing world, to be vessels of honour, as the reprobate are called vessels of wrath and dishonour; set apart by God's election, chosen to be holy: Eph. i. 4, 'According as he hath chosen us in him before the foundation of the world, that we should be holy, and without blame before him in love.' But then in time they are regenerated, and so actually set apart. Sanctification is an actual election. By election they are distinguished from others in God himself, so by regeneration and sanctification they are distinguished from others in themselves, separated and set apart from the perishing world, to act for God, to seek the things that may make for his glory: James i. 18, 'Of his own will begat he us with the word of truth, that we should be a kind of first-fruits of his creatures.' The first-fruits were the Lord's portion. Or else by the consent of their own vows: Rom. xii. 1, 'I beseech you that you present yourselves a living sacrifice, holy, acceptable to God, that is your reasonable service.' They have dedicated and devoted themselves to God. God calleth for it when he saith, 'My son, give me thy heart.' God will have his own right established by the creatures' consent; it is a necessary fruit of grace.

(2.) Purged by degrees, and made free from sin; this is to be sanctified, to be purged from the corruption of sin and the world. We are not only accounted holy, but we are made holy, and that cannot be till we are purged, because we come into the world polluted with the stain of sin: 1 Cor. vi. 11, 'Such were some of you; but ye are washed, but ye are sanctified, but ye are justified, in the name of the Lord Jesus, and by the Spirit of our God.' There is a stain and an uncleanness sticketh to our natures and defileth all our actions; we need to be purged.

(3.) Endowed with God's image and likeness; not only cleansed from sin, but adorned with grace; as the priests under the law were not only washed, but adorned with gorgeous apparel. To be sanctified is more than to be purified, because it noteth not only the expulsion of sin, but the infusion of grace: 2 Tim. ii. 12, 'If a man therefore purge himself from these, he shall be a vessel unto honour, sanctified, and meet for the master's use, and prepared unto every good work.' Besides purging, sanctification addeth somewhat more; they are not only purged from the filthiness of sin, but prepared by the infusion of grace for every good work, made holy as God is holy.

[2.] Why we should chiefly mind it in prayer?

(1.) Because of the excellency of it. It is God's glory, angels' glory, saints' glory. God's glory: Exod. xv. 11, 'God is glorious in holiness.' Angels' glory, who are called, Mat. xxv. 31, 'Holy angels.' And the saints' glory: Eph. v. 26, 27, 'That he might sanctify them with the washing of water by the word, that he might present it to himself a glorious church, not having spot or wrinkle, or any such thing; but that it might be holy, and without blemish.' The church's honour lieth not in pomp and outward ornament, but in holiness.

(2.) Because God aimeth at it in all his dispensations. Election: Eph. i. 4, 'According as he hath chosen us in him before the foundation of the world, that we should be holy, and without blame before him in love;' 2 Thes. ii. 14, 'God hath from the beginning chosen you, through sanctification of the Spirit, and belief of the truth.' God chooseth us that we may be of a choice spirit.   As when Esther was chosen out among the virgins, then she was decked with ornaments, so when we are chosen by God we are beautified with holiness.   Redemption : Eph. v. 26, 'Christ loved the church, and gave himself for it, that he might sanctify and cleanse it with the washing of water, by the word.'   His promises : 2 Peter i. 4, 'Whereby are given unto us exceeding great and precious promises, that by these ye might be partakers of the divine nature, having escaped the corruption that is in the world through lust.'   His providences : Heb. xii. 10, 'They verily for a few days chastened us after their own pleasure, but he for our profit, that we might be partakers of his holiness.   Earthly parents correct their children out of mere passion, but he to renew our affections, to sanctify us for himself, that the husk may fly off.   He bestows blessings to encourage us in holiness : 1 Tim. vi. 17, 18, 'Charge them that are rich in this world that they be not high-minded, nor trust in uncertain riches, but in the living God, who giveth us richly all things to enjoy ; that they do good, that they be rich in good works, ready to distribute, willing to communicate ;' that your riches may be instruments of piety, not occasions to the flesh.   It is our corruption to turn all things to a carnal use.   His ordinances : 'That he might sanctify them by the washing of water, through the word.'   Eph. v. 26.   This is God's aim, and it should be ours.

Use. Is to teach us what to seek for ourselves and others ; not temporal felicity so much as sanctification ; not deliverance from afflictions, nor outward blessings, so much as the sanctified use of them. This is to pray for one another out of the communion of the Spirit, and for ourselves out of a principle of the divine nature.   Temporal blessings are only to be desired in order to spiritual ends.   Nature is allowed to speak, but grace must be heard first : Mat. vi. 33, 'Seek ye first the kingdom of God, and the righteousness thereof and all these things shall be added unto you.'   These are for overplus.

2. Observe from the matter, he had prayed for conservation from evil, now for sanctification.   It is not enough to keep from evil, but we must be holy, and do good : Ps. xxxiv. 14, Depart from evil, and do good ;' Isa. i. 16, 17, 'Cease to do evil, learn to do well.'   God hateth evil and delighteth in good ; as we must hate what God hateth, so we must love what God loveth.   *Eadem velle et nolle.*   I durst not sin, God hateth it ; I durst not omit this duty, God loveth it.   Our obedience must carry a proportion with the divine mercy ; not only be positive but privative.   Divine mercy spareth and saveth : 'God is a sun and a shield,' Ps. lxxxiv. 11.   Therefore we must not 'walk in the counsel of the ungodly, nor stand in the way of sinners, nor sit in the seat of the scornful ;' but our delight must be 'in the law of the Lord, and in his law must we meditate day and night,' Ps. i. 1, 2. We must have communion with Christ in all his acts, in his death and resurrection.   He mortifieth sin and quickeneth the heart : Rom. vi. 11, 'Likewise reckon ye also yourselves to be dead indeed unto sin, but alive unto God, through Jesus Christ our Lord.'   The same divine power that killeth the old man quickeneth the new.   In the word, which is the rule, there are precepts and restraints ; therefore we are not only to escape from sin, but there must be a delight in communion

with God; there must be an eschewing what God forbiddeth, and a practising what God commandeth. Thus are we obliged from our approver, our principles, our encouragements, our rule.

Use. Let it press us not to rest in abstaining from sin. Men are not vicious, but they are not sanctified. The pharisees' religion ran upon negatives.

1. Both are alike contrary to the new nature.

2. Both are alike disserviceable to the work of grace.

3. Both are hated by God.

1. Both are contrary to the new nature; it hateth evil and loveth good. There is a putting off and a putting on: Eph. iv. 22, 'That ye put off concerning the former conversation the old man, which is corrupt according to the deceitful lusts; and that ye put on the new man, which after God is created in righteousness and true holiness.' It is indeed a question where the trial of a christian lieth most sensibly, in mortification or vivification? in a hatred of sin or in the practice of duty? It may be alleged that our nature doth more easily close with precepts than prohibitions. We are many times content to do much; if the law require this or that, we yield and consent to it; but to be limited and debarred of our delights, this is most distasteful. Men that love sin cannot endure restraints: Oh! that there were no bonds! And therefore, to meet with man's corruption, the decalogue consists more of prohibitions than precepts; the fourth and fifth commandments are only positive. But then, on the other side, it may be alleged that many that live a civil life, and do no man wrong, have no care of communion with God, and that sins trouble the conscience more than want of grace. Natural conscience doth not use to smite for spiritual defects. Sins work an actual distemper and disturbance to reason. It is the new nature that maketh conscience of duties, and of obeying God's precepts, therefore the new nature is here most tried; but yet both must be regarded.

2. Both are alike disserviceable to the work of grace. It is another question whether we are more hardened by sins of omission or by sins of commission? For sins of commission, it may be alleged that they stun the conscience, like a great blow on the head, and cast grace into a swoon. David's adultery put all out of order: 2 Sam. xii. 14, 'Howbeit, because by this deed thou hast given great occasion to the enemies of the Lord to blaspheme, the child which is born of thee shall surely die.' He lay in a spiritual swoon till the child was born. But then on the other side, neglect of duty depriveth us of the influences of grace, and hardens us insensibly. An instrument, though never so well in tune, yet if you let it alone, it will soon be out of order, worse than if a string were broken. After some great and sudden fall into sin, there may be a recovery, as in David's case, but it is hard to recover out of long neglects; therefore sins of omission are more dangerous than sins of commission. And if your communion with God be not constant, the heart contracts rust. A key that is seldom turned is rusted in the lock; by neglect and omission of God and duties the heart is wonderfully hardened and estranged from God. Gifts and graces languish and perish in idleness: 2 John 8, 'Look to yourselves, that we lose not those things which we have wrought.'

Standing pools are apt to putrify ; and sins increase as well as unfitness for duties, the motions of the Spirit are quenched.

3. Both are odious to God. It is a question whether God hateth most the careless sluggish person or the outwardly vicious. A barren tree cumbereth the ground, and is rooted out, as well as the bramble. It is not enough that a servant do his master no hurt, but he must do his work. A husbandman is not contented that his land does not bear him briars and thorns, but it must yield him good grain. It is not enough to say, I am no swearer, no drunkard. What communion have you with God ? What motions and feelings of the power of holiness ? Want of grace depriveth a man of happiness. As you would not be damned in hell, so you should get evidences for heaven. Negative righteousness in abstinence from sin the brutes and inanimate creatures have ; it is improper and lame. Omission of good duties is a more general means of destruction than commission of evil ; but then commission of evil is ever accompanied with omission of good, but omission of good is not always accompanied with commission of evil. He that doth evil dishonoureth God more, but he that omitteth good disadvantageth himself more. Sin is more odious than want of grace in itself ; yet want of grace, considering our advantages, may provoke God as much as commission of sin.

Secondly, To whom he prays : ' Holy Father, sanctify them.'

Observe, it is God must sanctify us ; we cannot ourselves, and means will not without God.

1. We cannot ourselves. 'We could defile ourselves, but we cannot cleanse ourselves ; as little children defile themselves, but the nurse must make them clean. A sheep can wander of itself, but it is brought home upon the shepherd's shoulders. *Domine, errare per me potui, redire non potui.* God, that gave us his image at first, must again stamp it on the soul. Who can repair nature depraved but the author of nature ? When a watch is out of order we send it to the workman : Eph. ii. 10, ' We are his workmanship, created in Christ Jesus unto good works, that we might walk therein ;' Lev. xxi. 8, ' I the Lord that sanctify thee am holy.' It is God's prerogative.

2. The means cannot without God. It is by the truth, but God is the principal cause. Sanctification is ascribed to many causes. To God the Father, as he decreeth it : Jude 1, ' To them that are sanctified by God the Father.' To the Son, as he merited it : Eph. v. 25, 26, ' He gave himself for the church, that he might sanctify and cleanse it.' To the Holy Ghost, as he effects it : 2 Thes. ii. 13, ' God hath from the beginning chosen you to salvation, through sanctification of the Spirit.' To faith, as it receiveth the grace of God : Acts xv. 9, ' Purifying their hearts by faith.' To the word, as the instrument of begetting it : John xv. 3, ' Now ye are clean, through the word which I have spoken unto you ;' it is the external means, but all efficacy is of God, and grace is his creature ; else what should be the reason why the same word, preached by the same minister, worketh on some and hardeneth others, at least it amendeth them not ? Lydia alone is converted, because the Lord ' opened her heart,' Acts xvi. 14. Man's will doth not put the difference, but God's grace.

Use. It presseth us—

1. To wait and look for it from God. A plant thriveth better by the dew of heaven than when watered by the hand. We may say as Peter, Acts iii. 12, 'Why look ye so earnestly on us, as though by our own power and holiness we had made this man to walk?' 'Am I in the place of God?' saith Jacob to Rachel, Gen. xxx. 2. When you look only to the teacher's gifts, you lose the divine operation; it may fill your heads with fancies and notions, but not your hearts with grace.

2. To praise the Lord when it is accomplished: 1 Cor. iii. 5, 'What is Paul, or what is Apollos, but ministers by whom ye have believed?' as if children should thank the servants for what they have. Grace maketh us more in debt; you have received it from him, not from yourselves: 'Not I, but the grace of God in me;' 'Thy pound hath gained ten pounds.' If you have any holiness, any good work, it is not of yourselves, but of God. Every act, every degree of holiness, is from God.

Thirdly, For whom he prayeth, the apostles.

1. That were already holy: John xiii. 10, 'Ye are clean;' and in the verse immediately preceding, 'They are not of the world;' yet now, 'Sanctify them,' let their hearts be more heavenly, and their lives more pure every day.

Observe, those that are sanctified need to be sanctified more and more: Rev. xxii. 11, 'He that is righteous, let him be righteous still; he that is holy, let him be holy still.'

[1.] Our inward sanctification must increase, because of the weakness of present grace and the relics of corruption: 2 Cor. iv. 16, 'Though our outward man perish, yet the inward man is renewed day by day.' It is not a work to be done at once: 1 Thes. v. 23, 'And the very God of peace sanctify you wholly; and I pray God your whole spirit, soul and body, be preserved blameless unto the coming of our Lord Jesus Christ.' It is perfect in parts at first; the new creature doth not come out maimed; but not in degrees: there is need of more sanctification in spirit, in soul, in body; the kingdom of heaven increaseth by degrees.

[2.] Our outward man must be cleansed day by day, because of new defilements: John xiii. 10, 'He that is washed needeth not but to wash his feet, but is clean every whit.' It is an allusion to a man coming from the bath; his feet contract soil in the passage. Your persons are sanctified by the Spirit; but when you are never so holy, there are new defilements.

Use 1. Be not satisfied with any present degrees of grace. There is a holy covetousness: 'I count not myself to have attained,' Phil. iii. 14. Christ is so full that we cannot receive all at once.

2. It is a strange conceit in any to think they may be too good. When we begin to be unwilling to grow better, we begin to wax worse; it is a good degree of grace to know our defects.

3. Therefore let us use means to persist in holiness, to increase in holiness, especially prayer, which is the breath which God hath appointed to keep in the flame.

Again, For the persons once more: they were to preach the word; as a preparative, he prayeth for sanctification.

Observe, holiness is a good preparative to the ministry, and they are inwardly consecrated by the Spirit sanctifying them.

[1.] That they may have experience of the truth of the doctrine upon their own hearts. The apostles were to preach the truth to others; now saith he, 'Sanctify them through thy truth.' 'I believed, and therefore have I spoken,' Ps. cxvi. 10. We speak best when we speak by experience. This is the right way of getting sermons by heart. We are God's witnesses; now we should have sound experience: 1 John i. 1, 'That which was from the beginning, which we have heard, which we have seen with our eyes, which we have looked upon, and our hands have handled of the word of life; that which we have seen and heard, declare we unto you.' Ezekiel was first to eat the roll, Ezek. iii. 1–3; not only to see it, and to hear it, but to eat it. Ministers must first eat themselves, then feed others. We are not to speak by hearsay, to deliver God's message as a mere narration, but out of a deep impression on the heart. What cometh from the heart and from experience is quick and lively.

[2.] For the honour of God. Carnal ministers bring a reproach upon the ordinances: 1 Sam. ii. 17, 'The sin of the young men was very great before the Lord, for men abhorred the offering of the Lord.' Who will take meat out of a leprous hand?

[3.] To answer the types of the law. Aaron and his sons were sanctified for the Levitical priesthood, Exod. xxix. 4; to be washed with blood and oil, to be washed in the great laver, sprinkled with blood, anointed with oil, which denotes remission of sins, regeneration, the gifts of the Spirit: 1 John v. 8, 'There are three that bear witness in earth, the Spirit, the water, and the blood.' Every office should have a solemn consecration.

Use 1. Ministers should look to their inward call. They that are designed to serve God in a special manner must look after special purity. It breedeth atheism, when we do not live up to our doctrine. People will say they must say something for their living.

2. Let people look to their choice of ministers. There is a great deal of difference between an eloquent and an experienced pastor.

Secondly, We now come to the means or manner how Christ's request is is to be accomplished, 'by thy truth,' ἐν τῇ ἀληθείᾳ. It may be rendered *in* thy truth, or *by* thy truth, or *through* thy truth; as ver. 19, ἐν ἀληθείᾳ, without an article, 'that they may be sanctified through the truth;' or, as in the margin, 'truly sanctified;' but we better render it 'by the truth;' there is an article τῇ, not in truth, but in the truth; and it is presently added, 'Thy word is truth.' So that it noteth not the kind of their sanctification, but the instrument and means. Now these words 'by thy truth' may be understood either of God's faithfulness or his revealed will, both which are called his truth. Of God's faithfulness, as ver. 11, τήρησον ἐν ὀνόματι σοῦ; so here, ἁγίασον ἐν τῇ ἀληθείᾳ, as 'keep them by thy power:' so sanctify them by, or according to thy truth and faithfulness. But this exposition, though plausible, yet is not so proper, because it is presently added, 'Thy word is truth,' By truth, then, is meant, not his faithfulness, but his revealed will. Now God hath revealed his will by the light of nature, or by the light of his word. That will of God which is revealed by the light of nature is called truth; so the Gentiles are charged, Rom. i. 18, with 'holding the truth in unrighteousness,' τὸ γνῶστον; 'that which may be known of God,' ver. 19, is called truth. How came the Gentiles by the truth, who are strangers to the covenant of promise? The apostle answereth, much of God was known to them. But this truth that is here spoken of is the will of God made known in his word, or the knowledge of things necessary to salvation, concerning God and his worship, first delivered by the prophets, afterwards explained by Christ himself to the apostles, and by them consigned to the church. Now the truths delivered in the word may be referred to two heads—law and gospel. The distinction in Christ's time was law and prophets. In this place Christ chiefly intendeth the gospel; the truth which they were sent to preach to others, Christ would have them to have an experience of it themselves. And it is notable that in many places of scripture the gospel is called the truth, not only in opposition to human writings, but also with respect to the law and other parts of scripture, because it is truth by way of eminency, as we call the plague the sickness, as being the chief of the kind.

Before I come to the observations I must clear up the latter part of the text, 'Thy word is truth.' Why is this added? I answer— Either by way of explication, or by way of argument and reason.

1. By way of explication. Christ would pray intelligibly; some might ask, as Pilate did, 'What is truth?' John xviii. 38. Christ answereth, 'Thy word is truth.' The word is the authentic and public record of the church; the truth whereby we are sanctified is nowhere else to be found; all pretended truths are hereby to be examined.

2. Or else by way of argument and reason why Christ would have them to be sanctified by the truth, that they might have a saving experience of the power of it, and so the better preach it to others; then we know the truth of the word, when it sanctifieth.

This premised, I come to the point—

Doct. That God sanctifieth by his truth. I shall open the point in these propositions.

1. God's way of working is by light; and in infusing grace he beginneth with the understanding. He dealeth with man as a rational creature; and therefore not only teacheth, but draweth and sanctifieth the heart by enlightening the mind. As the rising of the sun doth not only dispel darkness but mists and vapours, so doth a saving light not only dispel ignorance but lusts. This way is spiritual life begun: Eph. v. 14, 'Awake thou that sleepest, and arise from the dead, and Christ shall give thee light.' A man would have thought the apostle should rather have said, And Christ, shall give thee life, than 'give thee light.' It is the apostle's word; ἀποφώσει σοὶ, he shall shine upon thee, rather than ζωποιήσει, he shall quicken thee. But light is enough; the power of grace breaketh in upon the soul by the light of the gospel; as it is said of the natural life, John i. 4, 'In him was life, and the life was the light of men.' Reason and understanding are the fountain of life to men, so is spiritual reason and spiritual understanding to the soul. If the mind of a man were once spiritual, enlightened, and possessed of the ways of God, the heart could not utterly reject them.

There is a notional illumination, that, like a winter sun, shineth but warmeth not, leaveth no comfort and profit upon the heart. But a spiritual light is always effectual; for though the will and the judgment are distinct faculties, and the will is averse as the understanding is blind, yet God doth never soundly and thoroughly convince the judgment, but he moveth and inclineth the will. If we know things as we ought to know, 'as the truth is in Jesus,' Eph. iv. 21, the, heart must needs close with the ways of God; for the will of man is not brutish, but reasonable, and acteth reasonably. Answerably to the discovery of good or ill in the understanding, there is a prosecution or aversation in the will. Therefore a thorough conviction of judgment must be the ground of grace in the heart; for God worketh in us, not only by a powerful and real efficacy, but agreeably to an intelligent nature, by teaching, persuading, counselling: nothing can be wrought in this moral way unless light and knowledge go before.

2. It must be a true, and not a false light. Truth sanctifieth, and error defileth: Titus i. 1, 'According to the acknowledgment of the truth that is after godliness.' Right thoughts of God and his ways preserve an awe in the heart, which both restraineth and reneweth. Τὰ ὄρθα δόγματα περὶ Θεοῦ λεγόμενα ἀγιάζει τὴν ψυχὴν, saith Chrysostom. It is truth that cleanseth the heart; error leaveth a stain and defilement. The understanding and the will are like the head and stomach; a corrupt heart blindeth the mind, and a blind mind corrupts the heart; they mutually vitiate one another: as in a ruinous house, the upper room being uncovered, lets down the rain to founder the supporters below, and the rottenness of the supporters below weakeneth all above. Erroneous persons are generally represented in scripture as vain and sensual: Jude 8, 'These filthy dreamers defile the flesh.' First there is dreaming, and then defilement; error maketh way for looseness, and a vain mind for vile affections. Partly by God's just judgment: some opinions seem to be remote, and lie far enough from practice, yet the persons that profess them are generally loose. Nay, some errors seem to encourage strictness, as doctrines concerning the power of nature, and the merit of good actions; but we find it is otherwise. Duty is best pressed upon God's terms: Phil. ii. 12, 13, 'Wherefore, my beloved, as ye have always obeyed, not as in my presence only, but now much more in my absence, work out your own salvation with fear and trembling; for it is God that worketh in you both to will and to do of his own good pleasure.' By the judgment of God, such are of loosest life. God will have his glory kept unstained. Idolatry is expressed by whoredom; bodily uncleanness ends in spiritual:[1] Hosea iv. 12, 13, 'My people ask counsel of their stocks, and their staff declareth unto them; for the spirit of whoredoms have caused them to err, and they go a-whoring from under their God. They sacrifice upon the tops of the mountains, and burn incense upon the hills, under oaks, and poplars and elms, because the shadow thereof is good. Therefore your daughters shall commit whoredoms, and your spouses shall commit adultery.' So Rom. i. 23, 24, 'They changed the glory of the incorruptible God into an image made like to corruptible man, and to birds, and four-footed beasts, and

---

[1] Qu. 'Spiritual uncleanness ends in bodily'?—Ed.

creeping things. Wherefore God also gave them up to uncleanness, through the lusts of their own hearts to dishonour their own bodies between themselves.' Partly by a natural efficacy; the spirit is embased by error, and all false principles have a secret and pestilential influence on the life and practice. We lose a sense and care of piety, if we have not a right apprehension of God's essence and will; a frame of truth keepeth an awe. Therefore, where there is so much truth as to sanctify, yet because it is mingled with falsehood, there is no such reverence of God, no such strictness. Unbelief is the mother of sin; misbelief is the nurse of it. In error there is a sinful confederacy between the rational and the sensual part, and so carnal affections are gratified with carnal doctrines.

3. Every true light will not serve the turn, but it must be the light of the word. God hath reserved this honour of sanctifying the heart to the doctrine of the scriptures, to evidence their divine original: James i. 18, 'Of his own will begat he us with the word of truth.' The great change that is wrought in the heart of man is by the word. A moral lecture may make a man change his life, but the word of God maketh a man change his heart, as Xenocrates' moral lectures made Pollemo leave his vicious and sensual course of life; but regeneration is only found in the school of Christ: 'He hath begotten us by the word of truth.' And the ordinance of preaching the word is consecrated to this purpose: Eph. v. 26, 'That he might sanctify them by the washing of water through the word.' There are other occasional helps, but this is the instituted means. God will work no other way in his ordinary and revealed course, and will accept no other obedience and sanctification but by the word. Holiness, or that piety which is proper and genuine, is wrought by a divine truth, otherwise it is superstition, not godliness; civility, not holiness of conversation. Though men have never so good an inclination, yet because they have not a divine revelation for their warrant, it is but a bastard religion, superstition, or framing a strictness of our own, accompanied with opposition against the truth. The word and Spirit are in conjunction: Isa. lix. 21, 'My Spirit that is upon thee, and my words which I have put in thy mouth, shall not depart out of thy mouth,' &c. These act in conjunction, and it is for the honour of the scriptures that God hath annexed them: 1 Thes. v. 19, 20, 'Quench not the Spirit; despise not prophesying.' Preaching of the word and pouring out of the Spirit go together.

4. Every part of the truth worketh not, but only the gospel, which is the truth, $\kappa a\tau'$ $\dot{\epsilon}\xi o\chi\grave{\eta}\nu$. The law showeth us our spots, and the gospel cleanseth and washeth them away. The work of the law is preparation, but that which hath a special and direct influence upon sanctification is the gospel: John xv. 3, 'Now ye are clean through the word which I have spoken to you;' and that was the gospel privilege. This pulleth in the heart to God, that we may be partakers of his grace. Moses brought them to the borders, but Joshua brought them into the land of Canaan. The apostle appealeth to the experience of believers: Gal. iii. 2, 'This only would I learn of you, received ye the Spirit by the works of the law, or by the hearing of faith?' Though the Spirit may be received by the preaching of any part of

canonical scripture, yet most usually by the preaching of the gospel.
The Lord would give us this sensible and authentic proof of the truth
and excellency of the gospel, that we receive the Spirit of regeneration
by it, and not by the law.   It is the instrument by which God useth
to confer the Spirit.   So 2 Peter i. 4, ' To us are given exceeding great
and precious promises, that by these we may be made partakers of the
divine nature.'   What part of the word worketh the heart to a conformity to God, likeneth us in holiness to God ?   The great and
precious promises.   It is not by moral strains, nor by terrible threatenings ; these have their use in their place ; but by the great and precious
promises, as God was in the still voice.

5. The gospel worketh not unless it be accompanied with the Spirit.
There is a great deal of difference between seeing things in the light
of reason, and seeing things in the light of the Spirit.   Truth represented in the light of reason begets but a human faith, leaveth a weak
impression, and hath but a weak operation upon the soul; but things
represented in the light of the Spirit worketh quite otherwise ; there
is not only a notional irradiation, but an experimental feeling ; they
see another manner of beauty and excellency in Christ, a vanity in
worldly delights, which they never saw before.   Running water and
strong-water differ not in colour, but in taste and virtue : John xvi.
13, ' When he the Spirit of truth is come, he will guide you into all
truth ;' 1 John ii. 27, ' The anointing which ye have received of him
abideth in you ; and ye need not that any man teach you, but as the
same anointing teacheth you of all things.'   Most men content themselves with a superficial belief ; they have but a human knowledge of
divine things, and therefore their souls are not carried out to holiness,
love, fear, trust, obedience ; they have a cold and naked apprehension :
literal knowledge is washy and weak, it worketh not : 1 Peter i. 22,
' Seeing ye have purified your souls, in obeying the truth through the
Spirit.'

6. This must not only be represented in the power and demonstration of the Spirit, but received and applied by faith.   Sanctification
is sometimes ascribed to the gospel, and sometimes to faith, which
receiveth the gospel : Acts xv. 9, ' Purifying their hearts by faith.'
Our hearts are purified by the word of truth : 1 Peter i. 22, ' Seeing
that ye have purified your souls in obeying the truth, through the
Spirit.'   Here they were purified by faith.   The word worketh not
without an act on our part as well as on God's : ' The word preached
did not profit them, not being mixed with faith in them that heard it,'
Heb. iv. 2 ; as a plaster worketh not till it be applied to the sore.
Nay, the apostle's word implieth more ; the word must not only be
applied to the soul, but mingled with the soul, $\sigma\upsilon\gamma\kappa\epsilon\kappa\rho\alpha\mu\acute{\epsilon}\nu\circ\varsigma$.   As in
a medicine, the ingredients must be mixed together to do good ; so if
we have the word, we must have the Spirit, and we must have faith ;
mix it altogether, and then it worketh.   Faith receiveth the word as
a divine and infallible truth, and that begets an awe.

In short, faith working to sanctification, apprehends the love of God,
the blood of Christ, the promises, precepts of the word ; and by all
these it is ever purging and working out corruption.   By apprehending
the love of God : Gal. v. 6, ' In Christ Jesus neither circumcision

availeth anything, nor uncircumcision, but faith that worketh by love.'
Shall I love that which God hateth?   'Oh! do not this abominable
thing that I hate,' Jer. xliv. 4.   Faith representeth God pleading
thus : Is this thy kindness to thy friend? do I thus requite God for
all his kindness to me in Christ?   There is an exasperation against
lusts.   It maketh use of the blood of Christ: 1 John i. 7, ' The blood
of Jesus Christ his Son cleanseth us from all sins ;' Heb. ix. 14, ' How
much more shall the blood of Christ, who through the eternal Spirit
offered himself without spot to God, purge your consciences from dead
works to serve the living God?'   That is an excellent purger.   In
outward purging it is the water and the soap cleanseth, but the hand
of the laundress applieth it, and rubbeth the clothes that are washed.
Faith apprehendeth the blood of Christ to purge the conscience, it
waiteth for the sanctifying virtue of his blood, and the grace purchased
thereby.   So faith maketh use of the promises; this giveth faith
encouragement to expect glorious rewards.   Assistance is purchased,
and acceptance is promised: 2 Cor. vii. 1, ' Having therefore these
promises, dearly beloved, let us cleanse ourselves from all filthiness of
the flesh and spirit, perfecting holiness in the fear of God.'   Then
faith constantly maketh use of the precepts and counsels of the word,
by which sin is discovered and taxed.   When the word is received by
faith, there goeth a light with it to see sin after another manner,
although a man did not know it before.   Faith persuadeth us that
the commands of God are just and equal.   There is a believing commands, as well as promises; this is a command from God : Ps. cxix.
66, ' Teach me good judgment and knowledge, for I have believed
thy commandments.'

SERMON XXVII.

Sanctify them through thy truth : thy word is truth.—JOHN XVII. 17.

THIRDLY, I now proceed to the reasons why God sanctifieth by his
truth.   It is most suitable to God's honour and to man's nature.

First, To God's honour.   It was meet that God should give a rule
to the creatures, or else how should they know his will?   And then it
was meet to honour this rule, by owning it above all other doctrines,
by the concomitant operation of his Spirit.   This is the authentic
proof; the efficacy of the word is a pledge of the truth of it: John
viii. 32, ' And ye shall know the truth, and the truth shall make ye
free,' from the bondage of sin, the devil, and death.   A wicked man
cannot have an absolute assurance of the truth of the word; he hath
no feeling of the power of it.   There is a great deal of do.   How do
you prove the scriptures to be the word of God?   A believer hath the
testimony in his own heart: 1 John v. 10, ' He that believeth in the
Son of God hath the testimony in himself.'   His conscience and his
heart are set at liberty by water and blood.   This made the apostles
bold, and should make ministers so : Rom. i. 16, ' I am not ashamed

of the gospel of Christ, for it is the power of God unto salvation.' We should not be ashamed to preach it, and you should not be ashamed to profess it: ' It is the power of God.' God will not associate and join the powerful operation of his Spirit with any other doctrine. So David, when he commendeth the law, by which he doth not mean the decalogue, but the whole word of God : Ps. xix. 7–9, ' The law of the Lord is perfect, converting the soul; the testimony of the Lord is sure, making wise the simple. The statutes of the Lord are right, rejoicing the soul; the commandment of the Lord is pure, enlightening the eyes; the fear of the Lord is clean, enduring for ever; the judgments of the Lord are true, and righteous altogether.' He had spoken before of the excellency of the sun, now of the word, intimating that the word of God is as necessary for the heart as the sun is for the world. We can as well be without the sun as without the bible. But how doth he evidence it ? From the effects upon the heart and conscience : comfort and grace are two great evidences of the perfection of the word. No doctrine in the world, save this divine truth set down in scripture, is able to discover the sin and misery of man, the remedy and relief of it in Christ. No doctrine save this alone can effectually humble a soul, and convert it to God, make it sensible of the loss by sin, and restore it to a better condition.

Secondly, It is more suitable to man's nature. The word is more morally accommodated to work upon the heart of man than any other instrument, means, or doctrine in the world.

1. The precepts of it. It is the copy of God's holiness, the light by which we see everything in its own colours. The light of nature is ἔργον νόμου, ' the work of the law,' Rom. ii. 14, 15. It taketh notice of gross acts of sin, and the outward work of duty; they made conscience to abstain from gross acts of sin, and to perform outward acts of piety and devotion, as offering sacrifices and prayers. But now there is an excellent spirit of holiness that breatheth in the word, and all matters of duty are advanced to their greatest perfection : Ps. cxix. 96, ' Thy commandment is exceeding broad;' of a vast extent and latitude, comprising every motion, thought, and circumstance in duties; not only the act is required, but the frame of heart is regarded; not only sins, but lusts are forbidden. If ever there were an instrument fitted to do a thing, the word is fitted to promote holiness, the true purity that is pleasing to God.

2. The patterns and examples of the word. We miscarry by low examples, and learn looseness and carelessness one by another. Therefore the word of God, to elevate holiness to the highest extent, presseth not only the examples of the saints, whose memorials are left upon record in the word, but the holiness of the angels, yea, the holiness of God himself. The highest aim doth no hurt; he will shoot further who aimeth at a star than he that aimeth at a shrub : ' Be ye followers of them who through faith and patience have inherited the promises,' Heb. vi. 12 ; ' Thy will be done on earth, as it is done in heaven,' Mat. vi. 10 ; ' Be ye holy, as I am holy,' 1 Peter i. 15. Communion begets conformity. We need all kinds of examples ; high examples, that we may not rest in any low degrees and beginnings of holiness ; low examples, that we may think it possible. We are not

angels, but men and women, ὁμοιοπαθεῖς, of like affections, that have
the same natural interests, natural wants with others.   It is a trodden
path ; in the way to heaven you may see the footsteps of the saints.

3. Excellent rewards, and fit arguments to induce us to the practice of holiness: 2 Cor. vii. 1, ‘ Having these promises, dearly beloved,
let us cleanse ourselves from all the filthiness of flesh and spirit, perfecting holiness in the fear of God ;’ 2 Peter i. 4, ‘ Whereby are given
unto us exceeding great and precious promises, that by these ye might
be partakers of the divine nature, having escaped the corruption that
is in the world through lust.’   God covenants with us, as if we were free-
born ; to interest our hearts in the love and practice of holiness, we have
as much propounded as we can wish for, nay, and more : 1 Cor. ii. 9,
‘ Eye hath not seen, nor ear heard, neither have entered into the heart
of man the things which God hath prepared for them that love him.’
Lactantius saith of the heathens, *Virtutis vim non sentiunt, cujus præ-
mium ignorant*—They feel not the power of virtue, because they are
ignorant of the reward of virtue.   Life and glory, and the great things
to come, are powerful motives ; can you meet with the like elsewhere ?
All creatures seek their own perfection.   Philosophy is to seek of a
sure reward and encouragement.

4. Our many advantages in Christ.   We have not only encouragement offered, but help and assistance.   Christ hath purchased grace to
make us holy : 1 Peter ii. 24, ‘ Who his own self bare our sins in his
own body on the tree, that we, being dead unto sin, might live to
righteousness ; by whose stripes ye were healed.’   He hath not only
purchased the rewards of grace, to wit, that God should not deal with
us in sovereignty ; but purchased the abilities of grace, ‘ redeemed us
from a vain conversation,’ 1 Peter i. 18.   By his death the covenant is
made a testament, and all the precepts are turned into so many promises and legacies.   Christ will give what he requireth.   All excuse
is taken away from laziness, and wickedness is no longer allowed the
plea of weakness.   There is help offered in Christ.

5. Terrible threatenings.   The word is impatient of being denied ;
it would have holiness upon any terms.   There is somewhat propounded to our fear as well as our hope ; not only the loss of happiness :
Heb. xii. 14, ‘ Follow peace with all men, and holiness, without which
no man shall see God,’ which is loss enough to an ingenuous spirit ;
but the forfeiture of the soul into eternal torments, without ease,
without end : ‘ Go, ye cursed, into everlasting fire.’   God hath a
prison for obstinate creatures, a worm that never dies, a fire that
never goes out.   Whose heart doth not tremble at the mention of
these things ?   We cannot endure the torment of one night under a
feverish distemper ; how shall we think of lying down in everlasting
burnings ?

6. The word presseth all this with such a majesty and power, that
it astonisheth the conscience, and maketh the hearts and souls of men
to quake within them.   Felix trembled at the mention of judgment to
come.   There is so much of God in the word, that if it doth not renew
men, it doth restrain them, maketh them tremble ; where it hath least
force, it cometh with a manifestation of divine authority upon the conscience.   Lactantius saith, *Nihil ponderis habent illa præcepta, quæ sunt*

humana. There is no such majesty in human precepts. *Nemo credit, quia tam se hominem putat esse qui audivit quam illum qui prædicat.* Man is not astonished by man. *Verba dedi, verba reddidi.* But now the word of God searcheth the heart, pincheth the conscience, and where it worketh least it maketh men to quake within themselves. It is said, Mat. vii. 28, 29, 'The people were astonished at Christ's doctrine, for he taught them as one having authority, and not as the scribes.' God's word cometh with evidence and conviction upon the conscience, that they admire the power of it; there is a sovereign majesty in it, the draught is like the author. Thus you see what a powerful instrument the word is, even in a moral way; therefore the fittest means whereunto God should join his assistance to work on the heart of man.

Use 1. Of information.

1. It informeth us what a treasure truth is, and what a value we should put upon it. There are two things in the world that God is very tender of—his truth, and his saints. In the controversy about toleration, men, on the one side, have urged the danger of meddling with saints; on the other side, others have urged the value of truth. If the whole controversy did depend upon this issue, which are to be most respected, the truth or the saints, since God is tender of both, it would soon be decided; for besides this, that it is strange that they only who are called saints should be afraid of a vigorous prosecution and defence of the truth, it is clear truth must have the pre-eminence, for it is truth that maketh saints, and we had need be more tender of the root than of the branches.

2. It informeth us that out of the true religion there is no salvation, because there is no true holiness, and without holiness no man shall see God: Heb. xii. 14, 'Follow peace with all men, and holiness, without which no man shall see God.' It is not without peace; the necessity is not laid upon that, but holiness; for peace is often broken for strictness' sake. A man that is faithful and sincere may have little of the world's respect; but now without the true religion there is no holiness, that is clear. Hence it is said, ' Sanctify them by thy truth.' There may be civility, and the exactness of a moral course, counterfeit grace; but there can be no true sanctification, because the heart can never be good that is ignorant of the truth and poisoned with error. There may be superstition, which is but a bastard religion; there may be a good life, but there cannot be a good heart, no true comfort, and true grace. *Anima, que a Deo fornicata est, casta esse non potest.* He that believeth ill, can never live well. Grace and truth are twins, that live and die together. Moral virtue is very defective in itself. *Sapientia eorum plerumque abscondit vitia ; non abscindit*—All their craft was to hide a lust, not to root it out.

3. That they have not a sound apprehension of truth that have no grace. There may be a naked and inactive apprehension that is not accompanied with power; they learn truth by rote, and rest in a vain speculation, but have no strength to perform their duty : 2 Tim. iii. 5, compared with Rom. ii. 20. What in one place is called ' a form of godliness,' is in the other called ' a form of knowledge.' Poor, slight, and superficial apprehensions of the truth ; they take up truth, not

upon any divine testimony or evidence of the Spirit, but upon the credit and authority of men, the practice and profession of the nation, or the injunctions of a civil state. This is the account of most men's truth and faith. Alas! truth thus received entereth not upon the heart. Men gain but a disciplinary knowledge; a literal knowledge and a spiritual knowledge differ: Eph. iv. 21, ' If so be that ye have heard of him, and have been taught by him, as the truth is in Jesus.' When a man receiveth it out of the hands of the Spirit of Christ, it frameth and disposeth the heart to godliness. So Col. i. 6, 'Since ye heard of it, and knew the grace of God in truth.' The tasting of a thing excelleth the reading of it; the true, inward, powerful, affectionate knowledge affecteth the heart, and altereth and changeth it. A man knoweth no more of Christ than he valueth, esteemeth, and affecteth, and which puts the whole inward man into a holy spiritual frame. Good principles, if heartily embraced, will breed a good conversation. The point needeth to be heeded in these times, when knowledge is increased, but practice and strictness suffereth an abatement and decay. *Boni esse desinunt, postquam docti evaserint.* What strength and power of religion possesses the heart? When you know the truth, doth it carry you to God and godliness?

4. They that are above scriptures have no true holiness. God sanctifieth by the truth. It is strange how charity overreacheth to saint antiscripturists and men above ordinances; whereas it is the true ground and reason of sanctification. As Bernard saith of some, that whilst they plead for the salvation of heathens, scarce show themselves christians; so I am afraid our excessive charity to men argueth little affection to God. God accepteth no holiness but word-holiness, and worketh holiness no other way. I doubt they that despise prophesying quench the Spirit. When men neglect and contemn the word of God, they dam up the fountain of holiness.

5. What is the true witness of the scripture's certainty? Not the testimony of the church, but feeling the sanctifying virtue of it. It is good to take the testimony of the church at first, as we take a medicine from others upon their experience; but we must not rest in it: 1 Thes. i. 5, ' For our gospel came not unto you in word only, but also in power, and in the Holy Ghost, and in much assurance;' this giveth certainty. At first we believe upon the church's saying, as the woman commended Christ to her citizens: John iv. 42, ' Now we believe, not because of thy saying, for we have heard him ourselves, and know that this is indeed the Christ, the Saviour of the world.' There is a preparative human faith; as in taking pills, we do not chew them, but swallow them. It is not good to be disputing away our hopes. But we should not rest in this, but labour to get an experience of the power of the truth upon our hearts.

6. The difference between civility and sanctification. Civility is wrought by mere moral education, according to natural principles, without any knowledge, or so much as a desire to be acquainted with the word of God. Thus many are careful of common honesty in matters of traffic and commerce, obedience to civil laws, being restrained from gross enormities, but have no true grace; but in true holiness we are inclined by the word: 1 Peter ii. 2, ' As new-born babes desire the

sincere milk of the word, that ye may grow thereby.' This is true holiness, when we conform and subject ourselves in heart and practice to the will of God, revealed in the word. The word of God must be reason and rule. Reason: 1 Thes. v. 18, 'This is the will of God concerning you;' and rule: Gal. vi. 16, 'As many as walk according to this rule, peace be on them.' Why do you do this? as the children must ask their parents, 'Why do ye keep the passover?' Still all must be examined by the word: John iii. 21, 'He that doth truth cometh to the light, that his deeds may be made manifest that they are wrought of God;' he trieth every action by it. Only the word is our rule in all our actions; we seek to it as our guide, obey it for truth's sake.

Use 2. Exhortation.

1. Beware of error. It is a defiling thing; the more mixture of falsehood, the less awe of God upon the soul, and the more carnal affections are gratified. A constant use of the word discovers sin.

2. To press you to wait upon God for the purifying of your hearts through the word, in the use of the word, through the Spirit, to look for the purification and sanctification of your souls. Here I should press you to take heed *that* you hear, *how* you hear, and *what* you hear.

[1.] That you hear. You need wait upon God, and hearken diligently. The apostle infers it: James i. 18, 'Of his own will begat he us by the word of truth.' What then? 'Therefore be swift to hear.' Continually you will find some new enforcement or new consideration to promote your holiness and sanctification.

[2.] Take heed what ye hear, Mark iv. 24. You must get the distinguishing ear; that as the mouth tasteth meats, so the ear may taste doctrines, and you may judge of things that differ.

[3.] Take heed how you hear, Luke viii. 18; that is, wait for the operations of the Spirit, do not hear carelessly, negligently. It is said, Acts x. 44, 'While Peter was speaking those things, the Holy Ghost fell upon them.' While we are speaking to you there are many good motions stirred up in your hearts. Take heed how you hear, that the blessing may not escape from you.

'Thy word is truth.'—The point which I am now to discuss is, the truth of the word. In managing this discourse I shall show—

1. What necessity there is that God should give us his word, or a declaration of his will.

2. Where we shall infallibly find this word or declaration of his will.

3. Of what concernment it is to be established in the truth of this word.

4. Whether it be possible that carnal men, remaining so, can have any assurance of this truth; or whether it be only left to be cleared up infallibly to the soul, by the light and working of the Spirit.

First, What necessity there is of God's word, or some outward signification of his will. An absolute necessity of an outward rule there is not. God might immediately reveal himself to the heart of man; he who made the heart can stamp it with the full knowledge of his will. But the written word is best for God's honour, and for the safety of religion, and because of the weakness of our nature.

1. For the honour of God, that he should give man a rule. You

know all creatures that God hath made, they have a rule without themselves, by which they are guided and directed in their operations. It is God's own privilege to be a rule to himself. The angels have a rule, that is distinct from their essence. And in innocency, though God stamped the knowledge of his will immediately upon man's heart, that Adam's heart was as it were his bible, yet his rule was distinguished from his essence, otherwise he could not have sinned against God. If man were his own rule there would be an impossibility of sinning, and so there would be an intrenchment upon God's own privilege. You know it is God's own privilege that his act is his rule, and therefore it is impossible that God should sin. Look, as when a carpenter choppeth and squareth a piece of timber, there is a line and rule without him, by which he is guided and directed: if it were to be supposed that his hand could never strike amiss, that would be his rule, he would need no line or rule without him. But this is proper to no creature, it is God's own privilege that his essence and his rule are not distinguished; but still a man should not share with him in his peculiar privilege, therefore he hath given him a rule. Besides, if man were a rule to himself, there would be no room for rewards; there is no commendation nor praise where there is a natural necessity of doing good ; as stocks and stones are not capable of a reward for not sinning, because they cannot sin.

2. For the safety of religion, now man is fallen, that he might not obtrude fancies on his neighbour: Isa. viii. 20, 'To the law and to the testimony : if they speak not according to this word, it is because there is no light in them.' Let it be voice or oracle, all is to be measured by the outward rule which God hath given to the church.

3. In respect of man, to repair the defects of nature, and to satisfy the desires of nature.

[1.] To repair the defects of nature. Fallen man is brutish, and knows not how to carve out a right worship for God, or a rule of commerce between him and us. We have not light enough in our own hearts for such a work. You see what sorry devices of worship man frameth when he is destitute of the knowledge of God's will, and left to the workings of his own heart. The apostle observes it of the philosophers, Rom. i. 22, 23 ; the wisest of heathens, when they sat abrood upon religion, it proved but a monstrous misshapen piece: 'Professing themselves to be wise, they became fools, and changed the glory of the uncorruptible God into an image made like to corruptible man, and to birds, and four-footed beasts, and creeping things.' You see how sottish man, if left once to himself, is ready to worship a stick, or straw, or piece of red cloth, instead of God. Though the knowledge of the law of God be written on man's heart, as it was on Adam's, who was his own bible, yet it is so blurred and defaced that we cannot read the mind of God in our own heart. It is true there are some scattered fragments and relics, and some obscure characters, that will teach us something of morality and duties, to fit us for commerce between man and man, but very little to teach us how to have commerce with God. The Gentiles have the work of the law written upon their hearts: Rom. ii. 14, 15, 'For when the Gentiles, which have not the law, do by nature the things contained in the law, these having not the law,

are a law unto themselves ; which show the work of the law written in
their hearts, their consciences also bearing witness, and their thoughts
in the meanwhile accusing, or else excusing one another ;’ that is, they
are sensible of the necessity of external obedience, but nature goes no
further.   There is no article of belief, if we consider it with all its
circumstances, and in that exact manner that is propounded to us in
the word of God, that could ever have entered into the heart of man.
And therefore, since man’s heart is so weak, we need a rule that we
might know God’s will.   His works indeed declare God’s glory, that
indeed there is an infinite, eternal, incomprehensible power, that made
all things and guides all things : Ps. xix. 1, ‘ The heavens declare the
glory of God, and the firmament showeth forth his handiwork ;’ but
they speak nothing of the fall, of the restitution by Christ, of the
mystery of the Trinity, and those glorious representations that are now
made of God in the scriptures ; and therefore there was a necessity in
this kind to repair the defects of nature.

[2.] To satisfy the desires of nature.   There are two things that
render us unsatisfied with the light of nature—an insatiable desire of
knowledge in the soul, and a trouble of heart about misery, sin, and
death.

(1.) An insatiable desire of more knowledge, and full satisfaction
concerning God and the way to enjoy him.   Reason, you know, is the
property and excellency of man, and his privilege above the beasts ;
now reason desires to replenish itself with knowledge and perfection in
its kind.   The stomach no more desires true food for sustenance than
a man doth knowledge.   Man that is born to know hath a strong desire
to it, and delight in it when it is increased.   This was Adam’s bait in
paradise : Gen. iii. 6, ‘ The tree was good for food, and pleasant to the
eyes, and a tree to be desired to make one wise.’   And it is a mighty
delectation, even to man’s natural soul, to view any truth ; the contemplation of it is a mighty rejoicing and delight.   Therefore the word
of God may beget, even in natural men, such a kind of delectation : Ps. xix. 10, ‘ More to be desired are they than gold, yea, than
fine gold ; sweeter also than the honey and the honeycomb.’   They
rejoice the soul because they fill it with light.   That there is such
an impatient thirst and desire after more knowledge than we have
in ourselves appears by the very idolatry of the Gentiles ; they were
unsatisfied with their own thoughts, they would know more, and that
was the reason they were so ready to close with every fancy that was
offered to them.   As a man that is very hungry, and almost famished,
will fasten upon any food that comes next to hand, many times that
which is most hurtful and noxious, so man, being desirous of some
more knowledge concerning the nature of God, when he can meet with
no other, he fastens upon gross superstitions and fables, whatever comes
next to hand.   Some outward rule and direction they will have, a bad
one rather than none at all, out of a despair to find a better.

(2.) As there is an impatient thirst and desire after knowledge, so
there is a trouble in conscience about misery, death, and sin.   This
bondage is natural, and we cannot be eased of it without some knowledge of a means of reconciliation.   Nature is full of inquiries which
way God will be pleased : Micah vi. 6, 7, ‘ Wherewith shall I come

before the Lord, and bow myself before the high God? Shall I come before him with burnt-offerings, with calves of a year old? will the Lord be pleased with thousands of rams, or with ten thousands of rivers of oil? shall I give my first-born for my transgression, the fruit of my body for the sin of my soul?' What shall I do to pacify God? This is the great inquiry of nature. Nature knows that some satisfaction must be given to offended justice; and until conscience have a firm ground of rest it will not be quiet. This put the heathens upon such barbarous actions as giving the first-born for the sin of their soul; and this made the Jews so unsatisfied; they looked no farther than the sacrifice: Heb. ix. 9, 'In which were offered both gifts and sacrifices, that could not make him that did the service perfect, as pertaining to the conscience; that is, their conscience had no firm ground of satisfaction and quiet by sacrifices. Therefore you shall see how God makes use of this advantage, this dissatisfaction, without some external rule, and the knowledge of means how to be reconciled: Jer. vi. 16, 'Thus saith the Lord, Stand ye in the ways and see, and ask for the old paths, Where is the good way? and walk therein, and ye shall find rest for your souls.' As if the Lord had said, There is now a dissatisfaction, a natural bondage upon man. Now look to all the religions in the world, see where you can find rest for your souls. God leaves it upon that issue and determination. These things show there must be some external rule for guiding of the creature. It is for God's glory, for the safety of religion, to repair the defects of nature and to satisfy the desires of nature.

Secondly, What is God's word? This is necessary to be cleared; for the question is not so much, whether God's word be truth? as whether this or that be the word of God or no? This will be easily granted by every one that hath the sense of a godhead, that what God speaks must needs be true; for God is so infinitely wise that he cannot be deceived, and so infinitely just and true that he will not deceive us, and so omnipotent that he cannot be jealous of our knowledge, and so gracious that he is not envious of our knowledge, as the devil would insinuate: Gen. iii. 5, 'For God doth know that in the day ye eat thereof, then your eyes shall be opened, and ye shall be as gods, knowing good and evil.' It will be no infringement to his interest if we should know his nature and his will. But the great question is, what we should take for the word of God? Now that we may have a sure ground in this kind, let us consider how he hath revealed himself to man. The dispensations of God are several:—(1.) To Adam; (2.) To the world; (3.) To the church.

1. To Adam. His bible was his heart; the law was written there, and God preached to him immediately, and by oracle gave him all extraordinary commands, and the book of the creatures for his contemplation; not so much to better his knowledge, as to increase his reverence.

2. To the world. To heathens God gave the book of nature, which was more than they made use of, and therefore he stopped there: Ps. xix. 1–3, 'The heavens declare the glory of God, and the firmament showeth his handiwork. Day unto day uttereth speech, and night unto night showeth knowledge. There is no speech nor language

where their voice is not heard,' &c. This revelation God hath made of himself, even to all nations; they have sun and moon to look upon, and the structure of the heavens to behold, which are so many pledges of the excellency and infiniteness of God: Rom. i. 19, 20, ' Because that which may be known of God is manifest to them, for God hath showed it unto them; for the invisible things of him from the creation of the world are clearly seen, being understood by the things that are made, even his eternal power and godhead; so that they are without excuse;' Acts xiv. 17, ' Nevertheless, he left not himself without witness, in that he did good, and gave us rain from heaven and fruitful seasons, filling our hearts with food and gladness.' In the book of nature there is the rough draught of God's will. Trismegistus said it was *liber unus divinitate plenus*—creation was nothing else but one book, that was full of the glory of God and his excellency. God spake to them by things, not by words. This, with some instincts of conscience, the relics of the fall, was all the heathens had. Conscience was God's deputy, to put them in mind of a judge; and the heavens put them in mind of a God. Look, as Job's messengers said, ' I alone am escaped to tell thee,' so there are some few relics and principles alone escaped out of the ruins of the fall, to tell us somewhat of God, and somewhat of a judge. That light proclaims everywhere, and speaks to every nation, and proclaims it aloud to all people, kindred, and tongues of the earth : Take notice there is one infinite eternal God, that made us, and you, and all things else. God's refreshing the parched earth with showers of rain shows how willing he is to be gracious to poor hungry creatures. Fruitful seasons show us the abundance of his mercy. The decking the heavens with stars, and the earth with plants, show us what glory he can put upon the creatures. This language may be gathered out of the creation, and thus did God speak to all creatures by the voice of his creatures.

3. To the church. And the dispensations of God to the church have been various and diverse : Heb. i. 1, ' God who at sundry times, and in divers manners, πολυμερῶς καὶ πολυτρόπως, spake in times past unto our fathers by the prophets,' &c. He spake his mind by pieces, that is signified by the word; now he gave a piece of his mind, and then a piece; and he hath spoken also in ' sundry manners,' by several ways of revelation. The church never wanted sufficient revelation nor means of knowledge to guide them to the enjoyment of God and true happiness. God's dispensations to the church may be reduced to three heads. There was—(1.) His word without writing; (2.) Then word and writing; (3.) Then writing only.

[1.] There was the word without writing, by visions, oracles, and dreams, by which he manifested himself to persons of the greatest sanctity and holiness, that they might instruct others, and impart the mind of God to others. Now mark, this dispensation was sure enough to guide them to communion with God. Why? Because the people of the world were then but few families, and the persons intrusted with God's message were of great authority and credit, therefore sufficient enough to inform that present age of God's counsel; and (which was another advantage) they lived long, to continue the tradition with certainty to others for hundreds of years. Vision and tradition was sure enough ; for, as it is observed by some, three men might continue the tradition of the counsel of God from Adam till Israel went down into Egypt. There was Adam first ; God taught him by oracle, and he taught others, he lived a long time. Methuselah lived with Adam two hundred forty-three years, and continued until the flood ; then Shem lived with Methuselah ninety-eight years, and flourished about five hundred years after the flood ; and Isaac lived fifty years with Shem, and died about ten years before Israel's descent into Egypt. So that Methuselah, Shem, and Isaac might continue the knowledge of God, and preserve the purity of religion from Adam's death, till Israel's going down into Egypt, for so many hundred years. This was God's dispensation to that church.

[2.] Afterwards there was both word and writing. God's word was necessary for the further revealing and clearing up of the doctrine of salvation, which was revealed by pieces. And writing was necessary, partly because in process of time precepts were multiplied, and it was needful for men's memories that they should be registered in some public record ; and partly because the long life of God's witnesses was much lessened, and the corruption of the world was increased, and Satan began to imitate God by oracles, visions, and answers, and idolatry and superstition crept into the best families. Into Terah's : Josh. xxiv. 2, 'Your fathers dwelt on the other side the flood, in old time, even Terah the father of Abraham and the father of Nachor, and they served other gods.' And Jacob's family was corrupt : Gen. xxxv. 2, 'Then Jacob said to his household, and to all that were with him, Put away the strange gods that are among you, and be clean, and change your garments.' The people were grown numerous enough to make a commonwealth and a politic body, and it was fit they should have a public record and common rule ; and therefore, to avoid man's corruptions, and to give a stop to Satan's deceits, the Lord thought fit there should be a written rule at hand, for the trial of all doctrines. God himself wrote the first scripture that ever was written with his own finger : Exod. xxiv. 12, 'And the Lord said to Moses, Come up to me into the mount, and be there, and I will give thee tables of stone, and a law, and commandments which I have written, that thou mayest teach them.' And then commanded Moses and the prophets to do the same : Exod. xvii. 14, 'And the Lord said unto Moses, Write this for a memorial in a book ;' and Exod. xxxiv. 27, 'And the Lord said unto Moses, Write thou these words ; for after the tenor of these words I have made a covenant with thee and with Israel.' So he bids Jeremiah, chap. xxxvi. 2, 'Take thee a roll of a book, and write therein all the words that I have spoken to thee.' And so God spake to all the prophets, though it be not expressed, and by inward instinct bids them write their prophecies, that it might be a public record for the church in all ages. Now this way was always accompanied with prophetical revelations until Christ's time, who, as the great doctor of the church, perfected the rule of faith, and by the apostles, as so many public notaries, consigned it to the use of the church. And so when the canon was complete, then John, as the last of the apostles, and outliving the rest, closed up all, and therefore closeth up his prophecy thus : Rev. xxii. 18, 19, 'For I testify unto every man that heareth the words of the prophecy of this book; if any man add unto these things, God shall add unto him the plagues that are written in this book; and if any man shall take away from the words of the book of this prophecy, God shall take away his part out of the book of life, and out of the holy city, and from the things that are written in this book.' Which sealeth up the whole canon and rule of faith, as well as the book of the Revelations. And therefore—

[3.] There is now writing only without the word, without visions and revelations. There needeth no more now, because here is enough to make us wise unto salvation: 2 Tim. iii. 15–17, 'And that from a child thou hast known the holy scriptures, which are able to make thee wise unto salvation, through faith which is in Christ Jesus. All scripture is given by inspiration of God, and is profitable for doctrine, for reproof, for correction, for instruction in righteousness; that the man of God may be perfect, thoroughly furnished unto all good works.' It is sufficient to make us wise to preach, and you wise to practise.

SERMON XXX.

As thou hast sent me into the world, even so have I also sent them into the world.—JOHN XVII. 18.

IN the context our Lord had prayed for conservation and sanctification; first he saith, 'Keep them through thine own name,' ver. 11; then, 'Sanctify them through thy truth,' ver. 17. In this verse is the reason of the latter request, why he prays for sanctification for the apostles; and the argument which he uses is, 'I have sent them into the world.' It was at hand, and therefore it is spoken of a thing done, I am about to send; or it referreth to his election and choice, I have called them, that I may send them to preach the word. The same office which thou hast put upon me as a prophet I have put upon them, and therefore 'sanctify them.' They that are sent abroad to preach the gospel need special preservation and special holiness; their dangers are great, and so are their temptations. So much holiness as will serve an ordinary christian will not serve a minister. The measures of the sanctuary were double to other measures, and so should the graces of ministers be double to the graces of others. It is not enough that ministers excel in gifts, but they must also excel in holiness; they are to bear forth the name of Christ before the world, and therefore they should resemble Christ more than others do. This is the reason of the context: 'Sanctify them through, or by, thy truth; for I have sent them into the world, as thou hast sent me into the world.'

In the text there are two things:—

1. The mission of Christ.

2. The mission of the apostles. Together with the comparison between them both; *as thou hast sent me into the world, even so, &c.*

First, The mission of Christ, 'Thou hast sent me into the world.' Here you may consider—(1.) Who sends; (2.) The nature of this mission, or what this sending is; (3.) The ends and purposes why Christ was sent.

1. Who sends. Christ saith to his Father, 'Thou hast sent me.' The Holy Ghost sends as well as the Father, yea, the Son sends himself. The Trinity are one in essence and in will, and their actions are undivided; why then doth he say to the Father, 'Thou hast sent me into the world'? I answer—It is chiefly ascribed to the Father, because it is his personal operation. In the economy of salvation, the original authority is said to reside in God the Father; he sent Christ, and the Spirit fits and qualifies him, and the Son he takes human nature, and unites it to his own person. Now there is a great deal of comfort in this, that the Father sends Christ. The Father, being first in the order of the persons, is to be looked upon as the offended party, and as the highest judge. All sin is against God, and it chiefly reflects upon the first person, to whom we direct our prayers, and who is the maker of the law, and therefore requires an account of the breach of it. It chiefly reflects upon the first person, to whom Christ tendered the satisfaction. Sin, it is a grieving of the Spirit, it is a crucifying of Christ, there is wrong done to all the persons of the Godhead; but in the last result of all, it is an offence to God the Father, and an affront to his authority; for all that is done to the other persons redounds to him. It is his Spirit that is grieved; and our Saviour thus reasoneth, Luke x. 16, 'He that despiseth me, despiseth him that sent me;' so that he is the wronged party. And again, he is the supreme judge. All the persons in the Godhead are co-essential and co-equal in glory and honour; but in the economy and dispensation of salvation, the Father is to be looked upon as judge and chief. Therefore Christ doth say, 'My Father is greater than I.' And all addresses are made to him, not only by us but by Christ: 'Father, forgive them; they know not what they do.' And Christ is said to be 'an advocate with the Father,' 1 John ii. 1. I say, in that court and throne that is erected the Father is supreme; and if it passeth God the Father, the business is done. So John xiv. 16, 'I will pray the Father, and he will give you another Comforter, that he may abide with you for ever.' Pardon, comfort, grace, all comes from the Father, as the fountain and first cause. It is true it is said, Mat. ix. 6, 'That the Son of man hath power on earth to forgive sins;' but this is by commission from God the Father. Well, then, the Father sendeth Christ. Eli saith, 1 Sam. ii. 25, 'If one man sin against another, the judge shall judge him; but if a man sin against the Lord, who shall entreat for him?' There may be an umpire to compromise the difference between man and man, and award satisfaction to the party offended; but now who shall state the offence and compound the difference between us and God? Can there be an umpire above God, that can give laws to God? The sin is committed against the judge himself, the highest judge, from whom there is no appeal; and who is a fit person to arbitrate the difference? This is a doubt that would have remained to all eternity unsatisfied, a question that never could be answered. Where should we find an umpire between God and us, to have awarded a meet satisfaction? But now God himself is pleased to find out the remedy. Christ saith to the Father, 'Thou hast sent me;' his act is authoritative and above

contradiction. If God had not given us a mediator out of his own bosom there could have been no satisfaction, and we had for ever lain under the guilt and burden of our sins: Gal. iv. 4, 'God sent forth his Son, made of a woman,' &c.; he consecrated him for this great purpose. Therefore he is said to seal him: John vi. 37, 'Him hath God the Father sealed;' a metaphor taken from them that give commissions under hand and seal. Christ is a mediator, confirmed and allowed under the broad seal of heaven, by God the Father, as the supreme judge. God hath awarded satisfaction to himself, and sent his own Son to make it.

2. What is this sending? It implies three things—(1.) The designation of the person; (2.) His qualification for the work; (3.) His authority and commission.

[1.] The designation of the person. This was an act of divine and voluntary dispensation, according to which the second person in the Trinity, the Son of God, not the Father, nor the Holy Ghost, was sent to take our nature, and the office of a redeemer upon himself. In this choosing of Christ was the original and first rise of elective love. Augustine hath observed, in choosing Christ, what was the reason Christ was the person designed: Col. i. 19, 'It pleased the Father that in him should all fulness dwell.' What is the reason we are elected and chosen above others? that God reveals himself to babes? and the things of his grace are hidden from the wise and prudent? 'Even so, Father, for so it seemed good in thy sight,' Mat. xi. 26. The same reason is given for the election and choice of Jesus Christ to be the redeemer, that is given for our election; 'It pleased the Father;' that is all. That Christ might be the first pattern of free grace the Father chose the Son, that he might be the redeemer. It was congruous and very fit that the Son and heir of all things should give us the adoption of sons: Gal. iv. 4, 5, 'God sent forth his Son, made of a woman, made under the law, to redeem them that were under the law, that we might receive the adoption of sons.' He sent his Son that we might have the same relation to God by grace which Christ had by nature. By nature, he is the only-begotten Son of the Father; and this is that which is purchased for us, that we should become the sons of God; and the middle person of the Trinity is the fittest to be the mediator between us and God.

[2.] This sending implies his fitness and qualification to do the work for which he was sent. (1.) He had fit natures; (2.) He had fit endowments.

(1.) Fit natures. He was God-man: God, else how could he send? man, else how could he be sent into the world? This sending implies he was a person truly existing before he came into the world, as a man must be before he is sent, and therefore he is said to be 'sent forth from God;' Gal. iv. 4, 'God sent forth his Son, made of a woman.' 'Sent forth,' that shows his being before he took flesh; Christ was somewhere from whence he was sent forth. And then, 'made of a woman,' that implies his incarnation. This sending doth suppose his divine nature, and imply his incarnation, or God's bestowing upon him a human nature. God he was, in the bosom of the Father, from whence he was sent forth into the world. Such an errand as Christ came about required a God, no inferior mediator would serve the turn. Nothing but an infinite good can remedy an infinite evil. Sin had bound us over to an eternal judgment, and nothing can counterpoise eternity but the infiniteness and the excellency of Christ's person. His divine nature was requisite in many regards. Partly to give efficacy and virtue and value to his sufferings ; and therefore it is said that we are ' purchased by the blood of God,' Acts xx. 28 ; the meaning is, the blood of that person to whom the divine properties belonged. God is a spirit, and hath not flesh, blood, and bones, as we have ; how then are we said to be redeemed with the ' blood of God ' ? that is, the blood of him who was God ; which makes it to be of infinite value, and enough to counterpoise that eternity of torment which we should have endured. Again, the dignity of his person conduced to the acceptance of one for all : 2 Cor. v. 15, ' And that he died for all,' &c., in the room and stead of all the elect ; and therefore that there might be such a value in his sufferings, his person must be thus worthy ; as they said to David, ' Thou art worth ten thousand of us,' 2 Sam. xviii. 3. A general or commander given in ransom will redeem thousands of private soldiers ; so the worth of Christ's person made him equivalent in dignity to the persons of all those whom he sustained ; yea, much more, God was more satisfied from Christ, than if all the world had suffered, and all angels and men had been made a sacrifice. Again, God he must be, because of the exuberancy of his merit. Christ's suffering was not only a ransom from death, but the merit of eternal life. By his death he satisfied the old covenant, and ratified the new. The scriptures do not only set forth the death of Christ as a ransom for souls, but as a price given to purchase everlasting glory. A surety to an ordinary creditor, if he pay the debt, he only frees the creditor from bonds, but doth not bring him into grace and favour. But now Christ hath merited happiness for us, and not only freed us from wrath to come, and delivered us from bondage ; there was a price paid to divine justice. Again, the dignity of his person was necessary by way of compensation for those circumstances of punishment which did not beseem Christ. The civility of nations remits to princes and nobles some disgraceful circumstances ; though the punishment is inflicted, yet the kind of death is changed, because of the dignity of their birth, and place in the commonwealth. So here ; the sentence which passed upon men was eternal death ; the sentence itself is not reversed, that would lessen the authority of the law, and the glory of God's justice. The truth is, there are some circumstances abated which stood not with the worthiness of Christ's person ; as for instance, the eternity of the punishment is abated. Christ suffered but a few hours, because of the greatness of his sufferings, and the dignity of his person. A payment in gold is as full and valid as a payment in silver, though it may take up less room, because of the excellency of the metal ; so here, the suffering and death of Christ was of full value, though it was despatched in a lesser time ; the eternity, that is abated, because of the dignity and worth of his person. Once more, the godhead of Christ was necessary, that he may be able to discharge the office of a priest, as that he might satisfy on the cross, and know all those whom he did personate and represent before the tribunal of God. As the high priest had the names of the twelve tribes upon his shoulders and upon his breast, Exod. xxviii. 12–29,—upon his shoulders, to represent them to God, and upon his breast, to show how dear they were to himself,— so Jesus Christ hath, as it were, the names of all those for whom he was to suffer and intercede ; he was to know them man by man. And it was meet that he should know all the sins that were imputed to him ; and therefore the person thus sent, for such a work as this was, must needs be God. Again, he must be God, that he might support his human nature, and overcome his sufferings. Jesus Christ was to be raised, and also to raise himself ; he was to be raised by God the Father as a judge. As the apostles would not go out of prison till the magistrates came to fetch them out themselves, so God as judge is said to raise Christ, and exalt him ; he must give him power to rise. But now Christ was also to raise himself : John ii. 19, 'Destroy this temple, and in three days I will raise it again.' He was to raise himself, to declare the glory of his person. Christ was to rise by his Father's authority, and to rise by his own power. He was to rise by the Father's authority ; therefore, as a pledge of it, an angel is sent to roll away the stone, and open the prison-door, and let our surety out of prison, the debt being paid. And Christ was to rise also by the strength of his own godhead. Why ? This was necessary for our satisfaction. He that would undertake our case, with comfort and satisfaction to the creature, had need be able to overcome divine wrath, for the creature could never have satisfied. If our surety were kept in prison, and held under wrath, we could have no security that the debt was paid ; the great assurance that is given to the world is the resurrection of Christ : Acts xvii. 31, ' Whereof he hath given assurance to all men, in that he hath raised him from the dead ; ' this was his public acquittance and discharge. Again, it was necessary he should be God, for so much of his prophetical office as he accomplished upon earth. Christ came to bring the everlasting gospel out of the bosom of God, and to ratify it with miracles, to choose disciples to preach it, to give the Holy Ghost, to give them power to work miracles, suitable to the tenor of the gospel ; as raising the dead, giving sight to the blind, &c. Thus his godhead was necessary to his work.

But now, upon his sending (and that is more formally and expressly intended in the phrase), he had new qualifications and a new power ; for as God he could not suffer, therefore the manhood is bestowed upon him : Ps. xl. 7, ' A body hast thou prepared for me.' This is formally implied in that expression, ' He sent him ; ' that is, prepared a body for him. God's sending of Christ doth not imply his change of place ; for Christ, as God, before was everywhere ; ' the heaven of heavens could not contain him ; ' but it implies the assumption of another nature. He was *sent*, that is, took flesh, assumed another nature into his own person. Now this was necessary, that Christ should be man, that he might have an interest in us, and have compassion on us, and be in a capacity to die for us. That he might have an interest in us, and be of our blood : the next of blood had a right to redeem, Ruth iii. 9. Therefore Christ, he took our nature, that he might be of our blood, that so he might have a right to redeem us, having an interest in us ; and therefore he was not only man, but the Son of man. Christ might have been true man, if God had formed him out of the dust of the ground, as he did Adam, he might have given him a true human nature. But Christ was not only man, but was of our stock and lineage; and therefore it is said, Heb. ii. 14, 'Forasmuch then as the children are partakers of flesh and blood, he also himself likewise took part of the same;' and ver. 11, 'For both he that sanctifieth, and they that are sanctified, are all of one.' They are 'all of one.' How is that? Of one stock. Justice required that the same nature that had sinned should be punished. It was not fit our sins should be punished in the nature of an angel, nor in the nature of man that was made out of nothing, or out of the dust of the ground; but in one that was of the same stock. Again, that he might have compassion on us, as well as an interest in us. Christ hath a nature that inclines him to his office; besides his essential mercy as God, there is a human compassion, which ariseth from feeling and from experience: Heb. iv. 15, 'For we have not an high priest which cannot be touched with the feeling of our infirmities; but was in all points tempted like as we are, yet without sin.' He took our nature, that he might have experience of our sorrows, miseries, temptations, and so entender his own heart by an experimental pity and compassion. As man, Christ had a feeling what it was to be in the state of men, that we might have an assurance of his pity. As a man that hath felt the racking of the gout and stone is more fit to pity others in the same case, so Jesus Christ, having had a feeling of the buffetings of Satan, and wrath of God, and of the neglects and scorns of men, feeling of all conditions that are miserable, his heart is the more entendered, his human compassion is increased; and God would have it to be so for our greater assurance. Again, his human nature gave him a capacity to suffer. As God he could not suffer; and therefore when God would have no more sacrifices, but all were to be abolished; he prepared Christ a body: Heb. x. 5, God invested him with a human nature, that he might offer one sacrifice to abolish all the rest. Thus you see Christ was sent, that is, fitted by his two natures; his divine nature, that is supposed, and his human nature is formally included in that expression, 'He was sent;' that is, assumed a body, did not change place, but assumed a nature in his own person, that so he might be fit to deal with God for us.

(2.) And then he had fit endowments; he came to be loaded with graces and blessings, and with all kind of qualities to do men good: John x. 36, 'Him hath the Father sanctified, and sent into the world;' that is God's sending, his anointing of Christ as our head, 'with the oil of gladness above his fellows.' As the head of the high priest was anointed, and thence the oil dropped down to all the members: Ps. cxxxiii. 3, 'It is like the precious ointment upon the head, that ran down upon the beard, even Aaron's beard, that went down to the skirts of his garment;' so our head is anointed with the oil of gladness for our sakes. Christ received the Spirit without measure in our nature, as holiness, pity, and the treasures of wisdom and knowledge. Look, as when an ambassador is sent forth, there is not only a designation of his person, but he is furnished for his employment and work; so is Jesus Christ sent forth, that is, his person not only designed and chosen in grace, and yet in wisdom, but also furnished with all manner of endowments in our nature, grace and strength for his work as our head.

[3.] This sending implies authority, and noteth a commission sealed to him, so that he was an authorised mediator, or an ambassador with letters-patent from heaven. This is the principal thing intended in this sending, the call and authority Christ had to do his office: Heb. v. 4, 5, 'No man taketh this honour to himself, but he that was called of God, as was Aaron. So also Christ glorified not himself to be made an high priest; but he that said unto him, Thou art my Son; this day have I begotten thee.' He was designed in the council of the Trinity; and as every ambassador hath letters of credence under the hand and seal of him from whom he is sent, that he may be acknowledged as his deputy to act for him, so Christ is sent as God's deputy into the world, to act and deal for him; and the apostles they are thus sent from Christ, to act and deal for Christ. Here the comparison chiefly holds: ' As thou hast sent me into the world,' that is, given me authority to execute the office of a mediator, 'so have I sent them ;' I have given them authority to preach in my name, and to deliver the gospel to others. This sending of Christ, it maketh all that Christ doth in the Father's name to be valid, which is much for the comfort of our faith. Christ is not a mediator by the right, or merely by the desire of the creature, or by his own interposition; but he is sent and authorised; you may plead it with God, he hath sent him to save sinners. You know Moses, when he interposed on his own accord: Exod. xxxii. 32, 'Forgive their sin; and if not, blot me, I pray thee, out of thy book which thou hast written.' Though it was a high act of zeal in Moses, yet God refused it: ver. 33, ' And the Lord said to Moses, Whosoever hath sinned against me, him will I blot out of my book.' So if Christ had been set up as mediator by the right and desire of the creature only, he might have been refused; but he was authorised by God; he did not glorify himself by invasion of the mediatory office, but had a patent from the council of the Trinity, indited by the Father, accepted by himself, sealed by the Holy Ghost, evidenced to the world by his personal endowments, and by his miracles. Thus you see what this sending is; it implies the designation of the Father, the qualification of his person for the work, and his authority to execute it in his name.

3. To what purpose was he sent into the world? I answer—To perform the whole duty of the mediator, but principally to redeem and instruct the world; those two offices of prophet and priest Christ performed upon earth. The apostle toucheth upon them: Heb. iii. 1, ' Consider the apostle and high priest of our profession, Jesus Christ.' Mark, the apostle mentioneth but two offices, but they were the highest in both the churches: the high priest was the highest officer in the Jewish church, therefore he saith he was the ' high priest of our profession ;' and an apostle was the highest officer in the christian church, therefore he saith he was ' the apostle of our profession.' And he mentions but these two, because these were the two offices Christ chiefly performed on earth. He came to preach the gospel which we profess, so he is 'the apostle of our profession ;' and he came to ratify it with his blood, so he is ' the high priest of our profession.' In short, he

came to deal with God and with men: to deal with God, and so is a high priest, to pacify God, to offer such a sacrifice as might satisfy God; and he came to deal with men, and so he is an apostle, to open the everlasting gospel, to bring it out of the bosom of God to our hearts. His kingly office was but little exercised upon earth; we have a glimpse of his kingly office, or rather of his divine nature, in turning the money-changers out of the temple; but it was little exercised upon earth. Why? Because this was the time of Christ's humiliation. Now the kingly office suits more with the exaltation of Christ; when he comes the second time, then he comes to exercise his kingly office, to reign, and scatter his enemies, and show his kingly power; but now he came to teach and to suffer. That is the reason why his kingly office is made the consequent of his resurrection: Acts v. 31, 'Him hath God exalted with his right hand, to be a prince and a saviour, for to give repentance to Israel, and forgiveness of sins.' Was not Christ king of the church, and king before his resurrection? I answer—As God, so he was a king from all eternity; and in the days of his flesh he was our mediator, therefore certainly king, priest, and prophet; but in the world he did not come to possess his kingdom, but only to preach it and divulge it. Therefore he saith to Pilate, John xviii. 36, 'My kingdom is not of this world; if my kingdom were of this world, then would my servants fight, that I should not be delivered to the Jews; but now is my kingdom not from hence.' Christ came to bear witness that he was king, but did not come to possess his kingdom and act as a king. As soon as ever he was consecrated to be a mediator, he was king, priest, and prophet of the church. Look, as David was king before God as soon as he was anointed, long before he possessed the throne and was crowned at Hebron, 1 Sam. xvi. 13, for he was king when he wandered up and down, and was hunted like a flea or like a partridge upon the mountains; so Christ in the time of his humiliation was a king, but did not exercise his kingdom. Chiefly, then, he was sent into the world the first time to redeem and instruct the world. To redeem the world: 1 John iv. 10, 'God loved us, and sent his Son to be the propitiation for our sins.' This was Christ's first errand, to make satisfaction for sins; afterwards he will come to destroy his enemies at his second coming. And to instruct the world; that is of special consideration in this place: 'As thou hast sent me into the world, so have I sent them into the world.' Christ sent disciples as a prophet, and in this sense he is the 'apostle of our profession;' an ambassador sent from heaven, God's representative; in this sense he is called 'the angel of the covenant,' Mal. iii. 1. The solemnest messenger that ever God sent into the world: Isa. lxi. 1, 'The Spirit of the Lord God is upon me, because the Lord hath anointed me to preach good tidings unto the meek,' &c. Christ was anointed principally for this work, to preach the gospel; he came from heaven to show us the way of life: Heb. i. 1, 2, 'God, who at sundry times and in divers manners spake in time past unto the fathers by the prophets, hath in these last days spoken unto us by his Son.' He hath spoken to us by apostles, pastors, and teachers. Why doth he make mention only of Christ? Because in the roll of gospel preachers, Christ is the first, Christ's name is first enrolled, he was first in commission, and he sent forth apostles, and the apostles others. The mystery of redemption was never clearly known till Christ came to preach it; then all the deep counsel of God for man's salvation came out, which was hidden before. Christ brought out of God's bosom the doctrine of the gospel.

APPLICATION.

We learn hence many things. As—

1. The distinction of the persons in the Trinity. Christ is a distinct subsistence from the Father; for he that sendeth and he that is sent are distinct. Mark, it implies a distinction, but not an inferiority; against the Arians. Persons equal by mutual consent may send one another; as the elders of Antioch sent out Paul and Barnabas, but it doth not follow that they were inferior to the elders of Antioch. So here it implies distinction, but not inferiority.

2. The knowledge of Christ's person; he was 'sent into the world,' therefore is God-man. He was one that was sent, therefore had a being before he was incarnate; and was 'sent into the world,' therefore there was an assumption of the human nature.

3. It showeth us the love of God; he would not intrust an angel nor archangel with our salvation, but sent his Son: 1 John iv. 10, 'Herein is love, not that we loved God, but that he loved us, and sent his Son to be the propitiation for our sins.' There is nothing too near nor too dear for us. It will take the more with us, if we consider the infinite complacency and contentment God had in Christ, yet he sent his Son. Man's love is defensive; he loves his children out of design of immortality, because he lives in them. God had no reason to do so; he had many reasons to the contrary, yet he sent his Son to die for us, when we were enemies. And his Son is sent; what to do? Not only to treat with us, not only to borrow a tongue to speak to us, but to take a body to die for us, to be substituted in our room and stead.

4. It informs us of the great condescension of Christ, that he submitted to be sent: Ps. xl. 7, 8, 'Then said I, Lo, I come; in the volume of the book it is written of me, I delight to do thy will, O my God; yea, thy law is within my heart.' He was ready, when God would send him, like a servant ready to be despatched upon his errand. That Christ would be sent, that he would take our nature, not while it was innocent, but when it was guilty, liable to the wrath of God, when all mankind were proclaimed traitors and outlaws, and whoever partaked of our nature was to partake of our sorrow; yet then was Christ sent: he came 'in the similitude of sinful flesh,' Rom. viii. 3. Christ did not partake of the infection of our nature; he was not a sinner, by being born of our stock; the infection was stopped by the Holy Ghost; but he took our nature, when it was sinful, tainted with sin, and in this message and errand he laid aside his majesty, and by an unspeakable dispensation he abstains from the full use and exercise of the godhead, not from the godhead itself. Therefore, he prays, John xvii. 5, 'And now, O Father, glorify thou me with thine own self, with the glory which I had with thee before the world was.' He begs for his glory again, which he had laid aside for a while. It cannot be meant of the divine nature, for to that nothing can be given;

it cannot be meant of human nature, because that is not capable of
the glory which Christ had before the world was.   The meaning is,
he desires to be restored to the full use of the godhead, from which
he had abstained by an unspeakable dispensation a long time, and by
the interposition of his human nature, the glory of the godhead was,
as it were, eclipsed, as a candle in a dark lantern; and therefore he
desires that the veil might be taken away, and he might return again
to the full use of the godhead, having done his work.   It is irksome to
us to go back a few degrees in pomp and pleasure, even upon just
and convenient reasons; but how did Christ condescend and stoop,
when he was thus sent into the world by God for our sakes!

5. Here is some ground of comfort to them that believe; you may
offer to God a mediator of his own choosing, one that was authorised
by himself.   When you plead with God, you may say, 'Lord, thou
hast sent thy Son.'   Or when you plead with your own hearts, you
may urge them with this, 'God sent him to be helpful to my soul.'
These things may be observed from the first thing, the mission of
Christ.

SERMON XXXI.

*As thou hast sent me into the world, even so have I also sent them into
the world.*—JOHN XVII. 18.

SECONDLY, I come to the mission of the apostles, ' So have I sent them
into the world, as thou hast sent me.'   The words intimate a comparison between God's sending of Christ into the world, and Christ's sending the apostles into the world.

But how doth the comparison hold good?   Christ was sent to redeem, they to preach, the apostles were no redeemers.   Christ was
sent, not only as a prophet, but as a priest, as we have seen before.
And again, for the manner, Christ was sent by being incarnate, God-
man in one person, he must be man, if sent; but they were men, and
therefore there is a difference.   Christ was sent as the supreme officer
of the church, as God with original authority, they as ministers and
servants.   Christ could teach immediately, outwardly by his word,
inwardly by his Spirit; they only outwardly.   How then could it be
said, 'As thou hast sent me into the world, so have I sent them into
the world'?

I answer—There is an ὁμοιότης, not an ἰσότης, some likeness, but
not an equality.   As the union of the apostles is compared with the
unity of the Trinity, so the mission of the apostles with the mission of
Christ.   The similitude holdeth in several things.   They were authorised ministers and officers of the church, as Christ was.   Christ was
authorised by God, and the apostles by Christ; they were his deputies
and representatives, as he was God's; that is the notion of *apostle*, or
one sent, in the New Testament; not as bare messengers, but as
proxies (see Hammond); and we read of ' messengers of the churches,'
ἀπόστολοι, the church's deputies and representatives.   Yea, they had

power to send others, as Christ had. The world was bound to acknowledge them for such. To despise Christ was to despise God, whose deputy he was; and to despise them was to despise Christ; to hear them was to hear Christ, and to hear Christ was to hear God: Mat. x. 40, 'He that receiveth you, receiveth me; and he that receiveth me, receiveth him that sent me;' and Luke x. 16, 'He that heareth you, heareth me; and he that despiseth you, despiseth me; and he that despiseth me, despiseth him that sent me.'

But why doth Christ urge this argument in this place, 'They were sent,' and 'sent as I was sent'?

I answer—It is an argument as to God, and it is a ground of hope to the apostles. An argument fit to be urged to God in prayer, 'they are sent as I was.' Thou didst send me to redeem the world out of thy grace, and they are sent to preach this redemption, and therefore it is fit they should be preserved and sanctified. It is a fit ground of hope for the apostles to meditate upon; they were sent as Christ was. If they be in great poverty, want the help and assistance of the world, so did Christ. All God's witnesses prophesy in sackcloth.

Well, then, here we have the first rise of a gospel ministry. Christ was sent by God, the apostles by Christ, and others are their successors, authorised and sent by them.

The points which I shall handle are two:—

1. The necessity of a call to the ministry.

2. The dignity of those that are so called. Both are implied in the word *sent*.

Before I enter upon the discussion, let none take offence that I apply that to the ministry in general which is spoken of the apostles in the text, 'I have sent them;' which I do for two reasons:—

1. Partly because we may compare ordinary ministers and the apostles together, if their mission be compared with Christ's. As Christ's mission had something extraordinary and peculiar, by which it was distinguished from the mission of the apostles, so the apostles' mission hath something peculiar; but both agree in this, that they must be sent; this they have in common: Rom. x. 14, 'How can they preach except they be sent?' Mark, the apostles were sent as Christ was sent (though Christ was sent to redeem, as well as to prophesy and teach), and so ministers are sent; they must be authorised, as well as the apostles, though the apostles had somewhat peculiar and proper to that office, as the infallibility of doctrine, power of working miracles, the largeness of their circuit, which was the whole world, whereas ordinary ministers are set over one church, and fastened to one place. Again, the apostles were appointed to write scriptures, and pastors and teachers to apply scripture. The apostles were authorised by Christ himself, received their call immediately from his mouth; ordinary ministers are called by a power derived; yet they both agree in this, that they serve in the work of the gospel, and that they are officers that must be called and sent; as not only they are the king's officers, who are immediately appointed by the king, but those also that are appointed by subordinate powers.

2. Partly because a part of the comparison lieth in this, that as Christ was sent by God, and had power to call others, so the apostles

were sent by Christ, and had a power to send and constitute others, and so the succession was to continue. That this was a part of their power appeareth, because Christ, when he gave them their commission, saith, ' He will be with them to the end of the world,' Mat. xxviii. 20 ; that is, with them in their persons and their successors, who are taken into the same patent and commission, and have a power to call others to the end of the world ; and therefore the ' apostles ordained elders in every city,' Acts xiv. 23 ; and those elders ordained others, as the apostle giveth leave to Titus so to do : Titus i. 5, ' For this cause left I thee in Crete, that thou shouldst set in order the things that are wanting, and ordain elders in every city, as I had appointed thee.' Christ was not only sent to be a prophet himself, but to authorise others ; so the apostles not only were sent to preach the gospel themselves, but to authorise others, and they others, even to the end of the world.

This being premised, I come to handle—

First, The necessity of a call. That none can enter upon this work, or upon the office of the ministry, without a call, is, I suppose, out of controversy. All the difficulty will be to show you what a call is. Gifts merely do not make a call, but something else. Now a call is either extraordinary or ordinary.

1. Extraordinary, and that is an immediate call from God himself, by voice, vision, or oracle, or by Christ in person. So was Moses called to his office ; so the Baptist, so the apostles ; and so also was Paul called, because he not seen Christ in person, which it seemeth was necessary to the call of an apostle ; he was called by Christ appearing from heaven ; and therefore he saith, Gal. i. 1, ' Paul an apostle, not of men, neither by man, but by Jesus Christ,' &c. Now this extraordinary call may be pretended, but cannot be expected in these latter days. Many have pretended to an extraordinary call. Eusebius in his sixth book tells us of some that pretended they had a book sent from heaven, according to which they were to instruct their disciples ; and Sozomen speaketh of a monk that pretended that the instruction that he offered to the church was written by an angel ; and since in all ages, especially in ours, do men pretend to illuminations, teachings, and voices within. Thus it may be pretended, but it cannot be expected ; for an immediate extraordinary calling hath only place in establishing a new doctrine ; but now the canon of faith is closed up : ' This doctrine of the kingdom is to be preached to all nations, till the end come,' Mat. xxiv. 14. And the ordinances of the church are settled, and put into a stated course till Christ come ; and therefore we cannot reasonably expect new miracles and new calls. And besides, every extraordinary call is manifested by some vision, miracle, or special effect and gift of the Holy Ghost, by which the truth of that calling may be made out to others, and hath been always sealed with extraordinary effects, which are ceased in these days.

2. The ordinary call then is that which we should chiefly regard, and that is twofold—either inward or outward.

[1.] The inward calling, that is to be regarded in the first place. Be sure you be ministers of Christ's making. There can be no true calling unless you see God in it as well as men. And the Lord taketh it to be his prerogative to bestow officers upon the church, *dabo evangelistam ;* 'I will give to Jerusalem one that bringeth good tidings,' Isa. xli. 27. He did not only appoint the office, but doth design the persons. Now, what is this inward call? I answer—God calleth us when he maketh us able and willing; the inclination and the ability is from God. The inclination : 'He thrusts out labourers into his harvest,' Mat. ix. 38; and the ability: 'He makes us able ministers of the New Testament,' 2 Cor. iii. 6; and both these are required of us. Ability there must be. Look, as princes count it a point of honour, when they send out ambassadors to foreign nations, to employ those that are fit, so it is for the honour of God that all his messengers should be gifted and fitted. Gifts and abilities are our letters of credence that we bring to the world, that we are called of God and authorised to this work. Certainly if the Spirit of God fitted Bezaleel and Aholiab for the material work of the tabernacle, much more doth spiritual work require proportionate abilities. It is true there is a latitude and difference in the degree of abilities, but all that can look upon themselves as called of God must be able and apt to teach. The apostle took this for a call : 1 Tim. i. 12, 'I thank Christ Jesus our Lord, who hath enabled me, for that he counted me faithful, putting me into the ministry.' If ever God put us into the ministry, he first enableth us, and bestows suitable gifts and graces. But that is not all; a man must be willing too : 1 Tim. iii. 1, 'If a man desire the office of a bishop, he desireth a good work.' There must be a strong inclination, that carries us out to such a course of life, if the Lord shall give us a call; yea, in some cases, in the conscience of the inward call, a man may offer himself, his gifts to trial, and his person to acceptance, so it be done modestly, and not in a vainglorious confidence. As Antisthenes said in the case of magistracy, that a man should deal with magistracy as with fire ; a man would not come too near the fire lest he burn himself ; nor stand at too great a distance, lest he grow stiff with cold ; so of the ministry, a man must not be too forward nor too backward. In some cases it is good to expect the fair invitation of providence ; an inclination there must be, if the Lord vouchsafe a call. In some cases we may offer ourselves to the acceptation of the church, if the Lord see fit that we be chosen. But to return ; he hath the inward call who is able and willing ; I mean upon spiritual grounds, having first counted the charges, difficulties, duties, dangers of this calling. Well, then, if men be willing, but not fit, they are not called of God ; or if fit, yet not willing, they have not warrant enough to undergo the difficulty ; much more they that are neither fit nor willing, but only thrust themselves upon the office by the carnal importunity of friends, or corrupt aims at honour and secular advantage. Thus you see what the inward call is.

[2.] There is an outward call. The inward call is not enough ; to preserve order in the church, an outward call is necessary. As Peter, Acts x., was called of God to go to Cornelius; and then, besides that, he had a call from Cornelius himself. So must we, having an inward call from the Spirit, expect an outward calling from the church, otherwise we cannot lawfully be admitted to the exercise of such an office and function. As in the Old Testament, the tribe of Levi and house of Aaron were by God appointed to the service of the altar, yet none could exercise the calling of a Levite, or serve as a high priest, till he was anointed and purified by the church: Exod. xxviii. 3, 'And thou shalt speak unto all that are wise-hearted, whom I have filled with the spirit of wisdom, that they may make Aaron's garments, to consecrate him, that he may minister to me in the priest's office.' The like is repeated, Num. iii. 3. So the ministers of the gospel, though called by God, must have their external separation, and setting apart to that work by the church; as the Holy Ghost saith, Acts xiii. 2, 'Separate me Barnabas and Saul for the work whereunto I have called them.' Mark, the Spirit of God had chosen them, and yet calls upon the church, the elders of Antioch, to separate them for the work of the ministry. But now, in what order this is to be done, and by whom this separation is to be made, is the great controversy. Politicians, and with them Erastians, make it to be the magistrate's right; the Anabaptists, with some others, make it the people's right; papists and others give it to the bishops; others, to presbyters and elders of the church. To examine every claim at large would take up a great deal of time; let us compound the difference as well as we can. In short, there are three pretenders to the power of the external call—the people, the elders, the magistrate; and we may divide it among them, and give every one their share, and then the call will be complete. I say, there are but three pretenders, for we need not to speak of the bishops' plea, for bishops, and presbyters, or elders, in the scripture are all one. The apostle writes 'to the bishops and deacons at Philippi,' Phil. i. 1. The apostle taketh notice of no other officer in that church. And Chrysostom's gloss is of weight, What is the reason, the apostle saith to bishops? were there more than one of one city? The reason is, saith he, because bishops and elders or presbyters are the same. So when the apostle bids Titus, chap. i. 5, 6, 'Ordain elders in every city, if any be blameless,' &c., he adds, ver. 7, 'For a bishop must be blameless, as the steward of God.' To lay aside this, then, we shall speak to the claim of the people, the elders, and the magistrate, and give every one its due; for in the external call there are three parts— election, ordination, and confirmation. Election, that belongeth to the people; ordination, which standeth in examination of life and doctrine, together with authoritative mission, that is the right of the presbytery; and confirmation, that belongs to the magistrate.

(1.) Election is the people's right. This appeareth because their consent and suffrage is required in all offices, even in the choice of an apostle. Acts i. 15, 26, the one hundred and twenty nominate Matthias in the room of Judas, and God decided it by lot; and in the choice of a deacon: Acts vi. 3, 'Look ye out among you seven men of honest report, full of the Holy Ghost,' &c.; and of an elder: Acts xiv. 23, 'And when they had ordained them, χειροτονήσαντες, elders in every church, and had prayed with fasting, they commended them to the Lord.' I know I tread upon thorns, but yet this seemeth to have been the constant practice of the church in after ages. Leo the great, in an epistle of his, is for *vota civium*, the vote of the people, in the election of ministers. And Cyprian more clearly before him, lib. i. epist. 4, *Videmus de authoritate divina descendere ut sacerdos, plebe præsente, sub omnium oculis deligatur, et dignus atque idoneus publico judicio ac testimonio comprobetur*—The minister should be propounded to the people, and approved by their vote and suffrage. And just before, *Plebs illa maxime habet potestatem vel eligendi dignos sacerdotes, vel indignos recusandi*—The people have a power to choose those that are worthy, and refuse those that are unworthy. Certainly all allow some consent to the people, a full use of the judgment of discretion 'to try the spirits,' 1 John iv. 1, and to distinguish 'the voice of a stranger from the voice of a shepherd,' John x. 5. It seemeth to be most agreeable to scripture that the people should by suffrage propound the person, and then he is to be authoritatively determined by the presbytery: Acts vi. 3, 'Look out from among you seven men of honest report, &c., whom we may appoint over this business.' The apostles did not take to themselves an absolute power, but referred the nomination to the people, though still they reserve the determination and ordination to themselves. Election is the people's right, because he is chosen for their good ; but ordination is the elders' right, because that is done in the name of Christ, and therefore must be done by his deputies and proxies, as an evidence that the matter is confirmed by Christ, and that he accepts him for his servant in the work of the ministry. Christ himself, as head of the church, had his ordination from God, and his election from the church. God hath appointed him to be head of the church : Eph. i. 22, 'And hath put all things under his feet, and gave him to be the head over all things to the church.' And the church ratifies it by her consent : Hosea i. 11, 'Then shall the children of Judah and the children of Israel be gathered together, and appoint themselves one head,' &c. And it is notable that in Paul's vision the call is managed by a man of Macedonia, that represented the people of that place : Acts xvi. 9, 'A vision appeared to Paul in the night: there stood a man of Macedonia, and prayed him, saying, Come over into Macedonia, and help us.' Not *Go thou*, but *Come over and help us.*

(2.) Ordination, which consists in the trial of gifts and authoritative commission, that is the right of the elders. That appeareth, because to them is the power of the keys given for the people's good ; and Acts xiii. 2, 'The Holy Ghost saith, Separate to me Paul and Barnabas unto the work whereunto I have called them.' Who were those that were to separate ? They were prophets and teachers of Antioch, as appeareth ver. 1. And elsewhere the scripture speaketh of 'the laying on of the hands of the presbytery,' 1 Tim. iv. 14. Approbation of doctrine and life is the elders' right, who are best able to judge of men's fitness and abilities. To Titus, an officer, is this given : Titus i. 5, 6, 'To ordain elders in every city : if any be blameless, the husband of one wife,' &c. And then for imposition of hands, it is a custom most conform to apostolical practice ; it is not founded on a precept, but only on apostolical practice.

(3.) Confirmation is the magistrate's right. The christian magistrate hath his share, to see that all things are done orderly by the people and elders. Now magistrates are concerned, not only as principal members of the church, and of the first rank, but as *episcopi ad extra*, as nursing fathers, to whom care and inspection belongeth, that all things be done decently, and according to the mind and will of God. The christian magistrate is *custos utriusque tabulæ.* And upon this ground would the apostle have us to pray for the conversion of magistrates, that they might be converted from paganism : 1 Tim. ii. 2, ' That under them we may lead quiet and peaceable lives, in all godliness and honesty.' The magistrate is not only to interpose when differences arise about honesty, but also about godliness ; there is *judex, index, vindex.* In all controversies the word is *judex,* in it the mind and will of God is declared ; the minister is *index,* it is his office to preserve knowledge, and out of the word of God to show his mind and will ; and the magistrate is *vindex,* he is to see that duty be not neglected, that the administrations of the church be not ill managed, and carried on contrary to Christ's appointment, because he is the ' nursing father of the church,' Isa. xlix. 23. Again, the magistrate is concerned as the head of the commonwealth, and so to consider who shall be encouraged by public maintenance, and allowed to preach publicly without disturbance, the commonwealth being concerned in it. And there wants not precedents in scripture for this. David and Solomon did exercise such a power. Solomon deposed Abiathar : 1 Kings ii. 26, ' And to Abiathar the priest said the king, Get thee to Anathoth, unto thine own fields, for thou art worthy of death,' &c. And ' Jehoshaphat sent Levites and priests to teach in every city,' 2 Chron. xvii. 8, 9. And as soon as magistrates turned christian in after ages, they were much concerned in the votes and suffrages of the church. The power of princes herein hath been much debated, especially by those that have pleaded the rights of princes against the encroachment of the Romish synagogue, who abundantly prove that the election of the pope himself is not valid without the consent of the emperor. So in ancienter history, Socrates showeth that when Ambrose was chosen by the people of Milan, the election was confirmed by the Roman emperor, lib. iv. cap. 25. And Theodoret showeth that when Athanasius had nominated one Peter for his successor, and the people had given consent, they solemnly asked the magistrate's leave and confirmation. I might heap up many other instances, but let these suffice.

Having spoken to the call, I come to show the necessity of a call. Now such a call, or authoritative mission is necessary—

1. In respect of God. God enableth those whom he employeth : 1 Tim. i. 12, ' I thank Jesus Christ my Lord, who hath enabled me ; for that he counted me faithful, putting me into the ministry.' And this is the ground upon which Christ builds his prayer in this place, ' Sanctify them through thy truth ;' for ' I have sent them into the world.' Αὐτόκλητοι, those that run of their own heads without a call, cannot expect God's blessing, but those only that are regularly sent can expect the increase of gifts and success of their ministry ; for the word worketh not by its own force, but by God's blessing. Blessing dependeth altogether upon the institution, and therefore the institution must be carefully observed if we would have the blessing. God is said to employ not only those who are called extraordinarily, but in the ordinary way. The elders of Ephesus had no extraordinary call, yet it is said, ' The Holy Ghost had made them overseers,' Acts xx. 28.

2. In respect of Satan. He will soon spy out our want of commission, as he did in the sons of Sceva: Acts xix. 14, 15, ' Jesus I know, and Paul I know; but who are ye ? ' I know Jesus as the Lord, Paul as an authorised minister, one that had a lawful commission, ' But who are ye ? ' And then the devil fell upon them, and wounded them, ver. 16. It is true, we have not such visible instances of the devil's power now as then, because God rules the world now by wisdom, not by power; but yet we may observe the secret power of the devil upon those that run of their own accord, and venture upon the office of the ministry without a call. None are more apt to be led aside into errors, and those of the grossest nature, than those that venture upon this office without a call. Origen's errors are by many ascribed to his neglect or want of ordination. And the Arians, saith the synod of Alexandria, were *famosi vitio suæ creationis,* infamous for want of a right call to the ministry, and therefore fell into that damnable error.

3. In regard of yourselves, that you may digest difficulties with the more patience. You can never endure anything with comfort but when you can thus say, I am in God's way, doing God's work. This is a great ground of patience. Conscience in a time of danger will take hold of the least faulty circumstance. Uzzah had little comfort in his stroke, because he was out of God's way: Jude 11, ' Woe unto them, for they have gone in the way of Cain, &c., and perished in the gainsaying of Korah.' Korah was a sad instance.

4. In respect of the church. This external mission is necessary, that the church may receive you comfortably. It is made a character of Christ's sheep, ' not to hear the voice of a stranger,' John x. 5, nor of such as ' do not enter in by the door,' ver. 1. And in the Old Testament it is often said, ' Hearken not to them, for I have not sent them.' In the primitive church this was strictly observed. When Chrysostom was banished, and Arsanius unduly succeeded him, the people would not so much as hear him. Theodoret witnesseth that some of them would rather go into banishment than join with him in public worship. So when Felix was set over Rome instead of Liberius, against the consent of the church, the people would not enter while he was present, though Felix was orthodox, and nothing could be objected against his doctrine. This instance is approved by Luther in his comment on the Psalms of Degrees, and (in his way of expression) he saith, the same should be done to an angel or archangel, though he came with never so good tidings, if we knew they came without lawful commission.

Use 1. Information in two things—that the ministry is an office, and a standing office.

1. The ministry is an office, not a work of charity, which every one must perform ; there must be fit persons sent ; therefore it is said, Acts x. 41, that Christ appeared ' not to all the people, but unto witnesses chosen before of God, whom he commanded to preach unto the people.' Therefore he that cannot say he is chosen of God for this work, must not take this honour upon him, lest he run before he be sent, and so they do but prattle, not preach, for preaching is an ordinance. So the Lord said to Ananias concerning Paul, Acts ix. 15, ' He is a chosen vessel before me, to bear my name before the Gentiles, and kings, and the children of Israel.' He is called ' a chosen vessel,' not in regard of

eternal election, but in regard of designation to the work of the gospel. Every one is bound by the law of charity to use his gifts to the edifica-tion of others, but still in a regular way. A king hath many subjects, but all his subjects are not courtiers and special servants. All members of the church are subjects of Christ's kingdom, but all are not officers, for these are chosen members.

2. That the ministry is a standing office. When Christ was about to depart, then he sendeth apostles with a promise that he would be with them to the end of the world. He sendeth them that they may send others, and so continue the succession. So that the apostles are not only sent by Christ, but the ministers of the gospel virtually, being sent by Christ's deputies; as they are the king's officers that are not only immediately created by the king, but by his power. Still God hath ever had an ordinary standing ministry in the church. In the Old Testament there were not only prophets, that were immediately called to deliver God's message, and to write scripture, but an ordinary ministry, to open the law and the prophets, and to preserve knowledge in the church: Mal. ii. 6, 7, 'The law of the truth was in his mouth, and iniquity was not found in his lips, &c. For the priest's lips should keep knowledge, and they should seek the law at his mouth, for he is the messenger of the Lord of hosts.' Therefore the ordinary Levites are called νομοδιδάσκαλοι, teachers of the law. In the New Testament, Christ gave not only apostles to write scripture, but pastors and teachers to open scripture: Eph iv. 11, 'He gave some, apostles; and some, prophets; and some, evangelists; and some, pastors and teachers.' The Bible is not enough for your edification without this institution; the same Christ that instituted apostles to write scripture, instituted pastors and teachers to open and apply scripture. This is always necessary, though religion be never so thoroughly planted in a nation, for we need continual remembrancers. And the end of preaching is not only to learn what we knew not before, but that we may have spiritual things always before our eyes, and in the view and considera-tion of conscience, and that the heart be always kept lively and soft and tender by the frequent droppings of the word, and that we may receive new influences of grace in God's way. Yea, for nations, how soon would they degenerate without a monitor and standing ministry, and all things would be wrapt up in error and darkness! This was the first occasion of idolatry among the nations, when their monitors ceased, and religion began to be confined to a few families. Experience will best show the necessity of such a standing office in the church.

Use 2. Reproof of those that invade the minister's office, and of those that countenance them. Jude says of them, 'They perished in the gainsaying of Korah,' Jude 11. God's judgments will overtake them. Korah's sin was levelling of offices in the church: 'All the Lord's people are holy;' why should any take a special office upon them? It is a horrible abuse. Remember the breach of Uzzah; God is jealous even of a circumstance in his institution. Christ himself had his call to authorise him: 'Thou hast sent me into the world;' therefore much more should you have a call to authorise you. If the work doth not lie within the compass of your office, you do not glorify God, and cannot please him; and it will be ill for your account; you cannot, when you die, say as Christ, John xiv. 7, 'I have glorified thee upon the earth, I have finished the work which thou hast given me to do.' You do not glorify God with anything but that which he hath given you to do. It is notable that Christ would not intermeddle out of his calling. When one came to entreat him to 'speak to his brother to divide the inheritance with him,' he said to him, Luke xii. 4, 'Man, who made me a judge or divider over you?' Who was fitter to judge than Christ? yet this was not the work he came about. If troubles arise, you cannot suffer them comfortably. All the disorders abroad will lie in a great measure upon your score. Invading of callings hath been the source of those mischiefs that abound among us. Augustine saith, *Pax est tranquillitas ordinis,* when all things keep their place. In natural things, elements, when out of their place, breed confusion; the sea out of its place makes an inundation; and the air out of its place, imprisoned in the bowels of the earth, causeth an earthquake. It is true in this case also; when men are out of their place it begets confusion and disorder. Never do I look for the peace of the church, and power of the gospel, till men have learned to keep within the compass of their callings. You pretend gifts and abilities; if you have a desire to the work for the work's sake, why do you not submit to the regular way of sending? The angel that appeared to Cornelius biddeth him send for Peter, Acts x. 5. Why did not the angel teach him himself? His commission was only to bring a message from God, not to preach the gospel; that was Peter's work, therefore he sent him to Peter. Nay, Christ himself sendeth Paul to Ananias, Acts ix. 6. If any should usurp the place of an ambassador, without the prince's leave and command, it would be accounted horrible pride. No prince can endure a servant whom he hath not chosen; and how then can Christ take it well at your hands? It is but an itch of pride, if we search it to the bottom. There are regular ways of exercising your gifts, in private meditation, and family instruction, and gracious conferences, by way of interchangeable discourse, with less pride and usurpation, and more spiritual profit and comfort, than in public sermons.

Use 3. Advice to ministers and people.

1. To ministers. Strive to make out your calling to your people, to evidence it to the consciences of your auditory, by your sincerity and success.

[1.] By your sincerity: 2 Cor. iv. 2, 'We have renounced the hidden things of dishonesty, not walking in craftiness, nor handling the word of God deceitfully; but by manifestation of the truth, commending ourselves to every man's conscience in the sight of God.' Success is not in our power, but yet our aim should be sincere. Delight not in vain applause; let not this satisfy thee, but that others may feel the power of truth. Let it not satisfy thee when thy hearers go away and say, Oh! how learnedly, how eloquently, with what subtlety and sublimity of reason doth he preach! what excellent gifts of memory, wit, elocution! This did not satisfy Christ. Christ had made an excellent sermon; a woman in the company cries out, Luke xi. 22, 28, 'Blessed is the womb that bare thee, and the paps that thou hast sucked! But he said, Yea, rather, blessed are they that hear the word of God, and keep it!' It is far better, when they go away from hearing, to be more mindful of themselves than of us; of what is spoken to their consciences, rather than what are our gifts; condemning themselves, rather than commending us; bewailing their own hearts and lives, rather than applauding and admiring our sermons; smiting their own breasts, and saying, not so much, How well hath he preached! but how ill have I lived! how carnal am I, subject to sin!

[2.] By success. This you should covet above all things; this is the seal of your ministry in the people's consciences. Every ambassador sent out from a prince hath not only instructions and commands, but his commission sealed; so a minister must not only look to his instructions to preach the gospel, but for a seal of his ministry, as his letters of credence and recommendation. Now our seal is spiritual, as all other the parts of our administration are. What is this spiritual seal? God's owning and blessing our endeavours: 2 Cor. iii. 1–3, ' Do we begin again to commend ourselves; or need we, as some others, epistles of commendation to you, or letters of commendation from you ? Ye are our epistle, written in our hearts, known and read of all men. Forasmuch as ye are manifestly declared to be the epistle of Christ ministered by us, written not with ink, but with the Spirit of the living God ; not in tables of stone, but in the fleshly tables of the heart.' Success in the hearts of the people doth authorise our commission. So 2 Cor. xiii. 3, ' Since ye seek a proof of Christ speaking in me, which to you-ward is not weak, but is mighty in you.' This is a proof that we come to you in Christ's stead, and speak in his name and power. It is not who can speak most finely and plausibly, but most effectually to the heart: 1 Cor. ii. 4, ' My speech and my preaching was not with enticing words of man's wisdom, but in demonstration of the Spirit and of power.' That is the evidence, not luscious gifts. Carnal men may have these, for the good of the body, that have no inward calling. I remember Paul putteth the false teachers upon this experiment and proof of their calling : 1 Cor. iv. 19, ' I will come to you shortly, if the Lord will, and will know, not the speech of them which are puffed up, but the power.' I will not examine them by their speech, but by the spiritual efficacy of their ministry, which is the chiefest sign of God's approbation and blessing, not their pomp and eloquence. And therefore this is the seal that you should look after.

2. Here is advice to the people, to own them that are called, and sent to you in the name of Christ. Own their persons by a cordial submission to them : Heb. xiii. 17, ' Obey them that have the rule over you, and submit yourselves; for they watch for your souls as they that must give an account.' In the particular places where you are disposed by the care of providence, they are sent by God to you. There is much in the designation of God's providence, and cohabitation is an excellent friend to church communion. That is the sphere of your activity; where God hath appointed your dwelling, there you are in the greatest capacity to serve God, and to promote the ends of church-fellowship and communion. And do not only own the persons, but the calling of the ministers, as a gospel institution. Pray for it ;— how importunately doth Paul beg the people's prayers everywhere !—

and countenance and plead for it in the gates. Wicked men could never obtain that power they have over ministers, were there not some backwardness and faintness in the people of God to own them. Herod could have put John to death, 'but he feared the multitude, because they counted him for a prophet,' Mat. xiv. 5. The putting down the ministry will not only be imputed to the violence of others, but to your coldness and ingratitude. Therefore let the world know by some public vindication that you are not afraid to own Christ's institutions. If we have a charter given us by a prince, how zealous are we that it might not be infringed! Whatever the world thinks of it, this is Christ's royal gift in the day of his inauguration: Eph. iv. 11, 'When he ascended up on high, he gave some, apostles; and some, prophets; and some, evangelists; and some, pastors and teachers.' Therefore stand, and plead for it more. Paul took notice, 2 Tim. iv. 16, 'At my first answer no man stood with me; but all men forsook me.' It is a crime to forsake ministers in their defence, much more to forsake the ministry. Are we so backward that we do not think Christ's gift worthy a public vindication? Nothing hath been accounted so near and dear to the church of God, that hath put them upon such frequent prayers and zealous endeavours, as this, that their ministers may not be taken from them. Therefore own their calling, and own the institution.

Before I come to speak to the dignity of ministers, I shall answer an objection or two against what hath been said.

Object. 1. If none but such as have an outward call are to preach, what call had the first reformers? I answer—

1. The first reformers, most of them had a lawful call, being pastors and teachers before the reformation; and though they had it from antichrist, as some plead, or the popish clergy, yet that did not make it less valid. The apostles say of Judas, Acts i. 17, 'He was numbered with us, and had obtained part of this ministry.' Wicked Judas, *in foro ecclesiæ,* was a true and lawful apostle, and whatever he did by virtue of his office was valid and lawful. So the Roman clergy, they have obtained part of this ministry with us, and *in foro ecclesiæ,* at least before the reformation, were lawful ministers; it is disputable whether as yet God hath given such a total divorce, that all their ecclesiastical acts are nullities.

2. Others were stirred up by the special instinct of the Holy Ghost to undertake the work, and being received of their own churches, their call was valid; for things of order must give way to things of absolute necessity, and where an ordinary calling cannot be had, God calleth men out of order. It is the duty of all saints to contend for the faith; and when God, by a special instinct, stirreth up holy men to do this work, they are thereby authorised; especially when there is a general defection and corruption among the officers of the church. Who would expect the reformation of stews from bawds and panders? It is necessary the church should have pastors and teachers; and where ordination cannot be had, the election and consent of the people sufficeth, God especially accompanying them with his presence, and the men being furnished with gifts and necessary qualifications, both as to life and doctrine, for that office.

Object. or Case. 2. What shall be done in case of propagating the gospel, where no lawful call can be had, or all die at a time?

I answer—In extraordinary cases, God supplieth the want by extraordinary ways; that may be done at one time that is not lawful at another, especially in matter of order, as eating the shew-bread in case of necessity. Edesius and Frumentius, travelling into the Indies, had an opportunity of spreading the gospel; though the last afterwards returned, and was ordained by Athanasius. Natural bodies have their ordinary qualities; yet *ad fugam vacui*, they act contrary to them, as water will ascend contrary to the gravity of it. Before deacons were instituted, the apostles served tables, though it was a thing not meet for them: Acts vi. 2, 'It is not reason that we should leave the word of God and serve tables.' Philip, of a deacon, was made an extraordinary evangelist, Acts viii.

<hr>

SERMON XXXII.

As thou hast sent me into the world, even so have I also sent them into the world.—JOHN XVII. 18.

SECONDLY, I now come to speak of the dignity that is put upon them that are called to the work of the ministry; they are sent by Christ as his deputies and ambassadors, as those who impersonate Christ, and represent him to the world: 2 Cor. v. 20, ὑπὲρ Χριστοῦ οὖν πρεσβεύομεν, 'Wherefore we are ambassadors for Christ; as though God did beseech you by us, we pray you, in Christ's stead, be ye reconciled to God.' Ministers are sent out as Christ's proxies.

Here I shall show—(1.) Who are sent; (2.) From whom; (3.) To whom; (4.) Why, or about what business.

1. Who are sent? Principally the apostles, but secondarily the ordinary ministers of the gospel; the apostles as ambassadors extraordinary, but we as liegers and agents. The apostles were immediately sent by Christ, and furnished with extraordinary gifts, as infallibility of doctrine, gifts of miracles, gifts of tongues; as ambassadors are sent forth with more pomp and state than agents. But now ministers are sent by a power derived and delegated from Christ; and we have not like authority and infallibility as the apostles had, but the substance of the commission and of the work is the same; we are to open the mind of God to men, and in Christ's name and authority to pray you to be reconciled to God. And therefore both apostles and ordinary ministers of the gospel, ordinary pastors and teachers of the church, are sent.

2. From whom they are sent. From Christ, who is the king of the church, though with the consent of all the persons in the Trinity. The Father sendeth, Christ sendeth, the Holy Ghost sendeth: Gal. i. 1, 'Paul an apostle, not of men, neither by men, but by Jesus Christ, and God the Father, who raised him from the dead.' Paul raiseth up his commission as far as the grant and consent of God the Father. And the Holy Ghost sendeth: Acts xx. 28, 'Take heed therefore unto

yourselves, and to all the flock over which the Holy Ghost hath made you overseers.' So Acts xiii. 2, 'As they ministered to the Lord, and fasted, the Holy Ghost said, Separate me Paul and Barnabas for the work whereunto I have called them.' In short, then, we are sent by the decree and will of the Father, qualified by the Holy Ghost, and commissioned by the authority of Christ as king of the church. And therefore the apostles were to tarry at Jerusalem till Christ was ascended, and seated on the throne, and seized upon the kingdom, and poured out the Holy Ghost upon them. None are sent but such are also called and chosen by the Holy Ghost, by whom also they are gifted, with respect to God the Father's consent, and Christ's authority.

3. To whom are they sent? I answer—To all, without any distinction of nation, sex, person, or condition: Mark xvi. 15, 'Go ye into all the world, and preach the gospel to every creature.' Men send an embassy to kings and princes, but Christ to every mean creature, without any restraint. It is true, the motion and course of the gospel is directed by a special providence, to some places and not to others: Acts xvi. 7, 'After they were come to Mysia, they assayed to go into Bithynia; but the Spirit suffered them not.' But doth the Holy Ghost hinder the preaching of the gospel? We must distinguish between the grant of power and the exercise of it. Though there be a general grant, that the pale of the church shall be enlarged, yet this grant is to be made good as the Lord will. There is a general grant that the gospel shall be preached unto all nations, but as for the exercise and making good this grant, God will have the world to know that the preaching of the gospel is a privilege and a special favour, and therefore he sendeth it to some and not to others, as a token of his love. It is a thing that doth not come by chance, or by the counsels of men, but by his special grant and designation. Therefore it is notable that the apostles were guided by the Spirit, not only in their doctrine, but in their journeys; and the external means are distributed by the will of God, as well as internal grace, that wherever it cometh we may acknowledge it as a special favour; to some it cometh later, to others sooner, but to all as God will. He oweth it to none; and therefore, though the pale be enlarged, and there is a general grant that all creatures that live within the precincts of the round world shall have the gospel in their turn, yet to some it is sent before others: Acts iii. 26, 'Unto you first, God having raised up his Son Jesus, sent him to bless you.' The Jews had the first offer and liberty of choice or refusal. So Acts xiii. 26, ' Men and brethren, children of the stock of Abraham, unto you is the word of this salvation sent.' He doth not say, it is *brought* by me, but *sent*. The preaching of the gospel is governed by God's special providence and care; as the scriptures 'came not in old time by the will of man, but holy men of God spake as they were moved by the Holy Ghost,' 2 Peter i. 21. So it is not preached by the will of men. It is not your purses that procure it, nor your goodness that deserveth it, but good ministers are sent to you by Christ's special love and care, and so should you acknowledge it. I tell you, many have laboured for the gospel, fought for the gospel, and yet they have missed it,

because they do not consider him that hath the stars in his hand, and directeth and guideth their motions. God will have this mercy taken out of his own hand, as a special token of his love; therefore because they do not acknowledge God, though they fight, strive, and labour for it, yet the gospel is taken from them.

4. For what are they sent, or the end and scope of the gospel? Ever since the fall, there is a quarrel between God and man; and God might send heralds to proclaim war, as he sendeth ambassadors of peace 'to pray you to be reconciled,' 2 Cor. v. 20; that is the purport and drift of our message, to gain men to lay down the weapons of their defiance, and to accept of Christ, that in him they may find life and peace. God might send messengers into the world, as he sent Jonah to Nineveh, to warn the world of their destruction, or as he revealed the law upon Mount Sinai, to make men sensible of their bondage, and obnoxiousness to divine wrath and justice; but he sendeth messengers of peace, with an olive branch in their mouths, to tell the world of God reconciled, and God pacified by Christ, and invite them to be in favour and peace with God, that so they may enjoy communion with him in grace here and glory hereafter: Col. i. 27, 28, 'Christ in you, the hope of glory. Whom ye preach, warning every man, and teaching every man in all wisdom, that we may present every man perfect in Christ Jesus.' There is the subject of our ministry, communion with Christ, and reconciliation with God by Christ, as 'the hope of glory;' the manner of managing it, 'with wisdom warning' every man; the persons with whom we treat, 'every man,' without distinction; and our aim and scope, 'that we may present every man perfect in Christ Jesus.'

Use 1. It informeth us of four things :—

1. The excellency and dignity of the ministry. They are Christ's ambassadors; they are sent, not as a post or letter-carrier, but as honourable messengers. An ambassador usually is one of the nobility, sent by a prince, or the supreme power of a nation; not to private men, but to their fellow-princes or states; not upon a light cause, but to treat of matters of moment; and not in a low or base manner, but with an equipage and pomp answerable to the dignity of him that sendeth. Or, in short, an ambassador is an eminent person, sent from some chief prince, with dignity and authority to transact affairs of the greatest moment; and because he representeth the person from whom he is sent, therefore credit and honour is to be given to him suitable to his place and office. Now the greater the king or potentate is from whom he is sent, the more honour is done him; if from an emperor, it is more honour than from an ordinary prince; and the greater and more welcome the business is, still the greater honour. If the nature of the business be to require satisfaction for injuries, to denounce war, yet still he is respected according to his place; but if it be a matter of peace, he is more welcome; or if it be to establish a correspondence of traffic between nation and nation, much more if it be about a treaty of marriage, and to propound terms of the highest amity and friendship, he is much more respected; and yet more especially if the state or prince to whom he is sent be inferior to the other that sent him. Now these are the terms upon which the

ministers of the gospel are sent; they are Christ's ambassadors, they are sent from the greatest monarch that ever was, from Christ, who is the King of kings and Lord of lords; and they are sent to miserable and wretched men, to rebels to the crown of heaven; and their message is not to denounce war, but to propose terms of friendship and amity, to tell you that God is willing to be reconciled to, and to be at peace with, his creatures. Oh! 'how beautiful upon the mountains should their feet be that publish such glad tidings!' Isa. lii. 7. It is an allusion to the dirty feet of travellers, that come about weighty business; the dirt of the journey doth not render them defiled, but beautiful. Nay, this is not all; they are furnished with authority, with power of binding and loosing, of remitting and retaining sins: John ii. 23, 'Whosesoever sins ye remit, they are remitted unto them; and whosesoever sins ye retain, they are retained.' To them are given the keys of the kingdom of heaven, to open and shut; not as they please, but so as the Lord ratifies their regular proceedings in the court of heaven. They have a power, in God's name, to take up the controversy between God and you, and they bear God's name, that is, represent his person. And they are set forth with an answerable equipage, with plentiful gifts of the Holy Ghost, which are, as it were, their letters of credence, with gifts of knowledge, experience, and comfort, above the ordinary sort of christians.

2. It informeth us of the duty of the ministry, as well as their dignity; their duty both in their life and conversation, and in their ministry and calling.

[1.] In their life and conversation. Remember the gravity and state of ambassadors; you represent Christ's person, and you must be examples and patterns to others. You should not be guilty of levity, or be given to the pomp and vanities of the world, as others are; not only that you may not disparage your ministry, and hinder the ends of it, but that you may the better represent the person of him that hath sent you, and not disgrace Christ. An imprudent, vain, carnal minister is a disgrace to Jesus Christ: 2 Cor. iii. 18, 'We all with open face, beholding as in a glass the glory of the Lord, are changed into the same image, from glory to glory, even as by the Spirit of our God.' Principally that text concerns ministers; so Beza, Calvin, and others expound it; for there he is comparing the ministry of the New Testament with the ministry of the legal dispensation; that as Moses, by conversing with God, his face shone, so ministers of the gospel have their glory too; by conversing with Christ, they carry away his image. So that a minister should be a representative of Christ. It is a spiritual dignity, not a temporal, to be Christ's ambassadors; and therefore you must excel, not in place only, but in grace: 1 Tim. iv. 12, 'Let no man despise thy youth, but be thou an example of the believers, in word, in conversation, in charity, in spirit, in faith, in purity.' This is the duty of a minister, to appear like Christ's deputy, just as he was in the world. This will make way for your esteem, though young for age, and mean in birth and estate. The apostle doth not write to others, and say, 'See you do not despise Timothy;' but he writes to Timothy, 'Let no man despise thee.' Our disesteem cometh from ourselves, when we let fall the majesty of our conversations. Well, then, let the dignity of your office be in your eye, that you may not be a disgrace to him that sent you, but may walk with all religious circumspection, gravity, and prudence.

[2.] In their ministry and calling there is also required faithfulness, gravity, and sincerity.

(1.) Faithfulness. Propound nothing to others but what you have in command from God, and what you know to be certainly agreeable to his will; as an ambassador must not go beyond his commission, that is, upon his own score, and to his own peril. When Christ gave us our commission, this he gave us in charge' Mat. xxviii. 20, 'Teach them all things which I have commanded you.' The first mischief in the church came from dogmatising; men would be wise above the word, and that made way for foul abuses, and they for heresies; when you press things without warrant, others question all. You shall see the Lord Christ often avoucheth how punctually he kept to his commission: John xii. 49, 'For I have not spoken of myself; but the Father which sent me, he gave me commandment what I should say and what I should speak.' Christ would not go a tittle nor hair's-breadth from his instructions. When we are adding to the word, others will detract from it. It is sweet when we can say, John vii. 16, 'My doctrine is not mine, but his that sent me;' this I have in charge from God; when we have clear evidence from the word, and a strong instinct from the Spirit to deliver such a message; not the visions of our own brain, but the counsel of God to the people.

(2.) With gravity. God's message must be delivered like his message, speaking 'as the oracles of God,' 1 Peter iv. 11; with affection, as having experience of it in our souls, feeling the divine power of the word on our hearts. And with authority: thou art delivering Christ's message, in the presence of Christ and his holy angels; and therefore it must not be delivered with frothy gayish eloquence, but with majesty and power. Vainglorious preaching, such as is intermixed with strains of wit, and fancies, and idle speculations, ill becometh God's ambassadors. Such speak as if they were in jest, not as if they had a serious message to deliver from God; this becometh the stage rather than the pulpit.

(3.) With sincerity. It is required of an ambassador that he be faithful to him that sent him. He is not sent abroad to seek his own ends, and enter into a confederacy with foreign princes, to gratify his interest by secret combinations, but must be faithful to him that sent him: Prov. xiii. 17, 'A wicked messenger falleth into mischief, but a faithful ambassador is health;' health to himself, and health to the prince that sendeth him; and therefore we must not seek ourselves, but be faithful to God. You seek yourselves most when you do not seek yourselves, when you are faithful to God, when you do nothing for fear or favour of men, but are bold upon the Lord's commission. Your work is to go for another, not for yourselves. God himself will reward his own messengers, and will set the crown upon their heads with his own hand. And that is one reason why he permits them to have bad entertainment in the world, that they may not take up with men, and that he himself might crown them, and give them their reward

SERMONS UPON JOHN XVII.

SERMON XXXIII.

And for their sakes I sanctify myself, that they also might be sanctified through the truth.—John XVII. 19.

This is the second argument; he had urged their commission, now his own merit. Justice might interpose and say, They are unworthy; but Christ saith, 'I sanctify myself for them.' He dealeth with the Father, not only by way of entreaty, but merit; and applieth himself not only to the good-will of the Father, as his beloved one, but to his justice, as one that was ready to lay down his life as·a satisfaction.

In the text are two things :—

1. A meritorious cause, 'And for their sakes I sanctify myself.' Where—

[1.] *Quis,* the person, who is represented under a double notion—as an efficient cause, 'I sanctify;' and as the object-matter, 'Myself;' the person sanctifying and sanctified, the author and the object, the efficient and the material cause of this sanctification.

[2.] *Quid,* the action, what he did, ἁγιάζω, 'I sanctify.'

[3.] *Pro quibus,* the persons for whom this was done, 'For their sakes;' not for himself, he needed it not, but for their sakes, ὑπὲρ αὐτῶν.

2. The effect of Christ's sanctifying himself, 'That they might be sanctified through the truth.' Where—

[1.] The blessing intended, 'That they might be sanctified.' It is *bonum congruum,* for in all things Christ must πρωτεύειν, 'have the pre-eminence;' it is *bonum morale,* not that they might be rich, happy, glorious, but sanctified; it is *bonum specificativum,* such as maketh an evidence; for none can make comfortable application of the benefits of redemption but the sanctified, who have grace and holiness infused in them, and do devote and consecrate themselves to serve God in holiness and righteousness all their days.

[2.] The means, manner, or end, ἐν ἀληθείᾳ; it may be rendered *through* the truth, *in* truth, or *for* the truth; all which readings admit of a commodious explication.

(1.) As the means, 'Through the truth,' as the rule and instrument;

the word accompanied with the virtue of Christ's death is that which sanctifieth.

(2.) The manner, 'In truth,' or truly, in opposition to legal purifications by the use of the ceremonies of the law, which were but a shadow of true holiness: Heb. ix. 13, 14, 'For if the blood of bulls and goats, and the ashes of an heifer sprinkling the unclean, sanctifieth to the purifying of the flesh, how much more shall the blood of Christ, who through the eternal Spirit offered himself without spot to God, purge your conscience from dead works, to serve the living God?' And in opposition to counterfeit sanctification: Eph. iv. 24, 'And that ye put on the new man, which after God is created in righteousness and true holiness;' such as is sincere, true, and real.

(3.) The end, 'For the truth,' that they may be consecrated, set apart, and fitted for that function of preaching the truth. The context seemeth to justify this. From the whole observe—

Doct. That Christ did set himself apart to be a sacrifice for us, that we might be sanctified by the means appointed thereunto.

I shall explain this point by opening the text.

First, I begin with the meritorious cause, 'And for their sakes I sanctify myself.' Where—(1.) The agent, *I*; (2.) The act, *sanctify*; (3.) The object, *myself*; (4.) The persons concerned, *for their sakes.*

First, The agent, 'I sanctify myself.' In other places it is ascribed to the Father and the Spirit. To the Father: John x. 36, 'Him hath the Father sanctified, and sent into the world.' To the Spirit: Acts x. 38, 'How God anointed Jesus of Nazareth with the Holy Ghost and with power.' He did not only frame the human nature of Christ out of the substance of the Virgin, but adorned it with gifts and graces fit for his office and work. And here Christ saith, 'I sanctify myself.' All the persons in the divine nature concur to this work. The Father sanctifieth and sets him apart by his decree and designation; the Son sanctifieth himself, to show his willingness and condescension; the Spirit sanctifieth him by his operation, furnishing him with meet graces and endowments that were necessary for that singular person who should redeem the world. Christ's sanctifying himself falleth under our consideration, and doth show partly his original authority, as a person of the Godhead, coequal with the Father and the Spirit: 'Whatsoever the Father doeth, the Son doeth also,' John v. 19. Partly his voluntary submission; as the Father did consecrate the Son to the office of mediator, and the Spirit qualified him with all fulness of grace, so did Christ consecrate himself, as being a most willing agent in this work, and did really offer himself to become man, and to suffer all that misery, pain, and shame that was necessary for our expiation. The scripture often sets it forth to us: Eph. v. 2, 'Walk in love, as Christ also hath loved us, and hath given himself for us, an offering and a sacrifice to God for a sweet-smelling savour.' He did not do this work by constraint, but of a ready mind. When it was first propounded to him in God's decree, Heb. x. 9, 'Then he said, Lo, I come to do thy will, O God!' And before the time was come about when he should assume the human nature into the unity of his person, he feasted himself with the thoughts of that salvation which he should set afoot in the habitable parts of the earth:

Prov. viii. 31, 'Rejoicing in the habitable parts of the earth, and my delights were with the sons of men.' When the incarnation was passed, then he longed for the time of his passion: Luke xii. 50, 'I have a baptism to be baptized with, and how am I straitened till it be accomplished!' So willing was he to do and suffer that whereunto he was sent: Luke xxii. 15, 'With desire have I desired to eat this passover with you before I die;' that passover, because it was the last, the forerunner of his agonies. His heart was set upon that work. His behaviour in his death showed how willingly he did undergo it: John xiii. 1, 'Having loved his own that were in the world, he loved them unto the end;' then was his bitter work, but that did not abate his love. The heathens counted it a lucky sacrifice that went to the altar without struggling and roaring; certainly Christ did meekly suffer what was imposed on him for the expiation of our sins: Isa. liii. 7, 'He is brought as a lamb to the slaughter, and as a sheep before her shearers is dumb, so he openeth not his mouth.' A swine whineth and maketh a noise, but a sheep is dumb; this was the emblem chosen to represent Christ's meekness and patience. Salt cast into the fire danceth and leapeth with a kind of impatience, but oil riseth up in a gentle flame; so Christ suffered, not only with patience, but delight. He did not lay down his life by constraint, but died by consent: John x. 18, 'No man taketh my life from me, but I lay it down of myself; I have power to lay it down, and I have power to take it up again.' Now this endeareth our obligation to him, that he would consecrate himself to the work of the mediatory office, and to that end assume the human nature into the unity of his person, and so willingly condescend to all that sorrow and pain that he was to endure for our sakes, and offer himself up as a sacrifice for our sins ; being for a while without the actual sense of his Father's love: 'My God, my God, why hast thou forsaken me?' Mat. xxvii. 46.

But more distinctly let us consider the greatness of his sufferings, his willingness to endure them.

1. The greatness of his sufferings. His passions, take them in the very letter, were sore, but they were heightened by the delicacy of his temper; never any man suffered as he did, because never such a man. A blow on the head is soon felt because it is a principal member, and so more sensible than other parts of the body. A slave is not so sensible of blows and stripes as a nobleman of a tender and delicate constitution. Our Saviour Christ was of a more delicate constitution than any other; his body was immediately framed by the Spirit in the Virgin's womb. Lawrence on the gridiron, Stephen when stoned, could not be so sensible as Christ on the cross. None of the martyrs suffered what he did. Christ had a particular knowledge of all sins committed in the world, past, present, and to come, and a particular sorrow for them; which was the greater by how much the more he prized the honour of God. His love towards him was infinite, his hatred to sin infinite, his apprehension of his Father's displeasure clear ; all which made his soul heavy to the death. Our sins were more burdensome to him than his own wounds. No man's understanding is so great as to apprehend what Christ felt; Christ himself can only give us an account of the greatness of his sufferings. David confessed

'that his sins were more than the hairs upon his head;' yet he saith, 'Cleanse me from secret sins;' implying many had escaped his notice and knowledge. How great was the burden of Christ, that was the Lamb bearing the sins of the whole world! Neither did Christ suffer pains only for sins, but to make a purchase of spiritual blessings; and yet the price exceeded the value of that which was bought.

2. His willingness to suffer for us. Christ was so set upon his passion that he called Peter Satan for contradicting it: Mat. xvi. 23, 'Get thee behind me, Satan, for thou art an offence to me.' When Jonah saw the storm he said, 'Cast me into the sea;' this storm was raised for his own sake; but when Christ saw the misery of mankind he said, Let it come on me. We raised the storm, Christ was cast in to allay it; as if a prince, passing by an execution, should take the malefactor's chains and suffer in his stead. Christ bore our sorrows; he would have this work in no other hands but his own. His earnestness to partake of the last passover showeth his willingness; he had such a desire to see his body on the cross, that Judas seemed too slow, not diligent enough. Christ saith, John xiii. 27, 'That thou doest, do quickly.' It is not an approbation of his sin, but a testimony of his love; every day seems long. If Christ had been to suffer so much for every man as he did for all mankind, he would have done it; there wanted but a precept, there wanted not love; his heart was much beyond his sufferings, as the windows of the temple were greater and more open within than without, 1 Kings vi. 4. If Paul, that had but a drop of grace, could 'wish himself accursed from Christ for his brethren, his kindred according to the flesh,' Rom. ix. 3, how much more willing was Christ! Surely then we should as readily consecrate ourselves to his service. Christ saith, 'Lo, I come to do thy will, O God,' Heb. x. 9; and it becometh every christian to make an unbounded resignation of himself to God: Acts ix. 6, 'Lord, what wouldst thou have me to do?'

Secondly, The act, $\dot{\alpha}\gamma\iota\dot{\alpha}\zeta\omega$, 'I sanctify.' Things are said in scripture to be sanctified when they are set apart, and fitted and prepared for some holy use.

1. As it signifies to separate, or set apart from a common to a holy use, as the sacrifices under the law were separated and chosen out of the flock or herd, the best and the fairest, such as were without spot and blemish, and then designed for this holy use of being an offering to God, so was Christ separated for this use, to be the great sin-offering, or sacrifice of atonement for the whole congregation: 1 Peter i. 19, 20, 'Ye were redeemed with the precious blood of Christ, as of a lamb without blemish and without spot.' When was Christ so sanctified? He did sanctify himself when he accepted the conditions of the covenant of redemption, Isa. liii. 10–12; and visibly at his baptism he did present himself among sinners as our surety, and offer himself to the Father to pay our ransom, which God accepted, for he declared himself well pleased with Christ, as standing in our room: Mat. iii. 17, 'Lo, a voice from heaven, saying, This is my beloved Son, in whom I am well pleased.' Ordinary baptism is a dedication to God. So Christ's baptism was a dedication of himself to the recovering of the lost world to God. And then a little before his death in this prayer, 'I sanctify

myself;' afterwards in his agonies, 'Not my will, but thine be done;' at his death he offered up himself, Heb. ix. 14, 'Who through the eternal Spirit offered himself without spot to God.'

2. It signifieth his qualification and fitness; he did fit the human nature with all habitual and actual holiness. In this sense Christ did sanctify himself; as God, he fitted himself for this work.

[1.] There was the innocency and purity of his human nature, without any stain of corruption, and therefore he is called 'that holy thing,' Luke i. 35. This holiness was necessary in regard of himself, otherwise his human nature could not be assumed into the unity of his person, for God can have no communion with sin, no more than light and darkness can agree together. It was necessary in regard of his office, that he might satisfy for our sins: Heb. vii. 26, 'Such an high priest became us, who is holy, harmless, undefiled, separate from sinners.' The priest of the gospel must be sinless, because of the excellency of the sacrifice, that the priest may not be worse than the sacrifice. While things were carried in type and figure, and a beast was offered in sacrifice, a sinful man sufficed; but now the satisfaction was really to be made for us, and sin done away, and we were to be made really holy, our priest was to be holy, harmess, undefiled. It is for our comfort that Christ was sanctified; his original sanctity is a remedy against our original sin and impurity. When we are troubled with our natural deformity, it is comfortable to think that God looketh upon us in Christ, who was holy by nature; it is a comfortable hope that the corruption of our nature is covered in God's eyes, and shall be diminished more and more.

[2.] His actual holiness in his conversation. The business of the mediator was to commend obedience, and he hath done it by his own example, and the way that he took to recover us to God: Rom. v. 19, 'As by one man's disobedience many were made sinners, so by the obedience of one shall many be made righteous;' Phil. ii. 5, 'Let the same mind be in you that was in Christ Jesus.' Some dislike such a particular application; we have need of all Christ's properties, and we should make use of all. Why doth the scripture set it down, but to show that he is fit to remove sin original and actual? As a covetous man looks on a piece of gold, or we on a thing that we delight in, we turn it on every side. The first Adam was by God's institution a common person, in him sinning the world sinned; the second Adam was a public fountain of holiness, who is an infinite person as well as a public person.

Thirdly, The object, 'I sanctify *myself*;' not an angel to do this for us, but himself. Under the law the priests offered bulls and goats, while they themselves remained untouched, but Christ offered himself. As God he was priest, as man the sacrifice. As there was love in the priest, so there is worth in the sacrifice. Christ was both priest and sacrifice; it was himself that he offered as a recompense to angry justice. Otherwise we might say, Here is the person sanctifying, but where is the sacrifice? As Isaac said to his father, Gen. xxii. 7, 'Behold the fire and the wood, but where is the lamb for the burnt-offering?' It is good to see in what nature Christ was the priest, and in what nature the sacrifice. In his divine nature the priest, for 'he offered himself through the eternal Spirit to God,' Heb. ix. 14.   In his human nature principally he was the sacrifice; for it is said, Heb. x. 10, 'We are sanctified through the offering of the body of Jesus Christ once for all.' The godhead could not be offered, for who can offer himself, or any other thing to himself?   And, besides, the thing sacrificed must be slain, for it is blood shed which was given to God upon his altar. In this respect it is said by Christ, John vi. 51, 'The bread which I will give is my flesh, which I will give for the life of the world.' And when he had instituted the eucharist in memory of this great sacrifice, he mentioneth his body broken and given, and his blood shed. Yet because the priest and the sacrifice is one, the value of this sacrifice ariseth from the divine nature.   It is 'the blood of God,' Acts xx. 28, that is, of the person who was God.

Fourthly, The persons interested, 'For their sakes.'

1. Negatively, not for himself; he needed it not, he had no sin to expiate, nor happiness to purchase anew.   The scripture never speaks of Christ's doing anything for his own sake, but still of his love to us. His incarnation was for us: Isa. ix. 6, 'To us a child is born, to us a Son is given.'   His obedience was for us: Gal. iv. 4, 5, 'But when the fulness of time was come, God sent forth his Son, made of a woman, made under the law, to redeem them that were under the law, that we might receive the adoption of sons.'   His death was for us: Dan. ix. 26, 'The Messias shall be cut off, but not for himself.'   Our Lord died, not for himself, but for his people: Isa. liii. 4, 5, 'Surely he hath borne our griefs, and carried our sorrows.   He was wounded for our transgressions, he was bruised for our iniquities: the chastisement of our peace was upon him, and by his stripes we are healed.'   He was made nothing for himself, but all things for us.   Christ's merit for himself is an unworthy doctrine.   Bellarmine saith, *Christus præter ea bona quæ suis laboribus peperit, meruit etiam sibi corporis gloriam, et nominis exaltationem.*   But if Christ were to merit for himself, his obedience was not voluntary, but due; and what could be merit which was not from his conception due to him?   It is true Christ solaced his human soul with the consideration of consequent glory: Heb. xii. 2, 'For the glory which was set before him, he endured the cross, and despised the shame, and is set down at the right hand of the throne of God.'   But we cannot thence infer a merit.   A prince disguised in a foreign country may solace himself with the honour and happiness he shall enjoy at home: Phil. ii. 9, 'Wherefore God hath also highly exalted him.'   *Διὸ,* 'wherefore,' noteth a consequent in order of time: Christ was 'first to suffer, and then to enter into glory,' Luke xxiv: 26.

If you say, Christ, as man, was bound to be subject, as a reasonable creature, to God his maker; as the son of Abraham, he was comprehended in the covenant made with that people:—I answer—

[1.] If his human nature was bound to be subject, yet not his person, *actiones sunt suppositorum.*   The human nature was taken into his person, and the divine nature could do more to free the human nature than the human nature to oblige the person to obedience. Christ pleadeth his freedom as God's son: Mat. xvii. 26, 'If of strangers, then are the children free.

[2.] The human nature, as a creature, was to be subject to God, and guided by him, as being an inferior; but whether to a law of God is justly doubted; for the law is given to mere men for their weakness, for the instruction of good and the restraint of bad; and therefore his being subject to the law was voluntary, and not necessary; if it were necessary, there could be no merit in it: Luke xvii. 10, 'So likewise ye, when ye shall have done all those things which are commanded you, say, We are unprofitable servants; we have done that which was our duty to do.'

[3.] Again, Christ voluntarily brought himself into this condition merely for our sakes; as a man that removeth his dwelling into another country for his friend's sake, while he is in that country, he is bound by the laws of it, but merely for his friend's sake; or, as a surety, free before, when he cometh into bonds, he must discharge the debt, but all is for his friend's sake; so Christ 'was made under the law' Gal. iv. 4. He that makes himself a servant to free his friend is bound to service; yet his making himself a servant is meritorious. In short, if Christ had done aught for himself, he had been his own redeemer, mediator, and saviour. Christ came into the world, sanctified his nature, lived and died for our sakes; it is for our benefit and behoof, to effect our salvation. His human nature needed nothing but what might accrue to him by the dignity of his person.

2. Positively, 'For their sakes.' The apostles are chiefly concerned in the context, who were sent into the world upon a peculiar message and errand; but all the elect are intended, partly because it is presently added, ver. 20, 'Neither pray I for these alone, but for all that shall believe in me through their word;' partly because it is a common benefit, and what doth not concern the apostles as apostles, but is common to them with others, must be extended to all; for their sakes he doth wholly consecrate himself, and set himself apart for his people's benefit, that he might be theirs; it was for their weal, not for his own, that he might be their mediator and sacrifice. Christ was wholly set apart for our use; as mediator, he had no other work and employment but to procure our salvation. How doth this engage us to make use of Christ, for otherwise his undertaking is in vain, if we do not improve him for those ends and purposes for which he doth set apart himself; even as the sun would shine in vain if we did shut up ourselves in a dark place, and did not enjoy the light and comfort of it, and the brazen serpent would in vain be lifted up upon the perch and pole, if none that were stung would look upon it. Oh! let not Christ be a Christ in vain: 2 Cor. vi. 1, 'We then, as workers together with him, beseech you that you receive not the grace of God in vain.' If he wholly gave up himself to be a fountain of grace, holiness, comfort, and glory in our nature, and did fit himself to justify and sanctify us, and we never look after the benefit, we make him to be a Christ in vain.

Secondly, We come now to the end, effect, and fruit of it, 'That they might be sanctified through the truth.'

First, The benefit, or blessing intended, 'That they also might be sanctified.' Where—

1. Observe, it is *bonum morale*, not that they might be rich, happy,

great, glorious in the world, but 'that they might be sanctified.' When Christ was on the cross, he neither wanted wisdom to choose, nor love to intend, nor merit to purchase the highest benefits, and those which were most necessary for us ; but that which he had in his eye was our sanctification: Eph. v. 26, 'He loved the church, and gave himself for it, that he might sanctify and cleanse it ;' and Heb. xiii. 12, ' Jesus, that he might sanctify the people, suffered without the gate.'   All his aim was to recover us to God, and dedicate us to God ; for he came to repair the ruins of the fall, and save that which was lost : Luke xix. 10, ' The Son of man came to seek and to save that which was lost.'   And we were first lost to God before we were lost to ourselves ; as appeareth, Luke xv., by the parable of the lost sheep, which was lost to the owner ; and the lost groat, which was lost to the possessor ; and the lost son, which was lost to the father.   Our misery is included ; but the principal thing intended was, that God hath lost the honour of the creation.

2. It is *bonum congruum :* 'I sanctify myself, that they may be sanctified.'   The scripture delighteth in these congruities : Heb. v. 8, 9, 'He learned obedience by the things that he suffered : and being made perfect, he became the author of eternal salvation to all them that obey him.'   As there is a suitableness between the seal and the impression, so between Christ and his people.   In all things Christ must πρωτεύειν, he must have the pre-eminence.   We have the blessings of the covenant, not only from him, but through him.   Christ was elected : Isa. xlii. 1, ' Behold my servant whom I have chosen, my elect in whom my soul delighteth ;' so are we.   Christ was justified : 1 Tim. iii. 16, ' God manifested in the flesh, justified in the spirit ;' so are we.   Christ was sanctified, and we, in conformity to him, are sanctified also, as in the text.   Christ rose again, ascended, and was glorified ; so do we—he as the elder brother and first heir, and we in our order.

3. It is *bonum specificativum.*   It showeth the parties, or that sort of men to whom Christ intended the benefit : Heb. x. 14, ' For by one offering he hath perfected for ever them that are sanctified ;' them and no other : the godly themselves, while unconverted, and lying in their sins, have not the actual benefit of Christ's redemption.

But in what manner are we sanctified ?   Christ consecrated and sanctified himself as a sin-offering ; but we are sanctified and consecrated as a thank-offering ; Christ to do the work of a redeemer or mediator, we to do the work of the redeemed.   We are set apart for the Lord, to glorify him in all holy conversation and godliness.

Secondly, The means of applying and conveying this benefit : 'Through the truth,' ἐν ἀληθείᾳ.   It may be rendered ' through the truth,' ' in the truth,' or ' for the truth ;' all which readings admit of a commodious explication.

1. In the truth, or truly, in opposition to legal purifications, which were but a shadow of true holiness : Heb. ix. 13, 14, ' For if the blood of bulls and goats, and the ashes of an heifer sprinkling the unclean, sanctifieth to the purifying of the flesh, how much more shall the blood of Christ, who through the eternal Spirit offered himself without spot to God, purge your conscience from dead works to serve the living God ?'   Or in opposition to counterfeit sanctification : Eph. iv. 24,

'And that ye put on the new man, which after God is created in righteousness and true holiness.' Some only are sanctified externally, as they are in visible covenant with God: Heb. x. 29, 'And hath counted the blood of the covenant, wherewith he was sanctified, an unholy thing.' They live among his peculiar people ; others are really renewed and changed by his Spirit, and turned from a sinful life to God, making conscience of every commanded duty, and aiming at his glory in all things.

2. For the truth, that they may be consecrated, set apart, and fitted for that function of preaching the gospel. This is agreeable to the context, which limits this part of the prayer to the apostles.

3. Through the truth, as we render it, and fitly, considering the 17th verse, 'Sanctify them through the truth; thy word is truth;' through the word, by which the virtue of Christ's death is applied to us. There are certain means and helps by which Christ bringeth about this effect: Eph. v. 26, 'That he might sanctify and cleanse it by the washing of water, through the word.' The word offereth this grace, the sacraments seal and confirm it to us. So John xv. 3, 'Ye are clean, through the word which I have spoken to you.' The word of command presseth it : Ps. cxix. 9, 'Wherewithal shall a young man cleanse his way ? by taking heed thereto according to thy word.' The word of promise encourageth us: 2 Cor. vii. 1, 'Having therefore these promises, dearly beloved, let us cleanse ourselves from all the filthiness of flesh and spirit, perfecting holiness in the fear of God.' And the doctrine of Christ's blood holds out the virtue whereby it may be done: 1 John i. 7, 'The blood of Jesus Christ his Son cleanseth us from all sin.' And it exciteth faith, by which the heart is purified : Acts xv. 9, 'Purifying their hearts by faith.'

Use 1. Information. It informeth us of divers important truths.

1. That in ourselves we are polluted and unclean, or else what needed there so much ado to get us sanctified ? This is needful to be considered by us : Job xv. 14, 'What is man that he should be clean ? and he that is born of a woman, that he should be righteous?' That is, man by nature is neither clean nor righteous, destitute of purity by nature, and uprightness of conversation. They are ill acquainted with man who think otherwise ; for if we consider his earliness in sinning, his easiness in sinning, his constancy in sinning, and the universality of sinners, we may soon see what his nature is ; and the fountain being so corrupt, the streams or emanations from it are defiled also.

2. That nothing can cleanse us but the blood of Christ. Can man cleanse himself ? Job xiv. 4, 'Who can bring a clean thing out of an unclean ? not one.' Can that which is corrupt cleanse itself ? or that which is enmity to holiness promote it ? Or can the word do it without Christ ? Good instructions may show a man his duty, but cannot change the bent of his heart. Christ needed not only to be sent as a prophet, ver. 18, but must sanctify himself as a priest and sacrifice, before this benefit could be procured for us, as in the text. There was no possible way to recover holiness, unless a price, and no less a price than the blood of the Son of God, had been paid to provoked justice for us. He must **sanctify himself, give himself, before we can be sanctified and cleansed.**

3. That they do not aright improve the death of Christ that seek comfort by it, and not holiness. He died not only for our justification, but sanctification also. There are two reasons why the death of Christ hath so little effect upon us; either he is a forgotten Christ, or a mistaken Christ. A forgotten Christ: men do not consider the ends for which he came: 1 John iii. 5, 'Ye know that he was manifested, to take away our sins;' and ver. 8, 'To this purpose was the Son of God manifested, to destroy the works of the devil;' to give his Spirit to sinful miserable man. Now things that we mind not do not work upon us. The work of redemption Christ hath performed without our minding or asking; he took our nature, fulfilled the law, satisfied the lawgiver, merited grace without our asking or thinking; but in applying this grace, he requireth our consideration: Heb. iii. 1, 'Wherefore, holy brethren, partakers of the heavenly calling, consider the apostle and high priest of our profession.' Our faith: 'Believest thou that I am able to do this for thee?' Our acceptance: John i. 12, 'To as many as received him, to them gave he power to become the sons of God.' But the other evil is greater, a mistaken Christ; when we use him to increase our carnal security and boldness in sinning, and are possessed with an ill thought, that God is more reconcilable to sin than he was before, and by reason of Christ's coming there were less evil and malignity in sin, for then you make Christ a minister and encourager of sin: Gal ii. 17, 'For if, while we seek to be justified by Christ, we ourselves also are found sinners, is Christ therefore the minister of sin? God forbid!' You set up Christ against Christ, his merit against his doctrine and Spirit; yea, rather you set up the devil against Christ, and varnish his cause with Christ's name, and so it is but an idol-Christ you dote upon. The true Christ 'came by water and blood,' 1 John v. 6; 'Bore our sins in his body on the tree, that we, being dead unto sin, should live unto righteousness,' 1 Peter ii. 24. And will you set his death against the ends of his death? and run from and rebel against God because Christ came to redeem and recover you to God? Certainly those weak christians that only make use of Christ to seek comfort, seek him out of self-love; but those that seek holiness from the Redeemer have a more spiritual affection to him. The guilt of sin is against our interest, but the power of sin is against God's glory. He came to sanctify us by his holiness, not only to free our consciences from bondage, but our hearts, that we may serve God with more liberty and delight. This was the great aim of his death: Titus ii. 14, 'He gave himself for us, that he might redeem us from all iniquity, and purify to himself a peculiar people, zealous of good works.' Thus did Christ, that the plaster might be as broad as the sore; we lost in Adam the purity of our natures, as well as the favour of God, and therefore he is made sanctification to us, as well as righteousness, 1 Cor. i. 30.

SERMON XXXIV.

Neither pray I for these alone, but for them also which shall believe on me through their word.—JOHN XVII. 20.

HERE Christ enlargeth the object of his prayers, which is propounded
    (1) Negatively; (2) Positively.

First, Negatively; by which the restraint is taken off. Which showeth—

1. Christ's love. He had a care of us before we were yet in being, and able to apply these comforts to ourselves. We were provided for before we were born, there is a stock of prayers laid up in heaven. Christ, as God, foresaw that the gospel would prevail, notwithstanding the world's hatred, and that many would yield up themselves to the obedience of the faith; therefore to show that they have a room in his heart, they have a name in his testament. As parents provide for their children's children yet unborn, so doth Christ remember future believers, as well as those of the present age, and pleadeth their cause with God, as if they were standing by, and actually hearing his prayers for them. It was Esau's complaint, 'Hast thou but one blessing, O my father?' when he came too late, and Jacob had already carried away the blessing. We were not born too late, and out of due time, to receive the blessing of Christ's prayers. Hath he no regard to us? are his thoughts wholly taken up with the believers of the first and golden age of the church? Certainly not. 'I pray not for these only, but for them also which shall believe on me through their word.' We, that now live hundreds of years after they are dead and gone, have an interest in them. 'Increase and multiply,' was spoken to the first of the kind of all the beasts; and to the end of the world all creatures do produce and bring forth after their kind by virtue of this blessing. Christ doth not only speak of the first of the kind; but, that we might be sure to be comprised, he telleth us so in express words. Certainly much of our comfort would be lost if we were not comprehended in Christ's prayers, for his prayers show the extent of his purchase.

2. The honour that is put upon private believers; their names are in Christ's testament; they are bound up in the same bundle of life with the apostles. Here is a question, whether this passage relateth to the foregoing requests, or else to these that follow? What part of the prayer hath this passage respect to? Answer—I suppose to the whole; it looketh upward and downward. The middle part of the chapter doth chiefly concern the apostles and disciples of that age; some things are proper to them, yet there are many things in common that concern us and them too. He had lately said, 'I sanctify myself for their sakes;' he would not have that restrained. In the latter part of the chapter all believers are more especially concerned; yet some passages are intermingled that do also concern the apostles: ver. 22, 'The glory which thou hast given me, I have given them;' ver. 25, 'They have known that thou hast sent me;' ver. 26, 'I have declared my name to them, and will declare it.' Thus you see we are partly concerned in all the prayer. It is a great favour that he would make mention of us to God. As David, when about to die, did not only pray for Solomon his successor, but for all the people, so doth Christ not only pray for the college of the apostles, to whom the government of the church was committed upon his departure, but for all believers to the end of the world. He prayeth for the apostles, as intrusted with a great work, and liable to great danger and hatred; but yet he doth not neglect the church.

Secondly, Positively; the persons for whom he prays. They are described by their faith, and their faith is described by the object of it, 'That believe in me;' and by the ground and warrant of it, 'Through their word.'

And so the points will be two:—

1. That believers, and they only, are interested in Christ's prayers.

2. That, in the sense and reckoning of the gospel, they are believers that are wrought upon to believe in Christ through the word.

Doct. 1. That believers, and they only, are interested in Christ's prayers.

Though Christ doth enlarge the object of his prayers, yet he still keepeth within the pale of the elect. He saith, ver. 9, 'I pray not for the world;' and now, περὶ τῶν πιστευσόντων, 'for them that shall believe in me.' He doth not pray for all, whether they believe or no, but only for those that shall believe. Now this Christ doth, partly because his prayers and his merit are of equal extent: ' I sanctify myself for their sakes;' and then, 'I pray not for these only, but for them that shall believe in me through their word;' Rom. viii. 33, 34, 'Who shall lay anything to the charge of God's elect? It is God that justifieth; who is he that condemneth? It is Christ that died, yea rather, that is risen again, who is even at the right hand of God, who also maketh intercession for us;' 1 John ii. 1, 2, 'If any man sin, we have an advocate with the Father, Jesus Christ the righteous, and he is the propitiation for our sins.' His prayers on earth do but explain the virtue and extent of his sacrifice: he sueth out what he purchased, and his intercession in heaven is but a representation of his merit; both are acts of the same office. Partly because it is not for the honour of Christ that his prayers should fall to the ground: John xi. 42, 'I know that thou hearest me always.' Shall the Son of God's love plead in vain, and urge his merit, and not succeed? Then farewell the sureness and firmness of our comfort. Now Christ's prayers would fall to the ground if he should pray for them that shall never believe.

Use 1. It is much for the comfort of them who do already believe. You may be sure you are one of those for whom Christ prayeth, whether Jew or Gentile, bond or free. Particulars are under their general. How do we prove John or Thomas to be children of wrath by nature? All were so. So Christ prayeth for all those that shall believe, as much as if he had brought them forth, and set them before God by head and poll. And if Christ prayed for thee, why is not thy joy full? Why did he speak these things in the world? It is a copy of his intercession. Christ would show, a little before his departure, what he doth for us in heaven; he sueth out his purchase, and pleadeth our right in court. It is a sign we have a room in his heart, because we have a name in his prayers. And what blessings doth he seek for? Union with himself, communion with him, in grace here, in glory hereafter. It is a comfort against all temptations, doubts, dangers; you are commended to the Father's care.

Use 2. It is an engagement to others to believe. If he had commanded some great thing, ought we not to have done it? This comfort cannot be made out to you till you have actual faith; however it is with you in the purpose of God, yet you cannot apply this comfort till you believe. If a man should make his will, wherein rich legacies should be left to all that can prove a claim, by being thus and thus qualified, would not every one put in for a share? Believe, believe; this is the condition.

Use 3. It showeth the excellency of faith. Those that have an interest in Christ's prayers are not described by their love, their obedience, or any other grace (though these are necessary in their place), but by their faith; and the godly are elsewhere called ' of the household of faith.' Wherever our implantation into Christ, or participation of the privileges of his death, or our spiritual communion in the church is spoken of, the condition is faith. It is a grace that sendeth us out of ourselves, to look for all in another. It is the mother of obedience. As all disobedience is by unbelief, so all obedience is by faith. First he said, ' Ye shall not die ; ' and then, ' Ye shall be as gods.' First he seeketh to weaken their faith in the word ; they could not be proud and ambitious till they did disbelieve. Therefore, above all things let us labour after faith. Our hearts are taken up with the world, the honours and pleasures of it ; these cannot make us happy, but Christian privileges will ; all which are conveyed to us by faith.

But let us come to the second point.

Doct. 2. That, in the reckoning and sense of the gospel, they are believers that are wrought upon to believe in Christ through the word.

Here is the object, Christ ; the ground, warrant, and instrumental cause, and that is the word. The warrant must be distinguished from the object ; the warrant is the word, and the proper object of faith is Christ, as considered in his mediatory office. Sometimes the act of faith is terminated on the person of Christ, and sometimes on the promise, to show there is no closing with Christ without the promise, and no closing with the promise without Christ ; as in a contract there is not only a receiving of the lease or conveyance, but a receiving of lands by virtue of such a deed and conveyance. So there is a receiving of the word, and a receiving of Christ through the word ; the one maketh way for the other, the promise for our affiance in Christ. Faith that assents to the promise doth also accept of Christ ; there is an act terminated on his person. Faith is not *assensus axiomati,* a naked assent to the propositions of the word, but a consent to take Christ, that we may rely upon him, and obey him as an all-sufficient Saviour.

But now let us speak of these distinctly.

First, Of the object, that is, to believe in Christ. There is believing *of* Christ, and believing *in* Christ. He doth not say, Those that believe me, but, Those that believe in me through their word. Believing Christ implieth a credulity and assent to the word ; and believing in Christ, confidence and reliance. Once more, believing in Christ is a notion distinct from believing in God : John xiv. 1, ' Ye believe in God, believe also in me.' Since the incarnation, and since Christ came to exercise the office of a mediator, there is a distinct faith required in him, because there are distinct grounds of confidence ; because in him we see God in our nature, we have a claim by justice as well as mercy, we have a mediator who partaketh of God's nature and ours, and so is fit to go between God and us.

Briefly to open this believing in Christ, it may be opened by the implicit or explicit acts of it.

1. There is something implicit in this confidence and reliance upon Christ, and that is a lively sense of our own misery, and the wrath of God due for sin. All God's acts take date from the nothingness and necessity of the creature, and from thence also do begin our own addresses to God. God's acts begin thence, that he may be all in all; from the creation to the resurrection God keepeth this course, and then the dispensation ceaseth, for then there is no more want, but fulness. Creation is out of nothing; providence interposeth when we are as good as nothing; at the resurrection we are nothing but dust; God worketh on the few relics of death and time. So in all moral matters, as well as natural, it is one of his names, ' He comforteth those that are cast down.' When he came to convert Adam, he first terrified him: ' They heard the voice of God in the garden, and were afraid,' Gen. iii. 10. He delivered Israel out of Egypt when their souls were full of anguish. We are first exercised with the ' ministry of the condemnation,' before ' light and immortality are brought to life in the gospel.' And still God keeps his old course ; men are first burdened and sensible of their load before he giveth them ease and refreshment in Christ. At the first gospel sermon preached after the pouring forth of the Spirit, Acts ii. 37, ' They were pricked in their hearts.' Christ's commission was to preach the gospel to the poor and broken-hearted and bruised : Luke iv. 18, ' The Spirit of the Lord is upon me, because the Lord hath anointed me to preach the gospel to the poor ; he hath sent me to heal the broken-hearted, to preach deliverance to the captives, the recovering of sight to the blind, to set at liberty them that are bruised.' This is the roadway to Christ. And all our addresses to God begin too thence. Man is careless : Mat. xxii. 5, $\dot{a}\mu\epsilon\lambda\dot{\eta}\sigma a\nu\tau\epsilon\varsigma$, ' They made light of it ;' and proud : Rom. x. 3, $o\dot{v}\chi\ \dot{v}\pi\epsilon\tau\dot{a}\gamma\eta\sigma a\nu$, ' They have not submitted themselves to the righteousness of God.' The Israelites were not weary of Egypt till they were filled with anguish. Adonijah, when he found himself guilty of death, ' he laid hold on the horns of the altar.' The prodigal never thought of returning till he began to be in want, and to be soundly pinched. Therefore, till there be a due sense and conviction of conscience, it is not faith, but carnal security. In short, we can never be truly desirous of grace, we cannot prize it, ' we do not run for refuge,' Heb. vi. 18. We are not earnest for a deliverance till there be some such work.

There are two things keep the conscience quiet without Christ— peace and self, carnal security and self-sufficiency.

[1.] It is hard to wean men from the pleasures of sense, and to make them serious in the matters of their peace; before Christ and they be brought together, they and themselves must be brought together. This God seeketh to do by outward afflictions, that he may ' take them in their month,' as the ram was caught in the briars. In afflictions men bethink themselves : 1 Kings viii. 47, ' If they shall bethink themselves in the land whither they are carried captives,' &c. It makes them to return upon themselves, how it is between God and them. If affliction worketh not, he joineth the word ; it is ' a glass wherein we see our natural face,' James i. 21. God showeth them what loathsome creatures they are, how liable to wrath. Or if not, by the power of his Spirit upon their consciences; their reins may chasten them; they cannot wake in the night, or be solitary in the day, but their hearts are upon them; so great a matter is it to bring men to be serious.

[2.] Self. When the prodigal began to be in want, 'he joined himself to a man of that country,' Luke xv. 15. We have slight promises and resolutions, and all to elude the present conviction; long it is ere the proud heart of man is gained to take Christ upon God's terms. Convinced men are brought in, saying, 'What shall I do?' Acts ix. 6. Then let God write down what articles he pleaseth, they are willing to subscribe and yield to any terms; as softened pewter, let it be never so bowed and battered, is receptive of any shape and form. This is the implicit act, or that which is required in believing, that a man should be a lost undone creature in himself, ready to do what God will have him.

2. The explicit acts, when a soul thus humbled casts itself upon Christ for grace, mercy, and salvation. This may be explained with respect to the two great ordinances, *i.e.*, the word and prayer, which are, as it were, a spiritual dialogue between God and the soul. In the word, God speaketh to us; in prayer, we speak to God. God offereth Christ to us in the word, and we present him to God in prayer. So that the acts of faith are to accept of Christ as offered, and then to make use of him in our communion with God; and by this shall you know whether you do believe in him.

[1.] Accepting Christ in the word. Faith is expressed by receiving him: John i. 12, 'To as many as received him, to them gave he power to become the sons of God, even to them that believe in his name.' Receiving is a relative word, and presupposeth God's offer. Art thou willing to take Christ upon these terms? Yes, saith the soul, with all my heart; I accept him as a sanctifier, as a saviour, and I can venture all in his hands. Then you answer God's question. How often doth God lay forth the excellences of Christ, and none regard him? But a poor hunger-bitten conscience prizeth him, receiveth him with all his heart, and entertaineth him in the soul with all respect and reverence. This is to take Christ, to accept him as Lord and Saviour upon God's offer. As when Isaac was offered to Rebekah, 'Laban and Bethuel answered, saying, The thing proceedeth from the Lord; we cannot speak unto thee good or bad,' Gen xxiv. 50; they consented to take him, because they saw God in it. So they see God tendering Christ in the word, and they are willing to take him upon his own conditions.

[2.] By making use of him in prayer. The great use of Christ is that we may come to God by him: Heb. vii. 25, 'Wherefore he is able to save unto the uttermost all that come unto God by him.' We must make our approaches to God for supplies of grace, in the confidence of his merit. It is a great fault in christians that they do so little think of this act of faith. We are busy about applying Christ to ourselves. The great use of Christ is in dealing with God: Heb. x. 19, 'Having therefore boldness, brethren, to enter into the holiest by the blood of Jesus.' Every prayer that you make with any confidence and liberty of spirit, it cost Christ his heart's blood. He knew that guilt is shy of God's presence, as the malefactor trembleth to come before the judge : Eph. iii. 12, 'In whom we have boldness, and access with confidence, through the faith of him.' Surely the apostle speaketh *de jure*, not what is *de facto*. We have low and dark thoughts, as if we had no such liberty purchased for us; παῤῥησίαν ἔχομεν, we may be free with God. It is the fruit of Christ's purchase. Christ's name signifieth much in heaven.

Use. Can you thus believe in Christ, take him out of God's hand? No; I cannot apply Christ. I answer—Yet disclaim, when you cannot apply : Phil. iii. 9, 'And be found in him, not having my own righteousness, which is after the law, but that which is through the faith of Christ, the righteousness which is of God through faith.' And apply yourselves to Christ when you cannot apply Christ to you ; that is, cast yourselves upon Christ. You have warrant enough from the word. There is an adventure of faith when there is no persuasion of interest : 2 Tim. i. 12, 'I know whom I have believed, and I am persuaded that he is able to keep that which I have committed unto him against that day.' The venture is grounded on God's free offer of him to all sorts. When we rest on him, because we know he is ours, that is another thing ; there is trust, that is a fruit of propriety : 1 John v. 13, 'These things have I written unto you that believe on the name of the Son of God, that ye may know that ye have eternal life, and that ye may believe on the name of the Son of God.' But the adventure is grounded on the offer, as a child holds fast his father in the dark; mariners cast anchor at midnight. And ripen faith more; all faith draweth to particular application. The lowest degree is a desire to lay hold on Christ as our Saviour; this is the tendency and aim of the least faith, though we do not leap into full assurance at first ; as a man that climbeth up to the top of the tree, first he catcheth hold of the lowest boughs, and so by little and little he windeth himself into the tree till he cometh to the top.

Secondly, The next thing is the warrant or instrument, 'Through their word.' It is not meant only of those that heard the apostles in person. By 'their word' is meant the scripture, which was not only preached by them at first, but written by them; as Paul saith, Rom. ii. 16, 'In the day when God shall judge the secrets of men by Jesus Christ, according to my gospel;' that is, which I have published and delivered to the church in writing : John xv. 16, 'Ye have not chosen me, but I have chosen you, and ordained you that you should go and bring forth fruit, and that your fruit should remain.' By their 'fruit' is meant the public treasure of the church, the scriptures, and that remaineth in all ages until Christ come ; as the Jews were children of the prophets, that never heard them, Acts iii. 25. So were we converted by their word.

Now I shall handle the necessity, use, and power of the word to work faith.

1. The necessity of the word preached ; it is the ordinary means. It is a nice dispute whether God can work without it. God can enlighten the world without the sun. It is clear ordinarily he doth not work without the word ; we are bound, though the Spirit is free: 'How shall they believe on him of whom they have not heard? and how shall they hear without a preacher?' Rom. x. 14. It is the means to

convey faith into the hearts of the elect; it is as necessary to faith, as faith to prayer, and prayer to salvation. It is a means under a promise. You see how necessary it is; they that voluntarily neglect the means, put a scorn upon God's institution. Men will say, I can read at home. Are you wiser than he? Men think that, of all other things, preaching might best be spared; and of all offices, hearing is least necessary. The ear received the first temptation; sin and misery broke in that way; so doth life and peace. The happiness of heaven is expressed by seeing, the happiness in the church by hearing. This is our great employment, to wait upon the word preached; next to Christ's word, it is a great benefit to have the word written; next to the word written, the word preached. Christ sent 'first apostles, then pastors and teachers.' God could have converted Paul without Ananias, taught the eunuch without Philip, instructed Cornelius without Peter. Do not hearken to those that cry up an inward teaching, to exclude the outward teaching; as if the external word were but an empty sound and noise, as the Libertines in Calvin's time. Faith, confirmed by reading, is usually begotten by hearing.

2. The use of the word: it is our warrant. What have we to show for our great hopes by Christ but the word? It is our excitement, a means and instrument to show us God's heart and our own, our natural face, and the worth of Christ, the key which God useth and openeth our hearts by. Ministers are Christ's spokesmen; if we will not open the ear, why should God open the heart?

3. The power of the word is exceeding great. It is 'the power of God to salvation.' The first gospel sermon that ever was preached, after the pouring forth of the Spirit, had great success: Acts ii. 41, 'The same day there were added to the church about three thousand souls.' It was a mighty thing that an angel should slay 185,000 in one night in Sennacherib's host; but it is easier to kill so many than to convert one soul. One angel, by his mere natural strength, could kill so many armed men; but all the angels in heaven, if they should join all their forces together, could not convert one soul. There were single miracles of curing one blind or one lame; ay! but the apostle's word could work three thousand miracles: 1 Cor. iii. 5, 'Who is Paul, and who is Apollos, but ministers by whom ye believed, even as the Lord gave to every man?'

Why doth God use the word? I answer—Because it pleased him: 1 Cor. i. 21, 'It pleased God, by the foolishness of preaching, to save them that believe.'

[1.] It is most suitable to man's nature. Man is made of body and soul, and God will deal with him both ways, by internal grace and external exhortations. Man is a reasonable creature; his will is not brutish; God will not offer violence to the principles of human nature. Man is not only weak, but wicked; there is hatred as well as impotency. God will overcome both together, by sweet counsels, mixed with a mighty force; he useth such a remedy as our disease requireth; the gospel is not only called 'the power of God,' but 'the wisdom of God,' 1 Cor. i. 24. There are excellent arguments which the heart of man could not have found out.

[2.] It is agreeable to his own counsels to try the reprobate by an outward rule and offer, wherein they have as much favour as the elect; they shall one day know 'that a prophet hath been among them,' and so be 'left without excuse,' Rom. i. 20. The rain falleth on rocks as well as fields; the sun shineth to blind men as well as those that can see.

[3.] It commendeth his grace to the elect. Their faith must be ascribed to grace. When others have the same means, the same voice and exhortations, it is the peculiar grace of God that they come to understand and believe. Whence is it that the difference ariseth? that whereas wicked men are by the word restrained and made civil (there being a use of wicked men in the world, as of a hedge of thorns about a garden), they are by the same word converted and brought home to God? It is from the grace of God.

Use. Examination. Is our faith thus wrought? Every one should look how he cometh by his faith, by what means. True faith is begotten and grounded upon the word; it is the ordinary means to work faith. The word will be continued, and a ministry to preach it, as long as there are any to be converted. The gospel alone revealeth that which may satisfy our necessities; it giveth a bottom for faith and particular application, as being the declaration of God's will. It is the only means sanctified by Christ for that end: John xvii. 17, 'Sanctify them through thy truth, thy word is truth;' James i. 18. 'Of his own will begat he us, through the word of truth.' The condition of those is woful that want the gospel, or put it from them: Acts xiii. 46, 'Seeing ye put it from you, and judge yourselves unworthy of everlasting life, lo, we turn to the Gentiles.' If faith be of the right make, the word will show thee once thou hadst none, and that thou wert not able of thyself to believe. Beseech the Lord to work it in thee.

SERMON XXXV.

That they all may be one ; as thou, Father, art in me, and I in Thee, that they also may be one in us: that the world may believe that thou hast sent me.—JOHN XVII. 21.

WE have seen for whom Christ prayeth. Now let us see what he prayeth for; their comfortable estate in the world, and the happiness of their everlasting estate in heaven. With respect to their estate in the world, Christ mentioneth no other blessing but the mystical union, which is amplified throughout, ver. 21–23. Here he beginneth, 'That they may be all one ; as thou, Father, art in me, and I in thee.' He had before prayed for the apostles, 'That they may be one, as we are one,' ver. 11 ; and now, 'Let them *all* be one.' The welfare of the church is concerned, not only in the unity of the apostles, but of private believers ; you had need be one as well as your pastors. Many times divisions arise from the people, and those that have least knowlege are most carried aside with blind zeal and principles of separation ; therefore Christ prayeth for private believers, 'That they may be all one,' &c.

In which words there is—

1. The blessing prayed for, ' That they may be all one.'

2. The manner of this unity, illustrated by the original pattern and exemplar of it, ' As thou, Father, art in me, and I in thee ; ' the ineffable unity of the persons in the divine essence.

3. The ground of this unity, the mystical union with Christ, and by Christ with God, ' That they may be one with us.'

4. The end and event of this union, ' That the world may believe that thou hast sent me.'

First, From the blessing prayed for, I observe, that the great blessing Christ asketh for his church is the mystical union of believers in the same body ; ' Let them be one,' one in us, and ' as thou in me, and I in thee.' All these expressions show that the mystical union is here intended. ' Let them be one,'·$\dot{\epsilon}\nu$, that is, $\dot{\epsilon}\nu$ $\sigma\hat{\omega}\mu\alpha$, as it is else-where explained, that they may grow together in one body, whereof I am the head, or one temple. It is sometimes set out by ' one mystical body,' sometimes by ' one spiritual temple.' One body : Col. ii. 19, ' And not holding the head, from which all the body by joints and bands, having nourishment ministered, and knit together, increaseth with the increase of God ; ' Rom. xii. 5, ' We, being many, are one body in Christ, and every one members one of another ; ' Eph. i. 22, 23, ' And gave him to be the head over all things to the church, which is his body.' And one temple : Eph. ii. 20–22, ' And are built upon the foundation of the apostles and prophets, Jesus Christ himself being the chief corner-stone ; in whom all the building fitly framed together groweth unto an holy temple in the Lord : in whom you also are builded together for an habitation of God through the Spirit.' ' One, as thou in me, and I in thee.' Christ doth not say that they may be one in another ;[1] that $\dot{\epsilon}\mu\pi\epsilon\rho\iota\chi\acute{\omega}\rho\eta\sigma\iota\varsigma$ doth not agree to them ; but in the mystery of the Trinity it denotes the union between the divine persons. ' One in us,' that is, by the communication and in-habitation of that Spirit which proceedeth from us. Our union is from God, in God, and to God ; from the Spirit, with God, through Christ.

Let me now inquire—(1.) What it is ? (2.) Why it is so valued by Christ ?

First, What it is ? There is a union with Christ the head, and between the members one with another. I shall speak of both, though but little of the latter, because I handled it ver. 11.

1. There is a union with Christ the head. That ye may conceive of it, take these propositions.

[1.] The whole Trinity is concerned in this union. By the com-munion of the Spirit we are mystically united to Christ, and by Christ to God. The Father is, as it were, the root, Christ the trunk, the Spirit the sap, we the branches, and our works the fruits, John xv. This is the great mystery delivered in the scriptures. Christ doth not only ' dwell in us by faith,' Eph. iii. 17, but ' God dwelleth in us, and we in God,' 1 John iv. 16, and ' the Spirit dwelleth in us ; ' Rom. viii. 11. We are consecrated temples, wherein the whole Trinity take up their residence. We are children of God, members of Christ, pupils to the Holy Ghost ; God's family, Christ's body, and

---

[1] Qu. ' in one another ? '—ED.

the Spirit's charge. We are united to the Father as the fountain of grace and mercy, to the Son as the pipe and conveyance, and the Spirit accomplisheth and effecteth all. The Father sendeth the Son to merit this grace, and the Son sendeth the Spirit to accomplish it; therefore we are said 'by one Spirit to be baptized into the same body.'

[2.] Though all the persons be concerned in it, yet the honour is chiefly devolved upon Christ the second person. Christ, as God-man, is head of the church upon a double ground—because of his two natures, and the union of these in the same person. It was needful that our head should be man, of the same nature with ourselves: Heb. ii. 11, 'He that sanctifieth, and they that are sanctified, are of one;' the same stock. It were monstrous to have a head and members of a different nature; as in Nebuchadnezzar's image, the substance of the head and body differed; the head was of fine gold, the arms of silver, the belly and thighs of brass, the legs of iron, part of the feet of clay; here was a monstrous body indeed, made up of so many metals differing in nature and kind. But Christ took our nature that he might be a suitable head, and so have a right to redeem us, and be in a capacity to give himself for the body, and sympathise with us. All these are fruits of the Son's being of the same nature. And again, God he needed to be, to pour out the Spirit, and to have grace sufficient for all his members. Mere man was not enough to be head of the church, for the head must be more excellent than the body; it is above the body, the seat of the senses, it guideth the whole body, it is the shop of the thoughts and musings. And so Christ the head must have a pre-eminence; in him 'the fulness of the Godhead dwelt bodily, that we might be complete in him,' Col. ii. 8, 9; and 'it pleased the Father that in him should all fulness dwell,' Col. i. 19. The grace of God is most eminent in him, as life is most eminent in the head. Now there must be a union of these two natures in the same person. If Christ had not been God and man in the same person, God and we had never been united and brought together; he is 'Emmanuel, God with us,' Mat. i. 23. God is in Christ, and the believer is in Christ; we have a share in his person, and so hath God; he descendeth and cometh down to us in the person of the mediator; and by the man Christ Jesus we ascend and climb up to God. And so you see the reason why the honour of head of the church is devolved upon Christ.

[3.] Whole Christ is united to a whole believer. Whole Christ is united to us, God-man, and whole man is united to Christ, body and soul. Whole Christ is united to us; the Godhead is the fountain, and the human nature is the pipe and conveyance. Grace cometh from him as God, and through him as man: John vi. 56, 57, 'He that eateth my flesh and drinketh my blood dwelleth in me, and I in him. As the living Father hath sent me, and I live by the Father, so he that eateth me, even he shall live by me.' God is a sealed fountain, his humanity is the pipe, so that his flesh is the food of the soul. Christ came from heaven on purpose, and sanctified our flesh, that there might be one in our nature to do us good, that righteousness and life might pass from him, as sin and death from Adam; but our faith first pitcheth upon the manhood of Christ, as they went into the holy place by the veil. And then a whole christian is united to Christ, body and soul. The soul is united unto him, because it receiveth influences of grace, and the body also is taken in; therefore the apostle disputeth against fornication, because the body is a member of Christ: 1 Cor. vi. 15, 'Shall I then take the members of Christ, and make them the members of an harlot? God forbid!' It is a kind of dismembering and plucking a limb from Christ; you defile Christ's body, the disgrace redounds to him. And hereupon elsewhere doth the apostle prove the resurrection by virtue of our union with Christ: Rom. viii. 10, 11, 'If Christ be in you, the body is dead because of sin; but the spirit is life because of righteousness. But if the Spirit of him that raised up Jesus from the dead dwell in you, he that raised up Christ from the dead shall also quicken your mortal bodies by his Spirit, that dwelleth in you.' You may die, but you shall not be brought to nought, because the body hath a principle of life in it; it is a part of Christ, and he will lose nothing: John vi. 39, 'And this is the Father's will, which sent me, that of all which he hath given me, I should lose nothing, but should raise it up again at the last day.' As plants live in the root, though the leaves fade, and in winter they appear not, so doth the body live in Christ. So that it is a ground of hope, and a motive to strictness, that you may not wrong a member of Christ, nor seek to pluck a joint from his body.

[4.] The manner of this union. It is secret and mysterious: $\mu\acute{\epsilon}\gamma\alpha$ $\mu\upsilon\sigma\tau\acute{\eta}\rho\iota\upsilon\nu$, Eph. v. 22, 'This is a great mystery;' not only a mystery, but a great mystery; 'but I speak concerning Christ and the church.' It is a part of our portion in heaven to understand it: John xiv. 20, 'At that day ye shall know that I am in my Father, and you in me, and I in you.' When we are more like God, we shall know what it is to be united to God through Christ. Here believers feel it rather than understand it, and it is our duty rather to get an interest in it than subtly to dispute about it.

[5.] Though it be secret and mystical, yet it is real; because a thing is spiritual, it doth not cease to be real. These are not words, or poor empty notions only, that we are united to Christ; but they imply a real truth. Why should the Holy Ghost use so many terms; of being planted into Christ? Rom. vi. 5, 'For if we have been planted together in the likeness of his death, we shall be also in the likeness of his resurrection;' of being joined to Christ? 1 Cor. vi. 17, 'He that is joined to the Lord is one Spirit;' of being made partakers of Christ? Heb. iii. 14, 'For we are made partakers of Christ, if we hold the beginning of our confidence steadfast to the end.' Do these terms only imply a relation between us and Christ? No; then the emphasis of the words is lost. What great mystery in all this? Why is this mystery so often spoken of? Christ is not only ours, but 'he is in us, and we in him.' God is ours, and we dwell in God: 1 John iv. 13, 'Hereby know we that we dwell in him, and he in us, because he hath given us of his Spirit;' and ver. 15, 'Whosoever shall confess that Jesus is the Son of God, God dwelleth in him, and he in God.' It is represented by similitudes, that imply a real union as well as a relative, by head and members, root and branches, as well as by marriage, where man and wife are made one flesh. It is compared here with the mystery of the Trinity, and the unity of the divine persons, though not ἀκριβῶς. It is not a notion of scripture, but a thing wrought by the Spirit : 1 Cor. ii. 13, 'Which things also we speak,' &c. It worketh a presence, and conveyeth real influences.

[6.] It may be explained as far as our present light will bear, by analogy to the union between head and members. The head is united to the body primarily, and first of all by the soul. Head and members make out one body, because they are animated by the same soul, and by that means doth the head communicate life and motion to the body. Besides this there is a secondary union, by the bones, muscles, nerves, veins, and other ligaments of the body, and upon all these by the skin, all which do constitute and make up this natural union. Just so in this spiritual and mystical union there is a primary band and tie, and that is the Spirit of Christ: 1 Cor. vi. 17, 'He that is joined to the Lord is one spirit;' that is, is acted by the same Spirit by which Christ is acted, and liveth the same life of grace that Christ liveth, as if there were but one soul between them both. The fulness remaineth in Christ, but we have our share ; and 'he that hath not the Spirit of Christ is none of his.' But over and above there is a secondary bond and tie, that knitteth us and Christ together, which answereth to the joints and arteries, by which the parts of the body are united to one another, and that is faith, and love, and fear, and other graces of the Spirit, by which the presence is kept in the soul. Thus I have a little opened this mystery to you.

2. There is a union of the members one with another. A little of that.

[1.] The same Spirit that uniteth the members to the head uniteth the members one to another. Therefore the apostle, as an argument of union, urgeth the communion of the same Spirit : Phil. ii. 1, 2, 'If any fellowship of the Spirit, fulfil ye my joy, that ye be like-minded, having the same love, being of one accord, of one mind.' As Christ is the head of the church, so the Holy Ghost is the soul of the church, by which all the members are acted. As in the primitive times : Acts iv. 32, 'The multitude of them that believed were of one heart and of one soul.' And this is that that Christ prayeth for here, that they may all be one, in the communion of the same Spirit, that they may be of the same religion, and have the same aim, and the same affection to good things.

[2.] From the communion of the Spirit, there is a secondary union by love, and seeking one another's good, as if they were but one man ; wherever dispersed throughout the world, and whatever distinctions of nations and interests there are, they may love and desire the good of one another, and rejoice in the welfare, and grieve for the evil of one another : Ezek. i. 24, 'When the beasts went, the wheels went, and when the beasts were lifted up from the earth, the wheels were lifted up over against them ; ' and the reason is given, 'for the spirit of the living creature was in the wheels.' The same spirit is in one christian that is in another, and so they wish well to one another, even to those whom they never saw in the flesh: Col. ii. 1, 'For I would that ye knew how great conflict I have for you, and for them at Laodicea, and for as many as have not seen my face in the flesh.' What wrestlings had he with God, and fightings for their sakes, even for them that had not seen his face in the flesh ! So careful are the members one of another.

[3.] This love is manifested by real effects. Look, as by virtue of union with Christ there are real influences of grace that pass out to us, it is not idle and fruitless, so by virtue of this union that is between the members there is a real communication of gifts and graces, and the good things of this life one to another. If the parts of the body keep what they have to themselves, and do not disperse it for the use of the body, it breedeth disease, as the liver the blood, the stomach the meat; the liver imparts blood to the veins, and the stomach sends the food abroad into its proper vessels and channels; so God's children impart their spiritual or temporal gifts as the body needeth. When a famine was but prophesied, the disciples thought of sending relief according to their ability to the brethren of Judea, Acts xi. 29. It is never right but when there is this forwardness to distribute and communicate according to the necessities of the body.

Secondly, Why Christ valueth it so much as to make it his only request for believers in the present state? I answer—We can never be happy till we have a share in this union.

1. Because God hath instituted the mystical union to be a means to convey all grace to us, grace to us here, and glory hereafter; we receive all from God in it, and by it. Christ without us doth not save us, but Christ in us. Christ without us is a perfect Saviour, but not to you; the appropriation is by union. Generally we think we shall be saved by a Christ without us. He came down from heaven, took our nature, died for sinners, ascended up into heaven again, there he maketh intercession; all this is without us. Do not say there is a Saviour in heaven; is there one in thy heart? Col. i. 27, ' Christ in you the hope of glory.' He doth not say, Christ in heaven the hope of glory, though that is a fountain of comfort, but Christ in you : 1 Cor. i. 30, ' Of him are ye in Christ Jesus, who of God is made unto us wisdom, and righteousness, and sanctification, and redemption.' Whatsoever is imputed or imparted, light, life, grace, glory, it is still in him. Still look to Christ within you. It were a merry world to carnal men to be saved by a Christ without them. Christ without establisheth the merit, but Christ within maketh application : 2 Cor. xiii. 5, ' Know ye not your own selves, how that Christ is in you, except ye be reprobates ? ' Unless first or last he be in you, though disallowed for the present, he will be of no advantage to you. You have nothing to show till you feel Christ within you. All the acts of his mediation must be acted over again in the heart. His birth; he must be born and formed in us : Gal. iv. 19, ' My little children, of whom I travail in birth again, until Christ be formed in you.' His death : Rom. vi. 4, ' Therefore we are buried with him by baptism into death.' His resurrection : Col. iii. 1, ' If ye then be risen with Christ, seek those things that are above.' His ascension : Eph. ii. 6, ' And hath raised us up together, and made us sit together in heavenly places in Christ Jesus.' His intercession : Rom. viii. 26, ' Likewise the Spirit also helpeth our infirmities; for we know not what we should pray for as we ought, but the Spirit itself maketh intercession for us with groanings which cannot be uttered.' The acts without us do us no good unless we have the copy of them in our own hearts.

2. It is the ground of that exchange that is between Christ and us ; we communicate to him our nature, our sins, and troubles, and Christ communicateth to us his nature and merits and privileges. What hath Christ from thee ? Thy nature, thy sins, thy punishments, thy wrath, thy curse, thy shame ; and thou hast his titles, his nature, his spirit, his privileges. All this interchange between us and Christ is by virtue of union. All interests lie in common between Christ and the church ; he taketh our nature, and is made flesh, and we are made 'partakers of the divine nature,' 2 Peter i. 4. He is made the Son of man, we the sons of God ; he had a mother on earth, we a Father in heaven ; he is made sin, we righteousness : 2 Cor. v. 21, 'Who hath made him to be sin for us, that we might be made the righteousness of God in him.' He was made a curse that we might have the blessing of Abraham : Gal. iii. 13, 14, ' Christ hath redeemed us from the curse of the law, being made a curse for us ; for it is written, Cursed is every one that hangeth on a tree ; that the blessing of Abraham might come on the Gentiles through Jesus Christ.' Thus he imparteth his privileges to us, and assumeth our miseries to himself. He hath a share in all our sorrows, and we have a share in his triumphs ; he is afflicted in our afflictions, as we ascend in his ascension : Eph. ii. 6, ' He hath raised us up together, and made us sit together in heavenly places in Christ Jesus.' We live by his life : Gal. ii. 20, ' I live, yet not I, but Christ liveth in me,' &c. And we are glorified by his glory. He suffereth with us in heaven, and we reign with him on earth ; he suffereth with us, *non per passionem, sed compassionem*, not that glorified Christ feeleth any grief in heaven, but his bowels yearn to an afflicted member, as if he himself were in our stead ; and we are set down with him in heavenly places, because our head is there, and hath seized upon heaven in our right. It is a notable expression : Col. i. 24, ' Who now rejoice in my sufferings for you, and fill up, ὑστερήμα θλίψεων Χριστοῦ, that which is behind of the sufferings of Christ in my flesh for his body's sake, which is the church.' Christ and the church are considered as one person, whose afflictions are determined by providence ; thus much the head must suffer, thus much the members. Christ suffered his share, and we ours in our turn. In short, Christ suffereth no more in the body that he carried to heaven, but in his body that he left upon earth. Every blow that lighteth on a member, lighteth on his heart : Acts ix. 6, ' Saul, Saul, why persecutest thou me ? ' Christ was in heaven at that time ; how could he say, ' Why persecutest thou me ? ' Did he climb up into heaven, and war upon Christ in the midst of his glory ? No ; Saul persecuted the christians, and them Christ calleth *me*, his mystical body. As in a throng, if somebody treadeth upon your foot, the tongue crieth out, You have hurt me ; the tongue is in safety, but it is in the same body with the foot, and so their good and bad are common ; for though Christ's person be above abuse, he still suffereth in his members ; and he that persecuteth the church persecuteth Jesus Christ.

3. If once interested in the mystical union, then they are safe, preserved in Jesus Christ : Jude 1, ' Sanctified by God the Father, and preserved in Jesus Christ ;' ver. 24, ' Now unto him that is able to keep you from falling,' &c. The union is indissoluble ; that is a cabinet,

where God's jewels are kept safe. If a member could be lost, Christ's body could be maimed ; as the union between the two natures could not be dissolved ; it was the body of Christ in the grave ; there was a separation between his human body and human soul, yet both still remained united to the divine nature ; so this union cannot be dissolved. You may as well sever the leaven and the dough, when they are kneaded together, as separate Christ and the church when once united. *Impossibile est massam a pasta separare.* Christ will not suffer his body to be mangled ; the cutting off of a joint goeth to the quick.

Use 1. To press us to look after an interest in this great privilege. It is the main work of your lives. To move you, consider the honour and the happiness of them, that they are thus one with God through Christ.

1. The honour. What am I, to be son-in-law to the king? What are you, to be members of Christ? Christ counteth himself to be incomplete and maimed without us: Eph. i. 23, ' The church is his body, the fulness of him that filleth all in all.' How are we πλήρωμα αὐτοῦ, ' the fulness of him '? It relateth not to his personal perfection. Take Christ absolutely as God, and he is a person most perfect and glorious. Before the assumption of the human nature, before any creature in the world was made, there was enough in Christ to satisfy his Father's heart. Nay, take him relatively as mediator, what doth Christ want? Doth the body give aught of perfection to the head? No ; ' The fulness of the godhead dwells in him bodily,' and ' he filleth all things.' But taken in his mystical person, Christ mystical, as head and members are called Christ : 1 Cor. xii. 12, ' As the body is one, and hath many members, and all the members of that one body, being many, are one body ; so also is Christ.' So he is not perfect without his body, as a head without members is not perfect. Now, what an honour is this, that he accounteth himself imperfect without us ! And till all his members be gathered in, we are not grown up to the state wherein Christ.is full : Eph. iv. 13, ' Till we all come to the unity of the faith, and of the knowledge of the Son of God, unto a perfect man, unto the measure of the stature of the fulness of Christ.' Christ's mystical body hath not its complete stature till all the saints be gathered. This honour is not put upon the angels ; they are servants, but not members. He did not take their seed to be a head to them, nor die for them, nor took them for his members, as he doth us : Prov. viii. 31, ' Rejoicing in the habitable parts of the earth, and my delights were with the sons of men.' He left the company of angels to dwell with us ; his heart was set upon our good, that, next to the title of Son of God, he valueth this of being head of the church. He purchased it with his blood. He loveth his mystical body above his natural, for he gave his natural body to redeem the church, which is his mystical body ; as husbands love their wives as their own body. O christians ! is not this a mighty privilege ? We are not only his, but him, and Christ knoweth us and loveth us as parts of his own body, and will glorify us not only as his clients and servants, but members ; all the injuries and wrongs done to the church, Christ taketh it as done to himself. Wicked men they are his footstool ; Christ is over them, but not as a mystical head. As the head of a king is lifted up above all his subjects, and governeth them, and weareth the garland of honour,

but in a peculiar manner it governeth and guideth his own natural body; so Christ is 'head over all things to the church,' Eph. i. 22. Certainly this is a great honour put upon poor worms. What are the fruits of it? We are interested in all Christ's communicable privileges; we need not stretch it too far, it is ample enough of itself. Some things are incommunicably proper to Christ, neither given to man nor angel; as the name above all names, to be adored, to be set at the right hand of God, to be head of the church, the Lord our righteousness. But other things are communicated to us, first to Christ, and then to us. Christ is one with the Father, and a poor christian, though never so mean, is one with Christ. Christ is called 'God's fellow,' Zech. xiii. 7, and every saint is Christ's fellow: Ps. xlv. 7, 'Thou hast anointed him with the oil of gladness above his fellows.' The Father loveth him because he is the express image of his person, and delights in the saints because they are the image of Christ. God is his God and our God, his Father and our Father; where Christ is, they are, because they are a part of his body. Alas! we should count it blasphemy to speak so, if the word did not speak it before us.

2. The happiness: 'In him the fulness of the Godhead dwelleth bodily.' There is a sufficiency in Christ for all his members. We have all things in him, which is as good as if we had it in our hands, and better; for he is a better steward and keeper of the treasures of wisdom, grace, and comfort, than we are. If he hath it, it is for our use; for Christ is full as an officer to impart life, sense, and motion to all the body. It is the office of the liver to impart the blood to the veins; it were monstrous and unnatural to keep it. As a treasurer, it is his office to pay money out upon all just demands: Ps. xvi. 2, 3, 'My goodness extendeth not to thee; but to the saints that are in the earth, and to the excellent, in whom is all my delight.' Thou shalt not be forgotten, for the care of Christ extendeth to every member. To neglect a member is to neglect ourselves. If a man could forget a child, yet certainly he could not forget his members. This is your relation to Christ; if he hath bid the 'members to take care one of another,' 1 Cor. xii. 25, what will the head do? These grounds of comfort and faith you have.

Use 2. How shall we know that we have a share in this mystical union? I answer—By the Spirit of Christ: 1 John iv. 13, 'Hereby know we that we dwell in him, and he in us, because he hath given us of his Spirit.' There is a communication of the Spirit; so Rom. viii. 9, 'Now if any man have not the Spirit of Christ, he is none of his;' his creature, but not his member; a limb of Satan, not a member of Christ. Christ's Spirit is poured on all his brethren; it is shared among them, it is given to every member as soon as they are added to Christ's body.

Now, how shall we know whether we have the Spirit of Christ?

Ans. By life and conformity.

1. Life and stirring. A man may know whether the Spirit of Christ be dwelling in him, as a woman knoweth whether the child in the womb be quickened, yea or no, she knoweth it by the stirring; so you may know whether the Spirit of Christ be in you by its working. They are no members of Christ that are not quickened by the life of

grace; there is no withered member in his body. If a member of a lingering [1] body be dead and numb, we rub it and chafe it to bring heat and spirits into it again: so do you feel any grace, any spiritual love? Gal. ii. 20, 'I live, yet not I, but Christ liveth in me; and the life which I now live in the flesh, I live by the faith of the Son of God, who loved me and gave himself for me.' As we know there is life by the beating of the pulses, so there is spiritual life when there is a striving against corruption, complaining of it, sighing, groaning under it, seconded with a constant endeavour to grow better. These sighs and groans are in the greatest desertion.

2. Conformity. Where the Spirit of Christ is it fashioneth us into the likeness of Christ: 2 Cor. iii. 18, 'We all beholding as in a glass the glory of the Lord, are changed into the same image from glory to glory, even as by the Spirit of the Lord.' It maketh us to represent Christ, to be such as he was in the world, meek, holy, humble, useful, as if Christ were come again to converse with men. If you are acted with an unclean, proud, carnal, wrathful spirit, who is it that dwelleth in you? whose image do you bear? There is a changing, transforming power that ariseth from this union, that we delight to do the will of our Father, wherein the conformity lieth chiefly. We shall be humble, meek, gentle: Mat. xi. 29, 'Learn of me, for I am meek and lowly of heart;' thinking humbly of ourselves, not aspiring after greatness. This spirit is a spirit of obedience, enabling us to look to our Father's glory and commandment in all things. We shall have compassionate melting hearts to the miseries of others, as he had bowels yearning to see sheep without a shepherd.

SERMON XXXVI.

That they all may be one; as thou, Father, art in me, and I in thee, that they also may be one in us: that the world may believe that thou hast sent me.—JOHN XVII. 21.

SECONDLY, I am now to handle the second branch, the pattern of this unity, 'As thou, Father, art in me, and I in thee.' It is elsewhere compared three times in this chapter: ver. 11, ἵνα ὦσιν ἓν, καθὼς ἡμεῖς, 'that they may be one, as we are;' ver. 22, καθὼς ἡμεῖς ἓν ἐσμὲν, 'that they may be one as we are one;' and here, καθὼς σὺ πάτερ ἐν ἐμοὶ, κἀγὼ ἐν σοὶ, 'as thou, Father, art in me, and I in thee.' They are not only one, but in one another. It is that which divines call περιχώρησις, the intimate inhabitation or indwelling of the persons in one another, without any confusion of the several subsistences. Such is the unity of the divine essence, that the Father dwelleth in the Son, the Son subsisteth in the Father, and the Holy Spirit in both, without any confusion of the personalities. Now this is propounded as the pattern and original exemplar of the mystical union. The Arians conclude, out of this place, that there is not a unity of essence among the divine persons, but only a unity of love and concord, such

---

1 Qu. 'living'?—ED.

as is between us and Christ, and among believers one with another; ὁμοιούσια, not ὁμοούσια. *As* doth not imply an exact equality, but only a similitude or answerable likeness. In the mystical union there is a kind of shadow and adumbration of that unity which is between the persons of the Godhead. So when man is said to be made after the similitude and likeness of God, it doth not imply a universal and exact equality, but only some conformity and similitude of men to God. So, 'Be ye holy, as I am holy;' 'Be ye perfect, as your heavenly Father is perfect.' It is good to note that in the letter of the text Christ separateth his own unity with the Father from that of the creatures. He doth not say, 'Let us be all one;' but, 'Let them be all one.' Again, he doth not say, 'As thou art in us, and we in thee;' but, 'As thou, Father, art in me, and I in thee.' *Hic suam potentiam, et Patris a nobis secerneret.* Again, in the next clause, he doth not say, 'One with us,' but 'in us.' There is no common union wherein he and we agree. The note is—

Doct. That the mystical union carrieth some resemblance with the union that is between the Father and the Son.

Here I shall show—(1.) The unity between God and Christ; (2.) Wherein the resemblance standeth.

First, The unity between God and Christ. There is a twofold union between God and Christ. God is in him, and one with him, as the second person of the Trinity, and one in him as mediator.

1. As he is the second person of the Trinity, there is a unity of essence, intimated by this περιχώρησις, or mutual inhabitation. Christ is not the Father, but in the Father; to confound the persons is Sabellianism; to divide the natures is Arianism. He doth not only say, 'The Father is in him,' but, 'He is in the Father,' to note a consubstantial unity, that they both communicate in the same essence. At once he showeth the distinction that is between the Father and the Son, and the unity of essence that is between them. And as they are one in essence, so one in power: John x. 28–30, 'I give unto them eternal life, and they shall never perish, neither shall any man pluck them out of my hand. My Father which gave them me is greater than all, and no man is able to pluck them out of my Father's hand. I and my Father are one.' They work by the same power. They are one in will and operation, their actions are undivided; what the Father doeth, the Son doeth, though by an operation proper to each person: John v. 19, 'What things soever the Father doeth, these also doeth the Son likewise.' They are one in love; the Son lay in the bosom of the Father: John i. 18, 'No man hath seen God at any time; the only-begotten Son, which is in the bosom of the Father, he hath declared him.' It is a phrase that expresseth intimacy. There is a mutual complacency and delight in one another. They are equal in dignity and power, and must not be severed in worship: John v. 23, 'That all men should honour the Son as they honour the Father: he that honoureth not the Son, honoureth not the Father which hath sent him.' Thus God and Christ are one, as Christ is the second person. This is the great mystery, three and one, and one and three. Men and angels were made for this spectacle; we cannot comprehend it, and therefore must admire it. *O luminosissimæ tenebræ!* Light, dark-

ness! God dwelleth in both; in light, to show the excellency of his nature; and in darkness, to show the weakness of our apprehension. The Son is begotten by the Father,· yet is in the Father, and the Father in him; the Spirit proceedeth from them both, and yet is in both; all in each, and each in all. They were the more three because one, and the more one because three. Were there nothing to draw us to desire to be dissolved but this, it were enough: John xiv. 20, 'At that day ye shall know that I am in my Father, and you in me, and I in you.' It is no small part of our portion in heaven. For the present, how much cause have we to bless God for the revelation of this mystery! Let us adore it with a humble faith, rather than search into it by the bold inquiries of reason. It is enough for us to know that it is so, though we know not how it is. God were not infinitely great if he were not greater than our understanding.

2. Christ and God are one as mediator. There is a personal union of the two natures. The Father may be said to be in him, because the divine nature is in him; he is Emmanuel. In Christ there are two natures, but one person. His blood could not be the blood of God if the human nature were not united to the second person of the Trinity. It is so united that the human nature is the instrument. As the hand is man's instrument, not separated from the communion of the body, as a pen or knife; it is man's instrument, but yet a part of himself; so is Christ's human nature joined to his divine nature, and made use of as the great instrument in the work of redemption. So that the human nature is a temple 'in which the fulness of the Godhead dwelleth bodily,' Col. ii. 9. Now because of that union, the natures are in one another, and dwell in one another, as the soul dwelleth in the body, and the body is acted and enlivened by the soul. Hence the flesh of Christ is called the flesh of God, and the blood of Christ is called the blood of God: Acts xx. 28, 'Feed the Church of God, which he hath purchased with his own blood.' God was made man, but not man made God; because God was a person of himself, that assumed flesh, and united it to himself. All his actions are the actions of God-man, and so have a merit and a value. The human nature is a passive instrument, but the divine nature giveth it a subsistence, necessary gifts, and honour. Besides all this, there is a union and consent of will in the work of redemption; the Father's acts and Christ's acts are commensurable; God loveth Christ, and Christ obeyeth God.

Secondly, The resemblance between the mystical union and the unity of the persons in the divine nature. The Spirit is *indissolubile trinitatis vinculum*, as one saith, the eternal bond of the Trinity. So among believers, it is the Holy Ghost who joineth us to Christ. Christ, as one with the Father, liveth the same life that the Father doth; so do we, as one with Christ: John vi. 57, 'As the living Father hath sent me, and I live by the Father; so he that eateth me, even he shall live by me.' It is a close union, beyond conception, but yet real; ours is also close, hard to be understood: John xiv. 20, 'At that day ye shall know that I am in the Father, and you in me, and I in you.' There is the highest love wherewith the Father and the Son love one another. Believers have a room in Christ's heart, as Christ in the Father's bosom; they love Christ again, that loved them first. The union is everlasting, for in the divine nature there can be no change; Christ's mystical body cannot lose a joint. It is a holy union; be one as we are one, holy as we are holy; so must ours be with one another. An agreement in evil is like that of Herod and Pilate, who shook hands against Christ. In the divine persons there is order and distinction; the unity of the Trinity doth not confound the order of the persons; they are one, and still three, the Father, the Word, and the Spirit, from whom, in whom, and to whom are all things; they keep their distinct personalities, and distinct personal operations. The unity of the church doth not confound the order of it; there are diversity of gifts and ministrations, but one body. The persons of the Godhead mutually seek the glory of one another; the election of the Father maketh way for the redemption of the Son; and the redemption of the Son for the application of the Holy Spirit, and so upward: John xvi. 14, 'He shall glorify me, for he shall receive of mine, and shall show it unto you;' and John xiv. 13, 'And whatsoever ye shall ask in my name, that will I do, that the Father may be glorified in the Son;' Phil. ii. 9, 'Wherefore God hath highly exalted him, and given him a name above every name.' So in the spiritual union, Christ puts honour on the church, and the church honours Christ; they throw their crowns at the Lamb's feet, and the members are careful of one another: 1 Cor. xii. 25, 'That there be no schism in the body, but that the members should have the same care one of another.' To endear us one to another, Christ did not only leave us the relation of brethren, but of fellow-members; we are not only in the same family, but in the same body. Brothers that have issued from the same womb, and been nursed with the same milk, have defaced all the feelings of nature, and been divided in interests and affections; Cain and Abel, Jacob and Esau, are sad precedents; but there is no such strife between members of the same body. Who would use one hand to cut off another? or divide those parts which preserve the mutual correspondence and welfare of the whole? At least, brothers have not such a care for one another; each liveth for himself, a distinct life apart, and studieth his own profit and advantage; but it is not so in the body, each member liveth in the whole, and the whole in all the members, and they all exercise their several functions for the common good.

And the resemblance between the mystical and the personal union. In the hypostatical union, our nature is united with Christ's nature; in the mystical union, our person with his person. In the hypostatical union, Christ matched into our family; in the mystical union, the soul is the bride. It is an honour to the whole kindred when a great person matcheth into their line and family, but more to the virgin who is chosen and set apart for his bride. Thus Christ first honoured our nature, and then our persons; first he assumeth our nature, and then espouseth our persons. In the hypostatical union, two diverse substances are united into one person; in the mystical union, many persons are united into one body. In the hypostatical union, Christ was a person before he assumed the human nature; the body is a passive instrument, &c.; in the mystical union, on Christ's part active, on ours passive. Christ is in us, in that he liveth in us, governeth us, maketh us partakers of his righteousness, life and spirit; we are in him, as branches in the tree, rays in the sun, rivers in the fountain. The divine nature is a person by itself, and can subsist of itself; the other is only taken into the communion of his person. The human nature communicates nothing to the divine, but only serveth it as an instrument; so we communicate nothing to Christ, but receive all from him. Both are wrought by the Spirit; the body natural of Christ was begotten by the overshadowing of the Holy Ghost, so this union is wrought by God's Spirit. By the first, Christ is bone of our bone and flesh of our flesh ; by the second, we are bone of his bone and flesh of his flesh ; there cometh in the kindred by grace: Heb. ii. 11, 'For both he that sanctifieth and they that are sanctified are all of one ; for which cause he is not ashamed to call them brethren.' He is of the same stock with all men, but he calleth none brethren but those that are sanctified ; none else can claim kindred of Christ, he will own no others. The hypostatical union is indissoluble; it was never laid aside, not in death ; it was the Lord of glory that was crucified, it was the body of Christ in the grave. So it is in the mystical union ; Christ and we shall never be parted. In death, the union is dissolved between the body and the soul, but not between us and Christ; our dust and bones are members of Christ. In the hypostatical union, the natures are not equal; the human nature is but a creature, though advanced to the highest privileges that a creature is capable of; the divine nature assumed the human by a voluntary condescension and gracious dispensation; and being assumed, it always upholdeth it and sustaineth it ; so there is a mighty difference between us and Christ, between the persons united. Christ, as head and prince, is pleased to call us into communion with himself, and to sustain us, being united. In the hypostatical union, the human nature can do nothing apart from the divine ; no more can we out of Christ: John xv. 5, 'I am the vine, ye are the branches; he that abideth in me, and I in him, the same bringeth forth much fruit; for without me ye can do nothing.' In the hypostatical union, God dwelleth in Christ σωματικῶς, Col. ii. 9, 'In him dwelleth all the fulness of the Godhead bodily.' In the mystical union, God dwelleth in us πνευματικῶς, 1 John iv. 4, 'Greater is he that is in you, than he that is in the world.' The hypostatical union is the ground of all that grace and glory that was bestowed on the human nature, without which, as a mere creature, it would not be capable of this exaltation ; so the mystical union is the ground of all that grace and glory which we receive. By the hypostatical union, Christ is made our brother, he contracted affinity with the human nature; by the mystical union he is made our head and husband, he weddeth our persons. As by the hypostatical union there is a communion of properties, so here is a kind of exchange between us and Christ: 2 Cor. v. 21, 'For he hath made him to be sin for us, who knew no sin, that we might be made the righteousness of God in him.' As the honour of the divinity redoundeth to the human nature, so we have a communion of all those good things which are in Christ.

Use 1. Let us strive to imitate the Trinity in our respects both to the head and our fellow-members, that you may neither dishonour the head nor dissolve the union between the members. Christ useth this expression to draw us up to the highest and closest union with himself and one another.

1. In your respects to the head.

[1.] Let your union with him be more close and sensible, that you may lie in the bosom of Christ, as Christ doth in the bosom of God. Is Christ in us as God is in Christ? are we made partakers of the divine nature as he is of ours? that you may say to him, as Laban to Jacob, Gen. xxix. 14, 'Surely thou art my bone and my flesh;' that you may feel Christ in you: Gal. ii. 20, 'I am crucified with Christ: nevertheless I live, yet not I, but Christ liveth in me, and the life which I live in the flesh, I live by the faith of the Son of God, who loved me, and gave himself for me.' This mystery is not only to be believed, but felt.

[2.] In your care not to dishonour your head: 1 Cor. vi. 15, 'Know ye not that your bodies are the members of Christ? Shall I then take the members of Christ, and make them the members of an harlot? God forbid!'

[3.] By your delight and complacency. You should make more of the person of Christ: Cant. i. 13, 'A bundle of myrrh is my beloved unto me; he shall lie all night between my breasts.' Keep Christ close to the heart, delight in his company, and in frequent thoughts of him. This should be the holy solace of the soul.

[4.] By your aims to glorify him. The Father studieth the honour of Christ, so doth the Spirit. Thou art his, and all thine is his. Christ hath a title to thy wit, wealth, estate, strength, to all thou hast or canst do in the world. Dost thou spend thy estate as if it were not thine, but Christ's? use thy parts as if they were not thine, but Christ's? Use thy parts as Christ's.

2. To your fellow-members. Walk as those that are one, as Christ and the Father are one, seeking one another's welfare, rejoicing in one another's graces and gifts, as if they were our own; contributing counsel, assistance, sympathy, prayers for the common good, as if thy own case were in hazard; living as if we had but one interest. This is somewhat like the Trinity.

Use 2. Let it put us upon thanksgiving. No other union with us would content Christ but such as carrieth some resemblance with the Trinity, the highest union that can be. In love to our friends we wear their pictures about our necks; Christ assumed our nature, espouseth our persons; how should we be ravished with the thought of the honour done us! We were separated by the fall, and became base creatures; yet we are not only restored to favour, but united to him.

Thirdly, The ground of this union, 'One with us.' By the mystical union we are united to the whole Trinity. Our communion with the Father is spoken of, 1 John i. 3, 'That ye also may have fellowship with us, and truly our fellowship is with the Father, and with his Son Jesus Christ.' Communion with the Son: 1 Cor. i. 9, 'God is faithful, by whom we are called unto the fellowship of his Son Jesus Christ our Lord.' And communion with the Spirit: 2 Cor. xiii. 14, 'The grace of our Lord Jesus Christ, and the love of God, and the communion of the Holy Ghost be with you all. Amen.' To distinguish them accurately is very hard, only thus in general. We must have communion with all or none. There is no coming to the Father but by the Son: John xiv. 6, 'I am the way, the truth, and the life; no man cometh to the Father, but by me.' None can come to the Son but by the Father: John vi. 44, 'No man can come to me, except the Father, which hath sent me, draw him.' And none can come to both but by the Spirit. Unity is his personal operation: Eph. iv. 3, 'Endeavouring to keep the unity of the Spirit in the bond of peace.' The Father hath a hand in it, Christ hath a hand, the Spirit hath a hand.

Well, then, let us bless God that we have such a complete object for our faith as Father, Son, and Spirit. The Father bestoweth Christ on us, and us on Christ, as marriages are made in heaven. The meritorious cause of this union is Christ the mediator, by his obedience, satisfaction, and merit; otherwise the Father would not look upon us; and the Spirit is sent from the Father and the Son to bring us to the Father by the Son. The Spirit worketh this union, continueth it, and manifests it. All the graces of God are conveyed to us by the Spirit; the Spirit teacheth, comforteth, sealeth, sanctifieth; all is by the Holy Ghost. And so are all our acts of communion; we pray by the Spirit; if we love God, obey God, believe in God, it is by the Spirit, that worketh faith, love, and obedience. We can want nothing that have Father, Son, and Spirit; whether we think of the Father in heaven, the Son on the cross, or feel the Spirit in our hearts. Election is of the Father, merit by the Son, actual grace from the Holy Ghost: 1 Peter i. 2, 'Elect according to the foreknowledge of God the Father, through sanctification of the Spirit, unto obedience, and sprinkling of the blood of Jesus Christ.' Our salvation standeth on a sure bottom; the beginning is from God the Father, the dispensation through the Son, the application by the Spirit. It is free in the Father, sure in the Son, ours in the Spirit. We cannot be thankful enough for this privilege.

Fourthly, The end and issue, 'That the world may believe that thou hast sent me.' By the *world* is not meant the unconverted elect, for Christ had comprehended all the elect in these words, 'Neither pray I for these alone, but for them also which shall believe in me through their word,' ver. 20. The matter of his prayer is, 'That they may be one,' &c.; and the reason, 'That the world may believe that thou hast sent me.' So that by the world is meant the reprobate lost world, who shall continue in final obstinacy. By *believing* is meant not true saving faith, but common conviction, that they may be gained to some kind of faith, a temporary faith, or some general profession of religion; as John ii. 23, 24, 'Many believed in his name, when they saw the miracles which he did; but Jesus would not commit himself unto them, because he knew all men;' and John xii. 42, 43, 'Nevertheless among the chief rulers also many believed on him, but because of the pharisees, they did not confess him, lest they should be put out of the synagogue: for they loved the praise of men more than the praise of God.' There believing is taken for being convinced of the truth of his religion, which he had established, though they had no mind to profess it; or if so, yet they did not come under the full power of it.

But how is this the fruit of the mystical union?   The fruits of the mystical union are four, to this purpose :—

1. Holiness: ' Whosoever is in Christ is a new creature,' 2 Cor. v. 17.   Sanctification is a fruit of union : 1 Cor. i. 30, ' For of him are ye in Christ Jesus, who of God is made unto us wisdom, righteousness, sanctification, and redemption.'   And it is a means to convince the world : Mark v. 16, ' Let your light so shine before men, that they, seeing your good works, may glorify your Father which is in heaven ;' 1 Peter ii. 12, ' Having your conversation honest amongst the Gentiles, that whereas they speak evil of you as of evil-doers, they may by your good works, which they shall behold, glorify God in the day of visitation ;' 1 Peter iii. 1, ' Likewise, ye wives, be in subjection to your own husbands, that if any obey not the word, they also may, without the word, be won by the conversation of the wives.'

2. Unity: 1 Cor. xii. 13, ' For by one Spirit we are all baptized into one body.'   To endear us to himself, and to one another as fellow-members, Christ would draw us into one body : John xiii. 35, ' By this shall all men know that ye are my disciples, if ye have love one to another.'   *Aspice ut se mutuo diligunt christiani !*   Oh ! the mighty charity that was among the primitive christians : Acts iv. 32, ' And the multitude of them that believed were of one heart and of one soul.' Divisions in the church breed atheism in the world.

3. Constancy in the profession of the truth : Jude 1, ' To them that are sanctified by God the Father, and preserved in Jesus Christ, and called.'   We are preserved in Christ as wine in the hogshead, being in the cabinet where God's jewels are kept.   Now this is taking with the world.

4. Special care of God's providence.   God keepeth them as the apple of his eye : Dan. ii. 47, ' Of a truth it is that your God is a God of gods, and a Lord of kings, and a revealer of secrets, seeing he could reveal unto you this secret ;' 1 Cor. xiv. 25, ' And thus are the secrets of his heart made manifest, and so falling down on his face, he will worship God, and report that God is in you of a truth ;' Dan. iii. 28, ' Blessed be the God of Shadrach, Meshech, and Abednego, who hath sent his angel, and delivered his servants that trusted in him, and have changed the king's word, and yielded their bodies, that they might not serve nor worship any god, except their own God ;' Dan. vi. 27, ' He delivereth and rescueth, and he worketh signs and wonders in heaven and in earth, who hath delivered Daniel from the power of the lions ;' Josh. ii. 11, ' And as soon as we had heard these things, our hearts did melt, neither did there remain any more courage in any man, because of you ; for the Lord your God is God in heaven above, and in earth beneath ;' Acts v. 12–14, ' And by the hands of the apostles were many signs and wonders wrought among the people, and they were all with one accord in Solomon's porch ; and of the rest durst no man join himself to them : but the people magnified them, and believers were the more added to the Lord, multitudes both of men and women.'

SERMON XXXVIII.

And the glory which thou gavest me I have given them ; that they may be one, even as we are one.—JOHN XVII. 22.

CHRIST had prayed for the union of believers in one mystical body: here is an argument to enforce that request, ' The glory which thou hast given me, I have given them,' &c.   His act is urged as a reason, because of that consent of will that is between him and the Father; Christ would have his gift ratified by the Father's consent, as if he had said, Deny not what I have granted them.

For the meaning of the words, all the difficulty is, what is meant by the glory here spoken of ?   Some say by *glory* is meant the power of working miracles, that is called the glory of God: John xi. 40, ' Said I not, If thou wouldst believe, thou shalt see the glory of God ?' that is, a glorious miracle wrought by him.   When Christ wrought a miracle, John ii. 11, ' He manifested forth his glory.'   And so they limit it to the apostles, who had gifts of miracles, and were fitted to succeed Christ upon earth : thus many of the ancients.   By the glory of God is sometimes meant the image of God : Rom. iii. 23, ' All have sinned, and fallen short of the glory of God ;' so 2 Cor. iii. 18, ' We all with open face beholding as in a glass the glory of the Lord, are changed into the same image, from glory to glory.'   That glory which we lost in Adam and want by nature is restored to us in Christ.   Some by glory understand the Spirit, who is called ' a Spirit of glory,' and was given to Christ without measure, and from him to us, as a means of union between us and Christ, and between us and believers.   Others understand it of the honour of filiation ; as Christ was a son by nature, so are we by grace : John i. 14, ' We beheld his glory, the glory as of the only-begotten of the Father ;' and ver. 12, ' As many as received him, to them gave he, ἐξουσίαν, power to become the sons of God.'   It is an honour : it is a means of union.   Adoption maketh way for union with Christ, and Christ left us the relation of brethren, that we might love one another, for we are brethren.   But by glory I suppose is meant rather the happiness of the everlasting state, which is usually called glory in scripture ; and so it is taken, ver. 24, ' Father, I will that they also whom thou hast given me, may be with me where I am, that they may behold my glory which thou hast given me.'   And there is the most perfect union with Christ ; and we that expect one heaven, should not fall out by the way.   Eph. iv. 4, one of the bonds is ' one hope.'   All the difficulty is, how was this given them ?   The disciples were upon the earth, and the greatest part of believers were not then in being.   *Ans.* Christ acquired a right, and left us a promise; he would not go to heaven till he had made it sure to us by deed of gift ; this then I conceive to be the meaning.   It is not good to straiten the sense of scripture ; yet some one is more proper: adoption, gift of the spirit, new nature, eternal life, you may comprise all.

1. Observe, Christ's care to make us every way like himself, as far as our capacity will bear ; like, but not equal.   The reiteration showeth his care, ' Let them be as we are ;' and ' The glory which thou hast given me, I have given them.'

What resemblance is there between us and Christ?
1. Between us and Christ as the eternal Son of God.
2. Between us and Christ as mediator.

First, Between us and Christ as the eternal Son of God. Christ is the essential image of the Father, therefore called 'the image of the invisible God,' Col. i. 15, and the character or 'express image of his person,' Heb. i. 3; and we are God's image by reflection. If there be two or three suns appear, one or two are but a reflection. There are some strictures in us. Christ is one with the Father, and we with him; a poor christian, though never so mean, is one with Christ. Christ is called 'God's fellow,' Zech. xiii. 7, and every saint is Christ's fellow: Ps. xlv. 7, 'God, even thy God, hath anointed thee with the oil of gladness above thy fellows.' The Father loveth him because he is the express image of his person, and the Father delights in the saints because they are the image of Christ: 'The Father himself loveth you,' John xvi. 28. A man that loveth another, he loveth head and members with the same love. Christ is the Son of God, so are we; it was his eternal right and privilege; our title cometh by him: John xx. 17, 'I ascend unto my Father, and your Father.' First, he is Christ's father, and then ours; his by nature, ours by adoption, otherwise we could not have it.

2. But this likewise chiefly respects the glory that was given to Christ as mediator. As God communicateth himself to Christ as mediator, so doth Christ communicate himself to his members. Christ, as man, was begotten by the Holy Ghost; and the same Spirit begetteth us to the life of faith. The new nature is formed in us by the Spirit, as Christ was formed in the virgin's womb: Gal. iv. 19, 'My little children, of whom I travail in birth again, until Christ be formed in you.' All his moral excellences are bestowed on the saints: 2 Cor. iii. 18, 'We all beholding as in a glass the glory of the Lord, are changed into the same image, from glory to glory, even as by the Spirit of the Lord.' If a picture be well taken, it makes us know him whom it represents; we see the lineaments of his face as if he were present; so doth a christian express and show forth the virtues of Christ: 1 Peter ii. 9, 'Ye are a chosen generation, a royal priesthood, a holy nation, that ye should show forth the praises of him who hath called you out of darkness into his marvellous light.' There is an answerable impression to his mediatory actions, and a spiritual conformity to them: Rom. vi. 4, 'Therefore we are buried with him by baptism into death, that like as Christ was raised up from the dead by the glory of the Father, even so we also should walk in newness of life;' Phil. iii. 10, 'That I may know him, and the power of his resurrection, and the fellowship of his sufferings, being made conformable unto his death;' Eph. ii. 6, 'And hath raised us up together, and made us sit together in heavenly places in Christ Jesus;' a dying in his death, a living in his life, an ascending in his ascension; dying to sin, rising to newness of life; our ascension is by thoughts, hopes, and resolutions. We resemble him in his afflictions, it is a part of our conformity: 2 Cor. iv. 10, 'Always bearing about in the body the dying of the Lord Jesus, that the life also of Christ might be made manifest in our mortal flesh.' An afflicted innocence

and meek patience is a resemblance of Christ.   And as in this life we resemble Christ in his actions and passions, so that a christian is as it were a spiritual Christ, so in the life to come we resemble him in glory.   Christ, after he died, rose again, and so do we; the same Spirit raiseth us that raised Christ.   He ascended into heaven accompanied with angels; so are we carried by the angels into Abraham's bosom.   In heaven he liveth blessedly and gloriously, so do we; Christ hath a kingdom, so have we: Luke xii. 32, 'Fear not, little flock; it is your Father's pleasure to give you the kingdom.'   At the last day his human nature will be brought forth with a majesty and glory suitable to the dignity of his person: 'So shall he be admired in his saints,' 2 Thes. i. 10.   Then the mystery of his person shall be disclosed; so shall the mystery of our life: Col. iii. 3, 4, 'For ye are dead, and your life is hid with Christ in God.   When Christ who is our life shall appear, then shall ye also appear with him in glory.'   Christ judgeth the world; so do the saints: 1 Cor. vi. 2, 'Know ye not that the saints shall judge the world?'   Mat. xix. 28, 'Ye which have followed me, in the regeneration, when the Son of man shall sit in the throne of his glory, ye also shall sit upon twelve thrones, judging the twelve tribes of Israel.'   'The second time Christ shall appear without sin unto salvation,' Heb. ix. 28.   So we shall be then disburdened of all the fruits and effects of sin, 'which shall be blotted out when the times of refreshing shall come from the presence of the Lord,' Acts iii. 19.   We are like him in his offices, kings, priests, and prophets, but in a spiritual manner, to rule our lusts, to minister in holy things, and to instruct our hearts.   Thus you see there is a conformity in grace and glory.

Now Christ is thus earnest to make us like himself, partly out of his own love; he cannot satisfy his heart with giving us any inferior privilege.   Whatever he had and was, it was for our sakes; as man, he received it for us: Ps. lxviii. 18, 'Thou hast received gifts for men;' compared with Eph. iv. 8, 'He gave gifts unto men.'   His life, righteousness, and glory is for our sakes.   Wherefore doth Christ make himself like unto us, but that we might be like unto him?   Partly in obedience to God's counsels and decrees: Rom. viii. 29, 'For whom he did foreknow he also did predestinate, to be conformed to the image of his Son, that he might be the first-born among many brethren.'   There is wisdom in it, *primum in unoquoque genere est præstantissimum*.   Christ is the example and pattern set forth by God, and that in our nature; he is the second Adam, a new root, and it is meet that head and members should suit, otherwise it is monstrous.

Use 1.   It showeth who are Christ's, they that are like him; there is a conformity between them and Christ, first in grace, and then in glory.   Here we are like him in soul, in regard of disposition and moral excellences, and in body, in regard of afflictions and weaknesses. Hereafter we shall be like him in soul and body in a glorious manner; here in holiness, hereafter in happiness.   He beginneth with the change of the soul; the resurrection is παλιγγενεσία, a regeneration, Mat. xix. 28.   Then we shall be perfectly renewed; our carnality is done away by grace, our corruption and mortality by glory.   All things are there made new, new bodies, new souls.   Glory, it is but the full period of the present change and transformation into Christ's image:

2 Cor. iii. 18, 'We are changed into the same image, from glory to glory.' Glory is but the consummation of grace, or our full conformity to Christ, or that final estate which is suitable to the dignity of the children of God. Therefore every one that looketh for eternal life in Christ, must be like him in this life; they are partakers with him of glory hereafter, because followers of him here. Therefore see, art thou like Christ? hast thou the image of Christ? that is our title. Alas! many are not conformable, but contrary to Christ. Christ spent whole nights in prayer, they in gaming and filthy excess; it was meat and drink to him to do his Father's will, but it is your burden. Christ was humble and meek, you are proud and disdainful, vain in apparel and behaviour. Were you ever changed? Till you resemble Christ here, you shall never be like him hereafter.

Use 2. It presseth us to look after this conformity and likeness unto Christ. It is the ground of hope; you cannot otherwise think of death and judgment to come without horror: 1 John iv. 17, 'Herein is love made perfect, that we may have boldness in the day of judgment; because as he is, so are we in the world.' David was not ashamed to own his followers when he was crowned at Hebron, so neither will Christ be ashamed of us if we have followed him. If you profess Christ, and be not like him, Christ will be ashamed of you: Heb. ii. 11, 'For both he that sanctifieth, and they that are sanctified, are all of one; for which cause he is not ashamed to call them brethren.' He is not ashamed to own the saints: if one of your name were stigmatised, and branded with a mark of infamy, you would be ashamed to own him. To this end:—

[1.] Eye your pattern. Christ's life should be ever before your eyes, as the copy is before the scholars: Heb. xii. 2, 'Looking unto Jesus,' &c. He hath set forth himself in the word to this end and purpose.

[2.] Often shame thyself that thou comest so much short: Phil. iii. 12, 'I follow after, if I may apprehend that for which also I am apprehended of Jesus Christ.' Alas! we do but lag behind; Christ is a great way before. We have so excellent a pattern, that we may never want matter for humiliation and imitation. It is a good sign to desire to come nearer the copy every day.

2. Observe our glory for substance is the same that Christ's is. In the degree there is a difference, according to the difference that is between head and members. The head weareth the crown and badge of honour, and the eldest son had a double portion. So doth Christ πρωτεύειν, excel in degrees of everlasting glory, but the substance is the same; therefore we are said to be 'co-heirs with Christ,' and 'to be glorified with Christ,' Rom. viii. 17. Christ and we hold the same heaven: 2 Tim. ii. 11, 12, 'If we be dead with him, we shall also live with him. If we suffer, we shall also reign with him.' More particularly, our bodies are like his glorious body: Phil. iii. 21, 'Who shall change our vile body, that it may be fashioned like unto his glorious body, according to the working whereby he is able to subdue all things to himself.' When the sun ariseth, the stars vanish, their glory is obscured; but it is not so here. Christ's coming doth not eclipse, but perfect our glory; the more near Christ is, the more we shine. And so for our souls, they see God and enjoy him; though not in that same

latitude and degree which Christ doth, yet in the same manner they solace themselves in God: 'We shall be like him, for we shall see him as he is,' 1 John iii. 2. When we behold him in the glass of the gospel we are transformed, much more when we see him as he is. As the iron held in the fire is all fire, so we, being in God and with God, are more like him, have higher measures of the divine nature. So our privileges are the same with Christ's: Rev. iii. 21, 'To him that overcometh will I grant to sit with me in my throne, even as I also overcame, and am set down with my Father in his throne.' We sit upon his throne as he doth upon his Father's; there are two thrones mentioned for our distinct conceiving of the matter; as God is over all, so is Christ, and then we next.

Use 1. It is a great comfort :—

1. Against abasement. Will any one believe that these poor creatures, that are so slighted, and so little esteemed in the world, shall have the same glory that Christ hath? 1 John iii. 2, 'Beloved, now are we the sons of God, and it doth not yet appear what we shall be.' The world thinketh meanly and contemptibly of the condition of christians; in the world we are like him in afflictions, by that means we hold forth the life of Christ: 2 Cor. iv. 10, 'Always bearing about in the body the dying of the Lord Jesus, that the life also of Jesus might be made manifest in our mortal flesh.'

2. Against weaknesses and infirmities of the flesh; those saints that have now so many infirmities shall be made like Christ, and crowned with perfection. There is nothing less than grace at the beginning, it is as a grain of mustard-seed, a little leaven; but it groweth still, as a child groweth in favour more and more, and as the light increaseth to the perfect day. This should comfort us against all our weaknesses and infirmities: Ps. xvii. 15, 'As for me, I will behold thy face in righteousness; I shall be satisfied when I awake with thy likeness.'

Use 2. It informeth us :—

1. That our condition in Christ is in this regard better than our condition would have been if Adam had stood in innocency. Adam could only convey to us what he had received; but Christ is a better root; we have in Christ whatever we lost in Adam, the first root, and more, more than we lost. Christ, being God-man, must needs have the image of God in greater perfection; now we are not renewed to the image of the first Adam, but of the second. Oh! the depth of the divine mercy and wisdom, that hath made our fall to be a means of our preferment!

2. It informeth us what we may look for, even for what Christ is in glory; we have a glimpse of it in his transfiguration, in his giving the law. Let our thoughts be more explicit about this matter.

Use 3. It is an engagement to holiness. We expect to be as Christ is, therefore let us not carry ourselves sordidly, like swine wallowing in the mire: 1 John iii. 3, 'And he that hath this hope in him purifieth himself, even as he is pure.' We expect a sinless state, not a Turkish paradise. That body that is made an instrument of whoredom and drunkenness, shall it be like Christ's glorious body? Those affections that shall be ravished with the enjoyment of God, shall they be prostituted to the world? and that mind which is made for the sight of God, serve only to make provision for the flesh? shall it be filled with chaff and vanity?

3. Observe that glory is the fruit of union, as well as grace. The spiritual union is begun here, but it is accomplished in the next life. Here we are crucified, quickened, ascend, and sit down with Christ in heavenly places: Eph. ii. 5, 6, 'Even when we were dead in sins hath he quickened us together with Christ, and hath raised us up together, and made us sit together in heavenly places in Christ Jesus;' Col. i. 27, 'Christ in you the hope of glory.' Christ in us will not leave till he bringeth us to heaven. In this life we cannot come to him; the state of mortality is a state of absence; therefore Christ will come to us, but with an intent to bring us to himself, that we may be where he is: ver. 24, 'Father, I will that they also whom thou hast given me be with me where I am, that they may behold my glory.' He cometh to us where we are, that at length we may be where he is. It is the Lord's method to bring us from death to life, from misery to happiness, by degrees; thousands of years cannot make up that which was lost in an hour; till the resurrection all is not perfected, we do not fully discern the fruits of our union with Christ.

Use 1. To help us to conceive of the mystery of union. Some men fancy that as soon as we are united to Christ we are actually glorified in this life. It is true Christ is equally united to them upon earth as to them in heaven; he that reigneth with the church triumphant fighteth with the church militant; but there is a difference in the degree of influence and dispensation. In the blessings that he conferreth upon them, he respects their different condition, and poureth out of his own fulness as they are able to bear. The reason of this different influence is, because they are conveyed to us voluntarily, not by necessity: Phil. ii. 13, 'It is God which worketh in you, both to will and to do, of his good pleasure.' He gives more or less comfort, grace, joy, as he pleaseth; his grace floweth into his members, not by a necessity of nature, but according to his own pleasure. Give him leave to handle his mystical body as he handled his natural body. His natural body grew by degrees, and the capacity of his human soul was enlarged by degrees, else how could he 'increase in wisdom as well as stature'? Luke ii. 40. There was a perfect union between the divine and human nature at first, yet the divine nature manifested itself by degrees, not in such a latitude in childhood as in grown age. So though there is a perfect union between Christ and the soul at first conversion, yet the influence of grace and comfort is given out according to the measure of our capacity. All believers upon earth are united to Christ, yet all have not a like degree of manifestation and influence. As all the members of the body are united to the same head, and animated by the same soul, yet all the members grow according to the measure of a part; we cannot expect a finger should be as big as an arm. So all that are united to Christ receive influences according to their capacities; those that are glorified, glorious influences; those that are militant, influences proper to their state.

Use 2. It serveth to quicken those that are united to Christ to look for greater things than they do yet enjoy: John i. 50, 'Thou shalt see greater things than these;' another manner of union and communion with God through Christ. There is a mighty difference between our communion with God here and there. The saints in heaven have union with God by sight, as the saints on earth by faith: 2 Cor. v. 7, 'For we walk by faith, not by sight;' and faith cannot go so high as feeling and fruition. Now we are unfit for converse with God, because of our blindness and darkness, as men of weak parts are not fit company for the strong. But then our faculties are more enlarged. Grace regulates the faculty, but it doth not alter and change the faculty. God's communications are more full and free, and we are more receptive. Here we have dark souls and weak bodies; the old bottles would break if filled with the new wine of glory. At Christ's transfiguration, 'the disciples were astonished, and fell on their faces,' Mat. xvii. 6; but in heaven, the sight of Christ's glory will be ravishing, no terror. Here we are amazed at the sight of an angel; but there is a perfect suitableness between us and God, and therefore a more perfect union and communion. God more delighteth in the saints, as having more of his image; and the saints more delight in God, as being freed from sin. God loveth to look on what he hath made when he hath raised a worm to such an excellency. It is there continued without interruption; here our communion with God is sweet, but short, it cometh by glimpses; but there it is for ever and ever, not only in regard of duration, but continuance without ceasing. The Spirit of God came on Samson at times. In heaven there is nothing to divert us from the sight of God; we are withdrawn from all other objects, that we may study him alone without weariness

Use 3. It directeth us in what order we should seek these things; first grace, then glory: Ps. lxxxiv. 11, 'The Lord will give grace and glory;' Ps. lxxiii. 24, 'Thou shalt guide me with thy counsel, and afterwards receive me to glory;' Eph. v. 26, 27, 'That he might sanctify and cleanse it by the washing of water, by the word, that he might present it to himself a glorious church, not having spot or wrinkle, or any such thing, but that it should be holy and without blemish.' Here the first lineaments are drawn by the Spirit of sanctification, whilst the soul remaineth in the body, as a pledge of a more perfect state : 'God hath called us to glory and virtue,' 2 Peter i. 3. As they were to go through the temple of virtue to the temple of honour.

4. Observe, there is no privilege which we have but what Christ enjoyed first. Christ had it all, and from him we have it; he was the purchaser and the natural heir ; it is in us at the second-hand ; we are elected, sanctified, glorified in and through him. Whatever is in us that are members, it is in our head first; first God, then Christ as mediator, and then we. All good is first in Christ, he receiveth it, and conveyeth it. We ascend; why? because he ascended first; we sit in heavenly places, because he did first.

Use 1. In times of desertion, when we see nothing in ourselves, look upon Christ as a depositary, the first receptacle of grace; he is justified, sanctified, ascended, glorified; and encourage thyself to take hold of Christ, that thou mayest have all these things in him.

Use 2. To be thankful to God for Christ: 'Blessed be the God and Father of our Lord Jesus Christ, who hath blessed us with all spiritual blessings in heavenly places in Christ,' Eph. i. 3. Let us never bless God for what we enjoy, but still remember Christ.

Use 3. It presseth us to get a union with Christ: 1 Cor. iii. 22, 23, 'All are yours, for you are Christ's, and Christ is God's;' that we may not look on Christ as an abstracted head. All that Christ hath, he hath it for us.

5. Observe from those words, 'I have given them;' it may be objected that we see no such matter; Christ's members are poor despicable dust and ashes, more afflicted than others. How then can it be said, This glory 'I have given them'? *Ans.* Christ hath acquired a right. Observe, the glory that is given to us by Christ is as surely ours as if we were in the actual possession of it: John iii. 36, 'He that believeth on the Son of God hath everlasting life.' How hath he it?

[1.] He hath it *in capite*: it is done in regard of Christ, with whom we make one mystical body. The most worthy part of the body is in heaven, the head is there: Eph. ii. 6, 'And hath raised us up together, and made us sit together in heavenly places in Christ.' We are already glorified in Christ, though not in ourselves. Christians take possession in their head, as Christ hath taken possession in their names.

[2.] They have it in the promises. The promise is the root of the blessing; you have a fair charter to show for it. God standeth bound in point of promise. God is very tender of his word; you will see it in all the other promises when you put him to trial. The promise of God is but the declaration of his purpose: Heb. vi. 17, 18, 'Wherein God willing more abundantly to show unto the heirs of promise the immutability of his counsel, confirmed it by an oath: that by two immutable things, in which it was impossible for God to lie, ye may have strong consolation.' You have a lease to show for it; a man doth not carry his inheritance upon his back.

[3.] They have the first-fruits of it, which differ only in degree from glory: Rom. viii. 23, 'And not only they, but ourselves also, which have the first-fruits of the Spirit; even we ourselves groan within ourselves, waiting for the adoption, to wit, the redemption of our body.' We have the earnest in hand. That portion of the Spirit which we have received is given us for security. Wherefore this fitting and preparing, these groans, are grounds of confidence. If a vessel be formed, it is for some use. All this would else be lost. And do you think God will lose his earnest? The beginnings we have here are a taste and pledge; here we sip, and have a foretaste of the cup of blessing. Union with Christ, joys of the Spirit, peace of conscience, are the beginnings of heaven. They that live in the provinces next to Arabia have a strong scent of the odours and sweet smells of the spices that grow there; so the church is the suburbs of heaven; the members of it begin to smell the upper paradise. The comfortable influences of the Spirit are the taste, and the gracious influences are the pledge and earnest, of our future inheritance.

Use 1. Let us bless God aforehand: 1 Peter i. 3–5, 'Blessed be the God and Father of our Lord Jesus Christ, which, according to his abundant mercy, hath begotten us again unto a lively hope, by the resurrection of Jesus Christ from the dead, to an inheritance incorruptible and undefiled, and that fadeth not away, reserved in heaven for us, who are kept by the power of God through faith unto salvation.' The inheritance is kept for us, and we for it. We can never want matter to bless God; if we have nothing in hand, yet we have much in hope.

2. Let us wait with more confidence; we have no cause to doubt; we have God's word and pawn; as sure as Christ is in heaven, we shall be there.

3. Let us be there in affection, in earnest groans and desires, in frequent thoughts: Rom. viii. 30, 'Whom he did predestinate, them he also called; and whom he called, them he also justified; and whom he justified, them he also glorified.

4. Let us not fear changes; all changes will end in that which is best for us.

SERMON XXXIX.

I in them, and thou in me, that they may be made perfect in one; and that the world may know that thou hast sent me, and hast loved them, as thou hast loved me.—JOHN XVII. 23.

CHRIST'S request for union is again repeated, with the advantage of another expression, to declare the nature of it. So that in this verse we have—

1. The nature of the mystical union.

2. The end of it; with respect to believers and the world; their conviction of Christ's mission, and the Father's love to the disciples.

First, The nature of this union further declared, 'I in them, and thou in me.'

Here first observe, that one union is the ground of another. Christ and the Father are one, and then Christ and we are one, and then we are one, one with another. The assumed nature is united to the divine essence in Christ's person; and so he, as mediator, is one with the Father; and then we by the communion of the Spirit are not only united to the head, but to our fellow-members.

There are two unions spoken of in this verse.

1. With God, that is implied; the Father is a believer's as well as Christ: John xiv. 23, 'My Father will love him, and we will come to him, and make our abode with him.' Why then doth Christ say, 'I in them'? Not to exclude the Father; for he presently addeth, 'Thou in me.' Christ speaketh as mediator, to show that he is the cause, way, and means. He is the Jacob's ladder: John i. 51 'Verily I say unto you, Hereafter ye shall see heaven opened, and the angels of God ascending and descending upon the Son of man.'

2. There is a union with Christ immediately; that is formally expressed, 'I in them.' And then between us and others of the same body, 'That they may be made perfect in one;' all drawn up into

unity with God in Christ. First, God descendeth in the person of Christ, and then we all ascend by Christ, and come up to God again. Thus the personal union maketh way for the mystical, and the mystical for our joint communion with God in the same body. This is the great mystery that hath been driving on from all eternity, the Father is the beginning and ending, and Christ the means. All influence cometh from God through Christ, and our tendency is to him through Christ: 1 Cor. viii. 6, 'To us there is but one God, the Father, of whom are all things, and we in him; and one Lord Jesus Christ, by whom are all things, and we by him.' All mercies come to us, and our services and respects go to God, through Christ. The reason is, we are departed from God by sin; so that God is removed from us, and God is against us, at a distance, and at an enmity; and we are fugitives and exiles, as Adam ran away from God before he was banished out of his presence. Therefore Christ is not only a meritorious cause of the union that is between us and God, but also the bond and tie of it. To satisfy God offended, this he might do as a Saviour without us; but to be a means of influence on God's part, and respect and service on ours, to convey grace, and return service, he must be in us: 'I in them.' As exiles, we are taken into grace and favour by the merit of Christ; and as fugitives, we are brought into unity again by his Spirit working in us. Therefore it is said: Eph. i. 10, 'That in the dispensation of the fulness of times he might gather together in one all things in Christ, both which are in heaven, and which are on earth, even in him.' There God descendeth, and we ascend. All the scattered elect are brought into a body, to receive influences of grace from God as a fountain, through Christ as a conveyance. So Eph. ii. 18, 'For through him we have an access by one Spirit unto the Father.' All believers are united into a body by the communion of Christ's Spirit, that by Christ they may perform service to God, and receive grace from him.

Use. Is to prize Christ as mediator, and to make use of him in your addresses to God. Heathens had many ultimate objects of worship, and many mediators; we have but one.

1. If you perform anything to God, do it in and through Christ, 'in whom he is well pleased,' Mat. iii. 17. A holy God will accept nothing, but as tendered in Christ's name. We cannot endure the majesty of his presence: Col. iii. 17, 'And whatsoever ye do, in word or deed, do all in the name of the Lord Jesus, giving thanks to God and the Father by him;' by the assistance of his grace and dependence upon his merit, that is to do all in Christ's name. We are made amiable to God in Christ; out of Christ we are odious to God: Ps. xiv. 2, 3, 'The Lord looketh down from heaven upon the children of men, to see if there were any that did understand and seek God. They are all gone aside, they are altogether become filthy; there is none that doeth good, no, not one.' Once God looked on the creatures all good, but that was in innocency; after the fall he looked on the creatures, and all are become filthy; it is not meant of any particular sort of men, but all in their natural condition. The apostle bringeth that place to prove the universal corruption of nature, Rom. iii. 10, that is, out of Christ. **But as he looketh on us in Christ, so we are amiable; he is well-pleased**

in him: it is proclaimed from heaven, that we might not be afraid to go to God.

2. If you expect anything from him, you must expect it in Christ. Christ is not only the meritorious cause, but the means. All we look for is not only from him, but in him. As God first loveth Christ, then loveth us; he is the *primum amabile*, the first beloved of all; so he is first in Christ, and then in us; he is *primum recipiens*, the first object of blessing and grace: 1 Cor. iii. 22, 23, 'All are yours, for you are Christ's, and Christ is God's.' We have it at second-hand, Christ cometh between God and us, to convey the influences and bounty of heaven to us. Therefore it is said: 2 Cor. i. 20, 'All the promises of God in him are Yea, and in him Amen.' God doth whatever we desire him, in him. God doth not bless us as persons distinct from Christ, but as members of his body. There is as much need of the union of our persons to the person of Christ, as there was of the union of the human nature to the divine nature. Christ must be in us, as well as God in Christ; we must be Christ's as well as Christ is God's. The mediator hath an interest in God, and you must have an interest in the mediator. Look, as by the personal union, Christ merited all for us; so, by the union of persons, he conveyeth all to us. Christ could not suffer till he had united our flesh to his godhead; and we cannot receive the virtue of his sufferings till he unites our person to his person.

Secondly, Observe, Christ is in us, as God is in Christ. The two unions are often compared in this chapter; and here it is said, 'I in them, and thou in me.' How is God in Christ? By unity of essence, and by constant influence; and so is Christ in us. (1.) God is in Christ by unity of essence, or co-essential existency; Christ and He communicates in the same nature: 'The fulness of the godhead dwelt in him bodily,' Col. ii. 9. Now there is something which answereth to this in the mystical union; there is a communion of spirit between us and Christ, though not the same nature. The same Spirit dwelleth in Christ σωματικῶς, bodily, that is, essentially; in us πνευματικῶς, spiritually; we partake of the divine nature in some gifts and qualities. (2.) By constant influence. God is in Christ by a communication of life, virtue, and operation.

1. The Father is the perpetual beginning, foundation, and root of life to Christ as mediator: John vi. 57, 'As the living Father hath sent me, and I live by the Father; so he that eateth me, even he shall live by me.' So is Christ to us: Gal. ii. 20, 'Nevertheless I live; yet not I, but Christ liveth in me: and the life that I live in the flesh I live by the faith of the Son of God, who loved me, and gave himself for me.'

2. The divine essence sustained the person of Christ as mediator. The humanity could not subsist of itself, but by constant influence from the godhead: Isa. xlii. 1, 'Behold my servant, whom I uphold.' Christ had constant sustentation from the Father; he upheld him, and carried him through the work. So are we 'preserved in Jesus Christ,' Jude 1. We have not only the beginning and principle of life from Christ, but constant support. We can no more keep ourselves than make our-selves; all things depend upon their first cause.

3. The Father concurreth to all the operations and actions of Christ, and so the Father is in Christ as he worketh in him: John xiv. 10, 'Believest thou not that I am in the Father, and the Father in me? The words that I speak unto you I speak not of myself; but the Father, that dwelleth in me, he doeth the works.' The divine power was interested in Christ's works as mediator, especially in the miracles that he wrought to confirm the truth of his person. So is Christ in believers, as he worketh in them all their works for them: John xv. 5, 'I am the vine, ye are the branches: he that abideth in me, and I in him, the same bringeth forth much fruit; for without me ye can do nothing.' He doth not say, *nihil magnum*, no great thing; but, *nihil*, nothing at all. Thinking is the most sudden and transient act; sure the new nature there may get the start of corruption. But, 2 Cor. iii. 5, 'Not that we are sufficient of ourselves to think anything as of ourselves, but our sufficiency is of God.' Actions are more deliberate, there is more scope for the interposition of corrupt nature; but of ourselves we cannot think a good thought.

What use shall we make of this?

Use 1. If Christ be in us, as God was in Christ, let us manifest it as Christ did. Christ manifested the Father to be in him by his works: John x. 37, 38, 'If I do not the works of my Father, believe me not; but if I do, though ye believe not me, believe the works, that ye may know and believe that the Father is in me, and I in him.' Works and miracles exceeding the power and force of nature showed that Christ was a divine person; sure the Father is in him, or else he could not do these works. So St James puts hypocrites upon the trial, 'Show me thy faith by thy works,' James ii. 18. Do we do any works exceeding the power of corrupt nature? That would be a proof of Christ's working in you. When Jacob counterfeited Esau, Isaac felt his hands. So what are your works? If you walk as men, do no more than an ordinary man, that hath not the Spirit of God, where is the proof of Christ's working in you? Many boast of Christ in them; if Christ were in them, he would be there, as the Father was in Christ; they would bewray it by their operations. You may know what is within by what cometh out; if Christ be within thee, there will come out prayer, sighs, and groans for heaven, fruitful discourses, heavenly walking, a mortified conversation; all this cometh out, because Christ is within. But now, when ye belch out filthy discourses, rotten communication, there is nothing cometh out but vanity and sin, how dwelleth Christ in you? are these the fruits of his presence?

Use 2. Learn dependence upon Christ. All the power we have to work is from Christ. Whence hath the body the vigour it hath to work, and to move from place to place, but from the soul? And whence hath a christian his power but from Christ? We derive all our strength from Christ. We are as glasses without a bottom; they cannot stand of themselves, but they are broken in pieces. Christ can do all things without us, but we can do nothing without him, as the soul can subsist apart from the body; Christ hath no need of us, but we cannot live and act without him. *Sine te nihil, in te totum possumus* Phil. iv. 13, 'I can do all things through Christ, which strengtheneth me.' The apostle doth not speak it to boast of his power, but to profess **his dependence. It was never seen that a father would cast away the child that hangeth on him.**

Use 3. Examine whether Christ be in you or no. You may know it :—

1. By his manner of entrance. Christ is not wont to come into the heart without opposition. The devil is loath to be dispossessed : Luke xi. 21, 'When a strong man armed keepeth his palace, his goods are in peace.' Christ came into the temple with a whip to drive out the money-changers. He cometh to rule alone.

2. By the fruits of his abode—life, fruitfulness, tendency.

(1.) Life. It will stir and quicken you to good duties : Gal. iii. 20, 'I live, yet not I, but Christ liveth in me.' He is a living fountain of vital union.

(2.) Fruitfulness of soul : John xv. 2, 'Every branch in me that beareth not fruit, he taketh away; and every branch that beareth fruit, he purgeth it, that it may bring forth more fruit;' and ver. 4, 'Abide in me, and I in you : as the branch cannot bear fruit of itself, except it abide in the vine, no more can you, except you abide in me.'

(3.) Tendency—(1.) To heaven. Heaven is the place of our full enjoyment of him. They do not admire worldly excellences : Luke xix. 8, 'Behold, Lord, the half of my goods I give to the poor ; and if I have taken anything from any man by false accusation, I restore him fourfold.' The woman left her pitcher, John iv. 28 ; Matthew followed Christ. (2.) To God's glory as our last aim ; their aim is according to their principle.

Secondly, I come to the end of this union.

1. With respect to believers, 'That they may be made perfect,' &c.

2. With respect to the world, and their conviction, 'That the world may know that thou hast sent me, and hast loved them as thou hast loved me.'

First, With respect to believers, 'That they may be made perfect in one,' τετελειωμένοι εἰς ἕν. This oneness is either with God or with one another. Both are included in the mystical union ; we cannot be united to the head, but we must also be united to the members. The golden cherubims did so look to the ark and mercy-seat, that they did also look one towards another, Exod. xxv. 20. So in this union, as we respect God and Christ, so we must also look to our fellow-members : 'Let them be perfect in one ;' let them all centre in God, which is the creature's perfection.

Observe, our perfect happiness lieth in oneness, in being one with God through Christ. I shall evidence it to you in a few particulars.

1. Since the fall man's affections and thoughts are scattered : Eccles. vii. 29, 'God hath made man upright, but they have sought out many inventions.' When man lost his happiness, he sought out many inventions. A sinner is full of wanderings, as a wayfaring man that hath lost his direction turneth up and down, and knows not where to pitch ; or the needle in the compass, when it is jogged, shaketh and wavereth, and knoweth not where to rest, till it turneth to the pole again. There is a restlessness in our desires ; still we have new projects, and know not where to pitch ; are not content with what we do possess ; this is not the pole where we rest. *Quærunt in vanitate creaturarum quod amiserunt in unitate Creatoris.* A river, the further it runneth from the fountain, the more it is dispersed into several

streams. Blindness maketh us grope and feel about for happiness, as the Sodomites did for Lot's door. We change objects, striving to meet with that in one thing which we cannot find in another, as bees fly and go from flower to flower; we seek to patch up things as well as we can.

2. In all this chase and distraction of thoughts there is no contentment in the vast world, nothing that can satiate the heart of man. Transitory things may divert the soul, but they cannot content it. After Solomon's survey, Eccles. i. 2, 'Vanity of vanities, saith the preacher; vanity of vanities, all is vanity.' He had made many experiments, but still found himself disappointed, and disappointment is the worst vexation.

3. This distraction continueth till we return to God again: 1 Peter ii. 25, 'Ye were as sheep going astray, but are now returned unto the shepherd and bishop of your souls.' There is no safety but in the fold. God, who is the principle of our being, is the only object of our contentment. We began in a monad or unity, and there we end. God is the boundary of all things: Rom. xi. 36, 'For of him, and through him, and to him, are all things; to whom be glory for ever, Amen.' In him, or nowhere, the soul findeth content. He is our first cause and our last end. There are some scrictures and rays of goodness in the creature, but they cannot satisfy, because there we have happiness by parcels; it is dispersed. Nothing is dispersed in the creature but what is re-collected in the creator; there is all in him, because all came out from him.

4. The great work of grace is to return us to God again, that we may pitch upon him as the chief object and centre of our rest: Jer. xxxii. 39, 'I will give them one heart, and one way, that they may fear me for ever.' It is the great blessing of the covenant; this one heart is to pitch upon God as the chief object and centre of our rest, otherwise we are troubled with divers cares, fears, and desires. Thus grace worketh upon us. But the distance lieth not only on our part, but God's. Before God and the creature can be brought together, justice must be satisfied. Christ came to restore us to our primitive condition: 2 Cor. v. 19, 'God was in Christ, reconciling the world unto himself.' The merit of Christ bringeth God to us, and the Spirit of Christ bringeth us to God. It is as necessary Christ should be united to us, as we to God.

5. Our happiness in God is completed by degrees. In this life, the foundation is laid: we are reconciled to him upon earth; but the complete fruition we have in heaven; there we are fully made perfect in one. Here there is weakness in our reconciliation: we do not cleave to him without distraction; there are many goings a-whoring and wandering from God after our return to him. And here, on God's part, our punishment is continued in part. God helpeth us by means, at second and third hand. We need many creatures, and cannot be happy without them; we need light, meat, clothes, house. Our life is patched up by supplies from the creature. But there 'God is all, and in all,' 1 Cor. xv. 28. We find in God whatever is necessary for us without means and outward helps. There 'God is all, and in all;' he is our house, clothes, meat, ordinances. We have all immedi-

ately from God, and 'in all;' all are made perfect in one. We cannot possess any thing in the world except we encroach upon one another's happiness. Worldly things cannot be divided without lessening; and we take that from others which we possess ourselves. Envy showeth the narrowness of our comforts. But there the happiness of one is no hindrance to another, all are gratified, and none miserable; as the sun is a common privilege, none have less because others have more. All possess God as their happiness without want and jealousy.

Use. If to be drawn into unity and oneness with God be our happiness and perfection, then take heed of two things — (1.) Of sin, which divides God from you; (2.) Of doting upon the creatures, which withdraweth you from God.

1. Of sin, which maketh God stand at a distance from you: Isa. lix. 2, 'Your iniquities have separated between you and your God, and your sins have hid his face from you.' As long as sin remaineth in full power, there cannot be any union at all. 'What communion hath light with darkness?' And the more it is allowed, the more it hindereth the perfection of the union. What is the reason we do not fully grow up to be one with God in this life, that our communion with him is so small? Sin is in the way; the less holy you are, the less you have of this happiness, such unspeakable joys, lively influences of grace, and immediate supplies from heaven. In bitter afflictions, we have most communion with God many times; that is nothing so evil as sin; as afflictions abound, so do our comforts.

2. Of doting upon the creatures, which withdraweth your heart from God. The more the heart is withdrawn from God, the more miserable. Let the object be never so pleasing, it is an act of spiritual whoredom. Sin is poison, creatures are not bread: Isa. lv. 2, 'Why do you spend your money upon that which is not bread? and your labour for that which satisfieth not?' It cannot yield any solid contentment to the soul. These things are short uncertain things, beneath the dignity of the soul. There is a restlessness within ourselves, and envy towards others; they are not enough for us and them too. Not for us; if enough for the heart, not for the conscience. If God do but arm our own thoughts against us, as usually he doth when the affections are satisfied with the world, he will show you that the whole soul is not satisfied; therefore he awakeneth conscience; as children catch at butterflies, the gawdy wings melt away in their fingers, and there remaineth nothing but an ugly worm. Desertion is occasioned by nothing so much as carnal complacency. Many times the object of our desires is blasted; but if not, God awakeneth conscience, and all the world will not allay one pang.

You may understand this oneness with respect to our fellow-members; and so you may understand it jointly of the completeness of the whole mystical body, or singly of the strength of that brotherly affection each member hath to another. There is a double imperfection for the present in the church; every member is not gathered, and those that are gathered are not come to their perfect growth. So that 'let them be perfect in one,' is that the whole body may attain to the integrity of parts and degrees.

First, Let us take it collectively; that they may all be gathered into a perfect body, and no joints lacking.

Observe, that all the saints of all places and all ages make but one perfect body. In this sense the glorified saints are not perfect without us: Heb. xi. 40, 'God having promised some better thing for us, that they without us should not be made perfect.' It is no derogation, for Christ is not perfect without us. The church is called 'The fulness of him that filleth all in all,' Eph. i. 23. They are, as to their persons, perfect, free from sin and misery, made perfect in holiness and glory; but not as to their church relation. So Eph. iv. 13, 'Till we all come to the unity of the faith, and of the knowledge of the Son of God, unto a perfect man, unto the measure of the stature of the fulness of Christ.' All the body must be made up that Christ mystical may be complete. Now there are some joints lacking; all the elect are not gathered.

Use 1. See the honour that is put upon the saints; the saints on earth, and the saints in heaven make but one family: Eph. iii. 15, 'Of whom the whole family in heaven and earth is named.' In a great house there are many rooms and lodgings, some above, some below, but they make but one house; so of saints, some are militant, some triumphant, and yet all make but one assembly and congregation: Heb. xii. 23, 'We are come to the general assembly, and church of the first-born, which are written in heaven;' we upon earth are come to them. Our Christ is the same, we are acted by the same Spirit, governed by the same head, and shall be conducted to the same glory. As in the state of grace some are before us in Christ, so some are in heaven before us, their faces once as black as yours. We have the same ground to expect heaven, only they are already entered.

Use 2. It is a ground of hope, we shall all meet together in one assembly: Ps. i. 5, 'The ungodly shall not stand in the judgment, nor sinners in the congregation of the righteous.' Now the saints are scattered up and down, where they may be most useful; then all shall be gathered together; then shall be that great rendezvous, when the four winds shall give up their dead; then the wicked shall be herded, they shall be bound up in bundles, as straws and sticks bound up together in a bundle serve to set one another on fire, Mat. xiii. 40–42; adulterers together, and drunkards together, and thieves together, and so increase one another's torment. So all the godly shall meet in a congregation, and never be separated more. You do not only groan and wait for it, but the departed saints also: Rev. vi. 9, 10, 'I saw under the altar the souls of them that were slain for the word of God, and for the testimony which they held. And they cried with a loud voice, saying, How long, O Lord, holy and true, dost thou not judge and avenge our blood on them that dwell on the earth?' As in a wreck, those that get first to shore are longing for and looking for their companions. This is the communion between us and saints departed; they long for our company, as we for theirs; we praise God for them, they groan for us; we long and wait, by joint desires, for that happy day.

Use 3. It is an engagement to the churches of all parts to maintain a common intercourse one with another. All maketh but one body. We should pray for them whom we have not seen in the flesh, Col. ii.

2, and send relief to them, as the church at Antioch to Jerusalem when the famine was foretold, Acts xi., latter end; and, as God giveth opportunities, meet and consult for one another's welfare. But the world is not ripe for this yet.

Use 4. It giveth you assurance of the continuance of the ministry as long as the world continueth. As long as the world continueth there are elect to be gathered: 2 Peter iii. 9, 'The Lord is not slack concerning his promise, as some men count slackness, but is long-suffering to us-ward, not willing that any should perish, but that all should come to repentance.' The ship tarrieth till all the passengers be taken in, and then they launch out into the deep. The great aim of Christ in keeping up the world is to make his body complete; and as long as the elect are to be gathered, the ministry is to continue: Eph. iv. 11, 12, 'He gave some, apostles; and some, prophets; and some, evangelists; and some, pastors and teachers; for the perfecting of the saints, for the work of the ministry, for the edifying of the body of Christ.' The workmen are not dismissed till the house be built.

Secondly, Understand it singly and severally, 'That they may be made perfect in one;' that is, that there may be a perfect oneness between member and member of Christ's body, or a brotherly affection which one member hath to another.

Observe, no less union will content Christ but what is perfect. This was the aim of his prayers; then strive for it, wait for it.

1. Strive for it: 1 Cor. i. 10, 'Now I beseech you, brethren, by the name of our Lord Jesus Christ, that ye all speak the same thing, and that there be no divisions among you; but that ye be perfectly joined together in the same mind, and in the same judgment.' We should all strive together, as if we had but one scope, one interest, one heart. We should grow up to this perfection more and more. Oh! what conscience should we make of keeping the unity of the Spirit in the bond of peace! If we are not one in opinion, yet we should have one aim and scope. Let us concur in one object and rule, and as far as we have attained to the knowledge of it, let us walk together.

2. Wait for it. The perfection of our communion is in life eternal. Here it is begun, we are growing to the perfect day: Prov. iv. 18, 'The path of the just is as the shining light, that shineth more and more unto the perfect day.' *Ibi Lutherus et Zuinglius optime conveniunt.* We are going thither where Hooper and Ridley, Luther and Zuinglius, shall be of a mind. In heaven they are all of one mind, one heart, one employment; there is neither pride, nor ignorance, nor factions to divide us, but all agree in one concert.

Secondly, The end as to the world, their conviction, 'That the world may know that thou hast sent me, and that thou hast loved them as thou hast loved me.' When is the world convinced, and how? I shall answer both together—In part here, and fully hereafter.

1. In part here, by Christ's being and working in them, by the life of Christ appearing in their conversations.

2. Fully and finally at the last judgment, by the glory put upon them. The reprobate world shall know, to their cost, when they shall see them invested with such glory, that they were the darlings of God.

But of what shall the world be convinced? Of Christ's mission and the saints' privileges, that Christ was authorised by God as the doctor of the church, and the saints are dearly beloved of God.

Observe, there are two things God is tender of, and two things the world is ignorant of—his truth, and his saints.

1. God prizeth these above all things.

[1.] His gospel; and therefore would have the world convinced that Christ was sent as a messenger from the bosom of God.

[2.] His saints; and therefore he would have them convinced of his love to them, and that he hath taken them into his protection, as he did the person of Christ. What should people regard but these two, especially since God hath put his little ones to nurse, and bid them be wise to learn his truths?

2. The world is most ignorant of these two; of the divine authority of the gospel, and therefore they slight it, and refuse it as much as they do; and of the dearness of his saints, therefore they persecute and molest them, and use them hardly. The world may be well called ' darkness,' Eph. v. 8, because they are ignorant of two things which do most concern them.

But let us speak more particularly of that wonderful and mysterious expression, ' That thou hast loved them, as thou hast loved me.

Observe three things—(1.) That God loveth Christ; (2.) That God loveth the saints as he loved Christ; (3.) That Christ would have the world know so much, and be convinced of it.

Observe, first, that God loveth Christ as the first object of his love: ' This is my beloved Son, in whom I am well pleased,' Mat. iii. 17. He is his dear Son: Col. i. 13, ' Who hath delivered us from the power of darkness, and hath translated us into the kingdom of his dear Son.' God saw all the works of his hands that they were good. He delighteth in the creatures, much more in his Son. He loveth Christ as God, and as mediator, as God-man.

1. As God; so he is *primum amabile*, the first object of his love, as his own express image, that represents his attributes exactly. He is the first Son, the natural Son, as we are adopted ones; and so his soul taketh an infinite contentment in Christ, before hill or mountain were brought forth: Prov. viii. 30, 31, ' Then was I with him, as one brought up with him, and I was daily his delight, rejoicing alway before him, rejoicing in the habitable part of his earth,' &c. As two that are bred up together take delight in one another.

2. As mediator; he loveth the human nature of Christ freely. The first object of election was the flesh of Christ assumed into the divine person: Col. i. 19, ' It pleased the Father that in him should all fulness dwell;' it deserved not to be united to the divine person. When it was united, the dignity and holiness of his person deserved love. There was the fulness of the godhead in him bodily, the Spirit without measure, all that is lovely. And then, besides the excellency of his person, there was the merit of his obedience; he deserved to be loved by the Father for doing his work: John x. 17, ' Therefore doth my Father love me, because I lay down my life, that I might take it again;' that was a new ground of love. Christ's love to us was a further cause of God's love to him. Thus you see how God loveth Christ.

Use 1. It giveth us confidence in both parts of Christ's priestly office—his oblation and intercession.   His oblation: Mat. iii. 17, 'This is my beloved Son, in whom I am well pleased.'   God hath proclaimed it from heaven that he is well pleased with Christ standing in our room, though so highly offended with us, and with him for our sake: Eph. i. 6, 'To the praise of the glory of his grace, wherein he hath made us accepted in the beloved.'   All that come under his shadow will be accepted with God.   He is beloved, and will be accepted in all that he doeth; his being beloved answereth our being unworthy of love.   Surely he will love us for his sake, who hath purchased love for us.   His intercession: if the Father loveth Christ, we may be confident of those petitions we put up in his name: John xvi. 23, 'Whatsoever ye shall ask the Father in my name, he will give it you.'   Our advocate is beloved of God.   When we pray in the name of Christ, according to the will of God, our prayer is in effect Christ's prayer.   If you send a child or servant to a friend for anything in your name, the request is yours; and he that denieth the child or servant denieth you.   When we come in a sense of our own unworthiness, on the score and account of being Christ's disciples, and with a high estimation of Christ's worth and credit with the Father, and that he will own us, that prayer will get a good answer.

Use 2. It is a pledge of the Father's love to us; and if God gave Christ, that was so dear to him, what can he withhold? Rom. viii. 32, 'He that spared not his own Son, but gave him up to the death for us all, how will he not with him also freely give us all things?'   He spared him not; the Son of his love was forsaken and under wrath; and will he then stick at anything?   God's love is like himself, infinite; it is not to be measured by the affection of a carnal parent. Yet he gave up Christ.   Love goeth to the utmost; had he a greater gift, he would have given it.   How could he show us love more than in giving such a gift as Christ? John xvi. 22, 'The Father himself loveth you, because ye have loved me, and have believed that I came forth from God.'   God hath a respect for those that believe in Christ, and receive him as the Son of God.

Use 3. It is an engagement to us to love the Lord Jesus: 1 Cor. xvi. 22, 'If any man love not the Lord Jesus Christ, let him be Anathema maranatha.'   Shall we undervalue Christ, who is so dear and precious with God?   Let us love him as God loved him.

1. God loved him so as to put all things into his hands: John iii. 35, 'The Father loveth the Son, and hath put all things into his hand.'   Let us own him in his person and office, and trust him with our souls.   He is intrusted with a charge concerning the elect, in whose hands are your souls: 2 Tim. i. 12, 'I know whom I have believed, and I am persuaded that he is able to keep that which I have committed to him against that day.'

2. God hath loved him, so as to make him the great mediator to end all differences between God and man.   God hath owned him from heaven: Mat. iii. 17, 'This is my beloved Son, in whom I am well pleased.'   Do you love him so as to make use of him in your communion with God? Heb. vii. 25, 'Wherefore is he able to save to the uttermost all that come unto God through him, seeing he

ever liveth to make intercession for us.' That is the sum of all religion.

3. God loveth him so as to glorify him in the eyes of the world: John v. 22, 23, 'The Father judgeth no man; but hath committed all judgment to the Son, that all men should honour the Son, even as they honour the Father. He that honoureth not the Son, honoureth not the Father that hath sent him.' Do you honour him? Phil. i. 21, ἐμοὶ τὸ ζῆν Χριστός, 'To me to live is Christ,' should be every christian's motto. This is love, and not an empty profession. Christ will take notice of it, and report it in heaven; it is an endearing argument when the Father's ends are complied with: John xvii. 10, 'And all thine are mine, and mine are thine, and I am glorified in them.'

<hr>

SERMON XL.

I in them, and thou in me, that they may be made perfect in one; and that the world may know that thou hast sent me, and hast loved them, as thou hast loved me.—JOHN XVII. 23.

I COME now to the second observation, that God loveth the saints as he loved Christ.

The expression is stupendous; therefore divers interpreters have sought to mitigate it, and to bring it down to a commodious interpretation.

First, Καθώς, *as*, is a note of causality as well as similitude. He loveth us because he loved Christ. Therefore it is said: Eph. i. 6, 'He hath made us accepted in the beloved.' The elect are made lovely, and fit to be accepted by God, only by Jesus Christ; accepted both in our state and actions as we are reconciled to him; and all that we do is taken in good part for Christ's sake, who was sent and intrusted by the Father to procure this favour for us, and did all which was necessary to obtain it. The ground of all that love God beareth to us is for Christ's sake. There is indeed an antecedent love showed in giving us to Christ, and Christ to us: John iii. 16, 'For God so loved the world, that he gave his only-begotten Son—That whosoever believeth in him should not perish, but have everlasting life.' The first cause of Christ's love to us was obedience to the Father; the Son loved us, because the Father required it; though afterwards God loved us because Christ merited it. All consequent benefits are procured by the merit of Christ. The Father, that is first in order of persons, is first in order of working, and can have no higher cause than his own will and purpose. And besides, there is an obligation established to every person. Absolute elective love is the Father's property and personal operation; but then his eternal purpose is brought to pass in and through Jesus Christ. In the carriage of our salvation, Christ interposeth; so we are chosen in him as head of the elect, Eph. i. 4, pardoned, justified, sanctified, glorified in and through him. All these benefits and fruits of God's love are procured by Christ's merit; not only as it is the more for the freedom of grace that the reasons why man should be loved should be without himself, and so the obligation is increased; and not merely neither for the greater fulness of our comfort; for if God should love us in ourselves, it would be a very imperfect love, our graces being so weak, and our services so stained. / But whence should we have this grace at first, which is the object of his love? He could never find in us any cause why he should love us. God could not love us with honour to himself, if his wisdom had not found out this way of loving us in Christ. There was a double prejudice against us—our nature was loathed by God's holiness, and then God's justice had a quarrel against us.

1. For God's holiness. What communion could there be between light and darkness? God is holy by nature, and we are sinners by nature. Nature being corrupted, God cannot love it, unless he see it in such a person as Christ is: Ps. v. 4, 5, 'For thou art not a God that hast pleasure in wickedness, neither shall evil dwell with thee. The foolish shall not stand in thy sight, thou hatest all workers of iniquity;' not only the work, but the person. Therefore we are hidden in him, found in him; as when a man loathes a pill, we lap it up in something which he affects. God abhorred the sight of man till found in Christ.

2. God's justice had a quarrel against us. God dealt with man by way of covenant, and so hated man not only out of the purity of his nature, but out of justice; his righteous anger was kindled because of the breach of the covenant. When subjects are fallen into displeasure with their prince, such an one as the king loveth must mediate for them. So 'God was in Christ, reconciling the world unto himself,' 2 Cor. v. 19. How cometh God, who seemed to be bound in point of honour to avenge himself on sinners, to be reconciled? In Christ he received satisfaction. God was resolved to manifest an infinite love to man, but he would still manifest an infinite hatred against sin; which could not be more fully manifested than by making Christ the ground of our reconciliation. Thus the wisdom of God hath taken up the difference between us and his holiness, and between us and his justice, that so divine love may be like itself, not blind, but rational. This was the great prejudice—how could the holy God, the just God, who is not overcome with any passion, love such vile and unworthy creatures as we are? The question is answered—he loveth us in Christ, and for Christ's sake.

Secondly, Take the particle καθὼς, *as*, in the ordinary acceptation. So it signifieth smilitude and likeness; but then it signifieth not an exact equality, but some kind of resemblance: 'Be ye perfect, as your heavenly Father is perfect,' Mat. v. 48; 'One as we are one.' So here —(1.) There is a disparity; (2.) A likeness.

1. A disparity; for in all things Christ hath the pre-eminence, both as God and as mediator.

[1.] As God; he is most perfect, in whom God hath found all complacency and delight: Prov. viii. 30, 'Then I was by him, as one brought up with him; and I was daily his delight, rejoicing always before him.' He was God, we are creatures; he the natural Son: Ps. ii. 7, 'Thou art my Son; this day have I begotten thee.' We the adopted children: John i. 12, 'To as many as received him, to them gave he power to become the sons of God.' God's love to Christ was necessary, ours is a free dispensation: John iii. 16, 'God so loved the world, that he gave his only-begotten Son, that whosoever believeth in him should not perish, but have everlasting life.'

[2.] As mediator; so he is the first beloved. God loves Christ as the first object of his love; after Christ, he loveth those that are Christ's. The relation begins with him: John xx. 17, 'Go to my brethren, and say unto them, I ascend unto my Father and your Father, unto my God and your God.' He is loved as the head of the mystical body, we as members; the head first, then the members. He is loved for his own sake, we for his.

2. Yet there is a likeness. God loveth us with a like love.

[1.] Upon the same grounds—nearness and likeness.

(1.) Nearness. He loveth Christ as his Son, so he loveth us as his children: 1 John iii. 1, 'Behold what manner of love the Father hath bestowed upon us, that we should be called the sons of God.' There is a threefold *ecce* in scripture. (1.) *Ecce demonstrantis*, as pointing with the finger: John i. 29, 'The next day John seeth Jesus coming unto him, and saith, Behold the Lamb of God, that taketh away the sin of the world.' It referreth to a thing or person present, and it noteth the certainty of sense, as there he pointed at him as present; or to a doctrine, and then it noteth the certainty of faith: Job v. 27, 'Lo this, we have searched, so it is; hear it, and know thou it for thy good;' believe it as a certain truth. (2.) There is *ecce admirantis*, as awakening our drowsy minds more attentively to consider of the matter; as Lam. i. 12, 'Behold, and see if there be any sorrow like unto my sorrow.' So here, entertain it with wonder and reverence as an important truth. (3.) *Ecce exultantis, vel gratulantis*, as rejoicing and blessing ourselves in the privilege: Ps. cxxi. 4, 'Behold, he that keepeth Israel, he neither slumbers nor sleeps.' Now all these take place here. Behold it with faith and confidence, as a certain truth; behold it with reverence and wonder, as a high dignity; behold it with joy and delight, as a blessed privilege: as it is a certain truth, we should believe it more firmly; as it is an important truth, we should consider it more seriously; as it is a comfortable truth, we should improve it more effectually, to our great joy and satisfaction in all conditions. The wisdom of God findeth out relations between God and us, to establish a mutual love between us. He would be known, not only as our creator, but our father; and indeed none is so much a father as God is. Earthly parents have but a drop of fatherly compassion suitable to their finite scantling; never had any such bowels and affections as our Father which is in heaven. If we look to his fatherly bowels, none deserveth the title but he: Isa. xlix. 15, 'Can a mother forget her sucking child, that she should not have compassion on the fruit of her womb? yea, they may forget, yet will not I forget thee;' Mat. vii. 11, 'If ye then, being evil, know how to give good gifts unto your children, how much more will your Father which is in heaven give good things to them that ask him?' Ps. xxvii. 10, 'When my father and mother forsake me, then the Lord will take me up.' Certainly God excelleth all temporal relations; never father had such bowels and affections. We were never in the bosom of God, to know his heart; but the only Son of God, that came out of his bosom, he hath told us tidings of it, and hath bidden us come boldly and call him Father. 'When ye pray, say, Our Father.'

(2.) Likeness is another ground of love. God loveth Christ, not only as his Son, but as his image, he being 'the brightness of his glory, and the express image of his person,' Heb. i. 3. So he loveth the saints, who are by grace renewed after his image: Col. iii. 10, 'And that ye put on the new man, which is renewed in knowledge after the image of him that created him;' and who are thereby made 'partakers of the divine nature,' 2 Peter i. 4. We lost by Adam the image of God and the favour of God; now, first his image is repaired in us, then his love and favour is bestowed on us; without this we could not be lovely in his eye, for we are amiable in the sight of God by reason of that comeliness he has put upon us.

[2.] There are like properties.

(1.) It is free. So was God's love to Christ's manhood; as much of his substance as was taken from the virgin was chosen out of grace. Christ for his whole person deserved love, but as to his human nature, he was himself an object of elective love as we are; and this being assumed into the unity of his person, Christ was set apart by God for the work of mediation: Isa. xlii. 1, 'Behold my servant whom I uphold, mine elect in whom my soul delighteth; I have put my Spirit upon him.' Choice supposeth the preferment or acceptance of one, and refusal of another; so was Christ chosen as man. This the virgin acknowledgeth: Luke i. 48, 'He hath regarded the low estate of his handmaid.' He had done her an honour, the greatest that was done to any of his servants, among which she acknowledged herself the unworthiest. So much of the substance of the virgin as went to the person of Christ, and his human soul, was chosen out of mere grace. Nay, in his divine person there was a choice which is to be referred to the wisdom and pleasure of the Father: Col. i. 19, 'It pleased the Father that in him should all fulness dwell.' The same account as is given of our salvation: Mat. xi. 25, 26, 'I thank thee, O Father, Lord of heaven and earth, because thou hast hid these things from the wise and prudent, and hast revealed them unto babes. Even so, Father, for so it seemed good in thy sight.' So is God's love to us free and undeserved; his love is the reason of itself; he loved us because he loved us: Deut. vii. 7, 8, 'The Lord did not set his love on you, nor choose you, because ye were more in number than any people; but because the Lord loved you.' There is the last cause, God's act is its own law and reason, we can give no other account.

(2.) It is tender and affectionate. There is a full complacency and delight in Christ: Mat. iii. 17, 'This is my beloved Son, in whom I am well-pleased.' His heart was taken up with him, he was full of contentment in him; as a husband is called 'the covering of the eyes,' because a woman should look no further. So Prov. viii. 31, 'I was daily his delight, rejoicing always before him.' So tenderly affectioned is God to the saints: Isa. lxii. 5, 'As the bridegroom rejoiceth over the bride, so shall thy God rejoice over thee;' then affections are in their reign and height. So tender is God of his people: Zech. ii.

8, 'He that toucheth you, toucheth the apple of his eye.' The eye is the most tender part, and so is the apple of the eye. Can there be a more endearing expression?

(3.) It is eternal. Christ as mediator was loved before the foundation of the world in God's purpose: John xvii. 24, 'Father, I will that they also whom thou hast given me may be with me where I am, that they may behold my glory that thou hast given me; for thou hast loved me before the foundation of the world.' And in loving Christ he loved us; and in choosing Christ as head of the church, the members were included in that election, for head and body cannot be severed. This grace was given us in Christ before the world began: 2 Tim. i. 9, 'Who hath saved us, and called us with an holy calling; not according to our works, but according to his own purpose and grace, which was given us in Christ Jesus before the world began.' Some are not called as soon as others, but all are loved as soon as others, even from eternity. God's love is as ancient as himself, there was no time when God did not think of us, and love us. We are wont to prize an ancient friend; the ancientest friend we have is God, who loved us not only before we were lovely, but before we were at all. He thought of us before ever we could have a thought of him; after we had a being in infancy, we could not so much as know that he loved us; and when we came to years of discretion, we knew how to offend before we knew how to love and serve him; we cared not for his love, but prostituted our hearts to other things. Let us measure the short scantling of our lives with eternity, wherein God showed love to us. As to our beings, we are but of yesterday; as to the constitution of our souls, we are sinners from the womb; and when we are convinced of it, we adjourn and put off the love of God to old decrepit age, when we have spent our strength in the world, and wasted ourselves in deceitful and flesh-pleasing vanities. Now it should shame us when we remember God's love is as ancient as his being. Some look after God sooner than others; but if you look after God never so soon, God was at work before us; those that began earliest, as Josiah, John Baptist, find God more early providing for their eternal welfare.

(4.) It is unchangeable; as to Christ, so to us; from eternity it began, to eternity it continueth: it began before the world was, and will continue when the world shall be no more: Ps. ciii. 17, 'The mercy of the Lord is from everlasting to everlasting, upon them that fear him, and his righteousness unto children's children.' It is man's weakness to change purposes; we have good purposes, but they are suddenly blasted; but God's eternal purpose, that shall stand. We are mutable, and frequently change, out of the levity of our nature or the ignorance of futurity; therefore upon new events we easily change our minds; but God, that seeth all things at once, cannot be deceived; the first reasons of God's love to man are without man, and so eternal. Among the persons of the Godhead, the Son loveth because the Father required it; the Father, because the Son merited it; and the Holy Ghost, because of the purpose of the Father; and the purchase of the Son abideth in our hearts, to preserve us unto God's use, and to keep afoot his interest in us.

Thirdly, There are the like fruits and effects of it.   I shall instance in some which are like his love to Christ.

1. Communication of secrets.   All things are in common amongst those that love one another.   Said Delilah to Sampson, Judges xvi. 15, 'How canst thou say, I love thee, when thy heart is not with me? thou hast mocked me these three times, and hast not told me wherein thy great strength lieth.'   Now Jesus Christ knoweth all the secrets of God: John i. 18, 'No man hath seen God at any time; the only-begotten Son, which is in the bosom of the Father, he hath declared him.'   Christ, lying in the Father's bosom, knoweth his nature and his will.   So it is with the saints: John xiv. 21, 'He that hath my commandments, and keepeth them, he it is that loveth me; and he that loveth me shall be loved of my Father, and I will love him, and will manifest myself to him.'   As God manifested himself to Christ, so Christ will to us.   Christ hath treated us as friends: John xv. 15, 'Henceforth I call you not servants, for the servant knoweth not what his Lord doeth; but I have called you friends, for all things that I have heard of my Father, I have made known unto you.'   The knowledge of God's ways is a special fruit of his love.

2. Spiritual gifts.   God's love to Christ was a bounteous love: John iii. 34, 35, 'God giveth not the Spirit by measure to him: the Father loveth the Son, and hath given all things into his hands.'   God's love was showed to Christ in qualifying the human nature with such excellent gifts of grace.   As to us, God's love is not barren; as a fruit of God's love, Christ received all things needful for us.   You will perhaps say, as they replied to God when he said, 'I have loved you, Wherein hast thou loved us?' Mal. i. 2, because he hath not made you great, rich, and honourable.   If he hath given us such a proof of his love as he gave to Christ, namely, such a measure of his Spirit as is fit for us, we have no reason to murmur or complain.   The Spirit of illumination is better than all the glory of the world: Prov. iii. 32, 'The froward is an abomination to the Lord; but his secret is with the righteous.'   The Spirit of regeneration, to convert the heart to God and heaven: 1 Cor. ii. 12, 'Now we have received, not the spirit of the world, but the Spirit that is of God, that we might know the things that are freely given us of God.'   The Spirit of consolation, to evidence God's love to us, and our right to glory: 2 Cor. i. 22, 'Who hath sealed us, and given the earnest of his Spirit in our hearts;' 2 Cor. v. 5, 'Now he that hath wrought us for the self-same thing is God, who also hath given unto us the earnest of the Spirit.'   As the end of his love to Christ's human nature was to bring it to heaven, so the end of God's love to us is to sanctify us, and so to make way for glory.

3. Sustentation, and gracious protection during our work and service.   This was his love to Christ: Isa. xlii. 1, 'Behold my servant whom I uphold;' 'I am not alone, my Father is with me,' John viii. 16.   His enemies could not touch him till his time came: John xi. 9, 'Are there not twelve hours in the day?   If any man walk in the day, he stumbleth not, because he seeth the light of this world.'   As long as the time of exercising his function here lasted, there was such a providence about him as did secure him from all danger; and till that time was past, and the providence withdrawn, he was safe; and when that

was out, and he seemed to be delivered to the will of his enemies, all the creatures were in a rout, the sun was struck blind with astonishment, the earth staggered and reeled. So God will carry us through our work, and keep us blameless to his heavenly kingdom; but if we are cut off by the violence of men, all the affairs of mankind are put in confusion, and carried headlong, besides the confederacies of nature disturbed, and divers judgments (as in Egypt, and the land of the Philistines) ensue; *odium in religionis professores;* the world shall know how dear and precious they are to God.

4. Acceptance of what we do. God accepted all that Christ did; it was very pleasing to God: Eph. v. 2, 'Walk in love, as Christ also hath loved us, and given himself for us an offering and a sacrifice to God for a sweet-smelling savour.' In every solemn sacrifice for the congregation, the blood of it was brought unto the mercy-seat with a perfume; but Christ's sacrifice received value from his person, he being one so dear to God, so excellent in himself. This kind of love God showeth to us, the persons of the upright are God's delight; and then their prayers: Cant. v. 1, 'I am come into my garden, my sister, my spouse; I have gathered my myrrh with my spice, I have eaten my honeycomb with my honey.' Though our services are mingled with weaknesses and imperfection, they shall be accepted: 'But the sacrifice of the wicked is an abomination to the Lord, much more when he bringeth it with an evil mind,' Prov. xv. 8.

5. Reward. Christ was gloriously exalted; after his sufferings he entered into glory, and was conducted to heaven by angels, and welcomed by the Father, who, as it were, took him by the hand: Ps. ii. 7, 8, 'Thou art my Son; this day have I begotten thee. Ask of me, and I will give thee the heathen for thine inheritance, and the uttermost parts of the earth for thy possession.' So if we do what he did, we shall fare as he fared: John xii. 26, 'If any man serve me, let him follow me, and where I am, there shall my servant be: if any man serve me, him will my Father honour.' When we die, we shall be conveyed to heaven by angels: Luke xvi. 22, 'The beggar died, and was carried by angels into Abraham's bosom;' our souls first, then our bodies: Phil. iii. 21, 'Who shall change our vile bodies, that they may be like unto his glorious body, according to the working whereby he is able even to subdue all things to himself.' And at last we shall have a solemn welcome into heaven: Mat. xxv. 21, 'Well done, good and faithful servant; thou hast been faithful over a few things, I will make thee ruler over many things; enter thou into the joy of thy Lord.' Christ is not only purchaser, but first possessor, and is gone into heaven to prepare a place for us, to which he will at last bring us: John xiv. 2, 3, 'In my Father's house are many mansions; if it were not so, I would have told you: I go to prepare a place for you; and if I go to prepare a place, I will come again and receive you unto myself, that where I am, there ye may be also.'

Use 1. Information, to show what ground we have of patience, comfort, and confidence.

1. Of patience in afflictions from God. Would we be loved otherwise than Christ was loved? We see in the person of Christ that love may stand with fatherly correction. Christ was beloved by God,

yet under poverty, disgrace, persecution, hunger, thirst, &c.   When Christ was hungry, the devil came unto him: Mat. iv. 3, 'If thou be the Son of God, command that these stones be made bread.'   So he taketh advantage of our troubles and afflictions to make us question our adoption; but we may retort the argument: Heb. xii. 7, 8, 'If ye endure chastisement, God dealeth with you as with sons; for what son is he whom the father chasteneth not?   But if ye be without chastisement, whereof all are partakers, then are ye bastards, and not sons.'   Brambles are not pruned, but vines.   God loved Christ in the lowest degree of his abasement, as much as at other times.   Shall I desire to be otherwise beloved of God than Christ was?   Nay; God's love may stand with sad suspensions of soul-comforts: Mat. xxvii. 46, 'My God, my God, why hast thou forsaken me?'   The natural Son was in the love of God when at the worst; God loved him still, though he appeared to him with another face; as the sun is the same when it shineth through red glass, only it casts a more bloody reflection. God had one Son without sin, but none without suffering.

2. Comfort when we meet with ill-usage in the world.   Our Lord Jesus prayeth that the world may be convinced that God loved them as he loved Christ.   When the world entreated Christ ill, how was the world convinced that God loved him?   There was an eclipse at his death, which was a monument of God's displeasure: Mat. xxvii. 54, 'When the centurion, and they that were with him watching Jesus, saw the earthquake, and those things which were done, they feared greatly, saying, Truly this was the Son of God.'   So when Christ's members are evil-entreated, there are public monuments of God's displeasure, the courses of nature are altered, droughts, inundations, pestilences, famines, unseasonable weather, confusions, &c. If this be not, when God smileth, though the world frowneth, you will convince them by bearing up with courage and confidence.   The more the world is set against us, the more do the fruits of his love appear before men.

3. Confidence in the midst of dangers and temptations.   When once we are assured of God's love, what shall separate us from it?   Rom. viii. 38, 39, 'For I am persuaded, that neither death, nor life, nor angels, nor principalities, nor powers, nor things present, nor things to come, nor height, nor depth, nor any other creature, shall be able to separate us from the love of God which is in Christ Jesus our Lord.'   Can anything alienate God's love in Christ?   If it were God's love in us, that were an uncertain ground of hope; but it is God's love in Christ.   Get but an assurance of his love, and you will never be ashamed.   What can alienate the heart of God from you, while you are faithful to him, and have the sure pledge of his love, his Spirit in your heart?   Love or hatred is not known by anything that is before us.   But if you have a heart to seek him, fear him, obey his laws; this is the favour of his people, and this was his love to Christ.

Use 2. Direction.

1. Whereby chiefly to measure God's love; by his spiritual bounty: John iii. 34, 35, 'God giveth not the Spirit by measure to him.   The Father loveth the Son, and hath given all things into his hands.'   So the gifts and graces of the Spirit are the special effects of his love;

for he loved us as he loved Christ, and thus he manifested his love to Christ: Ps. cvi. 4, 'Remember me, Lord, with the love that thou bearest to thy people.' When one gave Luther gold, he said, *Valde protestatus sum, me nolle sic a Deo satiari.* Be not satisfied till God love you with such a love as he loved Christ. Inward excellences, though with outward crosses, these are the best fruits of his love; a heart to seek him, to fear his name, to obey his laws, an understanding to know his will. God's love is best known by the stamp of his Spirit, that is his mark set upon us. Let us leave outward things to God's wisdom. Love or hatred is not known by all that is before us. Let us labour for a share in his peculiar love: Ps. cxix. 132, 'Look thou upon me, and be merciful unto me, as thou usest to do unto those that love thy name.' Lord, I do not ask riches, nor glory, nor preferment in the world; I ask thy love, thy grace, thy Spirit. Doth our Saviour care for outward things? Other things are given promiscuously, these to his favourites. God's love is conveyed through Christ: Rev. i. 5, 'To him that loved us, and washed us from our sins in his own blood.' He loved us, and sanctified us: Eph. v. 25, 26, 'Husbands, love your wives, as Christ loved the church, and gave himself for it, that he might sanctify and cleanse it with the washing of water by the word.' Nothing more worthy, nothing more suitable to Christ's love.

2. It directeth us what to do when we are dejected through our own unworthiness. Look upon God's love in Christ. If God did take arguments and grounds of love from the creature, where would he have found objects of love? God hath proclaimed it from heaven: Mat. iii. 17, 'This is my beloved Son, in whom I am well pleased;' and 'We are accepted in the beloved,' Eph. i. 6. Jesus Christ is worthy; desire 'to be found in him, not having thine own righteousness.' Lord, for the merits of thy blessed Son, accept of me. Christ, being beloved of the Father, is the storehouse and conduit to convey that love to his people.

Use 3. Exhortation, to endeavour after the sense and apprehension of this love in our own hearts. Surely this is our duty; for Christ afterward saith, ver. 26, 'That the love wherewith thou hast loved me may be in them.' There is a love of God towards us, and a love of God in us; so Zanchy, citing the text. His love, *ergo nos,* towards us, is carried on from all eternity; but *nondum in nobis,* it is not in us, but in time. He loved us before the foundation of the world, though we know it not, feel it not; but now this love beginneth to be in us when we receive the effects, and God is actually become our reconciled Father in Christ. God's love from everlasting was in purpose and decree, not in act. God's love in us is to be interpreted two ways—both in the effects and the sense. In the effects, at conversion: Eph. ii. 4, 5, 'But God, who is rich in mercy, for his great love wherewith he loved us, even when we were dead in trespasses and sins, hath quickened us together with Christ.' In the sense, when we get assurance, and an intimate feeling of it in our own souls. Both are wrought in us by the Spirit: Rom. v. 5, 'And hope maketh us not ashamed, because the love of God is shed abroad in our hearts by the Holy Ghost, that is given to us.' A man may have the effects, but not the sense. God may love a man, and he not know it, nor feel it. But we are to look after both. Therefore I shall do two things—(1.) Press you to get the sense; (2.) Speak to the comfort of them that have indeed the effects but not the sense.

First, I shall press you all to get the sense and comfortable apprehension of this love, that God loved you as he loved Christ.

1. Motives. The benefits are exceeding great.

[1.] Nothing quickeneth the heart more to love God. Certainly we are to love God again, who loved us first, 1 John iv. 19. Now though it be true that *radius reflexus languet*, that God loveth us first, best, and most, yet the more direct the beam, the stronger the reflection ; the more we know that God loveth us in Christ, the more are we urged and quickened to love God again: 2 Cor. v. 14, ' For the love of Christ constraineth us.' And this consideration is the more binding ; if you expect those privileges which Christ had, you must express your love by suitable obedience : John vi. 38, ' I came down from heaven, not to do mine own will, but the will of him that sent me ;' John iv. 34, ' My meat is to do the will of him that sent me, and to finish his work ;' John viii. 29, ' And he that sent me is with me ; the Father hath not left me alone, for I do always those things that please him.' You must love him as Christ loved him. Will you sin against God, that are so beloved of him ? Thus we must kindle our hearts at God's fire, for love must be paid in kind.

[2.] It maketh us contented, patient, and joyful in tribulations and afflictions : Rom. v. 3, ' And not only so, but we glory in tribulations also ;' and 1 Peter i. 8, ' Whom having not seen, ye love ; in whom, though now ye see him not, yet believing, ye rejoice with joy unspeakable, and full of glory.'

[3.] Nothing more emboldeneth the soul against the day of death and judgment than to know that God loveth us as he loved Christ, and therefore will give us the glory that Christ is possessed of : 1 John iv. 17, ' Herein is our love made perfect, that we may have boldness in the day of judgment, because as he is so are we in the world ;' the greater apprehension we have of the love of God in Christ, the more perfect our love is.

2. Means that this may be increased in us.

[1.] Meditate more on, and believe the gospel. It is good to bathe and steep our thoughts in the remembrance of God's wonderful love to sinners in Christ : John xvii. 26, ' I have declared to them thy name, and will declare it, that the love wherewith thou hast loved me may be in them, and I in them.' Fervency of affection followeth strength of persuasion, and strength of persuasion is increased by serious thoughts.

[2.] Live in obedience to the Spirit's sanctifying motions ; for this love is applied by the Spirit : Rom. viii. 14, ' For as many as are led by the Spirit of God, they are the sons of God ;' compared with 16th verse, ' The Spirit itself beareth witness with our spirits, that we are the children of God.' The Spirit obeyed as a sanctifier will soon become a comforter, and fill our hearts with a sense of the love of God.

[3.] Take heed of all sin, especially heinous and wilful sins : Isa.

lxix. 2, 'Your iniquities have separated between you and your God, and your sins have hid his face from you that he will not hear;' Eph. iv. 30, 'And grieve not the Holy Spirit of God, whereby ye are sealed to the day of redemption.' Otherwise you may lose the sense of God's love once evidenced. Men that have been lifted up to heaven in comfort, have fallen almost as low as hell in sorrow, trouble, and perplexity of spirit. One frown of God, or withdrawing the light of his countenance, will quickly turn our day into night; and the poor forsaken soul, formerly feasted with the sense of God's love, knoweth not whence to fetch any comfort and support.

Secondly, I shall seek to comfort them that have but the effects, not the sense. For many serious christians will say, Blessed are they who are in Christ, whom God loveth as he loved Christ; but what is this to me, that know not whether I have any part in him or no? To these I will speak two things—(1.) What comfort yet remaineth; (2.) Whether these be not enough to evidence they have some part in Christ.

1. What may yet stay their hearts.

[1.] The foundation of God still standeth sure: 'The Lord knoweth those that are his,' 2 Tim. ii. 19. He knoweth his own, when some of them know not they are his own; he seeth his mark upon his sheep, when they see it not themselves. God doubteth not of his interest in thee, though thou doubtest of thy interest in him; and you are held faster in the arms of his love than by the power of your own faith; as the child is surer in the mother's arms than by its holding the mother.

[2.] Is not God in Christ willing to show mercy to penitent believers? or to manifest himself to them as their God and reconciled Father? Did not his love and grace find out the remedy before we were born? And when we had lived without God in the world, he sought after us when we went astray; he thought on us when we did not think on him, and tendered grace to us when we had no mind and heart to it: Isa. lxv. 1, 'I am sought of them that asked not for me; I am found of them that sought me not.'

[3.] Hast thou not visibly entered into the bond of the holy oath, and consented to the covenant, seriously at least, if thou canst not say sincerely? Or dost thou resolve to continue in sin rather than accept of the happiness offered or the terms required? Then thou hast no part in Christ indeed. But if thou darest not refuse his covenant, but cheerfully submittest to it, then God is thy God: Zech. xiii. 9, 'I will say, It is my people; and they shall say, The Lord is my God.' If thou consentest that Christ shall be thy Lord and Saviour, thou art a part of the renewed estate whereof Christ is the head.

[4.] If thou wantest a sense of his love, because of thy manifold failings, it is unreasonable to think that all will end in wrath, which was begun in so much love. If he expressed love to thee in thy unconverted estate, and hath brought thee into God's family, will he destroy thee, and turn thee out again upon every actual unkindness? The Lord doth gently question with Jonah in his fret: 'Dost thou well to be angry?' Jonah iv. 9. When the disciples fell asleep in the night of Christ's agony, he doth not say, Ye are none of mine, because ye could not watch with me one hour ; but rather excuseth it : Mat. xxvi. 41, 'The Spirit indeed is willing, but the flesh is weak.' This great love of God overcometh all the unkindness of his children.

2. What may evidence they are concerned in this love.

[1.] There is some change wrought in you ; thou art now no despiser of God and his holy ways ; the heart of thy sensuality, pride, and worldliness is broken, though too much of it still remaineth in thee. Now it is good to be in the way to a further progress ; and we begin with mortification : 2 Cor. v. 17, 'If any man be in Christ, he is a new creature : old things are passed away, behold, all things are become new.' Every change for the better is either the new creature or a preparation to it.

[2.] The gift of the sanctifying Spirit is more prized by thee than all the riches and honours in the world. Now without holiness we cannot esteem holiness, and practically prefer it about other things. God loveth Christ as he bore his image ; so he loveth us as we are sealed by the mark of the Spirit : Ps. cvi. 4, 'Remember me, O Lord, with the favour that thou bearest unto thy people : O visit me with thy salvation ;' and Ps. cxix. 132, 'Look thou upon me, and be merciful unto me, as thou usest to do unto those that love thy name.'

[3.] Thou lovest and preferrest Christ's people, and that for their holiness, and therefore seekest to discountenance all sorts of wickedness : Ps. xv. 4, 'In whose eyes a vile person is contemned ; but he honoureth them that fear the Lord.' He laboureth to discountenance all sorts of wickedness, and desireth to bring goodness and godliness into a creditable esteem and reputation, and payeth a hearty honour and respect to those that excel therein : so Ps. xvi. 3, 'But to the saints that are in the earth, and to the excellent, in whom is all my delight.' He doth value them, and esteem them, above the greatest men in the world, because they are so loved, prized, and set apart by God.

[4.] You labour more and more to be such, whom God loveth as he loved Christ. Jesus Christ was the express image of his person ; we strive to be such in the world as Christ was, 1 John iv. 17, hating what God hateth, and loving what God loveth ; then we make it our business to walk as he walked, 1 John ii. 6, doing his will, seeking his glory. God loved Christ for that spirit of obedience that was in him, who shrunk not in the hardest duties, but, whatever it cost him, was faithful in his work.

Observe, thirdly, that God would have the world know so much, and be convinced of this great love which he beareth to the saints : 'That the world may know that thou hast loved them,' &c.

1. The necessity of the world's knowledge.

[1.] Because the world is blinded with ignorance and prejudice against the children of God ; they cannot, or rather will not see : 1 Cor. ii. 14, 'But the natural man receiveth not the things of the Spirit of God : for they are foolishness unto him ; neither can he know them, because they are spiritually discerned.' They will not see, because they have a mind to hate.

[2.] The life that floweth from this union is a hidden thing : Col. iii. 3, 'For our life is hid with Christ in God.' It is hidden, because maintained by an invisible power ; the spiritual life is hidden under the veil of the natural life: Gal. ii. 20, 'The life which I now live in the flesh I live by the faith of the Son of God, who loved me, and gave himself for me.' It is obscured by infirmities. The best show forth too much of Adam, and too little of Jesus. It is hidden under afflictions: Heb. xi. 37, 38, 'They were stoned, they were sawn asunder, were tempted, were slain with the sword: they wandered about in sheep-skins, and goat-skins; being destitute, afflicted, tormented; of whom the world was not worthy,' &c.; and the world's reproaches: 2 Cor. vi. 8, 'By honour and dishonour, by evil report and good report; as deceivers, and yet true.'

2. The means whereby the world is convinced.

[1.] The promises of the word show God's great love to the saints, and hereby he hath engaged himself to do great things for them: 2 Peter i. 4, 'Whereby are given unto us exceeding great and precious promises, that by these ye might be partakers of the divine nature.' He hath engaged to pardon their sins, accept their persons, sanctify their natures, keep them blameless to his heavenly kingdom, and finally, to translate them to glory: Deut. xxxiii. 29, 'Happy art thou, O Israel: who is like unto thee, O people saved by the Lord, and who is the shield of thy excellency! thy enemies shall be found liars unto thee; and thou shalt tread upon their high places;' Ps. cxliv. 15, 'Happy is that people that is in such a case; yea, happy is that people whose God is the Lord.'

[2.] By the visible fruits of the mystical union. The gift of the Spirit cannot be hidden, they have a power and presence with them which others have not: 1 Peter iv. 14, 'The Spirit of glory and of God resteth upon you.' They live contrary to the course of this world, so as to become the world's wonder: 1 Peter iv. 4, 'Wherein they think it strange that you run not with them to the same excess of riot.' And reproof: Heb. xi. 7, 'By faith Noah, being warned of God of things not seen as yet, moved with fear prepared an ark for the saving of his house, by the which he condemned the world.'

[3.] By the wonderful blessings of God's providence; they are hidden in the secret of his presence, strangely preserved: Ps. iv, 3, 'But know that the Lord hath set apart him that is godly for himself;' not only as instruments of his glory, but as objects of his special favour and grace.

[4.] This is more fully seen for the utter confusion of the wicked at the last day: 2 Thes. i. 10, 'When he shall come to be glorified in his saints, and to be admired in all them that believe.' Now it is for their conviction or conversion, then for their confusion; these are those whose lives we judged madness, and ways folly!

3. Why Christ was so earnest that the world should know this.

[1.] To restrain their malice: 1 Cor. ii. 5, 'Had they known it, they would not have crucified the Lord of glory.' If God loveth believers, it should stop the violence and malice of the world against them; they are the beloved ones of God whom they malign, and against whom their heart riseth.

[2.] It stirreth them up to come out of their wicked condition, that is, out of a state of nature: Ps. vii. 11, 'God is angry with the wicked every day.'

[3.] To put in for a share in this blessed estate, that they may be some of those whom he loveth as he loved Christ.

Use 1. Caution to the carnal world. Do not hate those whom God thus loveth. To you they are accursed, but God counteth them precious : Isa. xliii. 4, 'Since thou wast precious in my sight, thou hast been honourable, and I have loved thee.' To you they are the scurf and offscouring: 1 Cor. iv. 13, 'We are made as the filth of the world, and the offscouring of all things to this day.' But to God they are jewels : Mal. iii. 17, 'They shall be mine, saith the Lord, in the day when I make up my jewels.'

Use 2. Advice to the children of God, to promote the conviction and conversion of the carnal : 1 Peter ii. 12, 'Having your conversation honest amongst the Gentiles ; that whereas they speak against you as evil-doers, they may by your good works which they shall behold, glorify God in the day of visitation.' Herein you imitate your master, and your own safety lieth in it.

<hr>

SERMON XLI.

Father, I will that they also whom thou hast given me be with me where I am ; that they may behold my glory, which thou hast given me : for thou lovedst me before the foundation of the world. —JOHN XVII. 24.

WE have hitherto seen Christ's prayers for the happiness of his church in the present world ; now he prayeth for their happiness in the world to come. His love looketh beyond the grave, and outlasteth the life that now is ; he cannot be contented with anything on this side a blessed eternity. Glory as well as grace is the fruit of his purchase, and therefore it is the matter of his prayers. Every verse is sweet, but this should not be read without some ravishment and leaping of heart. One saith he would not for all the world that this scripture should have been left out of the Bible. Certainly we should have wanted a great evidence and demonstration of Christ's affection. Every word is emphatical. Let us view it a little.

Here is a compellation, a request, and the reason of that request. The compellation, 'Father.' In the request there is the manner, how it is made, 'I will.' The persons for whom it is made, 'That they whom thou hast given me.' The matter of the request, in presence and vision, 'Be with me where I am, that they may behold my glory.' Or the matter is everlasting happiness, which is described by the place of enjoyment, and our work when we come thither. Now the reason of all is, the Father's eternal love to Christ, and in Christ to us, 'For thou hast loved me before the foundation of the world.'

First, The compellation, 'Father.' The titles of God are usually suited to the matter in hand. Christ is now suing for a child's portion for all his members, and therefore he saith, 'Father.' God is Christ's father by eternal generation, and ours by gracious adoption, whence our title to heaven ariseth. And therefore it is called an inheritance :

Col. iii. 24, 'Knowing that of the Lord ye shall receive the reward of the inheritance.' It is not simply wages, such as a servant receiveth from his master ; but an inheritance, or a child's portion, such as children receive from parents. And it is very notable the apostle there speaketh of servants, who are saved, as God's sons. So our waiting for glory is expressed by 'waiting for the adoption,' Rom. viii. 23, because then we have the fruit of it. We hold heaven not by merit, nor by our purchase, nor by privilege of birth, but by adoption. The ground of expectation is put for the matter of expectation, 'waiting for the adoption.' And now we wait, because now we have *jus hœreditatis ;* then we have possession.

Use 1. This notion represents the freeness of grace in giving us glory ; we do not receive it as a debt, but as a gift. Nothing is more free than an inheritance. It was purchased by Christ, but it was given to us ; we receive it by virtue of his testament, and the Father's promise. It is called an 'inheritance,' Eph. i. 18, 'What is the riches of the glory of his inheritance in the saints ;' an inheritance cometh freely, and without burden and incumbrance. Thus we hold heaven by all kind of titles ; we have it by purchase, and we have it freely. Christ maketh the purchase, and we possess the gift. It is a greater security to our hopes when we can look for heaven from a merciful Father and a righteous judge ; it is just, Christ having paid the price. Therefore it is called, 'The gift of God through Jesus Christ our Lord,' Rom. vi. 20. It is the Father's gift, but for the greater honour to God, and security to us, it is Christ's purchase.

Use 2. It showeth the neceessity of becoming sons to God if we expect heaven. Children can only look for a child's portion. The world is a common inn for sons and bastards ; but heaven is called ' our Father's house ;' none but children are admitted there : John iii. 3, 'Except a man be born again, he cannot see the kingdom of God.' *Seeing* is often put for *enjoying ;* yet the word is emphatical ; they shall not have so much as a glimpse of heaven, but are cast into everlasting darkness. A man should never be quiet till he be one of the family, and can evidence his new birth. As they were put from the priesthood as polluted that could not find their genealogy, Ezra ii. 62, so, if you cannot prove your descent from God, you are disclaimed, and reckoned not to God's, but to Satan's family.

Use 3. It teacheth God's children with patience and comfort to wait for this happy estate : Rom. viii. 23, 'And not only they, but ourselves also, who have the first-fruits of the Spirit, even we ourselves groan within ourselves, waiting for the adoption, to wit, the redemption of our bodies.' You do not yet know what adoption meaneth ; the day of the manifestation of the sons of God is to come : 1 John iii. 3, 'Behold, now are we the sons of God ; but it doth not appear what we shall be.' 'It doth not appear,' therefore wait. There is the spirit of an heir and the spirit of a servant, as we read of the ' Spirit of adoption.' A servant must have something in hand, pay from quarter to quarter ; they do not use to expect their master's possession ; but an heir waiteth till it fall.

You may look upon the compellation as an expression of Christ's hearty good-will. When he sueth for our glorification, he improveth all his interest in God, 'Father, I will.' When he pleadeth for him-self, he useth the same compellation, ver. 1, 'Father, glorify thy Son;' ver. 5, 'And now, O Father, glorify thou me with thine own self.' Thus here Christ's heart is much set upon the happiness of his mem-bers; if there be any more endearing title, the Spirit of God here will use it : Father, if I can do anything, or have any room in thy heart or affection ; 'Father, I will,' &c. When we would prevail, Christ biddeth us urge our interest : 'When ye pray, say, Our Father,' Luke xi. 2 ; so doth he. When we mediate for others, we are wont to mention our relation, as a circumstance of endearment ; so doth Christ expressly mention his relation when his requests are of great concernment.

Secondly, The next circumstance is the manner of asking, $\theta\acute{\epsilon}\lambda\omega$, ' I will,' a word of authority, becoming him that was God and man in one person, who knew the Father's will, who had made a thorough purchase, and so might challenge it of right. So some observe he doth not say $\dot{\epsilon}\rho\omega\tau\hat{\omega}$, but $\theta\acute{\epsilon}\lambda\omega$. But possibly it may bear a softer sense in this place ; and thus is $\theta\acute{\epsilon}\lambda\omega$ used elsewhere : Mark x. 35, $\theta\acute{\epsilon}\lambda o\mu\epsilon\nu$, ' Master, we will that thou shouldest do to us whatever we desire thee ;' if that look like an expostulation, or a capitulation rather than a request. See Mark vi. 26, $\theta\acute{\epsilon}\lambda\omega$, ' I will that thou give me by and by in a charger the head of John the Baptist;' Mark xii. 38, ' Master, $\theta\acute{\epsilon}\lambda o\mu\epsilon\nu$, we would see a sign from thee.' Briefly, then, it doth not express his authority so much as the full bent of heart ; only because he useth the word *will*, and because at least the manner of expression carrieth the force of a promise, which, if it be backed with his prayers, cannot fall to the ground ; we may thence—

Observe the certainty of our glorious hopes. If ' I will' be not a word of authority, it looketh like a testamentary disposition. Christ was about to die, and now he saith, ' I will.' When Christ made his will, heaven is one of the legacies which he bequeatheth to us. This was his last will and testament, ' Father, I will.' You have the very words and form of a testament : Luke xxii. 29, ' I appoint unto you a king-dom, as my Father hath appointed unto me;' $\delta\iota\alpha\tau\acute{\iota}\theta\eta\mu\iota$, the only word we have for a testament. Heaven is ours, a legacy left us by Christ.

But what power had Christ to dispose of it ? Let me clear that by the way, since he saith, Mat. xx. 23, ' To sit on my right hand, and on my left, is not mine to give ; but it shall be given to them for whom it is prepared of my Father.' Christ's power of disposing is not denied, but he showeth only to whom it is given, not for by-respects, but according to God's eternal will and purpose. In the original the words run otherwise than they do in our translation, $o\dot{\upsilon}\kappa$ $\ddot{\epsilon}\sigma\tau\iota\nu$ $\dot{\epsilon}\mu\grave{o}\nu$ $\delta o\hat{\upsilon}\nu\alpha\iota$, $\dot{\alpha}\lambda\lambda\grave{\alpha}$ $o\hat{\iota}\varsigma$ $\dot{\eta}\tauo\acute{\iota}\mu\alpha\sigma\tau\alpha\iota$ $\dot{\upsilon}\pi\grave{o}$ $\tauο\hat{\upsilon}$ $\pi\alpha\tau\rho\acute{o}\varsigma$ $\mu o\upsilon$. There is no ellipsis which some have fancied ; and it should be rendered thus, ' It is not mine to give, save to those for whom it is prepared of my Father.' He doth not deny degrees of glory, he doth not deny his own power to distribute them, but only asserts that he must dispose according to his Father's will ; not for outward and temporal respects of kindred and acquaintance, but as God hath given to every man his measure. Certainly Christ's will standeth good to all intents and purposes ; for as God he hath an original authority, and as mediator he doth nothing contrary to his Father's will; he is tender of that, as you see in the place alleged; so that the objection confirmeth the point.

Use 1. It is comfort to us when we come to die; thou hast Christ's will to show for heaven. When God's justice puts the bond in suit against us, then let faith put Christ's testament in suit. There is an old sentence against us, ' In the day thou eatest thereof, thou shalt die,' Gen. ii. 17, confront it with Christ's prayer. In life we should provide for death, and a comfortable departure out of the world. Hear for the time to come; it is good to have our comforts ready. Can a dying man have a sweeter meditation than Christ's words? ' Father, I will that those whom thou hast given me may be with me where I am.' We know not how soon we may go down to the chambers of death, and become a feast for the worms. When we come to make our own will, we should think of Christ's ' Father, I will,' &c.

Use 2. It is an engagement to holiness. That is a part of Christ's will: 1 Thes. iv. 3, ' For this is the will of God, even your sanctifica-tion.' How can I plead his will in one thing and not in another? *Hereditates habent sua onera.* Legacies have their burdens annexed. Christ will have an action against us if we do not fulfil his whole will; as a man that sueth for what is left him by will must take care that his claim be not invalidated. Did Christ ever say, I will that all that live as they list should at length come to heaven for all that? No; but, ' I will that all those whom thou hast given me,' &c. And therefore—

Thirdly, The next circumstance is the parties for whom he prayeth. It is as necessary to know for whom Christ prayed as for what; it is not enough to hear of a privilege, but we must consider which way our claim and interest doth arise. For ' those which thou hast given me;' that is, for all the elect, who are intended in this expression.

Observe, that there is a certain number given to Christ which cannot finally miscarry, but shall come to glory. But of that in former verses.

1. Who are given hath been already discussed. The elect are given, those that come to him from the Father: John vi. 37, ' All that the Father giveth me shall come to me.' They are given before all time, and therefore in time they come, and actually accept of grace. And as they come to him, so they keep there, for of those he can lose nothing: ver. 39, ' And this is the Father's will that hath sent me, that of all which he hath given me I should lose nothing.'

2. But how are they given? By way of reward, and by way of charge; the one as his work, the other as his wages.

[1.] By way of reward: John xvii. 6, ' Thine they were, and thou gavest them me.' They were given to be members of his body, subjects of his kingdom, children of his family; Christ hath a special and peculiar interest in them. This was the bargain which he made with God, that he should be head of the renewed state. This was all the honour and benefit accruing to Christ by the covenant of redemption: Isa. liii. 10, 11, ' He shall see his seed, he shall prolong his days, and the pleasure of the Lord shall prosper in his hands; he shall see of the travail of his soul, and shall be satisfied.' Christ was pleased with the bargain. Nothing could be added to the greatness of his person, who was the eternal Son of God, equal with the Father in glory and honour;

yet he was pleased to account it a good purchase to have a special title and interest in us, and rested satisfied, having gained sufficient by all his expense of blood and merit.   We are all Benonis, sons of sorrow to him.

[2.] By way of charge : John vi. 37–39, ' All that the Father giveth me shall come to me, and he that cometh to me I will in no wise cast out ; for I came down from heaven not to do mine own will, but the will of him that sent me ; and this is the Father's will which hath sent me, that of all which he hath given me I should lose nothing, but should raise it up again at the last day.'   God calleth Christ to account for the elect, and his number and tale must be full.   The elect are given to Christ, not by way of alienation, but oppignoration, that he may guide them safe to glory ; as the shepherd must give an account of the sheep to the owner that sets him awork.   And so doth Christ at the last day : Heb. ii. 13, ' Behold I and the children which God hath given me.'   God looketh narrowly what is become of the elect ; not one of the tale is wanting.

Use. Are you of this number ?   If you be given by God, you give up yourselves to him.   Our faith is nothing else but our consent to God's eternal decrees.   All the Father's acts are ratified in time by the creatures' consent.   God giveth by way of reward and charge ; so there is a committing and a consecrating both together.

1. Committing yourselves to Christ : 2 Tim. i. 12, ' I know whom I have believed, and I am persuaded that he is able to keep that which I have committed to him against that day ;' τὴν παρακαταθήκην μού, by an advised act of trust.   Can you put your souls into his hands ? The Father is wiser than we ; he knew well enough what he did when he left us in charge with Christ.   It argueth a sense of danger, a solicitous care about the soul ; and then an advised trust, grounded on the belief of Christ's sufficiency.   Many think their souls were never in danger, therefore they are not careful about putting them into safe hands.   Canst thou venture upon eternity on such assurances ?   Well, I have trusted Christ with my soul.   Oh ! it is the hardest matter in the world to trust Christ with our souls advisedly and knowingly.   Presumption is an inconsiderate act, a fruit of incogitancy, and therefore very easy.

2. Consecrating : Rom. xii. 1, ' I beseech you, brethren, by the mercies of God, that ye present your bodies a living sacrifice, holy, acceptable unto God, which is your reasonable service ;' yield up yourselves to Christ.   So David : Ps. cxix. 94, ' I am thine, save me.' Personal dedication showeth God's act is not fruitless.   In a serious self-surrender, we must give up ourselves to God ; not with any reservation, to use ourselves as our own, but absolutely to be at God's dispose, to live and act for him.   O christians ! if you would clear up your interest, this is your duty, for this is but making good his grant to Christ.   It goeth under the name of our deed, but it is God's work in us.   The altar, the sacrifice, the fire is sent down from heaven.   It is God's giving, still the receiving is on our part ; for by renouncing self, we enjoy self most.   Do we out of a sense of duty thus give up ourselves ?   Do we make good our vows ?   God lendeth us to ourselves, to be employed to his honour.

Fourthly, The next thing is the matter of the request. Presence, and the beatifical vision, as the fruit of that presence.

First, 'That they may be where I am ;' that is, where I am according to my humanity presently to be ; for he doth not speak of the earthly Jerusalem, where he was then visibly and corporally.

Observe, first, it is no small part of our happiness that we shall be there where Christ is. Now Christ is with us, but then we are with him. It is the inchoation of our happiness that he is with us graciously: 'I am with you to the end of the world,' Mat. xxviii. 20. It shall be the consummation of our happiness when we shall be with him. Thus it is often expressed: 2 Cor. v. 8, 'We are willing rather to be absent from the body, and to be present with the Lord.' So David expresseth our state of blessedness: Ps. xvi. 11, 'In thy presence is fulness of joy, and at thy right hand there are pleasures for evermore.' This makes heaven to be heaven, because Christ is there ; as the king makes the court wherever he is, it is not the court maketh the king : John xii. 26, 'Where I am, there shall my servant be.' It is our happiness to stand always in our master's presence, a happiness that wicked men are not capable of, because of their bondage and estrangement from God. Therefore Christ telleth the carnal Jews, John vii. 34, 'Where I am, thither ye cannot come.' Wicked men have no grant, no leave to come. Paradise is still closed up against them with a flaming sword ; and they have no heart to come, because they cannot endure the majesty and purity of his presence.

But when shall we be there where Christ is ? Presently after death our souls shall be there, and at the resurrection, body and soul together.

1. Presently after death the soul is where Christ is. So Paul thought: Phil. i. 23, 'I desire to depart, and to be with Christ ;' that is, with him in glory, otherwise it were a loss of happiness for Paul to be dissolved. It is a sorry blessedness to lie rotting in the grave, and only to be eased of present labours, for God's people are wont to reckon much on their present service and enjoyment of God, though it be accompanied with affliction. Paul was in a strait, and he saith it is πολλῷ μᾶλλον κρεῖσσον, much more better to be dissolved. A stupid sleep, without the enjoyment of God, is far worse ; what happiness were that, to be in such a condition wherein we do nothing and feel nothing ? God's children are wont to prefer the most afflicted condition with God's presence above the greatest riches and contentment in his absence : 'If thou goest not up with us, carry us not hence,' Exod. xxxiii. 15. Better be with God in the wilderness, than in Canaan without him. Therefore Paul would never be in such a strait, if this drowsy doctrine were true, that the soul lay in such an inactive state of sleep and rest till the resurrection. He would be no happier than a stone, or the inanimate creatures are. Again, Luke xxiii. 43, 'This day shalt thou be with me in paradise,' saith Christ to the good thief. Some, to evade this place, refer this day to λέγω ; but the pointing in all the Greek copies confuteth it, as also the sense of the place : σήμερον answereth to the thief's words, 'Remember me when thou comest into thy kingdom.' Christ promiseth more than he asketh, as God doth usually abundantly for us above what we can ask or think. He had reference to Christ's words to the high priest, 'The Son of man shall

come in his glory.'   Now, saith Christ, I will not defer thy desires so long ; heavenly joys attend thy soul.   And others seek to evade it by the word *paradise ;* it is a Persiac word, but used by the Hebrews for gardens and orchards, and by allusion for heavenly joys : the allusion is not only to the delights of an ordinary garden, but Eden, or that garden in which Adam was placed in innocency.   The fathers fancied, *secreta animarum receptacula, et beatas sedes.*   But it is put for heaven itself in other places : 2 Cor. xii. 2, ' He was caught up into the third heaven,' which he presently calls paradise, ver. 4.   So that presently souls, upon their departure out of the body, are immediately with Christ.   Thus it is said, Luke xvi. 22, ' The beggar died, and was carried by the angels into Abraham's bosom ;' presently, in the twinkling of an eye or the forming of a thought ; which is a great comfort to us when we come to die ; in a moment angels will bring you to Christ, and Christ to God.   The agonies of death are terrible, but there are joys just ready ; and as soon as the soul is loosed from the prison of the body, you enter into your eternal rest : it flieth hence to Christ, to be there where he is.   To be short, certainly men enter upon their final state presently as soon as they die : 2 Peter iii. 19, ' He went and preached to the spirits in prison ;' compare it with Heb. xii. 24, ' To the spirits of just men made perfect.'   How can souls be perfect if they lie only in a dull sleep, without any light, life, joy, or delight, or act of love to God ?   We see the very present refreshments of sleep are a burden to the saints, because they rob us of so much time, cheat us of half our lives.

2. Completely at the resurrection.   Believers consist of body as well as soul.   Now it is said, ' That they may be there ;' that is, their whole self shall be there where Christ is.   And so it proveth the resurrection, and the translation of our glorified bodies into heaven.   So our Lord showeth that our being there where he is shall completely be after his second coming: John xiv. 3, ' And if I go and prepare a place for you, I will come again and receive you to myself ; that where I am, there ye may be also.'   Christ and we that are one cannot always live asunder ; if he have any glory, we must have part of it ; and therefore he will come again and take us to himself, that as coheirs we may live upon the same happiness : Rom. viii. 17, ' And if children, then heirs, heirs of God, and joint-heirs with Christ ; if so be that we suffer with him, that we may be also glorified together.'   As Joseph brought his brethren to Pharaoh, he bringeth us to God.   As he took part with us in nature, so he will have us take part with him in glory.

Now the happiness of it will appear—

[1.] By the place, the third heaven, or paradise ; as there was the outward court, the holy place, and the holy of holies.   The spangled firmament is but the outside and pavement of that house where Christ and the saints meet.   When we look upon the aspectable heavens, we may cry out, as David in his night-meditation, Ps. viii. 4, ' Lord, what is man, that thou art mindful of him ? and the son of man, that thou visitest him ?'   The church is but προθύρον καὶ προαύλιον, the portal, as one saith, and entrance into heaven.   If the visible heavens so affect us, how glorious is it within !

[2.] The manner of bringing us thither : ' I will come again and

receive you to myself,' John xiv. 3.   Christ will not send for us, but
come in person to fetch us in state, which will make our access to
heaven the more glorious.   Christ will come to lead his flock into
their everlasting fold, to present his bride to God, decked and appar-
elled with glory.   How glorious a sight will it be to see Christ and all
his troops following him, with their crowns upon their heads ! to see
the triumphant entrance into those everlasting habitations, and to hear
the applauses of the angels ! Ps. xxiv. 7, 8, 'Lift up your heads, O ye
gates, and be ye lift up, you everlasting doors, and the King of glory
shall come in.   Who is this King of glory? The Lord strong and
mighty, the Lord mighty in battle.'   That was a private and a personal entry at his ascension; but now it shall be public and glorious;
now death the last enemy is destroyed, then he is the Lord mighty in
battle indeed.

[3.] Our perpetual fellowship with Christ in the presence and glory
of his kingdom.   Pray mark, there is a presence, and that is much,
that we are called to heaven as witnesses of Christ's glory.   The queen
of Sheba said of Solomon, 1 Kings x. 8, 'Happy are thy men, happy
are these thy servants, which stand continually before thee, and that
hear thy wisdom.'   They that stand before the Lord and see his glory
are much more happy.   Zaccheus pressed to see him ; the wise men
came from the east to see him.   It is our burden in the world that
the clouds interpose between us and Christ, that there is a great gulf
between us and him, which cannot be passed but by death ; that God
is at a distance ; that our enemies often ask us, Where is your God?
Now we shall be happy when we shall be in his arms, when we can
say, Here he is ; when our Redeemer is ever before our eyes, Job xix.
26, to remember us of the grace purchased for us, and we are as near
as we can desire.   Now we dwell in his family.   David envied the
swallows that had their residence in the temple : 'One day spent in
thy courts is better than a thousand spent elsewhere,' Ps. lxxxiv. 10.
Then we shall always be about his throne, and we shall for ever feed
our eyes with this glorious spectacle, Jesus Christ : his body shall be
in a certain place, where all shall behold it.   The three children
walked comfortably in the fiery furnace, because there was a fourth
there, the Son of God: Dan. iii. 25, ' Lo, I see four men loose, walking
in the midst of the fire ; and the form of the fourth is like the Son of
God.'   Again, this presence maketh way for enjoyment.   It is not a
naked sight and speculation ; we are in the same state and condition
with Christ: Rom. viii. 17, 'Heirs of God, and joint heirs with Jesus
Christ.'   We shall be like him.   Servants may stand in the presence
of princes, but they do not make their followers fellows and consorts
with them in the same glory.   Solomon could only show his glory to
the queen of Sheba, but Christ giveth it us to be enjoyed.   And all
this is perpetual and without change and interruption : 1 Thes. iv. 17,
' We shall be for ever with the Lord.'   We are then above fears, no
more eclipses of God's face, no more trouble because of God's absence.
Here we complain ; the spouse sought Christ about the city : Cant. iii.
3, 'Saw ye him whom my soul loveth ? '   Here we are forlorn orphans,
and often without his society.   Upon earth his converse was so acceptable, that the apostles were loath to hear of his departure.   Now it is

for a few days, he is not always abiding with us; then we shall never be glutted, God is always fresh and new to the glorified saints.

Use 1. To show us the love of Christ; his heart is not satisfied till we be in like condition with himself: Luke xxii. 30, ' Ye shall eat and drink at my table in my kingdom.' The greatest love that David could show to his friend was to admit his children to his table: 2 Sam. ix. 7, ' Thou shalt eat bread at my table continually,' said David to Mephibosheth; and to Barzillai, 2 Sam. xix. 33, ' Come over with me, and I will feed thee with me in Jerusalem.' And when he would honour Solomon, 1 Kings i. 33–35, ' He put him upon his own mule, and caused him to sit on his throne.' So we be at his table and on his throne: Rev. iii. 21, ' To him that overcometh will I grant to sit with me in my throne, even as I also overcame, and am set down with my Father in his throne.' We enjoy the same blessedness which Christ doth. Adam was in paradise, we in heaven; Adam with the beasts of the earth, we with God and holy angels; Adam might be thrown out, we never. It is no matter if the world deny us a room to live among them; they cast us out many times, but Christ will take us to himself.

Use 2. If the presence of Christ be no small part of our happiness, let us more delight in it here. We enjoy his presence in ordinances: Ps. xvii. 15, ' As for me, I will· behold thy face in righteousness; I shall be satisfied when I awake with thy likeness;' Ps. lxxxiv. 10, ' A day in thy courts is better than a thousand; I had rather be a doorkeeper in the house of my God, than to dwell in the tents of wickedness.' This is heaven begun, to be familiar with Christ in prayer and hearing, &c. Let us often give him a visit. Oh! shame thyself when thou art loath to draw near to God. Dost thou look for heaven?

Use 3. Be willing to die, Why art thou backward to go to Christ? Would Christ pray for an inconvenience? You shun his company when he desireth yours, and he desireth your presence for your own sakes, that you may be happy. Love brought Christ out of heaven, that he might be with us; he thought of it before the world was: Prov. viii. 31, ' My delight was with the sons of men.' He longed for the time; when will it come? We are to go from earth to heaven, from conversing with men to converse with angels; why are we so loath to remove? What could Christ expect but hard usage, labour, griefs, and death? He came to taste the vinegar and the gall; we are called to the feast of loves, to the hidden manna, to rivers of pleasures. If you love Christ, why should you be unwilling to be in the arms of Christ? Let him be unwilling to die that is loath to be there where Christ is. Love is an affection of union, it desireth to be with the party loved, and can you be unwilling to die? Death is the chariot that is to carry you to Christ: Gen. xlv. 27, ' When Jacob saw the waggons which Joseph had sent to carry him, the spirit of Jacob revived.' What is there in the world to be compared with heaven? Either there must be something in the world to detain us, or it is the terribleness of the passage, or else a contempt of what is to come, that you are unwilling to die. If you have anything in the world more worthy than Christ—father, or mother, or wife, or friend, or brother, or present delights—it is a sign of a carnal heart: Ps. lxxiii. 25, ' Whom have I in heaven but thee? and there is none on earth I desire besides thee.' Can you say so without dissembling? Quit them all then. It is not the company of angels, but Christ; it is not wife, children, relations (these must be loved in God, and after God); nothing within the circuit of nature, none so worthy as Christ. Now you are put to the trial when sickness cometh, and you see death a-coming; Christ hath sent his waggons, his chariots, to see if we be real. Or is it the terribleness of the passage? Doth nature recoil at our dissolution? Where is your faith? ' Death is yours,' 1 Cor. iii. 22. Christ hath assured you, and will you not trust his word? You love him little when you have no confidence in his word. Or else contempt of things to come; then why was all this cost to prepare a place for you? Why came Christ to lay down his life to purchase that which we care not for? What needeth all this waste? Christians! hear for the time to come. We know not how soon we may be sent for and put to the trial; it is good to be resolved, that we may say, The sooner the better.

Observe, secondly, Christ taketh great delight in his people's company and fellowship. His heart is much set upon it.

1. I shall give you some demonstrations and evidences of it.

2. Reasons.

First, Evidences.

1. His longing for the society of men before the creation of the world: Prov. viii. 31, ' I rejoiced in the habitable parts of the earth, and my delights were with the sons of men.' Though Christ delighted in all the creatures, as they were the effects of his wisdom, power, and goodness, yet chiefly with men, that are capable of God's image, and upon whom he should lay out the riches of his grace. He thought on us before the world was, and longed for the time of his incarnation : When will it come?

2. In that he delighted to converse in human shape before the incarnation : Zech. i. 10, ' The man among the myrtle trees;' who is also called, ' The angel of the Lord,' ver. 11.

3. He took pleasure to spend time busily among them, whilst he was with them in the days of his flesh: John ix. 4, 5, ' I must work the works of him that sent me while it is day: the night cometh, when no man can work. As long as I am in the world, I am the light of the world.' His affection to the service made him go up and down doing good to men; he would not leave this ministration to his servants, but would do it in person as long as he was in the world: John i. 14, ' The word was made flesh, and dwelt among us.' Christ did not assume our nature, as angels assumed bodies for the present turn, but lived a good space of time, and conversed with men.

4. When it was necessary he should depart, he had a mind to returning before he went away and removed his bodily presence from us; his heart is upon meeting and fellowship again, of getting his people up to him, as in the text, or his coming down to us: John xiv. 3, And if I go and prepare a place for you, I will come again, and receive you to myself, that where I am, there ye may be also.'

5. Until the time that that meeting cometh, he vouchsafeth us his

spiritual presence : Mat. xxviii. 20, ' Lo, I am with you always to the end of the world.' Whatsoever part or age of the world we fall into in this life, we are with Christ, and Christ with us; not only with the church in general, but with every believer. With the church or assemblies of his people : ' Where two or three are gathered together in my name, I am in the midst of them,' Mat. xviii. 20. With every particular believer: Christ is said ' to dwell in our hearts by faith,' Eph. iii. 17. There is a near familiarity between Christ and every believer; every sanctified heart is a temple wherein he keepeth his residence. As God he is everywhere ; as to his human nature, the heaven of heavens contain it ; as to his gracious operation, and especial influence, so he dwelleth in the hearts of his people. He is with us in our duties : Exod. xx. 24, ' In all places where I record my name, I will come unto thee, and bless thee.' Christ is present to entertain us ; we go to meet with Christ. In our dangers: Isa. xliii. 2, ' When thou passest through the waters, I will be with thee; and through the rivers, they shall not overflow thee : when thou walkest through the fire, thou shalt not be burnt, neither shall the flames kindle upon thee.' The Son of God was with the three children in the furnace. When left alone, they are not alone. He would never have gone from us if our necessities did not require it. It was necessary that he should die for our sins, that they might not hinder our believing and coming to him. It was necessary he should go to heaven. If our happiness lay here, he would be with us here, but it doth not ; it is reserved for us in the heavens ; therefore he must go there to prepare a place for us, that we may be ever with him.

6. When gone away he will tarry no longer than our affairs require; as soon as he hath done his work, he will come again and fetch us. When our souls are with him, that doth not fully content Christ; he will come and fetch us into heaven in our whole persons, and then Christ and we shall never part more : 1 Thes. iv. 17, ' And then shall we ever be with the Lord.' Thus Christ is never satisfied till our communion be perfect and perpetual, till we are all with him in one assembly and congregation : Ps. i. 5, ' Therefore the ungodly shall not stand in the judgment, nor sinners in the congregation of the righteous.' Then all the elect shall meet in one general assembly, that Christ's mystical body may be fully complete ; not one member of his mystical body is wanting.

Secondly, Reasons.

1. Negatively ; there is not any want in himself, nor any worth in us. We are worthless and wretched ; Ps. xiv. 3, ' They are all gone aside, they are altogether become filthy, there is none that doeth good, no not one;' Titus iii. 3, ' For we ourselves also were sometimes foolish, disobedient, deceived, serving divers lusts and pleasures, living in malice and envy, hateful and hating one another.' Christ hath no need of us, he was happy without us ; he lieth in the bosom of his Father, and hath been his delight from all eternity, and hath ten thousand times ten thousand angels to attend him. What want hath he of poor worms ?

2. Positively ; his affection and relation to them. Affection and self-inclination; they are the members of his body: John xiii. 1,

'Jesus having loved his own that were in the world, he loved them to the end.' There are both motives; he hath loved them, and they are his own.

[1.] He hath loved them, and love is all for union and near communion: Deut. vii. 7, 8, 'The Lord did not set his love on you, nor choose you, because ye were more in number than any people, but because the Lord loved you.' He hath no other reason but his own love; and therefore he will not leave till he hath brought them to their final happiness.

[2.] They are his own by election, purchase, resignation. They resign themselves to him, and so he hath a peculiar interest in them. He provideth for his own, they are members of his mystical body; 'The fulness of him that filleth all in all,' Eph. i. 23. Mystical Christ is not complete and full without them, though Christ personal be every way full and complete.

Use 1. Reproof. You see how Christ standeth affected to the society of his people, and so are all that have Christ's Spirit; as Moses chose rather to suffer affliction with the people of God, than to enjoy the pleasures of sin for a season,' Heb. xi. 25. It is better to be afflicted for a season with God's people, than to live with the wicked in pleasure for a season; both are for a season. But there are a sort of men whose spirit and practice is very contrary to this of Christ; who cannot abide the presence, much less the company and communion, of the saints. Christ cannot rest in heaven without the saints; and these men count themselves in a prison when they are in good company; it is their burden and trouble to have a restraint upon their lusts, to be confined to gracious discourse about heaven and heavenly things. Nay, their very presence is an eyesore. As in some of the commonwealths of Greece, they had their petalism and ostracism for men when they grew eminent and worthy, the baseness of popular government not consisting with conspicuous virtue; so these cannot endure holy strictness, or a size of grace above their dead-hearted profession.

Use 2. Comfort against the scorn and contempt of the world. Though you are cast forth as the sweepings of the streets, yet you are dear and precious with Christ. That company which is so disdained and rejected in the world is longed for by Christ; therefore 'let us go forth to him without the camp, bearing his reproach,' Heb. xiii. 13. The world casts us out, but Christ takes us to himself

Use 3. Let us prize the communion and fellowship of Christ. It is but reason that we should prize that company that is so necessary for us, such a blessing to us. If he value ours, he is worthy of love, and he is our head; let us long to be with him. But wherein?

1. By looking after communion with him for the present. Certainly there is such a thing; the world looketh upon communion with Christ but as a fancy, as many among the heathens pretended to a secrecy with their gods; but the saints know the reality of it: 1 John i. 3, 'And truly our fellowship is with the Father, and with his Son Jesus Christ.' Certainly there is such a thing as this. Now, this is either constant and habitual, or solemn and special.

[1.] Constant and habitual, as he dwelleth in our hearts by faith;

where Christ doth take up his abode and dwelling in the heart, renewing them by his Spirit, as the fountain of life: Gal. ii. 20, 'Nevertheless I live, yet not I, but Christ liveth in me.' And the seed and hope of glory: Col. i. 27, 'Christ in you the hope of glory;' maintaining and defending them against all temptations: 1 John iv. 4, 'Greater is he that is in you than he that is in the world.' There is no necessity, in order to the spiritual use, that his body be in the sacrament, received into the mouth and stomach; his human nature is locally present in heaven, but his Spirit is in us as a well of life. This is our constant communion with him.

[2.] Solemn and special, in holy ordinances. Our souls should run upon this, how we may find Christ there; as the spouse sought her beloved throughout the whole city: Cant. iii. 2, 3, 'I will arise now, and go about the city, in the streets, and in the broad ways; I will seek him whom my soul loveth. I sought him, but I found him not. The watchmen that go about the city found me, to whom I said, Saw ye him whom my soul loveth?' So doth the believing soul long to see Christ. If he longeth for our presence, we should desire his presence, and to enjoy as much as we can of it here in the world. It is heaven begun: 'As for me, I shall behold his face in righteousness,' Ps. xvii. 15. Not only to have bare ordinances, but to meet with God there, that we may never go from him without him. This is to begin heaven, to give Christ a visit, to be familiar with Christ in prayer, to seek after him in the Lord's supper, and never go from God without God: Ps. lxiii. 1, 2, 'O God, thou art my God, early will I seek thee: my soul thirsteth for thee, my flesh longeth for thee, in a dry and thirsty land, where no water is. To see thy power and thy glory, so as I have seen thee in the sanctuary.' That glimpse he had once found made him long for more: Ps. lxxxiv. 1, 2, 'How amiable are thy tabernacles, O Lord of hosts! My soul longeth, yea, even fainteth for the courts of the Lord; my heart and my flesh crieth out for the living God.' Spiritual communion will at last end in glory. You may change place, but not company.

2. Long to be with him, and to have immediate communion with him in heaven: Phil. i. 23, 'I desire to depart, and to be with Christ;' not to wish for death in a pet, to put an end to your troubles. Men look upon heaven as a retreat. Nay, do not merely look upon heaven as it freeth you from the torments of hell or the curse and vengeance of God, but as it giveth you communion with Christ: 2 Cor. v. 8, 'We are confident, I say, and willing rather to be absent from the body, and to be present with the Lord.' Therefore upon this account be more willing to depart. You that are old, and within sight of shore, wait for the happy hour. You that are sick, be forward to prepare for home. You that are young, you may live long, but you cannot live better than with Christ; be ready when God shall call you.

(1.) There is far more reason why we should long for Christ than Christ for us. He desireth your presence for your own sakes, that you may be happy; he is not solitary without you. You have all the reason in the world to be willing to go to Christ; the sooner the better.

(2.) If you have the hearts of christians, you will do so: Rev. xxii. 17, 'The Spirit and the bride say, Come.' If you have heartily consented to Christ, you will do so : Gen. xxiv. 58, 'They called Rebekah, and said unto her, Wilt thou go with this man ? and she said, I will go.' Christ saith, 'I will that they shall be where I am ;' and the soul saith, I will be ever in a posture longing, waiting for this happy time. The children of Israel eat the passover with staves in their hands.

(3.) Experience puts us to this ; such as have any communion with Christ here will long after the completing of it in heaven : Rom. viii. 23, 'And not only they, but ourselves also, who have the first-fruits of the Spirit ; even we ourselves groan within ourselves, waiting for the adoption, to wit, the redemption of our body.'

(4.) If we desire it not, it is a sign of some corruption, too great an inclination to the pleasures and contentments of the world. Lot lingered in Sodom, Gen. xix. 16. Or that you have lost your evidences, and so think to appear before him as malefactors before a judge.

SERMON XLII.

Father, I will that they also whom thou hast given me be with me where I am ; that they may behold my glory, which thou hast given me : for thou lovedst me before the foundation of the world.
—JOHN XVII. 24.

SECONDLY, Now I come to our work and employment in heaven, 'That we may behold his glory.'

Observe, our work, or rather our happiness in heaven, mainly consists in the sight of Christ's glory : 1 John iii. 2, 'Beloved, now are we the sons of God, but it doth not yet appear what we shall be ; but this we know, that when he shall appear, we shall be like him, for we shall see him as he is.' We see him now under a veil, then in person : 1 Cor. xiii. 12, 'Now we see but through a glass darkly, then face to face.'

Here I shall show—(1.) What is this glory ; (2.) What it is to behold this glory ; (3.) Why our happiness lieth in it.

First, What is this glory ?

1. The excellency of his person. The union of the two natures in Christ's person is one of the mysteries that shall then be unfolded : John xiv. 20, 'At that day ye shall know that I am in my Father, and you in me, and I in you.' How he is God-man in one person, how the Father, Son, and Spirit are one. We were made for the understanding of this mystery. God had happiness enough in himself ; he made creatures on purpose, angels and blessed men, to contemplate his excellency.

2. The clarity of his human nature. It is happiness enough to see Jesus Christ upon his white throne : Rev. xxii. 4, 'They shall see his face, and his name shall be in their foreheads.' We shall be eye-witnesses of the honour which the Father puts upon him as mediator. It will be a wonderful glory ; we want words to make it intelligible ; the visible sun hath scarce the honour to be Christ's shadow. We

may guess at it by his appearance on Mount Sinai, when he gave the law, Exod. xix., compared with Heb. xii. 18, 19 ; by the transfiguration, Mat. xvii., when the disciples were astonished ; by the glimpse given to Paul, when a light from heaven shined round about him, Acts ix. 3 ; Paul was three days without sight, and could neither eat nor drink ; by those emissions of light and glory, John xviii. 6, ' As soon as he had said unto them, I am he, they went backward, and fell to the ground.'   All these apparitions were formidable, but in heaven they are comfortable.   We are more able to bear it, the natural faculties being fortified ; and we come to consider it as a glory put upon him for our sakes.

Secondly, What is this beholding?   It is either ocular or mental.

1. Ocular ; our senses have their happiness as well as the soul ; there is a glorified eye as well as a glorified mind : 2 Cor. v. 7, ' We walk by faith, not by sight.'   He doth not mean present sense, and the present view of things ; the life of faith is sometimes opposed to that ; but now he meaneth our privileges in heaven.   Job pointed to his eyes : Job xix. 26, 27, ' Though after my skin worms destroy this body, yet in my flesh shall I see God ; whom I shall see for myself, and mine eyes shall behold, and not another.'   We shall see that person that redeemed us, and that nature wherein he suffered so much for us.   God intendeth good to the body, he hath intrusted it with the soul, and the soul with so much grace, that he will not lose the outward cask and vessel.   There is a glory to entertain our eyes in heaven ; not only the beautiful mansion, and the glorious inhabitants, but the face of the Lamb.   We shall be always looking on that book.

2. There is mental vision or contemplation.   The angels, that are not corporeal, are said ' always to behold the face of our heavenly Father,' Mat. xviii. 10.   Angels have no eyes, yet they see God. When we are said to see God, it is not meant of the bodily eye ; a spirit cannot be seen with bodily eyes.   And therefore God is called $\dot{\alpha}\acute{o}\rho\alpha\tau o\varsigma$, ' the invisible God,' Col. i. 15.   And seeing face to face is opposed to knowing in part : 1 Cor. xiii. 12, ' Now we see through a glass darkly, then face to face ; now we know but in part, then we shall know even as also we are known.'   The mind is the noblest faculty, and therefore it must be satisfied in heaven, or else we cannot be happy.   It is the mind maketh the man ; it is our preferment above the beasts that God hath given us a mind to know him.   Man is a rational creature, and there is as great an inclination to knowledge in the soul as in beasts to carnal pleasures.   Drunkards may talk of their pleasures, and the gratifications of sense ; but the pleasure and delight of the soul is knowledge.   And besides this general capacity, there is a particular inclination in believers by grace ; and therefore, that we may be completely happy, the mind must be satisfied with the sight of God.

Thirdly, Why our happiness lieth in beholding Christ ?

1. It is the cause of all our fruition and enjoyment in heaven.

2. All fruition and enjoyment is resolved into it again.

1. It is the cause of all our fruition in heaven.   Ocular vision maketh way for mental, and mental vision for complete holiness or

conformity to God, and conformity for love, and love for delight, and delight for fruition.

[1.] Ocular vision maketh way for mental. We go to heaven to study divinity in the Lamb's face: Rev. xxii. 4, 'They shall see his face, and his name shall be in their foreheads.' There is an assembly sitting round about the throne, and the Lamb is in the midst of them, and there, by looking upon his face, they learn more of God. We need no other books than beholding his glory. We converse with Christ that we may know more of God. Thus we come to knowledge without labour and difficulty; Christ in his glory and eminency is bible enough.

[2.] Mental vision maketh way for likeness and conformity to God. Knowledge in this life changeth us: Col. iii. 10, 'And have put on the new man, which is renewed in knowledge after the image of him that created him.' Much more are we sanctified and made holy by the light of glory. The sight that we have of Christ in the gospel transformeth us: 2 Cor. iii. 18, 'For we all with open face, beholding as in a glass the glory of the Lord, are changed into the same image, from glory to glory, even as by the Spirit of the Lord.' By looking upon Christ through the light of the Spirit we are made like him; but now in glory, when we see him face to face, we are more like him: 1 John iii. 2, 'We shall be like him, for we shall see him as he is.' Moses, by conversing with God, his face shone. As a glass held up against the sun, the image and brightness of the sun is reflected upon it; so the more we behold Christ, the more we do bear the image of the heavenly; τὴν ὄψιν ἀναχρωννύμενος, saith Basil, he dyeth his own spirit with a tincture of glory.

[3.] This light and conformity maketh way for love, that is, knowledge increaseth love. As light is, so is love; our affection is still according to the rate of our knowledge. In this world love is but weak, because light is imperfect; we love little, because we know little: John iv. 10, 'If thou knewest the gift of God, and who it is that saith to thee, Give me to drink, thou wouldest have asked, and he would have given to thee living water.' And conformity is a ground of love, it is the highest pitch of love to love God out of the communion of the same nature. The lowest love is to love him out of interest, as the highest love is to love him out of a principle of holiness, not because he is good and bountiful, but because he is holy. Whilst holiness is weak, love is imperfect. We wander and estrange ourselves from him, and go a-whoring from him, for there is some suitableness between us and the creature as long as flesh remaineth; but when we are perfectly holy, there is no suitableness between us and anything but God, and the saints and angels which partake with us of his image. And we love the creatures for the need we have of them, as well as the suitableness of them to us; but when we are likened to God in holiness and in happiness, we are above these wants, we are above all baits and snares, so that our love is entirely carried out to God.

[4.] Love maketh way for delight. Can a man cleave to God, and not rejoice in him? Rejoicing in God is not only a duty but a reward: Isa. lviii. 14, 'Then shalt thou delight thyself in the Lord.' The saints love God, and delight in him, in his essence and being, as much as in their own glory. This maketh heaven comfortable. It would be a torment to a carnal heart to be always thinking of God, and employed in acts of love and service to God; but the saints delight in him, they delight in his presence, and in their own happiness, because God is glorified in it. There is an inconceivable delight in seeing, knowing, and being beloved of God.

[5.] Delight maketh way for fruition; for the more we delight in God, the more doth God delight in us, and giveth us the actual fruition of himself for our blessedness, so that we are fully satisfied. It is fruition maketh us happy. We can only speak of it in general terms, the filling up of the soul with God, and of the 'glory that shall be revealed in us,' Rom. viii. 18. We are in God, and God in us; as fire in iron that is red hot, it seemeth all on fire. Thus can we prattle a little, and darken counsel with words.

2. Backward again. Fruition maketh way for delight. We enjoy God to the full, therefore we delight in him. We are bidden to rejoice in our pilgrimage: Phil. iv. 4, 'Rejoice in the Lord always, and again I say, Rejoice.' God hath made our work a part of our wages, to train us up by degrees. But now, when we come to heaven, we enter into our master's joy. It is our only work in heaven; painful affections have no more use. And joy maketh way for love; these mutual endearments pass between God and us to increase love. We delight in God, therefore we are never weary of him. And love maketh way for likeness, and light for likeness, *eadem velle et nolle*. There is the most perfect imitation and resemblance of God, because the most perfect love. And for light, there is light in this fire; blunt iron, if it be made red hot, pierceth deeper than a sharp tool: we have but one object. And likeness maketh way for knowledge: Mat. v. 8, 'Blessed are the pure in heart, for they shall see God.' A dusky glass doth not give a perfect representation. Ignorance is the fruit of sin. Man never knew less than since he tasted of the tree of knowledge. Holiness clarifies the eye: 'We shall be like him, for we shall see him as he is,' 1 John iii. 2. There is little proportion between God and men, and therefore we do not know him; when we are conformed to God, we are in a greater capacity to understand his nature. And then light, or mental sight, maketh way for ocular sight, that we may look upon Christ. It is a sweet employment to see the brightness of the Father's glory in Christ's face; there is God best to be seen at the rebound and by reflection; it is a delightful spectacle.

Use 1. To ravish your hearts with the contemplation of this happiness. Oh! what an affective sight is Christ's glory!

1. The sight itself is a privilege.

2. That we shall be able to see it with comfort.

1. The sight itself is a privilege. Abraham had a sight of his incarnation, when it was a thing long after to come, and it filled him with joy: John viii. 56, 'Your father Abraham rejoiced to see my day; and he saw it, and was glad.' Simeon saw him when he was a child, and then said, 'Now it is enough;' Luke ii. 29, 30, 'Now, Lord, lettest thou thy servant depart in peace, according to thy word; for

mine eyes have seen thy salvation.' Zaccheus climbed up into a tree to see him. When he was grown up, Luke xix. 4, yet then he went up and down as the carpenter's son. Many saw Christ in person that had no benefit by him. So to see him by faith and spiritual illumination fills the soul with joy: 1 Peter i. 8, 'Whom having not seen, we love; in whom, though now ye see him not, yet believing, ye rejoice with joy unspeakable and full of glory.' To know Christ by hearsay is lovely and glorious; but now what will it be to see Christ in the midst of angels and blessed saints face to face? He is another manner of Christ than ever we thought him to be. It is ravishing to behold him in ordinances; feasts are poor things to be spoken of to that; but yet there is a veil upon his glory. Oh! that there should be such a glorious spectacle provided for us! It is God's own blessedness to see himself and enjoy himself.

2. That we are able to behold it, and that with comfort. That we are able to behold it: The world is a dark place, and we are weak creatures; our eyes now are like the eyes of an owl before the sun; we cannot take in a full representation of his greatness, nor bear the lustre of his majesty. God is sometimes represented as dwelling in light, to show the lustre of his majesty: 1 Tim. vi. 16, 'Who only hath immortality, dwelling in the light which no man can approach unto.' And sometimes as dwelling in darkness, as noting the weakness of our apprehensions: Ps. xviii. 11, 'He made darkness his secret place; his pavilion round about him were dark waters, and thick clouds of the sky.' We are dark creatures, and can but guess; all is mystery and riddle to us. The children of Israel cried out, 'We cannot see God and live;' Deut. v. 25, 'Now therefore why should we die? for this great fire will consume us; if we hear the voice of the Lord our God any more, then we shall die.' God is fain to dwell in the heavens, and fix his throne there; his glory would drive us to our wits' end, the very happiness of heaven would not be a mercy upon earth. And then, that we may behold it with comfort. God in Christ is not formidable. Wicked men shall see Christ, but they shall see him as a judge; but, saith Job, with these eyes shall I see my redeemer: Job xix. 25–27, 'I know that my redeemer liveth, and that he shall stand at the latter day upon the earth. And though after my skin, worms destroy this body, yet in my flesh shall I see God; whom mine eyes shall behold, and not another's.' Every time we look upon Christ, we have the liveliest and sweetest sense of God's love, it bringeth to remembrance his passion and sufferings. Wicked men shall see him as a judge to their terror, as Joseph's brethren were ashamed to look on him, they cannot hold up their guilty heads; but we come to behold our best and beloved friend, to see him that laid down his life for us: John xv. 13, 'Greater love hath no man than this, that a man lay down his life for his friend.' To see such a friend will be comfortable.

SERMON XLIII.

*O righteous Father, the world hath not known thee: but I have known thee, and these have known that thou hast sent me.—*JOHN XVII. 25.

OUR Lord had laid down the object of his prayers and the matter of them, and now he comes to the reasons, though in such affectionate addresses to God we should not be anxious in stating the method. Some conceive this a doxology; as Mat. xi. 25, 26, 'I thank thee, O Father, Lord of heaven and earth, because thou hast hid these things from the wise and prudent, and hast revealed them unto babes. Even so, Father, for so it seemed good in thy sight.' He had fully discharged his office as a prophet, and therefore giveth thanks. But I rather look upon it as a part of the supplication. He had made his will and testament, and now allegeth the equity of it. Here—

1. A compellation, 'O righteous Father.'

2. The qualification of the disciples for that glory which he sought for them, saving knowledge. Which is illustrated—

[1.] By its opposite, the affected and obstinate ignorance of the world, 'The world hath not known thee.'

[2.] By its efficient and exemplary cause, 'But I have known thee.'

First, A compellation, 'Righteous Father.' In which there is an argument secretly couched, for always titles of God are suited to the matter in hand. It is brought to show the reason why the world is excluded the participation of heavenly glory, and the equity in bestowing it upon the elect. He had before called him 'Holy Father,' now 'Righteous Father.'

God is just and righteous two manner of ways—in a legal and in an evangelical sense. In a legal sense, his justice is rewarding men according to the merit of their actions. Thus he dealeth with the reprobate lost world. In the evangelical sense, God's righteousness doth not regard the merit of their actions, but the state of the person; and judgeth them rather according to what they have received than what they have done. And so God dealeth with the elect and reprobate; the one are rewarded according to their works, the other according to their state, evidenced by their works; to both God is just. So that I might—

Observe, first, that in the condemnation of the world, God is just, though they remain in blindness.

1. Because God hath done enough; God is aforehand with them; they have more means than they use well. The Gentile world had light enough from the creatures to convince them of the true God: Rom. i. 19, 20, 'Because that which may be known of God is manifest in them, for God hath showed it unto them. For the invisible things of him from the creation of the world are clearly seen, being understood by the things that are made, even his eternal power and godhead; so that they are ἀναπολόγητοι, without excuse.' Yet they would not acknowledge the true God. The Jewish world had miracles enough to convince them of the true Messiah: John xv. 24, 'If I had

not done among them the works that no other man did, they had not had sin ; but now they have both seen and hated me and my Father.'

The carnal world within the pale of the church have had means enough to be better ; and though it be blind in the things of God, yet the Lord is clear : Isa. v.'4, 'What could I have done more for my vineyard than I have done?' in point of external administration. The Lord loveth 'to be clear when he judgeth,' Ps. li. 4, compared with Rom. iii. 26. In all debates he loveth the victory: Isaiah lxv. 2, 'I have spread out my hands all the day unto a rebellious people, which walketh in a way which was not good, after their own thoughts.' None goeth to hell for want of warning : Mat. xxiii. 37, 'O Jerusalem, Jerusalem ! thou that killest the prophets, and stonest them that are sent unto thee ; how often would I have gathered thy children together, as a hen gathereth her chickens under her wings, but ye would not.'

2. They have not done their part. They dally with means, scorn wisdom ; their weakness is wilful, and their blindness affected. The things of God must be spiritually discerned. But they are folly to them : 1 Cor. ii. 14, 'For the natural man receiveth not the things of the Spirit of God, for they are foolishness unto him ; neither can he know them, because they are spiritually discerned.' There is not only an impotency, but a scorn ; there is a positive enmity, as well as an incapacity : John iii. 19, 'This is the condemnation, that light is come into the world, and men loved darkness rather than light, because their deeds were evil.' Man is in love with his own misery ; when we should hate sins, we hate the light that discovereth them. An ignorant people love a sottish ministry ; the faithful witnesses are the world's torment : Rev. xi. 10, 'These two prophets tormented them that dwelt on the earth.' The world would fain lie down upon the bed of ease, and sleep. Light is troublesome to sore eyes. Ignorant priests are the people's idols ; the blind lead the blind, and they both fall into the ditch. They do not only err in their minds, but err in their hearts ; the one is sad, the other worse. It is evil that we do not know, it is doubly evil that we desire not to know: Job xxi. 14, 'Therefore they say unto God, Depart from us, for we desire not the knowledge of thy ways.' Spiritual blindness is worse than bodily. When Elymas was stricken blind, he desired somebody to lead him by the hand, Acts xiii. 11. We count it our happiness to have fit guides ; but in spiritual blindness it is quite otherwise ; we cannot endure a faithful guide : 'the prophets prophesy lies and the people love to have it so.' Blind people are all for blind guides.

Use 1. Let it set God clear. He loveth to have it so. When he cometh to judgment, 'the books shall be opened,' Rev. xx. 12. We are apt to quarrel his justice, for leaving so great a part of the world in the dark. Remember he is aforehand with means, and they love the state they are in. God leaveth no man without a sufficient conviction and witness of himself.

Use 2. Let sottish men know that God is not all mercy and all honey. Usually our desires transform God into that shape which we fancy. A libertine would have God all mercy and all patience, because he desires him to be so. Affections make opinions : Ps. l. 21, 'Thou thoughtest that I was altogether such an one as thyself.' But be not deceived; to the blind world God will be severe, but just: Isa. xxvii. 11, ' It is a people of no understanding; therefore he that made them will not have mercy on them, and he that formed them will show them no favour.' Ignorance is fatal and deadly to the heathens: 2 Thes. i. 8, ' In flaming fire, taking vengeance on them that know not God, and that obey not the gospel of our Lord Jesus Christ.' We pity them, and say, Poor ignorant creatures! We hate a drunkard, but we pity an ignorant man. But God is very angry with them, because he knoweth the wickedness of their hearts, how many means they have withstood, and how much light they have abused. God doth not measure sins by the foulness of the act, but by the unkindness and ingratitude of it. The blind and the lame are equally an abomination to the Lord. To want knowledge is as bad as to want obedience; it will be no excuse.

Object. Ay! but they have good meanings, and surely God will not deal in justice and rigour with them: we are ignorant, but our heart is good.

Ans. Prov. xix. 21, ' Without knowledge the heart is not good.' Ignorance is so far from being the mother of devotion, as the Papists say, that it is the great hindrance of it. Simple credulity may be more awful and scrupulous, as men in the night have many fears; but God loveth rational service, not blind obedience: 1 Chron. xxviii. 9, ' And thou, Solomon my son, know thou the God of thy father, and serve him with a perfect heart and a willing mind.' Worship without knowledge is but a blind guess and loose aim, as Christ reproveth the Samaritans for worshipping they knew not what, John iv. 22. Certainly we are not so sensible of the danger of ignorance as we should be. Men live sensually, and die sottishly, and then perish eternally; they live by guess at best, and some devout aims; and when they come to die, they die by guess, in a doubtful uncertain way; like men that leap over a deep gulf blindfold, they know not where their feet shall light.

Observe, secondly, that God is not only merciful, but just, in the reward of the godly or glorifying the elect. Christ is praying and arguing for heavenly glory, and he giveth God the title of ' Righteous Father.' You shall see all your privileges are made to come from righteousness. Pardon of sins, which is one of the freest acts of God, and wherein he discovereth most of his mercy: 1 John i. 9, ' If we confess our sins, he is faithful and just to forgive us our sins, and cleanse us from all unrighteousness.' This is the mystery of divine grace. So also for eternal rewards: 2 Thes. i. 6, 7, ' Seeing it is a righteous thing with God to recompense tribulation to them that trouble you.' You will think that it is righteous indeed that God should punish the wicked; but read on: ' But to you who are troubled, rest with us, when the Lord Jesus shall be revealed,' &c.

But how is God's righteousness and justice interested in our rewards?

1. Partly it is engaged by Christ's merit. Though to us it be mere grace, yet as to Christ it is just, Christ's satisfaction being equivalent to the violation of God's majesty, and therefore it is just to pardon us. It is just for the creditor to forgive the debtor when the surety hath paid. So Christ's blood is not only λυτρὸν, a ransom, but ἀντάλλαγμα, a price. It is just with God to glorify us; Christ's

righteousness giveth us a right. This reason you have, Rom. iii. 24–26, 'Being justified freely by his grace, through the redemption that is in Jesus Christ; whom God hath set forth to be a propitiation, through faith in his blood, to declare his righteousness for the remission of sins that are past, through the forbearance of God. To declare, I say, at this time his righteousness; that he may be just, and the justifier of him that believeth in Jesus.' God being satisfied by Christ, can be gracious to the creature without disparagement to his justice; the mediator interposeth, his satisfaction is accepted. This was that the wise men of all times busied themselves in, how God could do good to the creature without disparagement to his justice. But all their devices were frustrate; Christ alone bringeth the blood to the mercy-seat.

2. God is fast bound by his own promise: James i. 12, 'Blessed is the man that endureth temptation; for when he is tried, he shall receive the crown of life, which the Lord hath promised to them that love him.' And it is a part of justice to make good his word. *Promittendo se facit debitorem.* The qualification being supposed, we may challenge him upon it: Ps. cxix. 49, 'Remember thy word unto thy servant, upon which thou hast caused me to hope.' He biddeth us put him in remembrance he hath drawn us to these hopes: 2 Tim. iv. 8, 'Henceforth there is laid up for me a crown of righteousness, which the Lord, the righteous judge, shall give me at that day, and not to me only, but unto all them also that love his appearing.' Upon which Bernard noteth, *Paulus expectat coronam justitiæ; sed justitiæ Dei, non suæ: justum est ut reddat quod debet, debet autem quod pollicitus est.* It is just with God to pay what he oweth, and he oweth what he promised. Therefore Chrysostom saith it was στεφανὸς ἐλεοῦς καὶ δικαιοσύνης. We may say to God, *Redde quod promisisti,* though not *Redde quod debes.*

3. By positive ordinance, that every man shall receive according to the kind of his work, the wicked according to their wicked actions, and the good according to their good actions: Mat. xvi. 27, 'Then he shall reward every man according to his works.' Now, lest any should think it is meant of wicked men only, the apostle tells us, 2 Cor. v. 10, 'Every one shall receive the things done in his body, according to that he hath done, whether it be good or bad.' God is not arbitrary in his judgment, it is the rule of process. All shall be rewarded in the general, *quoad genus,* according to the kind of their works; wicked men *quoad meritum,* because eternal punishment is due to evil works, out of the nature of the works; but for the godly, the kind of their works is judged, but not in rigorous justice; they shall not be weighed in the balance, then all would be found wanting, but brought to the touchstone. *Væ laudabili vitæ hominum, si (remota misericordia) discutias eam,* saith Gregory. And the apostle, James ii. 12, 'So speak ye, and so do, as they that shall be judged by the law of liberty.'

Use 1. See how careful God is to preserve the honour and the awe in us of his justice, even in his rewards of grace. God will be just; he is very careful to preserve the notions which the creature hath of his own essence inviolable. He will not exercise mercy to the prejudice of his justice; there must be some way to represent him still a righteous Father.' God would give his own Son to the death that he might appear righteous. God will not love [1] that honour. Therefore stand in awe, and sin not, lest thou come short of the grace offered in Christ; lest you find him just in a legal sense, while you abuse the mercy of the gospel.

Use 2. It is to give us a sure ground of hope: Heb. vi. 10, 'For God is not unrighteous, to forget your work and labour of love.' That which is most terrible in God is the pawn and pledge of our salvation. Conscience, which is God's deputy, is never satisfied till God be satisfied; for this thought cannot be plucked out of our minds, that God is an avenger. If we had not a sufficient satisfaction, we should always be troubled. Wherewith shall he be appeased? Micah vi. 6, 7, 'Wherewith shall I come before the Lord, and bow myself before the high God? Shall I come before him with burnt-offerings, with calves of a year old? Will the Lord be pleased with thousands of rams, or with ten thousands of rivers of oil? Shall I give my first-born for my transgression, the fruit of my body for the sin of my soul?' If a poor creature were in debt, and haling to prison, and a king should say, I will engage my whole revenue but I will pay it, how would this comfort him! Certainly Christ was responsible enough. We are not so cheerful in his service as we should be, now justice is made our friend. Make use of it in great dejections and pangs of conscience: Job xxxiii. 24, 'Then he is gracious to him, and saith, Deliver him from going down to the pit, I have found a ransom.' When the ram was taken, Isaac was let go. God will show mercy to our persons, for justice is satisfied in our surety. You have a double claim and hold fast upon him in every court; you may come before the tribunal of justice as well as the throne of grace. When you are fainting in service, encourage yourselves: 'Verily there is a reward for the righteous,' Ps. lviii. 11. One day or another the saints shall be rewarded, their labour and service shall not be lost.

Secondly, The qualification, saving knowledge 'These have known that thou hast sent me.' It is urged as a reason why they should behold his glory hereafter, because they make it their care to know God in Christ here. Here are two propositions:—

1. The only way to come to blessedness is by the knowledge of the true God.

2. There is no knowledge of the true God without the knowledge of Jesus Christ as mediator.

First proposition, That the only way to blessedness is by the knowledge of the true God. This I prove—

1. Because the foundation of the eternal state must be laid in this life. Now the foundation and superstructure must carry a proportion. What is the great happiness of heaven, and the blessedness of the creature? The beatifical vision; and therefore we must begin it here in knowledge, and in the study of God: John xvii. 3, 'This is life eternal, to know thee the only and true God;' that is, this is the beginning of life eternal. When there is a saving light in the soul, there is a spark kindled that will never be quenched. In the barn corn doth not grow, but in the field. Here we labour after knowledge, there we enjoy the perfection of it; and according to the degrees of

<hr>

[1] Qu. 'lose'?—ED.

knowledge and grace we attain in this life, so will be our happiness hereafter. The state of the wicked is a growing darkness : Mat. viii. 12, ' The children of the kingdom shall be cast out into utter darkness,' εἰς τὸ σκότος τὸ ἐξώτερον. What is that ? A darkness beyond a darkness—*in tenebras ex tenebris infœliciter exclusi :* they shall be cast out from one darkness into another. Here they are under the darkness of ignorance and sin, and there they shall be under the darkness of horror and terror for evermore. The state of the wicked in hell is a darkness that grows out of a darkness ; here they are dark, and care not to know God, or know his ways, and the mists of darkness are reserved for them for evermore. But now the state of the godly is an increasing light: Prov. iv. 18, ' The path of the just is as the shining light, that shineth more and more unto the perfect day.' Look, as the just do increase, and go on from knowledge to knowledge, till they attain the light of glory, as the sun climbeth up to the top of the meridian by degrees, so the way of the wicked is darkness ; they go on from darkness to darkness, and the mist of darkness is reserved for them. Ignorance makes way for sin, and sin for hell. They are hastening downwards from darkness to darkness, and we hasten to the perfect day, from grace to glory.

2. There is no serving or enjoying of God but by knowledge. I do not plead for a naked knowledge, and an inactive speculation, but such as is accompanied with faith, love, and obedience, otherwise it is no true knowledge. No knowledge, no faith : Rom. x. 14, ' How shall they believe in him of whom they have not heard ?' We must know what Christ is before we can trust him with our souls. Would a woman accept of a man when she knows not what he is, nor from whence he came ? Can the soul rest itself with Christ, and venture its salvation upon him, till it knows what he is? 2 Tim. i. 12, ' I know whom I have believed, and I am persuaded that he is able to keep that which I have committed unto him against that day.' Faith is an advised act, it is a child of light. Presumption is but a blind adventure, an act that is done hand-over-head, without advice and care ; but faith certainly presupposeth knowledge. The blind man speaks reason in this, when Christ asked him, ' Dost thou believe on the Son of God ?' John ix. 35. He answered, ver. 36, ' Who is he, Lord, that I may believe on him ?' And then for love. No knowledge, no love. An unknown object never affects us. Love proceeds from sight. Those that have a sight of the excellences of God, by the light of the Spirit accompanying the word, they love the Lord. And then where there is no love, there is no knowledge : 1 John iv. 8, ' He that loveth not, knoweth not God, for God is love.' And then for worship and obedience, that is also the fruit of knowledge ; that worship which is performed to the unknown God is never right. As those fruits that grow out of the sun are crabbed and sour, so all such acts of worship as proceed not from light and knowledge are not right and genuine. There cannot be a greater preservative from sin than knowledge : 3 John 11, ' He that doeth evil hath not seen God.' Certainly he that makes a trade and course of sin was never acquainted with God : 1 John ii. 4, ' He that saith, I know him, and keepeth not his commandments, is a liar, and the truth is not in him.' And there

can be no enjoyment of God without knowledge, neither in a way of grace nor in a way of comfort. Not in a way of grace: there can be no grace without knowledge; if we be renewed and changed, it is by knowledge: Col. iii. 10, 'And have put on the new man, which is renewed in knowledge after the image of him that created him.' If we be strengthened in affliction, and enabled for the duties of every condition, it is by knowledge: Phil. iv. 12, 'I know both how to be abased, and I know how to abound; everywhere and in all things I am instructed both to be full and to be hungry, both to abound and to suffer need.' All communications of grace are conveyed by light. Nor can there be any enjoyment of God in a way of comfort without light and knowledge. Fears are in the dark; till we have a distinct knowledge of the nature and tenor of the covenant we are full of fears and doubts, which vanish as a mist before the sun when knowledge is wrought.

Second proposition, There is no knowledge of the true God without the knowledge of Christ as mediator. For two reasons :—

1. Because God will accept no honour from the creature but in and through Jesus Christ : John v. 23, 'That all men should honour the Son, even as they honour the Father. He that honoureth not the Son honoureth not the Father that hath sent him.' God hath revealed himself in Christ, and you make God an idol if you think of him otherwise.

2. Because God out of Christ is not comfortable, but terrible. The fallen creature cannot converse with God without a mediator. As waters, which are salt in the sea, strained through the earth, are sweet in rivers, so are the attributes of God in and through Christ sweet and comfortable to the soul; for we cannot draw nigh to God without a screen.

Use. To press us to get knowledge. The more knowledge, the more a man; the more ignorant, the more brutish: Ps. xlix. 20, 'Man that is in honour, and void of understanding, is like the beasts that perish.' And again, as knowledge doth distinguish you from beasts, so the knowledge of God doth distinguish you from other men; to know God is your excellency above other men: Jer. ix. 23. 24, ' Let not the wise man glory in his wisdom, neither let the mighty man glory in his might, let not the rich man glory in his riches. But let him that glorieth, glory in this, that he understandeth and knoweth me, that I am the Lord,' &c. As if he had said, If you will needs glory, it is not who is most wealthy, nor most mighty, nor most wise, but who hath the greatest knowledge of God in Christ. Above all, know God in Christ, that is most comfortable. *Horrible est de Deo extra Christum cogitare.* It is a horrible thing to think of God out of Christ. God in Christ is the greatest mercy the world was ever acquainted with; this is a speculation fit for angels: 1 Peter i. 12, ' Which things the angels desire to look into ;' Eph. iii. 10, ' To the intent that now unto the principalities and powers in heavenly places, might be known by the church the manifold wisdom of God.' And therefore much more should it be the study of saints. But do not rest in a naked contemplation; there is 'a form of knowledge,' Rom. ii. 20, as well as 'a form of godliness,' 2 Tim. iii. 5, which is nothing else but an artificial speculation, a naked model of truth in the brain, which, as the winter sun, shines but warms not. But what is true knowledge? How shall we discover it? I answer—1. It must be a serious prudent knowledge, &c. [See on ver. 8.]

I now come to speak to the illustration of this qualification of saving knowledge. It is illustrated—

1. By its opposite, the affected and obstinate ignorance of the world, ' The world hath not known thee.'

2. By its efficient and exemplary cause, ' But I have known thee.'

The first illustration is from the opposite ignorance and obstinacy of the world, ' The world hath not known thee.'

Why is this alleged? I answer—Partly to show the reason why they should be otherwise dealt withal than the blind world. As if he had said, By thy righteous and wise constitution, thou hast appointed different recompenses to men of different states ; but now 'they have known thee,' but ' the world hath not known thee.' Partly to commend their acknowledgment of Christ, the world neither knowing nor believing, yea, rather hating and persecuting thee. In the original there is *και, though ;* so that, neither hindered by fears nor snares, the rulers and great men were against the acknowledging of Christ, the multitude blind and obstinate ; yet the disciples knew him, and owned him as the Messiah, or one sent of God.

Observe, first, that it is exceeding praiseworthy to own Christ when others disown him and reject him, to own him in the midst of the world's blindness and madness against him. Now he is publicly received among the nations, it is no great matter to own him now ; as those that followed Christ in his lifetime for the loaves, John vi. 26, when honours, and conveniences, and interests, look that way. But to own him then, when the powers of the world, the heads and rulers of the church are against him, when the stone. is refused by the builders, this is praiseworthy.

Now the reasons are two. It is a sign God hath a great love to them, and it is a sign of their great love to God ; of his choice, and their sincerity. There are two things hinder us from the sight of truth—prejudices and interests. Now it is a sign of the special direction of God's Spirit when we can overlook prejudices ; and it is a sign of our unfeigned zeal when we can deny interests.

1. It is an argument of God's love to us. This looketh like election: Mat. xxiv. 24, ' If it were possible, they shall deceive the very elect.' There are some favourites whom God taketh into his special care, that he may show them his counsel, and lead them into all truth. In times when error is so countenanced, and appeareth with a plausible face, it is a matter of great skill to find out the truth. There are some choice ones to whom God manifests himself, when others are left to perish in their own ways. So it is said, Ps. xxv. 14, ' The secret of the Lord is with them that fear him.' By the secret of the Lord is not meant the counsels of his providence ; they are revealed but to a few, to the prophets ; this is a promise common to all that fear him ; therefore by it is intended the counsels of the word ; those that are his favourites, that lie in his bosom, they shall know his secrets ; as the disciples, when they would know anything of Christ, pointed to

the disciple whom Jesus loved: John xiii. 23, 24, 'Now there was leaning on Jesus' bosom one of the disciples whom Jesus loved. Simon Peter therefore beckoned to him, that he should ask who it should be of whom he spake.'

2. It is an argument of our sincerity, to own God in times of public contest, when it is dangerous to own him. There are some times when God crieth, 'Who is on my side?' Exod. xxxii. 26, when he calleth upon us to manifest ourselves, and providence calleth for a public acknowledgment. Errors by God's permission are sent into the world to try us. The Lord trieth you to see if you will be led by every fancy, and swim with the stream. Many times the delusion is very strong, that our trial may be the greater; so 1 Cor. xi. 19, 'There must be heresies, that, δοκιμοὶ, they which are approved may be made manifest among you.' Winds are let loose to try who are chaff, who are solid grain; especially an error backed with power, as when a tree is shaken, rotten apples fall down; such times discover hypocrites: Prov. xxvi. 26, 'Whose hatred is covered by deceit, his wickedness shall be showed before the whole congregation.' But now it is a great argument of sincerity to own the truth, when the error is so plausible, and the inconvenience is great: 1 Kings xix. 10, 'I have been very jealous for the Lord God of hosts: because the children of Israel have forsaken thy covenant, thrown down thine altars, and slain thy prophets with the sword; and I, even I only, am left; and they seek my life to take it away.' When we are left alone to contest, that is a great trial.

Use 1. Information.

1. That true zeal is not seen so much in fighting with antiquated errors, as in being 'established in the present truth,' 2 Peter i. 12, ἐν τῇ παρούσῃ ἀληθείᾳ. The present truth of that age was to acknowledge Christ to be the Messiah. When truths are upon the stage, then to give our testimony to them, this is to be God's witnesses. To declaim against the errors of former ages is but a safe and wary zeal. The Jews that opposed Christ yet pleaded for the prophets slain by their fathers. Corah, Dathan, and Abiram were as hateful to them as Judas to us; but they had no eyes to see for the present. Christ taxeth the hypocrisy of them that maligned the living prophets, and garnished the tombs of the dead, Mat. xxiii. 29. It is no thank to own Christ in the day of his exaltation, as when he is opposed and slighted. Old truths are only opposed by natural prejudices, but present truths by carnal interests.

2. That it is a great folly in them that will profess nothing till the world be agreed. Laziness is apt to pretend want of certainty. This is the old prejudice. Chrysostom bringeth in a heathen disputing—I would fain become a Christian, but there are so many divisions among you, that I know not what to choose. Men are loath to put themselves to the trouble of prayer and search, and would have all fitted to their hands, and therefore, till all be agreed, keep themselves in a wary reservation. Should a traveller stand still because he meeteth with many ways? Jer. vi. 16, 'Thus saith the Lord, Stand ye in the way, and see, and ask for the old paths, where is the good way, and walk therein, and ye shall find rest for your souls.' Or should a man that is sick refuse physic till all physicians be of one mind? It is your

duty to search, and it is praiseworthy to own Christ in times of contest.

3. It informeth us that a multitude is no excuse, because all went that way. We should own Christ though the world know him not, though it hate him, though it persecute him. We should have an eagle eye. The old world was not spared for the multitude ; there were but eight persons of another judgment. We often presume that many eyes see more than one, and so spare the labour of examination ; but one man that hath the use of his eyes seeth more than a thousand blind men ; and often-times it falleth out that a few find the true way : Mat. vii. 14, 'Strait is the gate and narrow is the way that leadeth unto life, and few there be that find it.' Therefore it is brutish to follow the track. We should examine, because mostly the world is out, and the multitude followeth that which is evil ; nay, it is rather a ground of suspicion ; the most are not the best.

Use 2. It presseth us to be more earnest to get a clear and satisfactory knowledge in the controversies of the age, in the truths that are now upon the stage. To that end—

1. Desire the direction of Christ, and consult with him. As the woman of Samaria, John iv. 20, 'Our fathers worshipped in this mountain, and ye say that in Jerusalem is the place where men ought to worship.' Whether Zion or Gerizim? Present it often to Christ. Prayer is the best way to get satisfaction, and our doubts are best solved by consulting with the oracle. You can have no certain light from men without his illumination.

2. Search and prove all things : 1 Thes. v. 21, 'Prove all things, hold fast that which is good.' We should stand in the ways and see : Jer. vi. 16, 'Stand in the ways and see, and ask for the old paths, where is the good way, and walk therein, and ye shall find rest for your souls.' We should be able to render λόγον, 1 Peter iii. 15, 'A reason of the hope that is in you, with meekness and fear.' And we have ἴδιον στήριγμα, 'a steadfastness of our own,' 2 Peter iii. 17. We must not only regard the consent of others, but our judgments must be balanced with sound and weighty grounds, otherwise we shall be carried about with every wind of doctrine, when the posture of interest is changed, or a new opinion is started. *Non exploratis traditionum rationibus probabilem fidem portant.* Such men have no principles.

But must we not hold fast what we have received? must we always be searching, and keeping ourselves in a wary reservation, and be never settled? I answer—

[1.] For principles and fundamental doctrines, we are not to doubt of them : Deut. xii. 30, 'Thou shalt not inquire after their gods, saying, How did these nations serve their gods? even so will I do likewise.' It is dangerous to loosen foundation-stones, though with an intent to settle them better. Here we should be at a certainty.

[2.] For lesser truths, when they are already cleared, and God hath taught them, it is good to hold fast what we have already received, and not to loosen the assent, or keep the soul suspensive, out of a jealousy or supposal that something may be said against what we now hold. 'Ever learning, and never coming εἰς ἐπίγνωσιν, to the knowledge of the truth,' But in case of actual doubt, it is good to search.

Doubts smothered make way for atheism or hardness of heart. Therefore, in cases of anxiety, it is good to bring things to an issue. Smoke maketh way for flame.

[3.] In your choice, be not swayed with interests, nor vulgar prejudices, nor vile affections.

(1.) Not with interests. God puts us to trial, to see if we can love a hated truth. The world is a blinding thing: 2 Cor. iv. 4, 'The god of the world hath blinded the minds of them which believe not.' Why is Satan called 'the god of the world'? He throweth the dust of the world in our eyes, and then we cannot see. We easily believe what we readily desire, and are loath to search when we have a mind to hate. Let the weights be never so equal, yet, if the balances be not equal, you can never judge of the weight of anything. When the mind is prepossessed and infected with interests, we are not capable of making a right judgment; as the water, when it is muddied, doth not render and represent the face.

(2.) Not with vulgar prejudices, as prepossessions of custom and long tradition, the opinions of holy and learned men, general consent, pretences of a stricter way. Men would fain judge upon slight grounds, without entering into the merits of the cause, to save the pains of study and prayer. This is but to put a fallacy upon yourselves. Some are against novelty, and when the ways of God are revived, they are hardened, they will not change; as if there were no obstinacy as well as constancy, obstinacy in the bad angels, as well as constancy in the good. Others are swayed by the opinions of godly learned men, whose persons they have in admiration. There is no *ipse dixit* in the church but the Lord's. It is observed that the corruptions of the Roman synagogue were occasioned by admiration of some venerable pastors of that church. Paul withstood Peter to the face, Gal. ii. 12, when his credit and example was like to do hurt. Others are swayed by general consent; but it is dangerous following the multitude; the world hath been against Christ, when a few only have owned him. Others by pretences of a stricter way: Col. ii. 23, 'Which things have indeed a show of wisdom in will-worship and humility, and neglecting of the body.' This is to be wiser than God, and to judge the law.

(3.) Not by vile affections, pride, passion, envy. Pride, or an overweening opinion of our own wit and learning: John ix. 40, 'The pharisees said, Are we blind also?' Proud persons, as the great rabbies, will not seem to be in an error. Men choose rather to be wicked than to be accounted weak. So envy at others, when men cannot be admitted into such places as they affect; and that puts them upon error and opposition: 1 Cor. iii. 3, 'For whereas there is among you envying, and strife, and divisions, are ye not carnal, and walk as men?' So passion, revenge, and discontent. The devil worketh much upon spleen and anger, when offence is taken, whether justly, or upon supposed occasion, it mattereth not. Many in spite and stomach have turned atheists or heretics. Carnal Ham, when cursed of his father, began the way of atheism.

Observe, secondly, that the reprobate world can never have any true knowledge of God: 'The world hath not known thee.'

1. The reprobate world can go as far as nature can go : 1 Cor. ii. 14, 'The natural man receiveth not the things of the Spirit of God, for they are foolishness unto him, neither can he know them, because they are spiritually discerned;' ἄνθρωπος ψύχικος, not σάρκικος. There are two reasons urged by the apostle—a natural incapacity and a positive enmity. (1.) A natural incapacity. He supposeth a sufficient revelation: 'They are spiritually discerned.' There must be a cognation between the object and the faculty. Spiritual things must be seen by a spiritual light. Sense, which is the light of beasts, cannot trace the workings and flights of reason ; we cannot see a soul or an angel by the light of a candle. So that the object must not only be revealed, but there must be an answerable light in the faculty. There is light enough, but we have not eyes. There needeth not a plainer revelation. David prays, not that God would make a plainer rule, but open his eyes: Ps. cxix. 18, 'Open thou mine eyes, that I may behold wondrous things out of thy law.' The understanding must be opened, as well as the scriptures: Luke xxiv. 45, 'Then opened he their understanding, that they might understand the scriptures.' (2.) Positive enmity: 'They are foolishness to him.' He looketh upon the things of God and solid piety as frivolous and vain. When Paul came to Athens, they called him babbler: Acts xvii. 18, 'What will this babbler say?' The same disposition still remaineth in natural men. Though the truths of religion, by long tract of time, and by the consent of many ages, have obtained credit, yet men nauseate spiritual truths and the power of godliness. A stomach ill affected by choler casts up wholesome meats; so do they scorn strictness and the holy ways of God.

2. Experience shows it. Take mere nature itself, and, like plants neglected, it soon runneth wild ; as the nations that are barbarous, and not polished with arts and civility, have more of the beast than of the man in them : Jude 10, 'What they know naturally, as brute beasts, in those things they corrupt themselves.' Suppose they use the spectacles of art to help the native light of reason with industry, yet their eyes are blind. How erroneous in religion were the civil nations ! Rom. i. 22, 'Professing themselves to be wise, they became fools ;' very foolish in matters of worship. The Romans placed fear, human passions, and every paltry thing among their gods. The ruder and more brutish nations worshipped only the sun and thunder, things great and wonderful. And still now we see great scholars given over to fond superstitions. Nay, go higher ; suppose, besides the spectacles of art, nature be furnished with the glass of the word, yet we see great scholars very defective in the most useful and practical points. Nicodemus, a teacher in Israel, knew not regeneration, John iii. 10. Usually they delight rather in moral strains than mysteries of faith, and err in one point or another ; usually in the controversies of their age, they are blinded by pride or interest, are loath to stoop to truth revealed, and so are outstarted by the vulgar. *Surgunt indocti et rapiunt cœlum, &c.*—they dispute away heaven while others surprise it. Nay, suppose they had an exact model and proportion of faith, and do pry into all the secrets of religion, as it is possible to do with the common light and help of the Spirit, which is as far as a reprobate

can go; yet all this is without any change of affection, without any favour or relish of truth. This speculative and artificial knowledge doth not change the heart.

But here is an objection; many carnal men have great parts, and profess the knowledge of the true God. I answer—

[1.] The greatest part of the world lieth in ignorance; they are born in darkness, live in darkness, love darkness more than light, and are under the powers of darkness: Eph. vi. 12, ' The rulers of the darkness of this world.' The devil hath a large territory over all the blind nations.

[2.] Carnal men, that own the true God, and profess him, yet in a scripture sense they do not know him. For knowledge not being affective, it is reputed ignorance : John viii. 54, 55, ' Of whom ye say, that he is your God. Yet ye have not known him, but I know him : and if I should say, I know him not, I shall be a liar like unto you; but I know him, and keep his saying.' It is a lie to pretend to knowledge without obedience : 1 John ii. 4, 5, ' And hereby we know that we know him, if we keep his commandments. He that saith, I know him, and keepeth not his commandments, is a liar, and the truth is not in him.' For all their great parts, they are but spiritual fools; they have no true wisdom, ἀνόητοι. So are all carnal men: Titus iii. 3, ' We ourselves also were sometimes foolish,' out of our wits. They do not understand things spiritual, and such as tend to maintain communion with God; they love and do those things with delight that are against all reason, hurtful to body and soul. Natural men are sometimes represented as fools that judge amiss, sometimes as infants that know nothing: Isa. xxviii. 9, ' Whom shall he teach knowledge? and whom shall he make to understand doctrine? they that are weaned from the milk, and drawn from the breast.' Sometimes as beasts, that are incapable of understanding : Ps. xxxii. 9, ' Be ye not as the horse, or as the mule, that hath no understanding.' Fools they are in their choice that prefer a nut or an apple before a jewel; they spend all their time in looking after riches, and honours, and such kind of things as do not conduce to eternity; for carnal pleasures forfeit their souls, and yet think themselves very wise. In their course they make war with heaven, and enter into the lists with God, as if they were stronger than he. In their presumption, they give out themselves for the sons of God, when they are the devil's children; as if a man, born of a beggar, should pretend to be the son of a king. Fools and madmen challenge all lands as theirs, so do they all promises and comforts. Within a little while experience will show them to be fools; their eyes are never opened to see their folly till it be too late : Luke xii. 20, ' Thou fool, this night thy soul shall be required of thee;' Jer. xvii. 11, ' As a partridge sitteth on eggs, and hatcheth them not, so he that getteth riches, and not by right, shall leave them in the midst of his days, and at his end shall be a fool.' There is no fool to the carnal fool; godly men are only wise, that are wise to save their souls.

Use. It informeth us—

1. Of our misery by nature. For as the reprobate lost world are, so are we all by nature; we have no knowledge of the true God : Job

xi. 12, 'Vain man would be wise, though man be born like a wild ass's colt.' We are apt to think ourselves angels, but we are beasts. Every one affects the repute of wisdom; we would rather be accounted wicked than weak. If a man were born with an ass's head, or were monstrous and misshapen in his body, this were sad. It is worse to be born with the heart of an ass, to be born like a wild ass's colt, with such gross and rude conceits of God and holy things. This is our estate by nature.

2. The danger of ignorance; it is the state of the reprobate world. It is good to think of it, partly that we may avoid it ourselves, and strive for knowledge; partly that we may be thankful if we have obtained knowledge; and partly that we might pity others, as Christ wept over Jerusalem : Luke xix. 41, 42, ' And when he was come near, he beheld the city, and wept over it, saying, If thou hadst known, even thou, at least in this thy day, the things which belong unto thy peace ! but now they are hid from thine eyes.' It is one of God's ·sorest judgments; when the Lord hath left threatening other things, then he threatens a blind heart and a vain mind. The great reproach that Nahash would lay upon Israel was to put out their right eyes. The great design of the god of this world upon the men of this world is to put out their eyes, that they might not come to the knowledge of the truth.

3. Positive ignorance is a sign that we are of the world; I mean, where we have means and opportunities to the contrary, and do not come to the knowledge of God, and of his ways: 1 John ii. 13, ' I write unto you little children, because ye have known the Father.' God hath no child so little but he knows his Father. The blind world knows him not; when there is night in the understanding, or frost in the heart, it is a sign of a worldling; when men are ignorant, unteachable, and do not grow in knowledge. God's children many times may be ignorant, and do not profit according to their advantages : John xiv. 9, ' Have I been so long with thee, and yet hast thou not known me, Philip ?' that is, not known so distinctly God the Father, and me, as coming out from him. But God's children are not altogether unteachable.

4. We have no reason to trust the judgment of carnal men in matters of godliness, for they do not know God. Can blind men judge of colours? I urge it, that you may not be discouraged though the world scoff at holiness. Who would take notice of the judgment of fools ?

5. That ignorance is not only the badge of silly weak persons, but of great men, and those that are carnally wise: Mat. xi. 25, ' I thank thee, O Father, Lord of heaven and earth, because thou hast hid these things from the wise and prudent, and hast revealed them unto babes.' Whatever parts they have, they have no saving knowledge of God. The godly man is the only knowing and wise man ; all others they are but fools, however they swell with an opinion of knowledge, and count it a reproach to be so called.

The second illustration is by the efficient and exemplary cause of our knowledge, ' But I have known thee,' &c. All along our likeness to Christ and unlikeness to the world is asserted.

Observe, that Christ's knowledge is the pattern and cause of ours.

We have all things at the second hand: 'I have known,' and 'they have known.' All the candles are lighted at this torch; or, to use a comparison more celestial, all the stars receive their light from the sun. Therefore he is called, 'the Father of lights,' James i. 17, and 'the Sun of righteousness,' Mal. iv. 2.

Christ giveth us knowledge two ways—by his word and by his Spirit. Now none is fit to establish the word, none to pour out the Spirit, but Christ.

1. None can give us a sufficient revelation of the Father but Christ, that came out of his bosom, that knew all his counsels: John i. 18, 'No man hath seen God at any time; the only-begotten Son, which is in the bosom of the Father, he hath declared him.' Our knowledge is by the senses, by sight and hearsay. Now no man hath seen God, but Christ, that was God-man, who came out of his bosom. So Mat. xi. 27, 'No man knoweth the Son but the Father; neither knoweth any man the Father save the Son, and he to whomsoever the Son will reveal him.' To know him perfectly and comprehensively, so neither men nor angels know him. To know him originally, so as to establish a revelation with authority, and so as fit to offer the light and knowledge of him to the creature, so none but Christ knows him; our faith is built on God. Human authority begets but a human faith and credulity. It was necessary that in the bede-roll of gospel preachers the Son of God should have the first place, that in the latter times he should preach to us by his Son, that the ultimate resolution of faith might be into divine authority: John vii. 29, 'But I know him, for I am from him, and he hath sent me;' and John x. 15, 'As the Father knoweth me, even so know I the Father.' It is for our confidence that the full discovery of this doctrine was reserved for the Son of God.

2. None else can give us a capacity to learn. Jesus Christ is such a teacher, that he doth not only give the lesson, but the wit and skill to learn: 1 John v. 20, 'We know that the Son of God is come, and hath given us an understanding, that we may know him that is true.' No matter what the scholar is, when we have such a master. We use to inquire whether any one hath a capacity to learn. He openeth the scriptures, and openeth the understanding to learn: Luke xxiv. 27, 'And beginning at Moses, and all the prophets, he expounded unto them in all the scriptures, the things concerning himself;' and ver. 45, 'Then opened he their understandings, that they might understand the scriptures.' There is a double veil—upon the doctrine and upon the heart; Christ removeth both.

Use 1. If that the true knowledge of God is only to be had from Christ, it directeth us in the use of all ordinances to look up to him; there must our trust be fixed, in reading, hearing, meditating. We must use helps and means, else we tempt God, but our trust must be elsewhere. In reading, Ps. cxix. 18, 'Open thou mine eyes, that I may behold wondrous things out of thy law.' There are wonders in the law, but our eyes must be opened to see them, otherwise we shall have but a superficial and literal knowledge, when men think to find more in books than in Christ. So in hearing, *cathedram habet in cœlis:* Isa. ii. 3, 'Come ye, and let us go up to the mountain of the

Lord, to the house of the God of Jacob, and he will teach us of his ways.' You come to the word to be taught by man, and yet not to be taught by man; in obedience you use the means, but your confidence is on Christ, that you may hear his voice to the soul, that he that brought the gospel out of the bosom of God may bring it into your hearts. The dial is of no use without the sun; except the sun shine, you cannot see what is a-clock by the dial; so in meditation and study; Christ is 'Wonderful, counsellor,' Isa. ix. 6; Prov. viii. 14, 'Counsel is mine and sound wisdom; I am understanding, I have strength.' How are men befooled that go forth in the confidence of their own wit! Flesh and blood are apt to stumble in God's plainest ways. Carnal hearts turn all to a carnal purpose: Prov. xxvi. 9, 'As a thorn goeth up into the hand of a drunkard, so is a parable in the mouth of fools.' The same cloud that was light to the Israelites was darkness to the Egyptians. Luther calleth the promises 'bloody promises,' through our perverse applications. Truth is only renewing as taught by Christ: Eph. iv. 21, 'If so be that ye have heard him, and have been taught by him, as the truth is in Jesus.' We cannot tell how to master corruptions without this. The light of common conviction is like a March sun, that draweth up aguish vapours; it discovereth sins, but cannot quell them. We should be apt to forsake truth upon every temptation, unless it were for Christ's teaching: Ps. cxix. 102, 'I have not departed from thy judgments, for thou hast taught me;' 1 John ii. 20, 'Ye have an unction from the holy one, and ye know all things.' When men lead us into truth, others may lead us out again. Those that have made trial can best judge of the difference between being taught of God and men: 1 Cor. ii. 4, 'My speech and my preaching was not with enticing words of man's wisdom, but in demonstration of the Spirit and of power.' When the arrow cometh out of God's quiver, it sticketh in our sides. Then we see truths with application.

Use 2. It teacheth us how to direct our prayers to Christ. Seek to him with confidence, and with all earnestness of affection.

1. With confidence; we despair many times because of our blockishness: Col. ii. 3, 'In him are hid all the treasures of wisdom and knowledge.' Hidden, not that they should not be found out, but because they are seen by the eye of faith: hidden, because deposited there, to be dispensed to us. God made Christ a storehouse to furnish all our necessities: 1 Cor. i. 30, 'Of him are ye in Christ Jesus, who of God is made unto us wisdom, and righteousness, and sanctification, and redemption.' Wisdom to give us spiritual illumination. Be not discouraged; it is not the pregnancy of the scholar that prevaileth here, but the excellency of the teacher. If Christ be the teacher, no matter how dull the scholar be. Pride in parts hath been a hindrance, but simpleness hath never been a hindrance: Ps. xix. 7, 'The testimony of the Lord is sure, making wise the simple;' Jer. xxxi. 33, 34, 'I will put my law in their inward parts, and write it in their hearts; and will be their God, and they shall be my people: and they shall teach no more every man his neighbour, and every man his brother, saying, Know the Lord, for they shall all know me from the least of them to the greatest of them, saith the Lord;' Mat. xi. 25,

'I thank thee, O Father, Lord of heaven and earth, because thou hast hid these things from the wise and prudent, and hast revealed them unto babes.' God can give to shallow and weak people great understanding in spiritual things, as he cured him that was born blind, John ix.

SERMON XLIV.

And I have declared unto them thy name, and will declare it; that the love wherewith thou hast loved me may be in them, and I in them.—JOHN XVII. 26.

THIS is the second reason, taken from the benefits Christ had bestowed upon them. Here is his gift and his aim. In the first, what he had done, what[1] he will do. Where—(1.) *Quid*, the manifestation of his Father's name; (2.) *Quibus*, to whom, principally to the apostles, and from them to believers; (3.) *Quomodo*, 'I have,' that is, by his ministry upon earth; and 'I will,' in the pouring out the Spirit, and his discourses with them after the resurrection. All that needeth explication is, What is meant by God's name? *Ans.* The use of names from the beginning was a distinction to separate creature from creature by their appellations. At first Adam gave names to the beasts, that their species and kinds might be distinguished, for beasts are distinguished only by their herds and kinds. But the names which men bear are individual and particular; man being an excellent creature, made for rule and commerce, and therefore is to be known not by his kind, but name. But now, what is God's name? Where there are many, there is need of names; but where there is but one, the singularity is distinction enough. But yet God hath his name, by way of distinction from creatures; so we have a negative name, removing the imperfections of the creature, and to distinguish him from those λεγόμενοι θεοὶ, gods that are so called. And his name is a jealous God: Exod. xxxiv. 14, 'For thou shalt worship no other God; for the Lord, whose name is Jealous, is a jealous God.' And by way of notification, that we may conceive of him aright, as names are not only distinctive, but δηλώτικα τῶν πραγμάτων, as Damascene. So all that by which he is known or distinguished, that is his name; and so God hath many names, because one cannot enough express him. His works are a part of his name, but chiefly his word, the doctrine concerning his essence and will: Ps. cxxxviii. 2, 'Thou hast magnified thy word above all thy name;' there he hath made himself most known. In creation and providence we may read much of God, but in the bible more; and chiefly his word of promise and covenant, which is that theatre upon which his mercy and truth is discovered, which is the representation wherein God delighteth. And again, the covenant, as it is revealed in the gospel, is a chief part of his name, for his name was secret before the New Testament dispensation was set afoot: Judges xiii. 18, 'Why

---

[1] Qu. 'in the second, what, &c.'?—ED.

askest thou thus after my name, seeing it is secret?' There was little known of the Trinity, of the Son of God, the incarnation of the Son of God, &c.

First point, That one great privilege of the gospel is to know God by his right name.

1. I shall show you how God's name and title hath been often changed and altered, because he would acquaint his people with his full name by degrees: Exod. vi. 3, 'I appeared unto Abraham, unto Isaac, and unto Jacob, by the name of God Almighty, but by my name JEHOVAH was I not known to them.' First to Ahrabam, to distinguish him from idols and false gods, *El Shaddai ;* then 'Jehovah,' as giving being to his people, making good his promises; after, 'God of Abraham, God of Isaac, and God of Jacob,' as relating more to the covenant; then, 'God that brought them out of the land of Egypt,' Exod. xx. 2; then, 'God that brought them out of the land of the north;' then, 'the God and Father of our Lord Jesus Christ;' before that, 'the Lord our righteousness,' Jer. xxiii. 6. The Jewish church knew little of the doctrine of the Trinity, distinction of the persons, quality of the mediator. God proclaimed his name: Exod. xxxiv. 6, 7, 'The Lord, the Lord God, merciful and gracious, long-suffering, and abundant in goodness and truth, keeping mercy for thousands, forgiving iniquity, and transgression and sin.' But the way of pardon was not then so fully discovered. Some names God hath from everlasting, as Eternal, Infinite; some relate to the present state, as Creator, Lord, God in covenant, the God of Abraham, Isaac, and Jacob.

2. What the gospel especially doth discover more of God.

[1.] The distinction of the persons in the Godhead. At the baptism of Christ the whole Trinity was sensibly present; the Son in the body, the Father in the voice, and the Holy Ghost in the form of a dove. This was the mystery brought upon the stage.

[2.] The incarnation of Christ: 1 Tim. iii. 16, 'God manifest in the flesh.' The world was acquainted with this great help to piety. The Jews had a temple; here is a temple wherein the Godhead dwelleth bodily: Col. ii. 9, 'For in him dwelleth all the fulness of the Godhead bodily.'

[3.] The attributes of God are more amply declared. Every excellency of God hath its proper theatre where it is seen. In the gospel all are discovered, but chiefly mercy, justice, and truth. His power and his wisdom are seen in the world, but more in the gospel; the heavens do not declare half so much of the glory of God as the word and doctrine which Christ brought out of the Father's bosom: 1 Cor. i. 24, 'Christ the wisdom of God, and the power of God.' There is truth: 2 Cor. i. 20, 'For all the promises of God in him are Yea, and in him Amen.' The greatest assurance of his faithfulness was his sending Christ; that which we expect is nothing so difficult to believe as the incarnation of the Son of God; his second coming is not so unlikely as his first; if he came to suffer, and to purchase, he will come to reign. His wisdom in joining God and man together in the person of Christ, justice and mercy together, comfort and duty together in the covenant of grace; two natures, two attributes. God loseth no honour, man wanteth no encouragement. God showeth his justice : Rom. iii. 26, ' To declare, I say, at this time his righteousness, that he might be just, and the justifier of him which believeth in Jesus.' While the sacrifices continued, God only showed patience and forbearance ; his holiness and hatred of sin, by laying it on Christ, punishing it in Christ; his wrath, the most dreadful sight of God's wrath is upon Golgotha; God spared not his Son. But his grace, that was on the top : Titus iii. 4, ' But after that the kindness and love of God our Saviour towards man appeared.' This is the attribute that beareth sway in the gospel. Mercy is in office ever since the fall ; there was not so much kindness to man discovered in innocency ; God did good to a good man, there was no mercy to enemies then ; there man was made after God's image, here God is made after our image and likeness. Mercy and grace comes now to show itself to the world.

Use. Let us admire and study more the name of God in the gospel. The first letter of Christ's name is Wonderful. He is a mystery that is worthy our contemplation. The angels have known more of God since Christ was revealed : Eph. iii. 10, ' To the intent that now unto the principalities and powers in heavenly places might be known by the church the manifold wisdom of God.' Let it take up your thoughts, set your minds awork : Heb. iii. 1, ' Wherefore, holy brethren, partakers of the heavenly calling, consider the apostle and high priest of our profession, Jesus Christ.' There cannot be a more affective, humbling and heart-changing consideration.

Second point, That none can discover this name of God but Christ, none authoritatively, none perfectly.

1. None authoritatively can fix his name by which he shall be known among the creatures. The imposition of names implieth superiority ; the less is named of the greater. Adam had this favour to name the beasts, as having authority over them : Gen. ii. 19, 20, ' And out of the ground the Lord formed every beast of the field, and every fowl of the air, and brought them to Adam to see what he would call them, and whatsoever Adam called every living creature, that was the name thereof. And Adam gave names to all cattle, and to the fowl of the air, and to every beast of the field.' Now God is over all, there is no higher to name him, therefore he nameth himself. Jesus Christ, who is the very image of God, he cometh and declareth his name : ' My name is in him,' Exod. xxiii. 21. He is God, and therefore authoritatively fixeth the name of God, establisheth the gospel as the rule and direction of the church.

2. None can so perfectly discover him. Our hearts are too narrow to conceive of God, and our tongues too weak to express him : Prov. xxx. 4, ' What is his name? and what is his Son's name? if thou canst tell.' Who knoweth his pedigree exactly? Who knoweth his being? Who hath been in his bosom to discover him, so as Christ hath done? We must have a borrowed light to see him.

Use 1. Sit down with this revelation which Christ hath left in the church ; there is enough to instruct faith, though not to satisfy curiosity. In things not revealed, a simple nescience is better than a bold inquiry ; there is enough for service and adoration. Let not reason prescribe to faith. He were not God if he were not incomprehensible.

Should worms make their own apprehension the measure of divine truth? It is not so, because I cannot understand it; by a candle in the night, I cannot see it, therefore it is not. Some things are to be received from divine testimony, though we cannot fully conceive of them. Let us bless God for the word, and take heed unto it as to a light shining in a dark place. It is God's mercy that Christ came from heaven with a commission to discover so much to us. It is a ray of the face of God in Christ. Here, is God's heart discovered to us, and our hearts to ourselves.

Use 2. When you consult with the gospel, make use of Christ. He is to discover his Father's name; he taught the gospel, not only on earth, but in heaven: ' I have declared thy name, and will declare it.' *Non loquendum de Deo sine lumine.* There is no saving knowledge of God from ourselves. Christ is called Λόγος, the interpreter of his Father's mind. It is dangerous to set upon the knowledge of the mystery of the gospel in the strength of our own gifts and parts, to rest merely on the study of books and human helps. The gospel is God's riddle, which none but himself can expound. Beg the Spirit of revelation; you cannot have a knowledge of it without a revelation from Christ. We do not improve Christ's prophetical office so much as we should: we think he must .pacify our consciences, subdue our affections; but we do not look after knowledge, but think to get it by our own industry.

Third point, Christ doth not convey all knowledge, or the full notice of God's name at once. The knowledge that is originally in Christ is not communicated to us but by degrees, that it may increase more, like the good householder, that brought out the best at last: John i. 50, ' Because I said unto thee, I saw thee under the fig-tree, believest thou? thou shalt see greater things than these.' Partly to keep up our dependence and respect, lest a satiety grow upon us. When there is no more use of a thing, then we contemn it. Man is a creature that is led by hope rather than by memory. Still God keepeth the best till last; there is a perpetual use of Christ's prophetical office, that he may declare more. Partly to conform us to himself and to the church: ' Christ increased in wisdom and stature,' &c., Luke ii. 40, 52. His human capacity was enlarged by degrees. The church grew by degrees. There was a nonage; then it was ' the seed of the woman;' afterwards, 'in thy seed,' &c.; to ' Abraham, Isaac, and Jacob.' Then it was told what tribe, 'The sceptre shall not depart from Judah,' Gen. xlix. 10; afterwards of what family, to David; that ' a virgin shall conceive, and shall bear a son, and shall call his name Immanuel,' Isa. vii. 14. At last, ' Behold the Lamb of God,' John i. 29. Partly that he might suit his dispensations to our capacity. God will not violate the course of nature. Our life is hidden in Christ. You do not teach university learning to a boy; Christ dealeth with us as we are capable, according to our receptivity: ' We are made meet to be partakers of the inheritance of the saints in light,' Col. i. 12.

Use 1. Comfort against present defects. Though you are ignorant of some mysteries of religion, do not despond; Christ doth not give you all at once. There is a double comfort; God will accept our weakness, and we have a head in whom is all fulness. As our life is hidden in Christ, so is our wisdom hidden. In the text you see Christ hath undertaken for our growth ; we have a teacher that will carry us on from one degree of knowledge to another. Therefore let us not be discouraged, though we know little, and our parts be weak and insufficient.

Use 2. It presseth us to grow in knowledge : 2 Peter iii. 18, ' But grow in grace, and in the knowledge of our Lord and Saviour Jesus Christ.' There is more to be learned. Do not say, I know as much as they can tell me ; we never know so much but we may know more ; there is no stint to knowledge. If there be a measure of grace beyond which we cannot pass, the apostle would not say, ' Grow in grace and knowledge.' Therefore be conscionable and careful in the use of means. We must not rest in our low and imperfect measures, nor always keep to our A, B, C. We must grow till we come to heaven, and then there will be no more growing. A formal man is where he was (as a picture), doth not increase in stature. The way to keep what we have is to increase our store. Gifts that lie idle and inactive suffer loss and decay ; an active nature, such as man's, must either grow worse or better. It is an ill sign when we are contented with a little. Light groweth to the perfection of glory ; our reward is increased in the other world : Col. iii. 16, ' Let the word of God dwell in you richly in all wisdom.' It is the worst of poverty to have a poor understanding. Grace is multiplied through knowledge : 2 Peter i. 2, ' Grace and peace be multiplied unto you through the knowledge of God, and of Jesus our Lord.'

Fourth point, Christ maketh one mercy to be the pledge of another. I *have* declared, and I *will* declare. He is never weary of well-doing ; his love is infinite, and cannot be wearied, and his grace is infinite, and cannot be spent. Men waste by giving, their drop is soon spent ; but the oftener we come to God, the more welcome we are. Our faith is sooner tired than God's bounty, for he doth not waste by giving. I AM, is God's name ; he is where he was at first, he is never at a loss ; what he hath done, he can do, and will do : God's providence is new and fresh every morning : ' God is one,' Gal. iii. 21 ; he is always like himself. The creatures soon spend their allowance, but he is where he was at first. But it chiefly holdeth good in spiritual mercies ; the least drop of saving grace is an immortal seed ; it will grow, it will increase ; it is a spark that cannot be quenched, it is the pledge of more grace. Therefore where Christ hath begun to work for thee in some sparks of saving grace and knowledge, he will go on in his work ; where he is the Alpha, he will be the Omega ; where he is an author, he will be a finisher : Heb. xii. 2, ' Looking unto Jesus, who is the author and finisher of our faith.' The apostle would have us confident of this : Phil. i. 6, ' Being confident of this very thing, that he that hath begun a good work in you will perform it until the day of Christ.' God's first work is an earnest, and God will not lose his earnest ; it is the very first-fruits of the Spirit, and he gives it as a pledge of more grace to follow.

' That the love wherewith thou hast loved me may be in them, and I in them.' In the whole verse Christ showeth what he had done, what he would do, and with what aim. His end was twofold—to make way for application of God's love and his own presence as a vital principle in their hearts ; God's love and union with himself.

I shall speak now of the first. Whence—

Observe, that one great end why God's name is manifested in the gospel is that his love may be in us.

First, I shall inquire what it is to have his love in us. I shall give you several observations upon the phrase.

1. Observe, ' That the love,' &c. He doth not say, that they may have pardon, sanctification, or grace, or comfort in them, but love in them. *Obs.* God's love in Christ is the ground of all other favours and graces whatsoever. The spring of all is love, and the conveyance is by union, which containeth two truths :—

[1.] That all the goodness that is in us cometh from the love of God in Christ. We are loved into holiness, loved into pardon, loved into grace: Isa. xxxviii. 17, ' Thou hast in love to my soul delivered it from the pit of corruption,' or thou hast loved me from the pit. He loved his church, and sanctified it: Eph. v. 25, 26, ' Christ loved the church, and gave himself for it, that he might sanctify and cleanse it it with the washing of water by the word ;' Rev. i. 5, ' To him that loved us, and washed us from our sins in his own blood.' Our holiness is not the cause of love, but the fruit and effect of it. There can be no other reason for anything we receive. So 2 Thes. ii. 16, ' Now our Lord Jesus Christ himself, and God, even our Father, who hath loved us, and hath given us everlasting consolation, and good hope through grace,' &c. There was no other cause, there could be no other cause ; not necessity of nature, moral rule, or any former merit and kindness. Not necessity of nature ; God hath always the same love ; not bound by any external law and rule ; who can prescribe to him ? Not by any merit or debt, because of the eternity of his love, antecedent to all acts of the creature. There should be no other reason for the honour and majesty of God and our comfort.

[2.] That we have not only the blessings and benefits, but the love itself: 1 John iii. 1, ' Behold what manner of love is this that the Father hath bestowed upon us, that we should be called the sons of God !' Not showed us, but bestowed upon us. We have blessings from his heart, as well as his hand ; by his blessings in us, his love is in us ; we may gather thence that we are beloved of God, and no benefit is to be valued unless God's love be in it. What good will the possession of all things do us if we have not God himself ? The love is more to be valued than the gift, whatever it be. God giveth this love to none but special friends ; he giveth his outward love to enemies. He accepteth not our duties unless our hearts be in them, and our love be in them ; so we should not be satisfied till we can see love in the blessings that we receive from God, that they come from his heart as well as his hand. There are chastisements in love, and blessings given in anger, salted with a curse.

2. Observe, ' That the love wherewith thou hast loved me may be in them.' He had before said, ' Thou hast loved them as thou hast loved me ;' now, ' Let this love be in them.' The love of God is sometimes said to be in Christ, sometimes in us. Sometimes in Christ: Rom. viii. 39, ' Nor height, nor depth, nor any other creature shall be

able to separate us from the love of God which is in Christ Jesus our Lord.' Sometimes in us: 1 John iv. 9, 'In this was manifested the love of Christ towards us,' ἡ ἀγάπη τοῦ Χριστοῦ ἐν ἡμῖν, 'because that God sent his only-begotten Son into the world, that we might live through him.' We are the objects, and Christ is the ground. To make it sure, it is in Christ; and to make it sweet and comfortable, it is in us. God doth not love us in ourselves out of Christ; there would be no ground and reason for his love, but in Christ; and there is an eternal cause and reason why he should love us.

3. Observe, there is a love of God towards us, and a love of God in us. So Zanchy citing this text. His love *erga nos*, towards us, is from all eternity; his love *in nobis*, in us, is in time. These differ; there was a love of God towards us, so he loved us in Christ before the foundation of the world, though we knew it not, felt it not. But now this love beginneth to be in us, when we receive the effects of it, and God breaketh open the sealed fountain: 1 John iv. 16, ' And we have known and believed the love that God hath to us.' And therefore it must be distinguished. God's love from everlasting was in purpose and decree, not actual: Rom. ix. 11, ' That the purpose of God according to election might stand.' So Eph. i. 11, ' Being predestinated according to the purpose of him that worketh all things after the counsel of his will.' We are loved from eternity, but not justified from eternity. Certainly the elect are in a different condition before and after calling: 1 Cor. vi. 11, ' Such were some of you, but ye are washed, but ye are sanctified, but ye are justified in the name of the Lord Jesus, and by the Spirit of our God.' Secret things belong to God, but revealed things to us. Whatever thoughts God hath towards us, yet we know it not till his love be in us. We are to judge of our estates according to the law. It is true God is resolved not to prosecute his right against a sinner that is elect, but he is not actually acquitted from the sentence of the law till he actually believeth. We are not qualified to receive a legal discharge from the condemnation of the law till we be actually in Christ: Rom. viii. 1, ' There is no condemnation to them that are in Christ Jesus.' And whatever God's purposes may be towards us, we cannot but look upon ourselves as under a sentence of condemnation, and ' children of wrath,' Eph. ii. 3; that is the misery of our present estate. Before we know God as a Father in Christ, the love of God is towards us, but not in us.

4. Observe again, God's love is in us two ways—in the effects, and in the sense and feeling. These must be also distinguished; for God's love may be in us in regard of the effects, when it is not in us in regard of sense and feeling. It is in us in the effects of it at conversion, as soon as we begin to live in Christ. Where Christ liveth and dwelleth in us by faith, the love of Christ is there too. His love may be in us in the sense and feeling when we have the assurance of it: Rom. v. 5, ' The love of God is shed abroad in our hearts by the Holy Ghost, which he hath given to us,' that they may feel it in their hearts, that God loved them in Christ. There is the work of the Spirit, and the witness of the Spirit; both are intended in that expression; chiefly the latter, such a sense of God's love as stirreth up joy, and thankfulness, and hope. The precious ointment gave no savour while it was

shut up in a box, till it was poured out; so God's love, while it is kept secret, it yieldeth no reviving fragrancy. These two differ, for many have the effects of God's love, but not the sense; and the effects of love do always abide, for it is an immortal seed; but the sense of love is flitting and changeable. Nothing can separate us from the love of God in Christ, yet the love of God in Christ is often beclouded, overcast, and interrupted; and some have more effects, though less sense; the most shining years are not always the most fruitful; a man may have greater increase of grace though less comfort. Observe, for your comfort, that Christ prayeth for both; he hath prayed not only for grace, but for assurance, that we may feel ourselves beloved by the Father. The Lord delighteth not only to love us, but to assure us of his love. It is no comfort to a blind man to hear of a glorious sun or brave shows; he cannot see them. God would not leave us in the dark, but give us an experience of his love.

Secondly, How this ariseth from the manifestation of God's name in the gospel.

1. The knowledge of God is a means to kindle our respects to God.

2. To convey the influence of his grace to us.

1. It is a means to kindle our respects to God; as trust: Ps. ix. 10, 'They that know thy name will put their trust in thee.' Men are ignorant of God's goodness, mercy, and truth, and therefore they make so little use of him. Usually fears are in the night; doubts come from ignorance of the tenor of the gospel. If we did believe those things to be true which are revealed concerning his mercy and love to sinners, we should trust in him. Fire once kindled would burst out of itself into a flame; so did we once savingly know God's name, there would be more trust and confidence in God: Isa. l. 10, 'Who is among you that feareth the Lord, that obeyeth the voice of his servant, that walketh in darkness, and hath no light? let him trust in the name of the Lord, and stay upon his God.' We are overwhelmed with difficulties and straits, for want of studying God's name. So also for love: Cant. i. 3, 'Thy name is as ointment poured forth, therefore do the virgins love thee.' *Ignoti nulla cupido.* Love springeth from knowledge. In the beams of the sun there is a mixture of warmth and light. We know not the gift of God, and therefore our bowels are not troubled. Did we but see him as he is, it would set us all on fire.

2. It is the means to convey all the influences of grace to us: 2 Peter i. 2, 'Grace and peace be multiplied unto you, through the knowledge of God, and of Jesus our Lord.' God worketh upon us as rational creatures, agreeably to an intelligent nature, and so nothing can be wrought unless knowledge go before. A house, the more the windows stand open the more it is filled with light; so the more knowledge, the more is the capacity of the soul enlarged to receive comfort and grace. Guilty nature is full of fears, more presagious of evil than of good, and therefore it must have clear grounds of comfort and hope. But you will say, How comes it to pass that persons of great knowledge want comfort, and have no sense of God's love? I answer—It is not the light of parts, but of the Spirit: 'I have declared,' &c. It is God's prerogative to settle the conscience: ' I create the fruit of

the lips; peace, peace,' &c., Isa. lvii. 19.   The gospel is a sovereign plaster, but God maketh it work.   Our own thoughts do nothing, unless God put in with them.

Use 1. It informeth us of a double duty.

1. To study God's name.   It would settle the conscience to meditate upon those declarations which Christ hath made of his will.   Deep thoughts fasten things upon the Spirit, and musing maketh the fire to burn.   How hath God declared himself?   We may trust him upon his word: Ps. civ. 34, 'My meditation of him shall be sweet; I will be glad in the Lord.'   We should oftener find sweetness if we did oftener meditate of God.   It is sweet thus to enlarge our thoughts upon the promises and comforts of the gospel.

2. To apply it.   When God's name is proclaimed and made known to thee, urge thy own soul with it: Rom. viii. 31, 'What shall we say to these things?'   Job v. 27, 'Lo this, we have searched it, so it is, hear it, and know thou it for thy good.'   This is Christ's aim, that knowledge should beget love in them.   Knowledge without application doth no good; we must take out our share.   The riches of God's goodness are laid open to us for this end and purpose, that we may feel what is expressed: 'We have known and believed the love that God hath to us,' 1 John iv. 16.   It is no presumption; it is the great end why the gospel was written.   Wicked men are too forward and presumptuous of God's love; they continue their ungodly courses, do those things which offend him, and yet are persuaded that God loveth them.   God's children pray against their sins, and fight against their sins, and yet after all cannot be persuaded of it.   There is a fear of presumption, and a fear of security.   (1.) A fear of presumption; as some say, I am not worthy; it is as if you should say, I am too poor to ask or receive an alms, too filthy to be washed: say not so, for this is the way to make you worthy.   (2.) Of security; this is to say, If I take the physic, I shall be sick; whereas it is not by applying Christ that we are endangered, but by an insensibleness of our misery.   If thou feelest thy misery, there is no danger of security; it is not every-thing will satisfy a sensible sinner, not every slight comfort.

Use 2. Examination, whether you have gotten benefit by the gospel. Is God's love in you?   Have you any fruits or feeling of his love? Can you say God loveth you?   All God's children cannot feel his love; but have you the fruits of his love?   The feeling of his love is to be improved immediately to thankfulness, and the fruits of his love are to be improved by spiritual discourse to confidence.   The present argument will afford us ground of search and inquiry.

1. Things without us are excluded, they can be no evidence or argument of God's love.   It is love in them.   It is the common error of the world to be led with false evidences.   Many think God loveth them, because he spareth them, and followeth them with long-suffering and patience, and maketh them thrive in the world, and blesseth them with the increase and fatness of an outward portion.   Ay! but love and hatred cannot be known by the things that are without us; it must be something within us must discover it, Eccles. ix. 2.   All things come alike to all.   Some are fatted to destruction, and con-demned to worldly felicity, God will give them enough, Jer. xvii. 13.

'All that forsake thee, shall be ashamed; and they that depart from me shall be written in the earth, because they have forsaken the Lord, the fountain of living waters.' Worldly happiness may be God's curse; they shall be written in the earth, they shall have happiness here, that have none hereafter. On the other hand, there are some whose names are written in heaven; and though they have little of outward comforts, yet that is matter of joy: Luke ix. 20, 'Rather rejoice, because your names are written in heaven.' We must have a better evidence than things without us before we can see our names in those eternal records, and be assured that God loves us. When God only gives things without you, it is a sign you are only hired servants. You have your reward, and are satisfied; and when you die, your best days are at an end; there is no inheritance kept for you; as Abraham gave Ishmael and the rest of the sons of the concubines gifts and portions, but he reserved the inheritance for Isaac. This is so far from an evidence of love, that it is rather a sign of hatred, if your hearts are herewith satisfied. Nay, as it excludes and cuts off all outward things, so it cuts off all outward profession, as baptism and hearing of the word; for where the heart is not washed, baptism is but the monument of your unfaithfulness and breach of vows. And so for hearing of the word, it is but like Uriah's letters; he thought they contained matter of preferment, but when opened, they contained matter of danger, for he was to be set in the fore-front of the battle to be destroyed. So when you think to come to God with these pleasing excuses, it is matter of condemnation, because you have heard so much, and profited nothing. Here is no evidence without you of the love of God.

2. Things within are excluded. There are some moral inclinations, mere instincts of nature, which God hath left in men out of his common bounty and pity to human society: Rom. ii. 14, 15, 'For when the Gentiles, which have not the law, do by nature the things contained in the law, these, having not the law, are a law unto themselves, which show the work of the law written in their hearts.' These moral inclinations, by which we avoid gross sins, are not an evidence of God's love. Again, there are gifts for the use of the body. Hypocrites may have a great share in them. Achitophel and Saul had excellent gifts; but this is not an evidence of God's love. How did God love Christ? Herein was a great evidence of God's love to Christ; he loved him, and 'gave the Spirit to him without measure,' John iii. 33, 34. So we know his love by his Spirit, that he hath given to us to witness our justification, and to work our sanctification. The gift of the Spirit we may know by his witness, and by his work.

1. His witness. Hast thou a full testimony of thy adoption? Rom. viii. 16, 'The Spirit itself beareth witness with our spirits that we are the children of God.' It is such a certainty as ariseth from gospel grounds, working joy and peace, stirring up to thankfulness and love to God, which you have in God's way, by praying, reading, hearing, meditating. I confess there is something lower, that may be called the witness of the Spirit. There are expressions and impressions. Have you not some secret impressions of confidence and liberty in prayer, and resolutions to wait upon God? Doth he not stir you up to cry,

Abba Father, put you upon often calling upon God, and waiting upon God? There is something in your heart that carries you to God. These impressions are a kind of witness and testimony of the Spirit, though you have not those actual testimonies of God's favour.

2. His work. Have you the work of the Spirit? What is that? The work of the Spirit is to sanctify and cleanse: Eph. v. 25, 26, 'Christ loved the church, and gave himself for it, that he might sanctify and cleanse it.' It is the greatest sign of God's anger and wrath that can be to live and die under the power of sin, not to be sanctified, not to be cleansed, not to be washed from sin. And therefore are you sanctified, cleansed, and washed? Rev. i. 5, 'To him that loved us, and washed us from our sins in his blood.' Is there any care of obedience stirred up in your hearts? The Spirit will cause us to grow in obedience: John xiv. 23, 'If a man love me, he will keep my words, and my Father will love him, and we will come unto him, and make our abode with him.'

3. There is one thing more in the expression, 'that the love wherewith thou hast loved me may be in them,' and that is, If God love thee, thou canst not but love him again: 1 John iv. 16, 'For we have known, and believed the love that God hath to us. God is love, and he that dwelleth in love dwelleth in God, and God in him.' If thou lovest God, his people, his ordinances, and delightest in communion with him, his love is in thee. These are the fruits and effects of it.

Use 3. To press us to labour after the sense of his love. We should go to heaven as comfortably and as richly as we can ; not only creep thither, but labour after 'an abundant entrance,' 2 Peter i. 12. Though it is not always our sin to want it, yet it is our duty to strive after this sense of God's love in us. The sense of God's love, it is the flame of faith : Gal. ii. 20, 'I live, yet not I, but Christ liveth in me ; and the life which I live in the flesh, I live by the faith of the Son of God, who loved me, and gave himself for me.' It is the ground of our love to him again: 1 John iv. 19, 'We love him, because he first loved us.' The more full and direct the beams are cast upon any solid body, the stronger the reflection. It is the life of joy which enlargeth our hearts in thankfulness. It is our stay in afflictions, and our strength in duties, especially in prayer. How can we call God Father, unless in custom and hypocrisy, except we have some sense of our adoption? Therefore labour after the sense of his love, that it may be in you.

SERMON XLV.

And I have declared unto them thy name, and will declare it ; that the love wherewith thou hast loved me may be in them, and I in them.—JOHN XVII. 26.

'AND I in them.' This is the next aim of Christ, the mystical union. This is fitly coupled with the former privilege. God's love is the fountain of all mercy, and mystical union is the means of conveyance. The Father's love and the Son's inhabitation are elsewhere conjoined:

John xiv. 23, 'My Father will love him, and we will come unto him, and make our abode with him.' God's love cannot be in us unless Christ be in us, nor Christ be in us without the Father's love. God loveth the elect freely in Jesus Christ, and therefore giveth us his Spirit to work faith in our hearts, that Christ may dwell there, and be one with us, and we with him : love is the rise of all. And again, without the perpetual residence of Christ in the heart, we cannot have a sense of God's love. Again, from this conjunction we may learn the presence of the whole Trinity in the heart of a believer, as in a consecrated temple. The love of the Father it is in us, by the Holy Ghost given to us : Rom. v. 5, 'The love of God is shed abroad in our hearts by the Holy Ghost, which is given unto us.' Now we have not only the Holy Ghost to assure us of the love of God, but we have Christ as the head and fountain of vital influence. Once more, ' I in them.' Christ doth not only communicate gifts of grace to us, but himself.

Observe that the gospel is made known to us to this intent, that Christ may be in us ; or, this is one great privilege of the gospel, that Christ may be in us by a perpetual residence, as a principle and fountain of the spiritual life.

First, What is meant by Christ's being in us? How can one man be in another ? I shall answer—

First, Negatively ; how it is not to be understood, that we may remove all false, gross, and unworthy thoughts.

1. It is not contiguity that we speak of, but union. Two pieces of wood lying together are not united. Christ is in heaven, we on earth ; there is no contiguity, and if there were, it would not cause a union. There is indeed a union of contact, as when two hands are joined together, which may resemble this union ; for there is a mutual or reciprocal apprehension ; Christ apprehendeth us, and we him : Phil. iii. 12, ' If that I may apprehend that for which also I am apprehended of Christ Jesus.' He taketh hold of us by his Spirit, and we take hold of him by faith. But of this by and by.

2. It is not a congregation, as things may be gathered together ; as stones in a heap, they are united, or gathered into one heap, but they do not act one upon another. And therefore the Holy Ghost doth not resemble our union with Christ by stones in a heap, but by stones in a building, that afford mutual strength and support to one another, and Christ to the foundation and corner-stone, which beareth up all the rest : 1 Peter ii. 5, ' Ye also as lively stones are built up a spiritual house ;' and Eph. ii. 20-22, ' And are built upon the foundation of the apostles and prophets, Jesus Christ himself being the chief corner-stone, in whom all the building, fitly framed together, groweth unto an holy temple in the Lord ; in whom you also are builded together for an habitation of God through the Spirit.' Only here is the difference, that is but a union of art, not of nature ; and though stones orderly placed do give strength and beauty one to another, yet they do not communicate life and influence ; therefore the Holy Ghost saith, ' Ye are as living stones.'

3. It is not representation only, as all persons are in their common person and representation. This is a part of the privilege ; we are in Christ as our surety and common person. He impersonated and

represented us upon the cross, and doth now in heaven, where he appeareth for us as our agent and leiger with God. Thus what is done to him is done to us. This is the judicial union; but this is not all, for thus we may be said to be in Christ, but he cannot be said to be in us, ' I in them.' There is influence as well as representation.

4. It is not an objective union, *aut unio occupationis;* as the object is in the faculty, the star in the eye that seeth it, though at thousands of miles' distance; and what I think of is in my mind, and what I desire is in my heart, as a scholar's mind is in his books; when the mind is occupied and taken up with anything, it is in it. So when I fear God, my mind is with him; when I love God, my heart is with him. But this is not all, partly because such an objective union there is between Christ and hypocrites, they may think of him, and know him. But this union is rather subjective; it maketh us to live in Christ, and Christ liveth in us. Partly because then we should be no longer united to Christ than we do actually think of him, whereas Christ's being in us implieth a perpetual residence: Eph. iii. 17, ' That Christ may dwell in your hearts by faith.' Dwelling doth not note a transient thought, a short visit, but a constant stay and abode: John xiv. 23, καὶ μονὴν παρ' αὐτῷ ποιήσομεν, ' We will come unto him, and we will make our abode with him.' There Christ fixeth his seat and residence.

5. It is not merely a relation between us and Christ. He is not only ours, and we are his; but he is in us, and we in him. The resemblance of head and members doth not relate to a political body, but to a natural body. I am sure the case is clear in root and branches, John xv. 1–3. And relations do not need such bands and ties as constitute this union. There the Spirit and faith, and then secondarily other graces.

6. It is not only a consent or agreement; Christ agreeth to love us, and we to love him : ' My love in them,' and ' I in them ;' they are propounded as distinct. Confederation maketh way for union.

7. It is not a union of dependence merely, such as is between the cause and effect. The effect dependeth on the cause, and is in the cause, and the cause is in the effect. This is general to all creatures; for it is said, Acts xvii. 28, ' In him we live, and move, and have our being.' Such a union there is between God and all creatures. And not merely a dependence in regard of special and gracious influences. That doth much open the privilege; but that is not all, for then our union would be immediately with God the Father and the Spirit on whom we depend. And so a union there is between God and the holy angels. And Christ is in an especial manner the head of the church; it is a notion consecrated for our conjunction with him.

8. It is not merely a communion in the same nature. So he is Immanuel, God with us. But he saith, ' I in them.' He not only came into our natures, but he must come into our hearts. This union is common to all, though I confess it is only reckoned and imputed to the sanctified: Heb. ii. 11, ' For both he that sanctifieth, and they that are sanctified, are all of one ; for which cause he is not ashamed to call them brethren.' And to the children of God: Heb. ii. 14, ' Forasmuch then as the children are partakers of flesh and blood, he also himself took part of the same.'

9. It is not a mixture, as if Christ and we were confounded, and mingled our substances together. That is a gross thought, and suiteth with the carnal fancies of a corporeal eating his flesh and drinking his blood. We are not mixed, his substance with ours, and ours with his; he remaining still a distinct person, and we distinct persons.

10. It is not a personal union, as of the two natures in the person of Christ. We are not united to Christ so as to make one person, but one mystical body: 1 Cor. xii. 12, 'For as the body is one, and hath many members, and all the members of that one body, being many, are one body, so also is Christ.' The whole is Christ mystical, but every believer is not Christ.

Thus I have endeavoured to remove all gross and unworthy thoughts. But now—

Secondly, Positively. What it is. I answer—We cannot fully tell till we come to heaven; then we shall have perfect knowledge of it; then Christ is all in all: John xiv. 20, 'At that day ye shall know that I am in the Father, and you in me, and I in you.' Then our union is at the height. But for the present we may call it a union of concretion and coalition, for we are σύμφυτοι, 'planted into him,' Rom. vi. 5, and κολλώμενοι, 'joined to the Lord,' 1 Cor. vi. 17. It is immediately with Christ; we are united to Father and Spirit, but by Christ, as the foot is united to the head, but by the intervention of other members; so we are united to the Father and the Spirit, but by Christ; as an arm or foot of the Son belongeth to the Father, but as the Son belongeth to the Father. The love of the Father is the moving cause of it, the Spirit is the efficient cause of it, but it is with Christ. And it is by way of coalition, as things are united so as they may grow and live in another, as the branches grow in the vine, and the members, being animated and quickened by the soul, grow in the body; so are we united with Christ as our vital principle, that we may live and grow in him, that we might live in him: Gal. ii. 20, 'I live, yet not I, but Christ liveth in me;' and grow in him: Eph. iv. 15, 16, 'But speaking the truth in love, may grow up into him in all things, which is the head, even Christ. From whom the whole body fitly joined together, and compacted by that which every joint supplieth, according to the effectual working in the measure of every part, maketh increase of the body, unto the edifying of itself in love.' So that this is enough in general to call it a union of concretion and coalition, such a union whereby Christ remaineth and liveth and dwelleth in us as a vital principle. As the soul is τοῦ ζῶντος σώματος αἰτία καὶ ἀρχή, a cause and principle of life to the body, so is Christ to us. Before God breathed the soul into Adam, his body, though otherwise organised and formed, lay but as a dead lump, without breath and life; but no sooner was the soul put into him, but he began to live. So Christ, being mystically united, enableth us to live, to act, to grow, and increase more and more. More particularly to open it to you is hard, because it is a great mystery. Life natural is a mystery not sufficiently explained, much more life spiritual. But now—

1. I shall show how it is wrought and brought about, and in what order; for there is a difficulty there to be cleared. For since union is said to be by faith: Eph. iii. 17, 'That Christ may dwell in your

hearts by faith,' and faith is an act of spiritual life, it seemeth there is life before our union with Christ; so that this union seemeth to be the effect rather than the cause of the spiritual life; and some say it is the effect of the beginning, and the cause of the continuance and increase of it, and conceive the order thus: That Christ is offered in the gospel, and by receiving Christ we come to be united to him, and then to be possessed of his righteousness, and receive further influences of grace; and that the first beginning of spiritual life is not from union, but regeneration, by virtue of which faith is given to us, that we may be united to Christ. But I suppose this method is not right. Briefly, then, for the manner and order how it is wrought, take it thus: Union it is by the Spirit on Christ's part, and faith on ours; he beginneth with us as the most worthy, as having a quickening and life-making power in himself: 1 Cor. xv. 45, 'The last Adam was made πνεῦμα ζωοποιοῦν, a quickening spirit.' By the Spirit he infuseth spiritual life, the first act of which is faith; that is the first grace that acteth upon Christ, and maketh the union reciprocal, that so in him we may have righteousness and grace: Phil. iii. 9, 'And be found in him, not having mine own righteousness, which is of the law, but that which is through the faith of Christ, the righteousness which is of God by faith.' All graces flow from union with Christ, so doth faith. Believing is an act of the spiritual life, but it is at the same instant of time, and not before. The first band of union is the Spirit, for the gift of the Spirit is the cause of faith, and every cause is before the effect in nature, though not in time; for, *posita causa in actu, ponitur effectus.* But the Spirit is not given us in the least moment of time before the being of faith; for the Spirit being infused, immediately excites faith to take hold of Christ.

2. What is that act of faith by which we close with Christ? I answer—The apprehending, embracing, taking hold of Christ: 'To as many as received him,' &c., John i. 12, trusting him with our souls; that is the faith that gives us an interest in gospel privileges. But what is this receiving Christ? I answer—Receiving presupposeth offering; it is a consent to what is offered, an accepting of what is given. Receiving is a word used in contracts, and noteth the consent of one part to the terms which the other offereth. The scripture chiefly delighteth in the similitude of the matrimonial contract. As a woman accepteth a man for her husband, so do we receive Christ. When a man's affections are set upon a woman, he sendeth spokesmen to tell her of his love, and that he is ready to give her an interest in himself, and all that is his, if she will accept him for an husband. So Jesus Christ, the Son of God, the heir of all things, sendeth messengers to treat and deal with us about a spiritual marriage, to tell us how he loved us, gave his life for us, established an everlasting righteousness, whereby we may be accepted with God, and that he is ready to bestow it upon us, if we will receive, and honour, and obey him as Lord and husband; which if we do, then we are interested in this great privilege. Yea, Lord, I give up myself, body and soul, to thee, and I take thee for Lord and husband. For these are the terms: Hosea iii. 3, 'Thou shalt not be for another man, so will I also be for thee.'